MASTERPIECES
OF THE
RUSSIAN DRAMA

SELECTED AND EDITED
WITH AN INTRODUCTION
BY GEORGE RAPALL NOYES

Volume Two

DOVER PUBLICATIONS, INC.
NEW YORK   NEW YORK

WARNING

The plays in this volume are for reading purposes only. The fact that you have purchased this volume does not give you permission to produce any play in it unless you have received permission to do so.

The plays in this volume are fully protected by the copyright law. No performance, professional or amateur, no public reading, no radio broadcast, may be given without permission of Dover Publications, Inc., 180 Varick St., New York 14, N. Y.

Performances of each play in this volume are subject to royalty. Any one presenting any of these plays without the consent of the owner of the play, or his authorized agent, will be liable to the penalties provided by law:

"Section 4966—Any person publicly performing or representing any dramatic or musical composition for which copyright has been obtained, without the consent of the proprietor of said dramatic or musical composition, or his heirs and assigns, shall be liable for damages thereof, such damages in all cases to be assessed at such sum not less than one hundred dollars for the first and fifty dollars for every subsequent performance, as to the court shall appear to be just. If the unlawful performance and presentation be willful and for profit, such person or persons shall be imprisoned for a period not exceeding one year."

U. S. Revised Statutes, Title 60, Chapter 3

Library of Congress Catalog Card Number: 60-50844

Manufactured in the United Sates of America
Dover Publications, Inc.
180 Varick Street
New York, N. Y. 10014

To

MY WIFE

PREFACE

THE purpose of this volume is to group together a dozen of the best Russian plays in such a way as to illustrate the historic development of the Russian drama, its scope and variety. The period covered is from 1782 to 1921. Four of the plays selected are comedies, five are tragedies, two are of the intermediate sort common in Russian literature, one is an extravaganza. Five deal with country life and five with city life in the time of their authors; one is an historical tragedy of the sixteenth century. Nine are in prose and three in verse.

With the exception of *Wit Works Woe,* the translations in this volume are here printed for the first time. *The Young Hopeful, The Poor Bride, A Bitter Fate, Professor Storitsyn,* and *Mystery-Bouffe* have never before been translated into English. When two or more translators are named for one play, the main credit belongs to the first mentioned; the others added merely corrections or suggestions on style. Unless otherwise stated, the notes throughout the book are by the translators. I am indebted to Mr. Arthur A. Sykes for his courteous permission to use his excellent translation of *The Inspector (The Inspector-General,* London, 1896) in revising a few passages of the present translation: some notes on the text are also taken from his work.

The translation of Griboyedov's masterpiece by Sir Bernard Pares appeared under the title *The Mischief of Being Clever* in the *Slavonic Review* (London) for June and December, 1924, and was later published separately by the School of Slavonic Studies, London. Sir Bernard Pares has kindly consented to its inclusion in the present volume under the title, *Wit Works Woe,* and has approved some trifling changes in the style of printing and in the text.

The Introduction aims to explain the main lines of the development of Russian drama in relation to Russian literature as a whole, with special reference to the plays here printed.

The following books have been of particular service to me in writing the Introduction: Wiener, *The Contemporary Drama of Russia* (Boston, 1924); Sayler, *The Russian Theatre* (New York, 1922); Carter, *The New Theatre and Cinema of Soviet Russia* (London, 1924), and *The New Spirit in the Russian Theatre, 1917-28* (New York, 1929);

Mirsky, *A History of Russian Literature* (New York, 1927), and *Contemporary Russian Literature* (New York, 1926) ; Grossman, *Turgenev* (in Russian: Moscow, 1928) ; Znosko-Borovsky, *The Russian Theatre* (in Russian: Prague, 1925) ; Gorbachev, *Sketches of Contemporary Russian Literature* (in Russian: Leningrad, 1925) ; Evgenyev-Maksimov, *Sketch of the History of Recent Russian Literature* (in Russian: Leningrad, 1925) ; Piksanov, *Griboyedov* (in Russian, in Ovsyaniko-Kulikovsky, *History of Russian Literature of the Nineteenth Century,* Moscow, n.d.). Quotations from books in English are made by the kind permission of the publishers.

I am indebted to Professors G. Z. Patrick and A. Kaun for constant assistance in preparing this book; Professor Patrick has made particularly valuable suggestions for the Introduction. Finally, my greatest debt is due to my wife, who has aided me in all my work on the volume with tireless devotion.

G. R. NOYES.

Berkeley, California

CONTENTS

VOLUME TWO

ix

CONTENTS

MASTERPIECES
OF THE
RUSSIAN DRAMA

THE DEATH OF IVAN THE TERRIBLE

A Tragedy in Five Acts

By COUNT ALEXEY KONSTANTINOVICH TOLSTOY

(1865)

Translated by George Rapall Noyes

The king spake, and said, Is not this great Babylon, that I have built for the house of the kingdom by the might of my power, and for the honor of my majesty?

While the word was in the king's mouth, there fell a voice from heaven, saying, O King Nebuchadnezzar, to thee it is spoken: The kingdom is departed from thee. And they shall drive thee from men, and thy dwelling shall be with the beasts of the field. Daniel iv: 30-32.

CHARACTERS

Tsar Iván Vasílyevich iv
Tsarítsa Márya Fédorovna,* *his seventh wife, of the Nagoy family*
Tsarévich Fédor Ivánovich, *his son by his first wife*
Tsarévna Irína Fédorovna, *wife of* Fedor, *sister of* Borís Godunóv
Prince Mstislávsky
Nikíta Románovich Zakháryin-Yúryev, *brother of the tsar's first wife*
Prince Shúysky
Bélsky
Prince Shcherbáty
Prince Golítsyn
Prince Trubetskóy
Prince Sítsky
Sheremétev
Tatíshchev
Saltykóv
Mikháylo Nagóy, *brother of* Tsarítsa Márya Fédorovna
Borís Feódorovich Godunóv, *brother-in-law of* Tsarévich Fédor

} *Members of the Council of Boyárs*

Messenger *from Pskov*
Márya Grigóryevna, *wife of* Borís Godunóv
Grigóry Godunóv, *relative of* Borís
Grigóry Nagóy, *second brother of* Tsarítsa Márya Fédorovna

} *Officials of the Court*

Haráburda, *ambassador of* King Stefan Batory *of Poland*
Bityagóvsky,
Kíkin,

} *Nobles*

Hermit
Nurse *of* Tsarevich Dmitry Ivánovich
Steward *of the Kremlin Palace*
Steward *of the Alexandrov Suburb*
Steward *of* Godunóv
First Soothsayer
Second Soothsayer
Elms
Jacobi

} *Physicians*

First Patrolman

Second Patrolman
Jester
Seneschal
Commander of the Guards
Corporal of the Guards
Chamberlain
Shopkeeper
Serving Maid
Servant *of* Prince Shúysky

Boyars, officials of the court, watchmen, guardsmen, populace, minstrels, servants.

The action takes place in Moscow, in the year 1584.

---

* *Fedor, Fedorovna* are pronounced Fyŏ'dor, Fyŏ'do-ro-vna. This translation follows the original in varying between *Fedor* and *Feodor* (*Fe-ŏ'dor*), *Dmitry* and *Dimitry, Feodorych* and *Feodorovich.*

THE DEATH OF IVAN THE TERRIBLE

ACT I

SCENE I

Before the rising of the curtain the noise of angry disputes is heard. The curtain rises on a session of the Council of Boyars. The boyars are seated on benches arranged along the walls in the form of the Greek letter pi. On the center bench sit PRINCE MSTISLAVSKY, ZAKHARYIN-YURYEV, BELSKY, *and the other elder boyars; on the side benches are the younger men. At the end of the side bench on the right, near the front of the stage, sits* BORIS GODUNOV. *On the left side, opposite* GODUNOV, MIKHAYLO NAGOY *has seized* SALTYKOV *by the collar and is trying to drag him from his place.*

NAGOY: The tsar's my sister's husband; it fits not
That I should sit below the Saltykovs!
SALTYKOV: Drunkard, away! Your grandfather was but
A servitor of mine, his humble client!
NAGOY: That is not true! Ne'er did the Saltykovs
Have clients in their line! Did you attain
Your rank as a boyar because you aided
Golitsyn basely to surrender Polotsk
Into the hands of Stefan, King of Poland?
GOLITSYN: No, 'tis a lie! The outposts were my charge;
Shcherbaty held command within the city!
SHCHERBATY: Yes, held command! And during my command
In twelve days we repulsed seven strong attacks;
And if you had held firmly to the outposts
Fresh troops from Sokol would have come to us
And smote the Polish king upon the rear.
GOLITSYN: Am I to blame because the leaders of
Those troops delayed three days, fiercely disputing
How to divide among them posts of honor?
NAGOY (*continuing his dispute with* SALTYKOV): The tsar's my sis-
  ter's husband; at his marriage
I walked in front, bearing the imperial loaf!

SALTYKOV: I bore the platter with the golden cup!
My father was a governor. And yours—
Who was he? 'Tis a lofty honor that
By his seventh wife our tsar is kin to you!

NAGOY: Do not insult my sister—and your empress!

SALTYKOV: I mean no insult! Yet your sister's not
The first wife of the tsar, merely the seventh!
You boast of kinship to our Tsar Ivan!
Fine store of kinsfolk hath our tsar acquired!

ZAKHARYIN: Boyars, what do ye? Recollect your duty!
Unseemly is such strife!

NAGOY: Ready am I
To bow my head in homage to the tsar,
But always as befits my rank and state!

SALTYKOV: Aye, bow your head! And may the tsar deliver
That head to me!

MSTISLAVSKY: Enough, enough, boyars!
Though Sheremetev and myself surpass
You all in rank, we quarrel not about
To whom belongs precedence here!

VOICES: You higher
Than we? How so!

ZAKHARYIN: Oh, shame on you, boyars!
(To MSTISLAVSKY.) You, Prince Ivan Feodorych, as senior,
Restrain their angry spirits!

MSTISLAVSKY: How restrain them?
They have gone mad! You see, they wish to vie
With the Mstislavskys! Shall we bid the clerk
Bring in to us the books of heraldry?

ZAKHARYIN: Now is no time for heraldry, my prince!
(Stepping forward.) Boyars, do not forget the reason for
Our coming here! What! At the present time,
When, after slaying his belovèd son,
Our tsar is tortured by repentance, when
He purposes to leave this worldly life,
And bids us set aside his second son,
Feodor, since that prince is but a weakling,
And choose for him a worthier heir, to whom
He may transfer the burden of his rule—
When enemies from every side attack
Our native soil—when pestilence and famine
Rage in our land—at such a time do ye
Dispute on petty matters of precedence?

Come to your senses, brothers and boyars!
Now we must stand shoulder to shoulder, striving
Lest Russia perish! Now forget your ranks!
Setting aside precedence, let us now
Assume our gloomy task, and choose a prince!
Now we should all be equals!

BELSKY: Equals, then!

ALL: All equal! No precedence!

ZAKHARYIN: Prince Mstislavsky,
As senior of us all, speak first!

MSTISLAVSKY: Boyars
And members of the council, have ye heard
The heavy charge laid on us by Nikita
Románovich? Although the task be hard,
Yet must we yield to the imperial will.
Let us proceed to the election!

SHUYSKY: Hold!
Is that the last word of our lord and master?

MSTISLAVSKY: The last! In vain we strove to bend his will.
He charged us, not delaying, to elect
And bring to him our future tsar.

TRUBETSKOY: Grim news!

GOLITSYN: Beyond belief!

MSTISLAVSKY: Nor could I trust my ears
Until he stamped his foot, straitly commanding
That we convoke the Council of Boyars.

SHUYSKY: If such is then his will, can we oppose?

SHCHERBATY: Yes, if 'tis so, boyars, we have no right
To thwart his purpose!

SHEREMETEV: Aye, we have no right!

TATISHCHEV (*an old man*): It will be twenty years next Easter, since
Our mighty lord came to the same decision:
He purposed, even as now, to quit the throne
And to remove from Moscow to the Suburb.
The folk began to murmur. We resolved
That all of us should supplicate the tsar
Still to remain our ruler. This we did.
The tsar received us sternly; first refused
To harken to our prayers; then he relented,
Returned to Moscow, and once more assumed
The cares of state.

SITSKY: Aye, so indeed he did!
And then established the *oprichnina!* *
We well remember!
TATISHCHEV: That in very truth
Was such a time as may the Lord not bring
Again to afflict us! Yet without a tsar
Our case had been still worse! The turbulent
Folk would have stoned us, Russia would have perished,
The Tatars, Germans, Poles would have been victors—
No concord was there then among us nobles!
SITSKY: But now all men may envy our rare concord!
SHUYSKY (*to* TATISHCHEV): What was the aim of your discourse,
        boyar?
TATISHCHEV: I hazarded the hope, my lords, that now,
As at that former time, the tsar might yield.
MSTISLAVSKY: Nay, nay, boyar, the times have changed. The tsar
Is now another man. In soul and body
Now he is weak and frail. 'Tis not distrust
Of the boyars that drives him from his throne;
Sincere repentance bids him seek a refuge!
BELSKY: He neither eats nor drinks; he scarcely sleeps.
Of the negotiations that in secret
He was conducting with the English queen
No longer does he speak. Her envoy now
In vain requests of him an audience.
ZAKHARYIN: 'Tis true: he is no more his former self!
Three weeks before his crime, he wrote a letter
To Kurbsky, to the traitor, and reproached
Him fiercely; then, awaiting a reply
From Lithuania, he shook with wrath.
But now he has no further thought of Kurbsky;
His bearing now is mild, his speech is gracious.
SHUYSKY: 'Tis not our office to correct the tsar.
His wrath and clemency are given him
By God.—   Boyars and councilors, 'tis time
That we proceed to the election!
ALL: Yes!
(*Silence.*)
MSTISLAVSKY: Whom shall we choose, boyars?
NAGOY:
                        Whom can we choose,
If we must set aside the claim of Fedor,

---

* A body of guardsmen exempt from ordinary law and subject only to the
tsar's will. It was designed to hold in check the hereditary nobility.

Except his younger son, Prince Dmitry?
    MSTISLAVSKY: That mere babe?
    NAGOY: He has a mother, our tsaritsa!
And if my sister, the tsaritsa, be
Not competent, then we may join with her
A regent.
    SALTYKOV: So you nominate yourself?
    NAGOY: Yes, or my brother. We are both the uncles
Of Prince Dmitry!
    SALTYKOV: No such uncles need we!
    TATISHCHEV: May God forbid! We know what happened when
Our Tsar Ivan was in his childhood. From
Imperial uncles may the Lord deliver us!
    SHUYSKY: May God avert such fortune!
    ZAKHARYIN: God forbid!
We need a tsar who shall have power himself,
No regency!
    MSTISLAVSKY: Most true. And Tsar Ivan
Has now enjoined on us that we must choose
One of ourselves to rule.
    SHEREMETEV: Whom shall it be?
    SHCHERBATY: The candidate we choose must trace descent
From ancestors illustrious and noble,
That every man, feeling his worth, may bow
The head in reverence before him.
    SITSKY: No,
Boyar! Let him be tsar who has most merit!
Surely we need not seek him far: Nikita
Románovich Zakháryin is before you! (*Exclamations and murmurs.*)
Beside the blood-stained throne of Tsar Ivan
For thirty years he has stood pure and white.
By his bold words he has delivered thousands
Of guiltless men, when over them there flashed
The headsman's ax. Himself he has not spared.
Ever he looked into the face of death—
And yet, although we marveled, cruel death
Still spared his honored head. And now his life
Lies spread before our eyes, a snowy plain,
Unspotted!
    VOICES: Yes, Zakharyin, choose Zakharyin!
Zakharyin must we choose to be our tsar!
    TRUBETSKOY (*to* SITSKY): Who can oppose him! Innocent is he,
Pure and beyond reproach. We honor him

As his deserts require, but he is not
Of princely birth. To bow to his commands
Becomes not us, descendants of Gedimin.*

SHUYSKY: Still less fits us, who are of Rurik's † line.

GOLITSYN: No prince is he; we cannot be his subjects!

SALTYKOV: No prince, I grant—but kinsman to the tsar!

NAGOY: Not he alone! We too are the tsar's kin!

SALTYKOV: You are the brother of our tsar's seventh wife;
As his first bride he took Zakharyin's sister!

ZAKHARYIN: Am I the occasion of your quarrels, friends!
Prince Sitsky, much I thank you for the honor!
(*Bowing to several.*) You too I thank, boyars! And yet I must
Refuse such honor: yea, though all of you
Should wish to choose me, I could not accept it!
Too plain a man am I, boyars! The Lord
Denied me any gift for statesmanship.
But if you wish good counsel, then there is
One man who both by birth and service has
A claim superior to us all: 'tis Prince
Ivan Petrovich Shuysky, who defends,
While now we speak, our fortress Pskov, and thwarts
The armies of King Stefan Batory.
Choose him, my lords! To such a man as he
We all may join in doing reverence!

SHEREMETEV: No, Shuysky is impossible. The king
For five months now has been besieging Pskov,
And Prince Ivan must needs abide therein
Till death o'ertake him: such has been his oath
With all his valiant troops. God knows how long
The siege may be prolonged; but we cannot
Remain one hour without a ruler.

SHUYSKY: Then
What shall we do?

MSTISLAVSKY: That know I not, boyars!

SHUYSKY: The tsar is waiting. We must make our choice!

ZAKHARYIN (*to* GODUNOV): Boris Feodorych, you hitherto
Have sat in silence. Yet in time of stress

---

* Grand Prince of Lithuania, ruling 1315-41. To him some of the Russian princes trace their descent.

† A Scandinavian Viking who in 862 became ruler of Novgorod and founder of the Russian state. From him sprang various lines of Russian rulers, including those of Moscow. The greater part of the Russian princes claim to be descended from him.

Oft have you saved us from disaster. Now
Tell us your frank opinion.

GODUNOV (*rising*): How can I,
My foster father, venture to express
Myself in council, when the wisest here
In vain seek a solution. Yet if you
Bid me discourse, then I propose, boyars—

VOICES: Louder! Speak louder, pray! We cannot hear!

GODUNOV: Methinks, boyars—

VOICES: Louder! We cannot hear!

ZAKHARYIN: Boris, why have you taken a seat so low
And distant? Are you not aware of your
Own dignity? We cannot hear! Approach!
(*Takes him by the hand and leads him to the center bench.*)
Here is a seat more fitting to your worth!

GODUNOV (*bowing in all directions*): Boyars and scions of mighty
  ancestors—
And you, my foster father, you, Nikita
Romanovich, instructor whom I love—
Ne'er would I dare to utter here a word,
Had you yourselves not called on me to speak.

SALTYKOV: What is his aim?

NAGOY: The fox dissembles well!

SALTYKOV: See now, he has assumed the foremost place!

NAGOY: 'Twas not for naught he feigned humility!

VOICES: Sh! Quiet! Peace! Let us hear Godunov!

GODUNOV: Mighty boyars, each one of you knows well
What grave misfortunes now have come upon
Our native Russia. Polish Batory
Has taken from us city after city;
Already he has seized Usvyat, Velizh,
And Polotsk: he has crushed Velíkiya-
Lúki; and now our ancient Russian Pskov,
A town most dear to us, he has encircled
With an unnumbered host. Meanwhile the Swede
Has led his troops into Livonia
And seized Ivángorod and Kóporye:
While in the east and in the south the khan
Raises his horde once more: hundreds of thousands
Are threatening Tula and Ryazán. Disease
And famine devastate our land. And now
The Cheremis are raising a revolt!
  Boyars, amid such miseries, when Russia

Is on the brink of ruin, can we think
Of choosing a new tsar? Even if our choice
Should win support from all our council, are
You confident that he would also win
Acceptance from the people, that the land
Would welcome him? What if the populace
Should suddenly revolt? What then, boyars?
Is there such union and accord among us
That we could hope to stand in solid front
Against all foes, of our own house or foreign?
    Great is the strength of custom; usage is
A scourge to men, but may likewise restrain them.
A tsar who has hereditary right,
Whatever be his nature, always has
An easy claim to men's obedience;
Stronger is he even in an hour of stress
Than any newly-chosen unknown man
Could be in days of peace and harmony.
For fifty years Ivan Vasilyevich
Has ruled in Russia. Wrath and clemency
Oft have been mingled in his checkered reign;
But in his subjects deep have sunk the roots
Of limitless obedience, fostered by
Long habit and the terror of his name.
Boyars, for us that name is a strong fortress;
Only by it can we endure. Long since
We ceased to act or think with our own minds;
No longer are we a united whole.
The stern authority that shattered us
Is all that binds us now. If that grim force
Should perish, then all else would fall to ruin!
For us, boyars, there can be only one
Means of salvation: we without delay
Must come before the tsar in full assembly,
Fall prostrate at his feet, and with one voice
Implore him that he reascend the throne
And save our Russia in its hour of peril!
    VOICES: He's right!— Without Ivan Vasilyevich
We're lost!— We must proceed to him at once!
He is our lawful tsar!— When ruled by him
We feel no shame!— Aye, aye, let us straightway
Fall at his feet!— Let all the council join!

SITSKY: Friends and boyars! Have you no fear of God?
Have you forgot the nature of our tsar?
Compared to him the Germans, Poles, and Tatars
Are gentle foes! Famine and pestilence
Can harm us less than that wild beast Ivan!
   SHUYSKY: What words are these! He slanders Tsar Ivan!
   MSTISLAVSKY: Prince Sitsky, are you not perchance insane!
   SITSKY: Not I, but you, ye all are now insane!
Among you can I find a single man
For whom Ivan has not unjustly slain
A brother, father, relative, or friend?
Gazing upon you here, boyars, my heart
Grows sick and faint! I would not strive to rouse
Your fainting spirits, were it not the truth
That Tsar Ivan himself has now declared
His will to abdicate and leave us free.
I know my duty like the rest of you!
I do not urge you to rebel; but he,
He of his own accord consents to cease
From cruelty and slaughter: he declares
His will to take monastic vows and leave
Russia at rest from him—and you forsooth
Will beg him to continue slaughtering!
   GODUNOV: Prince Sitsky, 'tis not fitting that we hear
Such words against our tsar. You spoke in haste—
I trust that we have no informers here!
This I reply to you: We have no choice!
When two ills threaten him, what man is loth
To bear the less? Which is the better lot:
To see our Russian land subdued by foes
And Moscow captured by the Tatar khan,
Our churches ruined and despoiled; or else
To endure with due humility the rule
Of the stern tsar whom God has given us?
Our lives we love, but not so dearly as
Our native land! And furthermore: our tsar,
I grant, has shown himself a cruel and
Relentless ruler. But that time has passed:
Now he is changed—you know it well, my prince—
Now he is kind of heart and merciful.
If he resumes the cares of state, then he
Will be a terror only to our foes,
Not to our Russia, our belovèd land!

Voice: Yes, he is right!— He speaks the simple truth!

Sitsky: Boyar, thy tongue is honied, that I know!
By cunning eloquence you can gild all
That fits your purpose! We all know your aim:
You fear to lose your power if a man
Other than Tsar Ivan assumes the crown!
Boyars, beware! A soft bed doth he spread;
His sleep thereon may well prove hard for us!

Godunov: Honored boyars, I call upon you all
As witnesses that I have not deserved
Reproaches such as these! Ye know full well
That I have never sought for power or rule.
I did but utter what you thought yourselves—
And yet, boyars, perchance I was in error.
Prince Sitsky is an older man than I,
And wiser too: if you agree with him,
Then I am ready to bestow the crown
Upon Zakharyin, or what man you choose.

Voices: No, not Zakharyin: him we will not have.

Godunov: Perhaps Mstislavsky?

Voices: No, we will not have
Mstislavsky! We ourselves are good as he!

Godunov: Then Shuysky, lords?

Voices: Neither shall Shuysky reign!
We will not serve him; we demand Ivan!

Sitsky: Go! Go before him, every one of you!
Go to the slaughter, like a flock of sheep!
No longer will I tarry in your midst! (*Goes out.*)

Voices *and* Cries: He is a rebel! He insults us all!
He thwarts the common will of our state council!

Godunov: Boyars, pray be not roused to sudden wrath
Against a man who did but freely speak
The thought within him! If your wisdom bids
That this our council should attend the tsar,
Then come, let us make haste!

Zakharyin: Were not our land
In direst peril, I should not approve
This measure; but when danger threatens us,
The throne must needs stand firm. Let us at once
Beseech the tsar; there is no other choice!

Mstislavsky: But who shall be our spokesman?

Zakharyin: Thou, boyar!
Who is so fit? Of all the councilors

Thou art the eldest!

MSTISLAVSKY: I dare not accept
The weighty charge! I have this very day
Suffered my fill of the tsar's causeless wrath!

VOICES: Let Shuysky speak!

SHUYSKY: Reluctant too am I!

ZAKHARYIN: Then I consent to speak your will, boyars.
I do not fear his wrath; I fear naught but
The ruin of our land!

GODUNOV: Nay, foster father,
I will not let thee thus expose thyself
To such a risk of banishment and doom!
Let me voice our decision to the tsar—
I care not for myself!

MSTISLAVSKY: Then let us go!
Let Godunov be our interpreter!
Among us all he is most skilled of tongue.

(*All the boyars rise and follow* MSTISLAVSKY *out of the room.*)

SALTYKOV (*as he is leaving, to* GOLITSYN): Sitsky was right! Sly
Godunov aspires
To make himself the first man in the realm!

GOLITSYN: He took the lowest seat, but ended highest!

SALTYKOV: And yet we clamored: "No precedence"!

TRUBETSKOY: Wait!
Soon will that Tatar sit above us all!

(*They go out.*)

SCENE II

The Tsar's Bedchamber

IVAN, *pale and exhausted, clad in a black cassock, is seated in an arm-chair, holding his rosary. Beside him, on a table, is the Cap of Monomakh: * on his other side his imperial robes lie spread out upon a bench.* GRIGORY NAGOY *is offering him a cup.*

NAGOY: My liege! Refuse not, pray, to quaff a drop
Of wine! These many days thou hast tormented
Thy sacred frame! All food thou hast refused.

IVAN: The body needs no food, when grim remorse
Gnaws at the soul. Henceforth my nourishment
Shall be sincere repentance for my sins.

---

* The ancient crown of Russia, once worn, according to the legend, by Vladimir Monomakh (1053-1125).

NAGOY: Most mighty emperor, wilt thou indeed
Desert us thus? What fate will overtake
Thy loved tsaritsa and her son Prince Dmitry,
Thy cherished heir?

IVAN: The Lord will care for them.

NAGOY: But who has wisdom fit to guide the state
Save only thee?

IVAN: My mind is now diseased,
My heart is sick, my hands unfit to hold
The reins of rule. Already for my sins
The Lord hath given victory to the pagans,
And me he hath enjoined to yield my throne
To one more worthy. My transgressions are
More numerous than the sea's uncounted sands:
A murderer am I, a torturer,
An impure lecher, defiler of the Church:
I have exhausted God's long-suffering
And loving kindness by my latest crime!

NAGOY: My liege, thy brooding thoughts have magnified
A sin thou didst not plan. 'Twas not thy will
To slay the prince. By hapless chance thy staff
Inflicted such a wound.

IVAN: No, 'tis not so!
With malice, of mine own free will, I slew
My son and heir! Had I outlived my mind
That I knew not at whom I aimed my blow?
Not so! Maliciously I murdered him!
Prone on the floor he fell, drenched in his blood:
He kissed my hands, and, dying, he forgave
My mortal sin; but I myself can ne'er
Forgive myself a crime so villainous!

(*Mysteriously.*) Last night he came before me in a dream
And beckoned to me with his bloody hand;
He pointed to a cassock, calling me
To seek out with him that most blest retreat
On the White Lake, where lie at rest the bones
Of holy Cyril, wonder-working saint.

Even in former days I often loved
To find in that abode of monks a refuge
From the world's cares; there, far from vanity,
I oft would meditate on heaven's calm,
Forgetting men's unthankfulness, and all
The evil plots of my perfidious foes!

A blessed peace descended on my soul
When in the cell I rested from long standing
And followed with mine eyes the evening clouds,
While no sound reached mine ears save the wind's roar,
The screams of gulls, or the monotonous
Beating of the lake's waves upon the shore.
There quiet reigns! There passions stir men not!
There I will don the cowl, and by my prayers,
Perchance, by fasting all my days, by stern
Humility and penance I may gain
Forgiveness for my shameful life of crime.

   (*After a pause.*) Go, learn why the boyars so tediously
Prolong their council! Will they not soon reach
A just decision and report to me
Their choice of a new tsar, that promptly I
May place on him the crown and robes of power!

   (NAGOY *goes out.*)

   Now all is at an end! Such is the goal
Whereto the pathway of my greatness leads me!
What have I found thereon? Pain and naught else!
From boyhood I have never known repose:
Now on my steed, beneath the darts of foes,
Conquering the heathen hordes; now in the council,
Contending 'gainst mine own rebellious nobles,
Naught have I seen in all my reign, save only
Nights without sleep, and days full of alarms!

   No gentle ruler I! Nay, I confess
That I could never moderate my temper!
Father Sylvester,* my most gentle teacher,
Was wont to warn me: "Caution, my Ivan!
Within thee Satan seeks to make his home;
Yield not to him the empire of thy spirit!"
But I was deaf to all his warnings; I

---

* Priest Sylvester, Alexey Fedorovich Adashev (see page 484), and Prince Andrey Mikhaylovich Kurbsky (see page 474) were trusted counselors of Ivan during the earlier years of his long reign (1533-84). Falling into disfavor, Sylvester in 1560 withdrew from court to a monastery, where he died some years later. In 1560 Adashev also withdrew, to Livonia; the tsar had him placed under guard in Dorpat, where he died in the same year. In 1563 Kurbsky fled to Lithuania, where he became a subject of the king of Poland and fought against his former master; he died in 1583. His correspondence with Ivan (1563-79) is famous in Russian literature.— In his tragedy Tolstoy naturally enough does not hesitate to violate chronology for the sake of dramatic effect. The siege of Pskov by Batory, it may be mentioned, was in 1581, not 1584, the year of the death of Ivan.

Allowed the devil to rule my deathless soul.
No tsar am I; rather a wolf, a cur!
Tortures and torments I have loved. My son
I slew, a crime surpassing even the guilt
Of Cain himself! In mind and soul I am
A man of sin! My heart's iniquities
Cannot be numbered by man's feeble powers!
　　O God! O Christ! Heal me and comfort me!
Forgive me as thou didst forgive the robber!
Cleanse me of all the filth wherewith my soul
Is spotted and defiled, making me worthy
At last to be enrolled among thy saints!
　　(NAGOY *hastily returns.*)
　　NAGOY: My liege! A messenger has just arrived
From Pskov!
　　IVAN:　　　I am thy liege no more.— He must
Give his report to the new-chosen tsar!
　　NAGOY: He says that Shuysky sent him here with news
That will delight thine ears!
　　IVAN:　　　　　　Let him come in!
　　(NAGOY *admits the* MESSENGER.)
　　MESSENGER: Most mighty tsar! Thy voyevoda, Prince
Ivan Petrovich Shuysky sends thee greeting
From all thy faithful garrison of Pskov!
Supported by thy fervent prayers, and by
The intercession of God's holy saints,
And by the power of his holy cross,
We have repulsed our foes. A countless host
Of Poles have fallen. Their king has fled for aid
To Warsaw, leaving to his generals
The prosecution of a hopeless siege!
　　IVAN: Blest be the Lord! I would know more of this.
　　MESSENGER: Five weeks our enemies had pushed their mines
And trenches toward the town; meanwhile bombarding
Our walls with cannon! But our valiant Shuysky
Laid countermines to meet them. Underground
The soldiers met in conflict. Fierce the strife!
Our men exploded kegs of powder, and themselves
Were blown aloft together with the Poles.
Our losses were severe; but, thanks to God,
The Polish mines were all destroyed.
　　IVAN:　　　　　　What next?

MESSENGER: Seeing that underground their toil had failed,
They brought together all their many cannon
Upon a neighboring hill, and ere night came
Opened a breach through our stout walls. Straightway
We brought to it our guns, Panther and Smasher:
So, when the Poles advanced with eager shouts
To enter by the breach, we met them there
With cannon balls, and beat them back.

IVAN: What next?

MESSENGER: At dawn the king commanded an assault
With all his troops. Thereat we rang the bell,
And gathered all our men upon the walls,
Spreading the sacred banners; then we bore
The sacred relics of Prince Vsevolod
Around the ancient ramparts, and awaited
The onset of the Poles. There was a roar
Like thunder in hot summer. On all sides
We met the attack. From walls and battlements,
From towers and turrets we poured down a rain
Of missiles: stones, and logs, and burning flax.
Already they were weakening, when the king
Himself appeared and led his troops in person.
Like torrents swollen in spring, against the walls
Their warriors rushed once more. In vain with halberds
We beat them back. The Lithuanians
Closed round the Svinar tower and climbed like ants.
Upon the battlements we fiercely grappled:
New swarms of foes came fast; we long held firm,
But finally—

IVAN: Well?

MESSENGER: Finally they crushed
Our men and seized the tower!

IVAN: So it is thus
You kept your oath, ye godless perjurers!
What then did Shuysky do?

MESSENGER: Our Prince Ivan,
Seeing that now the tower was filled with foes,
With his own hand snatched at a lighted torch
And cast it in a mine. With a mighty roar
The tower rose skyward, and with stony rain
Bestrewed the Lithuanian host and camp.

IVAN: Hard won! What next?

MESSENGER: No more assaults there were.
The king withdrew from Pskov, charging Zamoyski
To carry on the siege.

IVAN: The Lord be praised!
Above me is God's mighty providence!
Ha, Batory! Thou thought'st to cope with me—
With me, a ruler by the grace of God,
Whilst thine authority was given by
The grace of Polish lords?* Now we shall see
Thee shatter 'gainst the ramparts of old Pskov
Thy butting brow!— What, say you, were the losses
Among the Lithuanians?

MESSENGER: Of slain
There were at least five thousand, and of wounded
Double that number.

IVAN: So then, Polish king,
Have I repaid thee now amply enough
For Pólotsk and Velízh?— How many of them
Have perished since the siege of Pskov began?

MESSENGER: In five assaults full twenty thousand fell,
And on our side but seven.

IVAN: Enough of you
Remain. You can resist five more attacks!

(CHAMBERLAIN *comes in.*)

CHAMBERLAIN: Most mighty tsar!

IVAN: Speak! Is their verdict ready?

CHAMBERLAIN (*handing him a letter*): A soldier, captured by our
    foes, was sent
To bring this message to your gracious hands.

IVAN: Give it to me! (*To* NAGOY.) Read it aloud, Grigory!

(CHAMBERLAIN *goes out.*)

NAGOY (*opens the letter and reads*): "To Tsar Ivan, the ruler of all
    Russia,
From Prince Andrey, the son of Prince Mikhaylo—"

IVAN: What? What?

NAGOY (*looking at the letter*): "—the son of Prince Mikhaylo
    Kurb—"

IVAN: From Kurbsky? Ah! So that most gracious lord
Deigns a response to my kind words of greeting!

(*To* MESSENGER.) Begone! (*To* NAGOY.) Now read it!

NOGOY: But, my sovereign—

---

* The king of Poland did not derive his authority from hereditary right, but
was elected by the gentry of the country.

IVAN: Read!

NAGOY (*reads*): "From Kurbsky, once thine humble servitor,
But now the Prince of Kovel, subject of
The Polish crown: Greeting! Attend my words!"—

IVAN: Well, what comes next?

NAGOY: I dare not read, my liege!

IVAN: Read it, I say!

NAGOY: (*continuing*): "To thine absurd and most
Bombastic letter I have given due heed.
In arrogant presumption, daring boldly
To exalt thyself above the stars of God,
And yet, even as a Pharisee, assuming
An humble mien, thou hast accused me, tsar,
Of treachery most foreign to my soul.
Thy foolish words, O tsar, arouse in me
Naught but a laugh, while thine unjust reproaches—"

IVAN: Well, "thy reproaches"?

NAGOY: "—are like drunken tales
Told by old women o'er a pot of ale!
Shame on thee that thou sendest thy rough-hewn
And most disordered words into this land
Where many men are schooled in the sweet arts
Of rhetoric! To thine unasked confession
It fits me not to pay the slightest heed!
I am no priest, but as a soldier now
Perform the service due mine own liege lord,
The exalted Stefan Batory, Grand Prince
Of Lithuania, and likewise King
Of Poland, a republic of free men.
Already by God's blessing we have seized
From thy dominions three of thy best cities,
Velízh, Usvyát, and Pólotsk, and we hope
That Pskov will soon be also in our grasp.
Where are thy victories of long ago?
Where are the wise and famous captains, who
With mailclad breasts once captured for thy realm
So many strongholds, bringing to thy feet
Kazan and Astrakhan? All thou hast slain,
Hast butchered and hast tortured. Now thine armies,
Bereft of generals worthy to command,
Flee from us like a silly flock of sheep,
Led by no shepherd. Dost thou not perceive,
Ivan, that all thy jesters and buffoons

Will ne'er replace the leaders whom thou hast
So foully put to death? Dost thou not know
That all thy wanton dancing in thy court,
Thy lewdness and thy lechery will never
Bring thee the same reward as valiant combat
Upon the open field? Thy mind, methinks,
Is now forgetful of all warlike deeds!
Thine host thou hast deserted!" . . .

IVAN: Read still more!
NAGOY: "Thine host thou hast deserted, and hast fled;
Within thine house thou hidest like a miser.
An evil conscience surely troubles thee,
Reminding thee of all thine impious deeds.
Repent thy folly now. And may—"

IVAN: Well, what?
What next? "And may!" Read on!

NAGOY: "And may thy brain
Recover from delusion and thy spirit
Once more be contrite.— Herewith I enclose
For thee two letters by the eloquent
Hero of Rome, the famous Cicero,
To Claudius and Marcus, his true friends.
Study his style and benefit thereby!
And finally, may these my humble words,
Be for thyself—"

IVAN: Conclude!
NAGOY: O gracious liege!
IVAN: "May these my humble words—"
NAGOY: "—be for thyself
A chastening and healing scourge! Amen!"

(*At the last words of* NAGOY, IVAN *snatches the letter from him,
gazes at it, and begins to crumple the paper. His face twitches and his
whole frame quivers with rage.*)

IVAN: Sitting in safety there beyond the border,
Thou barkest as a cur behind a fence!
Ah, prince, thou hast not deigned to accept from me
The crown of momentary earthly pain
And thus inherit heaven's lasting bliss!
But wilt thou not consent to visit me
In Moscow and repeat there face to face
The scornful words that thou hast written here? (*Looks around.*)
And none remains behind of the base men
Who sided with him! Not a single brother,

Or kin, howe'er remote—not even a slave!
Not one remains! All I have put to death.
And now I must endure his bitter taunts
In helpless silence! None are left to slay!
   (CHAMBERLAIN *comes in.*)
   CHAMBERLAIN: Great emperor! From council thy boyars
Have come to render thee a verdict!
   IVAN: Ah!
They are most welcome! They have come to say
Who shall replace me! Right glad are they, methinks!
"Away with him!" they cry! "That doting tsar
Has now outlived his usefulness; 'tis time
To cast him on the dustheap like a rag!"
It fills their hearts with merriment, no doubt,
When they imagine how I shall forsake
My palace, with my shoulders bent beneath
A beggar's wallet. Of their grace, perchance,
And in the name of Christ they will allow me
At least a humble garment for my back.
So let us see to whom it is my lot
To yield mine office. Show in the boyars!
   (CHAMBERLAIN *goes out.*)
   In very truth what emperor am I
To them? Beneath this coarse, black monkish garb
Will they perceive my power? Already I
Have taught them that they need no longer tremble
Before their ruler and his crown of state!
What is it Kurbsky writes? That I abandoned
Mine army in its need! That I now have
Become ridiculous! And that I write
An unliked style! That like a drunken crone
I babble idly! Ha! Is that the truth?
So let us see who is their sapient tsar
Who has presumed thus early to succeed me
While I still live!
   (*The boyars come in.*)
                     Mine homage to my lords!
Long have you sat in council, but at last
Have made your solemn verdict, and of course
Have chosen for me a most worthy heir
To whom I need not blush to yield my throne!
Doubtless he is of noble birth, no worse than mine?
In intellect, in warlike spirit, and

In piety he will surpass myself?
Now speak, boyars! To whom in humbleness
Must I now bend my knee? Before whose face
Must I prostrate myself? Is it before
Thyself, Prince Shuysky? Or perchance before
Thee, Prince Mstislavsky? Or, as you direct,
Before the champion of my foes, Boyar Nikita
Romanovich? Reply! I stand attentive.

GODUNOV: Most mighty tsar, obedient to thy will
We have taken counsel! Our unanimous,
Irrevocable verdict we have reached,
And on it we stand firm. Then harken, tsar!
Except thyself, no ruler will we have!
'Tis thou hast been our lord in years gone by;
Thou still must rule o'er us in years to come!
Such is our firm decision. Deal with us
Now as thou wilt! Punish or grant us grace!

   (*Kneels. All the boyars follow his example.*)

   IVAN (*after a long silence*): So you have thought to lay constraint
      on me?
Binding me like a prisoner, do you wish
To keep me on my throne by force?

   BOYARS: Our liege
And tsar! Thou art the ruler given us
By God!. None other do we wish save thee!
Punish or grant us grace!

   IVAN: My mantle is,
No doubt, too heavy for your feeble limbs!
You wish to cast the burden of the state
Again upon myself! So will it be
More comfortable for your souls?

   SHUYSKY: Great tsar!
Desert us not! Have mercy on us now!

   IVAN: God is my witness that I did not think
Or wish once more to place the irksome crown
Upon my weary head! Other designs
Had filled my mind. My soul yearned earnestly
For other blessings! But you have decreed
That this can never be. To a vessel tossed
And battered by the stormy waves of life
You have denied a harbor. Be it so!
I yield to my boyars! Under constraint
Of dire necessity I now resume

This golden crown, becoming once again
The tsar of Holy Russia and your lord!
   (*Puts on the Cap of Monomakh.*)
     BOYARS (*rising*) : Long live our tsar, Ivan Vasilyevich!
     IVAN: Give me my mantle! (*Puts on the imperial robes.*)
                     Now approach, Boris!
Bravely thou spakest. At the risk of death
Thou hast acted for the safety of our state.
Gladly I listen to a bold discourse
Flowing from heart so noble and sincere!
   (*Kisses* GODUNOV *on the head and turns to the boyars.*)
   Thus for the second time, against my wish,
Obedient to my council's verdict, I
Consent still to remain upon my throne.
Now woe to him among you who shall plot
Against my will, or who shall give relief
To any traitor; or who shall presume,
Even in his secret thoughts, to cast reproach
On aught that I have done, forgetful that
There is no judge who can condemn me, since
The powers that be have been ordained by God! (*Looks around.*)
   I see not Sitsky in your company!
     GODUNOV: My mighty liege, pray be not moved to wrath!
Pardon the madman!
     IVAN: What has Sitsky done?
     GODUNOV: Sitsky refused to join us in our prayer.
     IVAN: Refused? Behold the crafty man of guile!
What treachery he plots! When all the council
Had purposed to implore me—every man—
He must refuse! Ah ha! Is he in league
With Kurbsky and the Lithuanians?
And with the Khan of Perekop?— His head
Must fall!
     ZAKHARYIN: Our tsar and liege, permit me now
Upon this joyful day, to say a word
In his behalf!
     IVAN: Too late thou plead'st his cause,
Old kinsman. If thou wouldst show clemency
To traitors, then thou shouldst thyself have sat
Upon the throne—thou hadst a chance to-day! (*To the boyars.*)
   Inform the ambassador from Queen Elizabeth,
My sister, that to-morrow I assign
An hour for converse with him. Now we must

Resort to the cathedral, there to bend
Our humble knees in thankfulness to God! (*Goes out with the boyars.*)

ACT II

SCENE I

A room in IVAN'S *palace*

ZAKHARYIN *and* GODUNOV

GODUNOV: For a full hour has he been closeted
With England's envoy.   Stringently he bade
That no man be admitted to his presence.
  ZAKHARYIN: Boris, have you and I not sadly erred?
No gentle ruler has resumed his throne.
  GODUNOV: What other course had we?
  ZAKHARYIN: Boris, Boris,
May the results of this not prove far worse
Than was our former state!   Perchance you know
What they discuss?
  GODUNOV: Yes, father, though I should
Be happier if I knew it not.   Our tsar
Is eager to divorce his spouse; he woos
Through this ambassador the great queen's niece,
The Lady Mary Hastings.*
  ZAKHARYIN: God forbid!
Dares he desire to marry an eighth time?
Before his crime I knew he meditated
On such a plan.   But now, now when he has
But just renounced the cowl—now such a purpose
Is most unthinkable!   You know for sure?
  GODUNOV: To-day he told me so himself.
  ZAKHARYIN: And what
Was your reply?   Did you not tell the tsar
That thus he would commit a mortal sin?
That at his years, when Russia is beset

---

* The relationship was by no means so close.   Queen Elizabeth was the great-granddaughter of Edward IV.   Lady Mary Hastings (the "Princess Hastinskaya" of the Russian) was the youngest daughter of Francis Hastings, Earl of Huntingdon; on her mother's side she was the great-granddaughter of George, Duke of Clarence, brother of Edward IV.   Queen Elizabeth had neither niece nor nephew. Perhaps, however, Tolstoy uses *plemyanitsa* (niece) in its archaic sense of *kinswoman*.

By grievous ills, he should not think of marriage,
But how to save our land!

GODUNOV: No, father, I
Did not.

ZAKHARYIN: What, no? So then you failed to speak?

GODUNOV: No, father, it was not the time to speak.
The tsar remembered well that yesterday
He wished to lay aside his crown. The thought
That thus he might have been bereft of rule
Has made his soul love power all the more,
As though in it he sought a recompense
For wrongs he had endured. All that we now,
Working together, wish to effect through him
For the salvation of the state, we must
Conceal from him, that our own purposes
May ripen in his mind unconsciously,
And seem not ours but his.

ZAKHARYIN: Well said, Boris!
Always you best have understood his heart.
Do as you like; but at whatever cost,
Restrain him.

GODUNOV: Aye, such is my only thought.
By day and night, dear father, I have pondered
On that alone, how he may be restrained.
But all my plans are fruitless; I myself
Have no access to him!

ZAKHARYIN: So then, Boris,
We erred! His pride will lead us all to ruin,
Unless you can contrive to guide its course.

GODUNOV: Advise me!

ZAKHARYIN: Such advice is not for me
To proffer you, Boris. On you the Lord
Bestowed the potent gift of pliant wisdom.
'Twas not for naught you gained the tsar's affection
And yet remained untainted by his crimes
And secret sins. Cherish your skill and act
According to your lights. And yet beware!
Forget not that you do not serve yourself
Alone, but all our land; that wit and keenness
Are kindred to ambition, and that oft
Paths indirect and winding offer perils
To a man's own soul.

GODUNOV: How happy should I be,
My father, might I always choose the road
That leads directly to the goal. And yet,
How can I? You know well our Tsar Ivan;
You also know my adversaries, how
They seek to slay me or at least remove me.
What can I do? I must unceasingly
Detect their plots and match their cunning wiles
With mine, or else I must renounce forever
The service of our land.

ZAKHARYIN: May God preserve
And keep you! Unto Him you will give answer!
Boris, our Russia's fate is in your hands!

GODUNOV: Ah, if it did but rest within my hands!
I then could steer my course! If Tsar Ivan
Would let me rule the empire but a month,
In that one month I would make evident
To his own eyes what mighty strength lies hid
Within our Russian land! Then I would show
What miracles a ruler's power can work
When it rests not on fear of punishment,
But on his justice and his clemency!
But it is hard, my father, to behold
Such things as these, and helplessly remain
A silent witness of them!

(*The* CHAMBERLAIN *opens the door.*)

CHAMBERLAIN: The tsar comes!

IVAN (*entering with documents in his hands*):
Prince Shuysky writes to us: The royal camp
Is full of hunger, pestilence, sedition.
The Polish king, much wiser now, no doubt,
Has sent his envoy unto us from Warsaw.

ZAKHARYIN: God give long life to Prince Ivan Petrovich,
Thy general!

IVAN: In the beleaguered town
Our soldiers have renewed their sacred oath
To serve us and their God, to die before
They yield.— But now, methinks, the Polish Stefan,
My valued neighbor, must have lost his taste
For taking cities. If with a new army
He falls upon our hungry land, we'll catch
His soldiers with our caps like butterflies.

(*To* ZAKHARYIN.)   Go thou into the square: inform the people
That Polish Batory now begs for peace!

ZAKHARYIN: My liege, what if he sends his messenger
Upon a different errand?

IVAN: So your Grace is pleased,
I see, to give us kind instruction!   So
It was a blunder when the wise boyars
Returned to us the crown, not offering it
To thee!   Begone, old man!   In the great square
Inform the people that King Batory
Begs me for peace!

(ZAKHARYIN *goes out.*)

IVAN (*to* GODUNOV) : I have dispatched the business
With the envoy from Elizabeth.   But he
Proves obstinate and mightily exacting.
The English must, quoth he, have privileges
For trade.   Of such concessions I have now
No time for talk.   Invite him to thy house,
Give him a meal, discuss affairs with him,
And tell me what he says.

GODUNOV: Most mighty tsar,
But yesterday thou saidst that thou wert pleased
To hear bold words, if they did but proceed
From a heart sincere and true.   Once more permit
Me openly to speak my thoughts.   I fear
Lest the presumptuous envoy may assume
That thou too highly prizest this alliance
With the proud English queen, and so may prove
Even more obstinate.   Were it not better
Now to allow him to depart, his work
Still incomplete?   Then if perchance the queen—
As we need not expect—ventures to claim
New privileges for the English traders,
Then thou at any time canst send again,
And signify that thou wilt give them.

IVAN: Ah!
That is to say, Boyar Boris is loth
That Tsar Ivan should enter into kinship
With Queen Elizabeth!   Is that thy drift?
Speak out!   I see thee through and through!

GODUNOV: My liege!
In vain I sought by craft to gain my ends.
From thee no man can hide his secret thoughts.

My guilt is evident, my liege! Now let
My life be forfeit.— Yet attend my words!
Not I, great tsar—all Russia will resent
A marriage such as this. Yes, all the Russians
Love the tsaritsa for her piety;
Still more, because she is the mother of
Thy second heir, thy son Dimitry, who
In course of years will mount thine own high throne.
As for thyself, for thy tsaritsa too,
Thy people daily offer prayers in churches.
What will they say? What will the clergy say,
If thou divorce the mother of Dimitry,
And choose as thy new wife a foreigner,
Of alien faith? Great emperor, that would make
Eight nuptials for thee! Will not then thy folk
Proclaim that all the troubles and defeats
That we have suffered—and the future may
Bring us as many more—have been endured
Because of thine own errors? Mighty liege,
Condemn me now! I fall before thy feet! (*He kneels.*)
I pray thee! For in thee alone rest all
The hopes of Russia! Deign thou not to weaken
The confidence that Russia feels in thee!
Repulse not from thyself for an idle whim
Thy subjects' love!

IVAN: And hast thou done? I see
My heartening words have had too great effect!
In very truth, thy boldness is not small!
Knowing my kindness to thee, thou dost think,
Of course, I keep thee here as counselor
And guide! That all the freemen of our realm
Have delegated thee to praise or blame
My deeds! And that thou canst by subtle words
Direct my will as the wind bends a reed!
It is right laughable how all of you
Would like to play with me the worthy rôle
Of Priest Sylvester! On thy lips the milk
Was scarcely dry when I showed well that priest
And Alexéy that I had ceased to be
A child for them to tutor! Since that time,
Judging by mine own intellect how best
My realm shall prosper, so I have ordered it;
Nor do I grieve my heart, debating what

This man or that may think! Not for a day,
Not for a year do I make firm the props
Of the Russian throne, but for all future time.
And what I see before me, that your eyes,
Blinking like those of moles, can ne'er behold!
I keep thee—be informed!—only for this,
That thou mayst duly carry out my will:
Therein is all thy merit. Rise! This once
I pardon thee. Henceforth intrude thyself
No more as counselor! The envoy now
Thou wilt invite, and bring to me to-morrow
News of his last proposal! (*He withdraws into another chamber.*)
   GODUNOV (*alone*):   He is right!
Naught but his slave am I! And this I might
Well have foreseen! Did I not know him well?
I acted like a woman, like a boy!
I acted like a madman!— Such it is,
That bold, straightforward way by which Zakharyin
Bids me proceed! At my first step it is
Cut off, closed by the tsar's authority
As by a wall! Seeking the empire's good,
Defending the tsaritsa, I likewise
Strove to protect her kinsfolk the Nagoys,
My bitterest foes, who now, this very hour,
Are laying plans how to destroy myself.
Ready I was to save their lives to-day,
If but the tsar would cease from his rash plan
To ruin Russia. Such is the result!
Lightly you counsel younger men, Nikita
Romanovich, to travel the straight road.
No high ambition guides your own short steps.
Calmly, with gentle sadness, you look down
Upon this world! Even as the sun that shines
Upon a wintry day, shedding its light
But not its warmth upon the earth, so you
Decline in purity into your west!
But my soul yearns for action and for strife.
I cannot calm myself so readily—
See discords, plots, capricious arrogance—
And in my virtuous conscience, crowned therewith
As with a halo, be content, forsooth,
Since I myself was pure in deed and word! (*Goes out.*)

SCENE II

SHUYSKY's *house*

SHUYSKY, MSTISLAVSKY, MIKHAYLO NAGOY, *and* GRIGORY NAGOY
are seated at a table, drinking.

SHUYSKY (*pouring wine for them*) : I beg you drink, dear guests!
    Drink to the health
Of Godunov! At council it was he
Whose wisdom won the day! (*The guests drink unwillingly;* MSTI-
    SLAVSKY *does not drink at all.*)
                  What, Prince Ivan
Feodorych? Perchance this present wine
Pleases you not? Shall we not have some stronger?
    MSTISLAVSKY: No, prince, although I thank you. Not the wine—
It is the toast that is not to my liking.
    SHUYSKY: Why so? You will not drink to Godunov?
And you, boyars, you also frowned. Do you
Not love Boris?
    MSTISLAVSKY: An upstart, a base Tatar
Who has attained a place close to the throne!
    BELSKY: And we must lose our posts of influence!
    MIKHAYLO NAGOY: Soon he will be our tyrant!
    GRIGORY NAGOY: No, he is
Already so!
    SHUYSKY: Pardon, boyars! You speak
Of Godunov? It is by force that he
Is placed above us. He himself is loth
To have such dignity! He always pays
Due honor to our rank, and in the council
Is ready to be silent or to agree
With what we say!
    MIKHAYLO NAGOY: Aye, 'tis impossible
To quarrel with that loach! He gives assent;
He makes low bows, the devil, but in the end
He carries all before him!
    SHUYSKY: Well, this time
We owe him deepest gratitude.
    BELSKY: This time
Was not the first, nor will it prove the last.
Sitsky—Lord rest his soul!—spoke the plain truth:
Boris will crush us all!

MIKHAYLO NAGOY: If we do not
Contrive to crush him first!
    GRIGORY NAGOY: Crush him? But how?
    BELSKY: We might spread rumors of him!
    MSTISLAVSKY: Our poor gossip
Will never gain belief. By one slight word
He will destroy us, even as he destroyed
Prince Sitsky!
    MIKHAYLO NAGOY: No, such means will not avail.
We might use others.— Yet Prince Shuysky is
His loyal partisan.
    SHUYSKY: What, I? His friend?
To me Boris is neither kin nor crony!
I only said he was not worth our trouble!
    BELSKY: What, are you blind!
    SHUYSKY: I am not blind, boyars!
But when we need to act, then you yourselves
May change your purposes!
    BELSKY: Nay, do not fear!
    MSTISLAVSKY: We shall maintain our stand most loyally!
    GRIGORY NAGOY: Thereon we all consent to kiss the cross!
    SHUYSKY: Why will you fruitlessly thrust your own necks
Into the noose!
    BELSKY: Prince, pardon me my words!
Blind as a mole, forsooth, you are the first
Whom this false Tatar will contrive to ruin!
    SHUYSKY: Such are your thoughts?
    BELSKY: No thoughts, but **certainty**!
    SHUYSKY: Well, if such be the case, I change my mind!
    BELSKY: Then **you** agree?
    SHUYSKY: Can I alone oppose
Your common purpose? Yes, I will agree.—
But how shall we begin?
    MIKHAYLO NAGOY: This is our course:—
Throughout all Russia pestilence prevails.
The crops have failed. Disorders have occurred;
Across the Moscow river the populace
Has twice revolted. In such times as these
Our people are embittered. They are glad
To find a scapegoat, whosoe'er he be.
We must not let this fair occasion slip,
But whet betimes their wrath against Boris!

GRIGORY NAGOY: The plan has merit! Let the common folk
Free us from him—while our own hands are clean!
MSTISLAVSKY: Yes, clean! But how shall we arouse the mob?
We cannot haunt ourselves the public square!
MIKHAYLO NAGOY: 'Tis plain we need a man who can be trusted!
BELSKY: Or one whom we can always hold in leash
Through fear!
MSTISLAVSKY: Can such a man be found?
SHUYSKY (*opening the door into the next room*): Come in,
Danilych.* (BITYAGOVSKY *comes in.*)
          Here, boyars, is whom we need!
I've talked with him; he will be glad to serve us. (*General astonishment.*)
BELSKY: So you—! Aha, Prince Shuysky, you amaze me!
GRIGORY NAGOY: You have outplotted us, I must confess!
MSTISLAVSKY: And yet he drank the health of Godunov!
(SHUYSKY *laughs.*)
MIKHAYLO NAGOY (*pointing to* BITYAGOVSKY): So this man under-
    takes to do the work?
But who is he? We need to know him well!
SHUYSKY: A noble he, Mikhaylo Bityagovsky.
I pray you all to love and cherish him.
He never will betray us!
BELSKY: Prince, most surely
You have given proof to-day that you can plot.
On you we may rely. Yet still permit me,
Since the affair is perilous—I would
Not anger you nor cast reproach on him—
To ask you what is your security.
SHUYSKY: Boyars, the case is simple. This nobleman
At dice and cards has squandered all his substance.
He is in debt up to his ears; the prison
Now threatens him. Two courses lie before him:
If he serves us, we pay his debts; if he
Proves sly and faithless, then we shall employ
The law against him. Speak, Danilych: Is
The contract plain?
BITYAGOVSKY: Plain as the day, my lord.
SHUYSKY: If thou effect our purposes, we will
Reward thee well.
BITYAGOVSKY: Such are the terms agreed.

---

* The use of the patronymic is a sign of contemptuous familiarity.

SHUYSKY: My words were not in scorn; I merely wished
That the boyars should have more faith in thee.
And now sit down!
   BITYAGOVSKY: I am not loth to stand.
   SHUYSKY: Here, drink a cup!
   BITYAGOVSKY: That I will gladly do.
(*He drinks, bows, and replaces the cup on the table.*)
   BELSKY: So thou canst instigate and rouse the folk
Against Boris?
   BITYAGOVSKY: That I can do.
   MIKHAYLO NAGOY: With whom
Wilt thou begin?
   BITYAGOVSKY: With the rabble of the streets.
   GRIGORY NAGOY: Of what themes wilt thou speak?
   BITYAGOVSKY: Only of hunger.
   BELSKY: What wilt thou say?
   BITYAGOVSKY: Whatever occurs to me.
   MSTISLAVSKY: And wilt thou guarantee success?
   BITYAGOVSKY: I will.
   MIKHAYLO NAGOY: The people's mutiny must be no jest.
At first prepare thy ground. Say that Boris
Has caused the rise in prices! Tell them that
He leads the tsar by the nose! All suffering
Must seem to come from him. Malyuta's * daughter
He took to wife! 'Twas he that urged Ivan
To all his acts of cruelty! And then,
On a convenient day—a holiday,
When Godunov is on his way to church,
Or else returning, stir them up to madness!
It might be well for thee to find a comrade.
   BITYAGOVSKY: I need no comrade.
   BELSKY: Shouts and uproar will
Not serve our turn. When they see Godunov,
They needs must rush at him, tear him to bits!
   BITYAGOVSKY: They will.
   SHUYSKY: You may rely on him, boyars!
Words he likes not; but when it comes to deeds,
He has no match! Not his first test is this.
Meanwhile yourselves must work with the boyars—
Make trial of their thoughts. The greater is

---

* Malyuta Skuratov-Belsky was a favorite *oprichnik* (guardsman: see page 462) of Ivan, and the agent of some of his worst acts of cruelty. He is a prominent character in the Russian popular ballads.

Our party, the more easily we shall
Ruin Boris!

BELSKY: In any case I shall
Send further agents to excite the mob.
I now have one in view, a noble from
Ryazan, Prokofy Kikin.

SHUYSKY: If you can
Be sure of his fidelity, send him
Upon your own behalf. Thus our two agents
In different quarters will arouse the town.
If one man fail, the other may succeed.

MSTISLAVSKY: Your lips dispense sweet honey, Prince Vasily!

MIKHAYLO NAGOY: So now the work goes forward well! Lord, grant
Thy blessing on our acts!

(A SERVANT *comes in.*)

SERVANT: Boyar Boris
Feodorych is here!

(*The* SERVANT *goes out.*)

SHUYSKY (*to himself*): That cursed devil!

(GODUNOV *comes in. The guests rise in confusion.*)

SHUYSKY (*going to meet* GODUNOV *with extended arms*): Boris
    Feodorych! Most welcome guest!
I thank you for the kindness shown to us! (*They embrace.*)
Be seated, sir! Right here, beneath the ikons!*
Do honor to my humble house! What wine
May I now offer to you? Here is sack!
Here Alicant! Here Cyprus! And here Rhine wine!

GODUNOV (*bowing*): I thank you heartily, good Prince Vasily
Ivanovich! Have I perchance disturbed
Your company? Perchance you were engaged
On pressing business with your much-loved guests?

SHUYSKY: On business? No, boyar! We did but waste
Our time in idle chat. Be seated now,
I beg you humbly! Honor me, boyar,
At least by one small cup!

GODUNOV (*drinking*):   To your good health!

MSTISLAVSKY (*going up to* SHUYSKY): Kind host, I must depart
    without delay.
Farewell!

BELSKY: I too have home affairs. Farewell!

THE TWO NAGOYS: We too must be departing, Prince Vasily
Ivanovich.

---

* The seat of honor.

SHUYSKY: What, my dear guests? Why need
You leave so early?

MIKHAYLO NAGOY: I have work at home.

SHUYSKY: Farewell, boyars! I thank you kindly for
The honor you have done me! (*He accompanies his guests to the door
and returns to* GODUNOV.) Well, thank God!
They're gone! I am in very truth most grateful
That you have called! My joy at seeing you
Surpasses all belief! For long years now
We two have worked as one! Your purposes
Are mine as well!

GODUNOV: I thank you, Prince Vasily
Ivanovich! So I have come to seek
Your friendly counsel.

SHUYSKY: Sir, you may command me!

GODUNOV: Prince, as you know, the councilors of state
Cherish no love for me. I am a man
Of recent origin.

SHUYSKY: What matters that?
I stand for you most firmly. Yet 'tis true
That you have foes among us. Such may be
That rogue Mstislavsky—Belsky too—who knows!
They envy you because the tsar has shown
His love for you!

GODUNOV: Our Tsar Ivan has been
Gracious beyond my merits. Yet I tread
A slippery path. They may spread evil rumors!
In Russia men are easily disgraced!

SHUYSKY: But I am not involved! Ready am I
To hazard every peril for your sake.
I hold you dear as any brother!

(*The* SERVANT *comes in.*)

SERVANT (*to* SHUYSKY):   Prince,
The tsar has sent a summons for your Grace.

SHUYSKY (*rising*): For me? And now? Boyar, pray pardon me!
The tsar brooks no delay.

(*The* SERVANT *goes out.*)

GODUNOV: No ceremonies,
Prince!

(SHUYSKY *goes out hastily.* GODUNOV *remains alone with* BITYA-
GOVSKY *and gazes at him fixedly.* BITYAGOVSKY *becomes confused and
turns away from him.*)

GODUNOV: So thou art named Mikhaylo Bityagovsky—
Of noble birth. Is that not true?

BITYAGOVSKY: It is. (*He moves to leave the room.*)

GODUNOV: Stir not a step! Stand thou and hear my words!
At cards thou hast lost all. Thy creditors
Are now about to imprison thee. Thy state
Is bad, but it may prove still worse. A letter
Thou hast written to the Lithuanian camp,
Offering thy services to Pan Zamoyski.

BITYAGOVSKY: No, that is false! My foes have slandered me!

GODUNOV: Thy letter I have intercepted.— Here
It is, most clearly written! (*He takes the letter from his pocket.*
BITYAGOVSKY bends down and thrusts his hand into his boot.)
Thou wouldst draw
Thy knife? Thou needst not waste thy strength! Thy paper
Is far away, securely locked. This is
Merely a copy. Harken, friend! With thee
But yesterday Prince Shuysky made a bargain
To rouse the common folk against myself.
To-day, with Belsky, with the two Nagoys,
And with Mstislavsky, thou and he discussed
The matter farther. If I raise my hand
The ravens soon will pluck thy carrion!

BITYAGOVSKY: Boyar . . . I . . . I . . . did not intend—

GODUNOV: Enough!
Now thou must make pretenses that thou still
Art serving Shuysky. Go! Go haunt the squares!
The markets! Spread abroad the rumor that
Shuysky and Belsky plot to slay the tsar
With poison; that they plan likewise to kill
Prince Fedor and Prince Dmitry; that except
For Godunov they would before this day
Have wiped out all the imperial family;
That Godunov alone protects the tsar
And guards the empire in its hour of need.
Is all this plain?

BITYAGOVSKY: It is.

GODUNOV: Then come to-day
When darkness falls, unto the postern door
Of mine own house. From there my steward will
Conduct thee farther. Every evening thou
Must visit me. All the commands of Shuysky,
Of Belsky and the rest, thou wilt report.

And this remember: Wheresoe'er thou be,
I watch thy steps. Of flight thou canst not dream!
Know this: 'Twixt Shuysky and myself there is
A great distinction. Shuysky threatens thee
With prison, I with such a loathsome death
As even my late father-in-law Malyuta
Skuratov-Belsky could not have devised!
    (*He goes out.* BITYAGOVSKY *remains, stupefied.*)

ACT III

SCENE I

The apartment of TSARITSA MARYA FEDOROVNA

TSARITSA *and* NURSE *of* TSAREVICH DMITRY

TSARITSA: Tell me, good nurse, is Dmitry now in bed?
Has the tsarevich, mine own darling, gone
To sleep?
    NURSE: Aye, dear tsaritsa, that he has!
It warmed my old heart just to look at him.
He lies so peacefully, his eyes shut tight,
His little hands fast closed. My precious had
Grown weary with his play. A lively boy,
And quite unlike his older brother, Prince
Fedor Ivanovich! Fedor is calm
And crushed, not like a prince; quite different
From what his brother was—Lord rest his soul!
Ivan Ivanovich was nigh as rough
As his own daddy. Oh! oh! oh! To think
Of his sad fate! A horrid crime! Even now
I hardly can believe it's true!
    TSARITSA: Good nurse,
We will not speak of that. But has the tsar
Announced his coming? Has he deigned to ask
Whether my prince be well?
    NURSE: No, mother, he
Has not.
    TSARITSA: In former times he would each day
Make personal inquiries!
    NURSE: No, dear mother,
No messenger has come. But not long since,

While we were walking, Godunov approached.
He took Prince Dmitry in his arms and kissed him;
He fondled and admired him.

TSARITSA: Thou didst let
That man caress my son?* No one must dare
Do such a thing! Dost hear, good nurse?

NURSE: Aye, mother,
Boyar Boris said likewise. "Now take heed,"
He told me; "watch thy young tsarevich. Thou
Wilt answer for his every hair to God
And to our native land!"

TSARITSA: Listen, good nurse!
Such chatter is not seemly. In the future
Let no man speak with our belovèd child!

NURSE: But why so, mother? A few days ago
Boyar Zakharyin came to visit us.—
May I not speak a word even with him?

TSARITSA: With him thou mayst indeed! Him do I trust.
He is a father to me!

(A SERVING MAID comes in.)

MAID: Great tsaritsa,
Will you receive a visit from Nikita
Romanovich, Boyar Zakharyin-Yuryev?

TSARITSA: So he is here? Go bring him speedily!

(ZAKHARYIN comes in.)

ZAKHARYIN: Tsaritsa Marya Fedorovna, greetings!
How fares your health?

TSARITSA (going to meet him): Greetings to you, Nikita
Romanovich, my dearest friend! Now God
Has sent you here! I need your sage advice!
Nurse, leave us here alone! Go, watch your prince!

(The NURSE goes out.)

Much do I need to speak with you, Nikita
Romanovich! Sit down here, near to me.
I cannot tell the cause of my affliction,
But every day my aching heart forebodes

---

* The premonitions of the tsaritsa concerning Godunov were well founded.
In 1591, during the reign of Tsar Fedor Ivanovich, the Tsarevich Dmitry (born
in 1582) was found in the inner yard of the palace at Uglich, with a mortal
wound in his throat. An investigating commission, headed by Prince Vasily
Ivanovich Shuysky, reported that he had been playing with a knife and had
wounded himself during an attack of epilepsy. But his mother and many others
believed that he had been murdered by Bityagovsky, as the agent of Godunov,
who became tsar in 1598 on the death of the childless Fedor Ivanovich. The
opinion of modern historians on the question is divided.

Some woe to come! Tell me, have you heard naught?
What has occurred? What purposes the tsar?

ZAKHARYIN: Mother and empress, I have come to warn you!
Yet I myself am ignorant how best
To deal with him. Our woes are past belief!
Like a wild charger that has suddenly
Taken the bit in its teeth, or like a maddened
Aurochs that carries all before it in
Its rush, so he will now brook no restraint.
Like a spring torrent now his arrogance
Has overflowed its banks and sweeps away
All bounds!

TSARITSA: But tell me! What can be his plan?

ZAKHARYIN: God be his judge!

TSARITSA: Here in the palace they
Whisper of something awful. With the envoy
From Queen Elizabeth he long conversed
In secret. . . . I have guessed—I know that he
Is plotting marriage with a foreigner.
He is preparing to abandon me
And my son Dmitry!

ZAKHARYIN: Be prepared for all,
My child!

TSARITSA: My heart had grievous cause to ache!

ZAKHARYIN: This very morn he purposes, tsaritsa,
To call upon you. Make no faintest sign
That I have talked with you. I shall be here.
Listen to him with due humility;
Whate'er he say, make no retort: be dumb!
One word, one sigh, one movement on your part
Will cause your ruin! Let the storm pass by.
By your humility he still may be
Placated. Otherwise on mine own head
I will receive this blow and tell him frankly
That he acts wickedly!

TSARITSA: Boyar Nikita,
Save me! I fear not for myself! I toil
Not for myself—that you know well! When Tsar
Ivan Vasilyich married me, I felt
No joy in my high rank. Three years ago,
Had he divorced me, I should have thanked God.
But now, boyar, I am alone no longer!
I have become a mother! And if he

Should take another wife—ah, then my child—
I dread to think of it—my little son,
My Dmitry—oh, boyar!—I do not know
What I am saying, what I fear, but dimly
I sense a peril for my darling Dmitry!
Pray work upon the tsar! Rebuke him! You
He honors! Let him but discuss his plan
With you!

ZAKHARYIN: Tsaritsa, dear and much-loved child,
Whom does he honor! It is true that I
Have never soiled my soul to do him pleasure,
But how I have remained alive I know not!
To but one counselor in all this world
At times he harkens—may the good Lord grant
Long life to Godunov! None but Boris
Can still put some restraint upon his will!

TSARITSA: Nay, my belovèd sire, trust not Boris!
No, he is not the man! His gentle mien,
His air of constant dignity, his gaze
That never alters with emotion, his
Calm and unchanging voice always inspires me
With a well-grounded fear! I cannot bear
To see that man caress my child!

ZAKHARYIN: What? what?
Tsaritsa, what can such words mean? Why should
You fear Boris?

(*The* MAID *runs in, out of breath.*)

MAID: Our Tsar Ivan is coming!
He will be here at once!

TSARITSA (*terrified*):   Oh, my dear sire!
I am afraid! I cannot bear—!

ZAKHARYIN: Compose yourself
This moment! He must not observe your grief
And agitation! Wipe away your tears!

TSARITSA: Ah, my heart sinks!

ZAKHARYIN: Then leave the room. Attire
Yourself, while I receive him!

(*The* TSARITSA *goes out.* IVAN *comes in, attended by* GODUNOV.)

IVAN (*to* ZAKHARYIN):   Why shouldst thou
Be here?

ZAKHARYIN: I wait for the tsaritsa, sire.

IVAN: And what hast thou to do with the tsaritsa?

ZAKHARYIN: I did but come to ask about her health.

IVAN: Where is she now?

ZAKHARYIN: Hearing thy voice, she went
To robe her ere she met thy Majesty.

IVAN: She might have stayed. No robes will make her fairer.
(*Seating himself, to* GODUNOV.) Continue! So thou tell'st me that
    thou hast
Talked with the envoys?

GODUNOV: Aye, with both, my liege.

IVAN: What then?

GODUNOV: The English envoy, Bowes, repeats
That Queen Elizabeth agrees to give
Her niece, the Lady Mary Hastings, as
Thy wedded wife, but adds that he has no
Authority to sign the treaty till
Thou publicly divorce thy present spouse.
He further stipulates that thou forbid
All trade in Russia to all foreigners
Except the English. On such terms, quoth he,
His queen will proffer friendship and alliance,
And also urge the German Emperor
To move his armies into Poland.

IVAN: I
Must thank my sister, Queen Elizabeth,
That she scorns not our friendship, and consents
To marriage with our humble line. But now
We can dispense with favors from her hand
And need not ask the Emperor for aid.
Soon we ourselves will lead our troops beyond
Our Russian borders.— And what didst thou learn
From the Polish envoy? Say, what lands will Stefan,
My warlike neighbor, offer me for peace?

GODUNOV: Over the wine, great emperor, I sat
With him till dawn arose. Haráburda,
Though not a Pole by birth, loves mightily
To drink and talk. Yet could I not discover
The terms wherewith he came. To thee alone
He will disclose them.

IVAN: So it is too soon
For us to boast!

GODUNOV: This morning from the king
A courier arrived posthaste. Yet I
Endeavored vainly in his eyes to read
What news he bore—no single feature moved.

Drinking a cup, the weary messenger
Dropped on the floor asleep.

IVAN: I wot that he
Had slept not all his road. His errand was
Such as brooked no delay!

GODUNOV: If only he—

IVAN: What? what?

GODUNOV: If only he report no news
That is unwelcome!

IVAN: I have had no news
That is unwelcome. What I know not, is not!

GODUNOV: Be cautious, sire!

IVAN: Wretched Boris, dost thou
Again intrude advice? I tell thee that
My neighbor Stefan is afraid, that he
Has sent instructions to Haráburda
To offer new concessions.— Marya, hey!
(*Pounding on the floor with his staff.*)
Wilt thou not finish prinking?

(*The* TSARITSA *enters in her imperial robes; and, after bowing to*
IVAN, *stands motionless before him, without speaking.*)

IVAN (*looking at her fixedly*): Why are now
Thine eyes so tearful? (*The* TSARITSA *remains silent, lowering her eyes.*)
                         Dost thou hear? What ails thee?

TSARITSA: My lord, pray pardon me! . . . I—

IVAN: Well?

TSARITSA: I dreamed
Of evil things.

IVAN: Of what?

TSARITSA: I dreamed, my lord . . .
I dreamed that I was separated from thee.

IVAN: That dream is true. I like thee not. I have come
To tell thee that henceforth thou art no wife
To me.

TSARITSA: And so is this the truth? The truth?
Wilt thou abandon Dmitry and myself?
My Dmitry? So thou wilt—

IVAN: Be still! I hate
Womanish tears and cries.

TSARITSA: No, my good lord,
I weep not! No!— Thou seest, I weep not.
But tell me why thou wouldst divorce me! What

Canst thou allege against me to the priests?
What fault canst thou impute to me?

IVAN: What's this?
Dost thou presume to question me? And who
Art thou? The daughter of what potentate?
To whom am I responsible for thee?
Art thou more fair and beautiful than others,
That I should cherish thee as something precious?
Have I no power in mine own house? Art thou
By thine own right tsaritsa?

TSARITSA: Pardon me,
My lord! Forgive me! I murmur not, nor pray
For grace! For all things I am ready.— But
My poor son Dmitry—how has he been guilty?

IVAN: Waste no anxiety on him! My son
Shall have as appanage the town of Uglich.
No sins of thine I need discover! I
Will have thee made a nun. Such a divorce
Suffices. And my priests, thank God, I have
Not taught to meddle in my private business,
Nor to require that I explain my actions!

ZAKHARYIN: My tsar and sovereign! Let me say a word!

IVAN: Old man, I see thine aim! None of my acts,
Whate'er they be, are ever to thy taste!
I know you all too well!

ZAKHARYIN: Great emperor!—

IVAN: I know you all! You fain would tie my hands
Once more, as they were tied of old by Priest
Sylvester and by Alexéy! Thou wast
Their friend! Aye, when I outlawed them, what woes
Thou prophesiedst would fall upon my head!
Hearing thee prate, a man would then have thought
The state was being ruined! But what happened?
Those times were twenty years ago!— Where now
Is thy Sylvester? Where is now Adashev?
And we meanwhile, thanks to God's blessing, have
In no way lessened our wide empire's confines!
Without instruction from our subjects we
Have still contrived to rule by our own wit;
Nor do we now, old man, ask guidance from
Thy wisdom!

ZAKHARYIN: Emperor and liege! What we
With sword have won, may be reft from us by

The sword. All-powerful is the will of God,
My liege! But God can bless good deeds alone;
While thou, great emperor, hast now designed
An evil deed! Blameless is thy tsaritsa,
Pure as the day! Sinful is thy desire
To cast her off and marry once again!
Rather than seek alliance with the English
Thou shouldst regard thy Russia! What a state
Is hers! Thou, sire—I must speak openly—
In thy young days wast terrified by faction,
And so throughout thy life hast never ceased
To dread revolts that had no real being.
Hence thou hast ever crushed our tortured land,
Destroying all its elements of strength.
Trampling upon all men of intellect,
Thou hast transformed thy subjects into brutes
Who lack the power of speech; and now thyself,
Like to an oak upon the open field,
Standest alone, and hast no arm whereon
To lean. And if—which God forbid!—thy fortune
Desert thee now, facing calamity
Thou wilt be poor and naked. Near at hand
Is now misfortune, sire! Exult thou not
In triumph over Batory! Our Russia
Must cope with other ills! The Tatar horde,
The Swedes are threatening us outside; within
Are famine, rank injustice, gross disorder!
Such woes will not be cured by an alliance
With England! Old am I, great emperor,
And near to death. Idly to thwart thy will
Would benefit me not. And thou thyself,
My liege, art now no longer young. 'Tis wrong
And sinful for thee now once more to think
Of a new marriage. Thou shouldst thank thy God
For this thy good tsaritsa, not seek out
Another wife!
    IVAN: Nikita, I have let
Thee finish thine oration! Nearer art
Thou to the grave than thou dost fancy. I
Am weary of indulgence for thine age.
Most easily could I reply at length
To such weak babble. But I only say:
Such is my will! Enough! Not one word more!—

'Tis time that I receive the envoy from
The Polish king. Follow me now! (*To the* TSARITSA.)   And thou
Prepare thyself for entrance to a convent!
(*Goes out, followed by* ZAKHARYIN *and* GODUNOV.)

SCENE II

The throne room

*All the members of the court enter in rich array and take their places
along the walls. At the doors and around the throne stand guards with
axes on their shoulders. Trumpets and bells announce the coming of*
IVAN. *He comes in from the interior rooms, attended by* ZAKHARYIN.

IVAN (*to* ZAKHARYIN) : Admit the envoy! He need have no honors.
No longer will I humor Batory.

(ZAKHARYIN *goes out.* IVAN *takes his seat on the throne.* HARABURDA
*comes in through the state door and, with a low bow, stops in front
of* IVAN.)

IVAN (*measuring* HARABURDA *with his eyes*) : Well I remember, Pan
Haraburda,
How once in former years thou didst present
Thyself before my throne. Zygmunt your king
Had died. The Sejm * had sent thee here on urgent
Affairs of state.

HARABURDA : 'Tis true, great emperor.

IVAN : The Polish lords, if I remember well,
Had offered me the crown?

HARABURDA :   'Tis true.

IVAN :   I then
Thought it unfitting that I should become
The king of Poland and yet not secure
Hereditary power to my descendants.
But such conditions you refused to accept.

HARABURDA : Great tsar, the ancient rights and privileges
Of our republic could not be infringed!
Our law requires that every Polish king
Be chosen by the Sejm.†

IVAN :   A noble law!
A worthy ruler did it give you in
Prince Henry of Valois!

---

* The Polish parliament.

† Tolstoy's account of Polish constitutional law, and of events in Poland,
is far from accurate.

HARABURDA: To hell with him!
He was a king beneath contempt! When he
Fled home to France, we washed our hands of him
And chose another.

IVAN: Aye, chose Batory,
Who once paid yearly tribute to the Sultan,
As Prince of Transylvania. So what now
Does he desire? What are the terms thou bringest?

HARABURDA: My great and most illustrious lord, the King
Of Poland, Prince of Transylvania, and
Grand Duke of Lithuania—

IVAN: Stay, is not
Thy church the Orthodox? I have been told
That thou hast come to mass in our cathedral.

HARABURDA: True, emperor.

IVAN: Why then dost thou term lord
A base schismatic of the Latin faith?

HARABURDA: Because, great tsar, he has confirmed for us
All our Ukrainian liberties. He honors
Our Holy Church and has permitted us
To expel the accursed Romish priests.

IVAN: For him
All faiths are equal, if they tell me truly;
Even to the Mohammedans he pays
Respect.—But tell me, what is his petition?
What now does neighbor Stefan deign to ask
Of me?

HARABURDA: He asks that for all future times
Thou, tsar, shouldst cease to call him merely neighbor,
But shouldst confer on him both orally
And in thy written messages, such titles,
Such honors and distinctions as befit
His august majesty!

IVAN: How the man jests!
Now? At the very hour when he has fled
Homeward from Pskov? A fine proposal! Next?

HARABURDA: Next, he demands from thee that thou withdraw
Thine armies from Livonia at once,
And yield forever to the Polish crown
Smolénsk and Pólotsk, Novgorod and Pskov. (*Murmurs in the as-
sembly.*)
On such terms he will graciously consent
To make peace with thee.

IVAN: Envoy, hast thou drunk
Too many cups of wine? How dar'st thou flaunt
Thyself before me in such drunken wise? (*To the* CHAMBERLAINS.)
Which of you ventured to admit a sot
Into my palace?

HARABURDA: If thy Majesty,
Great tsar, consent not to accept such terms,
King Stefan then would have me say to thee:
"Rather than shed for naught our people's blood,
Let us bestride our steeds and, hand to hand,
Contend with sabers as befits true knights,
Till one of us fall dead."— Thereon the king
Sends thee his gauntlet. (*He flings a steel gauntlet on the floor in front of* IVAN.)

IVAN: Which of you is mad—
Thou or thy king? What means that gauntlet? Shall
I not slap thee across the face with it?
Hast thou forgot, thou dog, that here before thee
Is no elected king? Dost thou presume
To challenge God's anointed to the field?
I will give thee a field! I'll have thee sewn
In a bear's hide and chased across the fields
By dogs!

HARABURDA: Nay, that is quite impossible,
Great tsar!

IVAN: What, does he not presume to jest
With me! Boyars, do I seem ludicrous?

HARABURDA: Nay, an ambassador may not be sewn
In a bear's hide!

IVAN: Hence from my eyes! With whips
Drive him away! Drive him at once with whips
Back to the king! Leave thou my palace! Hence,
Thou dog! Hence!

(*He snatches an ax from one of the guards and throws it at* HARABURDA.)

HARABURDA (*warding off the blow*): Hasty art thou, tsar! I see
Thou hast not yet heard tidings that King Stefan
With a new army has returned from Warsaw!
That on the border he has crushed thy soldiers
Into the dust! Thou hast not heard, I see,
That Swedish troops have taken Narva and
Prepare to join the king in a campaign
Against old Novgorod! Worthless are all

Thy voyevodas if they have not sent
Messengers hither with such weighty news!

IVAN (*rising from his throne*) : Thou liest, villain!

HARABURDA :   Nay, I swear to God
'Tis true! Why should I lie? Nay, lying is
A sin. So if, great tsar, thou dost refuse
An honorable combat with the king,
Then the illustrious king may come himself
To Moscow! Now farewell! (*He goes out. General consternation.*)

GODUNOV (*running in*) :   Great emperor,
What hast thou done to-day! Hast thou insulted
King Stefan's envoy?

IVAN :   Like a cur he lied!

GODUNOV: Nay, good my liege! His every word was true!
Couriers have just arrived from our own army—
I have seen and talked with them. The Swedes are now
In Narva and our troops are crushed!

IVAN :   'Tis false!
The couriers lie! Hang them! Hang all who say
That I am beaten! 'Tis impossible
That *my* brave armies should have been defeated!
Tidings of *my* success must soon arrive!
Go bid the priests in every church prepare
Thanksgiving services for victory! (*He falls back exhausted upon
    the throne.*)

ACT IV

SCENE I

A square in the tradesmen's quarter, beyond the Moscow river

*The square is crowded with carts. On one side are the flour shops.
The Kremlin can be seen across the river. Evening is coming on. An
excited throng of people is gathered in front of one of the shops.*

SHOPKEEPER: Begone! Why do you shove? I have already
Told you my price. Now it is seven kopeks
A bushel!

ONE OF THE CROWD: Help us in our misery!
Take off one kopek!

ANOTHER :   'Tis four days since we ate!

A THIRD : Remember God and fear him!

A FOURTH :   Mercy, friend!

Give me some credit! I will pay at Easter—
I swear by Christ!

SHOPKEEPER: Be off with you! At Easter!
Can I give credit for my master's goods?
Begone, I tell you! (*He attacks them.*)

THE FIRST: What, you bloodsucker!
Must we drop dead with hunger!

THE SECOND: Better take
A knife and cut our throats!

THE THIRD: Thief! Murderer!

THE FOURTH: You dirty Jewish dog! Will you yourself
Eat your supplies? Yourself?

SHOPKEEPER: Help ho! Police!
They break into my shop!

(*Two* PATROLMEN *come up.*)

FIRST PATROLMAN: What means this noise?
Where is the ruffian?

SHOPKEEPER: Help! They start to riot!
They break the door!

ONE OF THE CROWD: Aid us, kind officers!

A SECOND: Bid them abate the price, kind officers!

A THIRD: Do not permit us all to starve!

SHOPKEEPER: Those men
Were on the point of robbing me!

THE FIRST: He lies!
He uses violence himself! Almost
He maimed me!

FIRST PATROLMAN (*to the* SHOPKEEPER): Dare you thus assault and
    maim
The people? Ah!

SECOND PATROLMAN: Arrest him! Take him off
To jail!

SHOPKEEPER: Kind officers, why should I go
To jail? I merely would not let them take
My master's goods! (*Puts money in their hands.*)

FIRST PATROLMAN: If that's the case, so be it!

SECOND PATROLMAN: Why did you not tell us before?

FIRST PATROLMAN (*to the crowd*):   Away!
Away, you robbers! I will show you! Hence!

SECOND PATROLMAN: Take them to jail! Let each of them be
    questioned!

(*The crowd withdraws.*)
That's right! (*The two* PATROLMEN *pass on.*)

SHOPKEEPER (*gazing after them*): The Judases! Aha! They stroll
The market, seeking further men to plunder!

ONE OF THE CROWD: It served you right!

A SECOND: Plague take you and
    your stores!

A THIRD: We die of famine, while that greedy rat
Sits in his bin and licks his chops!

(*The* SHOPKEEPER *retires.*)

A FOURTH: Great profit
Have the police from this!

THE FIRST: Yet they are set
To watch and to keep order in the city!

THE FOURTH: Fine order this! Would that the tsar knew all!

THE FIRST: For bribes the tsar oft punished them of old!
I have myself seen how nine grafters dangled
Upon one gallows; on the neck of each
Was tied the filthy coin that he'd accepted!

THE SECOND: Aye, aye, the tsar would not allow his folk
To suffer wrong. Often he would come forth
Upon the palace steps; from each man's hands
He there would deign to accept humble petitions,
And to pass judgment. Short his trial was:
Though the offender were a voyevoda
Or prince, if proof were manifest, he lost
His head!

(KIKIN *comes up, disguised as a pilgrim. He is clad in a cassock
and carries a staff and a rosary.*)

KIKIN: Aye, so it was of old, my son!
Now all is changed! Now, for our sins, the devil
Has darkened the tsar's eyes. Now not the tsar
But Godunov rules all; the tsar regards
All matters with the eyes of Godunov!

(*The people throng about* KIKIN.)

You heard the shopman's words? The flour, quoth he,
Belonged to his master, not to him! But who
May be that master? Godunov again!
Who raises prices? Once more Godunov!
He well may say, seven kopeks for a bushel
Of common rye! Were it not for Boris,
One kopek would suffice!

(*Murmur among the crowd.*)

                                Ah, brothers, we
Have angered God! Our tortures are deserved!

We gaze on crimes with folded hands; meanwhile
That heretic misleads and tricks the tsar
At every step!
  (*The murmur increases.*)
                    The Lord hath righteously
Sent us a sign, that bloody long-tailed star!
I wot that you have seen it!
  ONE OF THE CROWD: That we have!
  A SECOND: Each night it rises there, above that tower.
  A THIRD: Again it will appear straightway, when once
The sky grows dark.
  KIKIN: The Lord makes manifest
His mighty wrath. That is a fiery sword
Upraised to punish us, since we have let
The tsar and all our land be wronged by this
Foul heretic.
  THE FIRST: How do you know such things?
  KIKIN: My son, I wander through the holy places.
I have seen Sólovki and visited
Mount Athos; I have seen Jerusalem
And heard all that men say. Upon the seas
I have made many a voyage, and have trod
The soil of many lands. These eyes have seen
The whale, the fair bird Evstrafil,
The Alatyr, that white and burning stone!
And now I come from ancient Kiev. There
Occurred a mighty marvel: from the cross
Of St. Sophia a great voice was heard
That prophesied the ruin of our nation
Since we still suffer Godunov to live!
  THE FIRST: Brothers, you hear the holy pilgrim's words!
  KIKIN: The voice proclaimed: Arise, ye Christian men,
And gird your loins 'gainst Godunov; from him
Come all calamities to Russia!
  THE SECOND: Harken!
Take notice! Godunov has caused our woes!
  KIKIN: Aye, my son, aye! He is the cause of all!
He hoards the grain, he sends the pestilence;
'Tis he who called the Poles to war on us;
He boasted that he would arouse the khan
To ravage Moscow!
  THE THIRD: Hey, my friends, may not
All this be true? If Godunov be really

To blame for all our ills, then we must kill him!

A FOURTH: But is it true?

KIKIN: The solemn truth! 'Tis sinful
To doubt the voice of God, my son!

A FIFTH: Did you,
My holy father, hear the voice yourself?

KIKIN: Myself! Just when the throng was pouring forth
From mass at dawn, the cross of St. Sophia
Glowed with a heavenly light, and from it pealed
That voice. Not I alone, but all the folk
Of Kiev heard it, and in terror fell
Face down upon the earth!

THE THIRD: Brothers, if all
The men of Kiev heard that voice, it must
Be true!

VOICES IN THE CROWD: Of course it is!— So Godunov
Betrays us!— Yes, he is a traitor and
A wizard!— He has clearly brought on us
The wrath of God!— He is an Antichrist!

ONE OF THE CROWD: Fie, what is this that you are saying, brothers!
Enough! Most sinfully you slander him!

A SECOND: It is a sin indeed! Of Godunov,
My brothers, we have ever heard good things!

CRIES AMONG THE CROWD: Ravens!— Why listen to their croaking?
        They
Support that wizard!— Have they good stout ribs?—
Beat all who venture to defend that thief!—
He hoards our grain!— He is an Antichrist!—
He is the cause of our calamities!—
We now must slay him!— Why should we delay!

(*The voice of* BITYAGOVSKY *is heard, singing a ribald song.*)

BITYAGOVSKY (*off stage, singing*):

> O drunken comrade, do not tarry
> Come, tell us what 'neath your coat you carry!

THE FIRST: Who is that yelling? Does he mock at us,
Singing an alehouse catch at such a time?

BITYAGOVSKY (*makes his appearance, his hat on one side, his caftan
thrown open. He sings*):

> The taverns I haunt both far and wide!
> A gusli * 'neath my coat I hide!

---

* A stringed instrument.

KIKIN (*to* BITYAGOVSKY): Sinful it is in these sad times, my son,
When the Lord's wrath at us is manifest,
When he shows portents in the sky, and sends
Upon the earth famine and grief—most sinful
It is that we serve worldly vanity
And comfort with our idle words and songs
The devil in hell.

BITYAGOVSKY: Well said, my wise old comrade!
Only I must regret that your advice
Is most untimely! When should we be glad
If not at present? Friends, have you not heard
What mercies the good Lord has shown to us?

VOICES IN THE CROWD: What mercies!— Tell us!— Of what sort?

BITYAGOVSKY: Attend
My words, good comrades! Those two traitorous
And base boyars, Belsky and Prince Vasily
Shuysky—may God send punishment on them!—
Plotted—now may they boil in pitch beyond
The grave!—foully designed to slay the tsar
With poison!

VOICES IN THE CROWD: Hark!— Fellows, do you hear that!
(KIKIN *makes signs to* BITYAGOVSKY.)

BITYAGOVSKY (*paying no attention to him*):
The Lord would not allow their sinful plans
To prosper! Godunov divined their purpose
And threw before a dog the pasty that
Those criminals had baked for the tsar's table.
Eating the meat, the dog at once fell dead!

VOICES IN THE CROWD: The villains!— Ah, the cursed men! But
    who?—
Who, did you say?— Who saved the tsar? Who cast
The pasty to the cur?

BITYAGOVSKY: All men know who!
Boyar Boris, wise Godunov! Who else?
Both day and night he watches o'er the tsar!
Except for him Shuysky and Belsky would
Long since have blotted out the imperial line!

ONE OF THE CROWD (*to* KIKIN): Did you not say that Godunov
    had proved
A traitor!

KIKIN: Yes, he is an arrant traitor!
Does God for naught send prodigies and famine

On his account? (*Aside to* Bityagovsky.) Have you gone mad,
    or are
You drunk?
    A Second (*to* Kikin) : How can he be a traitor, if
He saved the tsar from death?
    A Third (*to* Bityagovsky) : Brother, are you
Quite sure of that? In Kiev this good pilgrim
Heard how the voice of God spoke from the cross,
Accusing Godunov!
    Bityagovsky: A holy pilgrim?
What pilgrim? This old fellow? Ha, ha, ha!
A worthy pilgrim he! He is Prokofy
Kikin, a nobleman who came here from
Ryazán! With him I often have caroused
In the pothouses. From Ryazán he never
Strayed farther than to Moscow! (*Slaps* Kikin *on the shoulder.*)
    Hey, Prokofy,
Whom now are you deceiving? Why have you
Dressed in a beggar's tatters?
    Kikin (*aside to* Bityagovsky) : Are you daft?
    Bityagovsky (*aside to* Kikin) : What man do you support?
    Kikin (*aside to* Bityagovsky) :   What man?
    Why, Belsky!
Belsky it was who promised us rewards!
    Bityagovsky (*contemptuously*) : You should have risen earlier!
    Kikin: Ha, you Judas!
I will tell Belsky!
    Bityagovsky: Not a word! Hey, lads!
Come, bind him! Belsky and Prince Shuysky have
Sent him to us!
    Kikin: No, that's a lie! Bind *him!*
By Godunov was he sent here!
    Voices in the Crowd: 'Tis plain
One of the two is duping us!— Well, fellows,
No long debate for us! Let's hang them both!—
Why both?— One will suffice!— But which?— The first!—
The second!— No, the first!
    (*The sound of bells is heard.* Grigory Godunov *makes his appearance, on horseback, with two heralds. After him a new throng rushes in.*)
    Voices in the Crowd: Hold, lads! Be quiet!
See the boyar, the heralds!— Silence now!
He will address us! Silence!— All attend!

He speaks!

GRIGORY GODUNOV (*speaks without dismounting*) : Men of the trades-
    men's quarter, of
The suburbs and the slums! The servant of
The tsar, his true boyar and confidant,
Borís Feódorovich Godunóv,
Sends you his greeting! Mourning for your lot,
And knowing all your great calamities,
The pestilence and the high price of rye,
He has with his own money purchased all
The grain supplies in Moscow, and to-morrow
Has bade them be distributed to you
As a free gift; he does but ask that you
Pray for his health!

VOICES IN THE CROWD: He is a father to us!—
God grant him health!— He feeds us in our need!—
Hark! Godunov is giving us the grain
From his own purse!— May the Lord bless and save him!
May he reward Boris an hundredfold!—
Long life to Godunov!— Who was it said
He was our enemy?— Brothers, who tried
To stir our minds 'gainst Godunov?— Where is
That dirty cur? Let us lay hands on him
And tear him into bits!

(KIKIN *attempts to flee; the throng rushes after him, shouting*
    "Come, catch him! Beat him!")

BITYAGOVSKY (*tucking his hands into his belt*) :
Well, fool, you now have met your just deserts!
Henceforward watch to see whence blows the wind!

SCENE II

The tsar's private rooms

Night. The TSARITSA MARYA FEDOROVNA, *the* TSAREVNA IRINA
FEDOROVNA, *and* MARYA GRIGORYEVNA *are looking out of the window.
Against the starry sky are outlined the towers of the Kremlin and the
domes of the churches. Between the churches of the Annunciation
and of Ivan the Great the comet is visible.*

MARYA GRIGORYEVNA (*to* IRINA) : Look, sister, see how far the
    comet's train
Extends! It covers half the sky above
Our city!

IRINA: Every night it seems to grow
Brighter and larger!
(TSAREVICH FEDOR IVANOVICH *comes in.*)
FEDOR (*pulling* IRINA *by the sleeve*): Stop, my dear Irina!
Enough! Pray leave the window! 'Tis not well
To gaze too long at that portent! It bodes
No good!
IRINA (*to* FEDOR): Where is the emperor? Does he
Still fix his eyes upon the heavenly sign?
FEDOR: Yes, darling. Standing on the porch he still
Watches the star. I wished to speak with him,
But was afraid. In silence he observes,
While the boyars dare not uplift their heads
To look at him.
TSARITSA (*pensively*): How many evenings has
He gone to watch the star!
IRINA: And every time
He has come back more gloomy, saying not
One word!
FEDOR: Gloomy reports are troubling him.
IRINA: True is it that the Tatar khan already
Has reached the Oka?
FEDOR: Yes, Boris has said
That is the truth. 'Tis terrible to think of!
I long to make a pilgrimage on foot
To the famed Convent of St. Sergius *
And there enjoin the monks to offer prayers
For our success, but yet I venture not
To ask papa's consent.
IRINA: O God! Our woes
Come thick from every side! Did not the comet
Appear to herald them?
MARYA GRIGORYEVNA: The Lord best knows!
Not long ago they brought diviners here
And soothsayers, whom the tsar bade be summoned
That they might tell him why it had appeared.
TSARITSA: Soothsayers! God forbid! Has the tsar seen them?
FEDOR: No, darling, but Boris has told me that
In full assembly they have been divining,
And are this very day to inform my father
What they have learned.

---

* About forty miles from Moscow.

IRINA: And he, they say, has sent
For an ascetic.
FEDOR: Yes, Irina, I
Have heard Boris report that so it is.
A holy man is he. Fully thirty years
He has lived a hermit's life. Of him the tsar,
My father, would ask counsel.
TSARITSA: May the Lord
Grant that the hermit give it him!
IRINA: God grant it!
Why should our emperor gather diviners
And thus defile his soul with sin!
FEDOR (*looking around*):   Hush! Hush!
Irina! In the hall I think I hear
My daddy's steps!
CHAMBERLAIN (*opening the door hastily and speaking in a whisper*):
                    The tsar is coming!
(IVAN *comes in, supporting himself with one hand on his staff, with
the other on the shoulder of* BORIS GODUNOV. *He is followed by the*
BOYARS.)
IVAN (*to* FEDOR *and the women*): Hither!
Come hither all of you! Approach and listen! (*He seats himself.*)
I comprehend the sign! Those soothsayers
Whom I have summoned to our capital
Can tell me nothing new. I have myself
Divined its meaning!
(*Silence,* FEDOR *gently nudges* IRINA.)
IRINA (*timidly to* IVAN): Father tsar, permit
Me to inquire of thee: What is it that
Thou hast divined?
IVAN: You see the star? It is
The herald of my death!
FEDOR (*falling on his knees*): Nay, nay, good father!
What words are these thou say'st!
IVAN: Rise! Snivel not!
Thou wilt have time enough for sniveling. First
Thou must assume the cares of state. Arise,
I tell thee! (*The women begin to wail.*) Silence, women! Ample time
You'll have for that! Summon the doctor to me!—
Tsaritsa Marya, a few days ago
I spoke unseemly words to thee. Forget them!
Son Fedor! In an hour of grief and trouble

Thou mount'st the throne. Hast thou deliberated
What thou wilt do when I am here no more?

FEDOR: Father and tsar! When thou desertest us
I know not what I can perform!

IVAN: Thou shouldst
Know well! Soon thou wilt be the emperor.
Thou canst not ring the church bells all thy life.
Wilt thou continue war, or wilt thou make
A peace with Batory?

FEDOR: Father, be that
As thou wouldst have it!

IVAN: For my grievous sins
The Lord has punished me! Ivan! Ivan!
My eldest son Ivan! Not thus wouldst thou
Have answered me!— The doctor!

(JACOBI, *the doctor, comes in.*)

                              Ah! So here
Thou art! Well? Has thine art availed me much?
I am doomed to death! Tell me the moment of it!
Speak thou! I wish to know!

JACOBI (*feeling his pulse*):   Thou art ill, great tsar,
But death at present does not threaten thee!

IVAN: 'Tis false! I soon shall die. I am sure of it!
That bloody star! Think'st thou that I am blind?
I comprehend its message!

JACOBI: Great tsar, if by
Thine own vain apprehensions thou dost not
Injure thyself, thou wilt be well. With mine
Own head I will avouch the truth of this.

IVAN: Thou liest! The boyars have bribed thee; Kurbsky
And all mine enemies have bribed thee—ha!—
That I may die unshriven, unconfessed!
Who bribed thee?

JACOBI: Mighty tsar, thy long night vigils
Have overwrought thy brain; thy blood is heated.
Permit me to prepare a draught which thou
Mayst quaff before thou goest to rest. It will
Refresh thee!

IVAN: No, I will not die without
Repentance. Hear'st thou? I shall yet have time
To repent me. (*To the* BOYARS.) That I shall—to spite you! Call
The soothsayers! From them I shall discover
The fated hour. Meanwhile I still am tsar!

I shall contrive to punish those of you
Who long to see me die without repentance,
Like a foul cur!
    (*Two* SOOTHSAYERS *come in.*)
                Here are the men! Why are
There only two of you? Where are the rest?
    FIRST SOOTHSAYER: For three whole days, O tsar, we read the fates
In Rafli and Zodéy.* Now our assembly
Has sent us two with our reply to thee.
    IVAN: What then?
    SECOND SOOTHSAYER: O tsar, we dread to speak!
    IVAN: I know
It all. Is it my death? Answer directly!
    FIRST SOOTHSAYER: It is, my liege.
    IVAN: When?
    FIRST SOOTHSAYER: On St. Cyril's day.
    SECOND SOOTHSAYER: St. Cyril's day—on the eighteenth of March.
    IVAN (*to himself*): The eighteenth day of March! So soon! I thought
It would be later. I had not expected
To die so soon! (*To the* SOOTHSAYERS.) Whence come you?
    FIRST SOOTHSAYER: I by birth
Am a Korelian.
    SECOND SOOTHAYER: I from Lithuania.
    IVAN: And who instructed you to read the stars
And practice sorcery?
    FIRST SOOTHSAYER: From sire to son
The art has long descended.
    IVAN: Are you Christians?
    SECOND SOOTHSAYER: We were baptized.
    IVAN: Accursed men! Ye know
That sorcery has been forbidden by
Our Holy Church.
    FIRST SOOTHSAYER: 'Twas at thine own behest,
Great tsar, that we divined.
    IVAN: At my behest
Wizards are executed. For your words,
Ill-omened lips, you shall be buried deep
Beneath the earth while still you live!
    SECOND SOOTHSAYER: Great tsar,
The fault is not our own. Another power
Speaks through our lips to thee.

---

* Books of divination.

IVAN: Whose power?
FIRST SOOTHSAYER: Ask not!
SECOND SOOTHSAYER: Ask not of us, great tsar!— Thou knowest it.
IVAN: No! God is my sure witness—I renounce
That power! You, renegades from God, I will
Give over to the Church!— Fetter them both
And with their comrades take them to the prison!
   (*The* SOOTHSAYERS *are led out.*)
The eighteenth day of March! Not many days
Remain for me. My time to give account
Before the Almighty Judge has come. But I
Will not allow my foes to triumph; I
Will settle all my reckonings with this world. (*To* GODUNOV.)
   Boris, go thou into my chamber. There,
Upon the shelf beneath the ikons, lies
A list of souls for whom mass must be sung.
I have begun to write it. Bring it here.
   (GODUNOV *goes out.* IVAN *continues, looking askance at the* BOYARS.)
Not one of those whom for their treachery
I have had executed will I leave
Without remembrance—not a single man!
For the least slave I will assign a fund
To gain his soul repose!— You understand
My drift! (GODUNOV *returns with the paper.*)   Come here! Good!
      There thou hast the list.
Read it to me aloud! Here! Take this pen,
And if I now remember others, set
Them down!
   GODUNOV (*takes the pen and reads*): "Lord, deign to give rest to
      the souls
Of these thy servants: the Boyar Mikhaylo,
The Okólnichys * Ivan and Petr, Boyar
Vasily and his wife, and thirty of
Their slaves. Be merciful to Prince Grigory,
The voyevoda, and his princess, to
Their daughters—both of them—and to their son
Of tender years, likewise to all their slaves,
Sixscore in number; to Boyar Prince Yakov
And to his Princess Marya, to his daughter
Princess Elizabeth, and to his sons
Princes Nikita and Ivan, and of

---

* A court title in Muscovite Russia.

Their slaves twoscore; also to the Igúmens *
Korníly and Vasyán; to Leoníd
The archpriest—and with them to fifteen monks—"
 IVAN: But stay! Fifteen? Too few! Change it to twenty!
 GODUNOV (*writes and continues*): "Be merciful, O Lord, and give
  repose
To certain peasants of estates that once
Belonged to the Boyar Morozov, but
Were confiscated, to the number of
One thousand and two hundred; to three monks,
Beggars whom a bear slew; to nine poor women
Who were brought here from Pskov; to all the folk
Of Pskov who yielded to the king, and whom
He set at liberty—the number is
Two thousand—to the folk of Novgorod,
Twelve thousand more, who were all drowned and slain:
Their names thou knowest, Lord—"
 IVAN: Stay! At the door
Some one is speaking!
 (BELSKY *goes out and immediately returns.*)
 BELSKY: Sire, thy steward has
Come from the suburb.
 IVAN: At this time? At night?
What has occurred? Call him! (*The* STEWARD *comes in.*) What
  brings thee here?
 STEWARD: My liege, God's wrath has overtaken us!
Yesterday morn a thunderbolt descended
On thine imperial mansion and consumed
It to the ground!
 IVAN: Now? In the wintertime?
 STEWARD: It is God's wrath, my liege! Upon a frosty,
Unclouded morning came a thunderstorm.
Into thy bedchamber a bolt crashed down;
Straightway the palace was aflame. Among
Our oldest men none can remember that
A thunderstorm ever arose in winter!
 IVAN (*to himself*): Truly it is God's wrath. That was the chamber
Wherein I slew my son. There he fell down—
Between the window and the door. He screamed
But once and fell. Vainly he tried to catch
The bed curtains, but failed. Then suddenly
He fell—and from his gaping wound the blood

---
* Abbots.

Was spattered on the curtains.— (*Shuddering.*)   What was that?
Boris!— Lay thou aside that paper, put it
Away! There will be time enough to finish it!
Hear you? What is that scratching underneath
The floor? Can you not hear? Again it comes!
Again! And nearer! May God save us all!
I still am tsar! My time has not yet come!
I still am tsar! I still am capable
Of most sincere repentance! Fedor, Marya,
Irina! Stand you here, beside each other!
Nearer, boyars! That is the way! Stand all
Of you before me in a row! Come, what
Have you to fear! Nearer! Of all of you— (*He bows down to
      the floor.*)
Of all I ask forgiveness!
   BELSKY (*aside to* SHUYSKY): May the Lord
Have mercy on us!
   SHUYSKY (*aside to* BELSKY): Caution! It may be
He is but testing us!
   IVAN (*kneeling*):   My faithful slaves
And servants! Each and all of you have I
Injured most grievously by deed or word!
Forgive me now! Thou, Belsky—thou, Zakharyin—
Thou, Prince Mstislavsky—thou, Prince Shuysky—thou—
   SHUYSKY: But pardon, sire! Can it be fitting that
Thou shouldst ask our forgiveness?—
   IVAN: Silence, slave!
I may repent me and humiliate
Myself before what man I please. Be still
And harken! I repent. My evil deeds
Are boundless and innumerable. I
Am vile of soul, corrupt of intellect;
I have been tempted by the glittering
Of purple robes; my head I have defiled
By pride, my lips with blasphemy, my tongue
With shameful words, my hands with murder and
With seizure of men's gold, my belly with
Gross gluttony and drunkenness, my loins
By sins whereof I must not speak! Boyars,
I pray you all! Forgive me, all of you!
Forgive your tsar! (*He bows down to the floor.*)
   ZAKHARYN: My liege and tsar! If it
Be now God's will that thou depart from us

Into eternity, then thou shouldst think
Of what thou hast to do, and of the war
That thou must leave unto thy son and heir
As heritage.   Thy sins whole-heartedly
We all forgive, and zealously pray God
For thee!
   IVAN (*rising*) : Thou art right, old man.   Approach, son Fedor!
Ere many days thou wilt be emperor.
Now hear my last behests!   (*Lowers himself into a chair.*)
                              Rule lovingly
And piously.   Thou must not wantonly
Banish or execute.   Upon my foes,
By whom I once was driven from my throne,
And like an humble pilgrim sought a refuge
In this our Russian land, seek not to take
Vengeance because of me—'tis God alone
Can judge between us!   Thy stepmother, my
Tsaritsa, thou must love and guard.   With Dmitry,
Thy brother, live in harmony; seek not
To seize unto thyself his appanage.
For slaying Abel, Cain the fratricide
Received no heritage.   Strive to conclude
The war with Lithuania by a truce,
And then turn all thy forces 'gainst the khan.
Consult with Godunov and trust him: he
Knows well my projects; from his youth he has
Been trained by me in all affairs of state.
In thy first years of rule Boris will be
An able minister; later thou must
Thyself acquire skill in diplomacy,
In war and justice, that thou mayst not serve
The will of others, but command their wills.
Whether thou wilt rule all the land thyself,
Or once more introduce the *oprichnina,**
Depends on thee; thou wilt decide which course
Will profit best thy brother and thyself.
A model has been set for thee.   Hast thou
Given heed and understood?
   FEDOR :   Father, God grant
Thou mayst not die!   God grant that through my prayers

---

* That is: Will you reëstablish the *oprichnina* (see page 462) to help you
control the boyars, or will you undertake the task yourself? Tolstoy's view of
history is somewhat different from that of contemporary scholars, who regard
Ivan as maintaining the *oprichnina* until his death.

Thou mayst outlive me! Am I fit to rule?
Thou knowest well that I am not prepared
For such a task!

IVAN (*angrily*) : Fedor, they will not ask
Whether it pleases thee or no! Thou must
Ascend the throne when I am gone.

FEDOR :   Dear father,
Pray be not wroth—but I implore thee now—
Assign thy scepter to another! Are
There not in Russia many men more skilled,
More competent than I? And, father, I
Should be content with a small appanage.

IVAN : Thou sacristan! I speak with thee as with
A man; thou answerest with a woman's lips!
Woe! Woe to me! A brother now avenges
His brother's death upon the slayer of
A son! Ivan, my son! My murdered son!
For this have I passed all my days in strife,
Crushed the boyars, quenched each revolt, have strangled
Treason around me, and have set so high
On blood a throne for my descendants, only
To see at last all my accomplishment
Perish with me!

(GRIGORY NAGOY *comes in with papers.*)

GRIGORY NAGOY : Great emperor, here are
Two letters for thee!

IVAN :   Give them to Boris!—
Now let him read them both!

GODUNOV (*after glancing over the letters*) : From Serpukhov,
My liege, they send word that the Tatar khan
Already has begun to cross the Oka;
And from Kazan, that all the Cheremis
And the Nogáys have risen in revolt.

IVAN : No! no! So many woes cannot at once
Assail one head! No, I will not believe it!
Give me the letters!

(GODUNOV *hands him the letters;* IVAN *gazes at them for a long time,
then drops them and remains motionless. Silence. The* CHAMBERLAIN
comes in and whispers to BELSKY.)

BELSKY (*to* IVAN) : Sire, the hermit whom
Thou badst be summoned is already here.

IVAN (*with a shudder*) : Admit him. Leave me, all of you! I would
Remain with him alone. (*All go out.*)

IVAN (*alone*):   Almighty God,
Enlighten now my mind!
    (*He remains buried in his thoughts.   After a short interval the*
HERMIT *comes in.* IVAN *rises and bows his head before him.*)
    IVAN: Father, pray give
Thy holy blessing to me!
    HERMIT (*making the sign of the cross over him*) : In the name
Of Father, Son, and Holy Ghost!
    IVAN (*seating himself*):   I much
Have heard of thee. Long hast thou lived a hermit.
In thy retired cell thou hast barred thy sight
And hearing to all worldly vanity.
On men like thee the good Lord oft bestows
The gift of most miraculous prevision,
And by their lips he speaks the very truth.
    HERMIT: 'Tis so, my son; in lives of ancient saints
We read examples of it, but those men
Had powers far above mine own.
    IVAN: When didst
Thou take monastic vows? Long years ago?
    HERMIT: The very year when thou didst overcome
Kazan, great tsar. How long the time has been
I cannot tell.
    IVAN: Since then the interval
Is thirty years. And all that period
Thou hast lived immured, far from the world?
    HERMIT: To-day
Is the first time that I have seen it. From
My cell deep underground they brought me forth
By violence.
    IVAN: Forgive me, father, that
I thus disturb thy solitude and prayers.
I needed thine advice. Instruct me, say
How best I may avert the doom that threatens
Myself, my land, and throne!
    HERMIT: The doom? What doom?
    IVAN: Dost thou not know it?
    HERMIT: Nay, I know it not,
My son. No tidings have I heard of this.
    IVAN: Father, for my transgressions God has sent
Just retribution. On the King of Poland
He has bestowed a victory over me;
The Swedes are conquering Livonia;

The khan advances with his horde against
Our state; the Cheremis and the Nogáys
Revolt. What shall I do?

HERMIT: Great changes, son,
Have come upon thee since those olden days!
Then thou wast terrible to all thy foes.
On high thou stoodst, and no man dared erect
Himself against thee. Often I myself
Have called to mind the signs and portents that
I witnessed. At the very hour when thou
Wast born, the thunder rolled in heaven; all day
It pealed while brightly shone the sun. Even so
It was throughout all Russia. Anchorites
Came here from many lands to celebrate
Thy greatness and to bless thy cradle.

IVAN: Aye,
All that is true, my father. And long years
The Lord was merciful to me. But now
He has removed from me his mighty arm.
My throne is tottering; foes from every side
Are pressing on me!

HERMIT: Send thy generals
To meet them. Many voyevodas thou
Hast at thy call. For thee they are accustomed
To smite the infidels.

IVAN: My holy father,
The leaders whom thou knewest all are gone!

HERMIT: And not one left? Where is the humpback Shuysky,
Prince Alexander, he who on the Volga
Laid low Prince Yapanchá?

IVAN: He played me false,
And he was put to death.

HERMIT: The humpback? He?
He was thy faithful servant. And where is
Prince Ryápolovsky, who so many times
Over the khan won glorious victories?

IVAN: He too was put to death.

HERMIT: And Fédorov,
Thy groom, who crushed the Tatars near Ryazán
And made a prisoner of Mamay, their prince?

IVAN: I slew him for his base conspiracy
To wrest my throne from me.

HERMIT: Tsar, in thy words
I hear no truth! Most faithful servants of
Thy Majesty were all those men—I knew
Them all. And yet there still remains to thee
Mikhaylo Vorotynsky, the brave prince?
When our troops took Kazan, he was the first
To plant the cross upon the battlements.
Thy foemen know him well!

IVAN: He died in torture.

HERMIT: Prince Vorotynsky, tsar!— And where is Pronsky,
Prince Turuntáy, who in the famous battle
At Pólotsk broke the Lithuanian strength?

IVAN: Drowned.

HERMIT: May the Lord have mercy on thee, son!—
But Kurbsky, Prince Andrey Mikháylovich,
Thy friend and gallant comrade in the days
Of glory at Kazan?

IVAN: Ask not of him!
Me he abandoned—he betrayed me and
He fled to Lithuania, to my foes.

HERMIT: In former times I well remember how
Thy subjects loved thee. No man fled from thee;
From distant lands men gathered to thy service.
But say: Where are the princes: Obolensky,
Shchenyátev and Shcherbáty?

IVAN: Father, do
Not speak their names!— They are no more.

HERMIT: And Kashin?
And Búturlin? Serébryanny? Morózov?

IVAN: All executed.

HERMIT: What! Not every one?

IVAN: All, father, all.

HERMIT: So thou hast put them all
To death?

IVAN: Aye, all. (*Silence.*) I have repented, father.
The remnant of my life will not be long.
I soon must die—the fatal day is set.

HERMIT: Who set it for thee?

IVAN: Ask thou not, my father!—
Ask not, but give me counsel how I may
Preserve my realm.

HERMIT: If thou wert not both weak
And ill, I should reply: "Rise, tsar, and in

The holy cause lead forth thyself thy troops!"
But thou art bent by thine infirmities;
In thee I do not recognize the hero
Who won Kazan from paynim hands. Thou must
Entrust thine armies to a younger man
Whose name may fill with ardor Russian hearts.
Doubtless thy son Ivan is now a warrior
Mature and competent: send him!

IVAN (*rising quickly*):   Thou monk,
Didst thou name him to mock at me? How dar'st
Thou name my son Ivan? I will command
My servants to tear out thy tongue!

HERMIT: Great tsar,
Thy wrath affrights me not, although its cause
Is quite unknown. Long have I been prepared
For death, my son!

IVAN (*resuming his seat*): Forgive me, holy father!
Forgive me! But hast thou heard naught? Into
Thy quiet cell has no news penetrated?

HERMIT: Unto this day the door into my cell
Has been fast closed; to me beneath the ground
No slightest sound has come except the distant
Roar of God's storms and the faint peal of bells.

IVAN: Father, I cannot act on thine advice.
My son Ivan—has gone to rest!

HERMIT: Who then
Is now thine heir?

IVAN: Fedor, my second son;
But both in body and in spirit he
Is weak. Neither wise counsel nor brave deeds
May be expected of him.

HERMIT: Then—ask God
To aid thee!

IVAN: And thou hast no further counsel?

HERMIT: Tsar, bid them lead me back into my cell.

IVAN (*rising*): Pray for me, holy father!

HERMIT: May the Lord
In his great mercy send his peace unto
Thy tortured conscience!

IVAN (*accompanies the* HERMIT *to the door, opens it, and calls*):
                    Lead away the holy
Father once more to his abode!— And now
Return—the rest of you!

(FEDOR *and the* BOYARS *come in.*)
IVAN (*seats himself and speaks after a brief silence*): Mstislavsky!
    Belsky!
Zakharyin! Godunov! Here, kiss the cross
And swear that you will serve my son, Prince Fedor,
In every danger and until his death!—
Thou, Fedor, trust these four! Without their counsel
Undertake naught! But if the Lord permit
That Prince Ivan Petrovich Shuysky shall
Return alive from Pskov, let him be joined
With them, as a fifth minister. To all
These men I leave the solemn legacy
That they coöperate in thy great task
Of ruling Russia. (*He hands them the cross that he wears on his
    breast.*)   Kiss the cross!
MSTISLAVSKY, ZAKHARYIN, BELSKY, GODUNOV (*bending down to the
    cross*):   We do,
Great emperor!
    IVAN: To Lithuania send
Envoys this very night, and at all costs
Make a fair peace—or truce—with Batory.
You may employ such words as these: "I greet
My much-loved friend and brother, Stefan, King
Of Poland," giving all his titles to him.
And at the close call him the ruler of
Livonia—such is his wish: "I yield
All the Livonian land to my belovèd
Brother, and merely ask that he renounce
The town of Dorpat: let all the rest be his!"
Farther, I yield to him the following towns:
Velízh, Usvyát, Ozérishche and Pólotsk,
Izbórsk, Sebézh, Holm, Závolochye, Ostrov,
Gdov, Nével, Lúki, Krásny, and all other
Cities that he has captured!
    (*Murmur among the* BOYARS.)
    ZAKHARYIN: Pardon, sire!
'Tis shameful that we should propose such terms!
    MSTISLAVSKY: My emperor, bid all of us depart
To war with Batory, if only we
May not be put to shame!
    BELSKY: Great tsar, permit
That we make sacrifice of our estates!
    ALL THE BOYARS (*speaking in rapid succession*):

We all will die for thee!— We will sell all!—
Each one of us will pledge his own estate!—
We will be true until our deaths!— We will
Shed our last drops of blood!— We all will perish!—
Yet bid us not yield up our Russian towns,
Towns ours by right of blood!

IVAN: Silence, boyars!
Think you that I rejoice in this? Naught else
Remains to do! Have you forgotten that
The khan already is approaching Moscow?
That now the Cheremis are in revolt?
And that the Swedes are threatening to advance
On Novgorod?

ZAKHARYIN: But, tsar, we still hold Pskov!
Till it surrenders Batory cannot
Leave it behind him! He will go no farther!
His troops are insubordinate and famished,
Harried by plague, without supplies. Wait, sire!
Wait but a little time, and he will soon
Be forced to raise the siege and to return,
Yielding to us once more whatever he
Has conquered!

IVAN: No, I cannot, cannot wait!
That bloody star is calling me! From Fedor
The king would ask still more! I cannot wait!

BELSKY: Yet, emperor, thou hearest: plague and famine
Stalk through their disaffected troops! Why should
We now, when by united efforts we
Might overwhelm them, yield to them so many
Russian dominions?

IVAN: Victory is not
For us! Have you forgotten that the star
Foretells my ruin and not Batory's?

ZAKHARYIN: Tsar and liege lord! If thou in very truth
Wert doomed to perish, why shouldst thou desire
To ruin Russia with thyself?

MSTISLAVSKY: Why wish
To humiliate our honor?

IVAN (*proudly*):   When, redeeming
My mortal sins before my death, even I
Humiliate myself—even I, your ruler!—
Then you need have no thoughts about your honor!
Not a word more!— Shuysky, ere light appears,

Thou wilt prepare a letter to the king
In my behalf: bid Pushkin and his comrades
Make ready to set forth at early dawn;
And bid them in their conferences bear
Themselves with gentle worthiness and with
Humility: that they endure abuse
And insults with no protests; that they suffer
Every indignity with meekness—all!

BOYARS: No, emperor!— That is not possible!—
Our heads and our estates thou mayest rule
Freely and absolutely, but the honor
Of this our native Russia is above
Thine own control!— No, emperor! No man
Will sign such orders!

IVAN (*rising*): Do you thus observe
Your oath to me? And thus do you remember
The Holy Scriptures? On the day when I
Desired to leave my throne, why did you all
In full assembly pray me to remain
Upon that throne? Did I on that great day
Receive from you a power conditional
And limited? Am I not still the tsar
Whom God gave you and whom yourselves again
Elected? What responsibility
Is yours except to give obedience
Unto myself? Perhaps so short a season
Remains for me to live that loyalty
Seems to you worthless? Traitors that you are!
My time is not yet come! I still am tsar!
Who dares to say that I am not the tsar!
Down on your faces in the dust before me!
I am your lord! (*He totters.*)

GODUNOV (*supporting him*): The emperor is ill!
Summon the doctors!

IVAN (*supported by* GODUNOV): Under pain of death
Delay not to equip the envoys! Order
Them to bear all, to suffer all—aye, all!—
Even to beatings!

(*The* BOYARS *retire.*)

God Almighty! Lo,
Thou seest the tsar whom thou anointedst!— Is
He now sufficiently humiliated!

ACT V

SCENE I

The house of Godunov

GODUNOV *and* MARYA GRIGORYEVNA, *his wife, bowing low, are bidding farewell to the* TSAREVICH FEDOR.

GODUNOV: Farewell, tsarevich! Grateful are we both
That thou hast honored us! But grieve no more!
Thou seest: St. Cyril's day has come, yet brought
No woe with it. Thy sire to-day is stronger,
And only good reports have come to us.
The messenger sent by the tsar was able
To overtake and to turn back his envoys;
The flood has checked the khan in his attempt
To cross the Oka—while even earlier
The news that Batory had raised the siege
Of Pskov, gave new life to the emperor.
Ere many days have passed, our liege, thy father,
Will be restored to perfect health.
    MARYA GRIGORYEVNA: My lord,
Why dost thou hasten? I have had no time
To entertain thee with a bit of food!
    FEDOR: Forgive me, sister! Though the tsar my father
Feels easier to-day, nevertheless
My heart is not at ease. Brother-in-law,
My hopes rest all in thee: do not renounce
Thy promise! If—which God forbid!—aught happen,
Then in a forest I shall go astray!
Do thou direct me how to act!
    GODUNOV: Tsarevich,
Always I am thy faithful slave and servant;
But if aught happen, have a care! They will
Not let me serve thee; all will blacken me!
    FEDOR: Never will I believe their words! My father
Commanded me to heed thy counsel, and
In all things I rely on thee. Farewell,
Boris! Farewell, dear sister! Pray do not
Accompany me farther! (*He goes out, attended by* GODUNOV.)
    MARYA GRIGORYEVNA (*alone*): Oh, my God!
Would that this day might quickly pass! Whate'er
My husband may profess, he is uneasy.

And as for me, all night I dreamed of jewels
And precious pearls: with his own hands the tsar
Kept rummaging in them—he strewed forth jacinths,
Delighting in their beauty. Dreams like that
Are omens of disaster! (*She begins to muse.*)
    GODUNOV (*returns and gazes at her*): Marya, what
Is it that troubles you?
    MARYA GRIGORYEVNA: Forgive me, husband!
I dread this day! The soothsayers—
    GODUNOV: Told lies.
The tsar is now more cheerful. I myself
Have seen him.
    MARYA GRIGORYEVNA: Yet, what if the soothsayers—
Did not tell lies?
    GODUNOV (*lowering his voice*): If that should happen, Marya,
Tell me—for now we are alone—should you—?
    MARYA GRIGORYEVNA: No, no, my lord! I do not fear for him,
But for yourself!
    GODUNOV: And why for me?
    MARYA GRIGORYEVNA: Did not
Tsarevich Fedor tell you that if aught
Should happen, he could not direct his course?
That you must guide his steps unceasingly?
Boris, what if there fall on you to-day
The heavy burden of the empire? If
For each rebellion, for the famine, for
The war, for all things you must bear the blame
Before our native land?
    GODUNOV: Truly, if that
Should happen which you fear, with no weak hand
Should I assume the reins of rule. From power
I shrink not, feeling that I am possessed
Of strength sufficient to uphold our Russia
In years of grievous trouble! Rather I dread
Lest incomplete authority be mine.
A regent, whatso'er his qualities,
Is but the shadow of an emperor;
He must contend with envious rivals, nor
Can give expression unreservedly
To his most cherished aims, as I might do,
Had I been born to ascend the throne—not to
Remain a subject always!

MARYA GRIGORYEVNA: Ah, we should
Thank God that we are not of lofty birth!
Tsars for their acts must render strict account!

GODUNOV: This present tsar's account will be most strict
Of all.   But now you waste anxiety.
He has recovered from his illness and
May still have many years to live, before
He renders that account.

MARYA GRIGORYEVNA: You are not calm
Yourself.

GODUNOV: Nay, I am calm.   I feel that all
Is for the best.   The soothsayers have lied.
Leave me now, Marya; go to your own room.
I have some work to do.

(MARYA GRIGORYEVNA *goes out.*   GODUNOV *opens a side door and admits the two soothsayers, in chains.   Then he seats himself, and gazes at them, in silence.*)

GODUNOV (*in a tone full of meaning*) : To-day is the
Eighteenth of March, St. Cyril's day!

FIRST SOOTHSAYER: Aye, sire!

GODUNOV: To-day the tsar is stronger.

SECOND SOOTHSAYER: May God save him!

GODUNOV: Therefore you erred in prophesying that
His end would come to-day?

FIRST SOOTHSAYER: We merely told
What we had read in heaven's stars.

GODUNOV: Why then
Has his disease so suddenly departed?

FIRST SOOTHSAYER: That we know not.   Nevertheless, the day
Is long; the sun has not yet set.   (*Silence.*)

GODUNOV: As I
Gave orders, have you sought to guess my fate?

FIRST SOOTHSAYER (*looking about him*) : We have, my lord.

GODUNOV: You may
        speak openly;
In this room none can hear.   What have you learned?

FIRST SOOTHSAYER: Your constellations are most closely twined
With constellations of crowned rulers; yet
Three stars are casting shade upon your greatness.
Soon one of them will be extinguished.

GODUNOV: Speak
More clearly!

FIRST SOOTHSAYER: As your path goes forward, it
Grows ever broader and more bright.
GODUNOV: But whither
Will it conduct me?
SECOND SOOTHSAYER: What your soul has long
Desired, yet dared not make confession of
To your own self—shall be fulfilled for you.
GODUNOV: Soothsayers, tell me frankly! What awaits
Me in the future?
BOTH SOOTHSAYERS (*kneeling*): When you sit upon
The imperial throne, remember then, boyar,
Your humble slaves!
GODUNOV (*rising*): Are you in your right senses?
FIRST SOOTHSAYER: Such was our divination.
GODUNOV: Hush! Be still!
Walls may have ears! (*He goes to the doors, inspects them, and pauses
    in front of the* SOOTHSAYERS.)
GODUNOV: Ye sorcerers, if I
Did but suspect you of misleading me,
'Twere better for you had you ne'er been born!
FIRST SOOTHSAYER: We tell you what we see. In heaven we read
The signs of future years; our comrades have
Taken the omens given by blood and smoke—
And in the misty darkness all of us
Have seen you on the throne, wearing the crown
And the imperial mantle.—
GODUNOV: Hush! More softly!
When will your prophecy come true?
FIRST SOOTHSAYER: We know
Not when.
GODUNOV: And am I fated to be tsar
For many years?
SECOND SOOTHSAYER: For seven years, no more,
You will be tsar.
GODUNOV: Seven days would much rejoice
My heart! But how shall I attain such power?
FIRST SOOTHSAYER: We know not how.
GODUNOV: Whom should I fear?
SECOND SOOTHSAYER: Ask not!
GODUNOV: I fain would know what adversary I
Must fear the most.
FIRST SOOTHSAYER: Obscure are all his traits.
GODUNOV: Recount them!

FIRST SOOTHSAYER: He is weak, yet powerful.
SECOND SOOTHSAYER: Alone, yet not alone.
FIRST SOOTHSAYER: Blameless and gentle.
SECOND SOOTHSAYER: The enemy of all the land, and cause
Of many woes.
    FIRST SOOTHSAYER: Slain, yet alive.
    GODUNOV: There is
No sense in these your words!
    FIRST SOOTHSAYER: Our divination
Had this result. Farther to know has not
Been granted us.
    GODUNOV: At present even this
Will serve my purpose.— They will take you back
To prison. I myself will in good time
Have you released, and will reward you richly.
Yet have a care! Under the pain of death
I charge you both: Forget yourselves what you
Have here informed me! (*He opens the door; the* SOOTHSAYERS *go out.*)
    GODUNOV (*alone*):   "What my soul has long
Desired, yet dared not make confession of
To mine own self!"— Aye, so it is! I now
See clearly what an aim has ever shone
Before me! Forward, forward I must go
And bring their prophecy to swift fulfillment.
Not fate exalts us high above the crowd—
It merely brings the occasion to our hands;
Nor does a strong man idly wait until
A miracle uplift him; he must aid
His fate. A fair occasion is presented,
And I must act accordingly! (*He stamps his foot. The* STEWARD
        comes in.)
                              Call hither
One of the tsar's physicians! (*The* STEWARD *goes out.*)
                              But seven years!
Only seven years! Nor have I any knowledge
Whether that day be far or near. Meanwhile
The hours fly by. The madness of Ivan
Is bringing on us all calamity;
For mine own empire nothing will remain
Save ruins. "But the sun has not yet set,"
The soothsayers spake. Who knows? Perchance if that
Wild beast should die, my little-witted kinsman
This very day would give into my hands

His power—then *I* shall be the master!
                                        Yet
Was that the prophecy they made me? No!
They saw me crowned, wearing the mantle, on
The throne—aye, crowned and clad in robes of state!
They said: "Three stars are casting shade upon
Your greatness!" Three! One of them is Ivan;
The second, the Tsarevich Fedor: who
Can be the third except Dimitry? That
Mighty opponent whom I aye must dread—
Who can he be except that babe Dimitry?
He, he it is that thwarts me. "He is weak,
Yet powerful; blameless, and yet the cause
Of many woes; alone, yet not alone."
All this applies exactly to Dimitry!
But what could mean the words, "Slain, yet alive"?
Ah, those ill-omened, problematic words
Sound strangely in mine ears! * By whom will he
Be slain? Impossible! And if some man
In very truth should dare to raise his hand
Against that babe, then how could the slain child
Revive? I seem to gaze into a dark
Abyss! Mine eyes are clouded and my thoughts
Confused. . . . Enough! Away with fruitless guesses!
Alive or slain—his fate is in the future.
I prize above all else the present moment.
    (*The* STEWARD *comes in.*)
    STEWARD: Boyar, the tsar's physician has arrived.
    GODUNOV: Let him come in! (JACOBI *comes in.*) Román Eleazárych,
I sent for you, seeking to learn exactly
How far improved is the tsar's health to-day.
May we now hope the danger is averted?
    JACOBI: The tsar's disease, boyar, is most complex.
His suffering is not of the flesh alone;

---

* To a Russian audience those words would be no mystery. In 1603, during the reign of Boris Godunov, there appeared a pretender to the throne, who claimed to be the Prince Dmitry who had been reported murdered in 1591 (see page 494). With an army partly composed of Poles and Cossacks, this "False Dmitry" attacked· the Muscovite state in 1604. When Tsar Boris died in April, 1605, the Muscovites, discontented with his rule, murdered his wife and son, and received the "False Dmitry" into Moscow, where he ruled from June, 1605, to May, 1606. He was overthrown and slain in an uprising engineered by Prince Vasily Ivanovich Shuysky, the opponent of Godunov in this drama. Shuysky then became tsar and ruled until 1610. During his reign he had to contend with a second "False Dmitry." Still a third "False Dmitry" appeared in 1611.

His mind is also ill. Accustomed from
His youth to have all else give way before
His own imperial will, he could not bear
This last humiliation. But good news
Has given him courage and revives his strength.
And he will yet be well, if we succeed
In keeping him from further irritation.

GODUNOV: And if—which God forbid!—his spirit should
Be roused to wrath?

JACOBI: Then we could surely not
Answer for the result. The channels that
Conduct the blood out from the heart and back
Into the heart are under such a strain
That they may burst if he be agitated.

GODUNOV: But how can we prevent his being roused?

JACOBI: Remove in every way each least excuse
For agitation and vexation. Let
Him hear and see only such things as may
Divert his troubled mind.

GODUNOV: How did you leave him?

JACOBI: After his bath he laid him down to rest,
But bade the warden transfer all his treasures
From the main safe into a neighboring room,
That when he waked he might inspect his wealth.
Near him remains my comrade, Richard Elms.

GODUNOV: You have imposed a hard condition for
The healing of the tsar's disease—you know
Our tsar!

JACOBI: In order to distract his thoughts
From cares of state, Belsky, the wise boyar,
Has gathered here a troop of minstrels and
Buffoons. The plan is good. This day may pass
In games and laughter.

GODUNOV (*rising*):   We shall do our best
To carry out your least suggestions, doctor.

JACOBI: Farewell, boyar!

(*He goes out.* GODUNOV *stamps with his foot. The* STEWARD *comes in.*)

GODUNOV: Is Bityagovsky here?

STEWARD: He is, my lord.

GODUNOV: Then summon him to me.

(*The* STEWARD *goes out and soon admits* BITYAGOVSKY.)

GODUNOV: Tell me of thy success amid the mob.

BITYAGOVSKY: Truly it is success, my lord!

GODUNOV: Are they
Enraged at Belsky and Prince Shuysky as
I might desire?

BITYAGOVSKY: They strain upon the leash.

GODUNOV: And so they will attack them when we give
The word?

BITYAGOVSKY: Perhaps before.

GODUNOV: Thou must be ready
To serve as witness that the insurrection
Was fostered secretly by the Nagoys.

BITYAGOVSKY: Ready am I.

GODUNOV: Also to swear thou heardst
With thine own ears them instigate their slaves
To rouse the mob.

BITYAGOVSKY: Swearing is easy work!

GODUNOV: To-day be close at hand. Perchance thou wilt
Be necessary for my purposes.
Now get thee gone!

(BITYAGOVSKY *goes out.*)

GODUNOV (*alone*): If I am not in error,
This day will settle things of great import! (*He goes out.*)

SCENE II

A richly furnished room in the palace

Servants are bringing in and arranging costly articles. The STEWARD
and the SENESCHAL *are superintending them.*

STEWARD (*to* SERVANTS): Make haste! Make haste! Finish your
   task betimes!
The emperor will be awake directly.

SENESCHAL (*to* STEWARD): Pray tell me why he is so set upon
Inspecting all this stuff.

STEWARD: The rumor goes
That he would send some presents to his bride
Beyond the sea.

SENESCHAL: What? Did he not forswear
The thought of marriage with her.

STEWARD: So indeed
He did; but now, it seems, he has resumed
His former plan. To-day his Majesty
Is in far better health!

SENESCHAL: Well, he must judge
Of his own acts! I grieve for the tsaritsa,
For Marya Fedorovna! She is good
And kind!

STEWARD (*looking out of the window*): What crowds! What crowds!
They throng the square!

SENESCHAL: Yes! Every day from early dawn they surge
About the palace, seeking to gain news
Of the tsar's health!

STEWARD: Those soothsayers, praise God!
Were clearly in the wrong! St. Cyril's day
Has come, and with it new health for the tsar! (*To the* SERVANTS.)
Ha? Is all ready?

SENESCHAL (*looking at the list*): Everything set forth!

STEWARD (*to the* SERVANTS): Well then! Begone! (*The* SERVANTS
go out.)
See how the goods are sorted!
Treasures of every kind! Bright sparkling stones,
And gold, and silks, and rich brocades! The room
Glows with the radiance!

SENESCHAL: Hush! Some one comes!

STEWARD: Ah! Lord! Is it the tsar?
(BELSKY *comes in.*)

SENESCHAL: No, it is Belsky.

BELSKY: Have you made all things ready?

STEWARD: Aye, my lord.

BELSKY: Straightway the tsar will grace us with his presence.
Take care that he be satisfied with all!
That he be caused no slightest irritation!
The doctors told us: "God forbid that he
Be stirred to wrath by aught this day!" (*Loud laughter is heard.*)
Whose is
That laughter?

(*The* JESTER *comes in. He is followed by a throng of* MINSTRELS,
*in fantastic costumes, carrying rebecks, bagpipes, cymbals, and clash-
ing instruments of various sorts.*)

JESTER (*to* BELSKY): I have brought my chorus, Uncle
Bogdán! Hark while they sing their merry songs!

MINSTRELS (*dance and sing*):
Hey, burn, burn, burn!
Open the gate to us, granny!
Pull the goat by his horn!
Hey, burn, burn, burn!
Granny, fly off to the moon!

JESTER: Well, do they please you?

BELSKY (*inspecting the* MINSTRELS): Excellently well!
Attention, clowns! Give no rest to your heels!
You must turn handsprings for the mighty tsar!
Meanwhile, into that room and hide yourselves!
When I shout, "Fellows!" all of you run in
And let your song ring joyously!

   (*The* MINSTRELS *pass over the stage and go out by a side door.*)

   BELSKY (*to the* JESTER):   Thy place
Shall be close by the tsar. Gaze at his eyes,
And if he merely knit his brows, fling out
Some merry jest!

   JESTER: Aye, fling it out! Should not
You like the task? But he will fling you out
From the high window! (*The door opens.*) Here he comes! Success,
My jests!

   (IVAN *is brought on the stage in a chair. He wears a dressing
gown. His face is exhausted by disease, but has a triumphant expression. The bearers set down the chair in the center of the room, and
place in front of it a small triangular table.* IVAN'S *entrance is followed by that of* GODUNOV, MSTISLAVSKY, SHUYSKY *and the rest of
the* BOYARS, *with the exception of* ZAKHARYIN.)

   IVAN (*seated in his chair, to* GODUNOV): To-day we cannot see
      again
England's ambassador. To-morrow he
May come to take his leave, without his sword
And cutlass. In our sleeping room we will
Informally receive him. Meanwhile we
Will see what presents we may designate
For Queen Elizabeth our sister and
Her niece, our future bride!

   BELSKY: Perhaps, great tsar,
These flowered silks of Persian workmanship,
Of varied patterns, might be pleasing to
The English queen.

   IVAN: No, rags will never win
Her admiration. She has not the traits
Of other women. Písemsky has written
To us from London that she loves to chase
The antlered stags amid the forests; that
In hawking also does she find delight,
And baiting of the bear. She needs must have
A gift more suited to her manly tastes.

Hand me that turquois harness, with the bridle
Set thick with lustrous pearls; therewith may go
That horsecloth strewn with jacinths!

(*They hand to* IVAN *the objects that he desires. He looks them over and motions to have them set to one side.*)

Next we will
Present to her two bears, alive, in chains
Of gold, and six Siberian falcons. Let
Our sister sport with them and call to mind
Our generosity! For Lady Mary—
She is a different sort—for her we choose
Rare jewels. Give me here the necklaces
And rings!

(*They hand* IVAN *various precious articles. He takes them in his hands and looks them over, one after another.*)

This string of diamonds, combined
With azure sapphires and with rubies, we
Will send our bride. The clear blue sapphire, when
One looks into its depths, brings to the soul
A lasting peace and banishes all griefs;
The ruby watches over wifely vows,
Because in hue it rivals the heart's blood.
Among our rings this we select for her:
Most precious is it of them all. The stone
Therein is called the "lal": * from India
The gem is brought; hard is it to procure,
Since griffins, frightful monsters, guard it there.
It heals the bite of serpents. Let our bride
Place it upon her finger, as a token
Of love from us. As for the fabrics, I
Know little of them: ask Tsaritsa Marya!
Women are keen at all such things; what she
Prefers, send to the Lady Mary!

JESTER: Tsar
And daddy!

IVAN: What, fool?

JESTER: When dost thou intend
To marry?

IVAN: What is that to thee?

JESTER: Just this! (*Pointing to* MIKHAYLO
        NAGOY.)

---

* Balas ruby.

I wish to do a service for friend Mishka.
Court life for the Nagoys is ended now,
And I would gain him funds for his last days!
(*He takes off his cap and with it walks about the assembly, as if
begging alms.*)

IVAN: What art thou doing, fool?

JESTER: A thread from each
I gather, tsar, to weave a shirt for naked
Mishka Nagoy!

IVAN: Ha ha! A priceless fool!
He never will be called Nagoy!* (*To the* NAGOYS.) You there!
If you still give me faithful service, I
Will not desert you! (*Glancing over his treasures.*) Thank the Lord,
I have
Treasure enough! I may reward what man
I please; my coffers will not soon be empty!
(*Cries are heard from the square.*)
What cries are those?

GODUNOV: The people shout, great tsar,
And make them merry since thou art restored
To health!

IVAN: Let them make merry now! Roll out
Into the square an hundred casks of mead
And wine! To-morrow morning they shall have
A novel sport. All of the soothsayers
And stargazers who falsely prophesied
That I should die to-day, shall on a pyre
Be roasted. Go, Boris! Inform them of
Their doom! Then come again to me and tell me
Of their grimaces! (GODUNOV *goes out.*)
Ha! So they would jest
With me! They strove to frighten me by naming
St. Cyril's day! No man can ever learn
The day whereon his death must come! Not one!
You! Do you hear?

SHUYSKY: We hear, great emperor.

IVAN: Why are you silent? Is it possible
For a man to prophesy, "So long I have
To live!" or say, "Thus I shall end my life!"?

MSTISLAVSKY: No, sire!

---

* "Nagoy" means "naked."

IVAN: Aye, 'tis the truth! So then, why do
You hold your peace?

SHUYSKY: Great emperor, we all
Both day and night implore the Lord to give
Thee health!

MSTISLAVSKY: May God restore thee soon, my liege!

IVAN: But am I not already healed? What mean
Your words? Think you that I am ill? The sun
Is setting, but I am more vigorous
Than in the morning. I have years enough
Before me to restore my shattered realm!
At my last mortal hour, when by my couch
The metropolitan and all his priests
Raise up their prayers, I shall speak boldly to them:
"Weep not, for I am comforted, since now
My son receiveth from mine hands a light
And easy task!" And thus I shall depart
Unto my God!

(BELSKY *makes a sign to the* JESTER, *who has been looking at various
articles on the tables. The* JESTER *takes the box of chess men and
offers it to* IVAN.)

JESTER: Dear tsar! Behold these playthings!

IVAN (*to the* BOYARS): For their false prophecies I have condemned
The soothsayers to death. What think you? Is
My sentence just?

BOYARS: It is, great tsar!

IVAN: If then
'Tis just, what strange restraint has tied your tongues?

BOYARS: Great emperor, have mercy on us, but
We know not what to say!

IVAN: You know not? So
I have condemned innocent men to death?
And so those sorcerers did not lie?

BOYARS: They lied,
Great tsar!— They lied!— They well have earned their tortures!—
For their transgressions death would not suffice!

IVAN: I wrung that from you!— These men fear to speak!
Words must be torn forth from their mouths with tongs! (*Silence.*)
What are you whispering there?

SHUYSKY: Nay, emperor,
We did not whisper!

IVAN: Are you waiting for
Some new event to-day? What look you for?

JESTER: Fair sun, our tsar, pray turn thine eyes upon
These playthings here!

IVAN: What holds he in his hands?

BELSKY: A set of chess men, sire, sent as a gift
To thee by Persia's shah.

JESTER (*looking over the pieces*): How gayly decked!

BELSKY (*taking the board from the table*): Here is the board!

IVAN: Show
it to me! (*Looking over the chess set.*) 'Tis long
Since I have played the game. (*To* BELSKY.) Seat thee, Bogdán,
And we shall see which is the better man!

(*The* SERVANTS *bring in candles.* IVAN *arranges his pieces.* BELSKY
seats himself opposite him on a stool and arranges his own.)

JESTER (*to* IVAN, *pointing to the chess men*): Just like thine own
         boyars; I tell thee what!
Lay all thy living counselors aside,
And set these chess men in their places. Then
Affairs will go no worse—and they'll not ask
For food or drink!

IVAN: Ha, ha! Our jester seems
No fool at all to-day!

(*He moves a pawn. The game begins. All the company stand in a
semicircle behind the tsar's chair and watch.*)

JESTER: Or, if not they,
Let me supply the place of thy boyars!
I'll sit alone in council—all alone,
And never will dispute with mine own self!
Or, honored tsar, dispatch me instantly
To Lithuania, as thine august
Ambassador; let me congratulate
The king!

IVAN: On what?

JESTER: That he has smashed his skull
Against the walls of Pskov!

IVAN: Indeed it were
No bad idea to send thee forth. To me
He sent his gauntlet by Haráburda!
I wot that now no longer they intend
To strike at Novgorod!

SHUYSKY: That is beyond them!

IVAN: Their Sejm has now refused to vote supplies!
Ridiculous indeed! A ruler's faithful
Subjects decline to give him funds!

JESTER: We here
Have no such customs. When a thing is wanted—
"Come, come!"—it is on hand.

BELSKY (*moving his queen*): Check, emperor.

IVAN (*protecting his king with a bishop*): Check to thy queen!

SHUYSKY (*to* BELSKY, *laughing*):   Now you are caught, boyar!
Your queen is lost!

IVAN: Yes, so indeed it seems!

BELSKY: In very truth, my queen is lost!

IVAN: 'Tis plain
We are not yet bereft of all our skill
At chess! Our ailment has not yet deprived us
Of all our intellect! St. Cyril's day!
What notions they contrived, the cursed knaves!
Where is Boris? Why comes he not with their
Reply!

(BELSKY *takes the tsar's bishop.* IVAN *is about to take* BELSKY'S
queen with his king, but drops the king on the floor. The JESTER
hastens to pick it up.)

JESTER: Aha, the tsar has cracked his crown!

IVAN (*with a flash of temper*): Fool, thou mayst lie, but not too
        much! (*To* BELSKY.) Thy turn!

(*The game continues.* GODUNOV *appears at the door.*)

GODUNOV (*pointing to* IVAN; *aside to a* BOYAR *who is standing in
the rear of the others*): How is he?

BOYAR (*aside to* GODUNOV): Very prone to wrath! His temper
Already twice has all but overcome him!

(GODUNOV *comes up and stands opposite* IVAN.)

IVAN (*raising his head*): Thou here? What then? Thou hast seen
        the sorcerers?
What did they answer? Why now art thou silent?
Why speak'st thou naught?

GODUNOV: Hm, emperor and liege!

IVAN: Why dost thou gaze at me in such a manner? (*Moving away
        from* GODUNOV.)
How canst thou dare gaze thus?

GODUNOV: Great emperor!
The soothsayers bade me reply to thee
That faithful are their arts.

IVAN: How so?

GODUNOV: That they
Cannot mistake, and that—St. Cyril's day
Is not yet past!

IVAN (*rises, tottering*): Not past?— St. Cyril's day?—
Thou dar'st— Knave, dar'st thou look me in the eye!—
Thou—thou— I understand thy glance!— Thou hast come
To slay me—slay me!— Traitor!— Headsmen!— Son!—
Feodor!— Trust him not!— He is a thief!—
Nay, do not trust him!— Ah! (*He falls face downward on the floor.*)
   SHUYSKY (*rushing to him and supporting his head*): God! He is
     dying!
   BELSKY: Call the physicians! Call them speedily!
   IVAN (*opening his eyes*): Bring my confessor!
   BELSKY: Run and fetch a
     priest!
Make haste! Run swiftly! Fellows! Fellows! Hey!
   (*The* MINSTRELS *run in, singing, whistling, and dancing.*)
   MINSTRELS (*sing*):

> Hey, burn, burn, burn!
> Pull the goat by his horn!

   BOYARS: What! What is this! Back, in the name of God!
   BELSKY (*rushing at the* MINSTRELS): Back! Back! Ye impious
     fools, get back! The tsar
Is dying!
   MSTISLAVSKY: Call the doctor!
   (IVAN *dies. Several of the* BOYARS *rush out of the room. The*
MINSTRELS *scatter in all directions.* ELMS *and* JACOBI *come in.*)
   JACOBI: Where is he?
Where is the emperor?
   BELSKY (*pointing to the corpse*): There!
   JACOBI (*bending down and feeling* IVAN's *pulse*): The pulse is still!
   ELMS (*taking the other hand*): It is not beating—no!
   JACOBI (*feeling the heart*):   The heart beats not!
   ELMS: Dead!
   JACOBI: Life is now extinct!
   GODUNOV (*approaches and lays his hand on* IVAN's *heart*): He has
     expired! (*He opens the window and shouts into the square.*)
Moscow, our Tsar Ivan Vasilyevich
Is now deceased!
   (*Uproar and loud talking are heard from the square.* GODUNOV *leaves
the room. The* BOYARS *surround* IVAN *and gaze at him without speaking.* ZAKHARYIN *comes in and stops in front of the corpse.*)
   ZAKHARYIN: The end has come! And thus,
Our Tsar Ivan, before whom Russia long
Has trembled—powerless thou liest now,

Helpless and motionless and poor amid
Thy treasures! Yet why stand we here and wait,
Boyars? Shall he lie prone in dust before us,
Before whom we ourselves lay in the dust
For half a century? Or do you dread
To touch him even now? Fear not! No more
Will he unclose his eyes! His nerveless hand
No more will clutch that pointed staff, nor will
His chilly lips pronounce death sentences!

(*They lift* IVAN, *lay him on a bench, make a pillow for him, and cover him with brocade.* FEDOR, *the* TSARITSA, *and the* TSAREVNA IRINA *run in.*)

FEDOR (*rushing towards the corpse*): Father and tsar!
TSARITSA: The Lord
      have mercy on us!
IRINA: Oh, God!

(*All three wail and sob. The cries in the square increase. The* COMMANDER OF THE GUARDS *comes in.*)

COMMANDER (*to* FEDOR): Great emperor, the folk rebels!
Already they attack the palace!
FEDOR (*terrified*):   What
Do they desire?
COMMANDER: They shout that Belsky and
Prince Shuysky here have slain our tsar with poison!

(CORPORAL OF THE GUARDS *runs in.*)

CORPORAL: The mob has captured now the giant cannon.
They seek to batter down the palace walls!
BELSKY (*to* FEDOR): Order the troops to fire upon them!
FEDOR: Find
Boris! The brother of my wife! Boris!

(GODUNOV *comes in.*)

What shall I do?
GODUNOV (*to* FEDOR, *in a solemn voice, falling on his knees*):
                  Great tsar!
FEDOR (*rushing to him*):   Ah! Here thou art
At last!

(*Cries are heard from the square. Amid them the names of* SHUYSKY *and of* BELSKY *can be distinguished.*)

SHUYSKY (*to* FEDOR): Make thy decision, emperor!
FEDOR (*indicating* GODUNOV): This is the man who now must make
      decisions!
To him I delegate my power henceforth!

GODUNOV (*after bowing to* FEDOR, *goes to the window*):
All Moscow, hear! Fedor Ivanovich,
By grace of God Grand Prince and Tsar of Russia,
Bids me proclaim to you that Tsar Ivan
Died of an illness. Of his death no man
Is guilty. But both Belsky and Prince Shuysky
Long have oppressed you. Knowing this, Tsar Fedor
Exiles them far from Moscow!
  (*Uproar in the square.*)
  SHUYSKY: What, Boris
Feodorych! What words are these?
  BELSKY: Why send
Us into exile?
  GODUNOV: You are free to stay.—
Will you go forth upon the porch?
  SHUYSKY: No! They
Would rend us limb from limb!
  BELSKY: Tear us to bits!
  GODUNOV: I think so too. (*To the* COMMANDER OF THE GUARDS.)
                    Guard the boyars securely
And lead them forth from Moscow. At Pokróv
You will receive instructions where to take them.
  (GUARDSMEN *surround* SHUYSKY *and* BELSKY.)
  ZAKHARYIN (*to* GODUNOV): Swift are your acts, boyar! We still
      know not
Who roused the people to revolt.
  GODUNOV: Mstislavsky
And the Nagoys. (*Indicating* BITYAGOVSKY, *who comes in, well dressed
      and with the air of a noble.*)   Here is a witness of
The fact!
  THE TWO NAGOYS *and* MSTISLAVSKY: What? He?
  BITYAGOVSKY (*insolently*):   Yes, I!
  GODUNOV (*to* MSTISLAVSKY):   You, Prince Mstislavsky,
Deserve to lose your life, but the kind tsar
Merely exiles you to a monastery. (*To the* NAGOYS.)
You two, from love of the tsaritsa, he
Pardons, but orders that you both repair
To Uglich, with Prince Dmitry the tsarevich
And with herself. (*To the* TSARITSA, *indicating* BITYAGOVSKY.)
                    This man is delegated
To keep guard over you.

TSARITSA (*to* FEDOR): Nay, trust him not!
Feodor, trust him not! Tsar, do not send
Us into exile!
      FEDOR (*to* GODUNOV): Could not the tsaritsa
Remain in Moscow, brother?
      GODUNOV: Sire, it will
Be better for her there.
      ZAKHARYIN: I see, boyar,
That you display rare skill in state affairs!
For all you have found places—me alone
You have forgot! Tell me where I must go!
To exile? To a monastery? To
A prison? To the block?
      GODUNOV: Father, the tsar
Begs that you still remain with him.
      TSARITSA (*to* ZAKHARYIN):   Save me!
Save me, boyar! My son and I are lost!
      ZAKHARYIN: God grant, tsaritsa, that all be not lost! (*To* GODUNOV.)
The seed that you have sown, Boyar Boris,
Is evil; no good harvest do I augur
Will come thereof! (*Turning to the corpse of* IVAN.)
                    O Tsar Ivan! May God
Forgive thee! May the Lord forgive us all!
Such is the penalty for despotism!
Such the result of our degeneracy!
      FEDOR (*in tears, to the* TSARITSA): Weep not, tsaritsa mother! What
            else could
I do for thee! It seems this must be so!
      GODUNOV (*going to the window*): People of Moscow! The great
            Tsar Feódor
Ivanovich forgives you your revolt!
Now get you gone and pray for the salvation
Of your late Tsar Ivan!— To-morrow morn
Throughout all Moscow you shall every one
Receive most ample gifts of grain and wine!
      SHOUTS IN THE SQUARE: Long life to Tsar Fedor Ivanovich!
Long life to Godunov his true boyar!
      (FEDOR, *sobbing, throws himself on the neck of* GODUNOV. *They
stand, embracing each other.*)

THE POWER OF DARKNESS

OR

IF A CLAW IS CAUGHT, THE WHOLE BIRD IS LOST

By COUNT LEV NIKOLAYEVICH TOLSTOY

(1886)

*Translated by George Rapall Noyes
and George Z. Patrick*

CHARACTERS

PETR,* *a rich peasant, forty-two years old, married for a second time, in poor health*

ANÍSYA, *his wife, thirty-two years old, smartly dressed* (*in Acts I and II*)

AKULÍNA, *daughter of* PETR *by his first marriage, sixteen years old, hard of hearing and feeble-minded*

ANYÚTKA, *daughter of* PETR *and* ANISYA, *ten years old*

NIKÍTA, *their workman, twenty-five years old, smartly dressed*

AKÍM, *father of* NIKITA, *fifty years old, a pious peasant, unattractive in external appearance*

MATRÉNA,† *his wife, fifty years old*

MARÍNA, *an orphan girl, twenty-two years old*

FRIEND *of* ANISYA

MÁRFA, *sister of* PETR

MÍTRICH, *an old laborer, a soldier retired because of age*

NEIGHBOR (*woman*)

MATCHMAKER (*man*), *a glum peasant*

HUSBAND *of* MARINA

FIRST GIRL

SECOND GIRL

POLICEMAN

COACHMAN

MATCHMAKER (*woman*)

BRIDEGROOM *of* AKULINA

BEST MAN (*at wedding*)

VILLAGE ELDER

Peasants: men, women, and girls.

---

* Pronounced, Pyŏtr (one syllable).
† Pronounced, Ma-tryŏ'na.

THE POWER OF DARKNESS

ACT I

The action takes place in autumn in a large peasant village. The stage represents PETR'S *spacious cottage.* PETR *is seated on a bench, repairing a horse-collar.* ANISYA *and* AKULINA *are spinning.*

SCENE I

PETR, ANISYA, *and* AKULINA

ANISYA *and* AKULINA *are singing together.*

PETR (*glancing out of the window*) : The horses have got loose again. They'll kill the colt before you know it. Nikita! Hey, Nikita! He's deaf! (*Listens for a moment. To the women.*) Keep still, will you! I can't hear anything.

NIKITA (*from the yard, off stage*) : What?

PETR : Drive in the horses.

NIKITA (*same*) : I'll drive 'em in. Give me time.

PETR (*shaking his head*) : Drat these hired men! If I was well, I'd never think of keeping one. They do nothing but make trouble. (*Rises and sits down again.*) Nikita! I can't make him hear.— One of you go, will you? Akulina, go and drive 'em in.

AKULINA : The horses?

PETR : What do you suppose?

AKULINA : Right away. (*Goes out.*)

SCENE II

PETR *and* ANISYA

PETR : The fellow's a loafer, no good on the farm. If he'd only stir himself!

ANISYA : You're mighty spry yourself—just crawl from the stove to the bench. All you do is boss the rest of us.

PETR : If I didn't boss you, the whole farm'd be ruined in a year. Oh, what a lot you are!

ANISYA : You give us a dozen jobs and then growl. It's easy to lie on the stove and give orders.

PETR (*sighing*): Oh, if this sickness didn't have hold of me, I wouldn't keeρ him for a day.

AKULINA (*off stage*): Shoo! shoo! shoo! (*One can hear the colt whinny and the horses run into the yard. The gate creaks.*)

PETR: Fancy talk is all he's good for. Honest, I wouldn't keep him.

ANISYA (*mimicking him*): "I won't keep him." If you'd only get a move on yourself, you might talk.

SCENE III

The same and AKULINA

AKULINA (*coming in*): I had hard work to drive 'em in. The roan kept—

PETR: Where's that Nikita?

AKULINA: Nikita? He's standing in the street.

PETR: What's he standing there for?

AKULINA: What for? He's standing round the corner and chatting.

PETR: Can't get sense out of her! Who's he chatting with?

AKULINA (*not catching his words*): What? (PETR *brandishes his arm at* AKULINA; *she sits down at her spinning.*)

SCENE IV

The same and ANYUTKA

ANYUTKA (*running in. To her mother*): Nikita's father and mother have come to see him. They're taking him home to marry him—just think!

ANISYA: Aren't you lying?

ANYUTKA: Honest and true, may I die if it ain't! (*Laughs.*) I was going by, and Nikita says to me: "Now good-by, young lady," he says; "come and have some fun at my wedding. I'm leaving you," he says. And then he just laughed.

ANISYA (*to her husband*): Folks haven't much need of you. You see he was getting ready to leave himself. And you were saying: "I'll turn him out"!

PETR: Let him go; can't I find other men?

ANISYA: But haven't you paid him in advance?

(ANYUTKA *goes toward the door, listens to their words for a moment, and goes out.*)

SCENE V

Anisya, Petr, *and* Akulina

Petr (*frowning*) : He can work off the money next summer if necessary.

Anisya: Yes, you're glad to let him go—one less mouth to feed. But during the winter I'll have to tend to things all alone, like a work horse. The girl ain't awful eager to work, and you'll just lie on the stove. I know you!

Petr: What's the use of wagging your tongue for nothing when you ain't heard anything yet?

Anisya: The place is crowded with the animals. You haven't sold the cow and you've taken in all the sheep for the winter—it'll be hard enough to store up feed for all of 'em, and to water 'em. And now you want to let the hired man go. I won't do a man's work! I'll lie down on the stove just like you and let things go to smash—and you can do what you please about it.

Petr (*to* Akulina) : Go for the fodder, will you? It's time.

Akulina: For the fodder? All right. (*Puts on her coat and takes a rope.*)

Anisya: I won't work for you. I've had enough of it—I won't! Work for yourself.

Petr: Shut up! What are you mad about? You're like a wet hen.

Anisya: You're a mad dog yourself! There's no work or joy to be got out of you. You're just sucking the life out of me. A mad dog, that's what you are.

Petr (*spits and puts on his coat*) : Plague take you—Lord forgive me! I'll go and find out how things are. (*Goes out.*)

Anisya (*shouts after him*) : Rotten, long-nosed devil!

SCENE VI

Anisya *and* Akulina

Akulina: What are you scolding dad for?

Anisya: Shut up, you fool!

Akulina (*going toward the door*) : I know what you're scolding him for. You're a fool yourself, you cur. I ain't afraid of you.

Anisya: What's that? (*Jumps up and looks for something with which to strike her.*) Look out or I'll take the poker to you.

Akulina (*opening the door*) : You're a cur, you're a devil; that's what you are. Devil, cur, cur, devil! (*Runs out.*)

SCENE VII

ANISYA *alone*

ANISYA (*meditates*): "Come to the wedding," says he. So that's what they're up to—marrying him? Look out, Nikita, if that's your doings, I'll have my say too. . . . I can't live without him. I won't let him go.

SCENE VIII

ANISYA *and* NIKITA

NIKITA (*comes in and glances about. Seeing that* ANISYA *is alone, he approaches her quickly. Whispers*): Well, my girl, I'm in trouble! My father's come and wants to take me away—tells me I must go home. "We're marrying you off for good and all," says he, "and you'll have to stay at home."

ANISYA: Well then, marry. What do I care?

NIKITA: Oh, re-ally! I thought it'd be better to talk things over; but this is what she says: she tells me I must marry. What does this mean? (*Winks.*) Have you forgotten?

ANISYA: Go ahead and marry. You needn't—

NIKITA: What are you snorting at? You won't even let me pet you a bit.— Well, what's wrong with you?

ANISYA: I think you want to desert me. And if you do want to desert me, then I've no use for you either. That's the whole story!

NIKITA: Oh, stop, Anisya. Do you think I want to forget you?— Not so long as I live. So I won't leave you for good and all. This is the way I figure it: let 'em marry me, but then I'll come back to you— if only they don't make me stay at home.

ANISYA: Much I'll care for you if you're married.

NIKITA: But remember, my dear girl: I simply can't go against my father's will.

ANISYA: You put the blame on your father, but the scheme's your own. You've been plotting for a long time with your sweetheart, with Marina. She put you up to this. She didn't run over here the other day for nothing.

NIKITA: Marina? Much I care for her! . . . Many of her kind fall for me!

ANISYA: Why did your father come? You told him to! You've been deceiving me! (*Weeps.*)

NIKITA: Anisya, do you believe in God or not? I never even dreamed of any such thing. Honestly, I never thought of it. My old man made the plan out of his own head.

ANISYA: If you don't want to get married yourself, can any one pull you to it like a jackass?

NIKITA: All the same, I figure a fellow can't oppose his father. And I don't want to.

ANISYA: Just say you won't, and stick to it.

NIKITA: One fellow refused, and they thrashed him in the village jail. Then he understood. I don't want to go through that. I tell you, it's ticklish.

ANISYA: Quit your fooling. Listen, Nikita: if you're going to marry Marina, I don't know what I'll do to myself. . . . I'll kill myself! I've sinned and broken the law, but now I can't turn back. Just as soon as you leave me, I'll do it.

NIKITA: Why should I leave? If I wanted to leave, I'd have gone long ago. The other day Ivan Semenych offered me a job as coachman . . . and what an easy life! Yet I didn't take it. I think that everybody likes me. If you didn't love me, I'd act differently.

ANISYA: Just remember this. The old man may die any day; then I think we can cover up all our sins. I've planned to marry you; then you'll be the master of the house.

NIKITA: No use guessing. What do I care? I do the work as if it was for my own self. The master likes me, and his wife—well, she's in love with me. And if women love me, I'm not to blame; it's a simple matter.

ANISYA: Will you love me?

NIKITA (*embracing her*): Just this way! You've always been in my heart.

(MATRENA *comes in and for some time stands before the ikon in the corner of the room, crossing herself.* NIKITA *and* ANISYA *move away from each other.*)

SCENE IX

The same and MATRENA

MATRENA: Oh, what I've seen, I didn't see; what I've heard, I didn't hear. Been having fun with a nice little woman, have you? What of it? Even calves have their fun, you know. Why shouldn't you? You're still young. But the master is asking for you in the yard, my son.

NIKITA: I came in to get the ax.

MATRENA: I know, my boy; I know what sort of an ax you came for. You're likely to find that kind near a woman.

NIKITA (*bends down and picks up an ax*): Well, mother, are you really going to marry me? I think there's no reason for that at all. And then I don't want to marry.

MATRENA: Oh, my darling, why should we marry you? You're living and having a good time; it's only the old man's plan. Go ahead, my boy; we'll settle the whole business without your help.

NIKITA: This is queer: first you want to marry me, and then you say there's no need of it. I can't understand things at all. (*Goes out.*)

SCENE X

ANISYA *and* MATRENA

ANISYA: Well, Auntie Matrena, do you really want to marry him?

MATRENA: Why should we marry him, my precious? You know what our family's like. My old man keeps mumbling foolish stuff: "Marry him, must marry him." But he hasn't enough sense to judge. Horses don't run away from oats, you know, men don't quit one good thing for another: that's the way to look at it. Don't I see (*Winks.*) the turn things are taking?

ANISYA: It's no use for me to hide from you, Auntie Matrena. You know everything. I have sinned; I have fallen in love with your son.

MATRENA: Well, this is news! And Auntie Matrena didn't know! Oh, girlie, Auntie Matrena is an old bird, a sly old bird. Auntie Matrena, I can tell you, darling, can see a yard underground. I know everything, precious! I know why young wives need sleeping powders. I've brought some. (*Unties a corner of her kerchief and takes out a packet of powders.*) What I need to, I see; and what I don't need to, I don't know and don't want to know. That's the way. Auntie Matrena was young once herself. I've had to find out how to live with my own fool, you see. I know the whole seventy-seven tricks. I see your old man's withering away, darling, withering away. What sort of life can you have? Stick a pitchfork into him and the blood won't flow. I tell you: you'll be burying him next spring! You must get some one else to be the boss. And ain't my son up to the job? He's no worse than others. So what use would it be for me to pull my son away from a good soft place? Am I my own child's enemy?

ANISYA: If only he don't leave us!

MATRENA: He won't leave you, birdie. That's all nonsense. You know my old man. His wits are all gone by now; but sometimes, when he gets a notion into his noddle, you can't knock it out with a mallet.

ANISYA: But how did the business start?

MATRENA: You see, darling; you know yourself the lad is daft on women; and he's handsome too, I must say. Well, he was living on the railroad, you know, and there they had an orphan girl as cook. Well, that hussy began to chase after him.

ANISYA: Marina?

MATRENA: Yes, plague take her! Well, whether anything happened or not, my old man only knows. Whether people talked, or whether the girl herself got round him—

ANISYA: What impudence, the bold thing!

MATRENA: So my silly old fool got on his ear and kept saying: "We must marry him, marry him to cover up the sin. Let's take the lad home," says he, "and marry him." I argued all I could, but it was no use. "All right," thinks I, "I'll play another game." You have to know how to manage those fools, darling. Just pretend to agree, but when the time comes you can turn things your own way. You know a woman can fly up in the air and think seven and seventy thoughts, and how's a man to guess 'em! "Well, old man," says I, "it's a good plan, but we must think it over. Let's go call on our son," says I, "and ask the advice of Petr Ignatych. Let's see what he'll say." So we've come.

ANISYA: Oh, auntie, how's this? What if his father orders him?

MATRENA: Orders him? Stick his orders under a dog's tail! Don't you worry: this thing won't come off. I'll talk over the whole business with your old man right away; I'll sift it so there won't be anything left of it. I came along just to fix it up. Think of it: my son's living in happiness and expecting more—and I'm to marry him off to a vagabond girl! Do you think I'm a fool?

ANISYA: She's even been running over here to see him, that Marina.— Will you believe it, auntie: when they told me he was to be married, I felt a knife run through my heart? I thought that his heart was with her.

MATRENA: Eh, darling! Do you think he's a fool? He's not the man to love a homeless trollop. Nikita, you know, is a lad of some sense. He knows whom it's worth while to love. And don't you worry, darling. We'll never take him away as long as he lives. And we won't marry him. Just hand us a little money, and we'll let him stay here.

ANISYA: If Nikita left, I think I'd die.

MATRENA: Yes, you're young. Hard lines! For a woman like you, fresh and rosy, to live with that old scarecrow—

ANISYA: Believe me, auntie, I'm sick to death of that man of mine, that long-nosed cur; I don't want ever to see him again.

MATRENA: Yes, such is your lot. But look here. (*In a whisper, glancing around.*) I went to that old man for powders, you know, and he gave me two different kinds. Just look here. "This is a sleeping powder," says he. "Give him one of 'em," says he, "and he'll fall asleep so sound you could walk on him. And this," says he "is a sort that she must have him drink—there's no smell to it, but it's awful strong. Give it seven times over," says he, "one pinch at a time. Give it to him seven times. And then," says he, "she'll soon be free from him."

ANISYA: Oh ho ho! What's that!

MATRENA: "It won't leave any traces," says he. He charged a whole ruble. "Can't let you have 'em for less," says he, "for it's hard to get 'em, you know." I paid my own money for 'em, darling. I thought you could use 'em; if you can't, I'll take 'em to Mikhaylovna.

ANISYA: Oh! oh! But maybe there's something bad about 'em.

MATRENA: What's bad about it, darling? It'd be different if your man was in strong health, but now he just makes a bluff of being alive. He don't belong to the living, he don't. There are a lot of men like him.

ANISYA: Oh! oh! poor me! Auntie, I'm afraid it may be sinful. Oh, what have I come to!

MATRENA: I can take 'em back.

ANISYA: Do you dissolve the second sort in water, like the others?

MATRENA: It's better in tea, he says. "You don't notice 'em at all," he says; "there's no smell to 'em, not a bit." He's a clever man.

ANISYA (*taking the powders*): Oh! oh! poor me! I'd never meddle with such things if my life wasn't a torment worse than prison.

MATRENA: And don't forget the ruble; I promised to take it to the old man. He has troubles of his own.

ANISYA: Sure! (*Goes to the chest and hides the powders.*)

MATRENA: And keep 'em tight, darling, so that people won't know. And if he finds 'em—God forbid!—say that they're for cockroaches. (*Takes the ruble.*) They're good for cockroaches too. . . . (*Stops suddenly.*)

(AKIM *comes in and crosses himself before the ikon;* PETR *comes in and sits down.*)

SCENE XI

The same, PETR *and* AKIM

PETR: Well, how goes it, Uncle Akim?

AKIM: A bit better, Ignatych, a bit better, y'see; a bit better. Because I was afraid that there might— Foolery, you know. I'd like, y'see, I'd like to get the lad down to business. And if you'd agree, y'see, then we might. It'd be better if—

PETR: All right, all right. Sit down and let's talk. (AKIM *sits down.*) Well then? So you want to marry him?

MATRENA: We can wait about marrying him, Petr Ignatych. You

know how hard up we are, Ignatych. If we marry him, we can't make a living ourselves. How can we marry him!

PETR: Decide for yourselves what's better.

MATRENA: Well, there's no haste about the marrying. It'll wait. She's no raspberry; she won't fall off the bush.

PETR: Of course, it'd be a good thing if you married him.

AKIM: I'd like to, y'see. Because, y'see, I've some work in town; I struck a good job, y'see.

MATRENA: Fine job! Cleaning cesspools. When he came home the other day, I puked and puked. Ugh!

AKIM: That's true; at first it just knocks you over, y'see, the smell of it. But when you get used to it, it's no worse than malt dregs, and after all it suits me. And about the smell, y'see— Men like me needn't mind it. And then we can change our clothes.— I wanted to have Nikita at home, you know; he can tend to things there. He can tend to things at home, and I'll make some money in town, y'see.

PETR: You want to keep your son at home: very well then. But how about the pay he took in advance?

AKIM: That's right, Ignatych, that's right; you told the truth there, y'see. He's hired himself out and sold himself, so let the bargain stand. But we must just marry him, y'see; so you just let him off for a while.

PETR: Well, that's possible.

MATRENA: But we two don't agree about it. Petr Ignatych, I'll tell you the truth as I'd tell it to God. You judge between me and my old man. He keeps saying, "Marry him, marry him." But marry him to whom, may I ask? If she was a decent girl, I'd not stand in my boy's way, but she's a low-lived hussy.

AKIM: That's all wrong. You're wrong in slandering the girl, y'see; you're wrong. Because she—that girl, I say—has been injured by my son; she's been injured, I tell you. The girl has, you know.

PETR: What was the injury?

AKIM: She got mixed up with my son, Nikita, y'see. With Nikita, you know.

MATRENA: Don't you speak of it; my tongue's softer, I'll tell the story. Before he came to you, you know, our lad was living on the railroad. And there a girl got hold of him; you know, a stupid hussy named Marina—she was cook for the railroad gang. So she accused him, that hussy did, our own son, and said that it was he, Nikita, that deceived her.

PETR: That's a bad business.

MATRENA: But she's a low-lived creature herself, runs after the men. She's just a streetwalker.

AKIM: Old woman, you're telling wrong stories again, y'see; it ain't a bit so. I tell you it ain't, y'see.

MATRENA: All my old boy can say is, "y'see, y'see"; but what he means by it he don't know himself. Don't ask me about the hussy, Petr Ignatych, ask other folks; anybody'll tell you. She's just a homeless vagrant.

PETR (to AKIM): Well, Uncle Akim, if that's the case, then there's no use marrying him. The business ain't an old shoe that you can kick off by making him marry her.

AKIM (getting excited): It's an injury to the girl, y'see, old woman, an injury, y'see. Because the girl is a very decent sort, y'see, a very decent sort; and I'm sorry for her, sorry for the girl, you know.

MATRENA: You're just like a silly old woman; you waste your sorrow on the whole world, while your own folks go hungry. You're sorry for the girl, but you ain't sorry for your son. Tie her round your own neck and walk with her! Quit talking nonsense!

AKIM: No, it ain't nonsense.

MATRENA: Don't you get on your ear: I'll say my say.

AKIM (interrupting): No, it ain't nonsense. You turn things your own way—maybe about the girl, maybe about yourself—you turn things your own way, as it's best for you; but, y'see, God will turn 'em his way. That's how it stands.

MATRENA: Bah! No use wasting words on you.

AKIM: The girl's a hard worker, a decent sort, and she knows how to look out for herself, y'see. And we're poor, and she'll be an extra hand, y'see; and the wedding won't cost much. But the main thing's the injury done the girl, you know; she's an orphan, y'see, the girl is. And she's been injured.

MATRENA: Any girl'd say that.

ANISYA: Just you listen to us women, Uncle Akim. We can tell you things.

AKIM: But God, I tell you, God! Ain't she a human being, that girl? So, y'see, God cares for her. What do you think about that?

MATRENA: Oh, he's off again!

PETR: See here, Uncle Akim, you can't much believe those hussies either. And the lad's alive. He's close by! Let's send and ask him straight out whether it's true. He won't perjure his soul. Call the lad here! (ANISYA rises.) Tell him his father's calling for him.

(ANISYA goes out.)

SCENE XII

The same without ANISYA

MATRENA: You've settled the business, my dear, you've cleaned it up: let the lad speak for himself. And these times you can't marry off a lad by force. We must ask him what he thinks. He'll never want to marry her and shame himself. What I think is: he'd better stay with you and work for his master. Even in summer we won't need to take him; we can hire somebody. Just give us ten rubles and he can stay here.

PETR: We'll talk about that later: take things in order. Finish one job before you start another.

AKIM: I'm talking this way, Petr Ignatych, you know, because such things happen sometimes, y'see. You keep trying to better yourself, and you forget about God, y'see; you think it'd be better—you go your own gait, and find the load's on your own shoulders. We think it'll be better for us, you know; and then it's much worse, for we've left out God.

PETR: Of course! We must remember God.

AKIM: All of a sudden it's worse. But if you act according to the law, and as God wills, then, y'see, somehow everything makes you happy. So that's how you want to do. So I struck the idea, you know: I'll marry the lad and keep him out of sin. He'll be at home, y'see, just as he should be by rights; and I'll just go to work in the town, y'see. It's a pleasant job. Suits me. Do as God wills, y'see, and things are better. And then she's an orphan. For instance, last summer they stole some wood from the clerk—what a trick! They thought they'd fool him. They did fool the clerk, but y'see, they didn't fool God: so, y'see—

SCENE XIII

The same, NIKITA *and* ANYUTKA

NIKITA: Did you ask for me? (*Sits down and takes out his tobacco.*)

PETR (*in a low voice, reproachfully*): Look here, don't you know how to behave? Your father is going to ask you questions, and you're fooling with your tobacco, and you've sat down. Get up and come over here.

(NIKITA *takes his stand by the table, jauntily leaning against it, and smiling.*)

AKIM: Well, y'see, there's a complaint against you, Nikita; a complaint, y'see.

NIKITA: Who complained?

AKIM: Who complained? A girl, an orphan complained. It was she, that same Marina, who complained on you, y'see.

NIKITA (*grinning*): Mighty queer. What's the complaint? Who told you about it? Was it she?

AKIM: Now I'm asking you questions, y'see, and you've got to answer, you know. Did you get mixed up with the girl? Did you get mixed up with her, I say?

NIKITA: I simply don't understand what you're talking about.

AKIM: I mean, was there any foolery, y'see, between you and her? Foolery, foolery, you know.

NIKITA: Of course there was. You have fun with the cook to pass the time away; you play the accordion and she dances. What more foolery do you want?

PETR: Nikita, don't shuffle around: answer straight out what your father's asking you.

AKIM (*solemnly*): Nikita, you can hide things from men, but you can't hide 'em from God. Nikita, just think it over, y'see; don't you tell me lies! She's an orphan, y'see; it's easy to injure her. An orphan, you know. Tell me plain how it was.

NIKITA: But there's nothing to tell. I'm telling you the whole story, because there's nothing to tell. (*Getting excited.*) She'll say anything. She can spread all the stories she wants, as if a man was dead. What stories didn't she tell of Fedka Mikishkin? So I suppose nowadays you can't have any fun! Let her talk!

AKIM: Eh, Nikita, look out! The truth will be known. Was there something or wasn't there?

NIKITA (*aside*): They're pressing me hard. (*To* AKIM.) I tell you there wasn't anything. There was nothing between me and her. (*Angrily.*) I swear to Christ, may I die on the spot if there was! (*Crosses himself.*) I don't know anything about the business. (*Silence.* NIKITA *continues still more excitedly.*) How did you get the idea of marrying me to her! What's all this anyhow? It's an outrage. Nowadays you've no right to marry a man by force. It's simple enough. I've just sworn to you—I don't know a thing about it.

MATRENA (*to her husband*): That's it, you silly old fool: whatever rubbish they tell you, you believe it all. You've just put the lad to shame for nothing. And he'd better just stay on living here with the master. Now the master will give us ten rubles to help us out. And when the time comes—

PETR: Well then, Uncle Akim?

AKIM (*clucks with his tongue. To his son*): Look out, Nikita; the tear of an injured girl don't flow in vain, y'see; it drops on a man's head. Look out for what's coming.

NIKITA: What's there to look out for? Look out yourself. (*Sits down.*)

ANYUTKA: I'll go tell mama. (*Goes out.*)

SCENE XIV

PETR, AKIM, MATRENA, *and* NIKITA

MATRENA (*to* PETR): That's how it always is, Petr Ignatych. My old man just makes trouble with his talk; when he gets a notion in his nut, you can't knock it out. We've just bothered you for nothing. Let the lad stay on living here as he has done. Keep the lad—he's your servant.

PETR: How about it, Uncle Akim?

AKIM: Well, y'see, I didn't want to force the lad—I was just afraid—Y'see, I'd like to have—

MATRENA: You don't know yourself what you're meddling with. Let him live here just as he has. The lad himself don't want to leave. And what use have we for him? We'll manage alone.

PETR: Just one thing, Uncle Akim: if you're going to take him in the summer, I don't want him this winter. If he's to stay here, it must be for a year.

MATRENA: He'll promise for the whole year. At home, when the working time comes, if we need anybody we'll hire him; and let the lad stay here. And now you give us ten rubles.

PETR: Well then, for a year more?

AKIM (*sighing*): Well, seems like, y'see; I suppose it's so.

MATRENA: One year more, from the feast of St. Dmitry.* You won't beat us down on the price—and now give us ten rubles. You'll do us that favor. (*Rises and bows.*)

(ANISYA *comes in with* ANYUTKA *and sits down at one side.*)

SCENE XV

The same, ANISYA *and* ANYUTKA

PETR: Well? If that's all right, then—then let's go to the tavern and wet down the bargain. Come on, Uncle Akim, and have a drink of vodka.

AKIM: I don't drink vodka, I don't.

---

* The Saturday between October 18 and 26.

PETR: Well, you'll have some tea.

AKIM: Tea's my sin. Tea, sure.

PETR: The women will have some tea too. Nikita, see that you don't drive the sheep too fast—and rake up the straw.

NIKITA: All right.

(*All go out except* NIKITA. *Darkness is falling.*)

SCENE XVI

NIKITA *alone*

NIKITA (*lights a cigarette*): They nagged and nagged me to tell about my doings with the girls. Those'd make a long story. He told me to marry her. If I married 'em all, I'd have a lot of wives. No use of my marrying; I'm as well off now as a married man: people envy me. And how lucky it was that something or other just put me up to go and cross myself before the ikon. That way I cut the whole business short. They say it's scary to swear to what ain't true. That's all bosh. Nothing but words anyhow. It's simple enough.

SCENE XVII

NIKITA *and* AKULINA

AKULINA (*comes in, lays down the rope, takes off her coat, and goes to the storeroom*): You might give us a light, anyhow.

NIKITA: To look at you? I can see you without it.

AKULINA: Drat you!

SCENE XVIII

The same and ANYUTKA

ANYUTKA (*runs in and whispers to* NIKITA): Nikita, hurry up; somebody's asking for you. Just think!

NIKITA: Who is it?

ANYUTKA: Marina from the railroad. She's standing round the corner.

NIKITA: You lie.

ANYUTKA: Honest!

NIKITA: What's she want?

ANYUTKA: Wants you to come. "I just need to speak one word to Nikita," she says. I began to ask questions, but she won't tell. She just asked if it was true that you're leaving us. "It ain't true," says I, "his father wanted to take him away and marry him, but he refused and he's going to stay another year with us." And she says: "Just send him to me, for Christ's sake. I just must say one word to him," she says. She's been waiting a long time. You go to her.

NIKITA: Plague take her! Why should I go?

ANYUTKA: "If he don't come," she says, "I'll come into the cottage for him. Honest I'll come," she says.

NIKITA: Don't worry: she'll stand there a while and then go away.

ANYUTKA: "Do they want to marry him to Akulina?" she says.

AKULINA (*still spinning, goes up to* NIKITA): Marry whom to Akulina?

ANYUTKA: Nikita.

AKULINA: Really? Who says so?

NIKITA: Some people say so. (*Looks at her and laughs.*) Akulina, will you marry me?

AKULINA: You? Maybe I'd have married you a little while ago, but now I won't.

NIKITA: Why won't you now?

AKULINA: 'Cause you won't love me.

NIKITA: Why won't I?

AKULINA: They won't let you. (*Laughs.*)

NIKITA: Who won't?

AKULINA: Stepmother, of course. She keeps scolding; she watches you all the time.

NIKITA (*laughing*): Bright girl! What sharp eyes you have!

AKULINA: I? Course I see. Am I blind? She blew up dad sky-high to-day. She's a witch with a big snout. (*Goes into the store-room.*)

ANYUTKA: Nikita, just look! (*She looks out of the window.*) She's coming. Honest, it's she. I'll clear out. (*Goes out.*)

SCENE XIX

NIKITA, AKULINA (*in the storeroom*) *and* MARINA

MARINA (*coming in*): What's this you're doing to me?

NIKITA: What am I doing? I'm not doing anything.

MARINA: You're going to desert me.

NIKITA (*rising angrily*): Well, what do you mean by coming here?

MARINA: Oh, Nikita!

NIKITA: You girls are a queer lot. . . . What have you come for?

MARINA: Nikita!

NIKITA: Nikita, you say? I'm Nikita. What do you want? Get out, I tell you.

MARINA: I see you mean to desert me, to forget me.

NIKITA: Why should I remember you? You don't know yourself. You were standing round the corner and sent Anyutka to me, and I didn't come to you. So I haven't any use for you; that's all. Now get out.

MARINA: No use for me! You've no use for me now. I believed you when you said you'd love me. And now you've done with me and haven't any use for me.

NIKITA: This talk of yours is all no use, don't amount to anything. You even blabbed to my father. Clear out, please!

MARINA: You know yourself that I never loved anybody but you. You might marry me or not, as you please; I shouldn't care. Have I done you any wrong that you've stopped loving me? Why did you?

NIKITA: There's no use of our wasting time talking. Clear out! . . . These senseless girls!

MARINA: What hurts ain't that you deceived me and promised to marry me, but that you don't love me any more. And it don't hurt that you don't love me, but that you've changed me off for another woman. For whom? I know!

NIKITA (*steps towards her angrily*): No use talking with girls like you; they won't listen to reason. Clear out, I tell you, or you'll make me do something bad.

MARINA: Something bad? Well, are you going to beat me? Go on, do! What are you turning away your mug for? Oh, Nikita!

NIKITA: Of course, it won't do; people'd come. But talking's no use.

MARINA: Well, this is the end; what's done is done. You tell me to forget it all! Well, Nikita, remember this. I guarded my honor more than my very eyes. You just ruined me and deceived me. You had no pity for an orphan (*Weeps.*); you deserted me. You've killed me, but I don't bear you any grudge. Good-by; I don't care. If you find a better one, you'll forget me; if you find a worse one, you'll remember. You'll remember, Nikita! Good-by, if I must go. But how I *loved* you! Good-by for the last time! (*Tries to embrace him and clasps his head.*)

NIKITA (*tearing himself free*): Bah! I'm sick of talking with you. If you won't go, I'll go myself and you can stay here.

MARINA (*screams*): You're a beast! (*In the doorway.*) God won't give you happiness! (*Goes out, weeping.*)

SCENE XX

NIKITA *and* AKULINA

AKULINA (*coming out of the storeroom*) : You're a cur, Nikita!
NIKITA : Well?
AKULINA : How she yelled! (*Weeps.*)
NIKITA : What's the matter with you?
AKULINA : What? You wronged her. You'll wrong me the same way—you cur! (*Goes out into the storeroom.*)

SCENE XXI

NIKITA *alone*

NIKITA (*after an interval of silence*) : It's all a puzzle to me. I love those women like sugar; but if a man sins with them—there's trouble!

ACT II

The stage represents a street and PETR'S *cottage. On the spectators' left, a cottage with a porch in the center, and on each side of this a living room; on the right, the yard fence, with a gate. Near the fence* ANISYA *is stripping hemp. Six months have passed since the first act.*

SCENE I

ANISYA *alone*

ANISYA (*stopping and listening*) : He's growling once more. Most likely he's got off the stove.*
(AKULINA *comes in, carrying pails on a yoke.*)

SCENE II

ANISYA *and* AKULINA

ANISYA : He's calling. Go and see what he wants. Hear him yell!
AKULINA : Why don't you go yourself?
ANISYA : Go along, I tell you!
(AKULINA *goes into the cottage.*)

---

*In a Russian peasant cottage the best couch is on top of the oven. It is generally reserved for the old or infirm.

SCENE III

Anisya *alone*

Anisya: He's worn me out: he won't tell where the money is; that's all there is to it. The other day he was in the entry way; most likely he'd hid it there. Now I don't know myself where it is. It's lucky he's afraid to part with it. It's still in the house. If I could only find it! It wasn't on him yesterday. Now I don't know where it is myself. He's clean worn me out.

(Akulina *comes out, tying on her kerchief.*)

SCENE IV

Anisya *and* Akulina

Anisya: Where are you going?

Akulina: Where? He told me to call Auntie Marfa. "Send for my sister," he says. "I'm dying," he says, "and I need to tell her something."

Anisya (*to herself*): Sending for his sister! Oh, poor me! Oh! oh! Most likely he wants to give it to her. What shall I do? Oh! (*To* Akulina.) Don't you go! Where are you going?

Akulina: For auntie.

Anisya: Don't you go, I tell you; I'll go myself. And you go to the brook with the wash. Otherwise you won't finish it before night.

Akulina: But he told me to.

Anisya: Go where I'm sending you. I'll go for Marfa myself, I tell you. Take the shirts off the fence.

Akulina: The shirts? But I'm afraid you won't go. He told me to.

Anisya: I've told you I'll go. Where's Anyutka?

Akulina: Anyutka? She's herding the calves.

Anisya: Send her here; they won't stray.

(Akulina *gathers up the clothes and goes out.*)

SCENE V

Anisya *alone*

Anisya: If I don't go, he'll scold at me. If I go, he'll give his sister the money. All my toil will go for nothing. I don't know myself what to do. My head's all mixed up. (*Continues her work.*)

(Matrena *comes in with a staff and a small bundle, equipped for traveling on foot.*)

SCENE VI

ANISYA *and* MATRENA

MATRENA: God help you, darling.

ANISYA (*looks around, drops her work, and claps her hands for joy*): Well, I never expected you, auntie. God has sent me such a guest just in time.

MATRENA: Well then?

ANISYA: I was just going crazy. Trouble!

MATRENA: Well, he's still alive, they tell me?

ANISYA: Don't speak of it. He's half alive and half dead.

MATRENA: Has he given the money to anybody?

ANISYA: He's just sending for Marfa, his own sister. Must be about the money.

MATRENA: Sure thing. But ain't he given it to somebody without your knowing it?

ANISYA: Not much! I've been watching him like a hawk.

MATRENA: But where is it?

ANISYA: He won't tell. And I can't find out anyhow. He hides it first one place and then another. And Akulina hampers me. She's only a silly fool, but she too keeps spying round and watching. Oh, poor me! I'm all worn out.

MATRENA: Eh, darling, if he gives the money to some one without your knowing it, you'll weep forever. They'll turn you out of the house empty-handed. You've worn yourself out, my precious, worn yourself out all your life with a man you don't love, and when you're a widow you'll have to go begging.

ANISYA: Don't speak of it, auntie. My heart aches and I don't know what to do and I've nobody to advise me. I told Nikita. But he's afraid to meddle with the business. He just told me yesterday that it was under the floor.

MATRENA: Well, did you look to see?

ANISYA: I couldn't; he was there himself. I notice, sometimes he carries it on him, sometimes he hides it.

MATRENA: Just remember, girlie: if you slip up once, you'll never get straight again. (*In a whisper.*) Well, have you given him the strong tea?

ANISYA: O-oh! (*Is about to reply, but sees her friend, and stops short.*)

(*Another housewife, a neighbor of* ANISYA, *walks past the cottage, and stops to listen to the shouts from within it.*)

SCENE VII

The same and FRIEND OF ANISYA

FRIEND (*to* ANISYA): Hey, friend! Anisya, Anisya, I say! Your man seems to be calling you.

ANISYA: He keeps coughing that way, and it sounds as if he was calling. He's pretty low by now.

FRIEND (*coming up to* MATRENA): Good day, old woman, where in the world did you come from?

MATRENA: From home, of course, my dear. I came to see my son. I've brought him some shirts. He's my boy, you know, and I'm sorry for him.

FRIEND: That's natural. (*To* ANISYA.) I was going to bleach my linen, friend, but I think it's too soon. People haven't begun yet.

ANISYA: No use of hurrying.

MATRENA: Well, have they given him the Communion?

ANISYA: Sure; the priest was here yesterday.

FRIEND (*to* MATRENA): I had a look at him yesterday myself, my dear; and he seemed hardly alive. He'd just wasted away. And the other day, my friend, he seemed on the point of death; they laid him out under the holy ikons. They were already wailing for him, and getting ready to wash the body.

ANISYA: He's come to life again—got out of bed; now he's walking again.

MATRENA: Well, will you give him extreme unction?

ANISYA: People are urging me to. If he's alive, we're going to send for the priest to-morrow.

FRIEND: Eh, it must be pretty hard for you, Anisya dear. It's a true saying: The bed's soft for the sick man, but hard for those that tend him.

ANISYA: That's so, but there's more to it.

FRIEND: Of course, he's been dying for most a year. He's tied you hand and foot.

MATRENA: A widow's lot is hard too. It's all right when you're young, but when you're old nobody will pity you. Old age is no joy. Take me for instance. I haven't walked far; but I'm tired out—my legs are numb.— Where's my son?

ANISYA: Plowing.— But come in, we'll start the samovar. The tea'll refresh you.

MATRENA (*sitting down*): I'm certainly tired, my dears. But you simply must give him the unction. People say that it's good for the soul.

ANISYA: Yes, we'll send to-morrow.

MATRENA: That's right.— But we're having a wedding down our way, girlie.

FRIEND: What, in the spring?

MATRENA: It's a good old proverb: "A poor man hurries to marry before the night's over." Semen Matveyevich is going to take Marina.

ANISYA: She's in great luck!

FRIEND: He must be a widower; she'll have to look out for the children.

MATRENA: There are four of 'em. What decent girl would marry him? Well, he took her. And she's glad enough. They were drinking, you know, and the glass was cracked—they spilled the wine.

FRIEND: Just think! Was there gossip? And has the man some property?

MATRENA: They get along pretty well.

FRIEND: It's true, hardly any girl will marry a man with children. . . . Just take our Mikhaylo. My dear, he's a man who—

PEASANT (*off stage*): Hey, Mavra, what the devil are you up to? Go and drive home the cow. (FRIEND *goes out.*)

SCENE VIII

ANISYA *and* MATRENA

MATRENA (*while the* FRIEND *is going out, she speaks in a calm voice*): They've got her out of harm's way, girlie; at any rate my old fool won't think any more about Nikita. (*Suddenly changes her voice to a whisper.*) She's gone! (*Whispers.*) Well, I say, did you give him the tea?

ANISYA: Don't speak of it. He'd better die all by himself. He's not dying anyhow; I've just got the sin of it on my conscience. O-oh, poor me! Why did you give me those powders?

MATRENA: Powders? They were sleeping powders, girlie; why shouldn't I give 'em to you? They won't do any harm.

ANISYA: I don't mean the sleeping powders; I mean the others, the white ones.

MATRENA: Well, darling, those powders were medicine.

ANISYA (*sighs*): I know, but I'm afraid. He's worn me out.

MATRENA: Have you used much of it?

ANISYA: I gave it to him twice.

MATRENA: Well, he didn't notice?

ANISYA: I tasted it a bit in the tea, myself; it's a trifle bitter. And he drank it with the tea and said: "I can't stand that tea." And says I, "Everything's bitter to a sick man." And I felt my heart sink, auntie.

MATRENA: Don't think about it; thinking makes things worse.

ANISYA: I wish you hadn't given 'em to me and led me into sin. When I remember it, it makes me shiver. And why did you give 'em to me?

MATRENA: Eh, what do you mean, darling! Lord help you! Why do you throw the blame on me? Look out, girlie, don't shift the blame to some one else's shoulders. If any questions are asked, I'm not concerned; I don't know a thing about it: I'll kiss the cross and say I never gave her powders, never saw any, never even heard that there were such powders. Just think for yourself, girlie. We were talking about you the other day, saying how the precious woman was just tormented to death. Her step-daughter's a fool, and her husband's no good, just skin and bones. Such a life'd make a woman do anything.

ANISYA: Well, I don't deny it. My life'd make me do worse things than these; I'm ready to hang myself or strangle him. 'Tain't being alive.

MATRENA: That's just the point. No time to stand and yawn. Somehow you must find the money and give him some more tea.

ANISYA: O-oh! Poor me! What to do now I don't know myself; it makes me shiver. I wish he'd die all by himself. I don't want to have the guilt on my soul.

MATRENA (angrily): But why don't he tell where the money is? Does he expect to take it with him and not let anybody have it? Is that right and proper? God forbid that such a lot of money should be wasted. Ain't that a sin? What's he doing? May I have a look at him?

ANISYA: I don't know myself. He's worn me out.

MATRENA: What don't you know? It's a clear case. If you make a slip now, you'll repent of it forever. He'll give the money to his sister, and you'll be left out.

ANISYA: O-oh, he was sending for her—I must go.

MATRENA: Don't go yet awhile: we'll start the samovar first thing. We'll give him some tea and between us we'll find where the money is —we'll manage to get it.

ANISYA: O-oh! Something may happen.

MATRENA: What's the matter? What are you staring at? Are you just going to roll your eyes at the money and not get it in your hands? Get to work.

ANISYA: Then I'll go and start the samovar.

MATRENA: Go on, darling; do the business right, so that you won't be sorry afterwards. That's the way. (ANISYA moves away, MATRENA urging her.) Be sure and not tell Nikita about all this business. He's sort of silly. God forbid he find out about the powders. God knows what he'd do. He's very tender-hearted. You know, he never would kill a chicken for me. Don't you tell him. Trouble is, he won't understand it. (*She stops in horror;* PETR *makes his appearance on the threshold.*)

SCENE IX

The same and PETR

(PETR, *holding to the wall, crawls out on the porch and calls in a weak voice.*)

PETR: Why can't I make you hear? O-oh! Anisya, who's here? (*Falls on the bench.*)

ANISYA (*coming in from around the corner*): What have you come out for? You ought to lie where you were.

PETR: Well, has the girl gone for Marfa? . . . I feel bad. . . . Oh, if death would only hurry up!

ANISYA: She's busy; I sent her to the brook. Give me time and I'll attend to it. I'll go myself.

PETR: Send Anyutka. Where is she? Oh, I feel bad! Oh, my death!

ANISYA: I've sent for her already.

PETR: O-oh! Where is she?

ANISYA: Where can she be? Plague take her!

PETR: O-oh, I can't stand it! My inside is burning. Seems like an auger was boring me. Why have you deserted me like a dog? . . . There's no one even to give me a drink. . . . O-oh! . . . Send Anyutka to me.

ANISYA: Here she is.—Anyutka, go to your father.

(ANYUTKA *runs in and* ANISYA *retires around the corner.*)

SCENE X

The same and ANYUTKA

PETR: Go and tell—o-oh!—your Aunt Marfa that your father wants to see her; tell her to come here.

ANYUTKA: Is that all?

PETR: Wait. Tell her to hurry up. Tell her I'm most dead. O-oh!

ANYUTKA: I'll just get my kerchief and go right away. (*Runs out.*)

SCENE XI

Petr, Anisya, *and* Matrena

Matrena (*winking*) : Now, girlie, get down to work. Go into the cottage and rummage everywhere. Look for it like a dog looks for fleas; turn over everything, and I'll search him right away.

Anisya (*to* Matrena) : With you seems like I have more courage. (*Goes towards the porch. To* Petr.) Shan't I start a samovar for you? Auntie Matrena's come to see her son; you'll have tea with her.

Petr: Go ahead and start it. (Anisya *goes into the cottage.*)

SCENE XII

Petr *and* Matrena

(Matrena *comes towards the porch.*)

Petr: Hello!

Matrena: Good day, my benefactor! Good day, my precious! I see you're still sick. And my old man is so sorry for you. "Go and inquire," says he. He sent his regards. (*Bows once more.*)

Petr: I'm dying.

Matrena: Well, when I look at you, Ignatych, I can see that trouble haunts men and not the forest. You've wasted away, my precious, all wasted away; I can see that. Sickness don't bring beauty, I suppose?

Petr: My death's near.

Matrena: Well, Petr Ignatych, it's God's will. They've given you the Communion, and now, God willing, they'll give you the unction. Thank God, your wife's a sensible woman; she'll bury you and have prayers said, all as is proper. And my son too, while he's needed, he'll tend to things about the house.

Petr: There's no one that I can give orders to! The woman's heedless and spends her time on foolery; I know all about it—I know. The girl's half-witted, and young at that. I've gathered a good property, and there's nobody to attend to it. It's too bad. (*Snivels.*)

Matrena: Well, if it's money or anything like that, you can give directions.

Petr (*calls into the house, to* Anisya) : Has Anyutka gone yet?

Matrena (*aside*) : Oh my, he still remembers!

Anisya (*from indoors*) : She went right off. Come into the house; I'll help you.

Petr: Let me sit here for the last time. It's close in there. I feel bad. . . . Oh, my heart's burning! . . . If only death would come!

MATRENA: When God won't take a soul, the soul won't leave of itself. God's the judge of life and death, Petr Ignatych. You can never tell when death will come. Sometimes you recover. For instance in our village a peasant was just on the point of death—

PETR: No! I feel that I'll die to-day; I feel it. (*Leans against the wall and closes his eyes.*)

SCENE XIII

The same and ANISYA

ANISYA (*coming out of the cottage*): Well, are you coming in or not? Don't keep me waiting. Petr! Petr, I say!

MATRENA (*walking away and beckoning to* ANISYA): Well, how about it?

ANISYA (*coming down from the porch, to* MATRENA): Not there.

MATRENA: But did you look everywhere? Under the floor?

ANISYA: Not there either. Maybe in the shed. He went there yesterday.

MATRENA: Search, search, I tell you. Lick things clean. And it's my notion he'll die to-day anyhow: his nails are blue and his face like earth. Is the samovar ready?

ANISYA: It'll boil right off.

(NIKITA *comes in from the other side of the stage—if possible on horseback; he comes up to the gate without seeing* PETR.)

SCENE XIV

The same and NIKITA

NIKITA (*to his mother*): Hello, mother; are you all well at home?

MATRENA: Thanks to the Lord God, we're still alive; we can still eat.

NIKITA: Well, how's the boss?

MATRENA: Shh—he's sitting there. (*Points to the porch.*)

NIKITA: Well, let him sit. What do I care?

PETR (*opening his eyes*): Nikita; hey, Nikita, come here!

(NIKITA *goes to him.* ANISYA *and* MATRENA *whisper.*)

PETR: Why have you come home so early?

NIKITA: I finished the plowing.

PETR: Did you plow the strip beyond the bridge?

NIKITA: It was too far to go there.

PETR: Too far? It's still farther from the house. You'll have to go there specially. You ought to have finished it at the same time.

(ANISYA *listens to the conversation without showing herself.*)

MATRENA (*approaching them*): Oh, sonny, why don't you try to please the master? The master is ill and relies on you; you ought to work for him as for your own father. Just stir yourself and work hard for him as I've told you to so often.

PETR: Then—ugh!—haul out the potatoes; the women—o-oh!—will sort them over.

ANISYA (*to herself*): Well, I won't budge. He's trying to send everybody away from him once more; most likely he has the money on him. He wants to hide it somewhere.

PETR: Otherwise—o-oh!— It'll be time to plant 'em, and they'll have sweated. O-oh, I'm exhausted. (*Rises.*)

MATRENA (*runs up on the porch and supports* PETR): Shall I take you into the room?

PETR: Yes. (*Stops.*) Nikita!

NIKITA (*angrily*): What next?

PETR: I shan't see you again. . . . I shall die to-day. . . . Forgive me for Christ's sake if I've sinned against you. . . . Whether in word or deed . . . if I ever sinned. There were many times. Forgive me.

NIKITA: No need to forgive; I'm a sinner myself.

MATRENA: Oh, sonny, take this to heart!

PETR: Forgive me, for Christ's sake! . . . (*Weeps.*)

NIKITA (*in a choked voice*): God will forgive you, Uncle Petr. I've no cause to bear you a grudge. I've never been ill treated by you. You forgive me; maybe I've sinned more against you. (*Weeps.*)

(PETR *goes out, sniffling, supported by* MATRENA.)

SCENE XV

NIKITA *and* ANISYA

ANISYA: Oh, poor me! He didn't think of that for nothing; it's clear that— (*Goes up to* NIKITA.) Well, you said that the money was under the floor.— It ain't there.

NIKITA (*sobs, without replying*): He was always fair and square to me—and see what I've done!

ANISYA: Well, stop it. Where's the money?

NIKITA (*angrily*): How should I know? Look for yourself.

ANISYA: You seem to be awful sorry for him?

NIKITA: Yes, I am sorry for him, mighty sorry. How he wept! O-oh!

ANISYA: How kind you are—found somebody to pity! He treated you like a dog, like a dog. Just now he was telling us to turn you out. You might be sorry for me instead.

NIKITA: Why should I be sorry for you?

ANISYA: He'll die and hide the money. . . .

NIKITA: Maybe he won't hide it. . . .

ANISYA: Oh, Nikita dear! He's sent for his sister and wants to give it to her. Bad luck for us! How can we live if he gives away the money? They'll drive me out of the house! You might do something about it. Didn't you tell me he went to the shed last evening?

NIKITA: I saw him coming out of there, but nobody knows where he hid it.

ANISYA: Oh, poor me, I'll go and look there. (NIKITA *walks away.*)

(MATRENA *comes out of the cottage and goes over to* ANISYA *and* NIKITA.)

SCENE XVI

The same and MATRENA

MATRENA (*whispers*): You needn't go anywhere. The money's on him: I felt it; it's on a string around his neck.

ANISYA: Oh, poor me!

MATRENA: If you let it out of your sight now, you can look for it next door to nowhere. His sister'll come and you're done for.

ANISYA: She'll come and he'll give it to her. What shall we do? Oh, poor me!

MATRENA: What shall you do? See here: the samovar's boiling; go make the tea and pour it out for him, and (*In a whisper.*) sprinkle in all the powder out of the paper and make him drink it. When he's drunk a cupful, just pull the string. Don't worry; he'll never tell about it.

ANISYA: Oh, I'm afraid!

MATRENA: Don't argue, hurry up about it; and I'll take care of the sister if she comes. Don't make a slip. Pull out the money and bring it here, and Nikita will hide it.

ANISYA: Oh, poor me! How can I ever dare to . . . and . . . and . . .

MATRENA: Don't argue, I tell you; do as I say. Nikita!

NIKITA: What?

MATRENA: Stay here; sit down on the bench close to the house, in case—you're needed.

NIKITA (*with a wave of his hand*): Those women are crafty. They make a man dizzy. Plague take you! I'll go haul out the potatoes.

MATRENA (*clutching his arm*): Stay here, I tell you.

(ANYUTKA *comes in.*)

SCENE XVII

The same and ANYUTKA

ANISYA (*to* ANYUTKA) : Well?

ANYUTKA: She was at her daughter's in the garden; she'll come right away.

ANISYA: If she comes, what'll we do?

MATRENA (*to* ANISYA) : Don't bother about her now; do as I tell you.

ANISYA: I don't know myself—I don't know anything; my head's all mixed up. Anyutka, girlie, run off for the calves; they must have strayed away. Oh, I'll never dare!

(ANYUTKA *runs out.*)

MATRENA: Go along; the samovar's boiling over, most likely.

ANISYA: Oh, poor me! (*Goes out.*)

SCENE XVIII

MATRENA *and* NIKITA

MATRENA (*going up to her son*) : Well, sonny! (*Sits down beside him on the earth bench around the house.*) Now we must think over your business, not just let it drift.

NIKITA: What business?

MATRENA: Why, how you're going to get along and make your living.

NIKITA: Get along? Other people do, and so can I.

MATRENA: The old man's sure to die to-day.

NIKITA: If he dies, let him go to heaven! What do I care?

MATRENA (*during her speech she keeps glancing at the porch*) : Eh, sonny! The living must think of life. Here you need a lot of sense, my precious. Just think, for your sake I've run around everywhere; I've trotted my legs off working for you. And mind you: don't forget me later.

NIKITA: What sort of work were you doing?

MATRENA: For your sake, for your future. If you don't take pains in time, nothing ever succeeds. You know Ivan Moseich? I called on him too. I went over the other day, you know, and told him about a certain matter; I sat there and we got to talking. "Ivan Moseich," says I, "how could a case like this be fixed up? Suppose," says I, "a peasant is a widower, and suppose he takes another wife; and just suppose," says I, "he has children, one daughter by his first wife and one by the second. Well," says I, "if that peasant dies, is it possible," says I, "for another peasant to marry the widow and get the farm? Is it possible," says I, "for that peasant to marry off the daughters and stay on the farm himself?" "It's possible," says he, "only you need to take a lot of pains; and," says he, "you need to use money to fix things up. Without money," says he, "there's no use meddling with it."

NIKITA (*laughing*) : You needn't tell me that; just give 'em money. Everybody needs money.

MATRENA: Well, darling, I explained everything to him. "First of all," says he, "your son must get himself enrolled legally as a member of that village commune: for this he'll need money, to give a drink to the old men of the village. Then they'll agree to it and sign the paper. Only," says he, "you must do everything with some sense." Look here (*Takes a paper from her kerchief.*) : he wrote out a paper. Read it—you're smart.

(NIKITA *reads, and* MATRENA *listens.*)

NIKITA: The paper is a legal order, of course. No great amount of sense needed here.

MATRENA: But just hear what Ivan Moseich had to say. "The main thing is, auntie," says he, "look out and don't let the money slip past you. If she don't grab the money," says he, "they won't let her marry off her daughter. The money's the root of the whole matter," says he. So look out. The time's coming to act, sonny.

NIKITA: What do I care: the money's hers, let her worry about it.

MATRENA: Is that what you think, sonny! Can a woman make plans? Even if she gets the money, she won't know how to manage it. She's nothing but a woman, and you're a man. So you can hide it and do anything you choose. Anyhow, you have more sense if any hitch comes.

NIKITA: Oh, you women don't understand anything!

MATRENA: Don't we though? You get hold of the money. Then the woman will be in your hands. If she ever happens to growl or grumble, then you can take her down.

NIKITA: Oh, you make me tired! I'm going.

(ANISYA *runs out of the cottage, all pale, and goes around the corner to* MATRENA.)

SCENE XIX

NIKITA, MATRENA, *and* ANISYA

ANISYA: It was on him. There it is. (*Points under her apron.*)

MATRENA: Give it to Nikita; he'll hide it. Nikita, take it and hide it somewhere.

NIKITA: Well, give it here!

ANISYA: O-oh, poor me! Maybe I'd better do it myself. (*Goes towards the gate.*)

MATRENA (*clutching her by the arm*): Where are you going? They'll miss it; his sister's coming. Give it to him; he knows what to do. How silly you are!

ANISYA (*stops, undecided*): Oh, poor me!

NIKITA: Well, give it here; I'll hide it somewhere.

ANISYA: Where'll you hide it?

NIKITA: Are you afraid? (*Laughs.*)

(AKULINA *comes in with the clothes.*)

SCENE XX

The same and AKULINA

ANISYA: O-oh, poor me, poor me! (*Hands him the money.*) Look out, Nikita!

NIKITA: What're you afraid of? I'll tuck it away where I can't find it myself. (*Goes out.*)

SCENE XXI

MATRENA, ANISYA, *and* AKULINA

ANISYA (*stands terrified*): O-oh, what if he—

MATRENA: Well, is he dead?

ANISYA: Yes, seems dead. I pulled it out, and he didn't feel it.

MATRENA: Go inside; there's Akulina coming.

ANISYA: Well, I've sinned—and now he's got the money.—

MATRENA: That'll do; go inside: there's Marfa coming.

ANISYA: Well, I trusted him. What'll come of it? (*Goes out.*)

(MARFA *comes in from one side;* AKULINA *approaches from the other.*)

SCENE XXII

MARFA, AKULINA, *and* MATRENA

MARFA (*to* AKULINA): I'd have come long ago, but I'd gone to my daughter's.— Well, how's the old man? Is he dying?

AKULINA (*sorting out the clothes*): How should I know? I've been at the brook.

MARFA (*pointing to* MATRENA): Where's she from?

MATRENA: I'm from Zuyev; I'm Nikita's mother, from Zuyev, dearie. Good day to you! Your dear brother is very sick, very sick. He came

out here himself. "Send for my sister," says he, "because," says he—
Oh! Maybe he's dead already?

(ANISYA *runs out of the cottage with a cry, clutches the post of the porch, and begins to wail.*)

SCENE XXIII

The same and ANISYA

ANISYA: O-o-oh! O-o-oh! Why have you left—o-o-oh!—and why have you deserted—o-o-oh!—your wretched widow?— Forever and ever, he has closed his bright eyes!—

(FRIEND *comes in.*)

SCENE XXIV

The FRIEND *and* MATRENA *support* ANISYA *under the arms.* AKULINA *and* MARFA *go into the cottage. Peasants, both men and women, come in.*

VOICE FROM THE CROWD: Call the old women; they must lay him out.
MATRENA (*rolling up her sleeves*): Is there any water in the kettle? And I don't believe the samovar's been emptied. I'll help in the work myself.

ACT III

PETR'S *cottage. Winter. Nine months have passed since Act II.* ANISYA, *dressed in shabby workaday clothes, is seated at the loom, weaving.* ANYUTKA *is perched on the stove.*

SCENE I

(MITRICH, *an old laborer, comes in.*)

MITRICH: Oh, the Lord be with you! Well, hasn't the master come home?
ANISYA: What?
MITRICH: Hasn't Nikita come home from town?
ANISYA: No.
MITRICH: Seems like he's been on a spree. Oh, Lord!
ANISYA: Have you fixed up the threshing floor?
MITRICH: Sure. I fixed it all up proper, covered it with straw. I don't like a halfway job. Oh, Lord! Gracious St. Nicholas! (*Pecks at his callouses.*) Yes, it's high time for him to be here.

ANISYA: Why should he hurry? He has money; I suppose he's on a spree with some hussy.

MITRICH: He has money; so why shouldn't he go on a spree? What did Akulina go to town for?

ANISYA: Ask her why the devil took her there!

MITRICH: Why should she go to town? There are all kinds of things in town, if you only have the money. Oh, Lord!

ANYUTKA: Mama, I heard why. "I'll buy you a little shawl," says he, just think; "you can pick it out yourself," says he. And she dressed up just fine; put on her plush wrap and a French kerchief.

ANISYA: That's just it: maiden's modesty as far as the threshold; but when she's crossed it she forgets everything. She's a shameless hussy.

MITRICH: Really! Why be modest? If you have money, go on a spree! Oh, Lord! Is it too soon for supper? (ANISYA *is silent.*) I'll go warm myself meanwhile. (*Climbs on the stove.*) Oh, Lord! Holy Virgin Mother! St. Nicholas the Martyr!

SCENE II

The same and FRIEND

FRIEND (*coming in*): I see your man ain't back yet?

ANISYA: No.

FRIEND: Time for him. Hasn't he gone to our tavern? Sister Fekla said, my dear, that a lot of sleighs from town were standing there.

ANISYA: Anyutka! Hey, Anyutka!

ANYUTKA: What?

ANISYA: Run over to the tavern, Anyutka, and take a look. See if he's got drunk and gone there.

ANYUTKA (*jumping down from the stove and putting on her coat*): Right away.

FRIEND: Did he take Akulina with him?

ANISYA: Otherwise he'd have no reason to go. It's she who keeps him busy in town. "I must go to the bank," says he, "there's some money due me"—but she's really the cause of all this mess.

FRIEND (*shaking her head*): You don't say! (*Silence.*)

ANYUTKA (*at the door*): If he's there, what shall I say!

ANISYA: Just see if he's there.

ANYUTKA: All right, I'll fly like a bird. (*Goes out.*)

SCENE III

ANISYA, MITRICH, *and* FRIEND

(*A long silence.*)

MITRICH (*bellows*): Oh, Lord! Gracious St. Nicholas!

FRIEND (*starts from fright*): Oh, he scared me! Who's that?

ANISYA: Mitrich, our laborer.

FRIEND: O-oh, how he frightened me! I forgot about him. Well, friend, they say people have made proposals for Akulina?

ANISYA (*coming out from behind the loom and sitting down at the table*): People from Dedlov hinted about it, but they must have heard something—they hinted and then shut up, so the matter dropped. Who wants her?

FRIEND: How about the Lizunovs from Zuyev?

ANISYA: They sent to inquire. But that too came to nothing. He wouldn't receive them.

FRIEND: But you ought to marry her off.

ANISYA: We sure ought. I can hardly wait to get her out of the house, friend, but I've no luck. He don't want to, nor she either. You see he's not had fun enough yet with that beauty of his.

FRIEND: Eh-eh-eh! Sins! The idea of it! Why, he's her step-father.

ANISYA: Ah, friend! They tied me hand and foot too cleverly for words. Fool that I was, I didn't notice anything, didn't even think of it—and so I married him. I didn't guess one single thing, but they already had an understanding.

FRIEND: O-oh, how sad things are!

ANISYA: More and more, I see, they're hiding things from me. Oh, friend, my life has been miserable, just miserable. It'd be all right if I only didn't love him.

FRIEND: You needn't tell me!

ANISYA: And it hurts me, friend; it hurts me to suffer such an insult from him. Oh, how it hurts!

FRIEND: Well, they say he's even getting rough with his hands. Is that so?

ANISYA: Rough every kind of way. When he was drunk he used to be gentle; even in old times he used to take a drop, but it never made him turn against me. But now, when he gets liquor in him, he just flies at me and wants to trample on me. The other day he got his hands into my hair, and I had hard work to break loose. And the hussy is worse than a snake; I wonder how the earth can bear such spiteful creatures.

FRIEND: O-o-oh! You're in hard luck, friend, the more I think of it! How can you stand it? You took in a beggar, and now he's going to make sport of you like that. Why don't you take him down a bit?

ANISYA: Oh, my dear friend, with a heart like mine what can I do! My dead husband was mighty severe, but all the same I could manage him whatever way I wanted to; but here I can't, friend. When I see him, my heart just melts. Against him I haven't any courage; he makes me feel like a wet hen.

FRIEND: O-oh, friend, I can see that somebody's bewitched you. That Matrena—they say she practices such things. Must be she.

ANISYA: I think so myself, friend. Sometimes I'm fairly ashamed of myself. I feel as if I'd like to tear him in pieces. But when I see him, no, my heart won't rise against him.

FRIEND: There must be a spell on you. It's easy enough to ruin a person, my precious. When I look at you, I can see that something's happened.

ANISYA: My legs are thin as bean poles. But look at that fool Akulina. She was a frowsy, sluttish hussy, and now look at her! What's the reason of this change? He's given her finery. She's swelled up and puffed up like a bubble on water. And then, no matter if she is a fool, she's got notions into her head. "I'm the mistress here," she says; "the house is mine. Dad wanted to marry me to him." And what a temper! God save us! When she gets mad, she fairly tears the straw off the roof.

FRIEND: O-oh, I see what a life you have, friend! And yet people envy you! "They're rich," they say; but, my dear, tears flow even through gold, you know.

ANISYA: Much there is to envy! And even the wealth will scatter like dust. He squanders money something awful.

FRIEND: But haven't you given him a pretty free rein, friend? The money's yours.

ANISYA: If you only knew the whole story! I made one big mistake.

FRIEND: In your place, friend, I'd go straight to the chief of police. The money's yours. How can he squander it? He's no right to.

ANISYA: Nowadays rights don't matter.

FRIEND: Oh, friend, I can see that you've grown weak.

ANISYA: Yes, darling, weak as a rag. He's bound me hand and foot. And I can't see any way out of it. O-oh, poor me!

FRIEND: Isn't somebody coming?

(*She listens. The door opens and* AKIM *comes in.*)

SCENE IV

The same and AKIM

AKIM (*crossing himself, knocking the snow off his bast shoes, and taking off his coat*): Peace to this house! Are you all well? Good evening, auntie.

ANISYA: Good evening, daddy. Have you come from home?

AKIM: I thought, y'see, I'd come see my son, y'see; I'd call on my son, you know. I didn't start early, had my dinner, you know; I started and it was deep snow, y'see, hard going, hard going; and so, y'see, I'm pretty late, you know. But is sonny at home? Is he home?

ANISYA: No, in town.

AKIM (*sitting down on the bench*): I have some business with him, y'see; a bit of business. I was telling him the other day, you know; telling him about our needs, y'see: the old horse has given out, you know, the old horse. So we must get some sort of nag, y'see; some kind of nag. And so, y'see, I've come.

ANISYA: Nikita told me: when he comes, you can talk with him. (*Rises and goes to the oven.*) Have supper, and he'll come. Mitrich, hey, Mitrich, come and have supper.

MITRICH: Oh, Lord, merciful St. Nicholas!

ANISYA: Come and have supper.

FRIEND: I'll be going; good-by. (*Goes out.*)

SCENE V

AKIM, ANISYA, *and* MITRICH

MITRICH (*climbing down*): I never noticed how I went to sleep. Oh, Lord, St. Nicholas the Martyr!— Good evening, Uncle Akim.

AKIM: Huh! Mitrich! What're you doing here?

MITRICH: I'm working for Nikita now; I'm living with your son.

AKIM: Do say! So, y'see, you're working for my son. Do say!

MITRICH: I was living with a merchant in town, but I ruined myself by drink there. So I came to the country. I'd no home to go to, so I hired myself out. (*Yawns.*) Oh, Lord!

AKIM: Well, y'see, well, what's Nikita doing himself? Is he so fixed, y'see, that he has to hire a workman, you know?

ANISYA: How's he fixed? First he managed by himself, but now he don't want to: so he's hired a laborer.

MITRICH: He has money, so what does he care?

AKIM: That's wrong, y'see; that's all wrong, y'see.   It's wrong. He's just lazy.

ANISYA: Yes, he's got lazy, got lazy: that's the trouble.

AKIM: That's it, y'see; you think it'll be better, and, y'see, it turns out worse.   When a man's wealthy, he gets lazy, gets lazy.

MITRICH: Fat makes a dog go mad, so why shouldn't fat make a man lazy!   Fat was what was the ruin of me.   I drank for three weeks without stopping.   I drank up my last pair of pants.   When I'd nothing more, I just quit.   Now I've sworn off.   Plague take the stuff!

AKIM: And where's your old woman now, y'see?

MITRICH: My old woman, friend, has found a place of her own. She's in town; sits in the taverns and begs.   She's a beauty, too: one eye pulled out and the other knocked in and her mouth twisted sidewise. And—may she always have cakes and pie!—she's never sober.

AKIM: Oh ho!   What's that?

MITRICH: But where's there a place for a soldier's wife?   She's found her job.   (*Silence.*)

AKIM (*to* ANISYA): What did Nikita go to town for?   Did he take something, y'see?   Did he take something to sell, you know?

ANISYA (*setting the table and passing the food*): He went empty-handed.   He went for money, to get some money in the bank.

AKIM (*eating*): What do you want the money for, y'see?   Are you going to make some new use of it?

ANISYA: No, we don't spend much.   Only twenty or thirty rubles. We ran short, so we had to get some.

AKIM: Had to get some?   What's the use of taking it, y'see, that money?   To-day you take some, you know; to-morrow you take some, y'see: that way you'll use it all up, you know.

ANISYA: This was just extra.   But the money's all there.

AKIM: All there?   How can it be all there, y'see?   You take it and still it's all there?   See here: if you pour meal, y'see, or something, you know, into a chest, y'see, or a storehouse, and then go take the meal out of there—will it still be all there, y'see?   That means something is wrong, you know; they're cheating you.   You see to it, or they'll cheat you.   Much it's all there!   You keep on taking it, and it's all there.

ANISYA: I don't know about such things.   Ivan Moseich gave us some advice then.   "Put your money in the bank," says he, "and the money'll be safer, and you'll get interest."

MITRICH (*finishing his meal*): That's right.   I lived with a merchant. They all do that way.   Put your money in and lie on the stove and earn more.

AKIM: That's queer talk of yours, y'see.   You say, "earn more," y'see, "earn more," but how do they earn that money, you know; who do they earn it from?

ANISYA: They give 'em the money from the bank.

MITRICH: What a notion! Women can't understand things. Look here and I'll explain the whole thing to you. You pay attention. You, for instance, have money; and I, for instance, when spring comes, have an empty field and nothing to sow on it, or I can't pay my taxes, maybe. So I just come to you, you know: "Akim," says I, "give me ten rubles; and when I harvest my crop, I'll return it to you on St. Mary's Day in October, and I'll help you to harvest your field for your kindness." You, for instance, see that I have something to use as security, a horse or a cow, maybe, and you say: "Give me two or three rubles extra for my kindness and let it go at that." I have the halter round my neck and can't help myself. "All right," says I, "I'll take the ten rubles." In the autumn I make a turnover and bring you the money, and you skin me of those three rubles extra.

AKIM: That means, y'see, those peasants are acting crooked, y'see; that's how it is when a man forgets God, y'see; 'tain't right, you know.

MITRICH: Wait a bit. It'll work out the same way over again. Remember now, that's what you've done, skinned me, you know: well, Anisya too, for instance, has some money on hand. She's nowhere to put it; and, just like a woman, you know, don't know what to do with it. She comes to you and says: "Can't you make some use of my money too?" she says. "Sure I can," says you. And you just wait. Then I come again next spring. "Give me another ten," says I, "and I'll pay you for it." So you just look and see if the skin ain't all peeled off of me, maybe you can tear off a bit more, and you give me Anisya's money. But if, for instance, I haven't a rag left, nothing to seize on, you just know it at a glance, and see that there's nothing to squeeze out of me, and you say right away, "Go somewhere else, my dear man, and may God help you!" and you look for some other fellow: then you lend him your own money once more and Anisya's too, and so you skin him. That's what a bank amounts to. It just goes round and round. It's a clever scheme, friend.

AKIM (getting excited): What's that? That's just nasty work, y'see. Peasants do that way; but the peasants, y'see, they feel it's sinful. That ain't lawful, y'see; it ain't lawful. It's nasty work. How do those learned men, y'see—?

MITRICH: That's just what they like best, my friend. Just remember this. If there's a man stupider than the rest of us, or a woman, and he can't make any use of the money himself, he just takes it to the bank; and they—it's fine bread and butter for them—just grab at it; and with that money they skin the people. It's a clever scheme.

AKIM (*sighing*): Eh, I see, it's hard not to have money, y'see; and it's twice as hard if you have it, y'see. Anyhow God bids us toil. But you, y'see, just put your money in the bank and go to sleep; and the money, y'see, will feed you while you lie idle. That's nasty work, you know; 'tain't lawful.

MITRICH: Not lawful? That ain't what folks think nowadays, my friend. And how they do strip a man bare. That's the point.

AKIM (*sighing*): That's the kind of times we're coming to, y'see. I've seen privies in town, you know. The new kind, y'see. All polished and polished, you know; made fine as a tavern. But it's no use, no use at all. Oh, they've forgotten God! They've forgotten him, you know! We've forgotten God, forgotten God!— Thank you, friend Anisya, I'm full; I've had enough. (*Gets up and leaves the table; MITRICH climbs on the stove.*)

ANISYA (*putting away the dishes and eating*): If only his father would make him repent of his sins—but I'm ashamed to tell him.

AKIM: What?

ANISYA: I was just talking to myself.

(ANYUTKA *comes in.*)

SCENE VI

The same and ANYUTKA

AKIM (*to* ANYUTKA): Hello, girlie! Always busy? Got chilled, didn't you?

ANYUTKA: Just awful chilled. Hello, grandpa!

ANISYA: Well? Is he there?

ANYUTKA: No. Only Andrian was there, just come from town; he said he'd seen 'em in town, in a tavern. He said dad was drunk, drunk as a fish.

ANISYA: Are you hungry? There's something for you.

ANYUTKA (*going to the stove*): I'm so cold. My hands are numb. (AKIM *takes off his bast shoes,* ANISYA *washes the dishes.*)

ANISYA: Daddy!

AKIM: What do you want?

ANISYA: Tell me: is Marina getting on well?

AKIM: All right. She's getting on. She's a sensible, quiet little woman, y'see; she gets on, y'see; she tries hard. She's a good sort of woman, you know; clever and hard-working and patient, y'see. She's a good sort of little woman, you know.

ANISYA: Well, people from your village tell me, the kinsfolk of Marina's husband want to ask for our Akulina in marriage. Have you heard of it?

AKIM: The Mironovs? The women were saying something about it. But I didn't pay attention, you know. I don't know whether it's true, y'see. The old women were talking about it. But I've a poor memory, poor memory, y'see. Well, the Mironovs, y'see, are decent sort of folks, y'see.

ANISYA: I wish that we could marry her off in a hurry.

AKIM: Why so?

ANYUTKA (*listening*): They've come.

ANISYA: Well, let 'em alone. (*Continues to wash the dishes, without turning her head.*)

SCENE VII

The same and NIKITA

NIKITA: Anisya, wife, who's come?

(ANISYA *glances at him and turns away in silence.*)

NIKITA (*threateningly*): Who's come? Have you forgotten?

ANISYA: Quit your bullying. Come in.

NIKITA (*still more threateningly*): Who's come?

ANISYA (*going to him and taking his arm*): Well, my husband's come. Come into the room.

NIKITA (*resisting*): So that's it! Your husband. And what's your husband's name? Say it right.

ANISYA: Confound you: Nikita.

NIKITA: So that's it! Booby! Say the full name.

ANISYA: Akimych. Well!

NIKITA (*still in the doorway*): So that's it! No, tell me what's the last name.

ANISYA (*laughing and pulling at his arm*): Chilikin. How drunk you are!

NIKITA: That's so! (*Holds to the door jamb.*) No, tell me what foot Chilikin puts into the room first.

ANISYA: Oh, stop, you'll cool off the room.

NIKITA: Say what foot he puts into the room first. You must tell me.

ANISYA (*to herself*): I'm sick of this. (*Aloud.*) Well, the left. Come in, will you?

NIKITA: So that's it!

ANISYA: Just see who's in the room.

NIKITA: Father? Well, I don't despise my father. I can show respect to my father. Good evening, daddy. (*Bows to him and offers his hand.*) My respects to you!

AKIM (*not replying to him*): Liquor, liquor, that's what it does. Nasty business.

NIKITA: Liquor? Have I had a drink? I'm certainly guilty; I had a drink with a friend—drank his health.

ANISYA: You'd better go lie down.

NIKITA: Wife, where am I standing? Tell me!

ANISYA: Oh, that's all right. Go lie down.

NIKITA: I'm going to have some tea with my father. Start the samovar. Akulina, come in, will you?

(AKULINA, *gayly dressed, comes in with packages she has bought and goes to* NIKITA.)

SCENE VIII

The same and AKULINA

AKULINA: You've mislaid everything. Where's the yarn?

NIKITA: The yarn? The yarn's over there.— Hey, Mitrich, what're you doing there? Gone to sleep? Go and unharness the horse.

AKIM (*without noticing* AKULINA, *looks at his son*): Just see how he's acting. The old man's tired out, y'see; been thrashing, you know; and he's showing his authority, you know. "Unharness the horse!" Bah! nasty!

MITRICH (*climbs down from the stove and puts on his felt boots*): Oh, merciful Lord! Is the horse in the yard? It sure must be tired. How drunk he is, confound him! Beats all! Oh, Lord! St. Nicholas the Martyr! (*Puts on his sheepskin and goes outdoors.*)

NIKITA (*sitting down*): Forgive me, daddy. I had a drink, that's true; but how can a man help it? Even a hen drinks. Ain't that so? And you forgive me! What about Mitrich? He don't take it ill; he'll unharness.

ANISYA: Shall I really start the samovar?

NIKITA: Yes. My father's come, I want to talk with him; I'll have tea. (*To* AKULINA.) Have you brought in all the packages?

AKULINA: Packages? I took my own, but there are some left in the sleigh.— Here, this ain't mine.

(*She tosses a bundle on the table and puts away the rest of the packages in the chest.* ANYUTKA *watches her do so.* AKIM, *without looking at his son, sets his leg wrappers and bast shoes on the stove.*)

ANISYA (*going out with the samovar*): The chest was full already, and he's bought more.

SCENE IX

AKIM, AKULINA, ANYUTKA, *and* NIKITA

NIKITA (*assuming a sober air*): Don't be cross with me, dad. You think I'm drunk? I'm equal to anything whatever, because I can drink and not lose my senses. I can talk things over with you this very minute, dad. I remember the whole business. You gave directions about money; the horse was worn out—I remember. I can do the whole thing. I have it right on hand. If you needed a huge sum of money, then you might have to wait a bit; but I can attend to all this! Here it is!

AKIM (*continues to fuss with the leg wrappers*): Eh, my boy, y'see, spring's coming on, y'see; bad traveling.

NIKITA: What're you saying that for? There's no talking with a man that's drunk. But don't you worry; we'll have some tea. And I can do everything; I can fix up absolutely the whole business.

AKIM (*shaking his head*): Eh-eh-eh!

NIKITA: Here's the money. (*Puts his hand in his pocket and takes out his purse; he turns over the bills and pulls out a ten-ruble note.*) Take that for the horse. Take it for the horse; I can't neglect my father. I certainly won't desert you, for you're my father. Here, take it. It's easy enough; I don't grudge it.

(*He comes up and thrusts the money at* AKIM; AKIM *does not take the money.*)

NIKITA (*clutching his hand*): Take it, I say, when I give it to you— I don't grudge it.

AKIM: I can't take it, my boy, y'see; and I can't talk with you, you know, because there's no decency in you, y'see.

NIKITA: I won't let you off. Take it. (*Stuffs the money into* AKIM'S *hands.*)

SCENE X

The same and ANISYA

ANISYA (*comes in and stops suddenly*): Go ahead and take it. He won't let up, you know.

AKIM (*taking the money and shaking his head*): Oh, that liquor! A drunkard's not a man, you know.

NIKITA: There, that's better. If you return it, all right; and if you don't return it, I don't care. That's my way! (*Sees* AKULINA.) Akulina, show 'em your presents.

AKULINA: What?

NIKITA: Show 'em your presents.

AKULINA: Presents? Why should I show 'em? I've put 'em away already.

NIKITA: Get 'em out, I tell you; Anyutka'll like to see 'em. Show 'em to Anyutka, I tell you. Untie that little shawl. Give it here.

AKIM: O-oh, makes me sick to watch! (*Climbs on the stove.*)

AKULINA (*getting her presents and laying them on the table*):
There! What's the use of looking at 'em?

ANYUTKA: That's pretty! Good as Stepanida's.

AKULINA: Stepanida's? Stepanida's is nothing to this. (*Becoming animated and spreading out the things.*) Look here at the quality! It's French.

ANYUTKA: And what gay chintz! Mashutka has one like it, only hers is lighter-colored, with a blue background. That's awful pretty.

NIKITA: That's right.

(ANISYA *goes angrily into the storeroom, comes back with the table-cloth and the chimney for the samovar, and goes to the table.*)

ANISYA: Confound you! You've covered up all the table.

NIKITA: Just look here!

ANISYA: Why should I look! Haven't I seen 'em? Take 'em away. (*Brushes off the shawl on the floor with her hand.*)

AKULINA: What are you slinging round? Sling round your own things. (*Picks it up.*)

NIKITA: Anisya! Look out!

ANISYA: What should I look out for?

NIKITA: Do you think I forgot you? Look here! (*Shows her the roll and sits down on it.*) There's a present for you. Only you must earn it. Wife, where am I sitting?

ANISYA: Quit your bullying. I'm not afraid of you. Whose money have you spent on your spree, and on your presents for your fat hussy? Mine.

AKULINA: Much it's yours! You wanted to steal it and couldn't. Get out of my way. (*Tries to pass by her and bumps into her.*)

ANISYA: Who are you shoving? I'll give you a push.

AKULINA: A push? Come on now! (*Pushes against her.*)

NIKITA: Here, women, women! Stop it! (*Stands between them.*)

AKULINA: She picks on me. She'd better shut up and remember what she did. Do you think people don't know?

ANISYA: What do they know? Tell us, tell us what they know.

AKULINA: They know something about you.

ANISYA: You're a slut; you're living with another woman's husband.

AKULINA: And you put yours out of the way.

ANISYA (*rushes at* AKULINA): You lie!

NIKITA (*holding her back*): Anisya! Have you forgotten?

ANISYA: Are you trying to scare me? I'm not afraid of you.

NIKITA: Get out! (*Turns* ANISYA *around and starts to push her out.*)

ANISYA: Where'll I go? I won't leave my own house.

NIKITA: Get out, I tell you! And don't you dare come back!

ANISYA: I won't go. (NIKITA *pushes her;* ANISYA *weeps and shrieks, clutching at the door.*) What, are you going to kick me out of my own house? What are you doing, you villain? Do you think there's no law for you? You just wait!

NIKITA: Come, come!

ANISYA: I'll go to the village elder, to the policeman.

NIKITA: Get out, I tell you. (*Pushes her out.*)

ANISYA (*outside*): I'll hang myself!

SCENE XI

NIKITA, AKULINA, ANYUTKA, *and* AKIM

NIKITA: Don't worry!

ANYUTKA: Oh, oh, oh! Dear, darling mother. (*Weeps.*)

NIKITA: Well, I was awful scared of her. What are you crying for? She'll come home all right! Go and see to the samovar.

(ANYUTKA *goes out.*)

SCENE XII

NIKITA, AKIM, *and* AKULINA

AKULINA (*gathering up and folding the presents*): Nasty woman, how she dirtied it! Just you wait, I'll slit her frock for her. I sure will.

NIKITA: I've turned her out. What more do you want?

AKULINA: She's soiled my new shawl. The bitch—if she hadn't left I'd sure have clawed her eyes out.

NIKITA: Just calm down. What's there for you to be angry at? Think I love her?

AKULINA: Love her? Could anybody love that broad mug? If you'd only quit her then, nothing'd have happened. You ought to have sent her to the devil. But the house is mine anyhow and the money's mine. And then she says she's the mistress. Mistress! She was a fine mistress for her husband! She's a murderess; that's what she is. She'll do the same to you!

NIKITA: Oh, you can't stop up a woman's throat. Do you know yourself what you're talking about?

AKULINA: Yes, I know. I won't live with her. I'll turn her off the place. She can't live with me. She the mistress! She ain't the mistress; she's a prison rat.

NIKITA: Stop it. You needn't meddle with her. Don't even look at her. Look at me. I'm the master. What I wish, I do. I don't love her any more; I love you. I love whoever I want to. I'm the boss. And she'll have to mind. That's where I've got her. (*Points under his feet.*)   Oh, I haven't my accordion! (*Sings.*)

> On the stove are buns,
> Porridge in the oven;
> Now we'll live gaily,
> We'll take our pleasure.
> And then when death comes,
> Then we'll just be dying.
> On the stove are buns,
> Porridge in the oven.

(MITRICH *comes in, takes off his coat, and climbs on the stove.*)

SCENE XIII

The same and MITRICH

MITRICH: I see the women have been fighting again! Another quarrel! Oh, Lord! Gracious St. Nicholas!

AKIM (*sits up on the edge of the stove, gets his leg wrappers and bast shoes, and puts them on*): Crawl in, crawl into the corner there.

MITRICH (*crawls in*): I see they're still arguing over their property. Oh, Lord!

NIKITA: Get out the brandy; we'll drink it with the tea.

SCENE XIV

The same and ANYUTKA

ANYUTKA (*coming in, to* AKULINA): Sister, the samovar's going to boil over.

NIKITA: Where's your mother?

ANYUTKA: She's standing in the hall, crying.

NIKITA: All right: call her in, tell her to bring the samovar. And give us the dishes, Akulina.

AKULINA: Dishes? Well, all right. (*Takes out the dishes.*)

NIKITA (*brings brandy, biscuits, and salt herring*): This is for me, this is yarn for the woman, the kerosene's there in the hall. And here's the money. Wait. (*Takes the counting frame.*) I'll reckon it up right away. (*Moves the counters on the frame.*) Wheat flour eighty kopeks, vegetable oil . . . Ten rubles for dad. Dad, come and have tea.

(*Silence.* AKIM *sits on the stove and puts on his leg wrappers.*)

SCENE XV

The same and ANISYA

ANISYA (*bringing in the samovar*): Where shall I put it?

NIKITA: Put it on the table. Well, did you go to the village elder? Now then, talk ahead and have a bit to eat. Just quit being cross. Sit down and drink. (*He pours her out a glass of brandy.*) And here I've brought a present for you.

(*Hands her the roll on which he has been sitting.* ANISYA *takes it in silence, shaking her head.*)

AKIM (*climbs down and puts on his coat. Goes to the table and puts the ten-ruble note on it*): Here, that's your money. Take it.

NIKITA (*not seeing the note*): Where're you going to now you're all dressed?

AKIM: I'm going, I'm going, y'see. Bid me good-by, for Christ's sake. (*Takes his hat and girdle.*)

NIKITA: Do say! Where are you going by night?

AKIM: I can't stay in your house, y'see; I can't stay, you know. Bid me good-by.

NIKITA: But are you running away from tea?

AKIM (*tying on his girdle*): I'm going, y'see, because it ain't good in your house, you know; it ain't good in your house, Nikita, you know. Your life is bad, Nikita, y'see; it's bad. I'm going.

NIKITA: Come, quit your talk; sit down and have tea.

ANISYA: Why, daddy, we'll be ashamed to face folks. What're you taking offense at?

AKIM: I'm not offended at all, y'see, not at all; but I can just see, you know, that my son's going to ruin, you know, going to ruin.

NIKITA: What ruin? Show me.

AKIM: To ruin, to ruin, you're ruined now. What did I tell you last summer?

NIKITA: You told me a lot of stuff.

AKIM: I told you, y'see, about the orphan; that you injured the orphan: you injured Marina, you know.

NIKITA: The old story! Don't talk twice about last year's snow: that thing's past and gone.

AKIM: Past and gone? No, my boy, it ain't gone. One sin brings another, you know; it brings more; and you're stuck fast in sin, Nikita boy. You're stuck fast in sin, I see. You're stuck fast, deep in it, you know.

NIKITA: Sit down and drink tea; that's all I have to say.

AKIM: I can't drink tea, y'see. Because your wicked ways make me sick, you know, awful sick. I can't drink tea with you, y'see.

NIKITA: Oh! . . . He's just talking silly. Sit down at the table.

AKIM: Your wealth, y'see, has caught you in a net; in a net, you know. Ah, Nikita, you need a soul.

NIKITA: What sort of right have you to reproach me in my own house? And what are you bothering me for anyhow? Am I just a kid for you to pull my hair? The time for such things has past.

AKIM: That's true; I've heard that nowadays, y'see, men pull their fathers' beards, you know; and that brings ruin, you know, brings ruin.

NIKITA (*angrily*): We make our living and don't beg of you, and you come to us in distress.

AKIM: Money? There's your money. I'll go begging, you know; but that money I won't take, y'see.

NIKITA: Stop that. What are you cross for, breaking up the party? (*Holds him back by the arm.*)

AKIM (*screaming*): Let me go; I won't stay. I'd rather spend the night under a fence than in this filth of yours. Bah, God forgive me! (*Goes out.*)

SCENE XVI

NIKITA, AKULINA, ANISYA, *and* MITRICH

NIKITA: Well, well!

SCENE XVII

The same and AKIM

AKIM (*opening the door*): Come to your senses, Nikita! You need a soul. (*Goes out.*)

SCENE XVIII

NIKITA, AKULINA, ANISYA, *and* MITRICH

AKULINA (*taking the cups*): Well, shall I pour the tea? (*All are silent.*)

MITRICH (*bellows*): O Lord, be merciful to me a sinner! (*All start with terror.*)

NIKITA (*lying down on the bench*): Oh, life is hard, hard! Akulina! Where's my accordion?

AKULINA: Your accordion? Don't you know that you took it to be fixed? I've poured the tea. Drink it.

NIKITA: I don't want it. Put out the light. . . . Oh, life is hard for me, awful hard! (*Weeps.*)

ACT IV

A moonlit evening in autumn. The yard behind the cottage. In the center of the stage is the hall, to the right the warm side of the house and a gate, to the left the cold side of the house and the cellar. From within the house can be heard talking and drunken shouts. A NEIGHBOR comes out of the house and beckons to her ANISYA'S FRIEND.

SCENE I

NEIGHBOR *and* FRIEND

NEIGHBOR: Why hasn't Akulina joined the company?

FRIEND: Why not? She'd have been glad to, but it was no time for her, believe me. The matchmakers have come to look at the bride; and she, my dear woman, just lies in the cold room and don't show herself at all, the darling.

NEIGHBOR: Why so?

FRIEND: They say the evil eye has lighted on her belly.

NEIGHBOR: Really!

FRIEND: And you know— (*Whispers in her ear.*)

NEIGHBOR: What? That's a sin. But the matchmakers will find out.

FRIEND: How can they find out? They're all drunk. And they're mostly concerned with the dowry. It's no small amount, my dear, they're giving with the hussy: two coats, six silk gowns, a French shawl, and then a whole lot of linen, and—so they say—two hundred in cash.

NEIGHBOR: Well, in a case like this even money won't make a man happy. Such a disgrace!

FRIEND: Sh! There's the matchmaker. (*They stop talking and withdraw into the vestibule of the cottage.*)

SCENE II

MATCHMAKER (*man*) *alone*

MATCHMAKER (*coming out of the vestibule, alone, hiccuping*): I'm all in a sweat. Awful hot! I want to cool off a bit. (*Stands and catches his breath.*) And the Lord knows—! Something's wrong. It don't make me happy. Well, here's the old woman.

(*MATRENA comes out of the vestibule.*)

SCENE III

MATCHMAKER *and* MATRENA

MATRENA: And I was gazing round! "Where's the matchmaker? Where's the matchmaker?" says I. So here's where you are, my man. Well, friend, thank the Lord, all's going fine. Wooing's not boasting. And I never learned how to boast. But as you came on a good errand, so, God grant, you'll always be grateful. And the bride, you know, is a marvel. Hard to find such a girl in the district.

MATCHMAKER: That's all right, but we mustn't forget about the money.

MATRENA: Don't you worry about the money. All her parents ever gave her, she still has. By now it must amount to a hundred and fifty.

MATCHMAKER: We're well enough satisfied; but he's our own child, you know. We must do the best we can for him.

MATRENA: I'm telling you the truth, friend: if it wasn't for me, you'd never have found the girl. There was a party from the Kormilins that wanted to get her, but I held out against it. And as for the money I can tell you true and honest: When the deceased—heaven's peace be with him!—was dying, he gave directions that his widow should take Nikita into the house—I know all this through my son—but that the money should be Akulina's. Another man would have made his profit out of the thing, but Nikita is giving them up, every kopek. Just think what a lot of money!

MATCHMAKER: Folks say she was left more money. He's a sly fellow.

MATRENA: Oh, fiddle-faddle! The other man's slice always looks big: they're giving you all there was. I tell you: quit your reckonings. Make it a firm bargain. The girl's pretty as a spring cherry.

MATCHMAKER: That's so. My old woman and I were wondering about one thing in the girl: Why didn't she show herself? We think she may be sickly.

MATRENA: Huh? She sickly? There ain't her like in the district. The girl's so plump you can't pinch her. You saw her the other day yourself. And she's a marvel at working. She's a bit deaf, that's true. Well, one little wormhole don't spoil a red apple. And the reason she didn't show herself, you know, was because of the evil eye. There's a spell on her. I know what bitch contrived it. They knew a charm, you see, and worked it on her. But I know a cure for it. The girl will get up to-morrow. Don't you worry about the girl.

MATCHMAKER: Well, the bargain's made.

MATRENA: That's right—and now don't go back on it. And don't forget me. I worked hard on it too. Don't you leave me out.

(*The voice of a woman is heard from the vestibule:* "We must be going: come along, Ivan.")

MATCHMAKER: Right away. (*Goes out.*)

(*Peasants throng the vestibule and take their departure.* ANYUTKA *runs out of the vestibule and beckons* ANISYA *to follow her.*)

SCENE IV

ANISYA *and* ANYUTKA

ANYUTKA: Mama!

ANISYA (*from the vestibule*): What?

ANYUTKA: Mama, come here, or they'll hear us. (*Goes off with her to the side of the cart shed.*)

ANISYA: Well, what? Where's Akulina?

ANYUTKA: She's gone into the grain shed. It's awful what she's doing there! Just think, "No," says she, "I can't stand it. I'll scream with all my might," she says. Just think!

ANISYA: She can wait. We must see the guests off, you know.

ANYUTKA: Oh, mama! It's so hard for her. And she's cross. "They needn't drink me out of the house," she says. "I won't marry," she says. "I'm going to die," she says. Mama, what if she died? It's awful! I'm afraid!

ANISYA: It ain't likely she'll die; don't you go near her. Get along.

(ANISYA *and* ANYUTKA *go out.* MITRICH *comes in from the gate and sets to raking up the hay that is strewn about.*)

SCENE V

MITRICH *alone*

MITRICH: Oh, Lord! Merciful St. Nicholas! What a lot of liquor they put down! And they did raise a smell. Stinks even out of doors. No, I won't—I won't touch it. See how they've scattered the hay! They're like a dog in the manger. Just look at this bundle! What a smell! Right under your nose. Plague take it! (*Yawns.*) Time to go to sleep! But I don't want to go into the room. It fills up a man's nose. How it smells, damn it! (*One can hear the guests driving away.*) Well, they've gone. Oh, Lord! Merciful St. Nicholas! They hug each other and make fools of each other. But it don't amount to nothing.

SCENE VI

MITRICH *and* NIKITA

NIKITA (*coming in*): Mitrich! Go lie down on the stove; I'll rake it up.

MITRICH: All right; give some to the sheep.— Well, did you see 'em off?

NIKITA: We saw 'em off, but things didn't go well. I don't know what'll happen.

MITRICH: Rotten business! Too bad we have it here; that's what the Foundling Asylum's for. There you can spill anything you like, they'll pick it up. Give 'em anything; they ask no questions. And they give money too. But the girl has to turn wet nurse. It's simple nowadays.

NIKITA: Look out, Mitrich: if anything happens, don't blab.

MITRICH: What do I care? Cover your tracks as you like. Eh, how you stink of liquor! I'll go in the house. (*Goes out, yawning.*) Oh, Lord!

SCENE VII

NIKITA *alone*

NIKITA (*after a long silence, sitting down on a sleigh*): What a life!

SCENE VIII

NIKITA *and* ANISYA

ANISYA (*coming out of the house*): Where are you?

NIKITA: Here!

ANISYA: What are you sitting still for? There's no time to wait. You must take it away right off.

NIKITA: What are we going to do?

ANISYA: I'll tell you what—and you do it.

NIKITA: You women might take it to the Foundling Asylum, maybe.

ANISYA: Take it and carry it, if you want to. You're ready enough to do anything nasty, but you don't know how to get rid of it. I can see that.

NIKITA: Well, what's to be done?

ANISYA: Go in the cellar, I tell you, and dig a hole.

NIKITA: But you women might manage somehow.

ANISYA (*mimicking*): Yes, "somehow." You can't let things just slide. You ought to have thought of it in time. Go where you're sent.

NIKITA: Oh, what a life! What a life!

SCENE IX

The same and ANYUTKA

ANYUTKA: Mama! Grandma's calling you. Sister must have a baby; just think—it cried.

ANISYA: What lies are you telling, plague take you! The kittens are squealing in there. Go into the house and go to sleep. Or I'll thrash you!

ANYUTKA: Mama dear, honest to God!

ANISYA (*brandishing her arm at her*): I'll give it to you. Get out of here and don't show yourself again. (ANYUTKA *runs out.*) Go and do what you're told. Otherwise, look out! (*Goes out.*)

SCENE X

NIKITA *alone*

NIKITA (*after a long silence*): What a life! Oh, those women! What a mess! "Ought to have thought of it in time," she says. How could I have thought of it in time? When could I have thought of it? Well, last summer, when that Anisya began to nag me about it. What of it? Am I a monk? The master died, and so then I covered up the sin as was proper. I wasn't to blame for that. Such things often happen. And then those powders. Did I set her up to that? If I'd known of it, I'd have killed her on the spot, the bitch. I'd sure have killed her! She made me her partner in that dirty work, the good-for-nothing! And from that time on she was hateful to me. When my mother told me of it at the time, I began to hate her, to hate her; I didn't want to look at her. Well, how could I live with her? And then this thing started! . . . That hussy began to make up to me. What did I care? If it hadn't been me, it'd been somebody else. And this business now! Again I'm not to blame for it a bit. Oh, what a life! (*He sits down and reflects.*) Those women are nervy—see what they've thought of! But I won't join in.

(MATRENA *comes in out of breath, with a lantern and spade.*)

SCENE XI

NIKITA *and* MATRENA

MATRENA: What're you sitting here for like a hen on a perch? What did your wife tell you? Get down to work.

NIKITA: What're you women going to do?

MATRENA: We know what to do. You just attend to your share.

NIKITA: You're getting me mixed up in it.

MATRENA: What's that? Do you think of backing out? So it's come to this: you're trying to back out!

NIKITA: But think what this means! It's a living soul.

MATRENA: Eh, a living soul! Anyhow, it's barely alive. And what can we do with it? If you go and carry it to the Foundling Asylum, it'll die all the same, and there'll be talk; they'll spread the news and that girl'll be left on our hands.

NIKITA: But what if they find out?

MATRENA: We can do what we like in our own house. We'll do it so there won't be a trace. Just do what I tell you. It's our woman's work, but we can't manage it without a man. Here's the spade: now climb down and attend to things there. I'll hold the lantern.

NIKITA: What shall I do?

MATRENA (*whispers*): Dig a hole. And then we'll bring it out and stuff it in there quick. There she is calling again. Go on, will you! And I'll be going.

NIKITA: Well, is it dead?

MATRENA: Of course it's dead. Only you must hurry up. Folks haven't gone to bed yet. They may hear and see; the scoundrels meddle with everything. And the policeman passed by this evening. This is for you. (*Hands him the spade.*) Get down into the cellar. Dig a hole there in the corner, the earth's soft, and you can even it off again. Mother earth won't tell any one; she'll lick it clean as a cow with her tongue. Go on, go on, my boy.

NIKITA: You're getting me mixed up in it. Plague take you! I'm going off. Do the thing alone, as you please.

SCENE XII

The same and ANISYA

ANISYA (*from the door*): Well, has he dug the hole?

MATRENA: What've you come out for? Where did you put it?

ANISYA: Covered it with some burlap. Nobody'll hear it. Well, has he dug it?

MATRENA: He don't want to!

ANISYA (*rushing out in a rage*): Don't want to! Does he want to feed lice in prison? . . . I'll go right away and tell the whole thing to the policeman. We can go to ruin together. I'll tell it all right off!

NIKITA (*panic-stricken*): What'll you tell?

ANISYA: What? I'll tell everything! Who took the money? You!

(NIKITA *is silent.*) And who gave him the poison? I gave it to him! But you knew it, knew it, knew it! I was in conspiracy with you!

MATRENA: Oh, stop it! Nikita, why are you so stubborn? See here, what's to be done? You must get to work. Come on, darling.

ANISYA: Look what an innocent you are! Don't want to! You've been abusing me long enough. You've been riding over me, but my turn's come now. Go along, I tell you, or I'll do what I said! . . . Here's the spade: take it! Get along!

NIKITA: Well, what are you nagging me for? (*Takes the spade, but falters.*) If I don't want to, I won't go.

ANISYA: Won't go? (*Begins to shout.*) Hey, folks!

MATRENA (*stopping her mouth*): What are you doing? Are you daft! He'll go. . . . Go along, sonny; go along, my dear boy.

ANISYA: I'll cry for help right off.

NIKITA: Stop it! Oh, what a lot you women are! But you'd better hurry up. The sooner the better. (*Goes toward the cellar.*)

MATRENA: Yes, that's the way it is, darling: if you've had your fun, you must know how to cover up your tracks.

ANISYA (*still agitated*): He and his hussy have been taking out their spite on me, and I've had enough of it! I'm not going to be the only one. Let him be a murderer too. He'll find out how it feels.

MATRENA: Well, well, you're excited. Now, girlie, don't be cross: take it slow and easy, and it'll be better. You go in to the hussy. He'll do the work. (*She follows* NIKITA *with the lantern; he climbs down into the cellar.*)

ANISYA: I'll tell him to strangle his dirty brat. (*Still excited.*) I had my torture all alone, pulling Petr's bones. Let him find out, too. I'll do my best to make him; I tell you, I will.

NIKITA (*from the cellar*): Give me a light, will you!

MATRENA (*holding the light, to* ANISYA): He's digging; go and bring it.

ANISYA: You just watch him. Otherwise he'll run away, the wretch. And I'll go bring it out.

MATRENA: See that you don't forget to put a cross on it. Or I'll attend to that. Is there a cross for it?

ANISYA: I'll find one; I know about that. (*Goes out.*)

SCENE XIII

MATRENA, *and* NIKITA (*in the cellar*)

MATRENA: How the woman did get worked up! And I must say, it was rough on her. Well, thank God, we'll just hush up this business and hide the traces. We'll get rid of the girl without scandal. My son will rest easy now. The house, thank God, is rich and well-stocked. He won't forget me either. They couldn't get along without Matrena. They couldn't attend to things. (*Calls into the cellar.*) All ready, sonny?

NIKITA (*climbs up; only his head can be seen*): What are you doing there? Bring it, will you! What are you dawdling for? If you're going to do it, go ahead.

(MATRENA *goes towards the house door and meets* ANISYA. ANISYA *comes out with the baby, wrapped in rags.*)

SCENE XIV

The same and ANISYA

MATRENA: Well, did you put the cross on?

ANISYA: Sure! I had hard work to get the brat; she wouldn't give it to me. (*Comes up and holds out the baby to* NIKITA.)

NIKITA (*not taking it*): Bring it down here yourself.

ANISYA: Here, take it, I tell you. (*Throws the baby to him.*)

NIKITA (*picking it up*): It's alive! Darling mother, it's moving! It's alive! What shall I do with it?

ANISYA (*snatching the baby out of his hands and throwing it into the cellar*): Hurry up and strangle it and it won't be alive. (*Pushing* NIKITA *down.*) It's your business; you finish it.

MATRENA: He's too kind-hearted. It's hard for him, the dear boy. Well, no help for it! It's his sin too. (ANISYA *stands over the cellar.* MATRENA *sits down on the house step, watches her, and reflects.*) Eh, eh, eh! How scared he was! Well, even if it is hard, you couldn't do anything else. No way out. And then just think how sometimes people beg for children! And then, y'see, God don't give 'em; they're all born dead. Take the priest's wife for instance. . . . But here it wasn't wanted, and it's alive. (*Looks toward the cellar.*) He must have finished. (*To* ANISYA.) Well?

ANISYA (*looking into the cellar*): He's covered it with a board and sat down on the board. Must've finished.

MATRENA: O-oh! He'd be glad not to sin, but what can you do?

NIKITA (*climbing out, shaking all over*): It's still alive! I can't! It's alive!

ANISYA: If it's alive, where are you going? (*Tries to stop him.*)

NIKITA (*rushing at her*): Get out; I'll kill you!

(*He clutches her by the arm, she tears herself free; he runs after her with the spade.* MATRENA *rushes toward him and stops him.* ANISYA *runs off to the house.* MATRENA *tries to take away the spade from* NIKITA.)

NIKITA (*to* MATRENA): I'll kill you; I'll kill you too! Get out! (MATRENA *runs to the house, to* ANISYA. NIKITA *stops.*) I'll kill you; I'll kill you all!

MATRENA: That's because he's scared. Never mind; it'll pass off!

NIKITA: What's this they've done? What have they done to me? How it wailed! . . . How it cracked underneath me! What have they done to me! And it's still alive, alive sure enough! (*Is silent and listens.*) It's wailing! . . . Hear it wail! (*He runs towards the cellar.*)

MATRENA (*to* ANISYA): He's going; he must mean to bury it. Nikita, you need a lantern.

NIKITA (*listens at the cellar, without answering her*): I can't hear it. I just fancied. (*Walks away and stops.*) And how the little bones cracked underneath me! . . . Krr . . . krr. . . . What have they done to me? (*Listens once more.*) It's wailing again; it's sure wailing. What's this? Mother! Mother, I say! (*Goes up to her.*)

MATRENA: What, sonny?

NIKITA: Mother, darling, I can't do any more. I can't do anything. Mother, darling, have pity on me!

MATRENA: Oh, you're frightened, my dear boy. Come, come, drink a drop to give you courage.

NIKITA: Mother, darling, my time must have come. What have you done to me? How those little bones cracked, and how it wailed! Mother, darling, what have you done to me! (*Goes off and sits down on a sleigh.*)

MATRENA: Go have a drink, my lad. It's true enough, nighttime makes you shiver. But just wait, the dawn will come; and then, you know, a day or two will pass, and you'll forget to think about it. Just wait, we'll get rid of the girl and forget to think about it. But you have a drink, go have a drink. I'll attend to things in the cellar myself.

NIKITA (*shaking himself*): Is any liquor left in there? Can't I drink this down! (*He goes out.* ANISYA, *who has been standing by the door all this time, silently stands aside to let him pass.*)

SCENE XV

MATRENA *and* ANISYA

MATRENA: Come, come, darling, I'll get to work myself; I'll climb down and bury it. Where did he throw the spade? (*She finds the*

spade and descends half way into the cellar.)   Anisya, come here;
give me a light.

ANISYA: But what's the matter with him?

MATRENA: He got awful scared. You gave it to him pretty hard.
Don't meddle with him; he'll come to himself. Let him alone; I'll
get to work myself. Set the lantern here. Then I can see. (MATRENA
disappears into the cellar.)

ANISYA (*shouts at the door by which* NIKITA *has departed*): Well,
is your fun over? You've had your fling: now just wait, you'll find
out yourself how it feels. You won't be so lofty.

(NIKITA *rushes out of the house towards the cellar.*)

SCENE XVI

The same and NIKITA

NIKITA: Mother! Hey, mother!

MATRENA (*emerging from the cellar*): What, sonny?

NIKITKA (*listening*): Don't bury it; it's alive! Don't you hear it?
It's alive! There, it's wailing! . . . There . . . plainly. . . .

MATRENA: How could it wail? You squashed it into a pancake.
You crushed all its head.

NIKITA: What's that? (*Stops his ears.*) It's still wailing! I've
ruined my life, ruined it! What have they done to me? . . . Where
shall I go! . . . (*Sits down on the steps.*)

VARIANT

*Instead of Scenes XIII-XVI of Act IV the following variant may
be substituted.*

The same scene as in Act I

SCENE I

ANYUTKA, *undressed, is lying on a bench with a coat spread over
her.* MITRICH *is sitting on a bunk at the head of the room, smoking.*

MITRICH: Pah! They've raised a smell, good luck to 'em for it!
They spilled the goods. You can't drown it with tobacco. It gets
into a man's nose. Oh, Lord! I'd better go to sleep. (*Goes to the
lamp and is about to turn it out.*)

ANYUTKA (*sitting up with a start*): Granddad, dear, don't put it
out.

MITRICH: Why not put it out?

ANYUTKA: They're up to something in the yard. (*Listens.*) Do you hear? They've gone into the grain shed again.

MITRICH: What do you care? They aren't asking you about it. Lie down and go to sleep. And I'll turn down the light. (*Turns it down.*)

ANYUTKA: Granddad, precious! Don't put it way out. Leave just a tiny bit, or I'll feel creepy.

MITRICH (*laughing*): All right, all right. (*Sits down beside her.*) What makes you creepy?

ANYUTKA: I can't help feeling creepy, granddad! How sister struggled. She kept knocking her head against the chest. (*Whispers.*) I know—she's going to have a baby. . . . Maybe it's born already.

MITRICH: What a little imp, confound you! You want to know everything. Lie down and go to sleep. (ANYUTKA *lies down.*) That's the way. (*Covers her up.*) That's the way. If you know too much, you'll grow old too soon.

ANYUTKA: Are you going up on the stove?

MITRICH: Of course I am. . . . You're a silly little girl, I see. You want to know everything. (*Covers her up and rises to go.*) Just lie there like that and go to sleep. (*Goes to the stove.*)

ANYUTKA: It cried just once, but now I can't hear it.

MITRICH: Oh, Lord! Merciful St. Nicholas! . . . What can't you hear?

ANYUTKA: The baby.

MITRICH: There isn't any, so you can't hear it.

ANYUTKA: But I heard it; just think, I heard it. A little shrill voice.

MITRICH: You heard a lot. Did you hear how the bogy-man put a naughty little girl like you in a sack and carried her off?

ANYUTKA: What's the bogy-man?

MITRICH: Just the bogy-man. (*Climbs on the stove.*) The stove's fine and warm now. Nice! Oh, Lord! Merciful St. Nicholas!

ANYUTKA: Granddad! Are you going to sleep?

MITRICH: What do you think? That I'm going to sing songs? (*Silence.*)

ANYUTKA: Granddad! Oh, granddad! They're digging! Honest to God they're digging! Do you hear? Just think, they're digging!

MITRICH: What notions you have! Digging? Digging at night? Who's digging? It's the cow scratching herself. And you say, digging! Go to sleep, I tell you, or I'll put out the light right away.

ANYUTKA: Granddad, darling, don't put it out. I'll stop. Honest to God, I'll stop. It scares me.

MITRICH: Scares you? Don't you be afraid of anything, and then you won't be scared. Now you just feel afraid and you say that it scares you. Of course it scares you when you're afraid. What a silly little girl!

(*Silence. The cricket chirps.*)

ANYUTKA (*whispers*) : Granddad! Hey, granddad! Are you asleep?

MITRICH : Well, what do you want?

ANYUTKA : What's the bogy-man like?

MITRICH : I'll tell you what he's like. Whenever there's any little girl, like you, who won't go to sleep, he comes along with his sack, and he pops the little girl into the sack; and then he pops his own head in and lifts up her little shirtie, and he gives her a spanking.

ANYUTKA : What does he spank her with?

MITRICH : He takes a broom.

ANYUTKA : But he can't see, himself, can he, in the sack?

MITRICH : He'll see all right.

ANYUTKA : But I'll bite him.

MITRICH : No, girlie, you won't bite him.

ANYUTKA : Granddad, somebody's coming! Who is it? Oh, holy saints, who is it?

MITRICH : If somebody's coming, let him come. What do you care? . . . I think it's your mother coming.

(ANISYA *comes in.*)

SCENE II

The same and ANISYA

ANISYA : Anyutka! (ANYUTKA *pretends to be asleep.*) Mitrich!

MITRICH : What?

ANISYA : What have you a light burning for? We'll go to bed in the cold half.

MITRICH : I've just finished my work. I'll put it out.

ANISYA (*searching in the chest and grumbling*) : When you want something, you can't find it.

MITRICH : What are you looking for?

ANISYA : I'm looking for a cross, I must put one on him. He'll die unchristened, God have mercy on him! Without a cross! It's a sin, you know!

MITRICH : Of course, you must do things properly. . . . Well, have you found it?

ANISYA : Yes. (*Goes out.*)

SCENE III

MITRICH *and* ANYUTKA

MITRICH: That's lucky—otherwise I'd have given her my own. Oh, Lord!

ANYUTKA (*jumps up, trembling*): O-oh, granddad! Don't go to sleep, for Christ's sake! I'm so scared!

MITRICH: What are you scared of?

ANYUTKA: Won't the baby die, most likely? Grandma put a cross on Auntie Arina's too—and it died.

MITRICH: If it dies, they'll bury it.

ANYUTKA: But maybe it wouldn't die if Grandma Matrena wasn't here. You know I heard what grandma was saying; just think, I heard it.

MITRICH: What did you hear? Go to sleep, I tell you. Pull things over your head: that's all.

ANYUTKA: But if it was alive, I'd nurse it.

MITRICH (*bellows*): Oh, Lord!

ANYUTKA: Where'll they put it?

MITRICH: They'll put it where it's proper. It's not your business. Go to sleep, I tell you. Your mother'll come—she'll give it to you! (*Silence.*)

ANYUTKA: Granddad! That little girl you were telling about—they didn't kill her?

MITRICH: That one? Oh, that girl came out all right.

ANYUTKA: How was it you were telling me they found her, granddad?

MITRICH: They just found her.

ANYUTKA: But where did they find her? Tell me.

MITRICH: They found her in a house over there. The soldiers came to a village and began to search the house; and there that same little girl was lying on her belly. They were going to smash her. But I just felt lonesome and I took her in my arms—she struggled. She was as heavy as if she had two hundred pounds inside her; and she clutched at everything with her hands—you could hardly tear her away. Well, I took her and stroked her head, stroked her head. And she was bristly as a hedgehog. I stroked her and stroked her, and she quieted down. I soaked a biscuit and gave it to her. She caught on. She chewed it. What could we do with her? We took her with us. We took her and just fed her and fed her; and she got so used to us we took her with us on the march: she just went with us. She was a nice little girl.

ANYUTKA: Well, she wasn't christened, was she?

MITRICH: Nobody knows. Not altogether, they said. For her people weren't ours.

ANYUTKA: Germans?

MITRICH: "Germans," you say? Not Germans, but Asiatics. They are just the same as Jews, but they aren't Jews either. They're Poles, but they're Asiatics. They're called Krudly or Krugly: I've forgotten the name.— We called the little girl Sashka. Sashka—and she was pretty. I've forgotten everything else, you see; but that little girl—Lord bless her!—I can see before my eyes right now. That's all I remember of life in the army. I recollect how they flogged me, and then I remember that little girl. She used to hang round your neck when you carried her. You couldn't have found a nicer little girl nowhere. Later we gave her away. The sergeant's wife adopted her as her daughter. And she came out all right. How sorry the soldiers were!

ANYUTKA: See here, granddad, I remember how daddy died too. You hadn't come to live with us then. He called Nikita and says to him: "Forgive me, Nikita," he says—and he began to cry himself. (*Sighs.*) That made me sad too.

MITRICH: Well, that's the way things go.

ANYUTKA: Granddad; oh, granddad! They're making a noise again in the cellar. Oh, dearie me, holy saints! Oh, granddad, they'll do something to him. They'll destroy him. He's just a little thing.— Oh! oh! (*Pulls the clothes over her head and weeps.*)

MITRICH (*listening*): They really are up to something nasty—curse 'em! Those women are a nasty lot. The men ain't much to boast of, but the women—they're like beasts of the woods. They ain't afraid of anything.

ANYUTKA (*getting up*): Granddad! Hey, granddad!

MITRICH: Well, what next?

ANYUTKA: The other day, a passer-by spent the night here. He was saying that when a child dies its soul goes straight to heaven. Is that true?

MITRICH: How should I know? Most likely. What of it?

ANYUTKA: Why, then I'd like to die too. (*Whimpers.*)

MITRICH: If you die, nobody'll miss you.

ANYUTKA: Till you're ten years old you're still a child, and maybe your soul'll still go to God. After that you get spoiled, you know.

MITRICH: You certainly do get spoiled! How can girls like you help getting spoiled? Who teaches you anything? What do you ever see? What do you hear? Nothing but nastiness. I'm not very learned, but still I know something; not very well, but anyhow better than a village woman.— What is a village woman? Just mud. There's huge millions of your sort in Russia, and you're all like blind moles—don't know anything. How to keep cows safe from the evil eye—all kinds of charms—how to cure children by putting 'em under the hen roost—that's what women know how to do.

ANYUTKA: Mama used to put 'em there.

MITRICH: That's just it. How many millions of you women and girls there are, and you're all like beasts of the forest. You grow up and then you die. You don't see anything and don't hear anything. A man—even if it's in a tavern, or maybe in a fortress, accidentally, or in the army, like me—he learns something or other. But what about a woman? Don't ask her about God and what's right! She don't even know sensibly what Good Friday is. Friday's Friday, but ask her anything about it and she don't know. They crawl round just like blind pups and stick their noses in the manure.— All they know is their silly songs: "Ho, ho! Ho, ho!" And they don't know themselves what "Ho, ho!" means.

ANYUTKA: But, granddad, I know "Our Father" halfway through.

MITRICH: You know a lot! But then one can't expect much of you. Who teaches you? Only a drunken peasant teaches you now and then with a strap. That's all your training. I don't know who'll ever answer for you. They put a sergeant in charge of recruits and hold him responsible for 'em. But nobody's responsible for you girls. So you women are just like a herd of cattle—without a herdsman—that run wild; your kind is the stupidest that's made. Your kind is just hopeless.

ANYUTKA: But what can you do about it?

MITRICH: Not much. . . . Now pull the clothes over your head and go to sleep. Oh, Lord!

(*Silence. The cricket chirps.*)

ANYUTKA (*jumping up*): Granddad! Somebody's shouting, somebody's just yelling! Honest to God, he's shouting. Granddad, dear, he's coming this way.

MITRICH: I tell you, pull the clothes over your head.

SCENE IV

The same, NIKITA *and* MATRENA

NIKITA (*coming in*): What have they done to me? What have they done to me!

MATRENA: Have a drink, have a drink, darling. What's the matter? (*Gets liquor and sets it before him.*)

NIKITA: Give it here: I guess I'd better take some.

MATRENA: Shh! They aren't asleep, you know. Here, drink it.

NIKITA: What does this mean? Why did you want to act that way? You might have carried it off.

MATRENA (*in a whisper*): Sit here, sit here; have another drink, and then smoke a bit. That'll divert your thoughts.

NIKITA: Mother darling, my time must have come. When it wailed, and when those little bones cracked, krr . . . krr . . . my strength gave out.

MATRENA: E-eh! You're just talking silly stuff. It's true enough, nighttime makes you shiver. But just wait till the day comes; a day or two will pass and you'll forget to think about it. (*Goes to* NIKITA *and puts her hand on his shoulder.*)

NIKITA: Get away from me! What have you done to me?

MATRENA: What do you mean, sonny, anyhow? (*Takes him by the hand.*)

NIKITA: Get away from me! I'll kill you! I don't care for anything now. I'll kill you!

MATRENA: Oh, oh, how scared you are! Now go away and go to bed.

NIKITA: I've nowhere to go to. I'm a lost man.

MATRENA (*shaking her head*): Oh! oh! I'd better go fix things up myself; and let him sit here for a while till he gets rid of all this. (*Goes out.*)

SCENE V

NIKITA, MITRICH, *and* ANYUTKA

(NIKITA *sits still, covering his face with his hands.* MITRICH *and* ANYUTKA *are stiff with terror.*)

NIKITA: It's wailing, it's sure wailing: hark, hark, you can hear it. . . . She'll bury it, she'll sure bury it! (*Runs to the door.*) Mother, don't bury it, it's alive! . . .

SCENE VI

The same and MATRENA

MATRENA (*returning, in a whisper*): What do you mean, Christ help you! What fancies you have! How can it be alive! All its bones are crushed.

NIKITA: Give me some more liquor! (*Drinks.*)

MATRENA: Go along, sonny. Now you'll go to sleep and it'll be all right.

NIKITA (*standing and listening*): It's still alive. . . . Hark! . . . It's wailing. Don't you hear it? Hark!

MATRENA (*in a whisper*): Not a bit of it!

NIKITA: Mother dear! I've ruined my life. What have you done to me? Where shall I go? (*Runs out of the house,* MATRENA *following him.*)

SCENE VII

MITRICH *and* ANYUTKA

ANYUTKA: Granddad, dear, darling, they've strangled him!

MITRICH (*angrily*): Go to sleep, I tell you! Bother you, confound you! I'll take a broom to you! Go to sleep, I tell you.

ANYUTKA: Granddad, precious. Somebody's grabbing me by the shoulders, somebody's grabbing me, grabbing me with his paws. Dear granddad, just think: I'll be gone right away. Granddad, precious, let me up on the stove! Let me up for Christ's sake! . . . He's grabbing me . . . grabbing. . . . O-o-oh! (*Runs to the stove.*)

MITRICH: See how they've scared the poor little girl—those nasty women, confound 'em! Well, come up if you want to.

ANYUTKA (*climbing on the stove*): And don't you go away.

MITRICH: Where should I go to? Climb up, climb up! Oh, Lord! St. Nicholas the Martyr! Holy Virgin Mother of Kazan! . . . How they scared the little girl! (*Covers her up.*) You're a little fool, just a little fool. . . . They sure scared you, those nasty women, much good may it do 'em!

ACT V

SCENE I

In the foreground, on the left, a thrashing floor, and near it a stack of straw; on the right, a cart shed. The doors of the shed are open; straw is scattered about in the doorway. In the background farm build-ings can be seen; songs and the tinkling of tambourines are heard. Two peasant girls come walking along the path past the shed towards the farm buildings.

TWO GIRLS

FIRST GIRL: You see how well we got across, we didn't even soil our boots; but on the road it was awful, so dirty! (*They stop and wipe their feet with straw.*)

FIRST GIRL (*looks at the straw and sees something*): What's that there?

SECOND GIRL (*taking a look*): It's Mitrich, their workman. He's dead drunk.

FIRST GIRL: But he didn't use to drink at all, did he?

SECOND GIRL: Not till to-day, so it seems.

FIRST GIRL: Just look: he must have come here for straw. You see he has a rope in his hands, but he just went to sleep.

SECOND GIRL (*listening*): They're still singing the wedding songs. Most likely they haven't given 'em the blessing yet. They say Akulina didn't wail a bit.

FIRST GIRL: Mama told me she didn't want to be married. Her step-father threatened her; otherwise she'd never have consented. You know what talk there was about her!

SCENE II

The same and MARINA

MARINA (*overtaking the girls*): Hello, girls!

GIRLS: Hello, auntie!

MARINA: Going to the wedding, darlings?

FIRST GIRL: It must be over by now. We just came to look around.

MARINA: Call my old man for me, Semen of Zuyev. You know him, don't you?

FIRST GIRL: Of course we know him. He's some relative of the bridegroom, it seems.

MARINA: Sure: the bridegroom is a nephew of my boss.

SECOND GIRL: Why don't you go yourself? How can you miss the wedding!

MARINA: I don't feel like going, girlie; and then I haven't the time. I must be riding off. We weren't on our way to the wedding. We were carting oats to town. We stopped to feed the horses, and they called in my old man.

FIRST GIRL: Whose house did you stop at? Fedorych's?

MARINA: Yes. So I'll stand here a bit, and you go call my old man, darling. Make him come, precious. Say: "Your wife Marina says you must be going; the fellows are harnessing already."

FIRST GIRL: All right, very well, if you won't go yourself.

(*The girls go out along the path towards the farm buildings. Songs and the tinkling of tambourines are heard.*)

SCENE III

MARINA (*alone*)

MARINA (*muses*): It'd be all right to go, but I don't want to, for I haven't seen him since the very time that he refused me. That's more than a year ago. But I'd like to peep in and see how he gets along with his Anisya. Folks say they don't agree. She's a coarse, ill-tempered woman. He's remembered me many a time, I'll warrant. He must have had a liking for an easy life. He gave me the go-by. Well, God help him, I bear no grudge. It hurt then. Oh, how it pained me! But now it's worn off and I've forgotten. But I'd like to see him. . . . (*Looks towards the house and sees* NIKITA.) Just look! What's he coming here for? Did the girls tell him? Why's he left the guests? I'll be going.

(NIKITA *comes in, at first hanging his head, waving his arms, and muttering to himself.*)

SCENE IV

MARINA *and* NIKITA

MARINA: How gloomy he looks!

NIKITA (*seeing* MARINA *and recognizing her*): Marina! My dear, darling Marina! What are you here for?

MARINA: I've come for my old man.

NIKITA: Why didn't you come to the wedding? You'd have looked on and laughed at me.

MARINA: What do I want to laugh for? I've come for my boss.

NIKITA: Oh, Marina dear! (*Tries to embrace her.*)

MARINA (*turning away angrily*): Nikita, you quit those tricks. That's been and gone. I've come for my boss. Is he at your house?

NIKITA: So we can't call to mind old times? You won't let me?

MARINA: No use remembering old times. That's been and gone.

NIKITA: So you can't bring it back?

MARINA: It won't come back. But what have you strayed off for? You're the master, and you've deserted the wedding.

NIKITA (*sitting down on the straw*): Why have I strayed off? Oh, if you only knew and understood! . . . My life's hard, Marina, so hard that I don't want to look at it. I got up from the table and came away, came away from people so that I needn't see anybody.

MARINA (*coming nearer to him*): How's that?

NIKITA: Well, it's that I have no joy in food or drink, no rest in sleep. Oh, I'm sick of life, just sick of it! And what makes me sickest of all, Marina dear, is that I'm all alone, and have nobody that I can share my grief with.

MARINA: You can't live without grief, Nikita. I cried over mine and now it's gone.

NIKITA: You're talking about old, old times. Just think, dear! You've done crying over yours, and now it's come my turn.

MARINA: But how's that?

NIKITA: It's that I loathe my whole life. I loathe myself. Ah, Marina, you could not hold me fast, and so you ruined me and yourself too! Well, is this a life worth living?

MARINA (*stands by the shed, weeps, but restrains herself*): I don't complain of my own life, Nikita. God grant that everybody had as good as mine! I don't complain. I confessed right off to my old man. He forgave me. And he don't reproach me. I'm satisfied with my own life. He's a gentle old man. And I like him; I wash and dress his children! And he's kind to me too. I've no reason to complain. It must be what God intended for me.— But what about your life? You're a rich man.

NIKITA: My life! . . . I just don't want to break up the wedding, or I'd take a rope—this one (*Takes up a rope from the straw.*), and I'd throw it right over that crossbeam. And I'd fix up a nice noose, and I'd climb on the crossbeam and put my head in it. That's what my life is like!

MARINA: Stop, Christ help you!

NIKITA: You think I'm joking? You think I'm drunk? I'm not drunk. Nowadays even liquor don't affect me. But I'm sick of life, sick to death of it! I'm done for, in such misery that I care for nothing! Oh, Marina dear, do you remember how we lived together, how we spent happy nights on the railroad?

MARINA: Nikita, don't rub my sore spot. I'm married now and you are too. My sin's forgiven; don't bring back the past.

NIKITA: What can I do with my heart? To whom can I give it?

MARINA: What should you do? You have a wife: don't lust after other women, but care for your own. You loved Anisya; keep on loving her.

NIKITA: Ah, that Anisya is bitter wormwood to me. She's just tangled up my legs like witchgrass.

MARINA: Whatever she is, she's your wife.— But it's no use talking! You'd better go to the guests and call my husband.

NIKITA: Oh, if you knew everything!— But why talk about it!

SCENE V

NIKITA, MARINA, *her* HUSBAND, *and* ANYUTKA

HUSBAND (*coming in from the farm buildings, red-faced and drunken*): Marina! Wife! Old lady! Are you here?

NIKITA: Here's your boss coming and calling for you. Go along!

MARINA: And what'll you do?

NIKITA: I? I'll lie down here. (*Lies down in the straw.*)

HUSBAND: Where is she?

ANYUTKA: There she is, uncle, close to the shed.

HUSBAND: What are you standing here for? Come to the wedding! The hosts want you to come and pay your respects. The marriage party will soon start out: then we'll go.

MARINA (*coming to meet her husband*): But I didn't want to.

HUSBAND: Come on, I tell you. We'll drink a glass; you'll congratulate that rogue Petrunka. The hosts are taking offense—and we'll have time enough for everything.

(MARINA'S HUSBAND *embraces her and goes out with her, staggering.*)

SCENE VI

NIKITA *and* ANYUTKA

NIKITA (*sitting up on the straw*): Oh, when I saw her, I felt sicker than ever. The only real life I ever had was with her. I've wasted my days for nothing at all; I've ruined my happiness! (*Lies down.*) What shall I do with myself? Oh, if only damp mother earth would open!

ANYUTKA (*sees* NIKITA *and runs to him*): Daddy! Oh, daddy! They're looking for you. Godfather and everybody have given their blessing. Just think, they've given their blessing; they're cross.

NIKITA (*to himself*): What shall I do with myself?

ANYUTKA: What's that? What are you saying?

NIKITA: I'm not saying anything. Don't bother me!

ANYUTKA: Daddy! Come on, will you! (NIKITA *is silent;* ANYUTKA *pulls at his arm.*) Daddy, go and give your blessing! Honest, they're cross; they're scolding.

NIKITA (*pulls away his arm*): Let me alone!

ANYUTKA: Come on!

NIKITA (*threatening her with the rope*): Get out, I tell you. I'll give it to you!

ANYUTKA: Then I'll send mother. (*Runs out.*)

SCENE VII

NIKITA *alone*

NIKITA (*sitting up*): How can I go in there? How can I take the holy ikon in my hands? * How can I look her in the eyes? (*Lies down*

---

* In order to confer the blessing.

again.) Oh, if there were a hole in the earth, I'd crawl into it. People wouldn't see me; I'd see nobody. (*Sits up again.*) But I won't go. . . . Let 'em go to thunder. I won't go. (*Removes his boots and takes up the rope; he makes a noose and puts it around his neck.*) That's the way.

(MATRENA *comes in hurriedly.* NIKITA *sees her, takes the rope off his neck, and again lies down on the straw.*)

SCENE VIII

NIKITA *and* MATRENA

MATRENA: Nikita! Hey, Nikita! There you are, and you won't answer. Nikita, what's the matter with you? Are you drunk? Come on, Nikita dear; come on, my precious! Folks are tired of waiting.

NIKITA: Oh, what have you done to me? I'm no longer a man.

MATRENA: What do you mean? Come on, my boy; give the blessing as is proper, and then it'll all be over. Folks are waiting for you.

NIKITA: How can I give a blessing?

MATRENA: Just as usual. Don't you know how?

NIKITA: I know, I know. But who am I going to bless? What have I done to her?

MATRENA: What have you done? The idea of remembering that! Nobody knows: not the cat, nor the mouse, nor the louse in the house. And then the girl herself is willing to marry.

NIKITA: But how is she willing?

MATRENA: Of course, she's doing it out of fear. But she's willing all the same. What else can she do? She ought to have thought of it then. But now she has no other choice. And the matchmakers feel satisfied. They've seen the girl twice, and the money goes with her. All's covered up clean.

NIKITA: But what's in the cellar?

MATRENA (*laughing*): What's in the cellar? Cabbage, mushrooms, and potatoes, I suppose. Let bygones be bygones.

NIKITA: I'd be glad to, but I can't. Whenever you make me think, I can hear things. Oh, what have you women done to me?

MATRENA: What are you acting so queer for anyhow?

NIKITA (*turning over flat on his face*): Mother, don't torture me! I can't stand it any longer.

MATRENA: But you must, all the same. There's talk among the people anyhow—and then all of a sudden the father goes off and won't come back, don't dare give his blessing. They'll put two and two together right away. If you shrink from it, they'll guess what's up right away. If you walk the beaten path, nobody thinks you a thief. But if you run away from a wolf, you run into a bear. Above all, don't betray yourself; don't be timid, my boy, or they'll think worse of it.

NIKITA: Oh, you've tied me tight!

MATRENA: Stop it, come along. Come into the company and give your blessing; everything must be as is proper and usual, and then the thing's over.

NIKITA (*still lying on his face*): I can't.

MATRENA (*to herself*): What's happened? Everything was all right, all right, and all of a sudden it struck him. There must be a spell on him.— Nikita, get up! Look, there's Anisya coming; she's left the guests.

(ANISYA *comes in gayly dressed and flushed with drink.*)

SCENE IX

NIKITA, MATRENA *and* ANISYA

ANISYA: Ain't this fine, mother! So fine and proper! And how happy folks are over it! . . . Where is he?

MATRENA: Here, darling, here. He lay down in the straw and there he lies. He won't come.

NIKITA (*looking at his wife*): Huh, she's drunk too. When I see her, it makes my heart sick. How can I live with her? (*Turns over on his face.*) I'll kill her some day. It'll be still worse!

ANISYA: Look where he is, buried in the straw! Has he got over his drunk? (*Laughs.*) I'd like to lie down there with you, but I haven't the time. Come on; I'll lead you. And it's so nice in the house! It's a pleasure to see 'em. And the accordion! The women are singing songs, just splendid. Everybody's drunk; all's fine and proper!

NIKITA: What's fine?

ANISYA: The wedding, the merry wedding. Everybody says that it's just a marvel of a wedding. Everything's so fine and lovely. Come on! We'll go together. . . . I've had a drink, but I can lead you. (*Takes his arm.*)

NIKITA (*pulling away from her, with revulsion*): Go on alone. I'll come later.

ANISYA: What're you in such a temper for! All our troubles are over, we've got rid of the girl that stood between us, we can just live and enjoy ourselves. All's nice and proper, according to the law. I'm so happy over it that I can't tell you. It's just as if I was marrying you a second time. Ha ha! Folks are so pleased! They'll all thank us.

And the guests are all nice people. Ivan Moseich is there too, and the policeman. They joined in on the songs.

NIKITA: Well, go sit with them. What did you come out here for?

ANISYA: But you must come along. Otherwise it ain't decent: the hosts have left and deserted the guests. And the guests are all nice people.

NIKITA (*rising and brushing off the straw*) : Go on; I'll come directly.

MATRENA: The night cuckoo sings louder than the day bird. He wouldn't heed me, but he followed his wife right away.

(MATRENA *and* ANISYA *move away*.)

MATRENA: Are you coming?

NIKITA: I'll come right away. You go along, and I'll follow. I'll come and give my blessing. . . . (*The women pause*.)   Go on, and— I'll follow. Go along.

(*The women go out.* NIKITA *gazes after them, musing*.)

SCENE X

NIKITA *and* (*later*) MITRICH

NIKITA (*sitting down and taking off his boots*) : Not much I won't go! No indeed! No, you'd better look for me on the crossbeam. I'll straighten the noose and jump from the crossbeam, and then you can look for me. And here are some rope reins, that's lucky. (*Meditates*.) I'd get over my grief, however heavy it was; I'd get over it. But it's right here, it's in my heart; I can't drive it out. (*Looks towards the house*.)   Looks like she was coming again. (*Mimics* ANISYA.) "Fine, just fine! I'll lie down with you!" Ugh! the nasty hag! Wait a bit: embrace me when they take me off the beam! That's all that's left. (*Seizes the rope and pulls it*.)

MITRICH (*drunken, sits up, but does not let go of the rope*) : I won't let you have it. I won't let anybody have it. I'll bring it myself. I said I'd bring the straw, and I'll bring it. Is that you, Nikita? (*Laughs*.) Oh, the devil! Did you come for straw?

NIKITA: Give me the rope.

MITRICH: No, you wait. The folks sent me. I'll bring it. . . . (*He rises to his feet and begins to rake up the straw, but staggers, recovers himself, and finally falls down*.) The liquor's got the best of me. Too much for me!

NIKITA: Give me the reins.

MITRICH: I told you I wouldn't. Oh, Nikita, you're stupid as a blind jackass. (*Laughs*.) I like you, but you're stupid. You think I've been drinking. To hell with you! You think I need you. . . . Just look at

me! I'm a corporal! You fool, you can't even say it, "Corporal of
Her Majesty's very First Regiment of Grenadiers." I served tsar and
country with faith and truth. But who am I? You think I'm a soldier?
No, I'm not a soldier, but the very least of men; I'm an orphan, a
vagrant. I swore off drinking. And now I've started in again! . . .
Well, do you think I'm afraid of you? Not much! I ain't afraid of
nobody. When I start to drink, I drink! Now I'll swill for two weeks
and raise the devil. I'll drink away everything down to my cross,*
I'll drink away my hat, I'll pawn my passport—and I ain't afraid of
nobody! They flogged me in the regiment to keep me from drinking!
They laid it on and laid it on. "Well," says they, "will you drink any
more?" "Yes," says I. Why should I be afraid of 'em: that's the
kind of man I am! I'm the way God made me. I swore off drinking,
and I didn't drink. Now I've started again, and I drink! And I ain't
afraid of nobody. I'm not lying; that's the way it is. . . . Why should
I be afraid of 'em, such rot! "There," says I, "that's the kind of man
I am!" A priest was telling me: "The devil is the worst boaster. As
soon as you begin to boast," says he, "then you'll feel afraid right away.
And when you begin to be afraid of people, then the devil, with his
cloven hoof, will snatch you up right away and stick you wherever he
wants to." But seeing I'm not afraid of people, it's easy for me. I spit
on his beard, the lame cuss, the son of a swine. He won't harm me.
"Does my fist taste good?" says I.

NIKITA (*crossing himself*): But what's this I'm doing, anyhow?
(*Throws away the rope.*)

MITRICH: What?

NIKITA (*Getting up.*): You say not to be afraid of people?

MITRICH: Much you need to be afraid of 'em, such rot! Just you
look at 'em in the bath. They're all of the same dough. One has a
fatter belly, and the other a thinner; that's all the difference between
'em. They're a fine lot to be afraid of, good luck to 'em!

(MATRENA *approaches from the house.*)

SCENE XI

NIKITA, MITRICH *and* MATRENA

MATRENA (*shouts*): Well, are you coming?

NIKITA: Ugh! It *is* better that way. I'm coming! (*Goes off
towards the house.*)

---

* Worn next the skin by a Russian peasant.

SCENE XII

Change of scene. The cottage of Act I, filled with people, some sitting at tables, others standing. In the front corner are AKULINA *and the* BRIDEGROOM. *On the table are the ikons and bread. Among the guests are* MARINA, *her* HUSBAND, *and the* POLICEMAN. *The women are singing songs.* ANISYA *is passing wine. The songs subside.*

ANISYA, MARINA *and her* HUSBAND, AKULINA, *the* BRIDEGROOM, COACHMAN, POLICEMAN, MATCHMAKER (*woman*), *Bridegroom's* BEST MAN, MATRENA, GUESTS, PEASANTS

COACHMAN: It's high time we were going; the church is a long way off.

BEST MAN: Just wait a while; the stepfather will give his blessing. But where is he?

ANISYA: He's coming, he's coming directly, my dears. Have another glass all round; don't hurt our feelings.

MATCHMAKER: What makes him so slow? We've been waiting a long time already.

ANISYA: He's coming. He's coming directly. He'll be here in two shakes of a lamb's tail. Have some more, my dears. (*Passes wine.*) He'll be here, directly. Sing some more, my beauties, while you wait.

COACHMAN: They've sung all their songs while we've been waiting.

(*The women sing; in the middle of the song* NIKITA *and* AKIM *come in.*)

SCENE XIII

The same, NIKITA *and* AKIM

NIKITA (*holding* AKIM *by the arm and pushing him in front of him*): Go on, daddy; I can't do it without you.

AKIM: I don't like it, y'see.

NIKITA (*to the women*): That's enough; keep still. (*Looks around at everybody in the room.*) Marina, are you here?

MATCHMAKER (*woman*): Come, take the ikon and give us your blessing.

NIKITA: Wait a while; give me time. (*Looking around.*) Akulina, are you here?

MATCHMAKER (*woman*): What are you calling the roll for? Where should she be?— What a freak he is!

ANISYA: Holy saints! Why's he taken off his boots?

NIKITA: Daddy! Are you here? Look at me! Orthodox people, you are here, and I'm here! Here I am! (*Falls on his knees.*)

ANISYA: Nikita dear, what are you up to? Oh, poor me!

MATCHMAKER (*woman*): Well, well!

MATRENA: I'll tell you what: he's had too much of that French wine. Come to your senses, will you? (*She tries to raise him up. He pays no attention to anybody, but looks straight ahead.*)

NIKITA: Orthodox people! I am guilty; I wish to repent.

MATRENA (*pulling him by the shoulder*): What's the matter with you? Have you gone crazy? Friends, his head's turned; we must take him away.

NIKITA (*shoving her aside with his shoulder*): Let me alone! And you, daddy, listen to me. To begin with! Marina, look here! (*He bows down to her feet and rises again.*) I did you wrong; I promised to marry you, I seduced you. I deceived you, I cast you off: forgive me for Christ's sake! (*Bows down to her feet once more.*)

ANISYA: What are you prating about? This ain't decent. Nobody's questioning you. Get up: what are you making a row for?

MATRENA: O-oh, he's bewitched! How did it happen? He's out of his head.— Get up, what are you talking nonsense for? (*Pulls at him.*)

NIKITA (*shaking his head*): Don't touch me! Forgive me, Marina! Forgive my sins against you for Christ's sake!

(MARINA *covers her face with her hands and is silent.*)

ANISYA: Get up, I tell you: what are you making a row for? No use mentioning bygones. Stop your foolery. Shame on you! Oh, poor me! He's gone clean daft.

NIKITA (*pushing away his wife and turning to* AKULINA): Akulina, I'll talk to you now. Listen, orthodox people! I am an accursed man. Akulina, I did you wrong! Your father did not die a natural death. He was poisoned.

ANISYA (*shrieks*): Poor me! What does he mean?

MATRENA: The man's out of his head. Take him away, will you! (*Several men approach and are about to seize him.*)

AKIM (*shielding him with his arms*): Wait! Here, fellows, wait, y'see; wait, I tell you!

NIKITA: Akulina, I poisoned him. Forgive me, for Christ's sake!

AKULINA (*jumping up*): He lies! I know who did it.

MATCHMAKER (*woman*): What are you doing? Sit still.

AKIM: Oh, Lord! What a sin! What a sin!

POLICEMAN: Seize him! And send for the village elder, and witnesses. We must draw up the document. Get up and come here.

AKIM (*to the* POLICEMAN): But you, you know—Brass Buttons, y'see—just wait a bit, you know. Just let him tell the story, y'see.

POLICEMAN (*to* AKIM): Look out, old man; don't meddle. I must draw up the document.

AKIM: What a fellow you are, y'see. Wait, I tell you. Don't fuss about the document, y'see. God's work's going on here, you know. A man is repenting, y'see; and you talk about a document, you know.

POLICEMAN: Call the elder!

AKIM: Let God's work go on, you know; when it's over, y'see, then you do your business, y'see.

NIKITA: I did you another great wrong, Akulina; I seduced you. Forgive me for Christ's sake! (*Bows down to her feet.*)

AKULINA (*coming out from behind the table*): Let me go; I won't get married. He told me to, but now I won't.

POLICEMAN: Repeat what you have said.

NIKITA: Wait, please, policeman; let me finish.

AKIM (*in ecstasy*): Speak on, my lad; tell it all; it'll be easier for you. Repent in the sight of God; do not fear men. God! God! This is His work!

NIKITA: I poisoned the father; I ruined, cur that I am, the daughter. I had power over her; I ruined her and her baby.

AKULINA: It's true; it's true.

NIKITA: I crushed her child in the cellar with a plank. I sat on it. . . . I crushed it . . . and the little bones in it cracked. (*Weeps.*) And I buried it in the earth. I did it, nobody but me!

AKULINA: He lies! I told him to. . . .

NIKITA: Don't shield me! I'm not afraid of anybody now! Forgive me, orthodox people! (*Bows down to the earth.*)

(*Silence.*)

POLICEMAN: Bind him. Your marriage is broken up, that's plain. (*Men approach* NIKITA *with sashes.*)

NIKITA: Wait, you'll have time. . . . (*Bows down to his father's feet.*) Dearest father! Forgive me, accursed sinner that I am—you also! You said to me in the very beginning, when I began to meddle with this nasty whoredom, you said to me: "If a claw is caught, the whole bird is lost." I did not listen to you, cur that I was, and it has come out as you said. Forgive me, for Christ's sake!

AKIM (*in ecstasy*): God will forgive you, my beloved child! (*Embraces him.*) You have not spared yourself, He will spare you. God! God! This is His work!

SCENE XIV

The same and VILLAGE ELDER

ELDER (*coming in*): There are plenty of witnesses here already.

POLICEMAN: We'll have the examination right away. (*They bind* NIKITA.)

AKULINA (*coming up and standing beside him*): I'll tell the truth. Question me too.

NIKITA (*bound*): No use questioning. I did it all by myself. I planned it and I did it. Lead me wherever you want to. I shall say nothing more.

DOWN AND OUT

A Drama in Four Acts

By MAXIM GORKY

(1902)

*Translated by George Rapall Noyes
and Alexander Kaun*

CHARACTERS

MIKHAÍL IVÁNOV KOSTYLÉV,* *the proprietor of a night-lodging, fifty-four years old*

VASILÍSA KÁRPOVNA, *his wife, twenty-six years old*

NATÁSHA (NATÁLYA), *her sister, twenty years old*

ABRÁM IVÁNOVICH MEDVÉDEV,† *their uncle, a policeman, fifty years old*

VASÍLY (VÁSYA, VÁSKA) PÉPEL,‡ *a thief, twenty-eight years old*

ANDRÉY MÍTRICH KLESHCH,§ *a locksmith, forty years old*

ANNA, *his wife, thirty years old*

NÁSTYA, *a streetwalker, twenty-four years old*

KVÁSHNYA, *a peddler of dumplings, about forty years old*

BUBNÓV,‖ *a capmaker, forty-five years old*

KONSTANTÍN SÁTIN, *a card-sharper* ⎱ *Both about forty years old*
ACTOR ⎰

BARON, *thirty-three years old*

LUKÁ, *a wanderer, sixty years old*

ALÉSHKA,¶ *a shoemaker, twenty years old*

WRYMUG ⎱ *Porters*
TATAR ⎰

Several unnamed dwellers in the slum, without speaking parts.

---

* Pronounced, Ko-sty-lyŏff'. The name suggests *kostyl,* "crutch."
† The name suggests *medved,* "bear."
‡ "Ashes."
§ "Pincers."
‖ Possibly suggestive of *buben,* "tambourine."
¶ Pronounced, A-lyŏ'shka.

DOWN AND OUT

ACT I

A basement that suggests a cave. The ceiling is of heavy, smoke-stained stone vaulting, from which the plaster has half peeled away. Light is afforded by a square window set high in the right-hand wall, near the front of the stage. The right-hand corner is taken up by a room enclosed by a thin board partition; this is occupied by PEPEL. *Near the door to this room is* BUBNOV'S *bunk. In the left corner is a large Russian stove. In the left wall, which is of stone, is a door leading into the kitchen, where lodge* KVASHNYA, *the* BARON, *and* NASTYA. *Between the door and the stove, close to the wall, stands a wide bed, over which is a dirty chintz curtain. The walls are lined with bunks. In the foreground, near the left wall, is a block of wood, to which are fastened a vise and a small anvil and another block of wood, lower than the first. On the lower block, in front of the anvil, sits* KLESHCH, *fitting keys to old locks. At his feet are two large bunches of keys of all sorts and sizes, strung on wire rings, a battered tin samovar, a hammer and files. In the middle of the lodging are a large table, two benches, and a stool: all of them unpainted and dirty. At the table* KVASHNYA *is presiding at the samovar. The* BARON *is munching black bread; and* NASTYA, *seated on the stool, with her elbows on the table, is reading a tattered book. On the bed* ANNA *is lying, hidden by the curtain; she coughs continually.* BUBNOV, *sitting on his bunk, is measuring on a hat block, held between his knees, a pair of trousers that he has ripped up, considering how to cut them. Beside him is a torn hatbox (to be used for visors), bits of enamel cloth, and rags.* SATIN, *who has just waked up, is lying on his bunk and—bellowing. On the stove, unseen, the* ACTOR *is tossing about and coughing.*

The action takes place in the morning, in early spring.

BARON: Go on!

KVASHNYA: "No-o, my dear," says I; "you can give me a rest on that subject. I've tried it," says I, "and now I'll never get married again, not for a hundred broiled lobsters!"

BUBNOV (*to* SATIN): What are you grunting about?

(SATIN *bellows.*)

KVASHNYA: "To think of me, a free woman," says I, "and my own mistress, getting my name written down on somebody's passport; to think of my selling myself as a slave to a man—not much! Even if he's an American prince, I'll never even consider marrying him."

KLESHCH: You lie!

KVASHNYA: Wha-at?

KLESHCH: You lie. You're going to marry old Abram.

BARON (*snatches the book from* NASTYA *and reads the title*): "*Fatal Love!*" (*He bursts out laughing.*)

NASTYA (*stretching out her hand*): Give it to me! Give it back! Quit your fooling!

(*The* BARON *looks at her and waves the book in the air.*)

KVASHNYA (*to* KLESHCH) You red-haired goat! "You lie," do you say? How do you dare speak such an impudent word to me?

BARON (*striking* NASTYA *on the head with the book*): You're a fool, Nastya!

NASTYA (*pulling at the book*): Let me have it!

KLESHCH: What a fine lady! . . . But all the same you're going to marry Abram—that's all you're waiting for.

KVASHNYA: Of course! Sure! Certainly! Let me tell you that you've beaten your wife almost to death.

KLESHCH: Shut up, you cur! It's none of your business.

KVASHNYA: Ah, ha! You can't stand the truth!

BARON: They've begun! Nastya, where are you?

NASTYA (*without raising her head*): Huh? Get out!

ANNA (*putting out her head from behind the curtain*): The day's begun! For God's sake . . . don't yell . . . don't scold!

KLESHCH: She's begun her whining!

ANNA: Every single day! . . . At least let me die in peace!

BUBNOV: Noise don't hinder death.

KVASHNYA (*going up to* ANNA): My dear, how have you ever managed to live with such a poor wretch?

ANNA: Let me alone! Leave me in peace!

KVASHNYA: We-ell! Oh . . . you martyr! Don't your chest feel any easier?

BARON: Kvashnya, it's time to go to market!

KVASHNYA: We're going right away! (*To* ANNA.) Want me to give you some hot dumplings?

ANNA: Don't need 'em, thank you. Why should I eat?

KVASHNYA: You just eat some. Hot food softens things up. I'll put some in a bowl for you and leave 'em. . . . You can eat 'em when you feel like it! (*To the* BARON.) Come on, sir. (*To* KLESHCH.) Ugh, you evil spirit! (*Goes into the kitchen.*)

ANNA (*coughing*): Lord!

BARON (*giving* NASTYA *a gentle slap on the back of the head*): Quit, you silly!

NASTYA (*mutters*): Clear out! . . . I'm not in your way.

(*The* BARON, *whistling, follows* KVASHNYA *out of the room.*)

SATIN (*sitting up on his bunk*): Who was it thrashed me yesterday?

BUBNOV: Ain't it all the same to you?

SATIN: I suppose so. . . . But what did they thrash me for?

BUBNOV: Were you playing cards?

SATIN: Yes.

BUBNOV: That's why they thrashed you.

SATIN: Scoun-n-ndrels!

ACTOR (*hanging down his head from the stove*): One fine day they'll beat you to death.

SATIN: You're a blockhead.

ACTOR: Why so?

SATIN: Because you can't kill a man two fine days.

ACTOR (*after a short silence*): I don't understand why they can't.

KLESHCH: You get down off the stove and clean up the place. . . . What are you shirking for?

ACTOR: None of your business.

KLESHCH: Vasilisa'll be back soon: she'll show you whose business it is.

ACTOR: To hell with Vasilisa! To-day it's the Baron's turn to clean up. . . . Baron!

BARON (*coming in from the kitchen*): I've no time to clean up; I'm going to market with Kvashnya.

ACTOR: That's not my affair—you may be going to the penitentiary for all I care. . . . But it's your turn to sweep the floor; I won't do other men's work.

BARON: Oh, to hell with you! Nastya'll sweep. . . . Hey, you, Fatal Love! Wake up! (*Takes away the book from* NASTYA.)

NASTYA (*rising*): What are you up to? Give it here! You pest! And you call yourself a nobleman!

BARON (*giving her back the book*): Nastya, sweep up the floor for me. Will you?

NASTYA (*going into the kitchen*): Not much I won't!

KVASHNYA (*at the kitchen door, to the* BARON): You just start off! They'll clean up without your help. . . . Actor, come on; do the work, if they ask you! It won't break your back, I'll bet!

ACTOR: Well, it's always me. I don't see why.

BARON (*brings out of the kitchen two baskets on a yoke. In them are pots, covered with rags*): Somehow they're heavy to-day.

SATIN: Much good it did you to be born a baron!

KVASHNYA (*to the* ACTOR): Look out now; sweep up!

(*She goes out into the hall, allowing the* BARON *to precede her.*)

ACTOR (*climbing down from the stove*): It's bad for my health to breathe dust. (*Proudly.*) My organism is poisoned with alcohol. (*Seats himself on one of the bunks, and meditates.*)

SATIN: "Organism!" Organon!

ANNA: Andrey Mitrich!

KLESHCH: What do you want?

ANNA: Kvashnya left some dumplings for me in there. Take 'em and eat 'em.

KLESHCH (*going towards her*): Won't you?

ANNA: I don't want 'em. . . . What's the use of my eating? You're a workman; you need to.

KLESHCH: Are you afraid? Cheer up! You may yet . . .

ANNA: Go on and eat! I feel bad. It won't be long now. . . .

KLESHCH (*walking away*): Don't worry! . . . Maybe you'll get well. . . . Such things happen sometimes. (*Goes into the kitchen.*)

ACTOR (*in a loud voice, as if he had suddenly waked up*): Yesterday, in the hospital, the doctor said to me: "Your organism," says he, "is completely poisoned with alcohol."

SATIN (*smiling*): Organon.

ACTOR (*insists*): Not "organon," but *or-ga-nism.*

SATIN: Sicambri. . . .

ACTOR (*waving his hand at him*): Eh, rubbish! I'm speaking seriously, I am. If my organism is poisoned, then of course it's bad for my health to sweep the floor, to breathe dust.

SATIN: Macrobiotics . . . huh!

BUBNOV: What are you mumbling?

SATIN: Words. . . . And then there's another: tran-scendental.

BUBNOV: What's that?

SATIN: I don't know. . . . I've forgotten.

BUBNOV: Then what are you talking for?

SATIN: Just for fun. . . . I'm sick of all human words, my dear man; I'm sick of all our words! I must have heard every one of 'em— well, a thousand times at least.

ACTOR: In the tragedy of *Hamlet* there is a saying, "Words, words, words." That's a fine drama. . . . I played the gravedigger in it.

KLESHCH (*coming in from the kitchen*): Are you going to play with the broom soon?

ACTOR: None of your business. (*Strikes himself on his chest.*) "Ophelia, O remember me in thy orisons!"

(*Off stage, somewhere in the distance, is a dull uproar: shouts and a policeman's whistle.* KLESHCH *sits down to his work and rasps with his file.*)

SATIN: I like rare words that you can't understand. . . . When I was a little kid . . . I worked in a telegraph office. . . . I read a lot of books.

BUBNOV: Were you really a telegrapher?

SATIN: Yes. . . . There are very fine books . . . and lots of queer words. . . . I was an educated man. . . . Did you know that?

BUBNOV: I've heard it—a hundred times! What if you were! Much it matters! . . . Now I was a furrier—had my own shop. . . . My arms were yellow all over, from the dye; I used to dye furs. Yes, man, my arms were all yellow, up to the elbow! I used to think I could never wash it off all my life long, that I'd die with yellow arms. . . . But now these arms of mine are just dirty—that's a fact!

SATIN: Well, what of it?

BUBNOV: That's all.

SATIN: What do you tell us this for?

BUBNOV: Just—for instance. . . . You see: however much you color yourself on the outside, it will all rub off. . . . Yes, it will all rub off!

SATIN: Oh, my bones ache!

ACTOR (*sitting and hugging his knees with his arms*): Education is tommyrot; the main thing is talent. I knew one actor—he had to spell out his parts, but he could play the hero so that . . . the theatre fairly shook and rocked with the enthusiasm of the public.

SATIN: Bubnov, give me five kopeks!

BUBNOV: I've only two myself.

ACTOR: I say, talent is what one needs to play the hero. And talent consists in faith in yourself, in your own powers.

SATIN: Give me five kopeks, and I'll believe that you're a genius, a hero, a crocodile, a police captain. . . . Kleshch, give me five kopeks!

KLESHCH: Go to the devil! There are too many of you here.

SATIN: What are you cursing for? You haven't a copper yourself; I know that much.

ANNA: Andrey Mitrich! . . . I'm suffocating; it's hard for me. . . .

KLESHCH: What can I do about it?

BUBNOV: Open the door into the hall.

KLESHCH: All right! You're sitting on the bench, and I'm on the floor. . . . Change places with me and open it. . . . I have a cold as it is.

BUBNOV (*calmly*): It's not my place to open it. . . . Your wife is asking you.

KLESHCH (*glumly*): People can ask a lot of things.

SATIN: My head aches to split . . . ugh! Why is it people whack each other on their noddles?

BUBNOV: They whack their noddles, and all the rest of their bodies too. (*Gets up.*) I must go buy some thread. . . . Somehow our landlord and landlady are late in showing themselves to-day. . . . Looks as if they'd croaked. (*Goes out.*)

(ANNA *coughs.* SATIN, *resting his head on his folded arms, lies motionless.*)

ACTOR (*after a weary glance about the room, goes up to* ANNA): How are you? Poorly?

ANNA: Suffocated.

ACTOR: Want me to lead you out into the hall? Well, get up. (*Aids the woman to rise, throws some sort of old rag over her shoulders, and, supporting her, leads her into the hall.*) Now, now! . . . steady! I'm a sick man myself—poisoned with alcohol.

KOSTYLEV (*meeting them at the door*): Going for a walk? Oh, a pretty pair are you, a ram with a little ewe!

ACTOR: You get out of the way! . . . Don't you see sick folks are coming.

KOSTYLEV: Go along if you want to. (*Humming through his nose some sort of religious tune, he looks suspiciously over the lodging and inclines his head to the left, as if listening to something in* PEPEL's *room.* KLESHCH *rattles his keys furiously and rasps with his file, casting stealthy glances at the landlord.*) You're rasping?

KLESHCH: What?

KOSTYLEV: Are you rasping? I say. (*Pause.*) Well . . . eh . . . what was it I was going to ask you? (*Quickly, in a low voice.*) Hasn't my wife been here?

KLESHCH: Haven't seen her.

KOSTYLEV (*cautiously moving towards the door of* PEPEL's *room*): What a lot of space you take up here for two rubles a month! A bed . . . seat for yourself . . . think of it! The place is worth five, honest to God! I'll have to raise you half a ruble.

KLESHCH: You can raise me on a rope and hang me. . . . You'll croak before long, and still you're always thinking of half-rubles.

KOSTYLEV: Why should I hang you? What good would it do anybody? Lord help you: live and enjoy yourself! . . . But I'll raise you half a ruble; I'll buy some oil for the lamp—and my offering will burn before the holy ikon. . . . And my offering will be acceptable, in atonement for my sins, and for yours, too. You see you never think about your own sins—that's the trouble. . . . Ah, Andrey, my boy, you are an evil man! Owing to your evil deeds your wife is dying of consumption. . . . Nobody loves or respects you. . . . Your work is rasping and disagreeable to everybody.

KLESHCH (*shouts*): What do you want of me? . . . Have you come to bait me?

(SATIN *bellows loudly.*)

KOSTYLEV (*with a shudder*): Look here, my dear sir!

ACTOR (*coming in*): I've set the woman down in the hall and wrapped her up.

KOSTYLEV: What a kind fellow you are, my boy! That's good . . . that'll all be set down to your credit.

ACTOR: When?

KOSTYLEV: In the other world, my boy. . . . There they reckon up everything, every one of our deeds.

ACTOR: But you might reward me for my kindness right here. . . .

KOSTYLEV: How can I do it?

ACTOR: Knock off half what I owe you. . . .

KOSTYLEV: Hee-hee! You're always joking, my dear lad, always having your fun. . . . Can kindness of heart be reckoned in money? Kindness is the most lofty of all blessings. But your debt to me—well, it's just a debt! So you should repay it to me. . . . Your kindness should be shown to me, old man that I am, without hope of reward.

ACTOR: You're a rascal, old man. . . . (*Goes into the kitchen.*)

(KLESHCH *rises and goes into the hall.*)

KOSTYLEV (*to* SATIN): What's taken that noisy locksmith? He's run off, hee-hee! He doesn't like me.

SATIN: Who does like you—except the devil!

KOSTYLEV (*chuckling*): How you scold! But I like all of you. . . . I understand: you are my unfortunate brethren, worthless and fallen. (*Suddenly, quickly.*) But—is Vaska at home?

SATIN: Look and see.

KOSTYLEV (*goes to the door and knocks*): Vasya!

(*The* ACTOR *appears at the kitchen door. He is munching something.*)

PEPEL: Who's there?

KOSTYLEV: It's I. . . . I, Vasya.

PEPEL: What do you want?

KOSTYLEV (*moving away*): Open the door.

SATIN (*without looking at* KOSTYLEV): He'll open it, and she's there. (*The* ACTOR *snorts.*)

KOSTYLEV (*uneasily, in a low voice*): Huh? Who's there? What do you mean?

SATIN: What? Are you speaking to me?

KOSTYLEV: What did you say?

SATIN: I was just talking to myself.

KOSTYLEV: Look out, friend! Don't carry your jokes too far! (*Knocks violently on the door.*) Vasily!

PEPEL (*opening the door*): Well? What are you bothering me for?

KOSTYLEV (*glancing into the room*): I . . . you see . . . you . . .

PEPEL: Have you brought the money?

KOSTYLEV: I have some business with you.

PEPEL: Have you brought the money?

KOSTYLEV: What money? Wait a bit.

PEPEL: The money, seven rubles, for the watch. Have you?

KOSTYLEV: What watch, Vasya? . . . Oh, you . . .

PEPEL: Now you look out! Yesterday, in the presence of witnesses, I sold you a watch for ten rubles: I got three, and you were to give me seven later. What are you staring at? You loaf round here and bother people—and you don't know yourself what you're up to!

KOSTYLEV: Shh! Don't be cross, Vasya. . . . The watch . . . the watch was—

SATIN: Stolen.

KOSTYLEV (*sternly*): I don't receive stolen goods. . . . How dare you—?

PEPEL (*seizing him by the shoulder*): See here! What have you disturbed me for? What do you want?

KOSTYLEV: Oh! . . . I don't . . . want anything. . . . I'll leave if you're in *that* frame of mind.

PEPEL: Go and bring me the money!

KOSTYLEV (*going out*): What rude men! Oh! oh!

ACTOR: Fine comedy!

SATIN: Fine! That's what I like.

PEPEL: What did he want here?

SATIN (*laughing*): Don't you understand? He's looking for his wife. . . . Why don't you knock him on the head, Vasily?

PEPEL: Much I'll spoil my life for such trash as he is!

SATIN: Do it cleverly. Then just marry Vasilisa—and you'll be our landlord.

PEPEL: Great joy for me! Then you kind souls will drink up in the tavern not only all my property, but me myself. (*Sits down on a bunk.*) The old devil . . . woke me up. . . . And I was having a fine dream. I was fishing, and I'd caught a huge bream! Such a bream —the kind that you don't see except when you're dreaming! . . . And I was playing him on the hook and was afraid that my line might break! And I had got my net ready. . . . Now, thinks I, right away—

SATIN: That wasn't a bream; that was Vasilisa.

ACTOR: He hooked Vasilisa long ago.

PEPEL (*angrily*) : You fellows go to the devil—and she too!

KLESHCH (*coming in from the hall*) : It's beastly cold.

ACTOR: Why didn't you bring Anna in? She'll freeze.

KLESHCH: Natasha's taken her into the kitchen with her.

ACTOR: The old man'll turn her out.

KLESHCH (*sitting down to work*) : Well, Natasha'll bring her here, then.

SATIN: Vasily, give me five kopeks.

ACTOR (*to* SATIN) : Five, you say: bah!— Vasya, give us twenty!

PEPEL: I'll have to give 'em in a hurry—before you ask for a ruble. . . . Here!

SATIN: Giblartarr! No better people in the world than thieves!

KLESHCH (*glumly*) : They get money easily. . . . They don't work.

SATIN: Many people get money easily, but few part with it easily. . . . Work? Make work pleasant for me, and then maybe I'll work. . . . Yes, I will! Maybe! When toil is a pleasure, life is good! When toil is an obligation, life is slavery! (*To the* ACTOR.) Here you, Sardanapalus, come on!

ACTOR: Come on, Nebuchadnezzar! I'll get drunk like—forty thousand drunkards! (*They go out.*)

PEPEL (*yawning*) : Well, how's your wife?

KLESHCH: Can't be long now. . . .

(*A pause.*)

PEPEL: I can see your rasping with the file is no earthly use.

KLESHCH: What else can I do?

PEPEL: Nothing.

KLESHCH: But how shall I eat?

PEPEL: Men get along.

KLESHCH: These here? Are they men? Ragamuffins, hoodlums— not men! I'm a working man. . . . I'm ashamed to look at 'em. . . . I've been working ever since I was a small boy. . . . You don't think that I'll break away from here? I'll crawl out of here. . . . I'll skin myself, but I'll crawl out. . . . Just you wait! . . . My wife'll die. . . . I've lived here only six months, but it seems like six years.

PEPEL: You're no better than the rest of us here. . . . You're talking nonsense.

KLESHCH: No better than they! They live without honor, without conscience.

PEPEL (*indifferently*) : What use are honor and conscience? If you've no boots, you can't use honor or conscience instead. . . . The men who need honor and conscience are those who have power and authority.

BUBNOV (*coming in*) : Oo-oo! I'm chilled!

PEPEL: Bubnov, have you a conscience?

BUBNOV: Wha-at? Conscience?

PEPEL: Yes.

BUBNOV: What's conscience good for? I'm not rich.

PEPEL: That's what I say, too: only rich men need honor and conscience. That's the truth! But Kleshch is scolding at us: he says we've no conscience.

BUBNOV: What's he up to? Does he want to borrow some?

PEPEL: He has plenty of his own.

BUBNOV: So you have it for sale? Well, nobody here'll buy it. I'd be ready to buy broken pasteboard boxes—on credit at that.

PEPEL (*instructively*): You're a fool, Andrey! You'd better hear what Satin has to say about conscience—and the Baron too.

KLESHCH: There's no use of my talking with them.

PEPEL: They'll show more sense than you . . . even if they are drunkards.

BUBNOV: Who drinks and has wit, for two things is fit.

PEPEL: Satin says: everybody wants his neighbor to have conscience, but nobody has any use for it himself. . . . And that's true.

(NATASHA *comes in.* LUKA *follows her: he has a pack on his back, a kettle and teapot at his girdle, and carries a stick.*)

LUKA: Good health to you, honorable people!

PEPEL (*stroking his mustache*): A-ah, Natasha!

BUBNOV (*to* LUKA): I was honorable—spring before last.

NATASHA: Here's a new lodger.

LUKA: It's all the same to me! I like even rogues; my idea is, every flea is good for me: they're all black and they all jump . . . that's the truth. . . . Where shall I settle down here, dearie?

NATASHA (*pointing to the door of the kitchen*): Go in there, grandfather.

LUKA: Thank you, my girl! Well, I'll go in there. . . . An old man is at home wherever it's warm. (*Goes into the kitchen.*)

PEPEL: What an interesting old boy you've brought us, Natasha!

NATASHA: More so than the rest of you. . . . (*To* KLESHCH.) Andrey, your wife's in our kitchen; come for her in a little while, will you?

KLESHCH: All right. . . . I'll come.

NATASHA: Seems to me you might behave a little more decently to her now. . . . It won't be long. . . .

KLESHCH: I know.

NATASHA: You know! . . . Knowing's not enough, you must understand. Dying's a dreadful thing.

PEPEL: Well, take me—I'm not afraid of it.

NATASHA: Ain't you? . . . How brave!

BUBNOV (*whistling*): This thread is rotten.

PEPEL: Sure, I'm not afraid! I'm ready to die right away! Just take a knife and stick it into my heart—I'll die without a groan! I'll even be glad to, for it'll come from a clean hand.

NATASHA (*going out*): Oh, you can waste your words on somebody else.

BUBNOV (*drawling*): This thread here is rotten.

NATASHA (*at the door of the hall*): Don't forget about your wife, Andrey.

KLESHCH: All right.

PEPEL: Splendid girl!

BUBNOV: Decent sort.

PEPEL: What makes her treat me like that? She cuts me. . . . She'll go to ruin here all the same.

BUBNOV: She'll go to ruin through you.

PEPEL: Why through me? I'm sorry for her.

BUBNOV: As a wolf for a lamb.

PEPEL: You lie! I'm very . . . sorry for her. . . . She has a hard life here. I can see that.

KLESHCH: You just wait: Vasilisa will see you talking with her.

BUBNOV: Vasilisa? Yes, she won't give up her rights for nothing; she's a fierce woman.

PEPEL (*lying down on his bunk*): Both of you prophets can go to hell!

KELSHCH: You'll see. . . . Just wait!

LUKA (*in the kitchen, humming*): In the ni-ight time ne-ever can we fi-ind our wa-ay. . . .

KLESHCH (*going out into the hall*): Now he's howling—he too!

PEPEL: Oh, my heart aches—and why does it ache? You live and live and all's fine! Then all of a sudden you seem to get chilled: then your heart aches.

BUBNOV: Heart aches? M-m. . . .

PEPEL: That's true.

LUKA (*sings*): Yea, ne-ever can we fi-ind our wa-ay.

PEPEL: Hey, old man!

LUKA (*looking in at the door*): You calling me?

PEPEL: Yes, you. Quit your singing.

LUKA (*coming in*): Don't you like it?

PEPEL: I like good singing.

LUKA: So mine ain't good?

PEPEL: Looks that way.

LUKA: Well, well! And I thought I sang well. That's the way

things always go: a man thinks to himself, I do things well! And all of a sudden people find fault.

PEPEL (*laughing*): That's a true word.

BUBNOV: You say your heart aches, and now you're laughing.

PEPEL: What do you care? You crow!

LUKA: Whose heart aches?

PEPEL: Mine. Do you hear?

(*The* BARON *comes in.*)

LUKA: Well, well! And there in the kitchen sits a girl, reading a book and weeping! That's right! Her tears are flowing. . . . Says I to her: "What's the matter, dearie, eh?" "I feel sorry," says she. "Sorry for whom?" says I. "It's in the book," says she. . . . That's what people spend their time on, eh? Because their heart aches, I suppose.

BARON: She's a fool! . . .

PEPEL: Baron, have you had tea?

BARON: Yes. Go on!

PEPEL: Want me to set up a bottle?

BARON: Of course. Go on!

PEPEL: Get down on all fours and bark like a dog!

BARON: You fool! Do you think you're a merchant? Or are you drunk?

PEPEL: Well, go ahead and bark a little! It'll amuse me. . . . You're an aristocrat. . . . There was a time when you didn't think men like us were really human—and all that.

BARON: Well, go on!

PEPEL: What? Well, now I'll make you bark like a dog, and you will, too. . . . You will, won't you?

BARON: Suppose I will! Blockhead! What pleasure can it be to you if I know myself that I've sunk almost lower than you have. You ought to have tried to make me walk on all fours when I was higher up than you.

BUBNOV: That's right!

LUKA: That's what I say, too: that's good!

BUBNOV: What was, is gone; what's left is just rubbish. . . . There are no aristocrats here. . . . The feathers are all molted off; only the naked man is left.

LUKA: So we're all equal. . . . And you, friend—were you really a baron?

BARON: What's this? Who are *you*, scarecrow?

LUKA (*laughing*): I've seen a count, and I've seen a prince—but this is the first baron I ever ran across; and he's gone to seed.

PEPEL (*guffaws*): A baron! And just now you called me down!

BARON: It's time you had more sense, Vasily.

LUKA: Oh ho ho! Now I can see, lads, your life ain't what it should be!

BUBNOV: That's our style of life: we set to howling as soon as we get up in the morning.

BARON: Life used to be better, it did! I used to wake up and have my coffee in bed. . . . Coffee! With cream! Yes, I did!

LUKA: And still—we're all men! No matter how much you pretend, no matter how much you try to get out of it, you were born a man and you'll die one. . . . And, I can see, men keep growing cleverer, keep growing more entertaining. . . . And though they live worse and worse, they want better and better things. . . . Stubborn!

BARON: Who are you, anyhow, old man? . . . Where did you come from?

LUKA: I?

BARON: Are you a holy wanderer?

LUKA: We're all of us wanderers here on earth. . . . And they say —so I've heard—that even this earth of ours is a wanderer in the sky.

BARON (*sternly*): Maybe so—but have you a passport?

LUKA (*after a pause*): Who are you—a detective?

PEPEL (*exultantly*): Good for you, old man! Well, Baron, old boy, you caught it!

BUBNOV: Yes, the squire got what was coming to him.

BARON (*put out of countenance*): Well, what's the odds? I was just joking, old man! I haven't any papers myself, my boy.

BUBNOV: You lie!

BARON: That is . . . I have papers . . . but they're no good.

LUKA: All those papers are of the same sort—they're all no good.

PEPEL: Baron, come on to the tavern!

BARON: I'm ready! Well, good-by, old man! . . . You're a rascal!

LUKA: There are all sorts of folks, my friend.

PEPEL (*at the door of the hall*): Well, come on, will you! (*He goes out. The* BARON *follows him with quick steps.*)

LUKA: Was that man really a baron?

BUBNOV: Who knows? He's an aristocrat, that's sure. . . . Even now, before you know it, all of a sudden he shows himself a gentleman born. Hasn't lost the hang of it yet, you see.

LUKA: Maybe gentle birth is like the smallpox. . . . Even when a man gets over it, the marks remain.

BUBNOV: He's a good sort, all the same. . . . He just kicks out now and then . . . as he did about your passport, for instance.

(ALESHKA *comes in, tipsy, with an accordion in his hands. He is whistling.*)

ALESHKA: Hey, fellows!

BUBNOV: What are you yelling for?

ALESHKA: Excuse me. . . . Pardon me! I am a polite man.

BUBNOV: Been on a spree again?

ALESHKA: You bet! Police Sergeant Medyakin just drove me off his beat and says: "Don't let me see hide nor hair of you on the street," he says; "look out!" I'm a man of character. . . . And the boss snorts at me. . . . But what does a boss amount to? Bah! He's just off his nut. . . . He's a drunkard, the boss is. . . . But I'm the kind of man that . . . don't want anything! I just don't—that's all! Here, you can have me for a ruble and twenty kopeks! But I—I don't want anything. (NASTYA *comes in from the kitchen.*) Offer me a million— I don't want it! And I won't stand for it that I, a good man, should be bossed by my comrade, a drunkard! I don't want it!

(NASTYA, *standing by the door, looks at* ALESHKA *and shakes her head.*)

LUKA (*in a kindly tone*): Eh, my lad, you've got off the track.

BUBNOV: Human folly!

ALESHKA (*lying down on the floor*): Here, eat me up! But I—don't want anything. I'm a desperate character! Just explain to me who's any better than I! Why am I worse than the rest of 'em? There! Medyakin says: "Don't you come on the street, or I'll smash your mug!" But I'll go. . . . I'll go lie down in the middle of the street—let 'em crush me! I don't want anything!

NASTYA: Poor fellow! . . . He's young still—and what a spectacle he's making of himself already.

ALESHKA (*seeing her, he rises to his knees*): Young lady! Mamzel! Parlay fransay . . . preiscourant! I'm on a spree. . . .

NASTYA (*in a loud whisper*): Vasilisa!

VASILISA (*quickly opening the door, to* ALESHKA): You here again?

ALESHKA: How d'ye do! Come in!

VASILISA: You pup, I told you not to show your face here—and now you've come again?

ALESHKA: Vasilisa Karpovna . . . want me to play you . . . a funeral march?

VASILISA (*giving him a push on the shoulder*): Get out!

ALESHKA (*moving towards the door*): Wait! . . . Can't act that way! A funeral march . . . I've just learned it! Fresh music. . . . Wait! Can't act that way!

VASILISA: I'll show you "can't act that way"! . . . I'll set the whole street on you, you damned heathen! . . . You're too young to bark about *me*.

ALESHKA (*running out*): All right, I'll be going.

VASILISA (*to* BUBNOV) : See that he never sets foot here again! Do you hear?

BUBNOV: I'm not your watchman.

VASILISA: I don't care who you are! You're living here on charity: don't forget that! How much do you owe me?

BUBNOV (*calmly*) : Haven't reckoned it up.

VASILISA: Look out or I'll reckon it!

ALESHKA (*opens the door and shouts*) : Vasilisa Karpovna! I ain't afraid of you! . . . I ain't afrrraid! (*He disappears.*)

(LUKA *laughs.*)

VASILISA: Who are you?

LUKA: A passer-by, a traveler.

VASILISA: For the night or permanently?

LUKA: I'll see later.

VASILISA: Passport!

LUKA: All right.

VASILISA: Give it here!

LUKA: I'll bring it to you. . . . I'll present it at your lodging.

VASILISA: Passer-by—not much! You'd better call yourself a shady tramp—that'd be more like the truth.

LUKA (*with a sigh*) : Oh, you aren't very kindly, friend.

(VASILISA *goes towards the door of* PEPEL'S *room.* ALESHKA, *peeping out of the kitchen, whispers:* "Has she gone?")

VASILISA (*turning towards him*) : You still here?

(ALESHKA *disappears with a whistle.* NASTYA *and* LUKA *laugh.*)

BUBNOV (*to* VASILISA) : He's not here.

VASILISA: Who?

BUBNOV: Vaska.

VASILISA: Did I ask you about him?

BUBNOV: I see you're looking all round.

VASILISA: I'm looking to see if things are in order: do you understand? Why hasn't the room been swept up yet? How many times have I told you to keep things clean!

BUBNOV: The actor was to sweep.

VASILISA: I don't care who! Now if the sanitary inspector comes and fines me—then I'll turn out every one of you!

BUBNOV (*calmly*) : What'll you live on then?

VASILISA: See that there ain't a speck of dirt! (*To* NASTYA.) What are you hanging round for? Why's your mug swollen? What are you standing there for like a bump on a log? Sweep up the floor! Have you seen Natalya? Has she been in here?

NASTYA: I don't know. . . . I haven't seen her.

VASILISA: Bubnov, has my sister been here?

BUBNOV: Eh? . . . It was she who brought him.

VASILISA: That fellow—was he at home?

BUBNOV: Vasily? Yes. . . . She was talking here with Kleshch—Natalya was.

VASILISA: I didn't ask you who she was talking with! Dirt everywhere—filth! Oh, you—pigs! Clean it up! . . . Do you hear! (*Goes out quickly.*)

BUBNOV: What a lot of savagery there is in that woman!

LUKA: Serious little body!

NASTYA: Any one would turn into a wild beast in such a life. . . . Just hitch any living creature to such a husband as hers! . . .

BUBNOV: Well, she's not hitched very tight.

LUKA: Does she always . . . break loose like that?

BUBNOV: Always. . . . She came to see her lover, you see; and he's gone.

LUKA: And so she felt hurt. Oh ho ho! What a lot of different people there are, bossing folks about on this earth . . . and they terrify one another with all sorts of terrors, and still there's no order in life . . . and no cleanness!

BUBNOV: They all want order, but their wits are in disorder. However, we must sweep up. . . . Nastya, you might attend to it.

NASTYA: Not much I won't! Am I your chambermaid? (*After a pause.*) I'm going to get drunk to-day . . . oh, so drunk!

BUBNOV: Sounds reasonable.

LUKA: What do you want to drink for, girl? A little while ago you were weeping, and now you say you'll take to drink!

NASTYA (*aggressively*): I'll drink, then I'll weep once more. . . . That's all!

BUBNOV: It ain't much.

LUKA: But for what reason, tell me! Even a pimple don't come out without any reason at all.

(NASTYA *is silent, shaking her head.*)

LUKA: That's the way. . . . Ah ha! . . . How folks do act! And what will become of you? . . . Well now, suppose I sweep up here. Where's your broom?

BUBNOV: Behind the door, in the hall.

(LUKA *goes into the hall.*)

BUBNOV: Nastya dear!

NASTYA: Eh?

BUBNOV: What did Vasilisa come down on Aleshka for?

NASTYA: He told stories about her, that Vaska was sick of her, and that Vaska wanted to turn her off . . . and to take on Natasha. . . . I'm going to leave here . . . go to another lodging.

BUBNOV: Why? Where to?

NASTYA: I'm sick of it. . . . Nobody wants me here.

BUBNOV (*calmly*): Nobody wants you anywhere . . . or anybody else on earth. Nobody's wanted.

(NASTYA *shakes her head. She rises and quietly goes into the hall.* MEDVEDEV *comes in;* LUKA *follows him, carrying the broom.*)

MEDVEDEV: I don't seem to know you.

LUKA: But do you know all the rest of the people?

MEDVEDEV: I have to know everybody on my beat. . . . But I don't know *you.*

LUKA: That's because the whole earth's not on your beat, uncle. . . . There's a little left outside it. (*Goes out into the kitchen.*)

MEDVEDEV (*going up to* BUBNOV): It's true, my beat's not large—though it's worse than any big one. . . . Just before I went off duty, I took Aleshka the shoemaker to the police station. . . . He lay down in the middle of the street, you understand, played his accordion and kept yelling: "I don't want anything, I don't need anything." Horses were passing and there was a lot of traffic; they might have crushed him with the wheels and so on. . . . He's a lad that makes trouble. . . . Well, I grabbed him right away and . . . disposed of him. He's too fond of acting disorderly.

BUBNOV: Will you come and play checkers this evening?

MEDVEDEV: Sure! I'll come. And what about—Vaska?

BUBNOV: All right. . . . Just the same.

MEDVEDEV: So—he's getting on?

BUBNOV: Why shouldn't he be? He can make a living.

MEDVEDEV (*doubtfully*): Can he? (LUKA *goes out into the hall with a pail in his hand.*) Hm . . . there's talk going around . . . about Vaska. Haven't you heard?

BUBNOV: I hear lots of talk.

MEDVEDEV: About Vasilisa. They say . . . you haven't noticed?

BUBNOV: What?

MEDVEDEV: Just in general. . . . Maybe you know, but are lying about it? Everybody knows. . . . (*Sternly.*) You mustn't tell lies, my friend!

BUBNOV: Why should I lie!

MEDVEDEV: That's it! . . . Ugh, the curs! The talk is about Vaska and Vasilisa, you know. . . . But what's that to me? I'm not her father; I'm her uncle. . . . Why should they laugh at me? . . . (KVASHNYA *comes in.*) What people there are now! . . . They laugh at everybody. (*To* KVASHNYA.) Ah ha! So you've come!

KVASHNYA: My beloved man of war!— Say, Bubnov; at the market he began again to tease me to marry him.

BUBNOV: Go ahead! Why not? He has money, and he's a gentleman still in the prime of life.

MEDVEDEV: I? Ho ho!

KVASHNYA: Oh, you gray-coat! No, don't you touch me on that sore spot of mine! I've been there before, my dear man. . . . For a woman to marry is just like jumping into a hole in the ice in winter time: if you've done it once you remember it all your life.

MEDVEDEV: You just wait; there's a difference in husbands.

KVASHNYA: But I'm the same all the time! When my darling husband croaked—may he never have a soft bed to rest on!—I just sat quiet all by myself for a whole day from sheer joy; I sat there and couldn't believe my own happiness.

MEDVEDEV: If your husband beat you . . . for no cause at all, you ought to have complained to the police.

KVASHNYA: I complained to God for eight years—and he didn't help me!

MEDVEDEV: Wife-beating's forbidden now. . . . There are strict laws about everything now—law and order! You can't beat anybody without a reason. . . . They beat folks to keep order.

LUKA (leading in ANNA): Well, we've crawled in. . . . Here you are! How can you ever walk alone when you're in such a feeble condition? Where's your place?

ANNA (pointing to it): Thanks, grandfather.

KVASHNYA: There's a sample of a married woman. . . . Look at her!

LUKA: The little woman's in poor shape. . . . She walks along the hall, catches hold of the walls, and—groans. . . . Why do you let her out alone?

KVASHNYA: We didn't keep an eye on her, daddy: pray excuse us! And her maid must have gone out walking.

LUKA: You're joking—but can you desert a human being like this? Every one of us—no matter what sort he is—has a value of his own.

MEDVEDEV: You need to keep watch! What if she dies all of a sudden? That'll make a mess. . . . You must keep track of her!

LUKA: True for you, Mr. Sergeant.

MEDVEDEV: Ye-es—though I'm not yet quite a sergeant.

LUKA: Really? But your appearance is most heroic.

(There is an uproar in the hall; heavy steps and dull cries are heard.)

MEDVEDEV: Sounds like a row?

BUBNOV: Something of the sort.

KVASHNYA: I'll go and see.

MEDVEDEV: I must go to. . . . Ugh, this job of mine! Why do they ever separate people when they fight? They'd stop of their own accord

. . . for you get sick of fighting, you know. . . . I'd let 'em pommel each other all they wanted to, as much as they liked. . . . Then they'd fight less, for they'd remember their beatings longer.

BUBNOV (*getting down from the bunk*) : You'd better speak to the authorities about that.

KOSTYLEV (*bursting open the door, shouts*) : Abram, come here! Vasilisa . . . is killing Natasha. . . . Come here!

(KVASHNYA, MEDVEDEV, *and* BUBNOV *rush into the hall.* LUKA, *shaking his head, gazes after them.*)

ANNA : Oh, Lord! . . . Poor little Natasha!

LUKA : Who's fighting there?

ANNA : The landlady . . . and her sister.

LUKA (*going up to* ANNA) : What's their quarrel?

ANNA : They're both . . . so well-fed . . . and healthy.

LUKA : What's your name?

ANNA : Anna. . . . Now I can see . . . you're like my father . . . like daddy. . . . He was just so kind and . . . soft.

LUKA : I've been punched a lot; that's why I'm soft. (*He laughs with a quavering laugh.*)

ACT II

The same setting. Evening. On the bunks near the stove SATIN, *the* BARON, WRYMUG, *and the* TATAR *are playing cards.* KLESHCH *and the* ACTOR *are watching the game.* BUBNOV *on his bunk is playing checkers with* MEDVEDEV. LUKA *is sitting on the stool close to* ANNA'S *bed. The lodging is lighted by two lamps: one hangs on the wall near the cardplayers; the other stands on* BUBNOV'S *bunk.*

TATAR : Once more I play—no more I play.

BUBNOV : Wrymug, sing! (*Starts the tune.*)

> Though the sun is shining brightly—

WRYMUG (*taking up the air*) :

> No ray falls upon my floor.

TATAR (*to* SATIN) : Shuffle card! Shuffle good! We know what your kind.

BUBNOV *and* WRYMUG (*together*) :

> Day and night the sentinels they—oh, ah ha!
> Go their rounds before my door.

ANNA : Blows . . . insults . . . that's all I've ever had. . . . Nothing else at all!

Luka: Eh, little woman! Don't fret!

Medvedev: Where're you moving? Look out!

Bubnov: Ah ha! Yes, yes, yes.

Tatar (*shaking his fist at* Satin): Why want hide card? I see.
. . . Hey, you!

Wrymug: Quit, Asan! They'll swindle us anyhow.— Bubnov, start
the song!

Anna: I don't remember when I ever had enough to eat. . . . I shook
with terror over every bit of bread. . . . I have trembled all my life.
. . . I tormented myself—in order not to eat more than anybody
else. . . . All my life I have gone around in rags . . . all my unhappy
life. . . . What for?

Luka: Poor dear child! Are you tired? Never mind!

Actor (*to* Wrymug): Lead the knave . . . the knave, you devil!

Baron: But we have the king.

Andante molto tranquillo (ALL)

Though the sun is shin-ing bright - ly, No ray falls up - on my floor. (ONE VOICE)

Day and night the sen-ti - nels_____ they oh, ah,_____ ha! (ONE VOICE)

(ALL) Go their rounds be-fore my door. Guard me safe-ly, guard me sure - ly (ONE VOICE)

(ALL) But I nev-er shall break out, Though I'm _ long-ing for my

(ONE VOICE) free - dom, oh, ah,_____ ha! (ALL) For the chain is strong and stout.

KLESHCH: They'll beat every time.

SATIN: That's our habit.

MEDVEDEV: King!

BUBNOV: And I have one too.— There!

ANNA: And now I'm dying.

KLESHCH: Look, look at him! Prince, quit the game! Quit, I tell you!

ACTOR: Can't he understand without your help?

BARON: Look out, Andrey, or I'll chuck you straight down to hell!

TATAR: Deal once more! Pitcher went for water, broke itself . . . me too!

(KLESHCH, *shaking his head, moves over to* BUBNOV.)

ANNA: I keep thinking: "Lord, is it possible that I am doomed to torment even in the other world! Must I suffer there too?"

LUKA: There won't be anything of the sort! Lie still, now! Never mind! You will have rest there! . . . Suffer in patience a bit longer. Everybody suffers, my dear woman; everybody has to endure life in his own way. (*He rises and goes into the kitchen with quick steps.*)

BUBNOV (*begins to sing*):

> Guard me safely, guard me surely—

WRYMUG:

> But I never shall break out—

BOTH TOGETHER:

> Though I'm longing for my freedom, oh, ah ha!
> For the chain is strong and stout.

TATAR (*shouts*): Ah! Stuck card in sleeve!

BARON (*taken aback*): Well! Shall I stick it in your nose?

ACTOR (*impressively*): Prince, you're mistaken. Nobody ever—

TATAR: I saw. Sharper! Me won't play!

SATIN (*gathering up the cards*): You let up, Asan. . . . You know mighty well that we're sharpers. So why did you play with us?

BARON: He's lost forty kopeks, and he's making noise enough for three rubles. . . . And he calls himself a prince!

TATAR (*hotly*): Must play honest!

SATIN: What for?

TATAR: What for, you say?

SATIN: Yes. What for?

TATAR: Don't you know?

SATIN: No, I don't. Do you?

(*The* TATAR *spits, infuriated. All laugh loudly at him.*)

WRYMUG (*genially*): You're a freak, Asan! Just you understand! If they started to live honestly, they'd die of hunger in three days. . . .

TATAR: What I care! Must live honest!

WRYMUG: How you keep it up! Let's go and have tea. . . . Bubnov! (*Sings.*)

Ah, my chains, my heavy chains! . . .

BUBNOV (*continuing*):

Ah, my iron watchmen! . . .

WRYMUG: Come on, Asan boy! (*Goes out, humming.*)

I can never break or smash you.

(*The* TATAR *shakes his fist at the* BARON *and follows his comrade out of the lodging.*)

SATIN (*to the* BARON, *laughing*): Well, your And-so-forth, you again triumphantly sat down in a puddle! You're an educated man, but you can't smuggle a card.

BARON (*spreading out his hands in despair*): Devil knows how it—

ACTOR: You've no talent . . . no self-confidence. . . . And without that you can never accomplish anything.

MEDVEDEV: I have one king . . . and you have two. . . . Well!

BUBNOV: One king's all right, if he can fight. . . . Move ahead.

KLESHCH: You've lost the game, Abram Ivanovich!

MEDVEDEV: That's none of your business. . . . Understand? And shut up!

SATIN: My winnings are fifty-three kopeks.

ACTOR: Give me three. . . . Though what do I need three kopeks for?

LUKA (*coming in from the kitchen*): Well, you fleeced the Tatar. Now are you going to drink vodka?

BARON: Come on with us!

SATIN: I'd like to see what you're like when you're drunk.

LUKA: No better than when I'm sober.

ACTOR: Come on, old man! . . . I'll declaim some couplets for you.

LUKA: What's that?

ACTOR: Verses.— Do you understand?

LUKA: Ve-erses! What use do I have for your verses!

ACTOR: They're funny. . . . And sometimes sad, too.

SATIN: Well, coupletist, are you coming? (*Goes out with the* BARON.)

ACTOR: I'm coming. . . . I'll catch up with you! For instance, old man, here's a bit of a poem. . . . I've forgotten the beginning . . . forgotten it. (*He rubs his brow.*)

BUBNOV: Done for! Your king's lost. . . . Move!

MEDVEDEV: I made the wrong move. . . . Confound it!

ACTOR: In earlier years, when my organism was not poisoned by alcohol, I had a good memory, old man. . . . But now . . . it's over, friend! All's over for me. I always recited that poem with great success . . . thunderous applause! You . . . you don't know what applause is. . . . It's like . . . vodka, my friend! . . . I used to come out, stand like this. . . . (*Poses.*) I'd stand . . . and . . . (*Is silent.*) I don't remember anything. . . . Not a word. . . . I don't remember! My belovèd poem! . . . That's bad, old man, isn't it?

LUKA: It sure is bad to forget what you loved. All a man's soul is in what he loves.

ACTOR: I've drunk away my soul, old man. . . . I've perished, friend. . . . And why did I perish? I've had no faith in myself. . . . I'm done for. . . .

LUKA: Well, never mind! You . . . take a cure! They cure drunkenness nowadays, do you hear! They cure it free of charge, my boy. . . . There's been a special hospital established for drunkards—to cure them for nothing, you know. . . . You see they recognize that a drunkard is a man like other men, and they're even glad when he wants to be cured! Well then, get a move on! Go there!

ACTOR (*pensively*): Where? Where is it?

LUKA: Oh, it's . . . in a city . . . what's its name! It's name is— Well, I'll tell you the city later! . . . Only you do this! You get ready to start. Hold yourself in! . . . Take yourself in hand—and endure. . . . And later you'll be cured . . . and you'll begin to live once more. . . . Won't that be fine, friend, to start fresh? Well, make your decision . . . do it quick!

ACTOR (*smiling*): Start fresh! . . . from the beginning. . . . That's fine. . . . Yes. . . . Start fresh. (*Laughs.*) Well . . . yes! Can I do it! Can I do it, I say!

LUKA: Why not? A man can do anything . . . if he only wants to.

ACTOR (*seems to wake up suddenly*): You're a queer fellow! Good-by for the present! (*Whistles.*) Good-by, old boy. (*Goes out.*)

ANNA: Grandfather!

LUKA: What, mother.

ANNA: Come and talk to me.

LUKA (*going over to her*): All right, let's have a chat.

(KLESHCH *looks round, silently goes over to his wife, looks at her, and gesticulates with his hands, as if wishing to say something.*)

LUKA: What is it, friend?

KLESHCH (*in a low voice*): Nothing. (*He slowly goes towards the door into the hall, stands in front of it for a few seconds, and—goes out.*)

LUKA (*gazing after him*): It's hard for your husband.

ANNA: I don't worry about him any longer.

LUKA: Did he use to beat you?

ANNA: I should say so. . . . He's why I'm sick and dying, most likely.

BUBNOV: My wife . . . had a lover; he used to play checkers splendidly, the rascal. . . .

MEDVEDEV: Hm-m.

ANNA: Grandfather! Talk to me, dear! . . . I feel sick. . . .

LUKA: That's nothing! That means that death is coming, darling. That's nothing, dear! Just have hope. . . . So you'll die and be at peace. . . . You won't need anything any more and you'll have nothing to fear! Quiet, calm . . . and you just lie still! Death brings peace to everything. . . . It is gracious to us. . . . You'll die and be at rest, as they say. . . . That's the truth, my dear! Because—where can a man find rest in this world?

(PEPEL *comes in. He is slightly tipsy; his hair is disheveled and he has a gloomy air. He seats himself on a bunk near the door and remains there, silent and motionless.*)

ANNA: But what if over there, there'll be more pain?

LUKA: There'll be nothing of the sort! Nothing! You can believe that! Peace and—nothing else! They will call you before the Lord and will say: "Behold, O Lord, thy servant Anna hath come."

MEDVEDEV (*sternly*): How do you know what they'll say there? Oh, you! . . .

(*At the sound of* MEDVEDEV'S *voice* PEPEL *raises his head and listens.*)

LUKA: You see that I know about it, Mr. Sergeant.

MEDVEDEV (*in a conciliatory tone*): Hm . . . yes! . . . That's your business. . . . Though I'm not yet . . . quite . . . a sergeant.

BUBNOV: I take two men. . . .

MEDVEDEV: Oh, you! . . . Plague take you!

LUKA: And the Lord will glance at you gently and graciously and will say: "I know this Anna! Lead Anna into Paradise!" he will say. "Let her be at peace. . . . I know: her life was very hard . . . and she is very weary. . . . Give peace to Anna."

ANNA (*choking*): Grandfather . . . you're a dear . . . if it were only so! If . . . there were peace . . . so that I should feel nothing!

LUKA: You won't! There will be nothing! Believe that! You must die with joy, without anxiety. . . . Death, I tell you, is the same to us as a mother to little children. . . .

ANNA: But . . . maybe . . . maybe I'll get well?

LUKA (*grinning*): What for? To suffer again?

ANNA: Well . . . if I could live . . . just a little longer . . . just a little! If there will be no torture there . . . I could endure it a bit here. . . . I could!

LUKA: There will be nothing there! . . . Simply . . .

PEPEL (*rising*): That's true. . . . But maybe it isn't true!

ANNA (*in a frightened tone*): Lord! . . .

LUKA: Ah, my handsome man. . . .

MEDVEDEV: Who's yelling?

PEPEL (*going towards him*): I! What of it?

MEDVEDEV: You're yelling just for greens, that's the trouble! A man should behave peaceably.

PEPEL: Eh . . . you blockhead! And yet you're an uncle! Ho ho!

LUKA (*to* PEPEL *in a low voice*): Listen, don't shout! This woman is dying here. . . . The earth is already sprinkled on her lips. . . . Do not hinder her!

PEPEL: All right, grandfather, I'll heed you! You're a good sort, my boy! You tell fine lies . . . tell pleasant fairy tales! Go ahead and lie, my boy! There's precious little that's pleasant in this world!

BUBNOV: Is the woman really dying?

LUKA: Looks so, no joking.

BUBNOV: So she'll stop coughing. . . . She's been coughing just awfully. . . . I take two men!

MEDVEDEV: Oh, to the devil with you!

PEPEL: Abram!

MEDVEDEV: Abram's not my name for such as you.

PEPEL: Abe! Is Natasha ill?

MEDVEDEV: What business is that of yours?

PEPEL: No, tell me: did Vasilisa beat her up badly?

MEDVEDEV: That's not your business either! That's a family affair. . . . And who are you, anyhow?

PEPEL: Never mind who I am, but—if I take a notion—you won't see your little Natasha any more!

MEDVEDEV (*abandoning the game of checkers*): What are you saying? Who are you talking about? That my niece should—! Pah, you thief!

PEPEL: I'm a thief, but you've never caught me.

MEDVEDEV: Just wait! I'll catch you . . . and mighty soon.

PEPEL: If you catch me, it'll be bad luck for all your tribe. Do you think I won't answer the prosecutor? A wolf can bite! They'll ask who put me up to thievery and showed me where to go. "Mishka Kostylev and his wife!" Who received the stolen goods? "Mishka Kostylev and his wife!"

MEDVEDEV: You lie! They won't believe you!

PEPEL: They'll believe me, because it's true! I'll get you mixed up in it too! . . . Ha! I'll ruin you all, you devils; you'll see for yourself!

MEDVEDEV (*losing his composure*): You lie! And . . . you lie! And . . . what harm have I ever done you? You're a mad dog! . . .

PEPEL: And what good have you ever done me?

LUKA: That's so!

MEDVEDEV (*to* LUKA): What are *you* croaking about? What business is this of yours? This is a family affair!

BUBNOV (*to* LUKA): Let up! They're making nooses for other people than you and me.

LUKA (*humbly*): I meant no harm! All I say is: If one man don't do any good to another, then he acts badly.

MEDVEDEV (*not understanding*): That's the point! We here . . . all know each other. . . . But you—who are you? (*Snorting angrily, he goes out hastily.*)

LUKA: The military gentleman got angry. . . . Oh ho ho! I can see, friends, your affairs here are all in a muss!

PEPEL: He's run off to complain to Vasilisa.

BUBNOV: You're acting wild, Vasily. Somehow you've developed a lot of pluck. . . . Now see here: pluck's all right when you're going into the forest for mushrooms—but here it's no use at all. . . . They'll wring your neck in short order.

PEPEL: Not much! You can't catch us fellows from Yaroslav right off with your bare hands. . . . If there's going to be war, we'll fight. . . .

LUKA: But really, my lad, you'd better be leaving this place.

PEPEL: Where to? Come now, tell me!

LUKA: Go—to Siberia!

PEPEL: Oh ho! No, I'll wait till they send me off to Siberia at government expense.

LUKA: Listen: you go there of your own accord! You can make your own way there. . . . Out there they need men like you!

PEPEL: My way is marked out for me! My father spent all his life in one prison after another and left that legacy to me. . . . When I was only a little fellow—even then they called me thief, son of a thief.

LUKA: But Siberia's a fine country! a golden country! Any man who has strength and sense can prosper there like a cucumber in a hotbed.

PEPEL: Old man, why do you keep telling lies!

LUKA: Wha-at?

PEPEL: Are you deaf! Why do you tell lies, I say?

LUKA: But what do I tell lies about?

PEPEL: About everything. . . . You say it's good there, and good here. . . . You're lying, you know! What's the use of it?

LUKA: You just believe me: go and see for yourself. . . . You'll thank me. . . . What are you wasting your time here for? And— why are you so awfully anxious for the truth? . . . Just remember: that truth may be the hammer that'll strike you dead.

PEPEL: It's all the same to me! If it's a hammer, let it be one.

LUKA: You're a funny fellow! Why should you kill yourself?

BUBNOV: What are you both talking nonsense for? I can't understand. . . . What sort of truth do you need, Vasya? And what for? You know the truth about yourself. . . . And everybody else knows it too.

PEPEL: Wait, don't croak! Let him answer me.— Listen, old man: Is there a God?

(LUKA *is silent, smiling.*)

BUBNOV: Men all live . . . as chips float on a river. . . . When they build a house, they throw away the chips.

PEPEL: Well? Is there? Tell me!

LUKA (*in a low voice*): If you believe in him, there is; if you don't, there isn't. . . . What you believe in, exists.

(PEPEL *is silent, staring with surprise at the old man.*)

BUBNOV: I'll go and have tea. . . . Let's go to the tavern! Shall we?

LUKA (*to* PEPEL): What are you staring at?

PEPEL: Because . . . wait a minute! So—

BUBNOV: Well, I'll go alone. (*Goes towards the door and meets* VASILISA:)

PEPEL: And so . . . you—

VASILISA (*to* BUBNOV): Is Nastya at home?

BUBNOV: No. (*Goes out.*)

PEPEL: Oh! . . . So you've come!

VASILISA (*going over to* ANNA): Still alive?

LUKA: Don't disturb her.

VASILISA: Hello! What are you hanging round here for?

LUKA: I can leave . . . if necessary.

VASILISA (*moving towards the door of* PEPEL'S *room*): Vasily! I have some business with you.

(LUKA *goes to the hall door, opens it, and slams it to loudly. Then he cautiously climbs on a bunk, and from there to the top of the stove.*)

VASILISA (*from* PEPEL'S *room*): Vasya! Come here!

PEPEL: I won't! . . . I don't want to!

VASILISA: Eh? What's that? What are you angry about?

PEPEL: I'm bored. . . . I'm sick of all this mess.

VASILISA: And are you sick of me too?

PEPEL: You too.

(VASILISA *pulls her kerchief tightly over her shoulders, pressing her hands to her breast. She goes to* ANNA'S *bed, cautiously looks behind the bed curtains, and returns to* PEPEL.)

PEPEL: Well! . . . Speak out!

VASILISA: What's there to say? You can't force your love on any-body, and it's not in my character to beg for love. . . . Thank you for telling the truth!

PEPEL: What truth?

VASILISA: That you're sick of me. . . . Or ain't that true?

(PEPEL *looks at her in silence.*)

VASILISA (*moving towards him*): What are you staring at? Don't you know me?

PEPEL (*sighing*): You're a handsome woman, Vasilisa . . . (*The woman lays her hand on his neck, but he shakes it off with a motion of his shoulder.*) but my heart has never been with you. . . . I've lived with you and all that . . . but I've never liked you.

VASILISA (*in a low voice*): We-ell . . . The-en? . . .

PEPEL: Then there's nothing for us to talk about! Nothing at all! . . . Go away from me.

VASILISA: Have you taken a fancy to somebody else?

PEPEL: None of your business. . . . If I have, I won't ask you to arrange the match.

VASILISA (*meaningly*): You're quite wrong. . . . Maybe I *would* arrange it for you.

PEPEL (*suspiciously*): Who are you talking about?

VASILISA: You know. . . . What's the use of pretending? Vasily, I'm a person that speaks straight out. . . . (*In a lower voice.*) I won't hide it. . . . You've done me wrong. . . . Without any reason at all, you've just hit me with a whip. . . . You said you loved me. . . . And now all of a sudden—

PEPEL: Not suddenly at all. . . . Long ago I . . . There's no soul in you, woman. . . . A woman ought to have a soul. . . . We men are beasts. . . . We need . . . we need . . . somebody to teach us. . . . And you—what have you ever taught me?

VASILISA: What's gone is gone. . . . I know, a man can't control himself. . . . If you don't love me any more . . . all right! So be it.

PEPEL: Well, then it's all over! We've separated peaceably, without a row. . . . That's fine!

VASILISA: No, wait! All the same . . . when I lived with you . . . I kept expecting that you'd help me to get out of this pit . . . that you'd free me from my husband, from uncle . . . from all this life. . . . And maybe I didn't love you, Vasya, but . . . in you . . . I loved my own hopes, my own dreams. . . . Do you understand? I expected that you'd pull me out.

PEPEL: You aren't a nail, and I'm not pincers. . . . Here I thought that you, as a sensible woman—you are sensible, you know . . . you're clever!

VASILISA (*snuggling up to him*): Vasya, come on . . . let's help each other!

PEPEL: How's that?

VASILISA (*in a low, strong voice*): You like . . . my sister. I know it.

PEPEL: And so you beat her brutally! Look out, Vasilisa, don't you touch her!

VASILISA: Wait. Don't get excited! We can do everything quietly and decently. . . . Do you want to marry her? All right, then I'll give you money into the bargain . . . about three hundred rubles! I'll get together more—I'll give more.

PEPEL (*moving away*): Wait! . . . How's that? What for?

VASILISA: Free me . . . from my husband! Take that noose off my neck!

PEPEL (*with a low whistle*): So that's it! Oh ho ho! That's a clever idea of yours. . . . You mean: your husband, to the grave; your lover, to penal servitude; and yourself—

VASILISA: Vasya! Why penal servitude? You won't do it yourself . . . but through your companions! And even if you do it yourself, who'll find out? You'll have Natalya—just think of it! You'll have money . . . go off somewhere . . . set me free for ever. . . . And if sister is kept away from me, that'll be good for her. It's hard for me to see her . . . I feel spiteful to her on your account . . . and I can't restrain myself. . . . I torture the girl, beat her. . . . Yes, I beat her so that I myself weep from pity for her. . . . But—I beat her. And I'll keep on beating her!

PEPEL: You brute! You boast of your own brutality.

VASILISA: I'm not boasting, I'm telling the truth. Just think, Vasya . . . you've been in prison twice owing to my husband . . . owing to his greed. . . . He's been sucking my blood like a bedbug, sucking it for four years! And what sort of husband is he? He nags at Natasha, taunts her, tells her that she's a beggar! And he's poison to everybody!

PEPEL: You're making a cunning scheme.

VASILISA: Everything's clear that I say. . . . Anybody but a fool'd understand what I want.

(KOSTYLEV *comes in cautiously and steals forward.*)

PEPEL (*to* VASILISA): Well . . . be off with you!

VASILISA: Think it over. (*Sees her husband.*) What do you want?
Have you come for me?

(PEPEL *jumps up and looks wildly at* KOSTYLEV.)

KOSTYLEV: It's I . . . I! So you two are here . . . alone? Ah,
ha! . . . And so you were talking? (*He suddenly begins to stamp
and to shout.*) Vasilisa, you dirty slut! You beggarly—hag! (*He
grows alarmed at his own shouting, which the others meet with placid
silence.*) Forgive me, O Lord! . . . Vasilisa, you have again led
me into sin. . . . I've been looking for you everywhere. . . . (*Yelling.*) It's time to go to bed! You've forgotten to fill the lamps in
front of the ikons . . . confound you! You beggarly—swine! . . .

(*He brandishes his trembling arms at her.* VASILISA *slowly goes
towards the hall door, looking back at* PEPEL.)

PEPEL (*to* KOSTYLEV): Here, you! Get out! . . . Off with you!

KOSTYLEV (*shouts*): I'm the master here! Get out yourself! You
thief!

PEPEL (*hoarsely*): Go away, Mishka!

KOSTYLEV: Don't you dare! I'm here. . . . I'll give it to you!

(PEPEL *grabs him by the collar and shakes him. From the stove are
heard the sound of movements and a wailing yawn.* PEPEL *releases*
KOSTYLEV, *who with a yell runs into the hall.*)

PEPEL (*shouting*): Who's that? . . . Who's on the stove?

LUKA (*putting out his head*): Wha-at?

PEPEL: Is it you!

LUKA (*calmly*): Yes. . . . Just me. . . . Oh, Lord Jesus Christ!

PEPEL (*closes the hall door, looks for the bar, but cannot find it*):
Oh, hell! . . . Come down, old man!

LUKA: I'll come down . . . ri-ight away.

PEPEL (*roughly*): What did you climb on the stove for?

LUKA: But where should I go?

PEPEL: But—didn't you go out into the hall?

LUKA: It's too cold in the hall, my boy, for an old man like me.

PEPEL: Did you . . . hear?

LUKA: Eh? . . . Hear? Of course I heard. Think I'm deaf? Ah,
my lad, luck's coming your way. . . . Luck's coming!

PEPEL (*suspiciously*): What luck? Why so?

LUKA: Why? Because I climbed on the stove.

PEPEL: Well . . . why did you begin to make a fuss there?

LUKA: That, you see, was because I got heated up . . . lucky for
your wretched self! . . . And then again I got a notion: "Maybe the
lad'll make a mistake," says I to myself; "he may choke the old man."

PEPEL: Ye-es . . . I might have. . . . I hate him.

LUKA: That's not strange. Nothing queer about that. . . . Such mistakes often happen.

PEPEL (*smiling*): What's that you say? Maybe you made a mistake once yourself?

LUKA: See here, boy! Listen to what I tell you: let that woman alone! Don't you touch her! Don't let her come near you! . . . She'll put her husband out of the way herself, and she'll do a cleverer job than you would—she will! Don't you listen to her, the she-devil! . . . Look at me now. I'm bald-headed. . . . And why? Because of all sorts and kinds of those women. . . . Maybe I've known more of those women than there are hairs on my head. . . . But that Vasilisa—she's worse than a heathen!

PEPEL: I don't know whether to thank you . . . or whether you, too . . .

LUKA: Don't you talk! You won't say anything better than I can! Listen now: you just take by the arm whichever of 'em pleases you, and clear out of here at the double-quick! Get out! . . . Go somewhere else.

PEPEL (*glumly*): You can't understand people! Some are good and others are bad. . . . You can't make out anything.

LUKA: What's there to understand? A man lives any old way. . . . He lives according to his inclinations: to-day he's good, to-morrow he's bad. . . . But if that girl has got a strong hold on your heart . . . then take her and go away from here with her and put an end to things. . . . Or you might go alone. . . . You're still young; you can find a woman easily enough.

PEPEL (*seizing him by the shoulder*): No, you just tell me why you're saying all this!

LUKA: Wait, let me go. . . . I'll take a look at Anna; she's been wheezing frightfully. (*He goes to* ANNA's *bed, pulls back the curtain, looks, touches the woman with his hand.* PEPEL *watches him in a meditative, perplexed fashion.*) Jesus Christ, Most Merciful! Receive in peace the soul of thy servant Anna that now appeareth before thee!

PEPEL (*in a low voice*): Is she dead? (*Without approaching, he bends forward and looks at the bed.*)

LUKA (*in a low voice*): Her misery is over! And where's her man?

PEPEL: In the tavern, most likely.

LUKA: We must tell him.

PEPEL (*with a shudder*): I don't like dead people.

LUKA (*going to the door*): Why should you like them? . . . One must like—must love the living . . . the living.

PEPEL: I'll go with you too.

LUKA: Are you afraid?

PEPEL: I don't like 'em. (*They go out hastily. For some moments emptiness and silence prevail. Then beyond the hall door is heard a dull noise, confused and unintelligible. The* ACTOR *comes in.*)

ACTOR (*pausing at the threshold without closing the door, and holding to the jambs with his hands, he shouts*): Hey, old man! Where are you? I've remembered it: listen! (*Staggering, he makes two steps forward, assumes a pose, and recites.*)

> Hark, gentlemen! If holy truth be hidden
> From the world's searching gaze, then honor to
> The madman, who shall cast upon the brain
> Of all humanity a golden dream.

(NATASHA *appears in the doorway behind the* ACTOR.)
ACTOR: Old man!

> And if to-morrow's sun should e'er forget
> To light the pathway of our earth, straightway
> A madman's thought would light the wide, wide world!

NATASHA (*laughing*): Scarecrow! You've had a drop too much.

ACTOR (*turning to her*): Ah, is that you? But—where's the old man . . . that dear old boy? There don't seem to be anybody here. . . . Natasha, farewell! Yes, farewell!

NATASHA (*coming in*): You didn't say how do you do, and now you're saying good-by!

ACTOR (*standing in her path*): I am departing, I am going. . . . Spring will come, and I shall be here no more.

NATASHA: Let me in! . . . Where are you going?

ACTOR: To seek the city . . . to be cured. . . . You too must go . . . "Ophelia, get thee to a nunnery!" . . . You understand, there is a hospital for organisms . . . for drunkards . . . a splendid hospital . . . of marble . . . with a marble floor! Light . . . cleanliness, food . . . all free of charge! And the floor is of marble, it is! I'll find it, I'll get cured and . . . I'll make a fresh start. . . . I am on the way to regeneration . . . as King . . . Lear said. . . . Natasha . . . on the stage my name was Sverchkov-Zavolzhsky. . . . Nobody knows it . . . nobody! I have no name here. . . . Do you understand what an insult that is, to lose your name? Even dogs have names to go by.

(NATASHA *cautiously walks past the* ACTOR, *stops at* ANNA'S *bed, and gazes.*)

ACTOR: Without a name a man ceases to exist.

NATASHA: Look . . . my dear . . . she's died.

ACTOR (*shaking his head*): Impossible!

NATASHA (*stepping back*): It's true! Look!

BUBNOV (*in the doorway*) : What is there to look at?

NATASHA : Anna here . . . has died!

BUBNOV: So she's stopped coughing. (*Goes to* ANNA'S *bed, looks, then goes to his own place.*) We must tell Kleshch—that's his business.

ACTOR: I'll go . . . and say . . . she's lost her name! (*Goes out.*)

NATASHA (*in the middle of the room*): So I too . . . sometime, in the same way . . . will be brought to a basement . . . beaten to death.

BUBNOV (*spreading out some sort of rags on his bunk*): What? What are you mumbling?

NATASHA : Just to myself.

BUBNOV: Are you waiting for Vasily? Look out or he'll smash your head for you.

NATASHA : Isn't it all the same who smashes it? It might as well be he.

BUBNOV (*lying down*) : Well, that's your business.

NATASHA : Just think: it's a good thing for her that she's died . . . yet it makes you sorry. . . . Lord! . . . What was the use of her life?

BUBNOV: Same way with everybody: they are born, they live awhile, and then they die. I'll die too . . . and so will you. . . . What's there to be sorry for?

(LUKA, *the* TATAR, WRYMUG, *and* KLESHCH *come in.* KLESHCH *brings up the rear; he walks slowly, and seems crushed and shriveled.*)

NATASHA : Sh-h! Anna—

WRYMUG: We've heard it. . . . May she go to Heaven, if she's died!

TATAR (*to* KLESHCH): Must take out! Must take to hall! Here can't be no dead people; here live people will sleep.

KLESHCH (*in a low voice*): We'll take her out.

(*All go up to the bed.* KLESHCH *looks at his wife over the shoulders of the rest.*)

WRYMUG (*to the* TATAR): You think she'll smell? There'll be no smell from her! . . . She dried up all over when she was still alive.

NATASHA: Lord! If they would only feel a bit sorry! . . . If only somebody would say a kind word! Oh, you!

LUKA: Don't take offense, girlie—that's all right! Why should they —why should we—be sorry for the dead? Oh, my dear child! We are not sorry for the living. . . . We can't even feel sorrow for ourselves. What can you expect here?

BUBNOV (*yawning*): And then, death is not afraid of words. Sickness may be scared away by words, but death—no!

TATAR (*stepping aside*): Must call police.

WRYMUG: We must certainly call the police! Kleshch! Have you reported to the police?

KLESHCH: No. . . . She must be buried. . . . And all I have is forty kopeks.

WRYMUG: Well, in that case—borrow. . . . Or we'll raise some money. . . . One will give five kopeks, another as much as he can. . . . But report to the police. . . . Hurry up! Otherwise they'll think you killed the woman . . . or something.

(WRYMUG *goes to the bunks and prepares to lie down beside the* TATAR.)

NATASHA (*going to* BUBNOV's *bunk*): Well, now I shall dream of her. . . . I always dream of dead people. . . . I'm afraid to go out alone. . . . It's dark in the hall.

LUKA (*following her*): You'd better be afraid of the living. . . . That's all that I have to say to you.

NATASHA: Take me to my room, grandfather.

LUKA: Come on! . . . come on! . . . I'll go with you! (*They go out.*)

(*A pause.*)

WRYMUG: Oh ho ho! Asan! It'll soon be spring, my boy! . . . Then life will be warm and comfortable for us. By this time the peasants in the villages are fixing their plows and harrows . . . getting ready to plow. . . . Yes, they are! And we? Asan! . . . He's asleep already, the damned Mohammed.

BUBNOV: Tatars like to sleep.

KLESHCH (*standing in the middle of the lodging, with a dull, fixed gaze*): What shall I do now?

WRYMUG: Lie down and go to sleep. . . . That's all.

KLESHCH (*in a low voice*): But . . . she . . . how about her?

(*No one answers him.* SATIN *and the* ACTOR *come in.*)

ACTOR (*shouts*): Old man! Come here, my faithful Kent!

SATIN: Miklukha-Maklay is coming! . . . Ho, ho!

ACTOR: It is fixed and decided! Old man, where is the city? . . . Where are you?

SATIN: Fata Morgana! The old man lied to you. . . . There is nothing of the sort! There are no cities, no men . . . nothing at all!

ACTOR: You lie!

TATAR (*jumping up*): Where is landlord? I go, landlord! Can't sleep, can't take money. . . . Dead men . . . drunk! (*He goes out quickly,* SATIN *whistles after him.*)

BUBNOV (*in a sleepy voice*): Lie down, fellows; don't make a racket. . . . It's nighttime; we must get some sleep!

ACTOR: Yes! . . . Aha! . . . A corpse is in the room. . . . "Our nets brought in a corpse!" . . . That's a poem by B-Béranger! *

---

* The quotation really comes from a ballad by Pushkin.

SATIN (*shouts*): Corpses do not hear! Corpses do not feel. . . . Shout! . . . Screech! . . . Corpses do not hear!

(LUKA *appears at the door.*)

ACT III

A yard littered with all sorts of rubbish and overgrown with coarse, high grass. In the rear is a tall brick party wall that hides the sky. Close to it are some elder bushes. On the right is the dark, timbered wall of some yard building, a cart shed or a stable. On the left is a gray wall, covered with the remains of plastering; this belongs to the house in the basement of which is the Kostylevs' night-lodging. It slants so that the rear end of it almost reaches the middle of the yard. Between it and the red brick wall is a narrow passage. In the gray wall are two windows: one is on a level with the ground, the other some four feet higher and nearer the party wall. Near this wall lie an overturned sledge and a wooden beam some six feet long. Near the right-hand wall is a heap of old boards and joists. It is evening; the sun is setting, flooding the party wall with a reddish gleam. It is early spring; the snow has only recently melted. The black twigs of the elder trees have not yet budded. On the wooden beam NATASHA *and* NASTYA *are seated, side by side.* LUKA *and the* BARON *are sitting on the sledge.* KLESHCH *is lying on the heap of wood near the right-hand wall. In the window close to the ground* BUBNOV'S *countenance can be seen.*

NASTYA (*closing her eyes and swaying her head in time to the words, she recites in a singsong*): So he came by night into the garden, to the arbor, as we had agreed. . . . And there I had long been waiting for him, trembling with fear and grief. He too was trembling all over and was white as chalk, and in his hands was a dissolver. . . .

NATASHA (*cracking sunflower seeds with her teeth*): Well, well! People must be right when they say that students are desperate characters.

NASTYA: And he said to me in a terrible voice: "My priceless love!"

BUBNOV: Ho, ho! Priceless?

BARON: Wait! If you don't like it, don't listen; but don't interfere with her lying.— Go on!

NASTYA: "My charming love!" says he. "My parents," says he, "will not give their consent for me to marry you . . . and they threaten to curse me forever because of my love for you. And for that reason," says he, "I must take my own life." . . . And his dissolver was tremenjus and loaded with ten bullets. . . . "Farewell," says he, "delightful friend of my heart! I have decided beyond recall. . . . Life without

you is impossible for me." And I answered him: "My cherished dear
. . . Raoul . . ."

BUBNOV (*surprised*): What? How's that? Growl?

BARON (*guffaws*): But, Nastya! Last time, you know, it was
Gaston!

NASTYA (*jumping up*): Shut up . . . you wretches! Oh . . . you
stray mongrels! Can you . . . can you understand . . . love? Real
love? And I—I have had it . . . real love! (*To the* BARON.) You
good-for-nothing! . . . You're an educated man. . . . You say you
used to drink your coffee lying in bed.

LUKA: Here, you men, wa-ait! Don't you hinder her! Respect her
feelings! . . . The words don't matter; the point is, why the words
are said! Keep on with your story, my girl: that's all right!

BUBNOV: Preen your feathers, crow: go ahead!

BARON: Well—go on!

NATASHA: Don't listen to them! . . . What do they amount to?
They're doing it just because they're envious. . . . They haven't anything to tell about themselves.

NASTYA (*sitting down again*): I don't want to any more! I won't
speak . . . if they don't believe it . . . if they laugh at me. (*Suddenly, interrupting herself, she is silent for several seconds; then, shut-
ting her eyes once more, she continues in a loud, heated tone, waving
her hand in time to her words, and seeming to be listening to distant
music.*) And so I answered him: "Joy of my life! My bright moon!
I too without you find it utterly impossible to live in this world . . .
because I love you so madly, and because I shall ever love you while
the heart beats within my bosom! But," I said, "take not your young
life . . . since it is necessary for your dear parents, whose only joy you
are. . . . Rather abandon me! Rather let me perish . . . from grief
for you, my beloved . . . I alone . . . I, worthless wretch! Let me
. . . perish—it matters not! I . . . am of no use at all . . . there
is nothing left for me . . . nothing whatever. . . ." (*Covers her face
with her hands and weeps noiselessly.*)

NATASHA (*turning aside, in a low tone*): Don't cry! . . . You
mustn't!

(LUKA, *smiling, strokes* NASTYA'S *head.*)

BUBNOV (*guffaws*): Oh, ain't she the devil's doll, though?

BARON (*also laughing*): Do you think that's true, granddad? She
read it all in that book, *Fatal Love.* . . . It's all humbug! Let her
alone!

NATASHA: What's that to you? Shut up, you . . . God-forsaken
wretch!

NASTYA (*furiously*): Damned soul! Worthless creature! Where's your soul?

LUKA (*taking* NASTYA's *arm*): Let's go away, my dear! Never mind! . . . Don't be angry! *I* know. . . . *I* believe you! You are right and not they. . . . If you believe you had real love . . . then you had it! You did! And don't be angry at him, at your fellow-lodger. . . . Maybe he's laughing at you just from envy. . . . Maybe he never had anything real . . . nothing at all! Come on!

NASTYA (*pressing her hands tightly to her bosom*): It's true, grandfather, that all happened! . . . It's all true! . . . That student . . . was a Frenchman. . . . His name was Gaston. . . . He had a little black beard . . . and wore patent leather shoes. . . . May thunder strike me on the spot if it's not true! And he loved me so . . . loved me so!

LUKA: *I* know! Never mind! *I* believe you! In patent leather shoes, do you say? Oh, my; oh, my! Well, and you loved him too? (*They go out around the corner.*)

BARON: Well, that girl is certainly silly. . . . She's a good sort, but she's silly. I can't stand it!

BUBNOV: Why is it that people are so fond of telling lies? They always act as if they were answering the state prosecutor. . . . Honest!

NATASHA: Seems like lying must be pleasanter than the truth. . . . I too . . .

BARON: Too what? Go on!

NATASHA: Make things up. . . . I make 'em up and . . . wait.

BARON: Wait for what?

NATASHA (*confused, but smiling*): Just wait. . . . For instance, I think: To-morrow . . . some one will come . . . somebody . . . out of the ordinary. . . . Or something will happen . . . also something out of common. . . . I wait for a long time . . . wait all the time. . . . But in real life . . . what is there to wait for?

(*A pause.*)

BARON (*with a grin*): There's nothing to wait for. . . . *I* don't wait for anything! Everything's been already! . . . It's past and gone! . . . Go on!

NATASHA: Or again . . . I imagine that to-morrow . . . I'll die all of a sudden. . . . And that makes me feel creepy. . . . In summer it's fine to dream about death. . . . There are thunderstorms in the summer. . . . You may be struck by lightning any time.

BARON: Life's not easy for you. . . . That sister of yours has a devilish character!

NATASHA: But for whom is life easy? It's hard for everybody. . . . I can see that.

(*Up to this point* KLESHCH *has been motionless, indifferent to what is going on. He now suddenly jumps up.*)

KLESHCH: For everybody? You lie? Not for everybody! If it were so for everybody, it wouldn't matter! Then it wouldn't hurt! . . . No it wouldn't!

BUBNOV: What the hell stirred you up? What a howl you gave!

(KLESHCH *again lies down in his place and growls.*)

BARON: Well, I must go make up with little Nastya. . . . If I don't make up, she won't give me the price of a drink.

BUBNOV: Hm. . . . People love to tell lies. . . . Well, it's easy to understand about Nastya! She's used to painting her mug, so she wants to paint her soul too—put a blush on her soul. . . . But . . . why should the rest of 'em? Take Luka, for instance. . . . He tells a lot of lies . . . and without any profit to himself. . . . He's an old man already. . . . Why should he do it?

BARON (*going off, with a grin*): All people have gray souls. . . . Everybody wants to put on some rosy.

LUKA (*coming in from around the corner*): What do you tease the girl for, squire? You ought not to hinder her. . . . Let her weep and amuse herself. . . . She sheds tears for her own pleasure, you know. . . . What harm does that do to you?

BARON: That's silly, old man! I'm sick of her. . . . To-day it's Raoul, to-morrow it'll be Gaston . . . but it's always the same old bunk! However, I'm going to make up with her. (*Goes out.*)

LUKA: Go ahead, that's right. . . . Pet her a bit! It never does any harm to pet a person.

NATASHA: You're a kind man, grandfather! . . . Why is it that you're so kind?

LUKA: Kind, you say? Well . . . all right; if that's so, very well! (*Behind the red wall are heard the low notes of an accordion and a song.*) Somebody or other ought to be kind, girlie . . . one must pity people! Christ pitied all men and told us to do the same. . . . Let me tell you: if you pity a man in time . . . things go well! For instance, I worked as a watchman at a country house, for an engineer near Tomsk. . . . Well, all right! The house was in a forest, it was a lonely spot . . . and it was winter and I was all alone in the house. . . . That was fine and splendid! Only once I heard men breaking in!

NATASHA: Robbers?

LUKA: Exactly. So they were breaking in! . . . I took my gun and went out. . . . I caught sight of two men opening a window—and they were so busy with their job that they didn't even see me. I shouted to 'em: "Hey there, get out of here!" . . . And so they came at me with an ax. . . . I gave 'em fair warning: "Keep away!" says I, "or

I'll shoot right off!" . . . And I aimed the gun first at one and then at the other. So they fell on their knees: "Let us off!" says they. Well, I was pretty hot by that time—owing to the ax, you know! "I tried to drive you off, you scamps," says I, "and you didn't go. . . . And now," says I, "break off some branches, one of you." So they broke 'em. And then I gave 'em orders: "One of you lie down and the other flog him!" And so at my orders they flogged each other. And when they were through with the flogging, they said to me: "Uncle," says they, "give us some bread for Christ's sake! We've been going without a bite in our bellies," says they. That's the kind of robbers they were, dearie . . . (*Laughs.*) that's the kind of men that used an ax! Yes . . . they were good peasants both of them. . . . And I says to 'em: "You ought to have asked me for bread in the first place, you scamps." "We're sick of that," says they. "You ask and ask, and nobody gives you anything . . . that hurts!" So they stayed with me for that whole winter. One of 'em—his name was Stepan—would take the gun and stroll off into the forest. . . . But the other—that was Yakov—was always ailing, coughed all the time. . . . So the three of us guarded that house. When spring came, "Good-by, uncle!" says they. And they went off to Russia on their wanderings.

NATASHA: Were they escaped convicts?

LUKA: Just so—convicts; they'd got away from a penal settlement. . . . They were good peasants! . . . If I hadn't had pity on them, maybe they'd have killed me . . . or something like that. . . . And then would have come trial and prison, and Siberia—where's the sense in that? A prison can't teach you anything good, and Siberia can't teach you either . . . but a man can teach you . . . he can! A man can teach you goodness. . . . That's a plain fact!

(*A pause.*)

BUBNOV: Ye-es, maybe! . . . But now I . . . don't know how to tell lies! What's the use of 'em? I think you ought to blurt out the whole truth, just as it is! Why should you boggle about it?

KLESHCH (*suddenly jumping up again, as if burned, shouts*): What truth? Where is truth? (*Slapping his own rags.*) Here's truth! No work! . . . No strength! There's truth! Nowhere to turn, nowhere to turn! Just have to croak—that's what truth is! The devil! What . . . what use is truth to me? If I only had a breathing spell! . . . Only a breathing spell! How am I to blame? . . . Why should I be hit with truth? I can't live—devil take it!—I can't live! . . . That's what truth is!

BUBNOV: Well, well! . . . The fit's on him!

LUKA: Lord Jesus! . . . Listen, my dear fellow! You—

KLESHCH (*trembling with excitement*) : You keep saying: "Tru-uth!"
You comfort everybody, old man. . . . But I tell you, I hate everybody!
And that truth of yours—curse it, damn it! Do you understand? Take
that in! Damn truth! (*Runs around the corner, looking back as he
goes.*)

LUKA: Ho, ho, ho! How excited the man did get. . . . And where
did he run off to?

NATASHA: Looks as if he'd gone crazy.

BUBNOV: He got it off in great shape! Just as if he was playing
in the theatre. . . . That often happens with him. . . . He ain't used
to life yet.

PEPEL (*coming in slowly from around the corner*) : Peace to this
honorable company! Well, Luka, you sly old graybeard, are you still
telling stories?

LUKA: You ought to have seen . . . how that man was shouting
here!

PEPEL: That was Kleshch, wasn't it? What's he up to? He's running as if he'd been scalded.

LUKA: You'll run, if it ever . . . gets a grip on your heart like that.

PEPEL (*sitting down*) : I don't like him. . . . He's awful ill-tempered
and proud. (*Taking off* KLESHCH.) "I'm a workingman." And he
thinks that everybody else is below him. . . . Work ahead, if you like
to . . . but why should you be proud about it? If you value men just
by the work they do . . . then a horse is better than any man; it just
hauls and—keeps still!— Natasha, are your folks at home?

NATASHA: They've gone to the graveyard. . . . After that they were
going to the all-night service.

PEPEL: So, I see, you're at liberty. . . . That don't happen often!

LUKA (*pensively, to* BUBNOV) : So . . . you talk . . . about truth.
. . . That truth of yours don't always suit man's ailments. . . . You
can't always heal a soul with truth. . . . Take this case, for instance:
I knew a certain man who believed in the Land of Truth. . . .

BUBNOV: In wha-at?

LUKA: In the Land of Truth. Somewhere in the world, he said,
there must be a Land of Truth . . . and in that land, he thought, dwelt
a special kind of people . . . good people. They respected one another;
they aided one another in every little thing . . . and all was fine and
splendid in their country! And so that man kept intending to set out
. . . and look for that Land of Truth. He was a poor man and had
a hard life. . . . But even when he was so badly off that he was just
ready to lie down and die, he never lost courage, but just used to grin
and keep repeating: "Never mind! I'll stand it! I'll wait a little while

longer, and then—I'll quit all this life and—I'll go off to the Land of Truth. . . ." That was his only joy—that land.

PEPEL: Well? Did he go?

BUBNOV: Where to? Ho, ho!

LUKA: Well then, to that place—this happened in Siberia—they sent an exile, a learned man. . . . That learned man had books and maps and all sorts of stuff. . . . So this man I was speaking of said to that learned man: "Please be good enough to show me where lies that Land of Truth, and how do you get there?" At once the learned man opened his books and spread out his maps. . . . He looked and looked—but there wasn't any Land of Truth anywhere! It was all exact, all lands were put down, but there wasn't any Land of Truth!

PEPEL (*in a low voice*): Well? Isn't there any? (BUBNOV *guffaws*.)

NATASHA: Just you wait. . . . Well, grandfather?

LUKA: The man wouldn't believe it. . . . "There must be such a land," says he; "look harder! Otherwise," says he, "your books and maps are no good, if there's no Land of Truth." . . . The learned man took offense. "My maps are most exact," says he, "but there's no Land of Truth anywhere." Well, then the man got angry—how could he help it? He'd lived and lived, suffered and suffered, and still believed that there was one; but the maps showed that there wasn't! This was robbery! . . . And he says to the learned man: "Oh, you . . . scoundrel! You're a rascal, and not a learned man at all." . . . And he gave him a box on the ear! And then he gave him more, too! (*After a pause.*) And after that he went home and—hanged himself! (*All are silent.* LUKA, *smiling, looks at* PEPEL *and* NATASHA.)

PEPEL (*in a low voice*): Devil take you! . . . That's not a jolly story!

NATASHA: He couldn't stand being cheated.

BUBNOV (*glumly*): That's all fairy tales.

PEPEL: Well, well! . . . So much for the Land of Truth! . . . So it proved there wasn't any.

NATASHA: I'm sorry . . . for that man.

BUBNOV: That story was all made up too! Ho, ho! Land of Truth! What next? Ho, ho, ho! (*Disappears from the window.*)

LUKA (*nodding his head towards* BUBNOV's *window*): He's laughing! Hee, hee, hee! (*After a pause.*) Well, boys! . . . Health and wealth to you! I'm going to leave you soon.

PEPEL: Where are you going now?

LUKA: Down south to the Ukrainians. . . . I hear they've discovered a new religion there. . . . I must take a look. . . . Yes, I must! . . .

Men are always searching, always wanting to get something better.
. . . Lord grant them patience!

PEPEL: Do you think they'll ever find it?

LUKA: Who—men? They'll find it! He who seeks, shall find. . . .
He who wishes with all his heart, shall find!

NATASHA: If they'd only find something . . . think up something
better!

LUKA: They'll think it up! Only we must aid them, girlie . . . we
must respect them.

NATASHA: How can I aid them? I'm helpless myself.

PEPEL (*with decision*): Once more I . . . I'm going to talk to you
again . . . Natasha. . . . Now, in his presence. . . . He knows everything. Come . . . with me!

NATASHA: Where. to? One prison after another?

PEPEL: I've told you that I'll quit thieving! It's the truth—I will!
If I've said it, I'll do it! I can read and write. . . . I'll work. . . . He
says that we must go to Siberia of our own accord. . . . Well, let's go
there! Can't we? . . . Do you think I'm not disgusted with my own
life? Oh, Natasha! I know. . . . I see it all! . . . I comfort myself
with the thought that other men steal more than I do and live respected
by the world. . . . Only that don't help me! That ain't what I want!
It ain't that I repent. . . . I don't believe in conscience. . . . But—
I feel one thing: I must live . . . differently! I must live better! I
must live so . . . that I can respect myself.

LUKA: That's right, my dear boy! The Lord grant you that! . . .
Christ aid you! That's right: a man must respect himself.

PEPEL: I've been a thief since my earliest childhood. . . . Everybody has always called me thief Vaska, Vaska the son of a thief! Aha?
So? Well then—all right! Then I'm a thief! . . . Understand: perhaps I'm a thief merely out of spite . . . am a thief simply because
nobody ever took a notion to call me any other name. . . . Here,
Natasha, call me something else, will you?

NATASHA (*sadly*): Somehow I don't believe . . . what anybody says
. . . and I'm restless to-day. . . . My heart aches . . . as if I were
expecting something. You made a mistake to start this talk to-day,
Vasily.

PEPEL: When should I speak of such things? I'm not saying this
for the first time.

NATASHA: And why should I go with you? You see . . . after all
. . . I don't love you very much. . . . Sometimes . . . I like you . . .
but now and then it makes me sick to look at you. . . . It's quite plain
that I don't love you. . . . When a girl's in love, she can't see anything
bad in the man she loves . . . but I see plenty in you.

PEPEL: You'll come to love me: never fear about that! I'll teach you to like me. . . . You just fall in with me! For more than a year I've been watching you. . . . I see that you're a girl of principle . . . a good girl . . . a person that I can rely on. . . . I've come to love you very much!

(VASILISA, *dressed in her best, appears in the window and listens, standing close to the frame.*)

NATASHA: Yes. You've come to love me, but my sister—

PEPEL (*taken aback*): Well, what's she? There are plenty . . . of her sort.

LUKA: Don't you care, girl! If there's no bread, folks eat chaff . . . if there's no bread at all.

PEPEL (*gloomily*): Do have pity on me! My life's not sweet. . . . It's a wolf's life—gives me small joy. . . . I seem to be drowning in a bog: whatever I catch hold of is all rotten . . . nothing holds me up. . . . Your sister, I thought, was different. . . . If she weren't . . . so greedy for money, for her sake I'd . . . undertake anything! If she were only mine all over. . . . Well, she needs something else . . . she wants money . . . and she wants her own way. . . . And her own way . . . is to play the strumpet. She can never help me. . . . But you're like a young fir tree; you're prickly, but you hold a man up.

LUKA: Let me tell you, girlie: Marry him, marry him! He's a decent lad, a good sort! Just you keep reminding him every now and then that he's a good lad, so that he won't forget about it, you know! He'll believe you. . . . You just keep telling him: "Vasya, you're a good man —don't forget that!" Just think, darling, where have you to go if you don't marry him? Your sister is a wild beast, and I needn't speak about her husband: the old man is worse than any words! . . . And then all this life here! . . . Where have you to go to! But the lad is a strong fellow.

NATASHA: I've nowhere to go to. . . . I know that. . . . I've thought about it. . . . But the only thing is—I don't trust anybody. . . . But I've nowhere to go to.

PEPEL: There's one road. . . . Well, I won't let you start on that road. . . . I'd rather kill you.

NATASHA (*smiling*): There! I'm not your wife yet, and you want to kill me already.

PEPEL (*embracing her*): Stop it, Natasha! It makes no difference!

NATASHA (*snuggling up to him*): Well, let me tell you one thing, Vasily—I'll tell you the truth as I'd tell it to God!— The first time you strike me . . . or do me wrong in any other way . . . I won't hesitate; I'll either hang myself, or—

PEPEL: May my arm dry up if I ever touch you!

LUKA: That's all right: don't worry, darling! He needs you more than you do him.

VASILISA (*from the window*): So the match is arranged! Love and harmony!

NATASHA: They've come home! . . . Oh, Lord! They saw us! . . . Oh, Vasily!

PEPEL: What are you scared of? Nobody dares to touch you now!

VASILISA: Don't be afraid, Natalya! He won't beat you. . . . He can't either beat you or love you. . . . I know!

LUKA: Ah, that woman! . . . She's a venomous snake!

VASILISA: His bravery's mostly in words.

KOSTYLEV (*coming out of the house*): Natasha, you lazy slut, what are you doing here? Just gossiping? Complaining of your own family? And the samovar isn't ready, is it? The table isn't set?

NATASHA (*going out*): But you intended to go to church.

KOSTYLEV: It's none of your business, what we intended to do! You ought to attend to your work and do what you were ordered!

PEPEL: Shut up, you! She's not your servant any more. . . . Natalya, don't you go! . . . Don't you do anything!

NATASHA: Don't you give commands! . . . It's too soon yet! (*Goes out.*)

PEPEL (*to* KOSTYLEV): That'll do for you! You've bullied the girl . . . long enough! Now she's mine!

KOSTYLEV: You-urs? When did you buy her? How much did you pay? (VASILISA *guffaws.*)

LUKA: Vasya! You'd better be going.

PEPEL: You two gay birds, look out! You may weep soon!

VASILISA: Oh, I'm scared! Oh, I'm afraid!

LUKA: Vasily, go away! Don't you see she's egging you on? She's getting you mad—don't you understand?

PEPEL: Yes . . . aha! She lies! (*To* VASILISA.) You lie! What you want won't happen!

VASILISA: And what I don't want won't happen either, Vasya!

PEPEL (*shaking his fist at her*): We'll see. (*Goes out.*)

VASILISA (*disappearing from the window*): I'll give you a fine wedding!

KOSTYLEV (*going up to* LUKA): What have you to say, old man?

LUKA: Nothing, old man!

KOSTYLEV: All right. . . . You're leaving, they say?

LUKA: It's high time.

KOSTYLEV: Where to?

LUKA: Where my eyes lead me.

KOSTYLEV: That means tramping. . . . I see you don't find it convenient to live long in one place: ain't that so?

LUKA: Under a stone that lies still, they say, no water flows.

KOSTYLEV: That's a stone. But a man should live in one spot. . . . Men can't live like cockroaches. . . . Each of them crawls wherever it wants to. . . . A man should fit himself to one spot . . . not roam over the earth helter-skelter.

LUKA: But what if a man feels at home everywhere?

KOSTYLEV: Then he's a tramp . . . a useless man. . . . A man must be of some use . . . must work.

LUKA: You don't say!

KOSTYLEV: Yes. Of course. . . . What is a wanderer, a stranger? He's a strange man . . . not like other people. . . . If he's really strange, he knows something . . . he's found out something or other . . . something that nobody needs to know. . . . Perhaps he's even found out the truth on his wanderings. . . . Well, we don't need to know every sort of truth—no, we don't! He can keep it to himself . . . and shut up! If he's really . . . strange . . . he keeps quiet about it! Or else he talks so that nobody can understand him. . . . And he doesn't want anything, doesn't meddle with anything, doesn't stir people up for nothing. . . . How people live is none of his business. . . . He must lead a righteous life himself . . . must live in forests . . . in caves . . . unseen by other men! And he should hinder no man, condemn no man . . . but pray for all men . . . for all the sins of the world . . . for mine . . . for yours . . . for all sins! For this very purpose he flees from the vanities of the world . . . in order to pray. That is the right way. . . . (*After a pause.*) But you? . . . What sort of a wanderer are you? . . . You have no passport. . . . A good man should have a passport. . . . All good men have passports. . . . Yes, they do!

LUKA: Some people are just humans, and others are real men.

KOSTYLEV: Don't you try to be smart! Don't give me any riddles to guess. . . . I'm no stupider than you. . . . What do you mean by humans and men?

LUKA: There's no riddle in that. What I say is: There is land unfit for sowing . . . and there is fertile land; whatever you plant on it, grows. . . . That's the point.

KOSTYLEV: Well? What do you mean by that?

LUKA: Take you, for instance. . . . If the Lord God himself should say to you, "Mikhail, be a man!" all the same nothing would come of it. . . . You'd remain forever such as you are now.

KOSTYLEV: Huh? Huh? Do you know that my wife's uncle is a policeman? And if I—

VASILISA (*coming in*): Mikhail Ivanovich, come and have tea.

KOSTYLEV (*to* LUKA): Look here, you! Get out of here! Leave this lodging!

VASILISA: Yes, you clear out, old man! . . . Your tongue's altogether too long. . . . And who knows? Maybe you're an escaped convict.

KOSTYLEV: Look out that we don't see hide nor hair of you here after to-day! Otherwise I'll—! Look out!

LUKA: You'll call your uncle? Go ahead and do it! . . . Tell him you've caught a convict. . . . Your uncle may get a reward—three kopeks!

BUBNOV (*at the window*): What are you trading in here? What'll he get three kopeks for?

LUKA: They're threatening to sell me.

VASILISA (*to her husband*): Come on!

BUBNOV: For three kopeks? Well, look out, old man! . . . They'll sell you even for one.

KOSTYLEV (*to* BUBNOV): You're staring at us like a brownie from under the stove! (*He starts to go out with his wife.*)

VASILISA: What a lot of shady characters there are in this world— all kinds of swindlers!

LUKA: Hope you'll enjoy your tea!

VASILISA (*turning back*): Hold your tongue . . . you rotten mushroom! (*She goes out around the corner with her husband.*)

LUKA: I'll leave this very evening.

BUBNOV: That's right. It's always better to leave in good season.

LUKA: True for you.

BUBNOV: I know all about it. Maybe I saved myself from prison and hard labor by leaving on time.

LUKA: How's that?

BUBNOV: That's the truth. It was this way: my wife hitched up with the foreman. . . . The foreman, I must admit, was a man of talent. . . . He was a great hand at turning dogs into raccoons . . . cats too—into kangaroo fur . . . muskrat . . . any old thing. He was clever. So then: my wife hitched up with him . . . and they got so daft on each other that any moment they might either poison me or put me out of the way some other fashion. I started to beat my wife . . . and the foreman did the same by me. . . . He was a fierce fighter! Once he pulled out half my beard and broke a rib. And I got my temper up too. . . . Once I whacked my wife on the crown with an iron yardstick. . . . Altogether, a great war had begun! But I saw that I couldn't make anything that way . . . they'd be too much for me! And so I made up my mind that I'd murder my wife . . . made it up for sure! But I got hold of myself in time—and left.

LUKA: That was the better way! Let 'em stay there and turn dogs into raccoons!

BUBNOV: The only thing was . . . the shop was in my wife's name . . . and I was left as you see me now! Though, to tell the truth, I'd have been sure to drink away the shop. . . . I have drinking spells, you see.

LUKA: Drinking spells? A-ah!

BUBNOV: Fierce ones! When I begin to swill, I'm just consumed by drink, nothing's left but the skin. . . . And then, I'm lazy. I just hate to work!

(SATIN *and the* ACTOR *come in, quarreling.*)

SATIN: Stuff and nonsense! You won't go anywhere! . . . All that's tommyrot! See here, old man: What have you been stuffing into the ears of this poor old candle-end?

ACTOR: You lie! Tell him that he lies, grandfather! I'm going! I've been working to-day: I swept the street . . . and I didn't drink vodka! How's that? There's my pay—thirty kopeks, and I'm sober!

SATIN: That's all humbug! Give the money to me: I'll drink it up . . . or I'll lose the money at cards.

ACTOR: Get out of here! That's for the journey!

LUKA (*to* SATIN): What are you driving him wild for?

SATIN: "Now rede me, enchanter, beloved of Perun, The good and the ill that's before me." * I've been cheated all to smithereens, my boy. All is not lost, grandfather: there are cleverer sharpers in the world than I am!

LUKA: You're a jolly fellow, Konstantin; good company!

BUBNOV: You come here, actor!

(*The* ACTOR *goes to the window and squats in front of it. They converse in an undertone.*)

SATIN: When I was young, my friend, I was great fun! I like to remember those times! . . . I was a broth of a boy . . . danced splendidly, was a good actor, liked to make folks laugh. . . . It was fine!

LUKA: How was it that you lost your trail? Eh?

SATIN: How curious you are, old man? You'd like to know everything. . . . And what good will it do you?

LUKA: I want to understand the ways of man. . . . But when I look at you, I don't understand you! You're a splendid fellow, Konstantin . . . not stupid a bit—but then . . .

SATIN: It's the prison, grandfather! I stayed in prison four years and seven months. . . . And after the prison, there's no chance!

LUKA: Oh, ho, ho! What were you in prison for?

* From Pushkin, *The Lay of the Wise Oleg;* tr. Shaw.

SATIN: All on account of a scoundrel. . . . I killed a scoundrel in a fit of fury. . . . It was in prison that I learned how to play cards.

LUKA: And you killed him on account of a woman?

SATIN: On account of my own sister. . . . But you just let up! I don't like to have people question me. . . . And . . . all that was long ago. . . . My sister's dead. . . . Nine years have gone by . . . since then. . . . My dear man, that sister of mine was just a splendid girl!

LUKA: You don't make a burden of life! Now here just a few minutes ago . . . that locksmith fairly howled! . . . Wo-o-ow!

SATIN: Kleshch?

LUKA: Yes. "There's no work!" he shouted, "there's nothing at all!"

SATIN: He'll get used to it. . . . What shall I do to kill time?

LUKA (*in a low voice*): Look! There he comes!

(KLESHCH *comes in slowly, his head drooping.*)

SATIN: Hey, widower! What're you hanging your nose for? What're you trying to think up?

KLESHCH: I'm thinking . . . what I'll do now. I've no tools left . . . the funeral ate up everything!

SATIN: Let me give you some advice! Don't do anything! Just take up room on earth!

KLESHCH: That's right! . . . Talk away! . . . I'm ashamed to look people in the face.

SATIN: Drop that! People ain't ashamed because your life's worse than a dog's. . . . Just think! You won't work, I won't either. . . . Hundreds and thousands more . . . everybody—do you understand?— everybody will quit work! Nobody will consent to do anything.— What'll happen then?

KLESHCH: Everybody will croak from hunger.

LUKA (*to* SATIN): With talk like that you ought to join the Fugitives. . . . There are such people; they're called Fugitives.*

SATIN: I know. . . . They aren't fools, grandfather!

(*From the Kostylevs' window is wafted a scream from* NATASHA: "Why? Don't! . . . Why?")

LUKA (*uneasily*): Is that Natasha? Is she screaming? Eh? Oh, you—

(*From the Kostylevs' lodging comes a confused uproar, the sound of broken dishes, and the piercing shriek of* KOSTYLEV: "O-oh! . . . You heretic . . . you hag.")

VASILISA: Wait! . . . Hold on! . . . I'll give it to her! . . . There . . . there!

NATASHA: They're beating—they're killing me!

---

* The reference is to one of the Russian religious sects.

SATIN (*shouting into the window*) : Hey, you there!

LUKA (*bustling about*) : Get Vasily! . . . We must call that Vasya! . . . Oh, Lord! Boys! . . . Fellows!

ACTOR (*running out*) : I'll call him . . . right away!

BUBNOV: They've been beating her very often lately.

SATIN: Come on, old man! . . . We'll be witnesses!

LUKA (*following* SATIN) : Much good I am as a witness! What's the use! . . . If we could only get Vasily in a hurry.

NATASHA: Sister! . . . sister dear! . . . Vasi-i-i—!

BUBNOV: They've stopped her mouth. . . . I'll go and take a look.

(*The uproar in the Kostylevs' lodging subsides, evidently receding from the chamber into the hall. The old man is heard to shout: "Stop!" A door slams violently, and this sound suddenly cuts off all the uproar. The stage is quiet. It is evening twilight.*)

KLESHCH (*He has been sitting on the pile of wood, heedless of all about him, rubbing his hands violently. He begins to mumble something, at first unintelligibly: then come the words*) : Well then? . . . A man must live. . . . (*Aloud.*) I need a shelter. . . . Don't I? There is no shelter. . . . There's nothing at all! Man is alone . . . alone, all by himself. . . . There is no help!

(*He goes out slowly, bent over. There are some seconds of ominous silence. Then somewhere in the passage a dull noise begins, a chaos of sounds. It grows and approaches. Separate voices are audible.*)

VASILISA: I'm her sister! Let go of her!

KOSTYLEV: What right have you?

VASILISA: Convict!

SATIN: Call Vaska! . . . Hurry up! Wrymug, hit him!

(*A police whistle.*)

TATAR (*running in from the house: his right arm is in a sling*) : Is any law for you kill by daylight?

WRYMUG (*coming in, followed by* MEDVEDEV) : Well, I gave him one!

MEDVEDEV: What business have you to be fighting?

TATAR: And you? What your duty?

MEDVEDEV (*chasing* WRYMUG) : Stop! Give me back my whistle.

KOSTYLEV: Abram! Catch him! . . . Seize him! He's killed me.

(*KVASHNYA and NASTYA come in from around the corner, leading NATASHA, her hair disheveled. SATIN follows, walking backwards and keeping off VASILISA, who, waving her arms, keeps trying to strike her sister. Around her ALESHKA skips as if bewitched, whistles in her ears, shouts, and yells. Then come a few more tattered figures, men and women.*)

SATIN (*to* VASILISA) : Where are you going? You damned owl!

VASILISA: Get out of here, convict! I'll tear her to pieces if I have to kill myself.

KVASHNYA (*leading* NATASHA *away*): That's enough, Vasilisa; aren't you ashamed! What makes you so beastly?

MEDVEDEV (*seizing* SATIN): Aha! . . . I've got you!

SATIN: Whack 'em, Wrymug! . . . Vaska! . . . Vaska!

(*All crowd together into a heap around the passage, near the red wall. They lead* NATASHA *to the right and seat her on the heap of wood.* PEPEL *rushes in from the passage and silently, with vigorous movements, pushes everybody aside.*)

PEPEL: Where's Natalya? You—

KOSTYLEV (*taking refuge around the corner*): Abram! Grab Vaska! . . . Fellows, help him capture Vaska! He's a thief . . . a robber!

PEPEL: And you're an old wretch!

(*With a violent burst of fury, he strikes the old man.* KOSTYLEV *falls so that only the upper half of his body can be seen from around the corner.* PEPEL *rushes to* NATASHA.)

VASILISA: Beat Vaska! Darlings . . . beat the thief!

MEDVEDEV (*shouting to* SATIN): You can't meddle! . . . This is a family affair! They belong to each other—and who are you?

PEPEL: How did—? What did she hit you with? A knife?

KVASHNYA: Just look what beasts! They've scalded the girl's legs with boiling water!

NASTYA: They tipped over the samovar.

TATAR: Maybe accident. . . . Must know sure. . . . Mustn't speak hasty!

NATASHA (*almost fainting*): Vasily . . . take me . . . hide me somewhere!

VASILISA: Lord! Just look! See! He's dead! They've killed him.

(*All crowd together at the passage, around* KOSTYLEV. BUBNOV *emerges from the throng and goes to* PEPEL.)

BUBNOV (*in a low tone*): Vaska! The old man . . . well . . . he's done for!

PEPEL (*looking at him as if he failed to understand*): Go . . . call the . . . we must take her to the hospital. . . . Well, I'll settle with 'em!

BUBNOV: I tell you: somebody's laid out the old man.

(*The uproar on the stage subsides like a bonfire drenched with water. Individual hushed exclamations are heard:* "Really?" "Well, I declare!" "Wha-at?" "Let's beat it, man!" "Oh, the devil!" "Look out now!" "Clear out before the police come!" *The crowd diminishes. People leave.* BUBNOV, *the* TATAR, NASTYA, *and* KVASHNYA *rush to the corpse of* KOSTYLEV.)

VASILISA (*getting up from the ground, she shouts with a triumphant voice*) : They've killed him . . . killed my husband! There's the man who killed him! Vaska killed him. I saw him! Darlings, I saw him! Well now, Vasya? Police!

PEPEL (*walking away from* NATASHA) : Let me go! . . . Get away! (*Looking at the old man, to* VASILISA.) Well? Are you glad? (*Touching the corpse with his foot.*) He's croaked . . . the old cur! It's come out your way. . . . Well . . . hadn't I better finish you too?

(*He rushes at her.* SATIN *and* WRYMUG *seize him quickly.* VASILISA *disappears in the passage.*)

SATIN : Think what you're doing!

WRYMUG : Whoa! Where're you running to?

VASILISA (*reappearing*) : Well, Vasya, my precious darling? You can't escape your fate. . . . Police! Abram, whistle!

MEDVEDEV : Those devils have torn off my whistle.

ALESHKA : Here it is! (*He whistles.* MEDVEDEV *rushes after him.*)

SATIN (*leading* PEPEL *towards* NATASHA) : Vaska, don't be scared! Killing in a scuffle is a small matter! That comes cheap.

VASILISA : Hold Vaska! He killed him. . . . I saw it!

SATIN : I struck the old man three times myself. . . . He didn't need much! Call me as a witness, Vaska.

PEPEL : I don't want to justify myself. . . . I want to bring in Vasilisa . . . and I'll do it! She wanted this. . . . She stirred me up to kill her husband. . . . She stirred me up!

NATASHA (*suddenly, in a loud voice*) : Aha . . . I understand! . . . So that's the way, Vasily! Listen, kind people! They work together! My sister and he—they work together! They arranged all this business! Ain't that so, Vasily? . . . That was why you were talking with me a while ago . . . so that she could hear everything? Kind people! She's his mistress. . . . All of you know that. . . . Everybody knows it. . . . They work together! It was she—she who stirred him up to kill her husband. . . . The husband was in their way. . . . And I was in their way. . . . So they just mangled me.

PEPEL : What do you mean, Natalya! . . . What are you saying?

SATIN : What the devil!

VASILISA : You lie! She lies. . . . I . . . It was he, Vaska, that killed him!

NATASHA : They work together! Damn you! Damn you both!

SATIN : Well, what a mess! . . . Look out, Vasily! They'll drown you yet.

WRYMUG : This is beyond me! . . . Oh, what a business!

PEPEL : Natalya, can you . . . really . . . ? Can you believe that I . . . helped her? . . .

SATIN: For God's sake, Natasha, just . . . consider!

VASILISA (*in the passage*): They've killed my husband, your Honor. . . . Vaska Pepel, the thief—he killed him, Mr. Police Captain. . . . I saw it. . . . Everybody saw it.

NATASHA (*tossing about, almost unconscious*): Kind people! . . . My sister and Vaska killed him! Listen, police! It was she, my sister, put him up to it . . . stirred up . . . her lover. . . . That's he, damn him! . . . They killed him! Take 'em . . . bring 'em to trial. . . . Take me too. . . . Take me to prison! For Christ's sake . . . take me to prison!

ACT IV

The scene is the same as in Act I, but PEPEL'S *room has disappeared; the partitions have been removed. And in the place where* KLESHCH *formerly sat, there is no anvil. In the corner once occupied by* PEPEL'S *room, lies the* TATAR, *tossing about and occasionally groaning. At the table sits* KLESHCH, *repairing an accordion and occasionally testing the keys. At the other end of the table sit* SATIN, *the* BARON, *and* NASTYA. *In front of them are a bottle of vodka, three bottles of beer, and a large chunk of black bread. The* ACTOR *is tossing and coughing on the stove. It is nighttime; the lodging is lighted by a lamp that stands in the center of the table. Outside the wind is howling.*

KLESHCH: Ye-es . . . he disappeared at the time of that row here.

BARON: He vanished from under the eyes of the police—like smoke from the face of the fire.

SATIN: Thus sinners vanish away from before the face of the just!

NASTYA: He was a nice old man! . . . But you aren't men—you're just scum!

BARON (*drinking*): To your health, lady!

SATIN: He was a queer old boy . . . he was! Nastya here fell in love with him.

NASTYA: I did fall in love with him. . . . I love him dearly! That's the truth! He saw everything . . . understood everything.

SATIN (*laughing*): In general . . . for a lot of people he was . . . like soft bread for the toothless.

BARON (*laughing*): Like a plaster for boils.

KLESHCH: He . . . had some compassion. . . . You people . . . have no compassion at all.

SATIN: What good will it do you if I feel sorry for you?

KLESHCH: Satin, you can—if you can't feel sorry for anybody . . . at least you can keep from insulting him.

TATAR (*sits down on a bunk and dandles his sore arm as if it were a child*) : Old man was good . . . had law in his soul! Who has law in his soul, is good! Who has lost the law, is lost himself!

BARON: What law, Prince?

TATAR: The law. . . . Many kinds. . . . You know what law.

BARON: Go on!

TATAR: Not insult a man—that's the law!

SATIN: That's known as "Statute concerning Criminal and Corrective Penalties."

BARON: And further as "Ordinance concerning Penalties imposed by Justices of the Peace."

TATAR: They call it "Koran." . . . Your Koran must be the law. . . . Soul must be Koran. . . . Yes, it must!

KLESHCH (*trying the accordion*) : Oh, the devil! It wheezes! . . . But the Prince tells the truth. A man must live by the law . . . by the Gospel.

SATIN: Go ahead and live by it!

BARON: Just try!

TATAR: Mohammed gave Koran, said: "That's the law! Do what's written there!" Later will come a time: Koran won't be enough. . . . Time will give its law, new. . . . Every time will give its law.

SATIN: Sure! Time has come and given the "Statute concerning Penalties." . . . It's a strong law . . . won't wear out soon!

NASTYA (*striking on the table with a glass*) : And why? . . . What am I living here for? . . . With you? I'll go away. . . . I'll go off somewhere . . . to the end of the world!

BARON: Without your shoes, lady?

NASTYA: Naked! I'll crawl on all fours!

BARON: That will be a picturesque spectacle, lady . . . if you go on all fours.

NASTYA: Yes, I'll just crawl! If I could only escape from seeing your mug! . . . Oh, I'm so sick of everything! Of all life . . . all people!

SATIN: If you go, take the Actor along with you. . . . He's bound for the same place. . . . He's found out that only a half-mile from the end of the world there's a hospital for organons. . . .

ACTOR (*leaning out from his place on the stove*) : Or-ga-nisms, you fool!

SATIN: For organons poisoned by alcohol.

ACTOR: Yes! He'll go! He'll go! . . . You'll see!

BARON: Who's he, sir?

ACTOR: I!

BARON: *Merci,* servant of the goddess . . . what's her name? The goddess of the drama, of tragedy. . . . What was her name?

ACTOR: The muse, you blockhead! Not the goddess, but the muse!

SATIN: Lachesa . . . Hera . . . Aphrodita . . . Atropa—the devil knows what's her name!— The old man's responsible for all this. . . . He wound up the Actor . . . You understand, Baron?

BARON: The old man was silly.

ACTOR: Boobs! Barbarians! Mel-po-me-ne! Men without hearts! You'll see—he'll go away! "Devour yourselves, ye darkened minds!" . . . That's a poem by Béranger. . . . Yes! He will find himself a place . . . where there is no . . . no . . .

BARON: Where there is nothing, sir?

ACTOR: Yes! Nothing! "This cave shall be my tomb! Thus do I die, helpless and weak!" Why do you live? Why?

BARON: Hey, you! Kean or genius of tommyrot! Stop your yelling!

ACTOR: You lie! I will yell!

NASTYA (*raising her head from the table and waving her arms*): Holler! Let 'em hear you!

BARON: Where's the sense, lady?

SATIN: Let 'em alone, Baron! To hell with you! . . . Let 'em shout . . . and smash their heads! . . . Let 'em! There *is* sense in it! "Don't hinder people," as the old man said. . . . Yes, it was he, that old yeast, that leavened our fellow-lodgers.

KLESHCH: He beckoned them to come somewhere . . . but he himself didn't show them the road.

BARON: The old man was a charlatan.

NASTYA: You lie! You're a charlatan yourself!

BARON: Shut up, lady!

KLESHCH: He didn't love truth—that old man didn't. . . . He used to come down hard on the truth. . . . And he was dead right! Sure enough, what does the truth amount to here? Even without it—we can't breathe. . . . Take the Prince there: he squashed his arm at his work. . . . They'll have to saw the arm off—do you hear? . . . There's the truth for you!

SATIN (*striking the table with his fist*): Keep still! You're all swine! You blockheads—keep still about the old man! (*More calmly.*) Baron, you're the worst of all! . . . You don't understand anything . . . and you tell lies! The old man was not a charlatan. What is truth? Truth is *man!* He understood that . . . and you don't! You people are dull as brickbats. . . . I understand the old man. . . . Yes, I do! He used to lie . . . but it was out of pity for you, devil take you! There are lots of men who lie out of pity for their neighbor. . . . I know that! I've read books! They lie beautifully, with inspiration, in a way that arouses you! . . . There is a comforting lie, an atoning lie. . . . A lie justifies the weight that has crushed the arm of the laborer . . . and accuses men who die of hunger. . . . I know about lies! If a man is weak of soul . . . and if he lives by the sap of other men, then he needs a lie. . . . A lie supports some men, it gives a refuge to others. . . . But if a man is his own master . . . if he is independent and does not prey on his neighbor, then what use has he for a lie? Lies are the religion of slaves and masters. . . . Truth is the God of the free man!

BARON: Bravo! Finely said! I agree! You talk . . . like a gentleman!

SATIN: Why shouldn't card-sharpers talk well sometimes, if gentlemen . . . talk like card-sharpers? Yes . . . I've forgotten a lot, but I still know a few things! The old man? He was clever! . . . He acted on me like acid on a dirty old coin. . . . Let's drink his health! Fill my glass!

(NASTYA *pours out a glass of beer and passes it to* SATIN.)

SATIN (*grinning*): The old man lives his own life. . . . He looks at everything with his own eyes. Once I asked him: "Grandfather, what do men live for?" (*Trying to speak with* LUKA'S *voice and imitating his mannerisms.*) "Eh, men live for a better man, my dear fellow! Just for instance, a lot of carpenters are living, and they're all the scum of the earth. . . . And then among them is born a carpenter . . . a carpenter the like of whom the earth never saw before; he surpasses them all, and he has no equal among carpenters. He gives his own form to all carpenters' work . . . and all at once he moves the whole work twenty years forward. . . . In just the same way all other men . . . locksmiths, for example . . . shoemakers and all other working men . . . and all peasants . . . and even the gentry: they all live for a better man! Everybody thinks that he's just passing his life for himself, but it turns out that it's for a better man! For a hundred years . . . and maybe for even more they live for a better man!"

(NASTYA *stares fixedly at* SATIN'S *face.* KLESHCH *stops working on the accordion and also listens. The* BARON, *hanging his head, drums softly on the table with his fingers. The* ACTOR, *leaning out from his place on the stove, cautiously prepares to descend to one of the bunks.*)

SATIN: "Everybody, my dear fellow, everybody that exists, lives for a better man! And so we should respect every man. . . . We don't know who he is, why he was born, and what he can do. . . . Maybe he was born to bring us happiness . . . to be of great benefit to us. . . . Above all, we should respect the babes . . . the little children! Little children need room! Do not hinder the babes from living. . . . Respect the babes!"

(*A pause.*)

BARON (*pensively*): Hm! Yes! For a better man? That . . . reminds me of our family. . . . An old stock . . . of the times of Catherine . . . nobles . . . warriors! . . . émigrés from France. . . . They were in the state service, and kept mounting higher. . . . Under Nicholas I my grandfather, Gustav Debil . . . occupied an important post. . . . Wealth . . . hundreds of serfs . . . horses . . . cooks. . . .

NASTYA: You lie! There wasn't any such thing!

BARON (*jumping up*): Wha-at? We-ell . . . go on!

NASTYA: There wasn't any such thing!

BARON (*shouting*): A house in Moscow! A house in St. Petersburg! Coaches . . . coaches with coats of arms!

(KLESHCH *takes the accordion, rises, and walks to the side of the room, whence he watches the scene.*)

NASTYA: There weren't!

BARON: Shut up! I say . . . dozens of footmen!

NASTYA (*with enjoyment*): There we-eren't!

BARON: I'll kill you!

NASTYA (*preparing to run away*): There weren't any coaches!

SATIN: Quit it, Nastya! Don't tease him!

BARON: Just wait, you slut! My grandfather—

NASTYA: There wasn't any grandfather! There wasn't anything!

(SATIN *guffaws.*)

BARON (*sitting down on a bench, exhausted by anger*): Satin, tell her . . . tell that trollop . . . What—are you laughing too? Don't you believe it either? (*He yells with despair, beating his fists on the table.*) That was all true, devil take you both!

NASTYA (*triumphantly*): Aha, so you're howling? Now do you know how a man feels when they won't believe him?

KLESHCH (*returning to the table*): I thought there was going to be a fight.

TATAR: O-oh, people silly! Very bad!

BARON: I . . . I cannot allow myself to be mocked at! I have proofs—documents, you devil!

SATIN: Throw 'em away! And forget about your grandfather's coaches. . . . You won't drive far in a coach of the past.

BARON: But how does she dare!

NASTYA: Do-o tell! Don't I dare!

SATIN: You see she does dare! How's she any worse than you are? Though in her past you may be sure she didn't have even a father and a mother—not to speak of coaches and a grandfather.

BARON (*calming down*): Devil take you! . . . You . . . you know how to reason calmly. . . . But I . . . seems that I have no character.

SATIN: Get one. It's a useful article. . . . (*A pause.*) Nastya, have you been going to the hospital?

NASTYA: What for?

SATIN: To see Natasha.

NASTYA: The idea! She left there long ago. . . . Left and—disappeared! There's no trace of her.

SATIN: So—she's gone for good.

KLESHCH: It's interesting to see who'll put the other in the worst hole: Vaska, Vasilisa; or she him.

NASTYA: Vasilisa'll get off! She's sly. But they'll send Vaska to prison with hard labor.

SATIN: For murder in a scuffle, prison is all you get.

NASTYA: Too bad! Hard labor would be better for him. . . . I'd like to send all of you . . . to hard labor . . . to sweep you off, like dirt . . . somewhere into the pit!

SATIN (*startled*): What's the matter with you? Have you gone crazy?

BARON: I'll give her one on the ear . . . for her impudence!

NASTYA: Try it! Just touch me!

BARON: I'll try it all right!

SATIN: Quit! Don't touch her! . . . Don't do wrong to a man! I can't get that old man out of my head! (*Guffaws.*) "Don't do wrong to a man!" . . . But what if once on a time they did me wrong and—it's lasted all through my life! What can you do about it? Forgive? Not a bit. Nobody.

BARON (*to* NASTYA): You should understand that I'm not your sort! You're filth!

NASTYA: Oh, you poor boob! You . . . you live on me like a worm lives on an apple!

(*The men burst out laughing in unison.*)

KLESHCH: Oh . . . the fool! Little apple!

BARON: A man can't . . . get angry. . . . She's just an idiot!

NASTYA: Are you laughing? You lie! You don't think it's funny!

ACTOR (*gloomily*): Let 'em have it!

NASTYA: If I . . . only could . . . I'd give it to you (*Taking a cup from the table and throwing it on the floor.*) like that!

TATAR: Why break dishes? Eh, eh . . . silly girl!

BARON (*rising*): No, I'm going to teach her . . . good manners right away!

NASTYA (*running away*): Devil take all of you!

SATIN (*calling after her*): Hey! That's enough! Who are you scaring? What's the matter anyhow?

NASTYA: Wolves! Hope you croak! Wolves!

ACTOR (*gloomily*) : Amen!

TATAR : Oo-oo! Russian woman is bad woman! Bold . . . free! Tatar woman, no! Tatar woman know the law!

KLESHCH : She ought to be thrashed.

BARON : W-wretch!

KLESHCH (*trying the accordion*) : It's ready! But the owner hasn't come back yet. . . . The lad's on a spree.

SATIN : Now take a drink!

KLESHCH : Thanks! But it's time to rest my bones.

SATIN : Are you getting used to us?

KLESHCH (*after taking a drink, goes to a bunk in the corner*) : So-so. . . . Men are the same everywhere. . . . At first you don't see that. . . . Later, you take a look and find out that all men . . . are not a bad lot!

(*The* TATAR *spreads something or other on a bunk, kneels, and begins to pray.*)

BARON (*calling* SATIN's *attention to the* TATAR) : Look!

SATIN : Let him alone! He's a good fellow . . . don't hinder him! (*Guffaws.*) I'm in a pleasant humor to-day. . . . Devil knows why!

BARON : You're always in a pleasant humor when you've had a drink. . . . And sensible too!

SATIN : When I'm drunk . . . I like everything. . . . Yes I do. . . . He's praying? Fine! A man may believe or not believe—that's his business! Man is free . . . he pays for everything himself : for faith, for unbelief, for love, for intelligence. Man pays for everything himself, and therefore he is free! . . . Man—that is truth! What is man? . . . Not you, nor I, nor they—no! Man is you, I, they, the old man, Napoleon, Mohammed . . . all in one! (*With his finger he outlines in the air the figure of a man.*) Do you understand? Man is huge! In him are all beginnings and all ends. . . . All is in man, all is for man! Man alone exists; all else is the work of his hands and of his brain! Ma-an! That is magnificent! That has a proud sound! Ma-an! We must respect man! Not pity him . . . not humiliate him by pity . . . we must respect him! Baron, let's drink to the health of man! (*Rising.*) It is good to feel oneself a man! I'm a jailbird, a murderer, a card-sharper: oh yes! When I walk the street, people look at me as at a swindler . . . and they move aside and look round at me . . . and they often say to me: "Scoundrel! Charlatan! Get to work!" Work? What for? To be well fed? (*Guffaws.*) I've always despised men who are too anxious to be well fed. That's not the point, Baron! That's not the point! Man is higher! Man is higher than a full belly!

BARON (*shaking his head*) : You reason about things. . . . That's good. . . . Most likely that warms the heart. . . . That's not in me.

. . . I don't know how! (*Looks around and speaks in a low, cautious voice.*) Sometimes, my boy . . . I'm afraid. Do you understand? I'm cowardly. . . . Because—what comes afterwards?

SATIN (*pacing the room*): Rubbish! Whom should a man be afraid of?

BARON: Let me tell you: From the earliest time that I can remember . . . I've always had a sort of fog in my noddle. I never understood anything at all. I feel . . . sort of out of place. . . . It seems to me that all my life I've done nothing but change my clothes. . . . And what for? I don't understand! I went to school, wore the uniform of the Noblemen's Institute . . . and what did I study? I don't remember. . . . I married; put on a dress coat, and then a dressing gown . . . but I got a wretched sort of wife—and what for? I don't understand. . . . I squandered all I had—wore a sort of gray jacket and rusty-brown trousers. . . . But how did I get ruined? I never noticed how. . . . I served in the Department of Finance . . . wore a uniform and a cap with a cockade . . . embezzled government money. . . . Then they dressed me in prison garb. . . . Finally I put on these duds. . . . And it all . . . seems like a dream. . . . Well? This is funny.

SATIN: Not very. . . . Stupid is how it strikes me.

BARON: Yes. . . . I think it's stupid myself. . . . But . . . I must have been born for some purpose, I suppose?

SATIN (*laughing*): Probably. . . . "Man is born for a better man!" (*Nodding his head.*) That's a fine idea!

BARON: That . . . girl Nastya! . . . She's run off . . . where to? I'll go and see . . . where she is. All the same . . . she . . . (*Goes out.*)

(*A pause.*)

ACTOR: Tatar! (*A pause.*) Prince!

(*The TATAR turns his head.*)

ACTOR: Pray . . . for me!

TATAR: What?

ACTOR (*in a lower voice*): Pray . . . for me!

TATAR (*after a pause*): Pray yourself!

ACTOR (*climbs quickly down from the stove, goes to the table, pours out vodka with a trembling hand; drinks, and almost runs into the hall*): I am gone!

SATIN: Hey you, Sicambri! Where're you going?

(*He whistles.* MEDVEDEV, *wearing a woman's wadded jacket, comes in with* BUBNOV; *both are slightly tipsy. In one hand* BUBNOV *has a string of cracknels, in the other a few whitebait; under one arm he has a bottle of vodka, and in his coat pocket another.*)

MEDVEDEV: A camel . . . is something like . . . a jackass! Only he has no ears.

BUBNOV: Drop it! You're something like a jackass yourself.

MEDVEDEV: The camel has no ears at all. . . . He hears with his nostrils.

BUBNOV (*to* SATIN): My dear boy, I've been looking for you in all the taverns and dramshops! Take a bottle, will you? My hands are both full!

SATIN: Just set the cracknels on the table, and you'll have one hand free.

BUBNOV: True for you! Oh, you . . . Cop, look here! What about him? Clever lad!

MEDVEDEV: Swindlers are all clever. . . . I know that! They can't get along without brains. A good man is good even if he's stupid, but a bad one simply has to have brains. . . . But as to the camel, you're wrong. . . . He's a riding animal . . . he has no horns . . . and has no teeth.

BUBNOV: Where's the gang? Why is there nobody here? Hey, come out . . . and I'll treat you! Who's in the corner?

SATIN: How soon will you drink up everything you have? Scarecrow!

BUBNOV: I'll do it soon enough! This time I've accumulated some capital—just a bit. . . . Wrymug! Where's Wrymug?

KLESHCH (*coming up to the table*): He's not here.

BUBNOV: Oo-oo-rrr! Growler! Grrr, grrr, grrroo! Turkey cock! Don't bark, don't snarl! Drink and revel and hold your head high! . . . I'm treating everybody! I like to stand treat, lad! If I were a rich man . . . I'd . . . open a tavern free to all! I sure would! With music and a whole chorus of singers. . . . Come and eat and drink and listen to songs . . . refresh your soul! Come, all you poor devils . . . come to my free tavern! Satin! I'd . . . give you . . . take half of my whole capital! That's it!

SATIN: Give me all of it right away!

BUBNOV: All my capital? Right away? Here you are! There's a ruble . . . there's twenty kopeks more . . . nickels . . . coppers . . . all of it!

SATIN: That's fine! It will be safer with me. . . . I'll make money with it at cards.

MEDVEDEV: I'm a witness. . . . The money was deposited for safekeeping. . . . What's the total?

BUBNOV: You? You're a camel. . . . We don't need witnesses.

ALESHKA (*coming in barefooted*): Say, fellows, I've wet my feet!

BUBNOV: Come and wet your throat. . . . That's all you need! You're a good fellow. . . . You play and sing. . . . That's fine! But—you drink! That's all wrong! It's harmful, my lad . . . drinking's harmful!

ALESHKA: I can see that by you! It's only when you're drunk that you're like a man. . . . Kleshch, have you fixed my accordion? (*He sings, dancing in time to his song.*)

> Oh, if my face
> Were not so lovely,
> Then my darling
> Would not love me.

I've got chilled, fellows! It's c-cold!

MEDVEDEV: Hm! . . . But may I ask who your darling is?

BUBNOV: Let him alone! You can subside now, my man! You're not a patrolman any longer. . . . That's over! You aren't a patrolman, and you aren't an uncle.

ALESHKA: You're just auntie's husband.

BUBNOV: One of your nieces is in prison, and the other's dying.

MEDVEDEV (*proudly*): You lie! She's not dying; she's merely disappeared!

(SATIN *guffaws.*)

BUBNOV: It makes no difference, brother! A man without nieces is not an uncle!

ALESHKA: Your Excellency, you're drummer-boy to a goat that's left the service!

> My darling has money,
> And I not a penny;
> But you see I am jolly,
> And gayer than many.

It's cold!

(WRYMUG *comes in; later, to the very end of the act, other figures, both men and women, make their appearance, one after another. They take off their wraps and settle down on the bunks, grumbling.*)

WRYMUG: What did you run off for, Bubnov?

BUBNOV: Come here! Sit down! . . . Let's have a song, brother! My favorite . . . eh?

TATAR: Night, must sleep! Song must sing daytime!

SATIN: That's all right, Prince! You just come here!

TATAR: How all right? Will be noise. . . . When sing songs, then is noise.

BUBNOV (*going to him*): How's your arm, Prince? Have they cut off your arm?

TATAR: What for? We'll wait. . . . Maybe no need cut off. . . . Arm not iron, easy cut off.

WRYMUG: You're in a bad hole, Asan! Without an arm you're of no use! They value us fellows by our arms and backs. . . . If there's no arm, there's no man! Your name is mud! Go and drink vodka. . . . There's nothing else for you to do!

KVASHNYA (coming in): Ah, my dear fellow-lodgers! What weather it is outside! Cold and slush. . . . Is my patrolman here? Cop!

MEDVEDEV: Here!

KVASHNYA: Are you wearing out my jacket again? Seems as if you . . . were a little over the line, eh? What are you acting that way for?

MEDVEDEV: Because it's Bubnov's name-day.* . . . And then it's cold . . . and slushy.

KVASHNYA: You look out . . . before you speak of slush to me! Don't act like a fool! . . . Go to bed!

MEDVEDEV (going out into the kitchen): I can go to bed. . . . I want to. . . . It's time!

SATIN: What's the matter with you? . . . You're awful severe on him!

KVASHNYA: I can't act otherwise, my lad. You must keep a firm hand on such a man. I took him in to live with me; I thought that he'd be a help to me . . . since he's a man of war and you're a rowdy lot . . . and I'm only a woman. . . . But he's taken to drink! So it hasn't helped me at all!

SATIN: You made a poor choice of a helper.

KVASHNYA: No, it's better so. . . . You wouldn't want to live with me . . . you're not the right sort! And if you did live with me, it wouldn't be for more than a week at a time. . . . You'd squander me and all my fat at cards!

SATIN (guffaws): That's right, mistress! I'd squander you.

KVASHNYA: Sure!—Aleshka!

ALESHKA: That's me!

KVASHNYA: What are you blabbing about me?

ALESHKA: I? Everything! Everything, as I see things. "There's a woman," says I, "just marvelous! Flesh, fat, and bones—two hundred pounds; and brains—not a quarter-ounce!"

KVASHNYA: Oh, now you're lying! I have a whole lot of brains. . . . No: why do you say that I beat my patrolman?

ALESHKA: I thought you were beating him, when you were just pulling his hair.

KVASHNYA (laughing): Fool! . . . But you'd better pretend not to

* The day of a person's patron saint, for whom he is named, is a family holiday in Russia.

see it. What's the use of showing your own dirt to other people? . . .
And then, it hurts his feelings. . . . Your talk has driven him to drink.

ALESHKA: So it's true what they say, that the hen drinks too!

(SATIN and KLESHCH *guffaw*.)

KVASHNYA: Foh, you scoffer! . . . But what kind of a man are you, Aleshka?

ALESHKA: Finest ever! Up to anything! All that I see is of use to me!

BUBNOV (*standing near the* TATAR'S *bunk*): Come on! We won't let you sleep anyhow! We're going to sing . . . all night long! Wrymug!

WRYMUG: Sing? All right.

ALESHKA: And I'll play for you!

SATIN: We'll listen!

TATAR (*smiling*): Well, Bubnov devil of fellow . . . he set up wine! We'll drink, we'll be merry; death come—then we die!

BUBNOV: Pour him out a glass, Satin! Sit down, Wrymug! Eh, fellows! A man don't need much! Here I've had a drink—and I'm happy! Wrymug! . . . Start up the song . . . my favorite! I'll sing . . . and I'll weep!

WRYMUG (*starts the song*):

Though the sun is shining brightly—

BUBNOV (*taking up the air*):

No ray falls upon my floor.

(*The door opens quickly.*)

BARON (*standing on the threshold, shouts*): Hey! . . . you there! Come . . . come in a hurry! In the lot . . . out there . . . the Actor . . . has hanged himself!

(*Silence. All look at the* BARON. NASTYA *makes her appearance from behind him, and slowly, with wide-open, staring eyes, goes to the table.*)

SATIN (*in a low voice*): Ugh! . . . He's spoiled the song. . . . The foo-ool!

THE CHERRY ORCHARD

A Comedy in Four Acts

By ANTON PAVLOVICH CHEKHOV

(1904)

Translated by Camilla Chapin Daniels
and George Rapall Noyes

CHARACTERS

LYUBÓV ANDRÉYEVNA RANÉVSKY, *a landowner*
ANYA, *her daughter, aged seventeen*
VÁRYA, *her adopted daughter, aged twenty-seven*
LEONÍD ANDRÉYEVICH GÁYEV, *brother of* LYUBOV ANDREYEVNA
YERMOLÁY ALEXÉICH LOPÁKHIN, *a merchant*
PETR * SERGÉICH TROFÍMOV, *a student*
BORÍS BORÍSOVICH SEMEÓNOV-PÍSHCHIK, *a landowner*
CHARLÓTTA IVÁNOVNA, *a governess*
SEMÉN † PANTALÉYEVICH EPIKHÓDOV, *a clerk*
DUNYÁSHA, *a maid*
FIRS, *the butler, an old man of eighty-seven*
YÁSHA, *a young footman*
A WAYFARER
THE STATION MASTER
A POST OFFICE OFFICIAL
GUESTS *and* SERVANTS

The action takes place at the country estate of LYUBOV ANDREYEVNA RANEVSKY.

---

* Pronounced, Pyŏtr (one syllable).   † Pronounced, Se-myŏn'.

THE CHERRY ORCHARD

ACT I

SCENE I

A room that is still called the nursery. One of the doors leads into ANYA'S *room. Day is breaking. The sun will soon rise. It is May, and the cherry trees are in bloom, but it is cold in the orchard, and a light frost lies on the ground. The windows in the room are closed.* DUNYASHA *enters with a candle, and* LOPAKHIN *with a book in his hand.*

LOPAKHIN: The train has come, thank Heaven! What time is it?

DUNYASHA: Almost two o'clock. (*Blows out the candle.*) It's beginning to get light already.

LOPAKHIN: How late was the train, anyway? At least a couple of hours. (*Yawns and stretches.*) I'm a fine one! I surely made a fool of myself. Here I came over on purpose to meet them at the station, and then all at once I fell asleep . . . sitting up! What a nuisance! . . . You might have waked me.

DUNYASHA: I thought you had gone. (*Listens.*) I think they're coming now.

LOPAKHIN (*listens*): No, they have to collect their baggage and so forth. (*Pause.*) Lyubov Andreyevna has been living abroad now for five years, and I don't know how she may have changed. She's a good soul, a simple, easy-going woman. I remember when I was a young sprout, fifteen years old, my father—he's dead now, but he used to have a little shop in the village then—struck me in the face with his fist one day, and my nose began to bleed. We'd gone out of doors together for some reason or other and he was drunk. I remember just as though it were now, how Lyubov Andreyevna—she was still a slim young thing—led me over to the washbasin here in this very room, the nursery. "Come, come, don't cry your eyes away; you'll live to dance on your wedding day, little peasant," says she. (*Pause.*) Little peasant! . . . True, my father was a peasant, and here I am wearing a white waistcoat and yellow shoes. From the sow's ear to the silk purse. . . . I've grown rich, made a lot of money, but when you come

693

to think of it, to figure it out, I'm still a peasant. . . . (*Fingers the pages of the book.*) Here I've been reading this book, and haven't understood a word of it. I fell asleep reading. (*Pause.*)

DUNYASHA: Even the dogs haven't slept all night long. They seem to feel their masters are returning.

LOPAKHIN: What's the matter with you, Dunyasha? You're so . . .

DUNYASHA: My hands are trembling. I'm going to faint.

LOPAKHIN: You're a tender, spoiled little thing, Dunyasha. Why, you even dress like a lady, and comb your hair to match. It's not right. You ought to remember your place.

(EPIKHODOV *enters, carrying a bouquet. He wears a short coat, and highly polished boots, which squeak loudly. As he enters, he drops the bouquet.*)

EPIKHODOV (*picking up the bouquet*): The gardener sent these, and said to put them in the dining-room. (*Hands the bouquet to* DUNYASHA.)

LOPAKHIN: And bring me some kvass.

DUNYASHA: Yes, sir. (*Goes out.*)

EPIKHODOV: There's a frost this morning. Six degrees below freezing, and the cherry trees all in bloom. I can't praise our climate. (*Sighs.*) No, that I can't. It won't favor us even this once. Just listen to this, Yermolay Alexeich—I bought myself some boots day before yesterday, and I tell you, they squeak so loudly you wouldn't believe it. What shall I grease them with?

LOPAKHIN: Leave me alone. I'm sick of you.

EPIKHODOV: Every day some bad luck or other overtakes me, but I don't grumble. I'm used to it. I just smile.

(DUNYASHA *enters and hands* LOPAKHIN *the kvass.*)

EPIKHODOV: I'm going. (*Stumbles against a chair, knocking it over.*) There! . . . (*With apparent triumph.*) There, if you'll pardon the expression, you see the kind of circumstance that pursues me. This is positively remarkable. (*Goes out.*)

DUNYASHA: Did you know, Yermolay Alexeich, Epikhodov's made me a proposal?

LOPAKHIN: Aha!

DUNYASHA: I don't know how to . . . He's a quiet sort of fellow, only sometimes when he begins talking, you can't make out a word. It's first-rate and full of feeling, only you can't understand it. I half like him, too. He's madly in love with me. An unlucky man. Something goes wrong with him every day. We tease him, and call him two-and-twenty troubles.

LOPAKHIN (*listening*): I think they're coming now.

DUNYASHA: Coming! What's the matter with me! . . . I'm all goose-flesh!

LOPAKHIN: They're really coming. Let's go out and meet them. Will she recognize me? It's five years since we've seen each other.

DUNYASHA (*in agitation*): I'm going to faint. . . . Oh, I'm going to faint!

(*Two carriages are heard drawing up to the house.* LOPAKHIN *and* DUNYASHA *go out quickly. The stage remains empty. There is noise and stir in the adjoining room. Across the stage, leaning on his stick, hastens* FIRS, *who has met* LYUBOV ANDREYEVNA *at the station. He wears an old-fashioned livery and a tall hat. He is muttering to himself, but not a word is distinguishable. The noise behind the scenes continually increases. A voice is heard, saying, "Come in this way. . . ."* LYUBOV ANDREYEVNA, ANYA, *and* CHARLOTTA IVANOVNA, *all wearing traveling clothes, cross the room, accompanied by* VARYA, *clad in a heavy coat and kerchief,* GAYEV, SEMEONOV-PISHCHIK, LOPAKHIN, DUNYASHA, *with a bundle and an umbrella, and a servant carrying the bags.* CHARLOTTA IVANOVNA *is leading a little dog by a chain.*)

ANYA: Let's come in here. Do you remember this room, mama?

LYUBOV ANDREYEVNA (*joyfully, through her tears*): The nursery!

VARYA: It's so cold my hands are numb. (*To* LYUBOV ANDRE-YEVNA.) Mama, your rooms, the white one and the lavender, have been left just as they were.

LYUBOV ANDREYEVNA: The nursery, my dear, beautiful room! . . . It was here I slept when I was little. . . . (*Weeps.*) And now I feel as though I were a little child again. . . . (*Kisses her brother, then* VARYA, *and then her brother once more.*) And Varya hasn't changed a bit—she's just like a little nun. And if here isn't Dunyasha. (*She kisses* DUNYASHA.)

GAYEV: The train was two hours late. How did it happen? Do you call that punctuality?

CHARLOTTA (*to* PISHCHIK): My dog even eats nuts.

PISHCHIK (*surprised*): Just think of that!

(*They all go out, with the exception of* ANYA *and* DUNYASHA.)

DUNYASHA: Here you are at last. . . . (*She takes off* ANYA's *hat and coat.*)

ANYA: I didn't sleep the four nights we were on the road. . . . Now I'm chilled through.

DUNYASHA: You went away during Lent. There was snow on the ground then, there was frost—and now? My darling! (*Laughs and kisses* ANYA.) I've waited for you so long, my joy, my dear one. . . . I must tell you right now; I can't keep it a minute longer. . . .

ANYA (*listlessly*): What now? . . .

DUNYASHA: Epikhodov, the clerk, made me a proposal right after Easter.

ANYA: Always harping on the same thing. . . . (*Arranges her hair.*) I've lost all my hairpins. . . . (*She is very tired, can hardly stand.*)

DUNYASHA: I'm all of a flutter. He loves me—he loves me so!

ANYA (*glancing tenderly through the door into her own room*): My room, my windows—just as though I had never gone away. I'm at home! To-morrow morning I shall get up and run out into the orchard. . . . Oh, if I could only sleep! During the whole journey I couldn't sleep a wink. I was restless.

DUNYASHA; Petr Sergeich arrived day before yesterday.

ANYA (*joyfully*): Petya!

DUNYASHA: He's sleeping in the bath house, and living there too. He says he's afraid he'll inconvenience us. (*Looks at her watch.*) I'd wake him up, but Varvara Mikhailovna told me not to. "Don't waken him," said she.

(VARYA *comes in with a bunch of keys at her belt.*)

VARYA: Dunyasha, bring us some coffee right away. . . . Mama's asking for it.

DUNYASHA: Right away. (*Goes out.*)

VARYA: Well, thank Heaven, you're here! Once more you are at home. (*Caressing* ANYA.) My darling is here! My pretty one has come home!

ANYA: I was impatient, too.

VARYA: I can just imagine!

ANYA: I left home during Holy Week. It was cold then. Charlotta talked all the way, and did tricks. Why, why did you tie me to Charlotta's apron strings?

VARYA: You couldn't have traveled alone, my dear. Seventeen years old!

ANYA: When we arrived in Paris, it was cold. There was snow on the ground. I speak French horribly. Mama was living on the fifth floor. I went to find her. There were a few Frenchmen there, and some ladies, and an old priest with a prayer book, and it was full of tobacco smoke and uncomfortable. Suddenly I became sorry for mama, so sorry. I hugged her head, squeezed it tight, and could not let her go. And after that mama kept caressing me and weeping. . . .

VARYA (*through her tears*): Don't tell me any more, don't! . . .

ANYA: She'd already sold her country house near Mentone. She had nothing left, nothing. And I didn't have a kopek left—we just managed to get there. But mama doesn't realize! We had dinner at the station, and she ordered the most expensive things, and tipped the servants a ruble apiece. Charlotta did too. And Yasha demands his share also: it's just awful! You know mama has a footman—Yasha. We brought him back with us.

VARYA: I saw the good-for-nothing.

ANYA: Well, how are things? Is the interest paid up?

VARYA: Not much!

ANYA: Good heavens, how awful!

VARYA: The estate will be sold in August.

ANYA: God help us!

LOPAKHIN (*looks through the door and moos*): Moo-oo-oo! (*Withdraws.*)

VARYA (*through her tears*): I'd like to give him that! . . . (*Shakes her fist.*)

ANYA (*softly, embracing* VARYA): Varya, has he proposed to you? (VARYA *shakes her head.*) But he does love you. . . . Why don't you both speak out plainly? What are you waiting for?

VARYA: I don't believe anything will come of it. His business takes up so much of his interest—he hasn't time for me. . . . And he doesn't pay any attention to me. Deuce take him anyhow, I'm tired of seeing him. . . . Every one's talking about our marriage, wishing us well—but there's really nothing at all in it. It's like a dream. . . . (*In another tone.*) You have a little brooch shaped like a bee.

ANYA (*sadly*): Mama bought it for me. (*Goes into her own room and calls back in a happy, childlike voice.*) While I was in Paris I went up in a balloon!

VARYA: My darling has come home! My pretty one is here!

(DUNYASHA *has already returned with the coffeepot, and is making coffee.*)

VARYA (*standing near the door*): All day long, my darling, I go to and fro, looking after the housekeeping and daydreaming. We must marry you to a rich man, and then I'd be easier in my mind. I'd go to some hermitage, then to Kiev, then to Moscow. I'd go from one holy shrine to another. . . . I'd wander and wander. . . . How lovely! . . .

ANYA: The birds are singing in the orchard. What time is it now?

VARYA: It must be three. It's time for you to sleep, my darling. (*Going into* ANYA's *room.*) How lovely!

(YASHA *comes in with a steamer rug and a traveling bag.*)

YASHA (*tiptoeing across the stage*): May I come through this way?

DUNYASHA: Why, I wouldn't have recognized you, Yasha. You've changed so while you were abroad.

YASHA: Hm. . . . And who are you?

DUNYASHA: When you went away, I was just so high. . . . (*Holds out her hand.*) I'm Dunyasha, Fedor Kozoyedov's daughter. Don't you remember?

YASHA: Hm. . . . Little cucumber! (*Glances hastily around and embraces her. She screams and drops a saucer.* YASHA *goes out hurriedly.*)

VARYA (*in the doorway, annoyed*): What's the matter here?

DUNYASHA (*through her tears*): I broke a saucer.

VARYA: That's good luck.

ANYA (*emerging from her room*): We must warn mama. Petya is here. . . .

VARYA: I told them not to wake him.

ANYA (*musingly*): Six years ago father died, and a month later brother Grisha was drowned in the river—such a darling little seven-year-old boy. Mama couldn't stand the shock; she went away, went away without looking behind her. . . . (*Shudders.*) How I understand her, if she only knew it! (*Pause.*) And Petya Trofimov was Grisha's tutor—he may remind her. . . .

(FIRS *comes in. He wears a waiter's jacket and a white waistcoat.*)

FIRS (*going over to the coffeepot with a preoccupied air*): The Mistress is going to eat in here. (*Puts on his white gloves.*) Is the coffee ready? (*To* DUNYASHA *sternly.*) You there! Where's the cream?

DUNYASHA: Oh, good Lord! (*She goes out hurriedly.*)

FIRS (*bustling around the coffeepot*): Eh, you're a lummox. . . . (*Mutters to himself.*) So they're back from Paris. . . . The Master visited Paris once too . . . in a coach and four. . . . (*Laughs.*)

VARYA: What are you saying, Firs?

FIRS: Beg pardon? (*Joyfully.*) My Lady's come home! I've lived to see it. I might as well die now. (*Weeps with joy.*)

(LYUBOV ANDREYEVNA, GAYEV, *and* SEMEONOV-PISHCHIK *come in.* SEMEONOV-PISHCHIK *wears a sleeveless coat of light-weight material, and loose trousers.* GAYEV, *as he enters, goes through the motions of a pool player.*)

LYUBOV ANDREYEVNA: How does it go? Let me see if I can remember! Yellow into the corner! Cross the table to the center!

GAYEV: Graze it into the corner! You and I, sister, slept here in this very room once, and now I'm fifty-one, strange though it may seem. . . .

LOPAKHIN: Yes, time flies.

GAYEV: What's that?

LOPAKHIN: I say, time flies.

GAYEV: It smells of patchouli in here.

ANYA: I'm going to bed. Good night, mama. (*Kisses her mother.*)

LYUBOV ANDREYEVNA: My darling girlie! (*Kisses her hands.*) Are you glad to be home? Somehow I can't calm myself.

ANYA: Good night, uncle.

GAYEV (*kissing her face and hands*): God bless you! How you resemble your mother! (*To his sister.*) Lyuba, at her age, you were just like her.

(ANYA *gives her hand to* LOPAKHIN *and* PISHCHIK, *and goes out of the room, closing the door behind her.*)

LYUBOV ANDREYEVNA: She is very tired.

PISHCHIK: It must have been a long journey.

VARYA (*to* LOPAKHIN *and* PISHCHIK): Well, gentlemen? It's past two o'clock. Time to be decent.

LYUBOV ANDREYEVNA (*laughing*): You are still the same Varya. (*Draws* VARYA *close and kisses her.*) See, I'll drink my coffee and then we'll all disperse. (FIRS *places a cushion under her feet.*) Thank you, my friend. I've become addicted to coffee. I drink it day and night. Thank you, dear old man. (*Kisses him.*)

VARYA: I'll go and see whether they've brought in all your things. (*Goes out.*)

LYUBOV ANDREYEVNA: Is it really I sitting here? (*Laughs.*) I want to wave my arms and jump for joy. (*Covers her face with her hands.*) And all of a sudden I drop off dozing! God knows, I love my country, I love it dearly. I couldn't look through the train window —I cried all the time. (*Through her tears.*) However, I must drink the coffee. Thank you, Firs. Thank you, dear old man. I am so glad you are still alive.

FIRS: Day before yesterday.

GAYEV: He is hard of hearing.

LOPAKHIN: I must leave shortly, between four and five, for Harkov. What a nuisance! I wanted to have a look at you, and to chat a little. . . . You are just as handsome as ever.

PISHCHIK (*breathing heavily*): She's even more beautiful. She's dressed Paris style. "This is more than we could hope for, most astonishingly fine."

LOPAKHIN: Your brother there, Leonid Andreich, says I'm a low sort of fellow, a skinflint, but that doesn't bother me. Let him talk. I only want you to have faith in me as before, to see your marvelous, touching eyes look upon me as they used to. God is merciful! My father was the serf of your grandfather and your father, but you, you yourself, once did so much for me that I have forgotten all old wrongs, and love you as though you were my own kin—no, even more.

LYUBOV ANDREYEVNA: I can't sit still—I simply can't. . . . (*She springs up and walks about excitedly.*) I cannot survive this joy. . . .

Laugh at me—I'm a silly woman. . . . My darling bookcase! . . . (*Kisses the bookcase.*) My desk! . . .

GAYEV: Nurse died during your absence.

LYUBOV ANDREYEVNA (*sits down and drinks her coffee.*) Yes, God rest her soul! They wrote me about it.

GAYEV: And Anastasy died. Petrushka Kosoy has left me, and is living in the city now at the Police Inspector's house. (*Takes a little box of lozenges out of his pocket and sucks one.*)

PISHCHIK: My daughter Dashenka . . . sends you her regards.

LOPAKHIN: I have something very pleasant and heartening to tell you. (*Looks at his watch.*) I must go at once—there's no time to explain it. . . . Oh, well, here it is in a nutshell. You know already that your cherry orchard is to be sold for debts, and that the auction has been set for the twenty-second of August. But don't you worry, dear lady, put your mind at rest—there's a way out. . . . Here's my proposition: let me have your attention. Your estate is situated only thirteen miles from the city, the railroad runs past it, and if the cherry orchard and the land along the river were divided into plots for cottages and then leased, you would get an annual return of at least twenty-five thousand rubles.

GAYEV: Pardon me, what utter nonsense!

LYUBOV ANDREYEVNA: I don't understand you at all, Yermolay Alexeich.

LOPAKHIN: You'll receive from the cottagers annually at least twenty-five rubles per desyatina,* and if you advertise it now, I'll wager anything you please that you won't have a vacant plot left by autumn. They'll all be taken. In short—I congratulate you—you're saved! The site is marvelous, the river deep. Only, of course, you'll have to fix it up a bit, clear it off. . . . Tear down all the old buildings—for instance, this house, which is no use to any one now, cut down the old cherry orchard—

LYUBOV ANDREYEVNA: Cut it down? My dear friend, forgive me, but you don't understand at all. If there is anything interesting—I might say remarkable—in our province it is our cherry orchard.

LOPAKHIN: The orchard is remarkable only for its size. The cherries ripen only every other year, and even then there's no way to dispose of them. Nobody buys them.

GAYEV: Even the Encyclopedia mentions this cherry orchard.

LOPAKHIN (*looking at his watch*): Unless we devise some plan and arrive at a definite decision, the cherry orchard and the entire estate will be sold at auction on the twenty-second of August. Make up your

---

* Desyatina—about 2.7 acres.

minds then! I assure you there's no other alternative. There is absolutely none!

FIRS: In times past, forty or fifty years ago, they used to dry the cherries, preserve them, and spice them; they made jam of them, and sometimes—

GAYEV: Be quiet, Firs.

FIRS: And sometimes they sent the dried cherries by cartloads to Moscow and Harkov. Ah, they brought in the money! And the dried cherries were soft, moist, sweet, fragrant. . . . They knew a way then. . . .

LYUBOV ANDREYEVNA: But who has the recipe now?

FIRS: They've forgotten how. No one remembers it.

PISHCHIK (to LYUBOV ANDREYEVNA): What did you do in Paris? Tell us! Did you eat frogs?

LYUBOV ANDREYEVNA: I ate crocodiles.

PISHCHIK: Just think of that! . . .

LOPAKHIN: Only gentry and peasants have lived in the country prior to our time, but now the cottager makes his appearance. Every city— even the smallest—is now surrounded by cottages. And one may safely foretell that within twenty years the number of cottagers will have increased remarkably. Now he only drinks tea on the balcony, but the time may come when he will busy himself with farming on his one desyatina, and then your cherry orchard will become joyous, rich, and luxuriant. . . .

GAYEV (becoming indignant): What nonsense!

(VARYA and YASHA come in.)

VARYA: There are two telegrams for you here, mama. (She takes out a key and opens the squeaking lock of the old bookcase.) Here they are.

LYUBOV ANDREYEVNA: They're from Paris. (Tears them across without reading them.) I am through with Paris. . . .

GAYEV: Do you know, Lyuba, how old this bookcase is? A week ago I pulled out the bottom drawer, and there I saw figures burned into the wood. This bookcase was made just a hundred years ago. What do you think of that, eh? We ought to celebrate its jubilee. It's an inanimate object, but just the same, say what you will, it's a fine old bookcase.

PISHCHIK (surprised): A hundred years! . . . Just think of that!

GAYEV: Yes. . . . This object. . . . (Laying his hand on the bookcase.) Dear, venerated bookcase! I greet thine existence, which for more than a hundred years now has been consecrated to the bright ideals of goodness and justice; thy mute summons to fruitful labor has grown no weaker during the course of these hundred years, as thou hast upheld through generations of our stock (*Tearfully.*) courage, faith in a better future, and hast developed within us ideals of goodness and social conscience. (*Pause.*)

LOPAKHIN: Yes. . . .

LYUBOV ANDREYEVNA: You haven't changed a bit, Lenya.

GAYEV (*somewhat confused*): Right ball to the corner pocket! Close shot to the center!

LOPAKHIN (*looking at his watch*): Well, it's time for me to go.

YASHA (*handing* LYUBOV ANDREYEVNA *a vial*): You must take your pills now. . . .

PISHCHIK: You shouldn't take medicine, my dear. It does you neither harm nor good. . . . Give it to me, most honored lady. (*Takes the pills, pours them out on his palm, blows on them, puts them in his mouth and drinks some kvass.*) There now!

LYUBOV ANDREYEVNA (*frightened*): Why, you're crazy!

PISHCHIK: I swallowed every pill.

LOPAKHIN: What a glutton! (*They all laugh.*)

FIRS: He was at our house on Easter, and ate half a gallon of cucumbers. . . . (*Mutters.*)

LYUBOV ANDREYEVNA: What is he talking about?

VARYA: He's been mumbling that way for ten years now. We've grown used to it.

YASHA: In his dotage.

(CHARLOTTA IVANOVNA, *a very thin, tightly-laced woman, dressed in white, and with a lorgnette at her waist, crosses the stage.*)

LOPAKHIN: Excuse me, Charlotta Ivanovna, I haven't had a chance yet to greet you. (*Tries to kiss her hand.*)

CHARLOTTA (*drawing away her hand*): If I let you kiss my hand, you'll want to kiss my elbow next, then my shoulder. . . .

LOPAKHIN: I'm out of luck to-day. (*All laugh.*) Charlotta Ivanovna, show us a trick!

LYUBOV ANDREYEVNA: Charlotta, show us a trick!

CHARLOTTA: Not I. I'm too sleepy. (*Goes out.*)

LOPAKHIN: I'll see you again in three weeks. (*Kisses the hand of* LYUBOV ANDREYEVNA.) In the meantime, good-by. (*To* GAYEV.) Time to go. Good-by. (*Exchanges kisses with* PISHCHIK.) Good-by. (*Gives his hand to* VARYA, *then to* FIRS *and* YASHA.) I don't want to leave. (*To* LYUBOV ANDREYEVNA.) If you can come to a decision regarding the subdivision, and make up your mind, let me know. I'll get you a loan of fifty thousand. Think it over seriously.

VARYA (*angrily*): Do go and be done with it!

LOPAKHIN: I'm going, I'm going. (*He goes out.*)

GAYEV: A low fellow, that. But no—your pardon! . . . Varya's going to marry him. That's Varya's suitor.

VARYA: Don't talk nonsense, uncle.

LYUBOV ANDREYEVNA: Why, Varya, I should be very glad. He's a good man.

PISHCHIK: A most worthy man, one must admit. . . . Even my Dashenka . . . says also that . . . she says a lot. . . . (*Snores, but rouses himself immediately.*) But still, dear lady, loan me two hundred and forty rubles . . . to pay the interest on our mortgage.

VARYA (*frightened*): We haven't any, we haven't!

LYUBOV ANDREYEVNA: Really, I haven't any money.

PISHCHIK: You'll find some. (*Laughs.*) I never lose hope. Here I used to think that everything was lost, ruined, and then—the railroad was built across my land, and . . . they paid me. And so, just watch and see—something else will turn up, if not to-day, then to-morrow. . . . Dashenka is going to win two hundred thousand. . . . She has a lottery ticket.

LYUBOV ANDREYEVNA: The coffee's all gone. We can go to bed.

FIRS (*in a lecturing tone, as he brushes off GAYEV*): You've put on the wrong trousers again. What shall I do with you?

VARYA (*softly*): Anya's asleep. (*Opens the window gently.*) The sun has risen already. It's not cold any more. Look, mama, what wonderful trees! How glorious the air is! The starlings are singing!

GAYEV (*opening another window*): The whole orchard is white. Do you remember, Lyuba? There is that long vista; straight, straight as an arrow it shines on moonlight nights. Do you remember? You haven't forgotten?

LYUBOV ANDREYEVNA (*looks out of the window into the orchard*): Oh, my childhood, those pure and happy years! Here in this nursery I used to sleep; from here I looked out upon the orchard. Gladness awakened with me every morning, and it was just the same then—as now—not a bit changed. (*Laughs joyously.*) White, all white! Oh, my orchard! After the dark, rainy autumns and the cold winters, you are young again, full of gladness. The heavenly angels have not abandoned you. . . . If only I might cast from my shoulders and breast the heavy stone, if only I could forget my past!

GAYEV: Yes, and they'll sell the orchard to pay our debts. How strange it seems! . . .

LYUBOV ANDREYEVNA: Look, the spirit of our mother is walking in the orchard . . . in a white dress! (*Laughs joyously.*) It is she.

GAYEV: Where?

VARYA: Lord help you, mama!

LYUBOV ANDREYEVNA: There's no one there. I only thought it

looked so. On the right, at the turn to the summerhouse, a white tree was bent so that it resembled a woman. . . .

(TROFIMOV *comes in. He is dressed in a shabby student's uniform, and wears glasses.*)

LYUBOV ANDREYEVNA: What a wonderful orchard! White masses of flowers, the blue sky! . . .

TROFIMOV: Lyubov Andreyevna! (*She looks at him.*) I shall only pay you my respects, and then go immediately. (*Kissing her hand warmly.*) They told me to wait until morning, but I didn't have the patience. . . .

(LYUBOV ANDREYEVNA *looks at him in bewilderment.*)

VARYA (*through her tears*): It is Petya Trofimov.

TROFIMOV: Petya Trofimov, who used to be tutor to your Grisha. . . . Can I really have changed so?

(LYUBOV ANDREYEVNA *embraces him and weeps quietly.*)

GAYEV (*embarrassed*): That's enough, Lyuba, that's enough.

VARYA (*weeping*): But I told you, Petya, to wait till to-morrow.

LYUBOV ANDREYEVNA: My Grisha . . . my boy . . . Grisha . . . my son! . . .

VARYA: What's the use, mama? It's God's will.

TROFIMOV (*softly, through his tears*): There . . . there. . . .

LYUBOV ANDREYEVNA (*weeping quietly*): My little boy is dead, he was drowned. . . . Why did it happen? Why, my dear? (*More softly.*) Anya is asleep in there and I am talking in a loud voice . . . disturbing her. . . . What's the matter, Petya? Why have you lost your good looks? Why have you grown old?

TROFIMOV: On the train a village woman called me "a gentleman gone to seed."

LYUBOV ANDREYEVNA: You were just a boy then, a dear, young student, but now your hair is thin, and you're wearing spectacles. Is it possible you're still a student? (*Going toward the door.*)

TROFIMOV: I suppose I shall be a student forever.

LYUBOV ANDREYEVNA (*kisses her brother, then* VARYA): Well, let's go to bed. Even you have grown older, Leonid.

PISHCHIK (*following her*): So then, we must go to bed. . . . Oh, my gout! I'll stay the night. . . . Lyubov Andreyevna, my dear friend, if you could just get me two hundred and forty rubles by to-morrow morning!

GAYEV: That's all he can think of!

PISHCHIK: Two hundred and forty rubles . . . to pay the interest on the mortgage.

LYUBOV ANDREYEVNA: I haven't any money, my dear man.

PISHCHIK: I'll give it back, my dear, it's a trifling sum. . . .

LYUBOV ANDREYEVNA: Well, all right then. Leonid will give it to you. . . . Give it to him, Leonid.

GAYEV: I'll give it to him—you just watch me!

LYUBOV ANDREYEVNA: What's the use? Give it to him. . . . He needs it. . . . He'll return it.

(TROFIMOV, LYUBOV ANDREYEVNA, PISHCHIK, *and* FIRS *go out.* GAYEV, VARYA, *and* YASHA *remain.*)

GAYEV: My sister has not yet broken herself of the habit of squandering money. (*To* YASHA.) Get away, my dear fellow. You smell like a chicken.

YASHA (*with a grin*): And you haven't changed a bit, Leonid Andreyevich.

GAYEV: What's he talking about? (*To* VARYA.) What did he say?

VARYA (*to* YASHA): Your mother has come in from the village. She's been sitting in the servants' room since yesterday. She wants to see you.

YASHA: Devil a bit I care!

VARYA: Ah, you're a shameless fellow!

YASHA: Much use her being here. She might have come to-morrow. (*He goes out.*)

VARYA: Mama is just the same as always. She hasn't changed a bit. If you'd let her, she'd give away everything she had.

GAYEV: Yes. . . . (*Pause.*) When a great many remedies are suggested for some ailment, it means that the ailment is incurable. I think, rack my brains, I find many solutions, very many, which means that in reality there isn't one. It would be splendid if some one would make us a bequest, splendid if we could marry our Anya to a very wealthy man, splendid to go to Yaroslavl and try our luck with our aunt, the Countess. Auntie is very, very rich.

VARYA (*weeping*): If only God would help us!

GAYEV: Don't cry. Auntie is very rich, but she doesn't like us. My sister, in the first place, married an attorney, a man below her class.

(ANYA *appears in the doorway.*)

GAYEV: She not only married below her class, but conducted herself, I must admit, in a manner far from virtuous. She is a kind, admirable, fine woman, I love her very much. But however diligently you may think up extenuating circumstances, you must still admit that she is immoral. One feels it in her slightest movement.

VARYA (*in a whisper*): Anya is in the doorway.

GAYEV: Who? (*Pause.*) That's strange—I've got something in my right eye—I can't see out of it. And on Thursday, when I was in the district court—

(ANYA *comes in.*)

VARYA: Why aren't you asleep, Anya?

ANYA: I'm not sleepy. I can't go to sleep.

GAYEV: My darling! (*Kisses* ANYA's *face and hands.*) My child!
. . . (*Through his tears.*) You're not only my niece—you're my angel
—everything in the world to me. Believe in me, believe. . . .

ANYA: I believe in you, uncle. Every one loves you, respects you
. . . but, dear uncle, you must keep still—only keep still. What were
you just saying about my mother, your sister? Why did you say that?

GAYEV: Yes, yes. . . . (*Covers his face with her hand.*) This is
indeed terrible! My God! Save me, God! And just a little while ago
I delivered an oration over the bookcase . . . so silly! And it was
only when I had finished that I realized it was silly.

VARYA: Yes, uncle dear, you truly must keep still. Just keep still,
that's all.

ANYA: You'll be happier yourself if you just keep still.

GAYEV: I'll keep still. (*Kisses their hands.*) I'll keep still. Only
here's some news about money matters. I was at the district court on
Thursday. Well, people came in, the talk turned from one thing to
another, from this to that, and I gathered that we might arrange a loan
on a note, to pay the interest at the bank.

VARYA: If only God would help us.

GAYEV: I'll go over on Tuesday and talk it over with them again.
(*To* VARYA.) Don't sob so. (*To* ANYA.) Your mama will have a
talk with Lopakhin—of course he'll not refuse her. . . . And when
you've rested up a bit, you will go to Yaroslavl to see your great-aunt,
the Countess. So you see, we'll be working from three points, and the
trick is turned already. I'm sure we shall pay off the interest. . . .
(*Puts a piece of candy in his mouth.*) On my honor, I swear by whatever pledge you please, the estate shall not be sold! (*Excitedly.*) By
my happiness I swear! Here's my hand on it. You may call me a
wretched, dishonorable man if I let it be put up at auction. By my
whole being I swear it!

ANYA (*cheerfully, her composure restored*): How good and clever
you are, uncle! (*Embraces him.*) I am quite calm now, quite calm
and happy.

(FIRS *comes in.*)

FIRS (*reproachfully*): Leonid Andreich, you're conscienceless!
When are you going to bed?

GAYEV: Right away, right away. You may go, Firs. I'll take off
my things without your help. Well, children, bye-bye. . . . I'll give
you the details to-morrow, but now, go and sleep. (*Kisses* ANYA *and*
VARYA.) I'm a man of the eighties. . . . People don't praise those
times much, but just the same, I may say that I've suffered a lot for my

convictions. The peasant loves me with good reason. One must understand the peasant, one must understand what—

ANYA: There you go again, uncle!

VARYA: You must keep still, uncle dear!

FIRS (*angrily*): Leonid Andreich!

GAYEV: I'm coming, I'm coming. . . . Go to bed now. Off two cushions into the center! I'll turn over a new leaf. (*He goes out, FIRS shuffling behind him.*)

ANYA: My mind is at peace now. I don't want to go to Yaroslavl, I don't like auntie; but just the same, I feel calmer, thanks to uncle. (*She sits down.*)

VARYA: We must sleep. I'm going to bed. Things went all to pieces while you were gone. You know, only the old servants live in the servants' quarters: Efimyushka, Polya, Evstigney, and Karp, too. They began to let in tramps to spend the night. I didn't say a word. But then the rumor got around to me that they were saying I didn't let them have anything but peas to eat. Out of stinginess—you see? And Evstigney was to blame all the time. Very well, I thought. If that's so, I thought, you just wait! So I called Evstigney in. (*Yawns.*) He came. . . . "What's the matter with you, Evstigney? You're making a fool of yourself!" . . . (*Looks at ANYA.*) Anya darling! (*Pause.*) She's fallen asleep. (*Takes ANYA by the arm.*) Let's go to bed! Come! (*Leading her.*) My darling has fallen asleep! Come on! (*They start to go.*)

(*In the far distance beyond the orchard a shepherd plays on his pipe. TROFIMOV walks across the stage, and seeing VARYA and ANYA, stops still.*)

VARYA: Sh . . . sh. She's sleeping . . . sleeping. Come, dear.

ANYA (*softly, and half asleep*): I am so tired. . . . All the little bells . . . dear uncle . . . mama and uncle. . . .

VARYA: Come, dear, come on. . . . (*They go into ANYA's room.*)

TROFIMOV (*tenderly*): My sun! My springtime!

ACT II

An old, ruined, long-since-abandoned shrine. Near it a well; and a few big stones, evidently at one time tombstones. An old bench. The road leading to GAYEV's farmhouse can be seen. At one side poplar trees tower up, dark and tall; beyond them, the cherry orchard begins. In the distance a row of telegraph poles, and far off along the horizon are dimly visible the outlines of a great city, which can be seen only during fine, clear weather. It is nearly sunset. CHARLOTTA, YASHA, *and* DUNYASHA *are sitting on the bench:* EPIKHODOV *is standing nearby and playing the guitar. They are all thoughtful.* CHARLOTTA *is wearing a man's old cap; she has lowered a rifle from her shoulder, and is adjusting a buckle on the strap.*

CHARLOTTA (*thoughtfully*) : I haven't a real passport. I don't know how old I am, and I always feel I am young. When I was a little girl my father and mother used to travel from fair to fair and give performances—very good ones. And I used to do the salto-mortale, and other tricks. Then, when papa and mama died, a German woman took me to live with her and began to teach me. Well and good. I grew up, and later I became a governess. But who I am or where I come from—that I don't know. Who my parents were, I don't know. Perhaps they weren't married. (*Takes a cucumber out of her pocket and begins to eat it.*) I don't know anything. (*Pause.*) I long so to talk, but there's no one to talk to. . . . I haven't anybody at all.

EPIKHODOV (*playing on the guitar and singing*) :

> What care I for friends and foes?
> What care I for the noisy world?

How jolly it is to play on the mandolin!

DUNYASHA : That's a guitar, not a mandolin! (*Glances into a little mirror and powders her nose.*)

EPIKHODOV : To the poor idiot who's in love, it's a mandolin. (*Hums.*)

> With the flame of a mutual love
> Would that your heart were burning!

(YASHA *joins in.*)

CHARLOTTA : These men sing horribly. . . . Foh! Like jackals.

DUNYASHA (*to* YASHA) : Just the same, it must be fine to live abroad.

YASHA : Yes, to be sure. I can't contradict you. (*Yawns and lights a cigar.*)

EPIKHODOV : That's easy to understand. Things have been properly established abroad for a long time.

YASHA : Of course.

EPIKHODOV : I'm an educated fellow, I read many remarkable books; but I simply can't understand my own state of mind—what I really want—whether to live, or to shoot myself, so to speak. But just the same, I always carry a revolver around with me. Here it is. . . . (*Produces a revolver.*)

CHARLOTTA : Now I'm through. I'm going. (*Slings the rifle over her shoulder.*) Epikhodov, you are a very clever and very terrifying man. Women must fall madly in love with you. Br-r-r! (*Walks away.*)

Those smart boys are all so stupid that I haven't a soul to talk to. I'm always alone, alone, no one belongs to me, and . . . and I don't know who I am nor why I was born. (*She goes slowly out.*)

EPIKHODOV: Without mentioning other matters, I should, properly speaking, say of myself among other things that fate has treated me as mercilessly as a storm does a little ship. Supposing you say I am wrong—then tell me why it was that this morning, for instance, I waked up and saw on my chest a spider of terrific size? It was so big. . . . (*Illustrates with both hands.*) And then, when I took up some kvass to have a drink, why there I saw something in the highest degree indecent, in the nature of a cockroach. (*Pause.*) Have you ever read Buckle? (*Pause.*) May I speak a couple of words to you, Avdotya Fedorovna?

DUNYASHA: Speak up.

EPIKHODOV: I should prefer to speak with you alone. (*Sighs.*)

DUNYASHA (*disconcerted*): Very well. . . . Only bring me my cloak first. . . . It's near the bookcase. . . . It's a little damp here.

EPIKHODOV: Very well. I'll bring it to you. . . . Now I know what to do with my revolver. . . . (*Picks up the guitar and goes out, playing.*)

YASHA: Two-and-twenty troubles! Between you and me, he's a stupid fellow. (*Yawns.*)

DUNYASHA: God grant he doesn't shoot himself! (*Pause.*) I'm afraid. I'm all upset. They took me to live with gentlefolk when I was still a little girl, and now I'm not used to humble living. Why, my hands here are snowy white like a lady's. I've grown tender and delicate, and turned into a lady—I'm afraid of everything. It's terrible to be that way. And if you should deceive me, Yasha, then I don't know what would become of my nerves.

YASHA (*kisses her*): Little cucumber! Of course, every girl should respect herself, and I should be the first to despise one whose conduct was not above reproach.

DUNYASHA: I'm head over heels in love with you; you're well educated, you can discourse on every subject. (*Pause.*)

YASHA (*yawning*): Oh, yes. . . . To my mind it's this way: if a girl loves some one, that means she's immoral. (*Pause.*) It's nice to smoke a cigar in the open air. . . . (*Listening.*) Some one's coming this way. . . . It's the gentry. . . .

(DUNYASHA *embraces him impulsively.*)

YASHA: Go on home as if you'd been down to the river to bathe. Take that little path, or else they'll meet you and think I've had a rendezvous with you. I couldn't stand that.

DUNYASHA (*coughing softly*) : My head aches a little from the cigar smoke. (*She goes out.*)

(YASHA *remains sitting near the shrine*. LYUBOV ANDREYEVNA, GAYEV, *and* LOPAKHIN *come in*.)

LOPAKHIN: You absolutely must make up your mind—time will not wait. The question is perfectly simple. Are you willing to lease the land for cottages, or not? Answer me in a word: yes or no? One word only!

LYUBOV ANDREYEVNA: Who has been smoking disgusting cigars out here? (*Seats herself.*)

GAYEV: It's convenient since they built the railroad. (*Sits down.*) We rode into town and had lunch. . . . Yellow to the center! I'd like to go into the house first and play just one game. . . .

LYUBOV ANDREYEVNA: You'll have time.

LOPAKHIN: Only one word! (*Beseechingly.*) Please give me an answer!

GAYEV (*yawning*): What's that?

LYUBOV ANDREYEVNA (*looking into her purse*): Yesterday I had a lot of money, but to-day there's very little. My poor Varya is scrimping along, feeding every one on milk soup; they're giving the old people in the kitchen nothing but peas to eat, and here I'm squandering money senselessly. . . . (*Drops her purse, scattering gold coins. In vexation.*) Look, they're all scattered. . . .

YASHA: By your leave, I'll pick them up right away. (*Picks up the coins.*)

LYUBOV ANDREYEVNA: Yes, please, Yasha. Why did I go out to lunch anyway! . . . Your vile restaurant with its music, the table-cloths smelling of soap! . . . Why do people drink so much, Lenya? Why do they eat so much? Why do they talk so much? To-day in the restaurant you rambled on and on, and all about nothing. About the seventies, about the decadents. And to whom? Talking to the waiters about the decadents!

LOPAKHIN: Yes.

GAYEV (*waving his hand*): I'm incorrigible, that's obvious. . . . (*Exasperatedly to* YASHA.) What's the matter? Why are you always under our noses?

YASHA (*laughing*): I can't listen to your voice without laughing.

GAYEV (*to his sister*): Either he or I . . .

LYUBOV ANDREYEVNA: Go away, Yasha, get along with you.

YASHA (*handing* LYUBOV ANDREYEVNA *her purse*): I'm going right away. (*With difficulty restraining his laughter.*) This very minute. (*He goes out.*)

LOPAKHIN: Deriganov, the rich man, is planning to buy your estate. They say he's coming to the auction himself.

LYUBOV ANDREYEVNA: Where did you hear that?

LOPAKHIN: That's the rumor in town.

GAYEV: Our aunt in Yaroslavl has promised to send some money, but how much she will send, and when, we don't know. . . .

LOPAKHIN: How much will she send? A hundred thousand? Two hundred?

LYUBOV ANDREYEVNA: Well! . . . ten or fifteen thousand, and we'll be grateful for that.

LOPAKHIN: Pardon me for saying so, but I have never yet met such frivolous, unbusinesslike, queer people as you, my friends. People tell you in plain Russian that your estate is to be sold, but you don't take it in.

LYUBOV ANDREYEVNA: What can we do about it? Tell us, what?

LOPAKHIN: Every day I tell you. Every day I repeat the same thing. The cherry orchard, and the land as well, simply must be leased for cottages, and this must be done now, now, without delay! The date of the auction is almost here! You must realize this! Just make up your mind definitely once for all to accept the leasing plan, and people will loan you as much money as you wish. Then you'll be saved.

LYUBOV ANDREYEVNA: Cottages and cottagers—forgive me, that's so vulgar.

GAYEV: I agree with you perfectly.

LOPAKHIN: I shall either sob, or scream, or fall in a faint. I can't stand it! You've worn me out. (*To* GAYEV.) You old woman!

GAYEV: What's that?

LOPAKHIN: Old woman! (*He turns to go.*)

LYUBOV ANDREYEVNA (*frightened*): No, don't go away. Stay here, my dear friend, I beg you. Perhaps we shall find a way.

LOPAKHIN: What's there to think about?

LYUBOV ANDREYEVNA: Don't go away, I beg of you. It's more cheerful with you here anyway. . . . (*Pause.*) All the time I feel as though I were waiting for something—as though the house were going to fall in ruins above us.

GAYEV (*musing deeply*): Double into the corner . . . back shot to the center. . . .

LYUBOV ANDREYEVNA: We have committed many sins.

LOPAKHIN: What sins have you committed? . . .

GAYEV (*putting a piece of candy into his mouth*): They say I've gobbled up all my substance in sugar candy. . . . (*Laughs.*)

LYUBOV ANDREYEVNA: Oh, my sins! . . . I've always squandered my money like a mad woman, and I married a man who only created more debts. My husband died from too much champagne—he drank horribly—and I, to my own misfortune, fell in love with another man, and at the very same time—this was my first punishment, a mortal blow—my little boy was drowned here in the river. I went abroad, broke all ties, planning never to return, never to see that river again. I covered my eyes and fled in desperation, and *he* followed me, with brutal, merciless persistence. I bought a villa near Mentone, for *he* became ill there, and for three years I knew no rest day or night. The sick man exhausted me, my soul shriveled up. And then, last year, when they sold the villa for debts, I went to Paris, and there he plundered me, abandoned me, and took up with another woman. I tried to poison myself. . . . It was so stupid and shameful. . . . And suddenly I was drawn back to Russia, to my native land, to my little girl. . . . (*Wipes away her tears.*) Lord, Lord, be merciful, forgive my sins! Do not punish me any more! (*Takes a telegram out of her pocket.*) I received this to-day from Paris. He asks forgiveness, entreats me to come back. . . . (*Tears up the telegram.*) Don't I hear music somewhere? (*Listens.*)

GAYEV: That's our famous Jewish orchestra. Do you remember? Four violins, a flute, and a double-bass.

LYUBOV ANDREYEVNA: So it's still in existence? We ought to ask them over sometime and have an evening party.

LOPAKHIN (*listening*): I can't hear. . . . (*Humming softly.*) "Germans, if paid well enough, can make Russians Frenchmen." (*Laughs.*) What a funny thing I saw in the theatre yesterday! It was very amusing.

LYUBOV ANDREYEVNA: I'm sure it wasn't a bit funny. You shouldn't go to plays, but observe yourself more closely. What a drab life you live, how many unnecessary things you say!

LOPAKHIN: That's true enough. One must frankly admit that we lead a fool's life. . . . (*Pause.*) My dad was a peasant and a stupid one, he understood nothing, taught me nothing, but only beat me when he was drunk, and always with a stick. And in reality, I am just the same sort of blockhead and idiot that he was. I never studied anything, my handwriting is wretched. I write like a pig—I feel ashamed of it.

LYUBOV ANDREYEVNA: You ought to get married, my dear man.

LOPAKHIN: Yes, that's true.

LYUBOV ANDREYEVNA: And to our Varya? She's a good girl.

LOPAKHIN: True.

LYUBOV ANDREYEVNA: She's a simple-hearted child, she works the whole day long, and most important of all, she loves you. And you—you've liked her for a long time.

LOPAKHIN: Well? I've no objection. . . . She's a good girl. (*Pause.*)

GAYEV: They've offered me a place in the bank. Six thousand a year. . . . Did you hear about it?

LYUBOV ANDREYEVNA: To a man like you! . . . Just sit still. . . .

(FIRS *comes in, carrying an overcoat.*)

FIRS (*to* GAYEV): Please put this on, sir, or you'll feel the dampness.

GAYEV (*putting on the coat*): You're a bother, old man.

FIRS: Never mind. . . . You went off this morning without saying a word to anybody. (*Surveys him.*)

LYUBOV ANDREYEVNA: How old you've grown, Firs!

FIRS: Beg pardon?

LOPAKHIN: She says that you've grown very old.

FIRS: I've lived a long time. They were getting ready to marry me off before your daddy was born. . . . (*Laughs.*) And when the Emancipation came, I was already head valet. I didn't approve of the Emancipation then, I stayed with my masters. . . . (*Pause.*) And I remember, every one was happy, but *why* they were happy they didn't know themselves.

LOPAKHIN: It was fine before the Emancipation, all right. At least, there used to be flogging.

FIRS (*who has not understood him*): Yes, indeed. The peasants for the masters, the masters for the peasants, but now they're all split up. You can't make head or tail of it.

GAYEV: Be quiet, Firs. I've got to go to town to-morrow. They promised to introduce me to some general who may loan us some money on a note.

LOPAKHIN: Nothing will come of it. And you'll not pay your interest—you can depend on that.

LYUBOV ANDREYEVNA: He's talking nonsense. There aren't any generals.

(TROFIMOV, ANYA, *and* VARYA *come in.*)

GAYEV: Here come our people.

ANYA: Mama's sitting out here.

LYUBOV ANDREYEVNA (*tenderly*): Come here, come here, Anya. . . . My dear ones! . . . (*Embracing* ANYA *and* VARYA.) If you only both knew how I love you. Sit down beside me, so. (*They all sit down.*)

LOPAKHIN: Our eternal student is always with the young ladies.

TROFIMOV: That's none of your business.

LOPAKHIN: He'll be fifty pretty soon, but he's still a student.

TROFIMOV: Quit your idiotic jokes.

LOPAKHIN: What are you getting huffy about, you freak?

TROFIMOV: Let me alone.

LOPAKHIN (*laughs*): Well, what do you think of *me*, anyhow, pray tell?

TROFIMOV: Here's what I think of you, Yermolay Alexeich: You are a wealthy man, you'll be a millionaire soon. And just as a ravenous beast that devours everything crossing his path, is necessary to the transmutation of the elements, even so you are necessary. (*All laugh.*)

VARYA: You'd better talk about the planets, Petya.

LYUBOV ANDREYEVNA: No, please, let's continue our discussion of yesterday.

TROFIMOV: What were we discussing?

GAYEV: The proud man.

TROFIMOV: We talked at length yesterday, but we didn't come to any conclusion. There is, in your opinion, something mystical in a proud man. Possibly from your own point of view you are right, but if you reason it out simply, without evasion, what pride can there be, what grounds for pride can exist if a man's physiological structure is of a poor sort, if in the great majority of cases he is crude, stupid, profoundly unhappy? He must moderate his self-admiration. He must apply himself to work alone.

GAYEV: You'll die just the same.

TROFIMOV: Who knows? And what does it mean—to die? Perhaps a man has a hundred senses, and only the five we know are annihilated by death, while the remaining ninety-five continue to live.

LYUBOV ANDREYEVNA: How clever you are, Petya!

LOPAKHIN (*ironically*): Awfully!

TROFIMOV: Humanity advances, perfecting its forces. Everything that is unattainable for it now, will sometime become near and comprehensible; only we must work and help to our fullest ability those who are seeking the truth. Only a few are thus far working among us here in Russia. The vast majority of those intellectuals whom I know, are seeking nothing, do nothing, and are as yet incapable of labor. They call themselves intellectuals, but they speak condescendingly to their servants, and treat the peasants like animals. They are wretched students, they don't read anything seriously, they are utterly idle, they only talk about the sciences, and they understand little about art. They are all solemn, they pull long faces and discuss only portentous matters, they philosophize—but in the meantime the enormous majority of us— ninety-nine out of a hundred—are living like wild beasts, wrangling and fighting at the least pretext We have vile table manners, we sleep in filth, in stifling rooms, there are bedbugs everywhere, stench, dampness, moral impurity. . . . And evidently all our nice conversations have only the purpose of fooling ourselves and others. Show me the day nurseries of which people speak so frequently and at such length, and the reading rooms! Where are they? People only write about them in stories—they really don't exist at all. There's only dirt, vulgarity, Asiatic backwardness. I dislike and fear deeply serious faces, I dread serious conversations. Best to keep silence.

LOPAKHIN: You know, I get up before five o'clock, I work from morning till night. Well, I'm always handling money, my own and other people's, and I observe those around me. You need only start some project of your own to discover how few honorable, decent people there are. Sometimes when I lie in bed awake I think, "Lord, thou hast given us vast forests, boundless fields, remote horizons, and we, living in their midst, should really be giants."

LYUBOV ANDREYEVNA: You want giants? . . . They're only good in fairy tales—they'd frighten you.

(EPIKHODOV *crosses back stage, playing on his guitar.*)

LYUBOV ANDREYEVNA (*thoughtfully*): Epikhodov is coming.

ANYA (*thoughtfully*): Epikhodov is coming.

GAYEV: The sun has set, friends.

TROFIMOV: Yes.

GAYEV (*softly, as though declaiming to himself*): O marvelous Nature, serene and beautiful, thou gleamest with an eternal radiance; thou whom we call our mother unitest within thyself life and death, thou livest and destroyest—

VARYA (*entreatingly*): Uncle dear!

ANYA: Uncle! At it again!

TROFIMOV: You'd better make it, "Yellow across the table to the center."

GAYEV: I'll keep still, I'll keep still.

(*They all sit pondering. Silence. Only the soft muttering of* FIRS *is audible. Suddenly a distant sound, seemingly from the skies, is heard; a melancholy sound, which dies away like the snapping of a violin string.*)

LYUBOV ANDREYEVNA: What's that?

LOPAKHIN: I don't know. Maybe a cable snapped in a shaft somewhere far off. But it was very far away.

GAYEV: Maybe it's a bird—a heron, perhaps.

TROFIMOV: Or an owl.

LYUBOV ANDREYEVNA (*shudders*): It depresses me, somehow.

(*Pause.*)

FIRS: It was the same way before the great misfortune. An owl hooted, and the samovar hissed and hissed.

GAYEV: Before what misfortune?

FIRS: Before the Emancipation.

(*Pause.*)

LYUBOV ANDREYEVNA: Come, my friends. It's growing dark already. (*To* ANYA.) There are tears in your eyes. What's troubling you, little girl? (*Embraces her.*)

ANYA: Never mind, mama. Nothing's the matter.

TROFIMOV: Some one is coming.

(*A* WAYFARER *makes his appearance. He has on a long coat and a worn, white cap. He is a little tipsy.*)

WAYFARER: Pray tell me, does this road lead directly to the station?

GAYEV: Yes. Follow the road.

WAYFARER: I'm deeply grateful to you. (*Coughing.*) It's fine weather. . . . (*Dramatically.*) "My brother, my suffering brother!" . . . "Go to the Volga, whose groan—?" * (*To* VARYA.) Mademoiselle, please give a hungry Russian thirty kopeks. . . .

(VARYA *is frightened, and screams.*)

LOPAKHIN (*angrily*): There's a limit to every sort of impudence!

LYUBOV ANDREYEVNA (*panic-stricken*): Take this. . . . Here it is. . . . (*Searches in her purse.*) There's no silver. . . . Oh well, here's a gold piece for you. . . .

WAYFARER: I'm deeply grateful to you! (*Goes out.*)

(*They all laugh.*)

VARYA (*frightened*): I'm going, I'm going home. Oh, mama dear, there's nothing at home for the servants to eat, and there you gave him a gold piece!

LYUBOV ANDREYEVNA: What's to be done with poor, foolish me? When we get home I'll give you everything I have. Yermolay Alexeich, make me another loan!

LOPAKHIN: Very well.

LYUBOV ANDREYEVNA: Come, friends, it's time to go home. And see here, Varya, we've found a husband for you. I congratulate you!

VARYA (*through her tears*): Please don't joke about it, mama.

LOPAKHIN: Go to a nunnery, Okhmelia!

GAYEV: My hands are trembling. I haven't played pool for a long time.

LOPAKHIN: Okhmelia, nymph, remember me in your prayers!

LYUBOV ANDREYEVNA: Come, every one, we'll have supper soon.

VARYA: He frightened me. My heart's fairly pounding.

LOPAKHIN: Let me remind you, my friends: the cherry orchard will be sold on the twenty-second of August. Think that over! Think that over!

(*They all go out, with the exception of* ANYA *and* TROFIMOV.)

---

* The quotations are from poems by Nadson and by Nekrasov.

ANYA (*laughing*) : We're alone, now, thanks to the wayfarer who frightened Varya.

TROFIMOV: Varya's afraid that we'll suddenly fall in love with each other; and for days on end she hasn't budged from our side. Her trifling little mind cannot comprehend that we are superior to love. To avoid the petty and deluding things that prevent one from being free and happy—this is the aim and significance of our life. Forward! We shall press on irresistibly toward the bright star that shines beyond in the distance! Forward! Do not fall behind, friends!

ANYA (*clapping her hands*) : How splendidly you say it! (*Pause.*) It's marvelous here to-day.

TROFIMOV: Yes, the weather is wonderful.

ANYA: What have you done to me, Petya, that I no longer love the cherry orchard as I did before? I used to love it so tenderly. It seemed to me that there was no place on earth more beautiful than our orchard.

TROFIMOV: All Russia is our orchard. The land is vast and glorious, there are many marvelous places in it. (*Pause.*) Think of it, Anya! Your grandfather, your great-grandfather, and all your ancestors were serf-owners, ruling over living souls. Don't you hear voices and see human beings looking at you from every cherry in the orchard, from every little leaf, from every tree trunk? . . . Oh, it is terrible, your orchard is a fearful place, and when one walks through it in the evening or at night, the ancient bark is lit then with a dull gleam, and the cherry trees seem to be dreaming of things that happened a hundred, two hundred years ago, and grievous visions harass them. What's the use of talking! We are at least two hundred years behind the times, we have nothing of our own, no definite relationship with the past; we do nothing but philosophize, complain of our own unhappiness, or drink vodka. But it's all so clear: in order to begin living in the present, we must first redeem our past, make an end of it. But we may redeem it only through suffering, only through strenuous, constant labor. You must realize this, Anya.

ANYA: The house in which we are living has for a long time ceased to belong to us, and I will go away, I give you my word.

TROFIMOV: If you have the housekeeper's keys, throw them into the well and go away. Be as free as the wind.

ANYA (*in ecstasy*) : How well you said that!

TROFIMOV: Have faith in me, Anya, have faith in me. I am not yet thirty, I am young, I am still a student, but how much I have endured already! I'm as famished as the winter, sick, distraught, poor as a beggar, and wherever fate has driven me, I have gone. But always my soul has been my own; at every moment, day and night it has been filled with inexplicable premonitions. I feel that happiness is on its way, Anya; I already see it. . . .

ANYA (*thoughtfully*) : The moon is rising.

(EPIKHODOV *is heard strumming over and over on the guitar the same melancholy song. The moon rises slowly.* VARYA *is searching for* ANYA *somewhere near the poplars, and calling* "Anya, where are you?")

TROFIMOV: Yes, the moon is rising. (*Pause.*) Ah yes, happiness is coming, drawing ever nearer and nearer. Already I hear its footsteps. And if we do not see it, do not recognize it, what matter? Others will see it!

VARYA's *voice:* Anya! Where are you?

TROFIMOV: It's that Varya again! (*Angrily.*) Exasperating!

ANYA: Never mind. Let's go down to the river. It's nice there.

TROFIMOV: All right. (*They go out.*)

VARYA's *voice:* Anya! Anya!

ACT III

A drawing-room, separated by an arch from the ballroom. A lighted chandelier. The Jewish orchestra—the same orchestra mentioned in the second act—is heard playing in the hall. It is evening. They are dancing the grand rond *in the ballroom. The voice of* SEMEONOV-PISHCHIK *is heard, calling,* "Promenade à une paire!" PISHCHIK *and* CHARLOTTA IVANOVNA *are the first couple to enter the drawing-room;* TROFIMOV *and* LYUBOV ANDREYEVNA *follow; then* ANYA *and the* POST OFFICE OFFICIAL, *then* VARYA *and the* STATION MASTER, *and so on.* VARYA *is weeping softly, wiping away her tears as she dances.* DUNYASHA *and her partner form the last couple. They circle around the drawing-room.* PISHCHIK *cries out,* "Grand rond, balancez!" *and then,* "Les cavaliers à genoux, et remerciez vos dames!"

FIRS, *wearing a dress coat, is carrying about a tray with seltzer water.* PISHCHIK *and* TROFIMOV *reënter the drawing-room.*

PISHCHIK: I'm full-blooded, I've had two strokes already, it's hard for me to dance, but, as the saying goes, "If you join the pack and cannot bay, wag your tail, anyway!" I have the constitution of a horse. My dear father—may he rest in peace—was a great joker, and he used to say in speaking of our ancestry, that the ancient stock of the Semeonov-Pishchiks was descended from the identical horse appointed senator by Caligula. . . . (*Sits down.*) But here's the pity of it; I've no money! A hungry dog believes only in meat. . . . (*Snores, and suddenly rouses himself.*)   And so I, too . . . can think of nothing but money. . . .

TROFIMOV: True, there really is something about you that reminds one of a horse.

PISHCHIK: Well . . . a horse is a good beast. . . . You can sell a horse. . . .

(*The click of billiard balls is heard in the next room.* VARYA *appears in the hall under the archway.*)

TROFIMOV (*teasingly*) : Madam Lopakhin! Madam Lopakhin!

VARYA (*angrily*) : Gentleman-gone-to-seed!

TROFIMOV: Yes, I'm a gentleman gone to seed, and I'm proud of it!

VARYA (*musing bitterly*) : We've hired musicians, but who's going to pay them? (*Goes out.*)

TROFIMOV (*to* PISHCHIK) : If the energy you've wasted all your life digging up money to pay interest, had been directed to something else, I believe that eventually you could have turned the world upside down.

PISHCHIK: Nietzsche, the philosopher . . . most noted . . . most famous . . . a man of vast intellect, says in his books that one can make counterfeit money.

TROFIMOV: Have you read Nietzsche then?

PISHCHIK: Bah! Dashenka told me about him. But things have come to such a pass with me now, that I'd even make counterfeit money. . . . Day after to-morrow I must pay out three hundred and ten rubles. . . . I've scraped together a hundred and thirty already. . . . (*Feels through his pockets excitedly.*) It's gone! I've lost my money! (*In tears.*) Where's my money? . . . (*Joyfully.*) Here it is, under the lining. . . . Why, that raised a sweat on me! . . .

(LYUBOV ANDREYEVNA *and* CHARLOTTA IVANOVNA *come in.*)

LYUBOV ANDREYEVNA (*humming a Caucasian air*) : Why is Leonid so long in coming? What is he doing in town? (*To* DUNYASHA.) Dunyasha, give the musicians some tea.

TROFIMOV: Most likely the auction wasn't held.

LYUBOV ANDREYEVNA: And so we needn't have asked the musicians to come, and there was no reason for planning a ball. . . . Well, no matter. . . . (*She sits down and hums softly.*)

CHARLOTTA (*handing* PISHCHIK *a pack of cards*) : Here's a pack of cards. Think of a card.

PISHCHIK: I've thought of one.

CHARLOTTA: Now, shuffle the pack. Very good. Give it to me, my dear Mr. Pishchik. *Ein, zwei, drei!* Take a look now—it's in your hip pocket. . . .

PISHCHIK (*takes a card out of his hip pocket*) : The eight of spades. Quite right! (*In astonishment.*) Just think of that!

CHARLOTTA (*holding the pack of cards in her hands and speaking to* TROFIMOV) : Tell me quick! What's the top card?

TROFIMOV: Eh? Why, the queen of spades.

CHARLOTTA: Right! (*To* PISHCHIK.) Well, what's the top card?

PISHCHIK: The ace of hearts.

CHARLOTTA: Right! (*Claps her hands, and the pack of cards disappears.*) But what fine weather we've had to-day! (*A mysterious voice —a woman's—coming as though from beneath the floor, answers her:* "Oh yes, the weather is splendid, madam.") You are charming—my ideal type of person. . . . (*Voice:* "And I likes you fery much too, Madam.")

STATION MASTER (*applauding*) : Bravo, Madam Ventriloquist, bravo!

PISHCHIK (*in amazement*) : Just think of that! Most enchanting Charlotta Ivanovna! . . . I'm fairly in love with you! . . .

CHARLOTTA: In love? (*Shrugging her shoulders.*) Can you really love? *Guter Mensch, aber schlechter Musikant.*

TROFIMOV (*clapping* PISHCHIK *on the shoulder*) : What a horse you are!

CHARLOTTA: Attention, please! Here's another trick. (*Takes a steamer rug from a chair.*) Here's a very good rug, I want to sell it. . . . (*Shakes it.*) Doesn't some one want to buy it?

PISHCHIK (*in amazement*) : Just think of that!

CHARLOTTA: *Ein, zwei, drei!* (*She raises the rug quickly, behind it stands* ANYA. *She makes a low curtsey, runs over to her mother, embraces her, and flies back to the drawing-room amid general delight.*)

LYUBOV ANDREYEVNA (*applauding*) : Bravo, bravo!

CHARLOTTA: Once more now. *Ein, zwei, drei!* (*Raises the rug; behind it stands* VARYA, *bowing.*)

PISHCHIK (*marveling*) : Just think of that!

CHARLOTTA: That's all! (*She throws the rug over* PISHCHIK, *makes a low curtsey, and runs into the ballroom.*)

PISHCHIK (*hurrying after her*) : Rascal! . . . You would then? You would? (*Goes out.*)

LYUBOV ANDREYEVNA: And Leonid's not come yet. What's he doing in the city to keep him so long? I don't understand it. Why, everything must be finished there by now; the estate is sold, or else the sale didn't take place. Why must we be kept so long in ignorance?

VARYA (*trying to console her*) : Uncle has bought it, I'm sure.

TROFIMOV (*mockingly*) : Oh, yes!

VARYA: Auntie gave him authority to buy it in her name and transfer the debt. She did it for Anya. And I'm convinced that with God's help uncle will buy it.

LYUBOV ANDREYEVNA: Our aunt in Yaroslav sent fifteen thousand rubles with which to purchase the estate in her name—she doesn't trust us—but that sum wouldn't be enough even to pay the interest. (*Covers her face with her hands.*) To-day my fate is decided . . . my fate . . .

TROFIMOV (*teasing* VARYA): Madam Lopakhin!

VARYA (*angrily*): Eternal student! He's been expelled from the University twice already.

LYUBOV ANDREYEVNA: Why do you lose your temper, Varya? He's teasing you about Lopakhin—well, what of it? Marry Lopakhin if you want to, he's a nice, good man. If you don't want to, don't marry him. No one is forcing you, dear.

VARYA: To be frank, mother dear, I do regard this matter seriously. He's a good man, I like him.

LYUBOV ANDREYEVNA: Well then, marry him. I don't understand what you're waiting for.

VARYA: I surely can't propose to him myself, mama. Every one has been talking to me about him for two years, but he either says nothing or jokes. I understand. He's making money, taken up with business. He hasn't time for me. If I had some money, even a little, even a hundred rubles, I'd give up everything and go far away. I'd enter a convent.

TROFIMOV: Magnificent!

VARYA (*to* TROFIMOV): A student ought to have some sense! (*Softly, and weeping.*) How old and ugly you've grown, Petya! (*To* LYUBOV ANDREYEVNA, *drying her tears.*) Only I can't stand it to be idle, mama. I must have something to do every minute.

(YASHA *comes in.*)

YASHA (*with difficulty restraining his laughter*): Epikhodov has broken a billiard cue! . . . (*Goes out.*)

VARYA: And why is Epikhodov in here? Who gave him permission to play pool? I don't understand these people. . . . (*Goes out.*)

LYUBOV ANDREYEVNA: Don't tease her, Petya. You can see she's unhappy enough without it.

TROFIMOV: She takes a lot of pains minding other people's business. All summer she's given Anya and me no peace. She was afraid a romance might spring up between us. What business is it of hers? And moreover, I gave her no occasion—I am beyond such vulgarity. We are superior to love.

LYUBOV ANDREYEVNA: Then I must be inferior to love. (*Deeply agitated.*) Why isn't Leonid here? If only I knew whether the estate had been sold or not! The catastrophe seems so incredible to me that I don't even know what to think. I'm losing my mind. . . . I may cry out or do some idiotic thing. Help me, Petya; say something, do! . . .

TROFIMOV: Isn't it all the same whether or no the estate is sold to-day? The matter's been settled for a long time; there is no turning back, the path is overgrown. Be calm, my dear friend, no need to deceive yourself. For once in your life at least, you must look truth straight in the eyes.

LYUBOV ANDREYEVNA: What truth? You can see where truth and falsehood lie, but I have quite lost that vision, I see nothing. You settle all important questions boldly, but tell me, my dear boy, is this not because you are young, because you haven't had time to put to painful test a single one of your questions? You look bravely forward—but isn't it because you do not see nor expect any terrible thing, inasmuch as life is still concealed from your young eyes? You are more fearless, more honest, more profound than we, but take thought for a moment, be a tiny bit magnanimous, and have pity on me. You see, I was born here, my father and mother lived here, and my grandfather too. I love this house; without the cherry orchard life is meaningless to me, and if it must be sold now, why then, you must sell me along with the orchard. . . . (*Embraces* TROFIMOV *and kisses him on the forehead.*) You see, my son was drowned here. . . . (*Weeps.*) Pity me, my good, kind friend.

TROFIMOV: You know that I sympathize with all my heart.

LYUBOV ANDREYEVNA: But you must say it differently, differently. (*Takes out her handkerchief and a telegram falls to the floor.*) You cannot imagine how heavy my heart is to-day. Things are so noisy and confusing, my very being shudders at every sound, I quiver all over, but I can't go off by myself—when I'm alone the silence terrifies me. Do not condemn me, Petya. I love you as though you belonged to my own family. I would gladly let Anya marry you, I swear it. Only, my dear boy, you must study, you must finish your course. You aren't doing anything but let fate bear you from place to place, strange as that may seem. . . . Isn't it so? And you simply must do something with your beard to make it grow decently. (*Laughs.*) You're so funny!

TROFIMOV (*picks up the telegram*): I don't want to be a dandy.

LYUBOV ANDREYEVNA: That's a telegram from Paris. Every day I receive one. That wild man is sick again and in trouble. He asks forgiveness, begs me to come to him; and really, I ought to go to Paris to be near him. Your face is stern, Petya, but what can I do, my dear? What can I do? He is sick, he is alone, unhappy, and who is there to look after him, who will keep him from making mistakes, and give him his medicine at the right time? And why should I keep silence or conceal anything? I love him, that is clear to me. I love him, I love him. . . . This is the stone around my neck, I shall sink with it into the depths, but I love this stone and I cannot live without it. (*Presses* TROFIMOV's *hand.*) Don't think ill of me, Petya; don't say anything to me, don't say . . .

TROFIMOV (*through his tears*): Forgive my bluntness, for God's sake—but he robbed you!

LYUBOV ANDREYEVNA: No, no, no, you mustn't say that. . . . (*Covers her ears.*)

TROFIMOV: Why, he's a rascal—you're the only one who doesn't realize it. He's a petty thief, a good-for-nothing . . .

LYUBOV ANDREYEVNA (*restrained, but angry*): You're twenty-six or seven now, but you're still a high school sophomore!

TROFIMOV: Well?

LYUBOV ANDREYEVNA: You should be a man, at your age you should understand those who love. And you should be in love yourself . . . you must fall in love! (*Angrily.*) Yes, yes! And you're not virtuous, you're only a prude, a sort of freak and monstrosity. . . .

TROFIMOV (*horrified*): What is she saying?

LYUBOV ANDREYEVNA: "I am superior to love!" You're not superior to love, you're only what our Firs always calls a "lummox." To think of not having a mistress at your age!

TROFIMOV (*horrified*): This is horrible! What is she saying! (*He walks quickly into the ballroom, clutching his head.*) This is horrible! I can't listen, I'll go away. . . . (*He goes out but returns immediately.*) Everything is over between us! (*Goes out into the hall.*)

LYUBOV ANDREYEVNA (*calling after him*): Petya, wait! Foolish man, I was joking! Petya!

(*Some one is heard quickly ascending the stairway in the hall, then all of a sudden loudly falling downstairs. ANYA and VARYA scream, but immediately laughter is heard.*)

LYUBOV ANDREYEVNA: What's the matter out there?

(ANYA *runs in.*)

ANYA (*laughing*): Petya fell downstairs! (*She runs out.*)

LYUBOV ANDREYEVNA: That Petya's a funny boy.

(*The* STATION MASTER *stops in the middle of the ballroom and begins to recite Alexey Tolstoy's "The Magdalen." The others listen to him, but after a few stanzas the strains of a waltz are borne in from the hallway, and the recitation breaks off. They all dance.* TROFIMOV, ANYA, VARYA, *and* LYUBOV ANDREYEVNA *come back from the hall-way.*)

LYUBOV ANDREYEVNA: Well, Petya . . . well, pure soul. . . . I beg your forgiveness. . . . Come, let's dance. . . . (*She and* PETYA *dance.*)

(ANYA *and* VARYA *dance together.* FIRS *comes in and leans his stick up near the side door.* YASHA *has also entered from the dining-room and is watching the dancing.*)

YASHA: What's the matter, grandfather?

FIRS: I'm not well. In the old days generals, admirals and barons used to dance at our balls, and now we send for the postal official and the station master, and even they don't come very graciously. I'm not as strong as I used to be. My dead master, their grandfather, used to cure everybody of every disease with sealing wax. I've been taking sealing wax every day for twenty years now, and maybe more; maybe that's what's kept me alive.

YASHA: You make me tired, grandfather. (*Yawns.*) It's time you croaked.

FIRS: Eh, you lummox! . . . (*Mutters.*)

(TROFIMOV *and* LYUBOV ANDREYEVNA *are dancing in the ballroom; then they pass into the drawing-room.*)

LYUBOV ANDREYEVNA: *Merci!* I think I'll sit down. . . . (*Seats herself.*) I'm tired.

(ANYA *comes in.*)

ANYA (*excitedly*): Some man just told them in the kitchen that the cherry orchard was sold to-day.

LYUBOV ANDREYEVNA: Sold to whom?

ANYA: He didn't say to whom. He went away. (*She dances off with* TROFIMOV *into the ballroom.*)

YASHA: Some old fellow was gossiping about it a while ago. A stranger.

FIRS: And Leonid Andreich hasn't come yet. He was wearing a lightweight overcoat. He'd better look out or he'll catch cold. Eh, these green young things!

LYUBOV ANDREYEVNA: I shall die this very minute! Go, Yasha, and find out who's bought it.

YASHA: The old man's been gone a long time. (*Laughs.*)

LYUBOV ANDREYEVNA (*somewhat annoyed*): Well, what are you laughing at? What are you so happy about?

YASHA: Epikhodov's very amusing. A stupid fellow. Two-and-twenty troubles.

LYUBOV ANDREYEVNA: Firs, if they sell the estate, where will you go?

FIRS: I will go wherever you command.

LYUBOV ANDREYEVNA: Why do you look so strange? Are you sick? You ought to go to bed.

FIRS: Yes. . . . (*With a grimace.*) I'd go to bed, but when I'm gone, who'll hand things around and manage everything? The whole house depends on me.

YASHA (*to* LYUBOV ANDREYEVNA) : Lyubov Andreyevna, permit me to make a request. Be so good! If you go back to Paris, kindly take me with you! It's absolutely impossible for me to remain here. (*In a low voice and looking around him.*) What's the use of talking? You can see for yourself, it's an uncivilized country, the people are immoral, and besides that, it's dull, they give you wretched food in the kitchen, and that Firs is always walking around muttering all kinds of stupidities. Please do take me with you!

(PISHCHIK *comes in.*)

PISHCHIK: May I ask you . . . most lovely lady . . . for a little waltz? . . . (LYUBOV ANDREYEVNA *dances off with him.*) Bewitching one, I'm going to borrow a hundred and eighty little rubles from you, I'm going to borrow . . . (*Dancing.*) a hundred and eighty little rubles. . . . (*They pass out into the ballroom.*)

YASHA (*humming softly*) : "Oh, canst thou comprehend the tumult of my soul?"

(*Out in the ballroom a figure in a gray top hat and checkered pantaloons waves its arms and jumps about; cries of "Bravo, Charlotta Ivanovna!"*)

DUNYASHA (*stopping to powder her nose*) : My young mistress told me to come in and dance. There are many gentlemen, and only a few ladies, but my head whirls when I dance, my heart beats, Firs Nikolayevich, and the post office clerk just said something to me that quite took my breath away.

(*The music stops.*)

FIRS: What did he say to you?

DUNYASHA: "You're like a flower," says he.

YASHA (*yawns*) : The bumpkin! . . . (*Goes out.*)

DUNYASHA: Like a little flower. . . . I'm such a delicate girl, I just love tender words.

FIRS: You'll lose your head.

(EPIKHODOV *comes in.*)

EPIKHODOV: You refuse to look at me, Avdotya Fedorovna . . . as if I were a sort of insect. . . . (*Sighing.*) Ah, well, that's life!

DUNYASHA: What do you want?

EPIKHODOV: Of course, you're probably right. (*Sighs.*) But then, if you want to regard it from this point of view, it's you, if you'll pardon my bluntness, who have brought me to such a pass. I know my fate. Every day some misfortune befalls me, and I've long since grown so accustomed to it that I smile at my fate. You gave me your promise, and though I—

DUNYASHA: Please let's talk later and leave me in peace now. I'm musing. (*Plays with her fan.*)

EPIKHODOV: Every day a mishap befalls me, and I—if I may say so—only smile, I even laugh.

(VARYA *comes in from the hall.*)

VARYA: Haven't you gone yet, Semen? What a presuming fellow you are, anyway. (*To* DUNYASHA.) Leave the room, Dunyasha. (*To* EPIKHODOV.) First you play billiards and break a cue, and then you swagger around in the drawing-room as though you were a guest.

EPIKHODOV: You can't expect much of me, if I may say so.

VARYA: I'm not expecting much of you, I'm just telling you the truth. All you know how to do is to walk from place to place, but you don't tend to your business. We keep a clerk, but goodness knows what for!

EPIKHODOV (*offended*): Only my elders and people who know what they're talking about can pass judgment as to whether I work, or walk, or eat, or play pool.

VARYA: You dare speak to me so? (*Flying into a passion.*) You dare? You mean to imply that I don't know what I'm talking about? Get out of here! This instant!

EPIKHODOV (*cringing*): Speak more politely, I beg you.

VARYA (*beside herself*): Get out of here this instant! Out! (*He goes towards the door, she following him.*) Two-and-twenty troubles! Don't let me set eyes on you again! Go away and stay! (EPIKHODOV *goes out. His voice comes back from outside the door:* "I'll call you to account for this.") What, coming back? (*She snatches up the stick* FIRS *has left earlier near the door.*) Come on, then, come on, come on, I'll show you! Well, are you coming? Are you coming? Then take that! . . . (*She deals a blow with the stick just as* LOPAKHIN *enters.*)

LOPAKHIN: I thank you humbly.

VARYA (*angrily and mockingly*): I beg your pardon.

LOPAKHIN: Don't mention it. I thank you humbly for a pleasant welcome.

VARYA: It deserves no appreciation. (*She moves away, then looks back and asks softly.*) I didn't hurt you, did I?

LOPAKHIN: Oh no, that's all right. All the same, there'll be a big bump.

VOICE (*in the hall*): Lopakhin's come! Yermolay Alexeyevich!

PISHCHIK: We'll see with our eyes and hear with our ears! (*Exchanges kisses with* LOPAKHIN.) You smell of cognac, my dear fellow. Well, we've been having a jolly time here too.

(LYUBOV ANDREYEVNA *comes in.*)

LYUBOV ANDREYEVNA: So it's you, Yermolay Alexeich? Why were you so long? Where's Leonid?

LOPAKHIN: Leonid Andreich returned with me, he'll be in directly. . . .

LYUBOV ANDREYEVNA (*excitedly*): Well, what happened? Did the sale take place? Do tell us!

LOPAKHIN (*in confusion and fearing to show his joy*): The sale was over at four o'clock. . . . We missed the train and had to wait until half past nine. (*Sighing deeply.*) Uh! I'm a little bit dizzy. . . .

(GAYEV *comes in. His right arm is full of bundles; with his left hand he wipes away his tears.*)

LYUBOV ANDREYEVNA: Lenya, what's happened? Come, Lenya? (*Impatiently, through her tears.*) Quickly, for God's sake! . . .

GAYEV (*he does not answer her but only gestures; then to* FIRS, *weeping*): Come, take these things. . . . Here are anchovies, Crimean herring. . . . I haven't eaten a thing to-day. . . . What I've been through! (*The door into the billiard room is open; one can hear the click of balls and* YASHA's *voice saying,* "Seven and eighteen!" GAYEV's *expression changes, he stops weeping.*) I'm terribly tired. Help me change my clothes, Firs. (*Goes into his own room across the hall,* FIRS *following him.*)

PISHCHIK: What happened? Please tell us.

LYUBOV ANDREYEVNA: Was the cherry orchard sold?

LOPAKHIN: Yes.

LYUBOV ANDREYEVNA: Who bought it?

LOPAKHIN: *I* bought it.

(*Pause.* LYUBOV ANDREYEVNA *is stunned. She would fall were she not leaning against the table and the armchair.* VARYA *takes the bunch of keys from her belt, throws them into the middle of the drawing-room floor, and goes out.*)

LOPAKHIN: *I* bought it! Wait a little, ladies and gentlemen, have patience, my head's swimming, I can't talk. . . . (*Laughs.*) When we arrived at the auction, Deriganov was already there. Leonid Andreich had on hand only fifteen thousand, while Deriganov immediately bid thirty thousand above the amount of the mortgage. I saw I was going to have a tussle with him, and bid forty. He raised to forty-five. I bid fifty-five. So he kept raising me five and I raised him ten. . . . Well, it was over at last. I offered ninety thousand over the mortgage, and it went to me. The cherry orchard's mine now! Mine! (*Roars with laughter.*) O Lord my God, the cherry orchard's mine! Tell me I'm drunk, out of my head, or dreaming. . . . (*Stamps his feet.*) Don't laugh at me! If only my father and grandfather could rise from their graves and see all these things that have come to pass—how their Yermolay, beaten, illiterate little Yermolay, who used to go barefoot in the winter, has bought an estate—the most beautiful one in the world! I have bought the estate where my father and grandfather were slaves, where they weren't allowed even to set foot in the kitchen. I'm asleep, this is only a dream, an hallucination. . . . This is the fruit of my imagination, veiled with the mist of uncertainty. . . . (*Picks up the keys with a caressing smile.*) She threw away the keys, she wants to show that she's no longer housekeeper here. . . . (*Jingles the keys.*) Well, no matter! . . . (*The orchestra is heard tuning up.*) Come, musicians, play, I want to hear you! Come, every one, and watch Yermolay Lopakhin swing his ax through the cherry orchard, see the trees fall to the ground! We'll build cottages here, and our grandsons and great-grandsons will see a new life arising here. . . . Let the music play!

(*Music.* LYUBOV ANDREYEVNA *falls into a chair and weeps bitterly.*)

LOPAKHIN (*reproachfully*): Why, oh, why didn't you listen to me? My poor, dear friend, you cannot return to your home now. (*Weeping.*) Ah, if only this might swiftly pass by, if only we might swiftly change this unhappy, incoherent life of ours!

PISHCHIK (*in a low voice, taking him by the arm*): She is weeping. Let us go into the ballroom and leave her alone. . . . Come on! . . . (*Takes him by the arm and leads him into the ballroom.*)

LOPAKHIN: What's the matter? Mind your notes, musicians! Let my wishes be obeyed. (*With irony.*) The new proprietor is coming, the lord of the cherry orchard! (*He unexpectedly bumps against a table, almost upsetting the candelabra.*) I can pay for everything! (*He goes out with* PISHCHIK.)

(*The ballroom and the drawing-room are empty save for* LYUBOV ANDREYEVNA, *who is huddled in her chair, weeping bitterly. The music plays softly.* ANYA *and* TROFIMOV *come in quickly.* ANYA *goes over to her mother and kneels before her.* TROFIMOV *remains near the ballroom door.*)

ANYA: Mama! . . . Mama, are you crying? My dear, good, kind mama, my beautiful mama, I love you. . . . I bless you. The cherry orchard is sold, it is gone, that is true, true, but don't cry, mama. Your life to come is left you, your good, pure soul is left you. . . . Come with me, come away with me, darling, come away! . . . We'll plant a new orchard, a more beautiful one; you shall see it, shall understand it; and joy, deep and quiet, shall descend upon your soul like the evening sunlight, and you will smile again, mama. Come, darling, come!

ACT IV

The same as in Act I. There are no curtains at the windows, no pictures; a little furniture remains, which has been piled in one corner, apparently to be sold. There is a feeling of emptiness. Trunks, strapped bundles, etc., are piled near the outside door and back stage. The door to the left is open, and through it may be heard the voices of ANYA *and* VARYA. LOPAKHIN *is standing in the room, waiting.* YASHA *is holding a tray with glasses filled with champagne.* EPIKHODOV *is roping a box in the entry-way. There is a droning behind scenes—the voices of the peasants who have come to say good-by.* GAYEV'S *voice is heard, saying,* "Thank you, my lads, thank you."

YASHA: The peasants have come to say good-by. It's my opinion, Yermolay Alexeich, that the peasants are a good lot, but unintelligent.

(*The voices die away.* LYUBOV ANDREYEVNA *and* GAYEV *come in through the hall. She is not weeping, but her face is pale and quivering. She cannot speak.*)

GAYEV: You gave them your purse, Lyuba. You mustn't do such things, you must not.

LYUBOV ANDREYEVNA: I couldn't help myself! I couldn't help it! (*They both go out.*)

LOPAKHIN (*calling after them from the doorway*): Please, I beg of you! Come and have a farewell glass. I forgot to bring any from town, and I could only find one bottle at the station. Please do! (*Pause.*) Don't you really want any? (*Moves away from the door.*) If I'd only known, I wouldn't have bought it. Well, then, I shan't drink any either. (YASHA *places the tray carefully on a chair.*) Yasha, you have a drink anyway!

YASHA: To the departing! Good luck to them! (*Drinks.*) This isn't real champagne, I can tell you that.

LOPAKHIN: It's eight rubles a bottle. (*Pause.*) It's cold as the devil here.

YASHA: We didn't build any fires to-day—it's all the same, we're going away. (*Laughs.*)

LOPAKHIN: Why are you laughing?

YASHA: Because I'm happy.

LOPAKHIN: Here it is October, but it's as quiet and sunny as though it were summer. Good building weather. (*Glances at his watch and calls through the door.*) Well, ladies and gentlemen, remember, it's just forty-seven minutes before train time. That means you must leave for the station in twenty minutes. Hurry up!

(TROFIMOV, *wearing an overcoat, comes in from outside.*)

TROFIMOV: I think it's time to go now. The horses have been brought around . Where the devil are my galoshes? They're lost. . . . (*Calls through the doorway.*) Anya, I can't find my galoshes. They're gone!

LOPAKHIN: I've got to go to Harkov. I'll take the same train you do. I shall spend the whole winter in Harkov. I've been frittering away my time with you people, I'm miserable without work. I can't live without something to do. I don't know what to do with my hands. They fidget around as though they belonged to some one else.

TROFIMOV: We'll be gone soon, and you can turn to your useful labors again.

LOPAKHIN: Have a glass, do.

TROFIMOV: No, thank you.

LOPAKHIN: So you're going on to Moscow now?

TROFIMOV: Yes, I'll accompany them as far as town, and then to-morrow I'll go on to Moscow.

LOPAKHIN: Yes. . . . I suppose the professors are holding up their lectures, every one will wait until you get there!

TROFIMOV: That's none of your business.

LOPAKHIN: How many years have you been studying at the University?

TROFIMOV: Think up a new question. That one's old and worn. (*Looking for his galoshes.*) You know, we probably shan't see each other again, so permit me to give you one parting bit of advice: Don't flourish your hands so! Break yourself of that habit of flourishing. And then too—all this building of cottages and figuring that in time their tenants will become land-owners—that's just another way of flourishing your hands. But for all that, I like you just the same. You have slender, delicate fingers like those of an artist; you have a slender, delicate soul. . . .

LOPAKHIN (*embracing him*): Good-by, my dear fellow. Thank you for everything. If you need money for your trip, let me lend you some.

TROFIMOV: I don't need any.

LOPAKHIN: But you have none!

TROFIMOV: Oh yes, thank you. I received some for a translation. Here it is, in my pocket. (*Anxiously.*) But I can't find my galoshes!

VARYA (*from the other room*): Here, take your rubbish! (*Throws a pair of rubber galoshes out on the stage.*)

TROFIMOV: Why are you so angry, Varya? Hm. . . . Those aren't my galoshes.

LOPAKHIN: Last spring I sowed three thousand acres to poppies, and now I've cleared forty thousand on them. And when my poppies were in bloom, what a picture it was! As I was saying, I made forty thousand clear, and I'm offering you a loan because I'm able to. Why turn up your nose at me? I'm a peasant—a plain, blunt fellow.

TROFIMOV: Your father was a peasant, mine an apothecary, and that fact is of no consequence whatever. (LOPAKHIN *takes out his wallet.*) Hold on there, hold on—if you gave me two hundred thousand I wouldn't take it. I am a free man; and everything which you all, rich and poor alike, value so highly and dearly, has not the slightest power over me, even as thistledown borne upon the breeze. I can get along without you, I can pass you by. I am strong and proud. Humanity is moving towards the highest truth, towards the highest happiness attainable on earth; and I am in the front ranks.

LOPAKHIN: Shall you get there?

TROFIMOV: I shall. (*Pause.*) I shall get there, or else I will show others the road whereby they may arrive.

(*The sound of an ax striking against wood is heard in the distance.*)

LOPAKHIN: Well, good-by, my dear fellow. It's time to go. Here we stand chaffing each other, but life goes on just the same. When I work without stopping for a long time, then my thoughts grow clearer somehow, and it seems as though I too knew the reason for my existence. But how many people there are in Russia, brother, who do not know why they are alive! Oh, well—the world wags on just the same. They say Leonid Andreich has taken a position in a bank, six thousand a year. . . . Only you know he won't stay there, he's very lazy.

ANYA (*in the doorway*): Mama asks you please not to let them cut down the orchard before she goes.

TROFIMOV: Really, haven't you the consideration to . . . (*He goes out through the hall.*)

LOPAKHIN: Right away . . . right away. . . . What people! . . . (*Follows him out.*)

ANYA: Has Firs been taken to the hospital?

YASHA: I told them to this morning. They must have taken him.

ANYA (*to* EPIKHODOV, *who is passing through the hall*): Semen Panteleich, please find out if Firs has been taken to the hospital.

YASHA (*offended*): I told Yegor this morning. Why do you have to ask about it a dozen times!

EPIKHODOV: It's my firm opinion that that superannuated Firs isn't worth repairs. It's time he joined his forefathers. I can only envy him. (*Puts a trunk down on top of a hat box and crushes it.*) Well, of course, that had to happen—I knew it! (*Goes out.*)

YASHA (*mockingly*): Two-and-twenty troubles. . . .

VARYA (*outside the door*): Have they taken Firs to the hospital?

ANYA: Yes.

VARYA: Why didn't they take the letter to the doctor?

ANYA: We'll have to send it after him. (*Goes out.*)

VARYA (*from the next room*): Where's Yasha? Tell him that his mother has come and wants to say good-by to him.

YASHA (*waves his hand*): She bothers me to death!

(*All this time* DUNYASHA *has been bustling about the baggage. Now that* YASHA *is alone on the stage, she approaches him.*)

DUNYASHA: You might look at me just once more, Yasha. You're going away . . . leaving me. . . . (*She bursts into tears and falls on his neck.*)

YASHA: What's the use of crying? (*Drinks champagne.*) In six days I'll be back in Paris again. To-morrow we'll take the express and roll along so fast they can hardly see us flying by. I can scarcely believe it. Veev la France! . . . I don't like it here, I can't live here. . . . There's nothing to do. I have looked my fill at ignorance—that's enough for me. (*Drinks champagne.*) What's the use of crying? Act like a lady, then you won't cry.

DUNYASHA (*glancing in the mirror and powdering her nose*): Write me a letter from Paris. You know I've loved you, Yasha—oh, how I've loved you! I'm a tender little creature, Yasha.

YASHA: They're coming. (*Bustles around the trunks, humming softly.*)

(LYUBOV ANDREYEVNA, GAYEV, ANYA, *and* CHARLOTTA IVANOVNA *come in.*)

GAYEV: We ought to be on our way. Time's short. (*Glancing at* YASHA.) Who is it smells of herring around here?

LYUBOV ANDREYEVNA: In ten minutes we shall be sitting in the carriage. . . . (*Surveys the room.*) Good-by, dear house, old grandfather! The winter will pass, spring will return, and then you'll be here no longer, they will tear you down. How many things these walls have seen! (*Kisses her daughter warmly.*) My treasure, you are radiant, your eyes are dancing like two diamonds. Are you happy? Very?

ANYA: Very. A new life is beginning, mama!

GAYEV (*cheerfully*): Indeed, everything is all right now. Before the cherry orchard was sold, we were all restless, unhappy; but now that the question has been definitely and irrevocably settled, we have all become calm and even cheerful. I'm a bank official now, I'm a financier. . . . Yellow into the middle! While you, Lyuba, somehow look better, no doubt of it.

LYUBOV ANDREYEVNA: Yes, my nerves are quieter, that's true. (*Some one hands her her hat and coat.*) I'm sleeping well. Carry my bags out, Yasha. It's time to go. (*To* ANYA.) My little girl, we shall see each other soon. . . . I am going to Paris, I shall live there

on the money your great-aunt from Yaroslavl sent to buy the estate
—long life to auntie!—but that money won't last long.

ANYA: You'll come back very, very soon, won't you, mama? I'll
study to pass the high school examinations, and then I'll work and
help you. We'll read so many books together, mama . . . won't we?
(*Kisses her mother's hands.*) We'll read on the autumn evenings, lots
of books, and a wonderful new world will open up before us. . . .
(*Dreamily.*) Be sure to come, mama.

LYUBOV ANDREYEVNA: I will come back, my treasure. (*Embraces
ANYA.*)

(LOPAKHIN *comes in.* CHARLOTTA *is singing softly.*)

GAYEV: Happy Charlotta! She is singing!

CHARLOTTA (*picking up a bundle shaped like a swaddled baby*):
Bye-o-bye, my baby. . . . (*A child's cry is heard:* "Wah! wah!") Keep
quiet, my darling, my nice boy! ("Wah! wah!") Oh, too bad, too
bad! (*Tosses the bundle back to its place.*) Please find a situation
for me, I can't manage otherwise.

LOPAKHIN: We'll find one for you, Charlotta Ivanovna, don't you
worry.

GAYEV: They're all leaving us. Varya's going away. . . . All of a
sudden, nobody needs us.

CHARLOTTA: I've no place to live in town. I'll have to leave you.
. . . (*Hums.*) Oh, well! . . .

(PISHCHIK *comes in.*)

LOPAKHIN: Nature's miracle!

PISHCHIK (*panting*): Oh, let me get my breath! I'm all worn
out! Most dear and honored friends—give me some water. . . .

GAYEV: You've come after money, I suppose? Your humble servant! . . . But just the same I'm going to flee temptation. (*Goes
out.*)

PISHCHIK: I haven't been to see you for a long time, most lovely
lady. . . . (*To* LOPAKHIN.) So you're here. . . . I'm glad to see
you . . . man of vast intellect. . . . Here, take this. . . . (*Hands
LOPAKHIN *some money.*) Four hundred rubles. . . . Eight hundred
and forty left on my account. . . .

LOPAKHIN (*shrugging his shoulders in bewilderment*): I'm dreaming. . . . Where did you get it?

PISHCHIK: Wait a minute. . . . I'm too warm. . . . A most unusual circumstance. Some Englishmen came to see me and found
some white clay on my land. . . . (*To* LYUBOV ANDREYEVNA.) And
four hundred for you . . . most beautiful and marvelous lady. . . .
(*Hands her the money.*) I'll have the rest for you later. (*Drinks
some water.*) A young man told me on the train just a little while ago

how some great philosopher or other told a man how to jump off roofs. . . . "Just jump!" says he, and that's all there is to it. (*In wonderment.*) Just think of that! Water!

LOPAKHIN: But who are these Englishmen?

PISHCHIK: I've leased them the piece of land with the clay for twenty-four years. . . . But excuse me, I haven't time to tell you about it now. . . . I've got to hurry on. . . . I'm going to see Znoykov . . . and Kardamonov. . . . I'm in debt to every one. . . . (*Drinks.*) Your health! . . . I'll call in on Thursday. . . .

LYUBOV ANDREYEVNA: We're just leaving for the city, and to-morrow I'm going abroad.

PISHCHIK: What? (*In alarm.*) Why are you going to town? Ah, now I see the furniture . . . the trunks. . . . Well, no matter. . . . (*Through his tears.*) No matter. . . . People of great intelligence . . . these Englishmen. . . . No matter. Good luck. . . . God will take care of you. . . . No matter. . . . There's an end to everything on earth. . . . (*Kisses the hand of* LYUBOV ANDREYEVNA.) And should you ever happen to hear that my end has come, remember this old . . . horse, and say, "There used to live upon this earth a certain . . . Semeonov-Pishchik. . . . The heavenly kingdom to him!" . . . It's wonderful weather. . . . Yes. . . . (*He goes out deeply moved, but returns immediately and says from the doorway.*) Dashenka sent her regards! (*Goes out.*)

LYUBOV ANDREYEVNA: Well, we can go now. I'm leaving with two cares on my mind. The first one is poor, sick, old Firs. (*Looks at her watch.*) I have still five minutes to spare. . . .

ANYA: They've sent Firs to the hospital already, mama. Yasha saw to it this morning.

LYUBOV ANDREYEVNA: My second worry is Varya. She is accustomed to early rising and work; and now, with nothing to do, she's like a fish out of water. She's grown thin and pale, and she weeps, poor girl. . . . (*Pause.*) You know very well, Yermolay Alexeich, I have dreamed . . . of giving her to you, for it's quite obvious that you'll marry some one. (*She whispers to* ANYA, *who nods to* CHARLOTTA, *and they both go out.*) She loves you, she's congenial to you, and I really don't know why you avoid each other so. I don't understand it at all!

LOPAKHIN: To tell the truth, I don't understand it myself. It's all strange somehow. . . . If there's still time, why I'm ready now. . . . We'll make an end of it right away and have done with it. But without your help, I feel I shan't propose.

LYUBOV ANDREYEVNA: That's fine now. It'll take only a moment, you know. I'll call her right away.

LOPAKHIN: By the way, there's some champagne. . . . (*Looking at the glasses.*) They're empty. Some one's drained them dry already. (YASHA *coughs.*) That's real guzzling, that is!

LYUBOV ANDREYEVNA (*with animation*): Splendid! We'll go out. . . . Yasha, *allez!* I'll call her. . . . (*In the doorway.*) Varya, leave everything and come here. Come! (*Goes out with* YASHA.)

LOPAKHIN (*looking at his watch*): Yes. . . . (*Pause.*)

(*There is a restrained laugh behind the door, and whispering. At last* VARYA *comes in.*)

VARYA (*looking over the baggage carefully*): That's strange, I can't find it anywhere. . . .

LOPAKHIN: What are you looking for?

VARYA: I packed it myself, and now I've forgotten where. (*Pause.*)

LOPAKHIN: Where are you going now, Varvara Mikhaylovna?

VARYA: I? To the Ragulins. . . . I've agreed to take over the housekeeping—something like that. . . .

LOPAKHIN: Don't they live in Yashnevo? That's fifty miles from here. (*Pause.*) So life in this old house is finished. . . .

VARYA (*surveying the bundles*): Where can it be? . . . Or perhaps I packed it in the trunk. . . . Yes, life in this house is over—it will never return.

LOPAKHIN: And I'm off to Harkov now . . . on this same train. I've a lot to attend to. And I'm going to leave Epikhodov here. . . . I've hired him.

VARYA: You don't say!

LOPAKHIN: Last year at this time, if you remember, snow was already falling, but now it's quiet and sunny. Only it's cold . . . six degrees below freezing.

VARYA: I haven't looked to see. (*Pause.*) But then, our thermometer is broken anyway. . . . (*Pause.*)

VOICE (*at the door*): Yermolay Alexeich!

LOPAKHIN (*as though he had long been waiting that call*): Right away. (*He goes out quickly.*)

(VARYA, *sitting on the floor, lays her head on a bundle of wraps and sobs softly. The door opens and* LYUBOV ANDREYEVNA *tiptoes in.*)

LYUBOV ANDREYEVNA: Well? (*Pause.*) We must be going.

VARYA (*stops crying and wipes her eyes*): Yes, it's time to go, mama. I'll arrive at the Ragulins' to-day, if only I don't miss the train.

LYUBOV ANDREYEVNA (*standing in the doorway*): Anya, put on your things.

(ANYA *comes in;* GAYEV *and* CHARLOTTA IVANOVNA *follow her.* GAYEV *is wearing a warm overcoat with a cape. The* SERVANTS *and* COACHMEN *assemble.* EPIKHODOV *bustles around the baggage.*)

LYUBOV ANDREYEVNA: Now we can start on our way.

ANYA (*joyously*): On our way!

GAYEV: My friends, my dear, good friends! In leaving this house forever, can I possibly remain silent, restrain myself, and not express at parting the emotions that now fill my whole being? . . .

ANYA (*beseechingly*): Uncle!

VARYA: Uncle dear, you mustn't!

GAYEV (*mournfully*): Yellow across the table into the middle. . . . I'll keep still. . . .

(TROFIMOV *comes in, after him* LOPAKHIN.)

TROFIMOV: Well, ladies and gentlemen, it's time to go!

LOPAKHIN: Epikhodov, my coat!

LYUBOV ANDREYEVNA: I'll sit here just one moment longer. It's as though I'd never really seen these walls, these ceilings before, and now I look at them eagerly, with such tender love. . . .

GAYEV: I remember when I was six years old sitting in this window on Trinity Sunday, and watching father go to church.

LYUBOV ANDREYEVNA: Has everything been taken out?

LOPAKHIN: I think so. (*To* EPIKHODOV, *who is helping him on with his overcoat.*) Epikhodov, look and see if everything is all ready.

EPIKHODOV (*in a hoarse voice*): Put your mind at rest, Yermolay Alexeich.

LOPAKHIN: What's the matter with your voice?

EPIKHODOV: I just drank some water and swallowed it wrong.

YASHA (*contemptuously*): Bumpkin!

LYUBOV ANDREYEVNA: If we go, there won't be a soul left behind. . . .

LOPAKHIN: Not until spring.

VARYA (*pulls an umbrella out of a bundle and seems about to swing it.* LOPAKHIN *pretends to be frightened*): What's the matter? What's the matter? . . . I never dreamed of it.

TROFIMOV: Let's climb into the carriages, ladies and gentlemen. It's time to go. It's nearly train time.

VARYA: Petya, there are your galoshes, near that trunk. . . .(*Tearfully.*) And how dirty and old they are! . . .

TROFIMOV (*putting on his galoshes*): Well, let's be on our way!

GAYEV (*deeply moved, on the verge of unwilling tears*): The train . . . the station. . . . Back shot to the middle, white across the table to the corner. . . .

LYUBOV ANDREYEVNA: We must go!

LOPAKHIN: Is every one here? No one left? (*He locks the door on the left.*) There are some things stored here, we'll have to lock them up. Come on!

ANYA: Good-by, old house! Good-by, old life!

TROFIMOV: Welcome, new life! (*He goes out with* ANYA.)

(VARYA *casts a glance around the room and goes slowly out.* YASHA, *and* CHARLOTTA, *her lap dog in her arms, follow.*)

LOPAKHIN: Until spring then! Come on, my friends! Till we meet again! (*Goes out.*)

(LYUBOV ANDREYEVNA *and* GAYEV *are left together. They seem to have been waiting for this moment. They fall into each other's arms and sob softly, restrainedly, as though fearing lest some one hear them.*)

GAYEV (*in despair*): My sister, my sister! . . .

LYUBOV ANDREYEVNA: Oh, my dear orchard, my tender, beautiful orchard! My life, my youth, my happiness, farewell! Farewell!

ANYA'S *voice* (*joyously, appealingly*): Mama! . . .

TROFIMOV'S *voice* (*joyously and with ardor*): Yoo-hoo!

LYUBOV ANDREYEVNA: To look at the walls, at the windows, for the last time! . . . Our dead mother loved to walk to and fro in this room. . . .

GAYEV: My sister, my sister!

ANYA'S *voice*: Mama!

TROFIMOV'S *voice*: Yoo-hoo!

LYUBOV ANDREYEVNA: We're coming! . . . (*They go out.*)

(*The stage is empty. One can hear keys turning in the locks of all the doors, the carriages roll away. Then the sound of an ax striking against wood, a sad and lonely sound, rings out amid the stillness. Footsteps are heard.* FIRS *emerges from the door on the right. He is dressed as usual in a waiter's jacket and white waistcoat, with slippers on his feet. He is ill.*)

FIRS (*going over to the door and pulling at the knob*): Locked! They've gone away. . . . (*Sits down on the sofa.*) They've forgotten me. . . . No matter. . . . I'll sit here a little while. . . . And I suppose Leonid Andreich didn't put on his fur coat and went off in a light one. . . . (*Sighs anxiously.*) I never looked to see. . . . Young and green! (*Mutters something unintelligible.*) So life has gone by— just as though I'd never lived at all. . . . (*Lies down.*) I'll lie here a little while. . . . You've no strength in you, nothing's left, nothing. . . . Eh, you're a . . . lummox! (*Lies motionless.*)

(*A distant sound is heard, like the melancholy twang of a string, breaking in the heavens. It dies away. Silence, save for the dull sound of an ax chopping, far off in the orchard.*)

PROFESSOR STORITSYN

A Drama in Four Acts

By LEONID NIKOLAYEVICH ANDREYEV

(1912)

*Translated by Isaiah Minkoff, George Rapall Noyes
and Alexander Kaun*

CHARACTERS

VALENTÍN NIKOLÁYEVICH STORÍTSYN, *a professor*
ELÉNA PETRÓVNA, *his wife*
VOLÓDYA
SERGÉY } *their sons*
MODÉST PETRÓVICH, *brother of* ELENA PETROVNA
PROKÓPY EVSÉYEVICH TELEMÁKHOV, *a professor*
GAVRIÍL GAVRIÍLOVICH SÁVVICH
PRINCESS LYUDMÍLA PÁVLOVNA
MAMYKIN
DUNYÁSHA, *the* STORITSYNS' *maid*
FÉKLA,* MODEST PETROVICH'S *cook*
GENNÁDY, TELEMAKHOV'S *orderly*

---

* Pronounced, Fyŏ'kla.

PROFESSOR STORITSYN

ACT I

PROFESSOR STORITSYN *is a lean, tall, big-boned man about forty-five years of age. He holds himself very upright, walks quickly and noiselessly, his gestures are free and easy, but in moments of great fatigue or illness, he slightly stoops. He is not noticeably gray either in his dark, thin, slightly tousled hair, or in his close-clipped beard. His handsome face and the form of his head remind one of Thomas Carlyle; there are dark hollows under his cheek bones. He usually wears a loosely-fitting frock coat and a turned-down starched collar that does not cover the neck. The outward appearance of* STORITSYN *is rather harsh than mild; only in his conversation and actions does he show his true character.*

An autumn evening, about seven o'clock. The street windows are hung with heavy woolen draperies. The air in the professor's study is stifling, dull, and motionless as in a cave. Everywhere are books, just as if the library had overflowed its shores and deluged the room; on the tables are his manuscripts and proof sheets. There are traces of desperate efforts to systematize the chaotic state of the books and newspapers, but with little result. The bookcases are without keys; here and there lie old newspapers. The floor is covered with a dark carpet; on the walls are portraits of writers, in black frames, and some paintings, gifts of artist friends. On a big desk stands a writing lamp with an opaque shade; close by on a metal tray is an opened bottle of red wine and two glasses. In a tall glass goblet is one lonely rose. Aside, on a little table near a couch, burns an electric lamp, with the green shade removed in order to give more light. The proprietor, PROFESSOR STORITSYN, *is not quite well and* PROKOPY EVSEYEVICH TELEMAKHOV, *a friend and comrade of* STORITSYN *in his school days, now a professor in a medical military academy, is examining and tapping* STORITSYN *with much attention.* TELEMAKHOV *wears a doctor's uniform with a general's epaulets; he is grizzled and lean, with a wrinkled yellow face; his speech and gestures are abrupt and infrequent. On his thin, lean nose is a pince-nez which* TELEMAKHOV *uses only when writing prescriptions and when studying; usually he looks over his glasses, bending his head and wrinkling his forehead. He is not quite so tall as* STORITSYN. *In a corner, sitting very quietly in an armchair, is* MODEST PETROVICH; *hardly breathing, afraid to interfere with the examination, he anxiously watches the deliberate, serious movements of* TELEMAKHOV. *Now* TELEMAKHOV *has raised the shirt of his patient and has put his ear to the broad, shivering back.*

TELEMAKHOV: Take a deep breath.

STORITSYN: Like this? (*Takes a long breath.*)

TELEMAKHOV: So. That's enough. Bend down. Breathe again. That's good. And now put your right hand on your head.

STORITSYN: I don't understand how. Like this? Well, is that all?

TELEMAKHOV (*tapping on his chest*): Wait. (*Again listening attentively.*)

STORITSYN (*looking at himself*): What a wretched body; a pale, cold, lifeless skin! A rotten body, Telemasha?

TELEMAKHOV: A professor's. Turn around, will you? (*Tapping his chest.*)

STORITSYN: But you have tapped me already. Pardon, I won't fuss any more. But really, I am as healthy as a horse. I ought to be rolling stones on the road or be a wrestler in a circus. If it weren't for my heart—

TELEMAKHOV: Hush. Don't bother me.

STORITSYN: All right. Modest, if it's no trouble, my friend, pass me a cigarette from the table.

MODEST: Right away, Valentin Nikolayevich, with pleasure.

TELEMAKHOV: Can't you wait?

STORITSYN: Well, if it is necessary, I can, but all the same— He won't let me, Modest. Thank you, my boy. Are you through?

TELEMAKHOV: Yes. Go ahead; smoke, you furnace.

STORITSYN: May I dress myself also?

TELEMAKHOV: Yes, you may dress. Modest Petrovich, help him.

STORITSYN: Oh, no, don't. It isn't necessary a bit, my boy. I'll do it myself. (*Dresses himself, turning away from* TELEMAKHOV.) Well, how is it, Telemasha; shall I live a while yet?

TELEMAKHOV (*pouring out wine*): You will.

STORITSYN: Are you telling the truth?

TELEMAKHOV: Well, what do you think I'm doing? You'll not be allowed to ride on a bicycle, and you'll have to give up your circus. They'll have to announce that you're not engaged in wrestling any more.

STORITSYN: Are you joking, Telemasha? It would be interesting to know what the hearts of the Roman gladiators were like; yes, yes, most likely remarkable hearts. Anyhow, this was all nonsense; I didn't need to ask your help at all. You listened only from the outside, but I hear it within and I can give you bad news, Telemasha: I have a perfectly worthless heart.

TELEMAKHOV: Subjective sensations, fatigue.

STORITSYN: Really? Oh, you are a humorist, Telemasha.

TELEMAKHOV: Every heart gets weary toward the forties. Why do you work so much, why do you smoke so much?

STORITSYN: Yes, why? Well, I had better go and report to Elena that I have subjective sensations; she has worried so, the kind soul.

MODEST: Perhaps I had better call sister in here, Valentin Nikolayevich? I'll call her.

STORITSYN: No, Modest, I'll do it myself. Wait for me, my boy. I'll be quick. (*Goes out.* TELEMAKHOV, *clasping his hands behind him under his coat, walks back and forth across the room, casting angry sidelong glances at* MODEST PETROVICH. *He drinks another glass of wine, then stops before* MODEST PETROVICH *and silently, for a long time, looks intently at him over his glasses.*)

MODEST (*timidly*): So. How about it, professor?

TELEMAKHOV: Yes, it is bad, very bad. We'll have to watch him.

MODEST: But you said that he had only subjective—

TELEMAKHOV: Confound your "subjective," Modest Petrovich. I'll have to talk with your sister, and you try to convince her that it is quite time to end your indecencies. Do you understand?

MODEST: But how shall I convince her?

TELEMAKHOV: That's your business. You're her brother. It's time to stop it. This is no pigsty here, I say. No pigsty. Is Savvich here again?

MODEST: But imagine yourself in my position!

TELEMAKHOV: I haven't the slightest desire to do so. I never want to understand anybody's position. I have enough position of my own. What are you blinking at? It is past my endurance when you start to blink, Modest Petrovich.

MODEST: But my dear sir—

(STORITSYN *enters hurriedly.*)

STORITSYN: Savvich is in there, and that cursed writer, Mamykin. What a beastly name, Mamykin. When did they come? I didn't hear the bell. . . . Oh, how sick and tired I am of both of them!

TELEMAKHOV: Turn 'em out.

STORITSYN: Oh, bother, Telemasha, you are a regular soldier. But where are you going? Already home?

TELEMAKHOV: I have to. A patient is waiting.

STORITSYN: And I thought, Telemasha, old friend, that you'd spend the evening here. Oh, I'm so sorry! Perhaps you would have some wine? Do you like red wine as much as ever?

TELEMAKHOV: I'd be glad to. I could stay for another half hour. It's surprising that you don't get gray at all, Valentin Nikolayevich.

STORITSYN: But you yourself show wear and tear a good deal, you old goat-beard. How old are you, Telemasha? I can remember you for thirty years, and you had lived some time before that.

TELEMAKHOV: We are about the same age. Yes, I'm gray as a wolf! . . . How is your book getting on?

STORITSYN: Splendidly, my boy! I am preparing the fifth edition now.

TELEMAKHOV: Oho!

STORITSYN: Yes, it is beyond belief. Well, and how is yours?

TELEMAKHOV: Mine? (*Looking over his glasses.*) It stands stock-still on the shelves.

STORITSYN: What do you mean? You must have a bad publisher, Telemasha! This can't be allowed.

TELEMAKHOV: The publisher has nothing to do with it; the book's no good.

STORITSYN: An excellent book, a splendid book!

TELEMAKHOV: Oh, stop it! I don't like it. Listen, Valentin Niko-layevich, you must let up on your work. Yes, yes, brother, listen to what I am telling you. Why do you speak before the public? You mustn't. Success, admirers, especially among the ladies, all that is very good; but one has to think of his health also. You are no longer a young man.

MODEST: Valentin Nikolayevich works terribly hard, till he almost drops.

STORITSYN: But you know that I don't do it for success or for fair admirers. How absurd!

TELEMAKHOV: Well, but who doesn't like success! By the way, tell me, has anything wrong happened to you recently? You are rather gloomy. I almost thought that your book had stopped selling.

STORITSYN: Wrong? Nothing, I think. Where are you going, Modest?

MODEST: To the dining-room. I'll return presently. (*Goes out.*)

STORITSYN: What delicacy of feeling he shows!

(TELEMAKHOV *looks dubiously in the direction of* MODEST, *with obvious disapproval.* STORITSYN *laughs.*)

STORITSYN: When I look at you now that we are alone, I want to laugh like an augur. Have you changed any, Telemakhov?

TELEMAKHOV: Have you? It is high time you did. Hasn't life taught you anything?

STORITSYN (*smiling*): It teaches. But this is what I wanted to tell you: I have begun to miss some of my books. Some one is stealing them. The other day I found a book in a second-hand shop with my own *ex libris*.

TELEMAKHOV (*looking from under his eyebrows*): That's bad, professor.

STORITSYN: Very bad indeed. The question is not of books, though quite a few of them have disappeared, but the main thing is that a thief is concealed close by—and a very peculiar thief. It is a terrible feeling; it makes every room seem five degrees colder. So it goes, Telemakhov.

TELEMAKHOV: You have your *ex libris,* but no keys to your cases. Better the other way around, Valentin Nikolayevich. My books are only numbered, but I have keys and not a single book dares get lost. That's bad, professor. Does your maid know how to read? Whom do you suspect?

STORITSYN: Our Dunya can't read . . . and I don't suspect anybody. Why don't you understand it, Telemasha? I simply don't want to suspect a certain person. There are people who rejoice when they find a thief, catch a criminal, or disclose a liar—they have always amazed me. When I meet a liar I feel rather silly—rather embarrassed, so that sometimes I even help him to lie, even against myself. It's silly, Telemasha. Is it not?

TELEMAKHOV (*looking at* STORITSYN *searchingly*): No, wait; it is getting interesting. And the secretary, you know, the one who typed for you, is he still with you?

STORITSYN: No, do whatever you want, but for the Lord's sake don't play Sherlock Holmes. It is enough for me that instead of my usual thoughts and usual work, I have at odd moments to become a detective. Such crafty thoughts, combinations, suspicions! . . . Bah, degrading, professor, degrading!

TELEMAKHOV: You needn't do it yourself. Why should you? Inform the police, they'll send you an agent.

STORITSYN: Oh, stop it! Forgive me, Telemasha, I am a little abrupt, but all this agitates me . . . it makes me ill. Take a drink of wine. I believe it is the kind you like. You ask whether anything wrong has happened. Oh, things happen every day and you know it just as well as I do! Perhaps I am getting impatient and ill-tempered, but I am surprised, fairly stupefied by the frightfully ignoble character of our Russian life. So much coarseness and vulgarity—what a repulsive word!—scandal and shouting; and everywhere the fist is in evidence, everywhere the fist: sometimes it is in the form of a "fig," the more delicate form, as those people think, but mostly in the form of a sledge hammer! Take yesterday: my Sergey stood in the middle of the hall and cried out, "Hey Dunka,* hurry up my galoshes!" What rudeness! —and where did he learn it? I never called the little brat even "Serezhka," and he stood and roared out "Hey Dunka, hurry up!" . . . Or take my Elena Petrovna, the kindest of women—you know her— always busy with charities, but still I can't teach her to say "thank you" to the maid. *"Merci,"* she can manage, it comes out unconsciously, but "thank you" not on any account. But what is there hard about "thank you"? Just think of it!

TELEMAKHOV: It must be hard, if you have not been able to teach her in twenty years. How is it that she has begun to worry about you?

(*After softly knocking on the door,* MODEST PETROVICH *comes in, carrying a glass of tea.*)

STORITSYN: Is it you, Modest! Sit down, my boy.—She is always worrying.

TELEMAKHOV (*rising*): Well, I don't know. It's your own affair; I have enough of my own Dunyas. So I'll go, Valentin; and you, please, try not to get agitated.

STORITSYN (*embracing him*): Thank you, Telemasha, old friend.

TELEMAKHOV: I know that my advice may be absurd, but you must take it. What is to-day, Friday? I'll come in about a week's time; we'll have a talk.—Good-by, my boy! Don't see me to the door; I'll make a moment's call on Elena Petrovna. Good-by, Modest Petrovich! (*Goes out.*)

MODEST: A severe man, an unapproachable man. The judges were of just the same sort, when they sent me off to prison.

STORITSYN: He is a humorist.—Are they there?

MODEST: Yes, they are sitting there.

STORITSYN: Don't go away, my boy. I don't feel like working to-day, but neither should I like to have anybody come here. What is the matter, old man?

MODEST (*indecisively looks at his watch*): I am worrying about the train, Valentin Nikolayevich.

STORITSYN: Oh, you had better leave your Ozerki! Devil knows why you live there, off in Ozerki? Haven't you room in Petersburg? When is the last train, at one o'clock? You'll make it. Sleep right here on the sofa; you are not a girl, stay with me.

MODEST (*hurriedly pockets his watch*): I would with pleasure, Valentin Nikolayevich, only I'm afraid of being in your way.

STORITSYN: Oh, Modest! How embarrassing it was about the book, Modest! Oh, to the devil with it! I made the impression of wanting

---

* In proper names the *-ka* termination gives an air of contempt in Russian.

to boast of my own success. Awfully embarrassing! I am so fond of
Telemasha. . . . What prison are you talking about? Don't you get
tired, old man, of repeating the story over and over? It isn't your
fault that the house collapsed, but the contractor's. And it's time for
you to get used to the affair.

MODEST: Very well, Valentin Nikolayevich.— But he says: "I am
an ignorant fellow and you must keep an eye on me. If you don't keep
an eye on me," he says, "I may destroy the whole world!" That's the
way he talks, Valentin Nikolayevich.

STORITSYN: Stop it! (*Walks about.*) He is a humorist. I still
remember his wife; she was a beautiful woman, but of loose morals,
I think, or something of the kind.

MODEST: More beautiful than my former wife?

STORITSYN: Your wife, if you'll excuse me, was vulgar and common—and you ought to be only too glad that she chased you out in
time.— Are they there?

MODEST: I have told you already. They are having tea there.—
"I am an honest woman, and why should I clean my nails?"

STORITSYN (*walks about*): It is sad, very sad, strange and sad! Here
he says that every heart gets tired in the forties—that is not true,
Modest! How can a heart get tired? Nonsense! A heart may weep,
cry from pain; a heart may struggle as though it were in chains—but
weariness? I am forty-six years old, and sometimes a thousand and
forty-six, but each day I love life more and more, and I love my
work more tenderly. To the devil with weariness, old man!

MODEST: All Europe gazes at you, Valentin Nikolayevich.

STORITSYN: Easy now, old man! He is gray and yellow like parch-
ment: what does he understand about joy? He is like a deaf man at
an opera. How is he to know the power of unexpected charms, the
joy of tragedy, the magnificent horror of sudden meetings, unexpected
discoveries, failures and triumphs? Weariness! Imagine, old man, that
you are a scientist and that for a thousand years you have been
searching—

(ELENA PETROVNA *comes in. She is a tall, stout woman; she breathes
noisily and impetuously. Her face is still beautiful but very much
powdered; her eyes are especially beautiful.*)

STORITSYN (*restraining an expression of displeasure*): Well, how
is it? Have you calmed yourself at last, Elena?

ELENA (*feeling his brow*): Aren't you better?

STORITSYN (*carefully pushing away her hand*): What has the head
to do with it? Do you think I have the dysentery like a baby?

ELENA: Don't agitate yourself. Prokopy Evseyevich said that first
of all you must avoid excitement. Ah, Valentin, I am so worried!

Just listen to me: let's go abroad; you'll rest there, you'll have some diversion. We'll visit the museums, hear music.

STORITSYN: No, I have to work, Lena.

ELENA: Why do you complain then?

STORITSYN: I do not complain; it is just your imagination.

ELENA: Then you must not complain, if you refuse to undergo medical treatment. Well, do not agitate yourself, don't get excited; I long ago got used to doing everything your way. But since you are better, perhaps you'll come out to the dining-room. Gavriil Gavriilovich is very much worried and would like to talk to you personally about your health.

STORITSYN: Savvich? No, no; please, Lena, make excuses; be polite about it; tell him that I am a little tired.

ELENA: The Princess also has come.

STORITSYN (*slowly*): Lyudmila Pavlovna?

ELENA: Yes, and she insists on seeing you. I have told her already that you are not quite well, but she is so persistent.

STORITSYN: Persistent?

ELENA: Don't quarrel over words, please; I am nervous enough anyhow. If you wish I'll send her in here; she will divert you. Don't trouble yourself about the others; they belong to the family, and I'll tell them that it is on business. Is it not kind of me, Valentin dear?

STORITSYN (*kissing her hand*): But please, make excuses, Lena; be polite about it.

ELENA: Oh, Valentin dear, I have been crying the whole day! No, don't worry, it is nothing; I have the most terrible nerves. Be a good boy and don't agitate yourself, and I'll bring her in immediately. It seems that the girl is genuinely in love with you. Have pity on her. *Je ne suis pas jalouse.*

STORITSYN (*reproachfully and harshly*): Elena!

(*But* ELENA PETROVNA *is already going out.*)

MODEST: Lyudmila Pavlovna is a very proud person, a splendid girl!

STORITSYN (*indifferently*): Really? Where is my tie? Have you seen it, Modest? Give it to me quickly, my boy. If you ever want to say something absolutely vulgar, then speak French, a wonderfully convenient language. And if you ever happen to get ill, Modest, hide it, just as if you were a murderer and had killed somebody.

(ELENA PETROVNA *and the* PRINCESS *appear at the door.*)

ELENA (*ceremoniously*): Come in, Princess. Here is my sick man, divert him; poor man, he is lonesome. *Un moment! Venez ici, Modest!*

MODEST (*hurriedly*): I am coming, sister; I am coming.

(*After greeting the* Princess *he goes out.* Storitsyn *and the* Princess *are left alone.*)

Storitsyn: Lyudmila Pavlovna, I am very glad to see you. Be good enough to forgive me, there is such terrible disorder here. I'll put away the tray, I'll take away the papers and the proof sheets—like that. Now, please, sit down, Lyudmila Pavlovna.

Lyudmila: Are you ill, Valentin Nikolayevich?

Storitsyn: Oh, just a trifle; The less we talk about it the better.

Lyudmila: All right. Your study is different now from what it is during the daytime.

Storitsyn: Better?

Lyudmila: Yes. Am I not disturbing you?

Storitsyn: Oh no!— Have you been ill, Lyudmila Pavlovna?

Lyudmila: No, I have been well, and now I ride horseback every day to the islands.

Storitsyn: To the islands? Oh, yes, exactly. But I had got a little accustomed to having you accompany me home from college, and these two weeks—

Lyudmila: You got accustomed to having me see you home? I haven't felt like doing so.

Storitsyn: Of course you haven't. Won't you have tea, Princess?

Lyudmila: No, thank you. I don't drink tea at this time. Is Savvich sitting again in your dining-room? Does he sit there always?

Storitsyn: Yes, almost always. At any rate he has for five years.

Lyudmila: Do you let him into the study also?

Storitsyn: We'll not speak of Savvich. You haven't been here for quite a while. Why?

Lyudmila: I haven't felt like that either; I dislike your house. You don't object to my frankness, do you? I can adopt another tone.

(*Silence.* Storitsyn *laughs quietly and unwillingly.*)

Storitsyn: I look at your long gloves and feel like a student who has accidentally met a society young lady at a ball and doesn't know what to talk about with her. You have on an unusual dress. I never notice a woman's dress, but you have on an unusual dress and because of it I simply do not recognize my own room. It would be very interesting to see you in a riding habit. However, this is all nonsense, and you are doing very well to be silent. Tell me, Lyudmila Pavlovna, have you read the books that I recommended to you?

Lyudmila: No.

Storitsyn (*coldly*): Probably you have had no time for it.

Lyudmila: No, I kept thinking all the time and I had no time to read.

Storitsyn: Thinking of what?

LYUDMILA: I have been thinking of life; I have been thinking of you, too.

(*Silence.* STORITSYN *paces hurriedly.*)

STORITSYN: Do you know of what I have always been dreaming?

LYUDMILA: Your wife says that it is not good for you to agitate yourself.

STORITSYN: Stop! . . . I have been dreaming of beauty. It is perhaps strange, but I, a bookman, a professor in galoshes, a learned bourgeois, a street car traveler, I have always been dreaming of beauty. I don't remember when I have been at an art exhibition. I am almost entirely deprived of the greatest delight, of music; I have no time to read poetry. Finally, my home— Are you listening?

LYUDMILA: Yes.

STORITSYN: But the question is not of pictures, nor of music either. Here people say that one has to live in such and such a fashion. They say a lot of things on the subject; you'll find out later all about it. I know only one thing: one must live beautifully. Are you listening? Must think beautifully, feel beautifully; and naturally, also talk beautifully. It is absurd for a man to declare: "I have an ugly face, I have a hideous nose." Every person—do you hear?—every one must and can have a beautiful face.

LYUDMILA: Like yours?

STORITSYN: I am very grateful that you consider my face a beautiful one. I myself have made it so. But this is I; how about the others, then? Explain to me this enigma, this most sorrowful enigma of my life. Why is there so little beauty around me? I hope, I believe that some one of my auditors whom I do not know, whom I have never seen closely, has carried away my dream of a beautiful life and has already created a whole garden of beauty, but why is there around me such—an Arabian desert? Perhaps it is my fate only to search and talk, while to act and to enjoy is left to others. But this is hard, very hard, Lyudmila Pavlovna.

LYUDMILA: Our house is very beautiful, but that makes it all the worse. Who put the little rose here?

STORITSYN: Modest. That is to say, either your house is really not beautiful, or not so bad as you think it is?

LYUDMILA: Oh, no, it is very bad; I know it.

STORITSYN: But do you not come from that house? Pardon, Princess.

LYUDMILA: I don't like to have you call me princess. And do you sincerely think, Professor, that I am beautiful?

STORITSYN (*laughs*): Yes.

LYUDMILA: Later I shall be, yes. But now I am not. You know

I have given up painting. It is such a horror: I combined beautiful colors and suddenly something horrid would appear on the paper. And they praise it. And do you know why I ride to the islands? To think. Once, Valentin Nikolayevich, you looked at me with contempt.

STORITSYN: I?

LYUDMILA: Yes, you, Valentin Nikolayevich—and even with repulsion. And since then I have been thinking, but if you knew how hard it is! Sometimes I even cry, so hard it is; and sometimes I rejoice as if it were Easter. And I feel like singing: "Christ is arisen, Christ is arisen!" And you are wrong in thinking that one must live beautifully.

STORITSYN (smiling): Wrong?

LYUDMILA: Yes, one must live in order to think! Sometimes I begin to think of the ugliest things imaginable—for instance, in our yard lives a peasant, Karp by name—and the more I think, the less ugliness do I find, and I feel again like singing, "Christ is arisen!"

STORITSYN: My dear, this is exactly— (A knock on the door.) Oh, my Lord! Come in, who is it? What do you want, Modest?

MODEST (indecisively approaching): Excuse me, Valentin, but Gavriil Gavriilovich and Mamykin want to come in.

STORITSYN: What for? I won't have them.

MODEST: But they are already coming. Gavriil Gavriilovich is worried about your health.

(Enter SAVVICH and MAMYKIN, after a while ELENA PETROVNA. SAVVICH is a stout, large, handsome man with black, close-cropped mustaches.)

SAVVICH: Although you have strictly forbidden any one to enter your sanctuary, Professor, and although our knees are shaking with fear, yet—since you have made an exception for one person—Mamykin and I have decided to let the exception become the rule. Sit down, Mamykin.

STORITSYN (coldly): Sit down, Mamykin.

SAVVICH: Joking aside, how do you feel, your Eminence? Do not believe the doctors; all the doctors lie.

STORITSYN: I have been examined by Telemakhov.

SAVVICH: I know it, but what of it? Excuse me, excuse me. Although you are an eminent professor and I an absolutely unknown gymnasium teacher, yet I always allow myself to speak the truth. Your Telemakhov is an absolute nincompoop. Why didn't you apply to Ratayev? Didn't I advise you to? You don't take advice and then you sulk like an old woman; pardon me my friendly frankness. Here, I am forty years of age, but did you ever see me sick or complaining, "Oh, my head aches; oh, my heart palpitates"? Have you seen me, Mamykin?

MAMYKIN: No.

SAVVICH: And you will not see it; that's an historical fact. What are you sulking for, Mamykin; are you afraid of his Eminence? Don't get frightened; he doesn't bite.

MAMYKIN: I am not afraid of anybody.

SAVVICH: And do not be so. Take a cigarette.

MAMYKIN: I have my own.

SAVVICH: Oh, quit! How much do you pay for yours? Three kopeks a dozen, I bet, for you are a proletarian—but the professor's have an aroma.

STORITSYN: Please have a smoke, Mamykin.

ELENA: Princess, do you know the date of the first subscription performance at the opera?

SAVVICH: Professor, I have come with Mamykin to inquire about that manuscript of his. Pardon me, Princess, you said something.

LYUDMILA: Valentin Nikolayevich, are you free on Sunday? Let us go somewhere out of town.

STORITSYN: On Sunday? What will it be on Sunday?

SAVVICH (*with a guffaw*): Friday.

STORITSYN (*laughing*): That is, I meant that I have a meeting.

ELENA: No, no, Princess; for the Lord's sake, take him away. I'll be very grateful to you! He needs air so much. I shall get angry if you do not go, Valentin.

SAVVICH: Suppose I go with you too? I have not been out in the country for a long time either.

MAMYKIN: You forget, Gavriil Gavriilovich, that on Sunday I am to read a story at your lodgings.

SAVVICH: Oh, yes, yes, yes! I forgot, friend, and in the afternoon too. We'll hear, we'll listen to your precious satire.

STORITSYN: Splendid, fine! It is a wonderful idea, after all. But just wait, where shall we go? Let's see! Modest, what if we come to you at Ozerki? What do you think about it, Lyudmila Pavlovna?

LYUDMILA: I agree.

MODEST: Valentin, dear, if you are not joking—

STORITSYN: Easy now, old fellow. But wait, how can it be arranged? Shall I come for you, or (*Anxiously.*)—Modest, you had better give me the time-table. Have you the time-table?

LYUDMILA: Good night, Elena Petrovna.

ELENA: Where are you going?

LYUDMILA (*not responding*): Can you see me home to-night, Valentin Nikolayevich?

STORITSYN: To-night?

SAVVICH: To-night he mustn't.

ELENA: Of course he can, certainly; let him take a walk, it is so smoky here.

STORITSYN (*sternly*): With pleasure, Lyudmila Pavlovna. I'll come back right away, Elena.

(*The* PRINCESS *bows her farewell to the company, not shaking hands.* ELENA PETROVNA *accompanies her.* MODEST PETROVICH *and* STORITSYN *follow them.*)

STORITSYN (*on the threshold*): Oh, yes, don't forget to give me some change, Elena. I'll come back in a cab. But where is my cigarette case? Here!

(*They go out.* SAVVICH *and* MAMYKIN *are left alone.*)

SAVVICH: Just watch him! (MAMYKIN *giggles.*)

SAVVICH: Mamykin, you laugh; but to tell the truth, all of this professorial pornography exasperates me. What does a mere girl understand—and especially one of such a family?

MAMYKIN: Is he—?

SAVVICH: How do I know? I am not a spy.

MAMYKIN: She is leading him on.

SAVVICH: She doesn't understand; that is why she is leading him on.

MAMYKIN: She has a contempt for both of us, Gavriil Gavriilovich. Stuck up!

SAVVICH: That is, whom do you mean by "us"? Me?

MAMYKIN: Yes, you too. I watched all the time how she kept glancing at you; we are in the same boat.

SAVVICH: All right, I'll pluck out the feathers of this fair maid. She'll know better next time. They don't like the truth, Mamykin. Come here. Did you see what a writing set his Eminence has? Take a look at it.

MAMYKIN: What is there to see?

SAVVICH: Just you take a look. Pure bronze! No, you'd better weigh it in your hand. Well?

MAMYKIN: Yes.

SAVVICH: Worth two thousand rubles if it is worth a kopek. A proletarian like you has no notion of such money?

MAMYKIN: But just look at the worn-out faces of the servants, driven like a cabman's horse. Well, will he ever read my manuscript? How long shall I have to wait for it?

SAVVICH: He has no time.

MAMYKIN: But he has time to take ladies home. Men of distinction!

SAVVICH: That's all right, you can bear with it.

MAMYKIN: I'll bear it, I'll bear it! Yes; oh, my God! Before my talent was awakened I had thought that these were the real people, our men of letters, our scientists. But when I got familiar with them, what did I find? . . . They are a spiteful, envious, vulgar lot. They almost set the dogs on you, keep you for three hours in the hall with the footmen. That's all I see: one man gets hold of a sweet bite and fairly trembles for fear some one will snatch it from him. I have lived for a whole month with Sokhonin, the writer, famous over all Russia, "a singer of the nation's sorrow." . . .

SAVVICH: Your Sokhonin is played out; much good it did you to visit him.

MAMYKIN: A writer known to all Russia, but what is going on in his house? All you see is stuffing. They stuff and swill, night or midnight. (ELENA PETROVNA *comes in.*)

ELENA: Gentlemen, supper is served. Sergey and Modest are already at the table. Hurry up, Mamykin!

SAVVICH (*laughs*): Night or midnight!

ELENA: What are you laughing at? Mamykin, go in ahead, please. I have a few words to say to Gavriil Gavriilovich.

SAVVICH: What now!

ELENA: It must be important if I say so.— Go, go! Tell them I'll be in right away. (MAMYKIN *goes out.*)

SAVVICH: What a tone! How many times have I told you not to dare talk to me in such a tone? The idea of it!

ELENA: Gavriil, I have cried all day to-day. It is terrible; I am losing my senses. Gavriil, in the name of all that is holy, I implore you; sell the papers even for three thousand, even for two. I am going insane.

SAVVICH: I have already explained to you that now, with the present situation on the exchange, we cannot sell anything. Do you understand? Yes or no?

ELENA: I don't understand anything. They'll take me to the court. I'll commit suicide.

SAVVICH: Nonsense! You'll get out of it. Who do you take me for? A schoolboy? Do you really think I believe that you and your professor haven't two thousand rubles? Am I a schoolboy?

ELENA: We haven't two kopeks. There isn't anything for to-morrow's dinner.

SAVVICH: Search your old skirts. Maybe there is something sewed in?

ELENA: How dare you! I am crying, asking you as a gentleman, and you behave yourself like a hoodlum.

SAVVICH: What is that?

ELENA (*out of breath*): You are as rude as a drunken cobbler. I go crazy when I talk to you. What meanness! You must not dare talk to me so in this house! No, no, you must not! You forget what house you are in. You—are a cabman! What right have you to raise your voice to me? When even my husband, even my husband . . .

SAVVICH: The right of your lover, Elena Petrovna. And if I behave like a cobbler, then you scold like a kitchen maid. Therefore we are quits.

ELENA: You have robbed me.

SAVVICH (*threateningly*): What is that? Repeat it, please! What did you say, if you please?

ELENA: Forgive me, Gavriil, I won't do so any more. But I can't listen when you talk to me so. Why do you disdain me? Don't forget I am not a mere girl. . . . I am a mother, every one respects me. . . . Explain, if I fail to understand something; but why such roughness, such contempt, such mockery? After you talk to me so, I can't face anybody. It seems to me that I am not the wife of a professor, an educated woman, who reads books, who speaks various languages, but a kitchen maid, dressed in her mistress's clothes—to whom her friend has just given a beating. Show me at least a little respect, Gavriil. I can't do without respect. I'll commit suicide.

SAVVICH: Have you any respect for me? Just a moment, please: who was it that cried out "robber" just now? You can't treat me like this, lady! And if I hear such things again—well?

ELENA: Please forgive me. Well, explain!

SAVVICH: Explain? (*Turns away and poses.*) Fool!

ELENA: It is so hard! I understand nothing of your game. Why can't we sell at least two thousand rubles' worth of papers? I don't say we have to sell all of them.

SAVVICH: "Robbed them! Scoundrel!" But to whom will you go with your professor, when you begin to starve? To me! Who saves your money, takes risks together with you, and doesn't grudge *his* hard-earned money? If one did not look after you, you would let your children go naked on the streets to sell matches. What housekeeping! You pay ten rubles for a thousand cigarettes and subscribe to the opera. You don't know your head from your heels in music, but you must have a subscription! The first performance! Esthetics! Literature! Ideas! But if the bills for firewood are left unpaid for two years, then you come to me! You ought to thank God that you have met on your way an honest man with a strong character. (*The door opens.*)

SERGEY (*cries out from the threshold*): Well, what is the matter, mama? This is outrageous. We have been sitting at the table for two hours. I have to study.

SAVVICH: Don't you dare to shout, you rowdy! Get out!

SERGEY (*stepping back*): What does this mean, please? This is not your gymnasium, Gavriil Gavriilovich! You are in a private house and—

Savvich: Elena Petrovna!

Elena (*hastily*): Go away, go away, Sergey. Haven't they served you yet? I'll be there right away; I must have just two words . . . about papa's health. Go! (*The door closes with a bang.*)

Savvich: Rowdy! You'll see yet; he'll show his real character, sullen fellow!

Elena: Forgive me. Are you very agitated, Gavriil?

Savvich: Let go my hand.

Elena (*kissing him on the cheek*): Forgive me, only do not leave me. I am going insane.

Savvich: Get some on a note.

Elena: I'll try to.

Savvich: One cannot sell now.

Elena: All right. Kiss me, Gavriil dear. I am so lonely, I am so afraid of everything. Kiss me! Don't desert me!

Savvich (*kisses her unwillingly*): Why do you powder yourself so much; it is dangerous to touch you?

Elena: I do it because of my tears. Well, come on! The dinner must be burned already. Oh, Lord, Lord!

ACT II

Ozerki. A little old cottage with a veranda; the unpainted planks and half-decayed posts are dark with dampness; here and there they are covered with green moss. A calm September day, full of sun, silence, and golden peace. The birch grove in which the cottage is situated, the mountain ash trees, and the young maple trees, just lately planted near the fence, have turned golden and crimson from the autumn. The light blue fog creates an illusion of remoteness even at a distance of a hundred paces, and transforms everything heavy, all that is attached to the ground, into something light and airy as a cobweb. Behind the low fence are seen other cottages, just as small and cramped; they are now empty and peaceful as a dream. Only the large cottage across the way is still occupied; it is now full of Sunday guests, mostly young girls and students. The piano plays from time to time. From the station nearby the whistles of the passing trains are heard.

In the garden on a bench Volodya *is half reclining, lazily biting a maple leaf that he has picked up from the ground. He is dressed like a laborer, in a coarse gray linen blouse with a leather belt, and high boots strapped just below the knee. Rustling in the fallen leaves,* Modest Petrovich *is walking uneasily along the path. He wears a shabby but clean black woolen coat and a soft felt hat. With his gray*

*curls, which fall on his collar, he looks like an unsuccessful old artist.
Very often he consults his watch; altogether he seems to be much worried and agitated.*

MODEST (*mumbles*) : Oh, Lord, Lord! What did you say, Volodya?

VOLODYA : I? Nothing, I am lying down.

MODEST : Lying, lying. Volodya, do you ever stand or walk. You mustn't be so lazy, it is beyond endurance.

VOLODYA : I am not lazy. If the machine were not broken, I should have flown to-day without fail. Fifteen of us are studying and we have only one machine, and even that one somebody keeps breaking.

MODEST : How high would you fly? To frighten the birds? They will say scarecrows used to stand on the earth but now they have begun to fly. You won't fly anywhere; shut up!

VOLODYA : I have flown already.

MODEST : I don't believe you.

VOLODYA : For about forty-five yards. You'd better watch me instead of slandering me.

MODEST : Slandering? . . . But who are you, please tell me. Are you the son of Professor Storitsyn, or who are you? You are not a mechanic; you are not a chauffeur; devil knows who you are! What boots! Yet I remember you in a velvet blouse with curly hair like an angel. Oh, children, children! Oh, what a life! Good God!

VOLODYA : Don't take it hard, uncle. Not everybody can be a genius.

MODEST : Genius? They don't expel geniuses from the gymnasium, my boy; geniuses don't wear peasant's boots. . . . But anyhow, what do you know about geniuses, you jackass, you mooncalf, you flying broomstick? Even without you it is bad enough, and then you come and disgrace us. You're living with a drunkard; you have lowered yourself.

VOLODYA : You are slandering again. Mikhail Ivanovich is not a drunkard at all, and he'll give you a big handicap. Do you think it's dirty or disorderly in our house? Not a bit. Clean as on Christmas; we sweep the floor twice a day, and have almost as many books as papa has. Oh, for a book Mikhail Ivanovich is ready to tear a man to pieces.

MODEST : So you read also?

VOLODYA : I don't, but Mikhail Ivanovich does. This is our bargain; everything fifty-fifty, but kerosene goes separate: that would be too hard on me. Mikhail Ivanovich is a wonderful man, uncle. All you know how to do is to scold me, to call me mooncalf and broomstick, but Mikhail Ivanovich never scolds.

MODEST : Never?

VOLODYA : Never.

MODEST: No, really?

VOLODYA: Never. We even stand on ceremony with each other. I call him Mikhail Ivanovich and he calls me Vladimir Valentinovich.

MODEST: Just watch the gentlemen! Well, so live in peace, Lord bless you! Who can understand you, you high brows! Oh, Lord, Lord! (*Looks at his watch.*) They are coming now.

VOLODYA: But it seems, uncle, that you are not very glad of papa's arrival; I should be glad in your place.

MODEST: You say not glad. How can I be glad, when the devil only knows what's going on within me? And besides, the day is so marvelous, one ought to rejoice and exult, and instead of that comes the disgrace and murder of a man. Yes, the disgrace and murder of a man. That's it, Volodya. I am chatting here with you, but still I am watching the gate just the same. If Telemakhov appears to-day, then everything is over. Murder!

VOLODYA (*raising himself up*): I can't get anything out of you, uncle. Has Sergey done something—or mother?

MODEST: You are too young to know, and it's still too early for you to talk about your mother. Shame!

VOLODYA: I know everything anyhow.

MODEST: You know nothing. . . . To make it short, I scoured the entire city yesterday, in order to get two thousand rubles for Elena; but what could I accomplish? I didn't get them. That's all. All is over, Volodya!

VOLODYA: All is over with papa?

MODEST: How terrible it is to be powerless and a coward! I toss and weep as though in a nightmare, but I haven't even the strength to shout. How I implored Telemakhov, yesterday; I almost fell on my knees; I wept, but it was all in vain. "I'll give to Valentin Nikolayevich," he says, "but not a kopek to you, or to your sister. A severe, an unapproachable man! And if Elena doesn't get the money by twelve o'clock to-day, then— Volodya, my boy, do you know, perhaps, some man of property—some aviator, maybe? No? (*Silence.*)

VOLODYA: Uncle, I haven't had any support from mother for the last three months: in fact that's the reason I have come to you, to ask you to put in a word for me. I sent her a registered letter, but it was no use; she doesn't answer. I tried going hungry, but Mikhail Ivanovich caught me at it, and he's on my track now. And what money could he have? There is a strike coming, too. Then we shall see our finish.

MODEST: Oh! oh! oh! What are you saying? Why didn't you go and ask for some?

VOLODYA: I have renounced them, uncle; and that place shall see me no more till the very end of my life; unless, perhaps, I am wrecked over their house—and even then I'll try to tumble down beyond them. But don't worry about me. I'll manage it. Poor old papa!

MODEST: Did you write to him?

VOLODYA: To father? Oh, no! Why should I bother him? Judge for yourself. Well, I'll beat it; the train has whistled. Give me half a ruble.

MODEST: Here are five rubles; they are your father's money anyhow. But perhaps you'd better wait?

VOLODYA: No, why should I disturb him? Thanks, uncle. Oh, but why do you stare at me so? You embarrass me, uncle; I don't like it, really! Such fools! Broke the machine! We could have had a nice fly to-day. I'd better take that road, otherwise I'm liable to meet them. Your news has bowled me over, uncle; my head fairly swims.

MODEST: Oh! and on such a splendid day! (*They walk off.* MODEST PETROVICH *stops and whispers.*)

MODEST: Savvich.

VOLODYA: Is he?

(MODEST PETROVICH *silently nods his head. They walk on.*)

VOLODYA: He ought to be killed.

MODEST (*stops and whispers again*): He is my horror, Volodya, my nightmare. It has gone so far that I see him every night.—Always the same identical dream. Just listen. I seem to see your papa sitting somewhere in a large assembly; there are lots of garlands and flowers, you know; all are doing him homage; some even weep; and all of a sudden Savvich approaches papa and says to him while everybody is silent: "You have insulted me, professor; and I will allow nobody to insult me; I care not a straw for the fact that every one here burns incense before you. Just take this slap on the face!" And he slaps him, you know; slaps him right on the face.

VOLODYA (*breathing heavily and looking from under his eyebrows at* MODEST PETROVICH): And wasn't I there at that meeting? For such a dream, uncle, you yourself deserve a—

MODEST: Wait, I think it's his voice. They are coming. Well, hurry up; I have to get a smile ready. I must screw up my face and smile! Like this, like this.

(VOLODYA *goes out.* MODEST PETROVICH *remains alone; grins unnaturally; smiles; bows in a friendly way and opens his arms.*)

MODEST (*mumbles*): Oh, my dear! I am so glad! What a day! Princess, you are here at last. Oh, what a pack of nonsense! I am a fool, a ninny. I am so glad, Princess!

(STORITSYN *and* LYUDMILA PAVLOVNA *approach the gate.* MODEST PETROVICH *rushes to meet them.*)

MODEST: What a glorious day, Valentin, is it not? Please, please,

Princess; I'll open it, you don't know how. What a day! . . . How was the journey? Wasn't it crowded? On Sundays usually there are a lot of people. Please, Lyudmila Pavlovna! Did you see how many people went to the cottage over there! And they are all your college girls. Is it possible they didn't recognize you, Valentin Nikolayevich?

LYUDMILA: One student bowed to him, but very modestly. I liked that very much.

MODEST: Of course! . . . We'll have tea right away. Well, how does this strike you, Valentin?

STORITSYN: You have a splendid place! But look how many cottages there are, and all of them so small!

MODEST: It is noisy during the summer, but in autumn and winter it is very nice here. Well, so how was the journey? I have prepared tea in the house, Lyudmila Pavlovna, but perhaps you would like to have it on the veranda—I'll bring it over. You are not afraid of the cold, Princess? It's so warm.

STORITSYN: Just wait. . . . Is that music? Listen to it, Lyudmila Pavlovna! It's music.

MODEST: It's in that cottage. He plays wonderfully.

STORITSYN: It is marvelous here. You are a lucky man, Modest!

LYUDMILA: All right, Valentin Nikolayevich, you listen to the music, but I want to look around. . . . Modest Petrovich, show me how you have arranged everything. Is this the veranda where we are going to have tea? (*Takes his arm and leads him toward the house.*)

LYUDMILA: It is very nice here, Modest Petrovich. This is the veranda? Modest Petrovich, I simply must have a talk with Valentin Nikolayevich. Softer, it is for his sake. No, I'll have a look later, but now we must listen to the music. . . . Don't pay any attention to us, Modest Petrovich. Do you agree?

(*She goes up to* STORITSYN; *both listen to the music. On the veranda* MODEST PETROVICH *and the cook set the table; he often glances at the gate.*)

STORITSYN: When we have too much joy, it passes into grief. It is embarrassing for me to confess, it may be considered sentimentality; but I am touched, ludicrously so. Everything amazes me to-day: the air amazes me, and the sun, the autumn sun, the yellow leaves amaze me, their color, their design; when a leaf falls and alights on my shoulder, it seems to me unusual and full of sacramental significance. Either I never before have seen autumn, or this is not autumn at all, but some extraordinary miracle, a world event, a migration of peoples. Are you listening?

LYUDMILA: Speak on.

STORITSYN: I see that even people are different to-day; in their

eyes I see gold and azure. And why music? It amazes me. Did I
seek and find it here; or was it waiting for me?—But now we have met!
And everything is so marvelous, and I look at you, and in your eyes are
gold and azure!

(LYUDMILA PAVLOVNA *frowningly lowers her eyes. Silence.* STORI-
TSYN *smiles and attentively looks down at the girl.*)

LYUDMILA: Why do you torture me, Valentin Nikolayevich?

STORITSYN: Do I? (*Seriously.*) It must be so.

LYUDMILA: No, it must not. Do you doubt my strength?

STORITSYN: No, I believe in your strength; and I also believe in
your pride, Lyudmila Pavlovna.

LYUDMILA: Pride? I don't know about that. But since I began
to think, I have become the strongest person in the world. For you,
who are used to meditate, to see everything and understand; for you
it is difficult to comprehend what it means when a person begins to
think for the first time. I live as in a hurricane; everything goes to
pieces and falls more swiftly than during an earthquake. I see only
ruins around me, Valentin Nikolayevich! Are you still silent? If I
wish, I can go away to-morrow and nobody, neither father nor brothers,
will dare to look askance at me. Are you still silent? Why did you
turn pale so suddenly? To-day I have decided to tell you everything.

STORITSYN: Don't.

LYUDMILA: Don't you wish me to? Do I have to be silent? Well,
so I am. (*Silence.*)

LYUDMILA: Did she resemble me, that girl whom you never told
of your love?

STORITSYN: No. She was a poor girl in a ragged coat. She died
of consumption.

LYUDMILA (*earnestly*): I'd like to go to her grave and tell her . . .

STORITSYN: I don't know where her grave is. I don't know where
the graves of my hopes and joys are; they are scattered throughout
the entire world. At times the whole world seems to me but a graveyard, and I am the dumb guardian of the graves. But to-day something miraculous is going on within me. I am so full of joy that it
becomes painful and torturing, and therefore I turn pale. The graves
have opened and the dead have arisen. From the whole world a heavy
curtain has suddenly fallen away—and I see now the radiant palaces
of my fancy. These are words such as nobody has ever heard from
me before, words which must be forgotten as soon as they are heard.
. . . And you must forget them.

LYUDMILA: Yes.

STORITSYN: All my life, and in everything, in my science, in my
books, in people, in things, in my joys and in my sufferings, I have

sought one thing, Her, the pure immaculate Mother of God the Word. Whether it be in the form of a man, a girl, a woman, or of beauty itself—I do not know. To-day, from the world the curtain has fallen, and I see the incorruptible in all things. Perchance it is beauty, and perchance it is you. I think it is you.

LYUDMILA: I feel terror.

STORITSYN: Yes, terrible words, a tragic charge, and I feel like baring my head as soon as they sound in my thoughts, in my head. In this world there are mothers of many children who have remained virgins, and there are babes at the breast who are corrupt as prostitutes. Forgive me, Princess!

LYUDMILA: Speak on.

STORITSYN: Above us, in the heavens, I see the incorruptible, the incorruptible I see in your eyes . . . and may God preserve you, Lyudmila Pavlovna! When you marry . . . yes, yes, marry, then in the name of the man who will love you, in the name of my love, of the whole of my life, I tell you: Preserve the incorruptible. Remember that only immaculate women give birth to God the Word, but that otherwise they bear only—children.

LYUDMILA: Yes.

STORITSYN: Careful, your *yes* sounds like an oath!

LYUDMILA: Yes, and it is an oath! But now, after I have given an oath, do I still have to remain silent? I do not wish to be silent. Do you think that you alone have sought and suffered? So have I sought, a thousand thousand years I have waited and sought, and now when I have found it, you tell me: "No, keep still, forget!" I am not a little girl who would allow herself to die of consumption, and I will not die. You too are proud and to-day I have understood you. You fear a vulgar romance between a professor and a pretty college girl; you are afraid.

STORITSYN: No. (*Silence.*)

LYUDMILA (*frightened*): Excuse me; perhaps I have insulted you, Valentin Nikolayevich. Forgive me. To-day—

STORITSYN: To-day we meet for the last time. And I love you: why shouldn't I tell you this too? And I am hopelessly, incomprehensibly solitary in this world of my graves—and why should not I tell you that too? Everything may be said, I can tell you everything; and all of this has only one meaning: I see your countenance for the last time, Lyudmila Pavlovna.

LYUDMILA: I know, you desire something heroic of me. Is your beauty an heroic deed?

STORITSYN: Yes, my beauty of life is an heroic deed. You are young, live on. The one who seeks for an heroic deed will always find it, and when you find it and perform it, and your life becomes as beautiful as your countenance, then come to me. Let it be then only my grave—from my grave I shall answer you; I shall lift the gravestone and answer.

LYUDMILA: But if it is *my* grave?

STORITSYN: Then I shall come there and you will hear my voice. But now—do not take this as an insult, Princess—now I still . . . do not quite . . . believe in this beauty of yours. Yes, I see the incorruptible in your eyes, but, my God!—I am no longer young, Princess; I must speak the truth, and I shall feel ashamed, terribly ashamed, if— Even now I feel a little ashamed, Princess, and only that gold and azure justify me somewhat. On my word of honor, all of a sudden I felt like blushing. Forget! Does this hurt you, Lyudmila Pavlovna?

LYUDMILA: Yes, but no matter. Forgive me, I am much to blame.

STORITSYN: But can you not smile?

LYUDMILA: For you—yes.

STORITSYN (*angrily and passionately*): Oh, if you but knew! (*Restraining himself and almost jestingly.*) It is no matter; I also smile. Many consider me blind, Lyudmila Pavlovna, but I can never decide whether I am too blind, or have too keen eyesight. But after all both mean blindness.

MODEST (*at a distance*): Professor, Valentin, the tea is ready.

STORITSYN: Right away. (*In a low voice.*) What delicacy of feeling! You know he purposely left us alone, so that we might be able to talk. . . . Are you smiling? On my word of honor, I felt like blushing again; the situation is becoming silly. Well, go, my dear; I want to be left alone. When you are at my side the time flies fast as death, and there is so little of it. . . . Yes, yes, smile, because it has been said of this day: "Let there be light and let there be happiness!"

LYUDMILA: Right away, Modest Petrovich, I am coming.— And to-morrow?

STORITSYN: Who knows the morrow?— Go, my dear, for Modest is beginning to suspect something. What an awful old fellow! (*The PRINCESS goes to the veranda, becoming more gloomy and stern with every step. STORITSYN thinks intently; his face is calm and serene.*)

MODEST: Please, Lyudmila Pavlovna, the tea is ready. Is it too strong? I am not an experienced housekeeper, and I so seldom entertain guests that— What a beautiful day! What is the matter with him, Princess; why are you so—? Forgive me, perhaps I ought not to ask; but you look agitated.

LYUDMILA: With him? I don't know. But what is the matter with you? Are you ill, or has something happened?

MODEST: Yes.

LYUDMILA: In their house?

MODEST: Yes. Oh, if you only knew! I don't take my eyes off the gate. If a certain person should appear now, then— Princess, perhaps it is indelicate to say so, but you alone can . . . save him! Elena is my sister, but— (*In an unnaturally loud voice.*) Is the tea not too strong? I'll pour another glass.

LYUDMILA: But do you think he will allow anybody to save him? (*Laughing bitterly.*) Would you accept my life, Modest Petrovich?

MODEST: Not only I, Princess, but all Europe.— We must call him.

LYUDMILA: We must have a meeting. I'll let you know when, shall I? He refuses to discuss his own life, but I must know everything— for his sake, do you understand? (*With the same bitter laugh.*) Aren't people saved against their own will!

MODEST (*decisively*): Yes, indeed, certainly.— Valentin Nikolaye-vich, your tea has grown cold, my dear. Come on.

STORITSYN: I'm coming.

MODEST (*in a low, hurried voice*): But I'll tell you what: we'll step aside somewhere—let him look for us. Oh, God! What a day! Val-entin, it is not a day, not a day but a genuine—what can I say, what is a proper comparison?— Here is your glass. By the way, I forgot to tell you: Volodya was here to-day; a very peculiar fellow, but a very fine lad.

STORITSYN (*no longer smiling*): Vladimir? Why did he not remain and wait for me? It's too bad. He is my elder son, Lyudmila Pavlovna.

LYUDMILA: Do you love him?

STORITSYN: Yes.— But it's so beautiful here, old friend, that I begin to gaze at you with reverence. You are a magician and an enchanter; you cast spells—and that is why I am successful in everything to-day. Well, at home would they allow me to drink such lye instead of tea?—No, no, leave it.

MODEST: I never have seen you in such a mood, Valentin Nikolaye-vich.

STORITSYN: Really? But have I ever before been like this? It is impossible to be like this twice, just as it is impossible to be born twice, or to die twice. This day is inscribed in the Book of Fate, old friend!

MODEST: Shall we not take a walk to the grove?

STORITSYN: You ought not to think, now, Lyudmila Pavlovna!— All right, let it be to the grove. Haven't you a hill here, Modest, even a small one?

MODEST: Excuse me, Valentin Nikolayevich, there is no hill. There are some hillocks, but . . .

STORITSYN: It's too bad. To-day I feel like climbing the highest mountain and looking from there down upon the earth. If this little spot is so beautiful to-day, then how will the whole world be?

LYUDMILA: And to say something from there?

STORITSYN: From the mount? (*Stops smiling and looks gloomily at the* PRINCESS.) No. You have penetrated almost to the very depth of my thoughts; but, Princess, you are mistaken in your conclusions. No, I am not a prophet. I am a modest, gentle Russian, who was born with a great and probably fortuitous need for beauty, for a beautiful and purposeful life. Every one of us has his hangman; and my hangmen are the coarseness, ugliness, and ignobleness of our life. And am I, a man already covered with wounds, who has passed through the ordeal of fire and water, who has for the last ten years every hour been expecting some last terrible blow, am I to preach from the mount?— But no more of this, no more, dear. . . . To-day I am happy, to-day I rejoice in my fate, to-day I see incorruptible beauty; you also must be happy. Smile, laugh, conjure forth music and bid it play. Proclaim loudly to all Ozerki that to-day is our holiday. Look, Modest is already smiling.

MODEST: Yes, I am very glad. The day is really an unusual one. But is it not time to go to the grove? Soon it will begin to grow dark. Perhaps you'll have some more tea, Valentin Nikolayevich?

STORITSYN (*rising*): Let us go.

MODEST: Let us go. (*Whispers.*) The day is passing; the day is passing, Princess.

STORITSYN (*joyfully*): No, just take a look, Modest: who is there? It is Telemakhov breaking the gate. Oh, how splendid, Lyudmila Pavlovna; oh, how glad I am! (*Runs down to the garden.*)

LYUDMILA (*to* MODEST PETROVICH): Is this the one you were expecting?

MODEST: It is. The very man.

STORITSYN: Telemasha, old friend! Wait, do you see this old goat-beard, this ancient nose saddled with eye glasses! (*They kiss each other.*) Once more, once more! Hurry and get some red wine, Modest; Telemasha cannot exist without wine.

TELEMAKHOV: How do you do! Telemakhov is my name. This thing is no gate, Modest Petrovich, but a barbed wire fence, an entanglement. It isn't right, Modest.

MODEST: To keep cows out, Professor.

TELEMAKHOV: It isn't right. I have torn my sleeve.

STORITSYN (*delighted*): What a humorist, Telemasha! But how did you find me? The same way the music has found me, or the sun? Do you know that to-day all goes well with me?

TELEMAKHOV: I have found you only after searching Ozerki for two hours. To whom does the house belong?

MODEST: To Koroleva.

TELEMAKHOV: And I was told to Korableva; they can't even write down an address correctly.

STORITSYN: Oh, what a humorist! An awfully jolly fellow! So you have been at our house?

TELEMAKHOV: I have. Well, how are you? You look well.

STORITSYN: Very well. Ask them.

TELEMAKHOV: Oho! It is quite pleasant here, and the air is comparatively pure. For tea I don't care, but I should like some wine. Don't bother yourself; I am used to pour for myself.— What kind of students are over there? They are shouting.

MODEST: To-day is a holiday; some guests have come.

TELEMAKHOV: How much do you pay for this cottage?

MODEST: The rate for a whole year is twenty-five rubles a month. It isn't dear.

TELEMAKHOV: But isn't cheap. Is it damp? It smells of rheumatism here.

STORITSYN (*embracing* TELEMAKHOV): You are delightful, Telemasha! Did you once look around on your walk? Just look! Over there! Over here! Drink your wine in peace and keep still; there is no rheumatism here. But you are rather gloomy, friends. Do you know that I feel embarrassed by my own gayety!

(*The cook* FEKLA *comes in, dressed in holiday clothes.*)

FEKLA: Master, master! Some young lady has brought you a bouquet and has told me to give it to you. Here it is.

MODEST (*taking a big bouquet of autumn leaves and flowers*): Young lady? Whom shall I give it to?

FEKLA: I don't know, to some guest. I told her, "Go ahead and give it yourself," but she said: "No, how can I go into a strange house?"— I'll go to the kitchen.

MODEST (*rises and solemnly gives the flowers to* STORITSYN): This is for you, Valentin Nikolayevich. Now even my hut has become famous. I am sorry I have no flowers that I might add to this gift of innocent youth.

LYUDMILA: You have turned pale again, Valentin Nikolayevich!

(TELEMAKHOV *looks askance at* STORITSYN *and lowers his eyes.*)

STORITSYN: It would be well to kiss the hand which picked the flowers; it was probably a still small and a very silly hand; she has no strength to lift a stone, so here she brings flowers.

LYUDMILA: Why so malicious? They love you.

STORITSYN: And I? "The rest is silence," as Hamlet says. Where is my coat, Modest? It is getting cold. Aren't you cold, Telemasha?

TELEMAKHOV: I hate Hamlets, although some probably do not share my taste; excuse me. No, I am not cold.

MODEST: And so we shall not go to the grove?

TELEMAKHOV: Is it far?

STORITSYN: You are. tired, Prokopy; we don't have to go.

TELEMAKHOV: Why not? Please, young lady, take Modest Petrovich and go for a stroll with him, and we'll have a little talk meanwhile. Go for a stroll.

STORITSYN (astonished): What is this? Some pressing business? Peculiar! We saw each other only the day before yesterday.

TELEMAKHOV: Oh, just some trifles.

(STORITSYN looks at everybody, still more alarmed.)

STORITSYN: It's peculiar! So you have been looking for me. Peculiar! Please go, Princess. Are twenty minutes enough for you, Telemakhov?

TELEMAKHOV: Yes. I am hurrying to the city myself.— Why so pensive, Modest Petrovich?

LYUDMILA: Come on. I'll be near by, Valentin Nikolayevich. (Walks quickly to the gate. MODEST PETROVICH follows her. TELEMAKHOV gazes after them and avoids looking at STORITSYN.)

TELEMAKHOV: Is she really a princess?— A beautiful girl! Your pupil?

STORITSYN: What has happened? Something about Sergey? Speak.

TELEMAKHOV (beginning to look at him): Speak? I don't like it at all, Valentin Nikolayevich, to be the messenger of misfortune and to break into your . . . idyll. Yes, I have enough of my own affairs, and I am surprised when people have no desire to understand that. Well, well, don't agitate yourself; it is nothing exceptional, just a trifle! Have I told you, or not, that your wife, Elena Petrovna, ought not to engage in charity work? After all it doesn't matter whether I have told you or not. There has been a trifling defalcation in the society.

(Looks at STORITSYN; the latter remains motionless.)

TELEMAKHOV: About two thousand or so. A mere trifle.—

STORITSYN: And a forgery?

TELEMAKHOV: Yes, and a forgery; a mere trifle! The last date for payment is to-morrow, and at that only from respect for your name and social position. It has to be paid, Valentin Nikolayevich.

STORITSYN: I have no money.

TELEMAKHOV: Find it; it has to be found. Otherwise, court proceedings and disgrace!

STORITSYN: Let it be court proceedings and disgrace.

TELEMAKHOV: That's silly, Valentin Nikolayevich. I haven't the least desire to shelter swindlers and spendthrifts, but you must not bring it into court. Whom would your disgrace benefit? You must not let the street laugh and mock at Professor Storitsyn. Pay; you must pay; and you must have money. If I only earned as much, I should have had a house on the main boulevard. Get an advance from the publisher.

STORITSYN: I have done so up to the limit. But why is it a disgrace for me? Do you think, Telemakhov, it is a disgrace to be deceived and robbed by somebody?

TELEMAKHOV: I think it is a disgrace not to have eyes or—to close them on purpose. I'll be frank: I was asked to loan this money without telling you; they swore to me and so forth; but I refused. To you personally, Valentin,—I am ready to give all I possess. Take it and do whatever you please with it; I'll trust you. But on one condition: take it with open eyes. It's time you did.

STORITSYN: You have known me from my childhood, and still you think that I have deliberately closed my eyes?

TELEMAKHOV: I don't know. But you aren't really blind, are you? I don't want to instruct you, Valentin Nikolayevich, nor should a man with as little talent as I turn preacher, but this must not continue, my dear! A decent man cannot enter your house without a feeling of disgust. If the situation is beyond you, if you lack character for it, then go away, leave them, don't soil yourself. I could believe yet, but others won't. Finally, how can you help seeing Savvich? Say what you will—this I cannot comprehend; I cannot comprehend it, not if I were to be shot for it.

STORITSYN: Is this the first defalcation?

TELEMAKHOV: I don't know. And who made Savvich such as he is? I haven't forgotten the occasion when he appeared for the first time; even then he was a "handsome man," a boor and a scoundrel, a knight . . . oh, the devil take him! But now, such insolence and calmness! He roars at everybody, at your servants, and at your wife; he even tells your children how to behave. And who is now the real master of your house? It seems he has even given *you* instructions.

STORITSYN: You are also giving me instructions.

TELEMAKHOV (*furiously*): No comparisons, please!

(*Silence. It is growing dark. In some cottages appear the first evening lights. Near the station a train puffs and clanks heavily and slowly.*)

TELEMAKHOV: I don't understand it. Psychological problems are beyond me. Even every cat on the stairs knows; and you seem to have just tumbled down from heaven! However, I am a biologist and a realist. Please excuse me.

STORITSYN: Don't you believe me?

TELEMAKHOV (*shrugging his shoulders*): I do. Even scatterbrained Volodya has left you. But, anyway, it has to be paid, Valentin Nikolayevich. Will you allow me to advance the money for you?

STORITSYN: No, I won't.

TELEMAKHOV: Then come court proceedings, disgrace; let the street laugh! A Japanese vengeance, to cut one's belly open to shame another? I can't restrain myself from telling you as a friend, Valentin Nikolayevich, that it is foolish three times over. The prisoner's bench is much easier for them than the witness's chair for you—if it prove only the witness's!

STORITSYN: Is it? Anyway, I thank you for your kind offer.

TELEMAKHOV: You are welcome. Excuse me for disturbing you.

STORITSYN: Are you going right now? We are leaving on the next train—probably the same as yours. Once more I thank you, if not for your words—of which allow me to have my own opinion—then at least for your action, which was very kind. How cold it has grown, however.

TELEMAKHOV (*shrugging his shoulders*): I won't argue the question. And how is your heart?

STORITSYN: Very well. I have already taken two doses of the medicine you gave me. It is a sedative. Then I believe I have something to smell . . . I have forgotten.

TELEMAKHOV: Yes, in case you feel poorly. Shall I not call on you to-morrow?

STORITSYN: What for? By the way, how is your practice? I have heard that it is growing. Soon you'll become a fashionable doctor.

TELEMAKHOV: Thank you, it is quite all right. Here is Modest.

STORITSYN: We'll ask him for the time-table. (*Descends from the veranda.*) Pardon me, Lyudmila Pavlovna, I have to go home immediately, and we'll have to break up our holiday. If this day is really inscribed in the Book of Fate, it is with a rather different significance from what I supposed.

MODEST: May I go with you, Valentin?

STORITSYN: Certainly, we'll all go together. By the way, you'll take Lyudmila Pavlovna home. When is the train?

LYUDMILA (*in a low voice*): Don't go home!

MODEST: In half an hour. We'll be on time. I'll just put on my cloak; I'll be here directly.

TELEMAKHOV: I'll walk on slowly then, and wait for you on the platform. I am not a walker. How can people make such a gate!

(*Goes out.* STORITSYN *and* LYUDMILA PAVLOVNA *are left alone.*)

LYUDMILA (*hurriedly*): Valentin Nikolayevich, don't go home! Don't go!

STORITSYN: I must.

LYUDMILA: Well then—I love you! Do not forget that, do not forget!

(*Silence.*)

LYUDMILA (*desperately*): You remain silent? Then recollect the girl in the torn coat. You mustn't forget her; you must not!

(MODEST PETROVICH *appears. In his cloak and hat he resembles an old Italian bandit.*)

MODEST: Here I am. (*In a paroxysm of gayety.*) What a splendid evening! Please, don't hurry. We have time enough. . . . Wait, the flowers! We almost forgot the flowers. Immediately, one moment!

(*The two dark silhouettes of* STORITSYN *and the* PRINCESS *stand in silence near the open gate.*)

ACT III

The same day. STORITSYN'S *study. The lights are already turned on, but the window curtains are not drawn, and in spite of the double windows one can hear the Sunday evening noise of the street. Through one of the windows is seen on the façade of a house on the opposite side of the street the flashing of an electric sign, "skating rink." In the usual place of the Professor at his desk sits* SAVVICH *with a pencil in his hand, with which he plays during the conversation; nearby at the same desk* ELENA PETROVNA *sits in an armchair and attentively listens to him. Her eyes bear traces of tears and are swollen; she often sighs.*

ELENA: Speak, Gavriil Gavriilovich; I am listening.

SAVVICH: I repeat and insist that it is even better if the professor learns of your speculation on the stock exchange. Why? Because the abscess is already ripe and it ought to be cut open, as the doctors say in such cases. Of course he'll fret a little, because no one is pleased to have people dispose of his money without permission, but on the other hand we shall be able to speculate openly. I am sick and tired—

ELENA: But, Gavriil! . . . But you don't know his character!

SAVVICH: Do not interrupt, but listen to what I am telling you. I repeat, I am sick and tired of playing the part of a secret accomplice, who has to hide himself and blink like your brother Modest, the idiot. What am I, a swindler or an honest man? First, with you I risk my own hard-earned money; tell him so. Second, both when we win and when we lose I take my fair share of gains or losses.

ELENA: But he won't understand, Gavriil Gavriilovich! Excuse me;

I am listening to you very attentively, I respect every word of yours; but he won't understand. I stake my life on it. He appreciates and respects you very much, he believes in your disinterestedness. . . .

SAVVICH: He knows me.

ELENA: I am in such a hurry. . . . I can't!

SAVVICH: Tell him, there is still time. Of course he is a very clever man, I respect him myself; and one can always make a clever man listen to reason. Just let his first blaze of fury pass by.

ELENA: No, no. I assure you, Gavriil Gavriilovich, it's impossible! He has a terrible character, and if he doesn't want to understand something, then he can drive one crazy! He'll simply say that it is very bad, and then—I don't know.

SAVVICH: Bad? Well, if he *refuses* to understand, then send him over to me. I'll make him see things. Bad, look at that! People are doing their best for him and for his family, and he will only bluster and blush like injured innocence. "Ah! You mustn't! Ah! I won't have it! Ah! I shall die of shame." That's all right, he won't die. I know those fellows; I have seen enough of them. I am even glad there is an occasion to tell him the truth right to his face; let others sneak if they wish to, I don't care a damn if he is a professor. I should be a professor myself now, if I hadn't been carried away by women. . . . Not every one has such a fishy temperament.

ELENA: But two thousand? (*Shuddering.*) I shall lose my reason, Gavriil.

SAVVICH: No, you won't. There's none to lose. Wait, next week we'll have fifty thousand, and now because of a caprice, of a whim, do I have to throw the money out on the street? I won't give even a kopek. Tell him so, not a kopek He'll come to his senses; he'll even be grateful. But the money, the two thousand, let him get it from Telemakhov; and if he refuses to borrow of outsiders—do you understand?—then I can get it for him on a note. Thank God, I am not a swindler, and I won't let a man perish. Well, can you say all that? You won't mix things up?

ELENA: I don't know; I'll try. I am very agitated, Gavriil; I can hardly breathe, my whole chest is cramped.

SAVVICH: I should say so, you can hear your corsets squeak a mile off. It comes from too much blood. You eat too much. Only talk to him delicately, do you hear? Better cry, if you can't talk like a human being; but don't jump at him like a cow at a fence. (*Carelessly.*) Did you put the book on the table?

ELENA: Yes.

SAVVICH: Say that I saw it when I was passing a second-hand store.

I thought it might be useful to him, an interesting little book. And be sure to tell him about Sergey; let him know what a hooligan he is. Tell him that if it wasn't for me Sergey would have been expelled from the gymnasium a long time ago. They wouldn't have cared if his father was a professor. Do not forget that I—

ELENA: Oh! There's the bell, I think it's he. Go, go away, Gavriil.

SAVVICH (*looks at his watch*): Not yet, but he'll come soon; the train has arrived already. But still, I'll go. Listen, Lena, I'll go out with Mamykin for about ten minutes; by the way, I'll buy some ham for supper, and then I'll be in the dining-room.

ELENA: Yes, yes, thank you. But perhaps it's better that you should not come to-day at all. Come to-morrow instead; he'll have time to calm himself.

SAVVICH: Will he kill me? I am not a coward, Elena Petrovna. See here: don't agitate yourself; in case anything happens I'll be there. Hold up your forehead, I'll give you a kiss. (*Kisses her.*) So—like a father. And please do not be afraid, Lenochka: God will save us, a swine will not swallow us. I'll buy the ham on my own tick to-day. I can't be bothered now with accounts. Adieu.

(*Goes out. ELENA PETROVNA stands for a while by the window, looking at the street, then sits down at the table, in the Professor's place, and cries, covering her face with a handkerchief. She hears steps and has barely time to get up and put herself in order before STORITSYN comes in. In the Professor's hand are flowers, for which he tries to find a place, evidently not quite aware what he is doing. He comes to himself and throws the flowers on the table. Silence. ELENA PETROVNA undecidedly takes the bouquet.*)

ELENA: May I? (*Smells them for a long while.*) What a beautiful bouquet, and it smells so fragrantly of autumn. (*She carefully puts the flowers in place.*) Will you have some tea, Valentin?

STORITSYN: Yes. (*Rings the bell.*)

ELENA: What splendid weather it is to-day. It's difficult to stay indoors.

(*The MAID comes in.*)

ELENA: Dunya, bring tea for Valentin Nikolayevich.

STORITSYN: Please, Dunya, make it strong.

(*The MAID goes out. ELENA PETROVNA takes a seat on the very edge of the sofa just as indecisively as she does everything now.*)

STORITSYN: I believe Sergey has some guests?

ELENA (*animated*): Yes, two friends. One is Shchukin; he plays well on the balalaika, just marvelously, a real artist! Sergey has asked me for a balalaika too . . . but I wanted to tell you, Valentin, that Sergey—

STORITSYN: Later.

(*While the* MAID *brings in the tea and goes out, the room is full of tense silence. Through the open door are distinctly heard the balalaikas playing "Walking down the street"; when the door is closed, the sounds are weaker but are still heard.*)

STORITSYN: Thank you, Dunya.

ELENA: Close the doors, Dunya.

(*Silence.*)

ELENA: Well then, Valentin, I started to speak of Sergey. (*Almost shouts.*) Forgive me, Valentin, pity me, I feel so guilty before you! I am not worthy of you.

(*She falls on the sofa and weeps. Silence.* STORITSYN *paces the room, stops behind his armchair, and speaks almost in a whisper—as if from a great distance were wafted a voice, an echo of his former voice.*)

STORITSYN: Do you remember, Elena, that ten years ago—I shall not mention under what circumstances—I forgave you? Do you remember?

ELENA: I remember.

STORITSYN: And you swore then by the life and happiness of your children that your life would be forever pure and innocent. Do you remember, Elena?

ELENA: I remember.

STORITSYN: What have you done with your purity, Elena?

(*Silence.*)

STORITSYN: I believe that very soon I shall die, and who will be one of my murderers, Elena? And who is the murderer of our children, by whose life you swore, Elena? And who is the murderer of everything honest in this house, in this unhappy, terrible life? I ask you, Elena.

ELENA: Forgive!

STORITSYN: What has happened to you, Elena; why have you decayed so quickly and so terribly? I remember you while still a girl, a bride: you were then pure, worthy of ardent love and respect. I remember you as a wife in those first years: you then lived one life with me, you were pure; as a friend you supported me often in moments of grief. Even now I cannot utter to you words of unmixed blame, merely because of those two years of my exile, when you, as a valiant friend, as a comrade . . . I cannot!

(*Silence.*)

STORITSYN: What did you find in Savvich?

ELENA: I don't know. He is a scoundrel. Forgive me!

STORITSYN: Well—so that is true! It's true. . . . It's true. . . . Ah . . . that's it. . . . That's it . . . so . . .

ELENA (*terrified*) : Do you want some water?

STORITSYN: No. Even to-day Professor Telemakhov reproached me for either dishonesty or silliness, because I have consciously closed my eyes. . . . But could he, and all of you, could you understand that as an honest man I have refused to see and that I have not seen—all your abominations? Could you understand then that as an honest man I have denied the facts themselves? A fact! What is a fact, I have thought, with all its delusion of movements and words, when I have before my eyes such an immovable rock as your vow, the dignity of my whole life. Oh, what a fool, what a fool!

ELENA: Do not talk so about yourself! You have no right to talk so about yourself!

STORITSYN: Oh, what a fool, what a fool! Once I clearly saw Savvich squeezing your leg under the table . . . and I had enough pride—and the strength of a madman—to take it for the unfaithfulness of my sight, but not for your unfaithfulness. Let my whole house begin to hiss as a serpent, I thought, let me be suffocated in the arms of reptiles, still I will fully accept their kiss; before the whole world I will say they are human beings until they themselves come crawling and declare: "No, we are not human beings, we are reptiles." Oh, abominable creatures! . . . Then it is all true. Then everything that I denied— this whole world of treason and hideousness and lies—is the truth? But the vow to God is a lie? Self-respect also a lie? Everything is true, even the fact that Sergey steals and sells my books. . . .

ELENA: Do you know that?

STORITSYN: And also that everything around me has been plundered, and that . . . that you and Savvich—! Who else, speak! Students, chimney-sweepers, floor-polishers also come to our house.— Whom do you love more, then, students or floor-polishers? Speak! Whose son is Sergey?

ELENA: Yours, yours! I swear.

STORITSYN: And that they crucified God is also true? Tell me, tell me, did they crucify God or not?

(*Silence.*)

STORITSYN: Speak!

ELENA: You can . . . you can kill me, but it is a lie that Sergey is not your son. I swear it to you! . . . I know that I am a perjurer and that you ought not to believe me, but believe now for the last time. I swear by everything that is sacred to me that Sergey is yours . . . your son! Yes, I am a criminal, but why have you left me, why have you not pitied me, why have you—?

STORITSYN: I? I have not pitied you? What do you call pity, then?

ELENA: Yes! You expected too much of me, and I was not equal to it—you never were willing to forgive my weaknesses. I cannot be so intellectual as you, and you wished that I also should—

STORITSYN: It is not true, Elena! Recollect, how often I have talked to you, how much health, how much of my most vigorous strength I have spent on you. During these hours of endless toil I could have educated a whole generation of men, I could have thrown into the world dozens of books. . . . Do I speak then in any one of my books with such passion, with such desire to persuade, with such an effort of all my will as I have talked to you? Ah, if I could only write as I speak to you when I need to win over the very smallest fragment of your heart! What has remained of all my words, what have you understood, Elena?

ELENA: It is not my fault that I could not understand you. Have I not tried to? You have suffered, I know it; you have a weak heart, and I am your murderer: still you have had some joy in life—but have I? Sometimes you would be reading a book, and I would observe you, would see how it made you happy, but I? Many times I used to sit down at your desk, and open the book at the very same page, but what of it? It meant nothing, nothing to me! You withdrew from me farther and farther until finally I was left alone. Formerly I could speak three languages, but now . . . English I have entirely forgotten, and German I can hardly read. . . . With whom can I converse, on what subjects? Savvich is a swindler, it's true; but he was the only one who pitied me, who understood that I also was a human being. . . . When I came to you with some unpleasant trifles, or something about the servants, you drove me away. . . . Yes, you drive me away; I understand that you cannot be disturbed by such things, but Gavriil Gavriilovich . . . Take last year, when Sergey caught the diphtheria and there was a strike in your University, then who sent for the doctor, who almost broke in the front door of the pharmacy? Gavriil Gavriilovich. . . . And even now who is first to care about your health? . . .

STORITSYN: You have really gone insane! Savvich is the man who cares about my health! Bethink yourself, what are you saying, Elena?

ELENA: If I really have gone insane, then who is responsible for it? You have never respected me. Why didn't you expel Savvich at the very beginning?

STORITSYN: Oh, my Lord! again this absurd logic! Yes, yes, I respected you and that's why I didn't expel him and ought not to have expelled him.

ELENA: No, you have never loved me! How many times have I besought you: take care of Sergey, punish him. But what have you done? You might at least have shouted at him—to your mere words nobody pays any attention. You ought to have used the switch.

STORITSYN: Did Savvich say so?

ELENA: I don't know who said so, I don't care. You don't believe in God and I do; now please think, imagine how much happiness I have! You will die and go to heaven; but I, but I, where shall I go to? Without you I should be respected by others, as other women are respected, but beside you what do I amount to? Don't I understand it myself?

STORITSYN: Why did you swear then?

ELENA: Why did you demand that I should swear?

STORITSYN: I didn't demand it; that is not true!

ELENA: But anyway you wanted me to swear, and so I did. It was for your sake, to make you feel better, but as for myself— (*Weeps aloud.*) You never did care about me. Never!

STORITSYN: But this is a twofold deceit; twice you have deceived God. . . . Elena, Elena! What words shall I use to dissipate the darkness of your conscience—there are no such words! Now I swear! If there existed in this world one word that could open your eyes, I would give my life away for that word! For only one word! For only one spark of light in this terrible darkness! Wake up, Elena! Oh, Lord! how dark it is, how dark! . . . I feel that I am beginning to die.

ELENA: I'll bring you some water. You don't feel well, Valentin?

STORITSYN: Water? No. Oh, my gentle hangman, I kiss your hand. . . . (*He quickly approaches* ELENA PETROVNA *and kisses her hand—then harshly casts it away.*) You are doing only the will of him that sent you. . . . But who has sent you to this world, this lady laced in a corset, with powder on her beet face, with a breast which could have fed thousands of babies, thousands of martyrs and heroes, but which feeds only—Savvich? Who are you, most terrible woman? Are you the horrible nightmare of my whole life, or are you really existing, weeping, blowing your nose, complaining, and waiting that I may approach you and strike you, just as Savvich hits you!

ELENA: That is not true! Savvich has never struck me! If you would pity me just as he does, then I should be altogether different. And I say nothing at all about your college girls, about the hussies whom you—

STORITSYN: What? . . .

ELENA: Not I alone, but Savvich too will tell you that, even though you despise him.

STORITSYN: Silence!

ELENA: Don't you dare to roar at me, I am not a chambermaid; I am the mother of your children. . . . It is all the same to me now, to-morrow I shall lay hands on myself; but still don't you dare, don't you dare—I also have a weak heart, I may die sooner than you—don't you dare to roar at me! Roar at your hussies, but I am a mother; I brought forth your children in torment while you were reading books. We lost three children: who buried them, who bought the little coffins, you? . . . And what every coffin cost me, do you know it?

STORITSYN: You are not a mother, you are a harlot.

ELENA: Don't you dare!

(SAVVICH *comes in without knocking on the door.*)

SAVVICH: Heaps of noise and no fighting. This won't do, Professor; won't do. Gentlemen like you do not treat a woman in this manner.

ELENA: Don't you dare to roar at me!

STORITSYN: Get out!

SAVVICH: Softer, softer, my dear sir! I won't get out, and I never allow a woman to be insulted in my presence. If you wish to come to an explanation with your wife, of course it is your own family business; no one hinders you: but for this purpose you ought to have gentle manners, and not roar as if you were speaking to a coachman! You're a professor, you have to respect your own dignity.

(MODEST PETROVICH *walks in through the open door and, clutching his head, sits down in the armchair.*)

STORITSYN: Oh, what insolence, what insolence! What ought I to do then: strike you? Strike you!

SAVVICH (*lifting his shoulders*): We shall see yet who is going to strike whom, my dear sir. . . . Although you are a prominent professor, I will not allow any one to insult me. If you wish (*Takes a step forward.*), touch it, touch it, here is my face, won't you do it? . . . But what would be left of you, I should like to know?

ELENA: Don't do it, for God's sake, Gavriil Gavriilovich! Don't touch him! He doesn't know what he is saying; he won't do it any more.

SAVVICH: Of course, we are joking. Aren't we joking, Professor?

STORITSYN (*all of a sudden becoming absolutely quiet*): And do you really think that I am afraid of you?

SAVVICH: I don't know. But a man who can lift seventy pounds with his left hand ought to inspire a certain respect, that's what I know. Mamykin, come in here!

ELENA: I don't want Mamykin, please; for my sake don't call him, please; I beg you, I beseech you. This is my disgrace; I'll die of shame.

SAVVICH: Why, why don't you want him? Let him see how professors treat women, let him learn a little about humanism. He'll make use of it in his notebook. Mamykin! Take a look!

MAMYKIN (*comes in with a downcast air*): Oh, what is there for me to see here? I'd better go away.

SAVVICH: No, you will look if I tell you to! Here, look, a prominent professor, a man of talent, flowers, and adoration—did anybody ever greet you with such bouquets, Mamykin? (*Takes the bouquet from the table and thrusts it into* MAMYKIN'S *face, then throws it into a corner.*) But his wife he treats like a kitchenmaid! Perhaps, Professor, you would really have struck her just as you were about to strike me? She is a defenseless woman. Try it!

(MODEST PETROVICH, *tottering, walks back and forth across the room, covers his face and eyes with his hands, and mumbles.*)

MODEST: Oh, Lord, Lord, Lord!

ELENA: Sit down, Modest! Don't, Gavriil Gavriilovich; he is ill, he has not insulted me. I myself—

MODEST: Oh, Lord, Lord, Lord!

STORITSYN: Elena, I beg you, go away with these gentlemen.

SAVVICH: This is different talk. You see, Mamykin, how quiet our professor has become. Soon he'll call her Lena dear. But what if we really and urgently ask him to do so, will he call her so or not, what do you think? I'll bet you three rubles that he will. Professor, won't you be so kind as to call your wife Lena dear, since you have already called her Lena? (*Makes a face.*) Oh well, it is not worth while!

MODEST: Oh, Lord, Lord, Lord!

STORITSYN: Elena, once more I beg you, go away with these gentlemen; otherwise I shall have to go away myself. And send in Sergey to me.

ELENA: Oh, God, what is coming now? I am going insane. You'll kill him, I fear.

SAVVICH: And he will do a good thing, by the way. (*Shouts through the open door.*) Sergey, Serezhka, father wants you! Well, now our conversation is quite different, and I request you to leave the battle-field, Elena Petrovna. I myself reply courteously to courtesy, and I respect the rights of another man's dwelling no less than an English lord. Did you hear, Mamykin?— You were asked courteously. Have you seen enough, you fool? I am sorry to corrupt your innocence, but what can one do? Look, learn. Oh! what creatures men are!

(SERGEY *comes in and stops on one side, gloomily and indifferently looking at everything that is going on.*)

SERGEY: What do you want? What did you call me for?

SAVVICH: Well, you talk with your father; then you'll know what for. You jailbird! . . . Let's go, Elena Petrovna. And you, Professor, when you calm yourself and come down to normal, then I am entirely at your disposal. We may fight a duel if you want to try that foolish thing; but the best course will be to have a quiet, sensible talk, as is the custom among decent people. Adieu. What do you want, Modest Petrovich? What are you shaking and shivering around me for?

MODEST (*brandishing his clenched fists*): You are a scoundrel, Gavriil

Gavriilovich, a worthless scamp! Oh, Lord, Lord! What else shall I tell him? Scoundrel!

SAVVICH: What? Listen, Elena Petrovna.

MODEST: Elena, sister! As your elder brother, who knew you when you were still an innocent girl—

STORITSYN: Stop it, Modest. Leave us.

MODEST: All right, Valentin Nikolayevich! But he *is* a scoundrel, Valentin Nikolayevich! What else shall I tell him? . . . He is laughing.

SAVVICH (*full of contempt*): What a fool! It is true enough that they sow not, neither do they reap, but just naturally grow. (*Furiously.*) Get out, you booby; I'll throttle you! Oh, you old rascal, didn't you have enough of your own prison days, that you now want to get others into the same trouble. Get out!

(*With a slight push he thrusts out of the door* MODEST PETROVICH, *who incoherently but insistently repeats:* "Oh, Lord, Lord!")

ELENA: I'll remain here, Gavriil Gavriilovich; I won't go.

SAVVICH: No, you'll go. You will have time to-morrow for mutual explanations; you too are all used up now. Quiet yourselves, quiet yourselves, ladies and gentlemen—later you will talk business. Good-by, Professor—here is my most disinterested advice; don't be easy on the hooligan. Adieu.

(*Goes out.* STORITSYN *and* SERGEY *remain alone, the latter in the same pose at the door. In the darkness his face seems to be at times indefinite and gloomy, at times smiling just as indefinitely and peculiarly.* STORITSYN *strides back and forth across the room.*)

STORITSYN: Sit down.

SERGEY (*taking a seat*): What do you want, papa?

(STORITSYN *silently and impatiently waves his hand and continues walking. In the light* SERGEY'S *face is gloomy, but indifferent, almost bored.* STORITSYN *turns abruptly and sits down in his place at the table.*)

STORITSYN: I have noticed many times, Sergey, that you smell of liquor. Do you drink? Even to-day you smell of liquor.

SERGEY: Look here, papa. To-day is Sunday, I had some friends here and just as host . . . I can't understand what there is to make a fuss about. And anyhow, papa, you can absolutely rely upon me: I'll never allow myself to drink too much; I have character. I always behave myself decently. I'll take a cigarette. (*Stretches out his hand to a box of cigarettes; but* STORITSYN, *in a fit of anger, slaps his hand violently.* SERGEY *rises.*)

SERGEY: What does this mean! You are crazy!

STORITSYN: Don't you dare . . . thief! Lock the door and give me the key.

SERGEY: But that's silly! You are not going to— God knows what's going on in this place! But after all, I don't care!

STORITSYN: Sit down.

(SERGEY *sits down in the same place and looks at the ceiling.* STORITSYN *locks the door himself and puts the key in his pocket.*)

STORITSYN: Have you been stealing my books for a long time, Sergey?

SERGEY (*rising*): Did *he* report it to you?

STORITSYN: Sit down. (*In a weary tone.*) Do you know what a book is, Sergey? Many times I have told you about books, I have taught you to love and respect them. When you were still a little boy, while showing you the pictures I taught you to be careful in turning the pages, and to wash your hands, in order not to soil them. You have seen how I love books myself, how I care for them, how I rejoice over every new book in my library. . . . Even supposing that you don't love and understand them yourself, you have nevertheless seen my attitude toward them . . . and you have robbed me of my dearest possession. I could understand you if you had stolen money—but books! To sell some one's soul in order to make twenty kopeks, thirty pieces of silver! . . . That is the deed of Judas, Sergey.

SERGEY: I am not Judas.

STORITSYN: No, you are not Judas, you are my flesh and blood, my own son. . . . But where do I appear in all that? Wait, wait, it seems to me that I see your face for the first time. . . . Sit still, sit still, do not be embarrassed. So is this flat, crushed, narrow brow your forehead, the forehead of my son? Strange! How is it that you have this narrow, beastlike jaw. . . . I believe that you can crush with it very thick bones; can you not?

SERGEY: I don't care.

STORITSYN: And how is it that you have these young, but already dull and sullen, very sullen eyes! And that carefully pomaded parting in your hair, a smart parting! And that peculiar, cheap perfume . . . yes, oh, youth! You are a very sullen fellow, Sergey; I have never heard you laugh.

SERGEY: I have no reason to be gay. Judases are never gay.

STORITSYN: Yes, yes, strange! Let's talk plainly, Sergey: I am very tired of shouting and agitating myself; forget that I am your father, just as I do. . . . Come on, tell me, tell me of yourself. . . . On what do you spend money?

SERGEY: I am no Judas. It is not my fault that I have no talents. Not everybody can be a professor like you are. But if I really have no talents, what then?

STORITSYN: Yes, yes. What are your plans for life?

SERGEY: How do I know?

STORITSYN: But still one has to live!

SERGEY: So I will. You are mistaken, papa, in thinking that I am a frivolous fellow, a drunkard.

STORITSYN: Take a cigarette.

SERGEY: Thanks. I am a serious person, and my hair stands on end when I think of the future. I'll get married some time or other, I am a serious person; then come children, and how shall I bring them up? In other families the parents help out or they have some patronage, but what do I have? It's easy for you to talk, papa; but suppose you die, we'll all have to go begging.

STORITSYN: My life is insured, if I am not mistaken.

SERGEY (*grinning*): Ten thousand rubles? Don't make me laugh, papa.

STORITSYN: Yes, it isn't much.

SERGEY (*grinning*): It won't be enough even for Savvich alone! And there are two of us, Volodya and I. Volodya also needs sympathy. There you are! We live in grand style, people envy us, but I have been teasing mother for a balalaika these six months and can't get it. As for saving money, I have no salary.

STORITSYN: Is it necessary to save?

SERGEY: Everybody has to save. One needs character in life, papa; without character you'll die in the gutter. . . . Our Savvich is a scoundrel, I see through him: he is afraid that thieves will break into his house at night and slay him, but look what character he has! I'll take another cigarette, may I?

STORITSYN: Please. And so that is why you have been selling books?

SERGEY (*lighting his cigarette*): Well, since we have started to talk frankly, I hate these books! You like to look at them, but I can't stand them; it is awful to enter the house. "Oh, the pretty books; oh, the darlings; oh, the pets! Read them, Serezhka, you little fool!" But what if I don't want to read, don't want to be wise! I don't want to! You are wise and I am a fool, and let me stay so, and this is my right, and no one has the right to change me, if I don't want to. That is all! Judas! . . .

STORITSYN: Quiet, Sergey. Is this your principle?

SERGEY: Yes, principle. And what is a fool? For others, perhaps, I am a fool, but for myself I am wise enough and I don't want to be wiser. That's all. Judas! . . . How am I to blame that my father is a professor—soon they'll fairly drive me crazy. Even in the gymnasium that beast Savvich says: "Mamykin, come here, see what a fool the professor has for a son." Well, suppose I am a fool: I don't want to be wise. . . . That's all. I also have character.

STORITSYN: But do you care to be an honest man?

SERGEY: If I want to I will be; if I don't want to then I won't. A low brow, pomaded hair! . . . Bosh, papa!

STORITSYN: Strange, strange! . . . (*Paces the room in agitation.*)

STORITSYN: You are a terrible, an unbelievable creature, Sergey! Just with one movement of that forehead you have driven me down into such depths, into such infernal darkness. . . . I wonder that you have not yet struck me!

SERGEY: It's Savvich says that I am a jailbird. Much you need to repeat!

STORITSYN: I know what I must do. You are a forehanded fellow; you must have some liquor on hand.— Bring it, Sergey.

SERGEY: Are you going to drink? It's not healthy for you. And what's the use, papa? You won't change anything, anyhow, and you'll just get sick. You had better lie down, really.

STORITSYN: Am I to stand on ceremony with you? Now? Hurry up, quick, do you hear?

SERGEY: I hear—I don't care. The door is locked.

STORITSYN: Take this.

(*Gives him the key. SERGEY goes out. STORITSYN walks up and down the room, ejaculating loudly.*)

STORITSYN: Ah! Professor Storitsyn! Beauty and the incorruptible! Martyr and sufferer! Purity and stainlessness! Yes? But don't you want the low brow? Don't you want the pomaded hair? But don't you want the perfume?

ELENA (*on the threshold*): In the name of God, Valentin, if you're going to drink I'll throw myself out of the window; I'll send for Savvich! You have no right to mock at us so!

STORITSYN: Go away.

ELENA (*falling on her knees*): On my knees I beg you.— Modest brother!

MODEST (*weeping*): May I come in, Valentin? (*Comes in with* SERGEY.)

STORITSYN: No, no. Go away, all of you.

ELENA (*humbly rising and trembling*): All right; but remember, Valentin, that I . . . that I buried your children.

SERGEY: Well, go, go, mamma! . . . You can't help it now. Uncle Modest, take her. Well?

(SERGEY *locks the door and puts the key on the table.*)

SERGEY: Here is cognac, but don't drink much. I don't think you want anything to eat, or I would get it.

STORITSYN: No. Why only one wine glass? You must drink with me.

SERGEY (*glumly*): No.

STORITSYN: You won't?

SERGEY: No.

STORITSYN (*trying to laugh*): Well, perhaps you are right. What is this? Just a wine glass? No, boy, it won't do! This will be (*Throwing the remains of his tea out of his glass.*) my—what do you call it? —tub. You see, a little bit of wisdom never hurts.

SERGEY: This way you'll get drunk soon; you're not used to it.

STORITSYN: To the health of your principle! I am not joking. (*Drinks and coughs.*) So. I am not joking! Just imagine that my wisdom all of a sudden has become repugnant to me and that I don't want it. Why shouldn't it be so? To fools and to Professor Storitsyn! Fill it up!

SERGEY (*pouring*): I don't care.

STORITSYN (*drinks*): No, you do care. To-morrow tell everybody in the gymnasium that your father was drunk. The cognac is not strong! Tell them.

SERGEY (*becoming more and more sullen*): Why should I tell them?

STORITSYN: Oh, it's too bad that your balalaikas have gone! (*Sits down and laughs.*) Sergey, is the cognac working?— Peculiar! Fill it up again! Sergey, to-morrow I'll buy you a balalaika.

SERGEY: I don't need a balalaika. You'd better go to bed, papa.

STORITSYN (*fills and drinks*): You do need it! Oh, my dear Sergey, my poor little boy! . . . (*Bends down his head and becomes absorbed in thought.* SERGEY *silently looks at him.*) What?

SERGEY: Nothing. Go to bed.

STORITSYN: Stop! Sergey, my boy, tell me: you are probably in love with some one?

SERGEY: Yes, as usual.

STORITSYN: Yes?

SERGEY: Yes.

STORITSYN: But what a man I am! . . . Of course, of course, I have entirely forgotten that you are a boy.

SERGEY: Well, not quite.

STORITSYN: And that you are just now in the period when flowers bloom. Fill the glass. To-day I brought the flowers all the way home, and they threw them in the corner. Whom do flowers bother? Who can hate flowers enough to throw them into a dark corner? My flowers!

SERGEY: Papa, who is this princess who comes to visit us? She is a very proud one.

STORITSYN (*waves his hand*): Stop it! (*Drinks.*) Absurd! Why are my window curtains not drawn to-day? Strange! I drew them myself. It now seems to me that the entire street is gazing at me. . . . Well—look! What? Am I handsome? Aha!

SERGEY: Shall I draw them, papa? I will.

STORITSYN: Absurd! (*Bending over to his son.*) So who is she, Sergey; tell me. A schoolgirl?

SERGEY: Something of the sort.

STORITSYN: Flowers, flowers! . . . Well then, Sergey, are you happy? Tell me. Oh dear, how I want you to be even a little bit happy, my poor little boy! Forget the horrors of this house; tell me as you would a friend, that you have learned even a little of this . . . this . . . (*Tenderly and dreamily smiling.*) Do you understand? Foh, I am drunk!

SERGEY: I live with her, papa.

STORITSYN: Wha-at?

SERGEY: Don't worry, we take measures. Don't drink any more; it's silly. It's awful to look at you! Why do you make such a face at me? Don't you dare make such faces!— I'll call mother.

(STORITSYN *stops looking at his son and laughs, shaking his finger drunkenly.*)

SERGEY: If you don't know how to drink, then don't; nobody asks you to! I'll call mother.

STORITSYN: Sergey! And what if you and I go over there? You know—where all of them go? Ah? That will be high jinks. What does it mean, high jinks, Sergey! I insist! Initiate me into your worthlessness, into the great filth of this world. . . . Degrade me, Sergey, degrade me.

SERGEY: Stop it, please, I am tired of it. You are drunk.

STORITSYN: But I demand! Take me you know where. Drop me somewhere on the street like carrion, filthy garbage . . . for the gods to laugh at! Policeman, to the station with the professor . . . what's his name . . . Storitsyn! . . . Aha! Give me your hand, Serezhka.

SERGEY: Get away from me. You are drunk. Foh, how drunk, disgusting!

STORITSYN: To the devil and blue hell with him, with Storitsyn! . . . the chatterbox, the handsome man! On your knees, Storitsyn, before the low brow, because otherwise— (*Suddenly turns frightfully pale and clutches his chest. In his normal voice.*) Wait! My heart! Water!

(*Falls into the armchair, wheezing.*)

SERGEY (*not daring to approach*): Papa! You are drunk. Papa! Get up!

(*Desperate knocking at the door, and voices.*)

ACT IV

The rooms of PROFESSOR TELEMAKHOV, *the next evening; that is,*
Monday. It is about eleven o'clock; it is raining and it is very windy.
TELEMAKHOV'S *study. Judging by the size of the room and by the*
largeness of the doors and windows, the apartment is in one of the
government buildings. The ceiling is white, with almost no decoration;
the wall paper is of a light color, the furniture dark; the two couches
and the armchairs are covered with cheap leather or enamel cloth.
There are many books but their abundance is not so conspicuous as in
STORITSYN'S *study, on account of the strict order. There are some*
medical instruments and a small electric machine. One notices an abso-
lute lack of anything that might ornament or at least soften the straight,
heavy, and rigid lines. The windows, which face the garden or an
empty lot, have no curtains. In one of them a single large pane is
open. Besides the lamp on the table there are two small lamps burn-
ing, one of them a hanging lamp, both with white shades.

TELEMAKHOV *is reading something, but either it is hard to under-*
stand, or he is hampered by his thoughts: he often pulls his beard and
ruffles his grizzled hair, which is cut short in military style. He is
already quite intoxicated, but still continues drinking the red wine. His
gray military coat is half open.

On a leather couch, facing TELEMAKHOV, *lies* VOLODYA, *watching*
TELEMAKHOV *read, drink wine, and ruffle his hair. At strong gusts*
of wind both turn toward the window and listen. From time to time
a cannon booms from the fortress, warning people of a flood.

VOLODYA (*breaking the silence*): What a strong wind! It's a bad
time for flying now. You might break your neck and spoil the machine.
Yesterday the barometer was changeable, and to-day it went down below
storm level. How could it be, below storm level? That's queer!
Prokopy Evseyevich, have you looked at the barometer to-day?

TELEMAKHOV (*bellows*): M-hem! Don't bother me.

VOLODYA: Prokopy Evseyevich, are we going to have a flood to-day,
or not? Hear the cannon! (*They both listen.*)

TELEMAKHOV: I don't hear it. I am getting deaf. See here, did
you come to disturb me? If you want to lie down then do so, you
precious aviator!

(*Silence.*)

VOLODYA: Prokopy Evseyevich, what is going on in our house? Do
you know?

TELEMAKHOV (*angrily*): Do you want to talk?

VOLODYA: Yes.

TELEMAKHOV: Well, I don't. I don't know what is going on in your house. I don't know and I don't want to know.

VOLODYA: I called them up on the telephone from the bakery, but the receiver was taken off. I could hear nothing.

TELEMAKHOV: Could you hear them munching?

VOLODYA: Why munching?

TELEMAKHOV: They are eating up your papa. Didn't you hear? Then keep still.

(*Silence.*)

VOLODYA: Prokopy Evseyevich, are you a professor?

TELEMAKHOV: Yes.

VOLODYA: And a general?

TELEMAKHOV: And a general. What else?

VOLODYA: Why do you drink so heavily? Do you drink so heavily every evening?

TELEMAKHOV: And why do you fly?

VOLODYA: Well, I do it because it is useful. Oh, what a question!

TELEMAKHOV: So do I do it because it is useful. So you have decided not to let me read? Which one of us is visiting the other here, you or I? What a guest!

VOLODYA: You'd better quit reading. You'll have time enough; let's talk. What a strong wind!

TELEMAKHOV: Do you think that if you lie around here every evening, I'll spend every evening talking to you? But what can I talk about with you, you mooncalf? Have you ever thought of that, bright boy?

VOLODYA: Plenty of things. Prokopy Evseyevich, aren't you lonesome by yourself all the time? You have neither comrades nor friends, only an orderly; and even he always sleeps in the kitchen. That's the reason you drink, because you are alone.

TELEMAKHOV (*with a snort*): Is that why?

VOLODYA: Why else should it be? In your place even a cow would take to drink.

TELEMAKHOV: A cow? Have you ever heard of cows drinking alcohol?

VOLODYA: Bears do.

TELEMAKHOV: Bears? What a thinker! Bears! Doesn't understand anything in life, hasn't learned even how to bellow decently, poor calf, and puts his nose into discussions! "Because of this, because of that"! . . . You are a thinker, Volodya, aren't you? But I too am a thinker (*Laughs a long time.*)—from the word "think." Do you understand? A thinker, ha, ha! A Russian thinker!

VOLODYA: I am worried about papa. Sergey came to me to-day

and told me such strange stories. . . . (*Suddenly sobs loudly and turns his face to the wall.*) They'll gobble up my papa, don't you think so? You say yourself that they are munching.

TELEMAKHOV: Don't be an old woman. Stop it! When a man has a bass voice like an archdeacon, then it's too late for him to squall! You should have done your squalling long ago. Why have you left the house then, why have you left him alone?

VOLODYA: I couldn't bear it. (*Not turning around.*) I'll kill Savvich, Prokopy Evseyevich. My word of honor on it!

TELEMAKHOV: Aha! "I'll kill Savvich!" You've struck an idea. But what were you thinking about before, you thinker?

VOLODYA: I believed papa—that Savvich was not a bad man. Now I have my own ideas.

TELEMAKHOV: Your own ideas? But can any one rely upon your papa, when he praises people? Does your papa understand anything about men? Ah? Well, well, cheer up! It's good that you have your own ideas. I also was a good deal of a fool once on a time, dear Volodya, even more than was necessary! Have you heard anything about my wife? No sort of a woman, just a mannequin with the brain of a canary. All she liked was soap and perfumery, and she also liked massages; she thought that all the science of medicine consisted in massaging the face! Most likely she married me in hopes of free massage. She married me, and I for the last fifteen years have been sending her a hundred rubles every month, on the first day of the month—what do you say about that, thinker? I think the same. (*Roars.*) Gennady! . . . (*Rings a bell.*) I ought to be flayed for it, flayed like a gypsy's eel! I have begun to despise myself for those hundred rubles. Every month I write a check, not for a hundred rubles but for a hundred stripes for myself—stripes, stripes! (*After knocking,* GENNADY, *the orderly, comes in.*)

TELEMAKHOV: Snoozing? I ring for you and your nose keeps on snoring! Change it.

GENNADY: Not at all, your Excellency.

TELEMAKHOV: Change it!

GENNADY: Very well, your Excellency.

(*All the time that the orderly is walking about the room, bringing wine,* TELEMAKHOV *silently and angrily watches him through his glasses.*)

TELEMAKHOV (*pouring wine*): Well, well, thinker, I am a sensible man and support a parasite on my hard-earned money; every month a hundred rubles to the parasite: "Please take it!" And the parasite says: "Thank you, Mr. Telemakhov, won't there be any more?" She will get more, more, and more! (*Waves his hand before his throat.*)

I'd rather cut my throat with a razor than send money to that mannequin. (*Silence. A puff of wind and the sound of a distant shot.* TELEMAKHOV *looks at the open window and angrily slams it to with his stick.*)

VOLODYA (*sighing*): I'll kill him. (*A loud ring.* TELEMAKHOV *stops;* VOLODYA *quickly sits down, both listening.*)

VOLODYA: This is from the house.

TELEMAKHOV: Wait a while, not every one is from your house. There are some patients also. (GENNADY *comes in.*)

GENNADY: Your Excellency, Mr. Storitsyn wants to enter. He is in the hall.

(TELEMAKHOV *takes a few steps forward, but* STORITSYN *comes in, wearing his overcoat and hat. He is dripping wet from the rain; he wears no galoshes; his shoes and the bottoms of his trousers are dirty.*)

STORITSYN: I have come to see you, Telemakhov. Excuse me for breaking in at night; I believe it's very late. . . . May I?

TELEMAKHOV: I am very glad, I am glad from the bottom of my heart. . . . Gennady, take off his coat.

STORITSYN: Yes, please. . . . Gennady, I won't go back to the hall. And some hot tea, Gennady, if it isn't too late. I am chilled.

TELEMAKHOV: Tea! Some more wine!

STORITSYN: Is your name Gennady? Thank you. No, you needn't wipe my boots, it's no matter. . . . What a terrible rain! Are *you* here, Volodya? Hello, how did you get here? Is this your home?

VOLODYA: I am a guest here, papa.

STORITSYN: I am very glad. It looks as though there would be a flood; I was just walking along the bank of the Neva; it's pitch dark. . . . Wait, Telemasha, does the river come anywhere near your lodging?

TELEMAKHOV: It does. Sit down, my dear fellow; we'll have tea right away.

STORITSYN: Of course it does. But imagine, I suddenly forgot your address; I was walking and walking. . . . I couldn't even take a cab— where should he go? Once the cannon went off right close to my ear. . . . May I stay here, Telemakhov? I must tell you that I have left my own house for good.

TELEMAKHOV: I am very glad. You ought to have done so long since!

STORITSYN: Yes, yes, I ought to have. To-day, Telemakhov, I have had a terrible day, a hundred and twenty miles long. . . . Volodya, perhaps you would go home. I am very glad to see you, but just now I don't feel like having you here. . . . How tall you are now, Volodya. Kiss me good-by and go.

TELEMAKHOV (*with decision*): He'll stay here overnight. Go to the bedroom, Volodya. (*Takes his arm and leads him, talking to him and looking at him over his glasses.* STORITSYN *looks first at the dark window, then at the table.* TELEMAKHOV *returns, resolutely rubbing his hands.*)

STORITSYN: Still sipping red wine, Telemasha?

TELEMAKHOV: Yes. Won't you have a bite; you must eat something.

STORITSYN: No, I have eaten already. We have dined to-day. Telemakhov, I must tell you that I have left my house forever.

TELEMAKHOV: Yes, yes, I heard. Time long ago! Congratulations!

STORITSYN: Telemakhov, do you keep a revolver in your house? Can you imagine, I couldn't find a revolver in my house. . . . Show me the thing. I should like to see one. But how could I know that I should need such a plaything in my house. . . . Foh, what nonsense I am talking! I am joking, Telemasha. And I am chilly, I am shivering a bit.

TELEMAKHOV (*furiously*): Gennady!

STORITSYN: Don't, he'll come right away; it isn't ready yet. I'll drink some tea with pleasure. An unusually heavy rain. And such darkness on the Neva. . . . Yet how strange it is that the Neva is so close to you!

TELEMAKHOV: Give me your hand, Valentin!

STORITSYN: What for? (*Snatches his hand away.*) Ah, my pulse! Don't, don't, don't do it, for the Lord's sake, don't do it! When anybody inquires now about my health or tries my pulse, I always imagine that they are going to hang me, and are afraid that I am already dead. I am quite well.

TELEMAKHOV: You are delirious!

STORITSYN: Maybe, but do not be angry. And I beg you, Telemasha, if he comes here, don't let him in, I can bear it no longer.

TELEMAKHOV: Who is that *he?* Savvich?

STORITSYN: Yes.

TELEMAKHOV: Shall I not let him in? But maybe it's better to let him in?— Maybe it's better to take him by his little white hand and say to him: "Please come in, Mr. Savvich!"

STORITSYN: No, no, I cannot!

(TELEMAKHOV *opens the door to the bedroom and calls loudly.*)

TELEMAKHOV: Volodya, Mr. Savvich is expected here, and your father asks to have him kept out. . . . Can you do it or not?

VOLODYA (*slowly and, judging by his voice, lazily*): I can.

(TELEMAKHOV *loudly slams the door.* GENNADY *brings in the tea.* STORITSYN *thanks him and drinks it greedily.* TELEMAKHOV, *snort-*

ing louder and louder, paces the room, looking angrily askance at STORITSYN. *He laughs.*)

STORITSYN: It's hot. How cozy it is here. What are you laughing at, Telemasha?

TELEMAKHOV: I laugh because I laugh. Or maybe you will forbid me to laugh? Pardon me then—I can't help it. (*Stops laughing.*) I am laughing.

STORITSYN: At me?

TELEMAKHOV: I don't know, and nobody has the right to forbid me to laugh. I am laughing and that is all there is to it! And those to whom my laugh is not agreeable, I would ask not to listen. Yes!

STORITSYN (*making laborious attempts to understand*): Shall I leave, perhaps?

TELEMAKHOV (*stopping and looking furiously at* STORITSYN): It's silly! It was silly from three sides, but now it's silly from all four. Gennady! Some more tea!

(GENNADY *comes in hurriedly.*)

TELEMAKHOV: If you dare to fall asleep once more I'll fix you, you beast! . . . Some more tea!

STORITSYN: Why do you insult him?

TELEMAKHOV: Why do I insult him, why do you insult me?— Put it down, you blockhead! . . . I call him a blockhead, but what do you slap me in the face for? When Professor Storitsyn is chased out of his house, who do you think gets slapped? Savvich? No, *I* get slapped. That's the truth of it. Yes, *I* get slapped. I have laughed and I will laugh and no one shall forbid me! No, no one!

STORITSYN (*involuntarily smiling, slowly*): But wait awhile, Telemasha. . . . You accuse me? Do you consider *me* guilty?

TELEMAKHOV: I don't know who is guilty. But I won't allow anybody to slap me on the face! I won't! Let it be even Mr. Storitsyn with his most noble palm. And that settles it.

STORITSYN (*seriously*): Don't roar, Telemakhov; I am tired of roaring. Do you think that it is my fault? But you know yourself, that truly and honestly I have sown only good seed.

TELEMAKHOV: Yes? Only? But a sparrow came and picked them up?

STORITSYN: I am so sad that you . . . Telemasha, old friend! They don't understand anything, but I understand them: there is the whole story. And they can beat me, or act the way they do; but I can't, and I ought not to do so, because I understand them. . . . Wait, don't roar! My head aches and I feel ill, Telemakhov! I have made a terrible discovery. I was drunk yesterday, something was the matter with me; but that's all right, Telemakhov! . . . Yesterday I saw my son Sergey . . . the scamp Serezhka, as they call him. You are laughing? Don't, do not laugh.

TELEMAKHOV (*trying to be quiet*): I can be serious, why not? When Professor Storitsyn is chased out of his house, I can talk seriously, if that's your wish. It is a long time, Valentin Nikolayevich; many years have passed since I separated myself from your life, quite deliberately detached myself from your life and said to myself: "Live the way you please, but like Pilate, I wash my hands." But when you (*Shaking his finger.*) come to me on such a night, I'll tell you everything; I'll remind you, I won't remain silent any more. What do you think, Mr. Storitsyn—I ask you now, on this night of reckoning—what do you think are our precious fellow men and brethren; angels without wings, in stained but still white attire, or wolves? What? Tell me, you exile, you solitary, unfortunate man . . . you relic of a man!

STORITSYN (*rising*): You are solitary and unfortunate yourself. I am sorry for you.

TELEMAKHOV: Please do not be sorry for me. Yes, yes, suppose I am a solitary old dog, but I have a lair, I have a home—you see. (*Waves his hand.*) After all, who has come to whom: I to you or you to me? Of course, you live all your life in a world of ideal entities, you simply have no desire to lower your eyes to the earth— well, but I am a realist, I am a biologist and a realist! and I have no desire to know your unreal treasures! You may fly in the heavens, but I stand firmly on the earth, and I shall not leave my earth, and I know that we Professors Telemakhov and Storitsyn—are alone on this night, amid a pack of wolves. And let them gobble *you* up, but *I* do not want to be mere food for them; I will go at them with firebrands. Yes!

STORITSYN: It is a lie, Telemakhov! Storitsyn does not exist; he is a delusion, a deceit. Telemakhov, imagine! My son Sergey has a low brow.

TELEMAKHOV: A low brow? Why is it low? Low! (*Furiously.*) So let's shoot at that low brow! Shoot! Shoot!

STORITSYN (*loudly*): Keep still!

TELEMAKHOV: No, I won't keep still. I have obtained the right to talk and I can't keep still on such a night. (*Mocking him.*) "Gennady, my dear, please." . . . For twenty years I have been learning how to roar at Gennady: "Blockhead!" And I have learned it well. Twenty years I have been trying to lose the habit of pity. I have turned my soul inside out, I have taken a blood-bath in the Far East . . . and I have learned how! And now Professor Storitsyn comes to me, the exile who has been driven out of his home, and slaps me on the face with his most delicate palm. (*Mimicking him.*) "I feel kindly toward every one, I despise your fist, Telemakhov; but why didn't you defend me, why did you allow Savvich to devour my most delicate soul?"

STORITSYN: It's not true. I don't need your protection. I am a wanderer who has only asked for a night's lodging, who is a homeless vagabond, who goes—

TELEMAKHOV (*approaching close, bending down his head, and looking straight in* STORITSYN'S *eyes*): You don't need protection? Ha, ha! And Savvich? And who was looking for a revolver to-day? But can there be such a plaything in Professor Storitsyn's house? But I have one! I have and I'll always have it! The incorruptible! . . . Well, if you have it, then keep still, do not babble, do not drag it on the streets, do not feed the animals . . . with your incorruptible. Here is where I keep it (*Beats himself on the chest.*) . . . and I keep still. I won't say even one word; when I die, I'll fill my mouth with sand, so that my tongue may not babble it out. It's mine! Let Professor Storitsyn babble—but I shall shoot, yes! Low brow— let us shoot at the low brow! Shoot, shoot! Hang!

STORITSYN: I am going away. I won't spend another minute in a house where that terrible word has been uttered. (*Makes a step toward the door.*)

TELEMAKHOV (*as though nailing him down with his forefinger*): Are you going away? Go ahead, go. But where will you go?

(VOLODYA, *frightened, looks in at the door.*)

STORITSYN: I am going. Good night.

TELEMAKHOV: Good night. Gennady, see the professor off! But where will you go? You have no road to take!

STORITSYN: Where? (*Raising his hands.*) I'll find at least one auditor who has listened to me. To him! (*Goes to the door, but a loud ring stops him.*)

TELEMAKHOV: Gennady, wait! Volodya, go to the hall, open the door yourself.

VOLODYA: All right. (*Crosses the stage rather quickly.* TELE-MAKHOV *approaches* STORITSYN, *and speaks standing sidewise to him, and not looking at him.*)

TELEMAKHOV: I beg you to excuse me. I am slightly drunk this evening and that's why I—lost my temper! Remain here, I beg you. But if my presence is unpleasant to you, I'd better go to the hospital to attend to some business.

STORITSYN (*shaking his head*): No, I am going.

TELEMAKHOV: Please excuse me, the old dog! If you dare to leave my house to-day, then I'll go away too; I won't stay here another minute! To the devil with it!

VOLODYA (*coming in*) : I have opened the door. They are taking off their coats. It is Uncle Modest and the Princess.

TELEMAKHOV: Ah! The Princess! (*Goes to meet them, buttoning his coat and putting himself in order.*) I am very glad!

(*The* PRINCESS *and* MODEST PETROVICH *come in.* TELEMAKHOV *meets them ceremoniously, but very cordially, shaking and holding their hands for a long while, repeating several times: "I am very glad!" The* PRINCESS *is dressed in an evening gown, as though returning from a party or the theatre; she is agitated, but restrains herself.* MODEST PETROVICH *also restrains himself. He is evidently distraught, as if he had been through trials, but now he is beaming with happiness. At the first moment neither he nor the* PRINCESS *seem to take any notice of* STORITSYN, *greeting him the very last.*)

TELEMAKHOV (*again trying to button his coat*) : Heartily welcome. Please sit down, Princess! Please, Modest Petrovich, Volodya, sit down. Why don't you sit down, Valentin Nikolayevich? Gennady, bring in some wine! I beg your pardon: won't you have some tea and fruit? Gennady, bring some tea and fruit.

(*All sit down.* GENNADY *utters something under his breath, then aloud.*)

GENNADY: We have no fruit, your Excellency.

TELEMAKHOV (*restraining himself, looks furiously at him, and shouts*) : Tea! (*In a lower voice.*) Get the tea set, you know!

GENNADY: Certainly, your Excellency.

LYUDMILA: Please don't trouble yourself . . . Prokopy . . . ?

TELEMAKHOV: My name is Prokopy Evseyevich. For goodness sake, it is no trouble at all. I am very glad! Volodya, please give papa a cigarette.

STORITSYN: Thanks. I have some.

(TELEMAKHOV *sits down and remains silent.* STORITSYN *smiles.*)

STORITSYN: Where do you come from now, Princess?

LYUDMILA: From the theatre. I have been there with my mother and brothers.

STORITSYN: Has the performance ended already?

LYUDMILA: Yes, almost. But how terrible the Neva is! Modest Petrovich and I took the road across the bridge. . . .

MODEST (*smiling*) : Are your feet wet, Lyudmila Pavlovna?

LYUDMILA (*also smiling*) : A little bit. Are yours? We walked for quite a while through some yard or other, and he was continually afraid that I might wet my feet. Valentin Nikolayevich, do you know the news?—I have left my home for good.

STORITSYN (*smiling*) : When? I didn't know it.

LYUDMILA: To-day. I shan't return home any more. Do you approve of my action . . . (*Suddenly becomes frightened and finishes her sentence.*) Professor?

(*Silence.* TELEMAKHOV, *seeing* GENNADY *with the tray at the door, furiously waves his hand toward him and hisses:* "Go back.")

LYUDMILA (*still more confused and almost weeping*): You are silent? But I began to think long ago; though I have just begun to think, still I understand; I understand so well. But if . . . you don't approve of my act, then I absolutely don't know what to do.

MODEST (*rising*): Valentin! Valentin Nikolayevich! I swear to heaven, to-day I have turned gray again, Valentin Nikolayevich! And if I am still alive and have not thrown myself into the river, it's thanks to her, to her! I have so resolved, I swear to heaven that either with her, or . . . They didn't want to let me into the theatre without a ticket, so I raised a scandal and suddenly she came along the hall. I didn't recognize her, but she recognized me. . . . There was such a scandal, Valentin Nikolayevich, that if you do not approve of it . . . with your authority . . . There was her mother, and brothers, and there was such an awful scandal!

LYUDMILA: Stop it, Modest Petrovich. Go, go away from here.

MODEST: My dear darling, but that's happiness, the new life has come to us! You know, I have resolved to work: let the houses collapse, collapse, but I—I respect you, yet you . . . should fall on your knees . . . on your knees. . . . Hurrah!

TELEMAKHOV: That's silly, Modest Petrovich! Please let us go to the dining-room, Modest Petrovich, to have a bite of what we have been blessed with: a glass of liquor! . . . Gennady! . . . Volodya, please.

MODEST: Oh, suppose it is silly. . . . I'll get drunk and make a scandal. . . .

TELEMAKHOV: That's silly! Please, please! . . . (*Leads* MODEST PETROVICH *and* VOLODYA *away; closes the door.* STORITSYN *and the* PRINCESS *remain alone.*)

STORITSYN: Did he tell the truth? Forgive me, Lyudmila Pavlovna; I have had such a long day to-day—long as a whole life—that I have gone slightly insane. I do not understand. Did he tell the truth?

LYUDMILA: The truth, why? Over there I was not afraid and here I am afraid. Yes, I have left my home forever. But I haven't left it for you: don't think so! I wanted to do so a long time ago.

STORITSYN: So neither one of us has a home?

LYUDMILA: No.

STORITSYN: What a world! Yes, now I understand. We have left our homes, neither you nor I have a home. I understand now. For a very long time we pretended in vain to be . . . I to be a Professor Storitsyn, and you to be a princess, and it turned out a humbug. You are not a princess, you're the girl in the ragged coat. Do you hear?

LYUDMILA: Yes.

STORITSYN: And our home, that is yours and mine, is the whole world. Close your eyes, and look how large it is—the whole world! That's why the wind blows to-day—do you hear?—because we have left our homes, our little homes. And the river overflows its banks, do you hear?—that's the waves. Aren't you cold, little girl?

LYUDMILA: No. (*Blushing.*) I am ashamed that I am dressed so!

STORITSYN: You are all burning like the sun! But you understand, you understand, little girl, what an awful deed! He took your flowers and threw them in the corner! He threw your flowers! Then I realized for the first time that I had gone insane, and I left them there. So I left them, and so there they lie. I should have walked with them along the streets, I should have thrown myself into the river with them . . . silly old Ophelia.

LYUDMILA: Let us go to Modest Petrovich. I am horrified when I think how tired you are. There we'll find people who love us. Volodya will go with us.

STORITSYN: Yes, let's go; he is a good man, and I have to sleep, I have to sleep a long time. I am tired. To-morrow I'll go farther, I have to go.

LYUDMILA (*weeping softly*): May I come with you? I'll be your sister, your daughter, if you wish. I know that you don't love me.

STORITSYN: Yes, I do love you. Do you hear, what a wind? That is the eternal wind of the exiles, of those who have left their little homes and who are at night walking toward their great home, who are returning to their mother country. Only exiles hear the wind; it blows only above their heads. . . . (*Rises.*) I am afraid, I am afraid, my girl! This is not a wind. The spirit of God is passing by! Listen!

(*He closes his eyes and listens, stretching out his arms toward the windows, behind which the wind blows. He opens his eyes and smiles.*)

STORITSYN: That is like the cry of the watchman, "All's well." . . . I think that at times I talk somewhat strangely, Lyudmila Pavlovna; but I believe I have a fever. But why fever, and why strangely?— I see more clearly than ever before.

LYUDMILA: But how is it that you haven't even changed your clothes; they are all wet, and you'll catch cold! I'll arrange everything immediately.

STORITSYN (*indifferently*): One must not catch cold; in order not to, one must change his clothes.

LYUDMILA: I'll call them.— Modest Petrovich!

STORITSYN: Call them. Everything is just as it should be. I forgot my cigarettes to-day and I went into some store or other. . . . How peculiar! I had not gone into a store for the last ten years. . . . So peculiar!

(*All come in.* MODEST PETROVICH *is a little tipsy—very slightly so.*)

LYUDMILA: Modest Petrovich, we are going.

MODEST: How splendid! And just in time! And everything is and everything will be! Prokopy, my friend, send your man for cabs to take us to the station. Prokopy and I have drunk *Bruderschaft* with each other, and now he is a retired general. Prokopy, I like you!

TELEMAKHOV: But I don't like you.— Gennady!

LYUDMILA: No, wait a while, Prokopy Evseyevich; he has to change his clothes. Give him some underwear and your coat; he is wet all over.

TELEMAKHOV: All right. I am sorry I have only a uniform. (*To* GENNADY, *who has just come in.*) Gennady! Give Professor Storitsyn my new coat. . . . Hm? The one in the closet. Valentin Nikolayevich, please go to the bedroom; he'll bring you the clothes right away. Excuse him, Princess.

STORITSYN (*continuing to look at every one with a smile*): Is it necessary?

TELEMAKHOV: Yes; go, my dear fellow.

STORITSYN: All right. Volodya, come with me. All of you are so peculiar to-day and—strange! Come and help me change my clothes, Volodya.. I am told to do so.

VOLODYA: Come on, papa. (*They go off to the bedroom.*)

LYUDMILA: Prokopy Evseyevich, I fear for him. I think he has fever; he is slightly delirious.

TELEMAKOV: I don't know; I haven't noticed! But if you torture a man for a whole day, tear him to pieces, and—munch him!—of course he'll talk nonsense. I am also talking nonsense to-day. (*To* GENNADY, *who has just come out of the bedroom.*) Gennady! Hire two cabs to take my friends to the station, thirty kopeks. If I see before my eyes for only one hour the knightly mug of Mr. Savvich, I—shall forget how to speak. That's all! The trouble does not lie in fever, but—

(*A bell rings in the hall, and all become silent as the dead.*)

TELEMAKHOV: Gennady—wait. Volodya, please go to the hall; there is some business. Gennady, help Vladimir Valentinovich.* Princess, please sit down. Modest, sit down.

(VOLODYA *and* GENNADY *pass quickly into the hall. The door to the bedroom remains half-opened. Voice of* STORITSYN: "Who is there?")

---

* The real name of Volodya; "Volodya" is a diminutive, like "Bob."

TELEMAKHOV: Of no importance, just trifles; everything will be arranged immediately. Two words to Mr. Savvich. Please, Valentin Nikolayevich. (*Closes tightly the door of the bedroom.*) Sit down, Princess.

(*In a businesslike way* TELEMAKOV *turns off one of the hanging lamps; the room becomes darker. One can hear the noise of the bolt being drawn back on the hall door.* TELEMAKHOV, *stretching out his neck and twitching his beard, listens to what is going on in the hall. One can clearly hear the following dialogue:*)

SAVVICH: What's the matter that you didn't come to the door? Are you asleep, you beast! Is Professor Storitsyn here?— Tell him that persons from his house have come for him. Hurry up! . . . What's the idea, what's the idea? . . . Who gave you the right? I don't know you. Oh! that's you, Volodya?

VOLODYA: Yes.

(*A moment of silence.*)

SAVVICH: You'll pay for it! I won't allow any one to slap me on the face, you rasc— (*A moment of silence.*)

SAVVICH: And you here too! What's the idea of this? Two against one. But I'll—

(*The voice breaks off. A moment of silence and a loud sound of the door being closed. Two or three furious rings from the outside, then silence.*)

TELEMAKHOV (*paces the room with enjoyment, listening to the ringing of the bell and humming*): "Masha was a-walking in her garden, tra-la-la!" (*Drinks a glass of wine at one gulp, then says gently.*) Well, how was it, Volodya?

VOLODYA: All right. He went away. But I had to— (*He whirls around the room, furiously sniffing and snorting for a while, opening his eyes very wide, and feeling his body with his hands in a peculiar way. He rubs his right hand.*)

MODEST (*in a low voice*): Stop it, Volodya, sit down! Well, you have done it; now sit down. What a beast you are, anyhow!

TELEMAKHOV: No, why? Gennady . . . Gennady—thanks!

GENNADY: Glad to serve you, your Excellency.

TELEMAKHOV: Move along! No, why? (*Drinks a glass of wine.*) "Masha was a-walking . . ."

LYUDMILA: But he? He says nothing. Prokopy Evseyevich, he says nothing!

(*For a moment all turn with a certain fear toward the bedroom, where nothing is heard from* STORITSYN.)

TELEMAKHOV (*knocks and half opens the door*): Valentin, may I come in, or will you come out?

(*Silence.* TELEMAKHOV *peeks through the door and goes away angrily.* LYUDMILA PAVLOVNA *looks at him anxiously.* TELEMAKHOV *indicates by gestures that* STORITSYN *is sitting, resting his head on his hands. After this pantomime he furiously shrugs his shoulders on his own account.*)

LYUDMILA (*in a low voice*) : Did he hear it?

TELEMAKHOV: I don't know.   And I have no desire to know! Volodya, go to your father.

VOLODYA (*at the door*) : Papa, may I come in?   Papa?

STORITSYN: No, send Modest to me.

(MODEST PETROVICH *goes in quietly, leaving the door half opened.*)

TELEMAKHOV (*standing with determination by the half-opened door*) : Valentin Nikolayevich, I take the liberty to draw your attention to the fact that I arranged the matter and that I take the blame on myself!   I didn't want to profane your ear, but this is my house, and I can't allow Mr. Savvich to open his filthy jaws here without due punishment.   That's all!

VOLODYA: Papa, pa-pa, you are unjust.   If you can't understand even such a thing, then I'll go away too.   On my word I will.   Even if I too am left without a home, I do not want things to be like that, papa. Let me in, I tell you!

STORITSYN: Come in.

(VOLODYA *goes in sidewise, without turning back, bending over his head just as though the door were very low. The door closes.* TELE-MAKHOV *and the* PRINCESS *are left alone. Silence.* TELEMAKHOV *sits down in his armchair by the table, drinks a glass of wine, and looks askance through his glasses at the door. Then he turns his gaze on the* PRINCESS.)

LYUDMILA: What is it, Prokopy Evseyevich?   Do you want to say something?

TELEMAKHOV: Give me your hand.   (*He takes the outstretched hand, kisses it, puts it on the table, and bends down his face to it.*)

LYUDMILA: Prokopy Evseyevich, are you weeping?   You mustn't.

TELEMAKHOV (*raising his head and sitting up as usual*) : I am drunk, that's why I weep.   I weep and that's all!   Nobody has the right to forbid me to weep.   And that's all!   (*Shakes his finger at the bedroom.*) So be it! . . . And I am very sorry, I am sincerely afflicted that I my-self could not . . . with my own hand—   (*Shakes his fist almost before the* PRINCESS's *countenance.*)   That's all!—   Princess?

LYUDMILA: What, Prokopy Evseyevich?

(TELEMAKHOV *silently points at the door behind which is seated* STORITSYN, *continuing to look at the* PRINCESS, *and with his forefinger draws circles in the air.*)

LYUDMILA (*frightened*) : I do not understand you.

TELEMAKHOV (*leaning over and continuing to draw with his finger*) : He'll die soon. His heart is giving out. He'll die soon.

LYUDMILA : It is impossible!

TELEMAKHOV (*nodding his head*) : He will.— But what is this?

(VOLODYA *comes out from the bedroom on tiptoe; both his face and his gait express extreme terror. He stops, looking behind him.*)

LYUDMILA : What is the matter with him?

VOLODYA : I don't know. He must be dying. I don't know.

(MODEST PETROVICH *comes out of the room, almost repeating the gestures of* VOLODYA, *but covering his face with his hands. All look with terror at the door. Opening the door wide,* STORITSYN *comes out, quite blind to his surroundings, frightful in his expression of concentration and complete alienation from everything visible. He has on* TELEMAKHOV'S *uniform coat, which is too short for him; his boots are dirty. Slowly, without looking around, he goes to the door.*)

TELEMAKHOV (*becoming sober*) : Where are you going?

(STORITSYN *stops and for a moment looks back without seeing anything.*)

STORITSYN : I am going. (*Lifts up his hand.*) Do you hear? (*There is a moment of absolute silence in the room: the furious shrieks and deep sighs of the wind and the beating of the raindrops on the panes become more audible.* STORITSYN *turns around and walks with the same expression of concentration. The first few steps are firm, then his strength fails him; he staggers, almost runs two paces, and falls down right at the door. All run toward him.*)

VOLODYA : Papa! papa! papa!

TELEMAKHOV : Let me go to him. Lift his head! Open his shirt! No crying; quiet!

(*He listens, putting his head to* STORITSYN'S *heart, then goes to the middle of the room with decisive steps, and stops with his back to the corpse, with his feet resolutely together, and furiously pulling his beard.* VOLODYA *and* MODEST PETROVICH *weep.*)

TELEMAKHOV : It is a lie! A lie! A lie! (*Furiously shouts, shaking his fist toward heaven*). Murderer!

MYSTERY-BOUFFE

An Heroic, Epic and Satiric Representation of Our Epoch

By VLADIMIR VLADIMIROVICH MAYAKOVSKY

(SECOND VARIANT: 1921)

*Translated by George Rapall Noyes
and Alexander Kaun*

CHARACTERS

1. **Seven Pairs of the Clean**

   1. Negus of Abyssinia
   2. An Indian Rajah
   3. A Turkish Pasha
   4. A Russian Speculator (Merchant)
   5. A Chinese
   6. A well-fed Persian
   7. Clemenceau
   8. A German
   9. A Russian Priest
   10. An Australian
   11. The Australian's Wife
   12. Lloyd George
   13. An American
   14. A Diplomat

2. **Seven Pairs of the Unclean**

   1. A Soldier of the Red Army
   2. A Lamplighter
   3. A Chauffeur
   4. A Miner
   5. A Carpenter
   6. A Farm Hand
   7. A Servant
   8. A Blacksmith
   9. A Baker
   10. A Laundress
   11. A Seamstress
   12. A Locomotive Engineer
   13. An Eskimo Fisherman
   14. An Eskimo Hunter

3. **Compromiser**

4. **Member of the Intelligentsia**

5. **Lady with Bandboxes**

6. **Devils**

   1. Beelzebub
   2. Senior Devil
   3. First Courier
   4. Second Courier
   5. Watchman
   6. Twenty of the Clean with Horns and Tails

7. **Saints**

   1. Methuselah
   2. Jean Jacques Rousseau
   3. Lev Tolstoy
   4. Gabriel
   5. First Angel
   6. Second Angel
   7. Angels

8. **The Lord of Hosts**

9. **Actors of the Promised Land**

   1. Hammer
   2. Sickle
   3. Machines
   4. Railway Trains
   5. Automobiles
   6. Jack Plane
   7. Tongs
   8. Needle
   9. Saw
   10. Bread
   11. Salt
   12. Sugar
   13. Dry Goods
   14. Boot
   15. Board and Lever

10. **Man of the Future**

SCENES OF ACTION

1. All the Universe. 2. The Ark. 3. Hell. 4. Paradise. 5. The Land of Fragments. 6. The Promised Land.

MYSTERY-BOUFFE

PREFACE

The *Mystery-Bouffe* is a highway, the highway of the Revolution. No man can foretell with certainty what mountains we who are proceeding along that highway, must still lay low. To-day the name *Lloyd George* still rings harshly in our ears, but to-morrow it will be forgotten even by Englishmen. To-day the will of millions surges toward the Commune, and fifty years hence, perchance, the airy dreadnaughts of the Commune will rush to the attack against distant planets.

Hence in the present version of my drama, though I retain the same form, that of the highway, I have altered certain parts of the landscape.

In the future let all men who act, present, read, or print the *Mystery-Bouffe* change its contents, make its contents that of their own time, their own day, their own moment.

PROLOGUE

By One of the Unclean

In a moment
We shall show you . . .
The *Mystery-Bouffe*.
I must say two words to you:
This piece
Is something quite new.
To jump higher than your heads
Some man must aid you.
And so for this new piece
A short prologue is due.
First, why
Is the whole theatre so awry?
People staid and sensible
Will be startled much thereby.
But, pray, why do you go to shows?

To get pleasure at them,
I suppose.
Yet what pleasure penetrates your heart
If the pleasure's only on the stage?
The stage is only a third part.
And so, you see,
If now we can arrange our theatre
To help along the show,
The pleasure will be multiplied by three.*
And if the show's not interesting,
Then of course it were the best thing
Not to see a third of it.
In other theatres
The scenery's of small account:
For them
The stage
Is but a keyhole.
"Sit you in your chairs," they say,
"In front or at the side, and give
Heed how other people live."
Gaze and see!
On the sofa sit and loll
Uncle Vanya †
And Aunt Manya;
But you find no pleasure com-
ing from their words:
Uncles, aunts, you have at home!
We too will show you real life,
But it
By the theatre is made fit
For a most unusual show.
   This in short will be our first act:
The earth leaks.
Then it follows
All men flee the Revolution's flood.
Seven pairs of the Unclean
And seven of the Clean;
That is,
Fourteen ragged proletarians,
And fourteen sleek bourgeois are seen.

---

* A reference to the new practice of having the action take place not merely
on the stage, but in the whole auditorium.
† A jibe at Chekhov's play, *Uncle Vanya.*

And among them,
With tears upon his cheek,
A wretched Menshevik.*
The pole is drenched,
Ruined is their last refuge;
And so they all begin to build
An ark surpassing that of Noah at the deluge.
The second act will show them all
Within their ark upon the waves:
Here we shall see both an autocracy,
And a republic of true democratic slaves.
And finally,
While Mensheviks howl with emotion,
They throw the Clean headlong into the ocean.
The third act will prove well
That toilers need fear naught,
Although they may seem caught
By demons deep in Hell.
The fourth will then exhibit—
Now laugh unto the limit!—
The bowers of Paradise.
In the fifth act Confusion,†
Opening her cavernous maw,
Will swallow and will chaw.
Although we long have toiled
With insides almost spoiled
For lack of aught to eat, yet
Confusion we've defeated.
In the sixth act at last
The Commune!
All
The hall
Must sing with all its might!
Now gaze, open your eyes!
All ready?
Hell?
And Paradise?
(*Voice from behind the scenes:* "Ready!")
Curtain, rise!

---

* The Mensheviks were the more moderate faction of the Social Democratic Party of Russia. Unlike their more radical opponents, the Bolsheviks, they were in favor of compromise with the property-holding classes.
† The disorganization of transportation and industry following the Great War.

ACT I

In the glow of the northern lights the terrestrial globe is seen, its pole resting on the ice of the floor. Over the whole globe the ropes of the parallels and meridians are interlaced like the uprights and rungs of ladders. Between two walruses, which support the world, an ESKIMO HUNTER *sticks his finger into the earth, and shouts to an* ESKIMO FISHERMAN, *who lies near by, stretched out in front of a bonfire.*

HUNTER: Oh ho!
                    Oh ho!
FISHERMAN: He's yelling just because
                    He's nothing else to do
                    But stick his finger in the earth!
HUNTER: A hole!
FISHERMAN: Where's the hole?
HUNTER: It's leaking!
FISHERMAN: What's leaking?
HUNTER: The earth!
FISHERMAN (*jumping up, running to his companion, and looking under his tightly pressed finger*):
                    O-o-o-oh!
                    The work of unclean hands!
                    Hell!
                    I'll go and notify
                    The polar lands.

(*He runs off. From behind the edge of the world a* GERMAN, *wringing his sleeves, jumps out at him. For a moment he searches for a button on the* FISHERMAN'S *garments; finding none, he clutches the fur.*)

GERMAN: Herr Eskimo!
                    Herr Eskimo!
                    My business is most urgent!
                    Just a moment!
FISHERMAN: Well!
GERMAN: You see: to-day
                    I sat most comfortably in a café
                    Upon the Friedrichstrasse.
                    And through the panes the sun
                    Was most alluring.
                    And just like a bourgeois before the Revolution
                    The day

Was gay.
The public all were sitting
Most peacefully sipping
Their beer,
And talked in gentle Scheidemannic * tones.
So I dispatched my soup
And carelessly looked up
Upon the bottley Eiffels.†
I thought
What style of beef I ought
To choose,
Or if for beef I had much use!
I gazed with all my eyes,
And then my throat began to choke,
For to my great surprise
The *Siegesallee* was not as it should be.
The stony Hohenzollerns,
Standing amid the camomile,
Flew upward many a mile.
A roar!
Then I ran to the roof.
Surging around the building's frame
An inundation came,
Engulfing every quarter—
Yet not with water.
A stormy sea swept through Berlin;
Bass notes of unseen waves
Arose with awful din.
And to
And fro;
Aloft,
Below,
Dreadnaughts of houses!
Before I could be quite sure
Whether Foch had caused that—

FISHERMAN: Quick, sir!
GERMAN: I was wet as a rat!
I gaze:
It seems dry out of doors,

---

* The allusion is to Philipp Scheidemann, leader of the German Social Demo-
cratic Party, and from February to June, 1919, Chancellor of the Provisional
Government of Germany.
† Bottles arranged in towers on the bar.

But it pours and pours and pours.
And I behold
A picture now unfold
Like that of Pompeii of old.
Berlin was torn forth by the roots
And smelted in the hearth
Wherein had sunk our earth.
On the crest of seething villages I floated.
I gathered all the skill for which I had been noted
In our yacht club:
And so
Before you,
Dearest sir,
Is all
That now remains of Europe.

FISHERMAN: N-n-not much!
GERMAN: It will grow calm, of course,
              Within a day or two.
FISHERMAN: Speak plainly! Do not beat about the bush
              In European style!
              What do you want? This place is not for you.

GERMAN (*pointing in a horizontal direction*):
              Let me repose beside your honorable seals a while!

(*The* FISHERMAN, *irritated, waves his hand toward the bonfire, and walks off in the opposite direction, to notify the polar lands; he bumps into a couple of water-soaked Australians who run out from behind the other edge of the world.*)

FISHERMAN (*stepping back in surprise*):
              Were ever faces more disgusting!

AUSTRALIAN *and his* WIFE (*together*):
              We are Australians.
AUSTRALIAN: I am an Australian.
              We had all that befits us;
              For instance, thus:
              A platypus, a palm, a porcupine,
              A cactus.

WIFE OF THE
AUSTRALIAN (*sobbing with emotion*):
              And now
              We're lost!
              All's gone:
              The cactuses,
              And platypuses,

And palms!
All's perished in the sea,
All's drowned!

FISHERMAN (*pointing to the* GERMAN, *who has stretched himself out*):
Go and join him.
He's lonesome lying on the ground.

(*The* FISHERMAN *once more prepares to depart, but stops, listening to two voices that are heard from opposite sides of the globe.*)

FIRST VOICE: Derby, oh ho!
SECOND VOICE: Topper, oh ho!
FIRST VOICE: It's getting worse!
Hold to the northern parallel!
SECOND VOICE: It's getting furious!
Clutch at the south meridian!

(*Holding to the ropes of the parallels and meridians,* LLOYD GEORGE *and* CLEMENCEAU *clamber down from the globe. Each sets up the flag of his country.*)

LLOYD GEORGE: My banner is set up.
Now I command
This snowy land.

CLEMENCEAU: No, pardong,
You're wrong!
I was the first to plant a stake;
This land my colony I make.

LLOYD GEORGE (*laying out some wares*):
No, it is mine.
To trade I have begun.

CLEMENCEAU (*beginning to grow angry*):
No, it is mine.
Go get another one!

LLOYD GEORGE (*furious*):
What, what!
Oh, you be damned!

CLEMENCEAU (*furious*):
What, what!
I'll smash your nose!

LLOYD GEORGE (*running at* CLEMENCEAU *with clenched fists*):
England, hip, hip!

CLEMENCEAU (*running at* LLOYD GEORGE *with clenched fists*):
Vive la France!

AUSTRALIAN (*rushing to separate them*):
Well, what a gang!
Mere hooligans!

Empires have all gone by,
Imperial gold coins too: so why
Do they still punch each other's mugs?
FISHERMAN: Oh, you
Imperialists!
GERMAN: Quit, don't raise hell!
FISHERMAN: How they can yell!

(*Just as the* FISHERMAN *is again about to take his departure, a fat Russian* MERCHANT *drops down straight on his head.*)

MERCHANT: Respected sirs,
My blood this stirs!
Am I an Asiatic!
To crush the Yellow Peril
Is the decree of Heaven's Soviet,
But never have I been a Yellow Devil—
Not yet!
(*Becoming a trifle calmer.*)
But yesterday in Tula, where
I sat most calmly in my chair,
My door was broken open.
I thought: "Ah ha,
They've come from the Cheka!" *
And then, you cannot fail
To guess,
My cheek began to pale.
But God is still most kind:
Not the Cheka—the wind!
It dripped a bit,
Then torrents came
More and more,
Higher yet;
The streets were flowing,
The roofs were blowing
Off!
ALL: Hush, hush!
CLEMENCEAU: Do you not hear?
Do you not hear a trampling?

(*A multitude of* VOICES *is heard, coming ever nearer.*)

Deluge, deluge! The flood, the flood, the flood!
LLOYD GEORGE (*horrified*):
Oh, Lord!

---

* The Extraordinary Commission organized to combat counter-revolutionary movements.

Misfortunes pour as from a water main,
And here's that Eastern Question once again!

(*The* NEGUS OF ABYSSINIA *enters, followed by a* CHINAMAN, *a* PERSIAN, *a* TURKISH PASHA, *a* RAJAH, *a* RUSSIAN PRIEST, *a* COMPROMISER,* *a* DIPLOMAT,† *an* INTELLIGENT.‡ *The procession is closed by seven pairs of the* UNCLEAN *who pour in from all sides.*)

NEGUS: Although
I'm slightly blacker than the snow,
Yet I'm the Abyssinian Negus, all the same,
I'd have you know.
My respects!
I have just now forsaken Africa.
Through it the Nile, that boa constrictor stream,
went winding.
Then rose the Nile and swallowed up my realm,
And with it sank my Africa, past finding.
Though my luck's hard,
Yet none the less—

FISHERMAN (*with vexation*):
—yet none the less,
My respects!
We've heard all that, my Lord!

NEGUS: I beg you'll not forget
A Negus speaks with you,
A hungry Negus, too!
What's that?
A tasty dog, no doubt?

FISHERMAN: A dog, you ass!
A walrus, not a dog.

(*The* NEGUS *by a mistake tries to sit down on* LLOYD GEORGE, *who is the very image of a walrus.*)

FISHERMAN: Go and sit down, don't scatter ink on us.

LLOYD GEORGE (*in alarm*):
I'm not a walrus,
There is the morse!
I'm not a morse.
I am Lloyd George!

FISHERMAN (*turning to the others*):
What do you want?

---

* A cant name for a Menshevik.
† Not mentioned at this point in the original.
‡ That is, a member of the Intelligentsia, or educated liberal class of Russia. Also not mentioned here in the original.

CHINAMAN: Nothing!
               Nothing!
               My China has gone down!
PERSIAN: Persia,
               My Persia is beneath the ocean's streams!
RAJAH: And India,
               The heavenly India is no more!
PASHA: And Turkey now survives only in dreams!
   (*From the throng of the* CLEAN *a* LADY *bustles forth, carrying an infinite number of bandboxes.*)
LADY: Be careful!
               Don't you tear it!
               The silk's thin!

   (*To the* FISHERMAN.)
               Porter,
               Help me put down my boxes.
VOICE (*from the throng of the* CLEAN):
               What a darling!
               How piquant!
FISHERMAN: Just an idle parasite.
CLEMENCEAU: Madame, what is your nation?
LADY: My nation is most multifarious;
               I've roamed the earth with fortune various.
               At first I was a Russian.
               Those Bolsheviks are so nefarious!
               Since I'm a lady of tastes refined,
               And with a cultivated mind,
               Without delay I fled away
               And made Esthonia my home.
               The Bolsheviks came near the border—
               I turned Ukrainian in short order.
               They captured Harkov some ten times,
               But I escaped to southern climes,
               To a new republic in Odessa.
               They seized Odessa, but
               In the Crimea Vrangel * still had power—
               With him I found a refuge in that hour.
               They chased the Whites cross land and sea,
               But I had become a Turkish ladee,

---

* During 1920 General Vrangel (Wrangel), perhaps the most capable of the anti-Bolshevik leaders, carried on a campaign in southern Russia. In November he was defeated and forced to withdraw his army from Russian territory. Constantinople became filled with Russian refugees.

> And strolled Constantinople, dressed exquisitely.
> The Bolsheviks pressed farther, nothing daunted,
> But I had moved to Paris, where
> The boulevards I haunted.
> Of forty nations have I been, at least;
> Now in Kamchatka I intend to rest.
> But Polar summers bore me, I must say;
> None of my toilets can I here display.

FISHERMAN (*shouting at the* CLEAN):
> Hush! Hush!
> What is that wailing?

COMPROMISER (*hysterically extricating himself from the throng*):
> Just listen, please!
> Such things are most disheartening!
> Just listen, please!
> What is it that is happening?
> There's not a dry place in the world to-day!
> Just listen, please!
> Leave me in peace, I pray!
> Let me go home, I say,
> And read my peaceful books
> And meditate for hours!
> Just listen, please!
> This is beyond my powers!
> I thought the flood would be
> Like that foretold by Kautsky's pen,*
> With well-fed wolves
> And unhurt lambs.
> But now—
> Men slay their brother men.
> Dear Reds! Dear Whites!
> Listen, I faint and fall!

CLEMENCEAU: Don't rub your eyes or bite your lips:
> That's all!

(*To the* UNCLEAN, *who are approaching the bonfire: in a haughty voice.*)
> And you? What are your nations?

UNCLEAN (*together*):
> We wandering folk
> Must travel through the world
> And never find a station.

---

*Karl Kautsky (1854—), a German Marxist, denounced the Bolshevik Revolution and argued against Lenin's policies.

No nation ever claims us;
Toil is our only nation.

CLEMENCEAU: Ancient arias!

VOICES OF THE CLEAN (*frightened*):
Proletarians!
Proletarians!
Proletarians!

BLACKSMITH (*to* CLEMENCEAU, *slapping him on his plump belly*):
Does the roar of the deluge ring in your head?

LAUNDRESS (*also to* CLEMENCEAU, *in a mocking, squealing tone*):
You'd like to lie down and repose on your bed.
Go to the mines or the trenches instead!

SOLDIER OF THE RED ARMY (*threateningly*):
Get to the trenches, you,
Where it's wet and it drenches you!

(*Seeing a "conflict" brewing between the* CLEAN *and the* UNCLEAN, *the* COMPROMISER *rushes to separate them.*)

COMPROMISER: Dear friends! Pray don't! You must not raise a
rumpus!
Do not give way to angry looks and cross!
Open your arms,
Embrace like friends!
My comrades dear,
We must have harmony, of course!

CLEMENCEAU (*in an angry, bitter tone*):
Me be at peace with them?
This is too much!

(*Both the* FISHERMAN *and* CLEMENCEAU *punch the* COMPROMISER *on the neck.*)

Oh, mediator!
Mediator prater!

COMPROMISER (*in a whimpering tone, running away after his beating*):
Well, now,
Just see!
I speak him fair,
And he! . . .
It's always so:
When you cry, "Peace!"
Both sides give you a blow.

(*The* UNCLEAN *cross the stage, elbowing their way contemptuously through the close-packed throng of the* CLEAN, *and seat themselves at the bonfire. The* CLEAN *stand immediately behind, in a circle.*)

PASHA (*advancing to the middle of the stage*):
                    Men of the true faith!
                    We must consider what has taken place.
                    Let's understand the trend
                    Of all this row.
MERCHANT: The thing's quite simple—
                    The world's come to an end.
PRIEST: I think it is the flood.
CLEMENCEAU: No flood at all:
                    In that case rain would fall.
RAJAH: Yes,
                    We've had no rain, that's true.
DIPLOMAT: So that idea will never do.
PASHA: But still—
                    What has occurred, ye faithful?
                    Let's sift the matter till we find its reason.
MERCHANT: The people, seems to me, show signs of treason.
GERMAN: I think it is the war.
INTELLIGENT: No, to my mind that's far
                    From true.   I think
                    The basis must be metaphysical. . . .
MERCHANT (*not convinced*):
                    The war and metaphysical!
                    You have begun from Adam!
VOICES: Order!
                    Order!
                    Don't be raising a damn
                    Commotion.
PASHA: Sh!
                    Let us proceed with dignity.
                    Student, you have the floor!
  (*Justifying himself to the crowd.*)
                    You see his mouth froths more and more.
INTELLIGENT: At first
                    All was most regular:
                    The day was followed by the night,
                    Except
                    The sunset red was far too bright.
                    But then
                    Laws,
                    Beliefs,
                    Faiths,

The granite masses of great cities,
And e'en the sun's immobile orb,
All seemed to grow a trifle fluid,
Somewhat creepy,
Somewhat sticky.
And then the floodgates opened!
Streets were flowing;
One shattered house dissolved upon its neighbor.
All the world, all,
In the revolution's hot blast furnace smelted
And melted,
Poured like a waterfall.

VOICE OF THE CHINAMAN:
Gentlemen, attention!
Here comes the drizzle!

WIFE OF THE
AUSTRALIAN: The drizzle!
Fizzle!
We're drenched to our bones!

PERSIAN: Perhaps the day of doom is nigh,
While we
Hold meetings, shout, and cry.

DIPLOMAT (*snuggling up to the North Pole*):
Stand here!
Closer!
Here it does not drip.

MERCHANT (*shoving with his knee at the* ESKIMO HUNTER, *who all this time has been pressing down the hole, with the patience peculiar to his race*):
Hey, you!
Go join those walruses!

(*The* ESKIMO HUNTER *flies away, and from the open hole a stream strikes upon those present. The* CLEAN *scatter helter-skelter, yelling with one voice.*)

CLEAN (*together*):
Ee-ee-ee-ee-ee!
Oo-oo-oo-oo-oo!
A-a-a-a-ah!

(*After a moment all rush toward the stream.*)
Stop it!
Plug it!
Squeeze it!

(*They fall back. Only the* AUSTRALIAN *is left by the terrestrial*

globe with his finger in the hole. In the general confusion the PRIEST
mounts a couple of logs.)

PRIEST:	Brothers!
	We are deprived of our last refuge!
	The water covers the last inch of soil!
VOICES OF THE UNCLEAN (*softly*):	
	Who's that?
	Who is that bearded cask of oil?
PRIEST:	This is for forty days and forty nights!
MERCHANT:	Well said!
	The Lord has given him a grain of sense.
INTELLIGENT:	In history for this there have been precedents—
	Remember Noah's notable experience.
MERCHANT (*mounting up into the* PRIEST'S *position*):	
	That's bunk—
	Both history, and precedent, and so forth.
VOICES:	Come to the point!
MERCHANT:	Well, brothers, let us build an ark.
WIFE OF THE AUSTRALIAN:	He's right! An ark!
INTELLIGENT:	What an idea!
	Let's build a steamboat.
RAJAH:	Two steamboats!
MERCHANT:	That's right!
	I will contribute all my capital!
	Those men were saved; and we, I think, are quite as bright.
GENERAL SHOUT:	Long live,
	Long live technique!
MERCHANT:	Raise your hands!
	Those in favor!
GENERAL SHOUT:	Useless labor!
	By acclamation!

(*Both the* CLEAN *and the* UNCLEAN *raise their hands.*)

CLEMENCEAU (*usurping the place of the* MERCHANT, *and gazing wrath-
fully at the* BLACKSMITH, *who has raised his hand*):

	You voting too?
	Don't *you* butt in!
	Gentlemen,
	We must not take any Unclean!
	We must teach them manners!
VOICE OF THE CARPENTER:	
	But can *you* use saws and hammers!

CLEMENCEAU (*crestfallen*):
I've changed my mind.
Even the Unclean may come along.

MERCHANT: Only we'll choose the sober and the strong.

GERMAN (*climbing up into* CLEMENCEAU'S *place*):
Hold, gentlemen, you're wrong!
Perhaps with those Unclean we need not bother.
We're fortunate enough still to be ignorant
How the fifth part of the world is getting on.
You loudly prate,
But have not troubled to investigate
Whether we have not some Americans at hand.

MERCHANT (*joyfully*):
I see
No common man is he,
But Chancellor of Germany!

(*His joyful words are interrupted by a cry from the* WIFE OF THE
AUSTRALIAN.)

WIFE OF THE
AUSTRALIAN: What's this?

(*An* AMERICAN *speeds in on a motorcycle, while the crowd gazes
fixedly at him.*)

AMERICAN: Respected sirs,
I hear you have begun to build an ark.

(*Flourishes a bit of a paper.*)
Then mark:
From drowned America I bring a check
For full two hundred thousand millions.

(*A moment of silent dejection is followed by a sudden wail from the*
AUSTRALIAN, *who is stopping the flow of water.*)

AUSTRALIAN: What are you looking at?
Stop your staring there!
I will let go, I swear.
My fingers have grown stiff.

(*The* CLEAN, *in confusion, huddle close to the* UNCLEAN.)

CLEMENCEAU (*to the* BLACKSMITH):
Well, comrades,
Shall we begin to build?

BLACKSMITH (*without a trace of malice*):
What do I care?
As for me—

(*Waves his hand to the* UNCLEAN.)
Come, comrades,

Let's start in!
(*The* UNCLEAN *stand up, lifting their saws, planes, and mallets.*)
COMPROMISER: Hurry, my comrades!
Hurry, my dear men!
To work!
Take saws and axes!
INTELLIGENT (*moving away*):
Work!
Work I will not!
I'll sit right here and practice sabotage.
(*Shouts to the men at work.*)
Speedy, my lads!
Strike while the iron is hot!
CARPENTER: But you, why do you sit with folded hands?
INTELLIGENT: I am a learned specialist, you know,
Quite necessary for the show.

ACT II

The deck of the ark. In all directions there is a panorama of lands sinking into the waves. Into the low clouds towers a mast, equipped with stays and cordage; on it is a rope ladder. On one side is the roundhouse and the entrance to the hold. The CLEAN *and the* UNCLEAN *are grouped along the bulwark nearer to the spectators.*

FARM HAND: Whew! To-day
I should not like to fall into the deep!
SEAMSTRESS: Look there, I say:
The wave is high and steep!
MERCHANT: I was a fool to mix with you.
It's always so—
A perfect fake!
Sailors you claim to be!
A fine sea dog I'll make!
LAMPLIGHTER: The sea is rising to drown us,
Roaring and groaning!
SEAMSTRESS: Those waves close fast around us!
CLEMENCEAU: Yes,
'Twas very silly, that's a fact!
I speak to you with bitterness and dole.
We might have stayed there still.
The earth remains intact;

A poor thing, but the pole.

FARM HAND: The waves sure howl like wolves!

Both ESKIMOS, *the* CHAUFFEUR, *and the* AUSTRALIANS (*together*):

Look!

What's that?

What's happening to Alaska?

NEGUS: It rushed away

Like a stone from a sling!

GERMAN: Gone down, I say!

HUNTER: Gone down!

FISHERMAN: Gone!

ALL: Farewell! Farewell! Farewell!

CLEMENCEAU (*bursts into tears, overwhelmed by his memories*):

Mon Dieu!

Mon Dieu!

In old times

All our dear family

Would gather comfortably

For tea,

For muffins,

For caviar!

BAKER (*measuring off the tip of his finger nail*):

It's queer, I swear!

Well, I don't care

That much.

SHOEMAKER:* I brought along some vodka.

Have you a glass?

SERVANT: I'll get one.

MINER: Fellows, to the hold!

Let us pass

Below!

HUNTER: Well, how's the walrus?

I hope it is not tough.

SERVANT: Not tough at all,

And roasted just enough.

(*The* CLEAN *are left alone. The* UNCLEAN *descend into the hold, singing.*)

UNCLEAN (*sing*): What have we to lose?

Shall we fear the deluge?

Our legs we had tired;

Some rest we required.

---

* Not mentioned in the list of characters; carelessly retained from the "First Variant."

So let's rest on this boat
While we still are afloat!
We'll eat juicy walrus steak
And our thirst we shall slake
On wine that's not thin.
To act thus is no sin!

(*The* CLEAN *encircle the sniveling* CLEMENCEAU.)

PERSIAN: Shame on you, fellow!
Do not yell so!

MERCHANT: We'll make our way somehow
Up to Mount Ararat.

NEGUS: You'll croak with hunger before that.

AMERICAN: I have heaps of cash on hand,
But I'm so famished I can't stand.
For a pound of bread I offer
Half a million bank notes from my coffer,
Of Tsar Nicholas's money,
And two pounds of diamonds.

MERCHANT: I was a speculator, man,
So the Cheka three times jailed me.
Now my money seems to have failed me!

CHINAMAN: Throw it in the garbage can!

PASHA: Diamonds are of no use!
Now, if a man has even gallstones,
Even that somehow atones
For the emptiness within.

AUSTRALIAN: For gluttony it's late!
We've nothing but an empty plate!

COMPROMISER: And now they've closed the market in the slums!

MERCHANT (*to the* PRIEST):
Care not, my humble father: in every square
Now there's a veritable Novgorod fair.*

LADY: In the market are milk and butter and cream,
But how to procure them I cannot dream.

MERCHANT: You'll do without your milk, you fool!
Now's the workman's time of rule.
The workman always has some goods:
He brings them out,
And barters.

LADY: But I will barter my hats for eggs.

---

* Referring to the free exchange of goods at the time when Russian currency became absolutely worthless.

INTELLIGENT: You will barter your last straw,
And then you'll sit and suck your paw.

PRIEST (*listening to the uproar in the hold*):
Hear 'em gabble!

INTELLIGENT: What's it all to them?
They've caught fish and gobble.

PRIEST: Let's take a net or a harpoon
And try our luck as well as they.

GERMAN: H-a-r-p-oo-n?
How do I know the way
To use the tool, my lord?
I know but how to stick a sword
In the body of a man.

MERCHANT: I cast a net
And thought I'd get
As a reward
Plenty of fish.
I toiled, toiled hard,
But pulled on board
Naught but seaweed.

PASHA (*dejectedly*):
Such is the world: there is no help;
Even millionaires
Must feed on kelp.

LLOYD GEORGE (*to* CLEMENCEAU):
Eureka!
Let us abandon all our fuss.
Can differences now exist
Between an English and a French imperialist?
The main thing is that each of us
Depends upon his belly.

COMPROMISER: I have a belly too.

CLEMENCEAU: How sad this is:
At such a charming gentleman
I almost dealt a blow.

LLOYD GEORGE: But now we must not quarrel so;
We have a common foe.
I'd like a word with you. . . .

(*Takes him by the arm and leads him away.   After whispering together, they return.*)

CLEMENCEAU: Gentlemen,
We all alike are clean;
Our hands we must not soil.

Why should such persons work so hard
And sweat beneath the sun?
From such things we recoil.
Let's make the Unclean toil
For us, while we reap the reward!

INTELLIGENT: I'd make 'em quick!
But I can't;
I'm sick!
And each of them has shoulders like a bull.

LLOYD GEORGE: The Lord forbid all violence!
Fighting is not my plan.
But while they munch their tasty food,
While they sit there below,
And drink and yell in merry mood,
We'll trick them well, you know.

CLEMENCEAU: Let's choose a tsar for them.

COMPROMISER: A tsar! But why?
A policeman would suit me.

CLEMENCEAU: Because the tsar will issue a decree
That all supplies belong to him.
The tsar will eat
And we will eat:
His faithful subjects, we!

ALL: Splendid!

PASHA: Fine! That hits the mark!

GERMAN (*joyously*):
I told you so;
That man's a second Bismarck!

AUSTRALIANS: The tsar must be elected right away.

SEVERAL VOICES: But who?
Who? I say.

LLOYD GEORGE *and* CLEMENCEAU:
The Negus.

PRIEST: Correct!
To him the reins!

MERCHANT: What reins?

GERMAN: Why, what you call 'em:
The reins of rule.
Don't be a fool,
For you know what I mean!

(*To the* NEGUS.)
Here, take this stool
And mount upon the roundhouse!

LADY: Kind gentlemen,
                   Inform me:
                   Say, will this tsar be genuine
                   Or only something shady?
VOICES: Most genuine, the real thing!
LADY: Ah!
                   Then I'll be a real court lady!
LLOYD GEORGE: Hurry up quick,
                   And draw up the decree:
                   "By the grace of God,
                   We"—
PASHA *and* AUSTRALIAN:
                   And we will help compose the draft,
                   Before the Unclean observe our craft.

(*The* PASHA *and the rest draw up the manifesto. The* GERMAN
and the DIPLOMAT *stretch out a rope in front of the gangway to the
hold. Staggering, the* UNCLEAN *climb out. When the last of them
has crawled to the deck, the* GERMAN *and the* DIPLOMAT *exchange
places, and the* UNCLEAN *are thus tied up.*)

GERMAN (*to the* SHOEMAKER):
                   Hey!
                   You!
                   Approach and swear!
SHOEMAKER (*absolutely bewildered*):
                   I'd better lie down there.
DIPLOMAT: I'll lay you down
                   So you'll get up again
                   The Lord knows when!
                   Mr. Officer,
                   Aim your pistol here!
CLEMENCEAU: Aha!
                   They've sobered up!
                   Now things will run quite smoothly.
SOME OF THE UNCLEAN (*sadly*):
                   Fellows, we are caught
                   Like chickens in the soup.
AUSTRALIAN: Hats off!
                   Whoever has a hat!
CHINAMAN *and* RAJAH (*nudging the* PRIEST, *who stands beneath the
   roundhouse, on which the* NEGUS *is perched*):
                   Read it!
                   Read while they stand in terror there!

PRIEST (*reading from the paper*):
>"By the grace of God,
>We,
>Tsar of those chicks
>Which the Unclean have fried,
>And grand duke of all eggs they may have laid,
>Mercifully flaying no man seven times—
>We stop at six
>And leave the seventh hide—
>Proclaim to all our faithful subjects:
>Bring in everything,
>Both fish and toast and good seal meat,
>And all else that man can eat.
>And the August Executive Senate
>Will not delay a single minute,
>But take account of all the store,
>And give us what we need—and more."

PASHA *and* RAJAH (*who form an improvised Senate*):
>We hear and obey,
>Your Majesty!

PASHA (*directing operations: to the* AUSTRALIAN):
>You to the cabins!

   (*To the* WIFE *of the* AUSTRALIAN.)
>And you to the larder!

   (*To the company in general.*)
>Let the Unclean with the supplies run fast!
>And on the way see that they fast!

   (*To the* MERCHANT, *setting free the* BAKER *for his convenience.*)
>Now you go down with him into the hold,
>While with the Rajah I survey the whole
>Expanse on deck.
>Send the stuff here
>And then come back
>Yourselves.

THE CLEAN (*with a joyful roar*):
>We'll bring along whole mountains for our shelves.

PRIEST (*rubbing his hands*):
>And then we will divide the booty,
>As is our Christian duty.

(*Guarded closely by the* CLEAN, *the* UNCLEAN *descend into the hold. In a moment they return and tumble out all sorts of edibles in front of the* NEGUS.)

MERCHANT (*joyfully*):
>We've searched the whole place,
>Left nothing there.
>The products are most plentiful,
>But rare
>Beyond compare!
>In fact,
>Of standard quality.
>Well, fellows, whet your teeth!

AMERICAN: But the Unclean?

GERMAN: They must be locked beneath
>The hatches, most stiffly.

PRIEST: Well then, your Majesty,
>Just wait a jiffy.

(*He chases the* UNCLEAN *into the hold; while he is engaged with them, the* NEGUS *eats up all that has been brought to him. The* CLEAN *return.*)

CLEMENCEAU: Are you coming, Lloyd George?

LLOYD GEORGE: Coming, coming!

THE CLEAN (*hustling forward*):
>Hurry, hurry!
>It's time
>To dine!

(*They climb up beside the* NEGUS. *In front of the* NEGUS *is only an empty platter.*)

THE CLEAN (*in unison, with threatening voices*):
>What's this?
>Has Mamay's Tatar horde
>Laid waste our festive board?

PRIEST (*furious*):
>One man!
>But one!
>And he could swill so much!

PASHA: I'd like to give him one
>Upon his well-filled paunch!

NEGUS: Silence!
>I am the Lord's Anointed.

GERMAN: Anointed!
>Anointed!
>May you lie down like us—!

DIPLOMAT: —with empty belly,
>Disappointed!

PRIEST : Judas!
RAJAH : Oh, damn!
I never thought of his deceiving.
MERCHANT : Let's stretch out.
To-morrow we shall rise, no doubt,
A trifle wiser than this evening.

(They compose themselves for rest. Night. The moon passes swiftly across the sky. The moon is setting. Dawn. In the gray of the dawn the DIPLOMAT rises. On the other side the GERMAN rises.)

DIPLOMAT : Are you asleep?

(The GERMAN shakes his head.)

DIPLOMAT : Woke up so early?
GERMAN : How could I rest?
My belly's all a hurly-burly.
Well, talk away!
COMPROMISER : I dreamed of juicy steak.
PRIEST *(from a distance)* :
What else was there to dream of?

(Pointing to the NEGUS.)

That cursed wretch is fat and sleek.
AUSTRALIAN : It's cold.
INTELLIGENT *(pointing to the NEGUS)* :
He has no spiritual doubts
Beneath his cap; he
Has eat his fill
And now feels happy.
CLEMENCEAU *(after a short pause)* :
Gentlemen,
Just let me tell you that
I feel that I've turned democrat.
GERMAN : That's no great news to impart!
I've always loved the people
With all my heart.
PERSIAN *(venomously)* :
But who proposed to reverence his Majesty?
DIPLOMAT : Drop all those poisonous taunts! You must not prate;
Autocracy in politics is surely out of date.
MERCHANT : It will be out of date, and hollow,
If there remains no bit of food to swallow.
GERMAN : Now in good earnest!
A constitution ripens.
Let us have done with strife
And live a peaceful life.

COMPROMISER: Hurrah!
Hurrah for the Constituent Assembly!
ALL (*opening the hatch*):
Hurrah! Hurra-ah!
(*To one another.*)
Make haste!
Pull hard!
(THE UNCLEAN, *awakened, climb out of the hatch.*)
SHOEMAKER: Well, are you drunk?
BLACKSMITH: What! Is the ship capsizing?
MERCHANT: Citizens, attend the meeting.
(*To the* BAKER.)
Citizen, you favor a republic?
THE UNCLEAN (*in chorus*):
Meeting?
Republic?
What may that be?
CLEMENCEAU: Stand still, gen-
tlemen,
The Intelligent
Will tell
You well.
(*To the* INTELLIGENT.)
Hey you, Intelligent!
(*The* INTELLIGENT *and* CLEMENCEAU *mount the roundhouse.*)
CLEMENCEAU: The session has begun.
(*To the* INTELLIGENT.)
You have the floor!
INTELLIGENT: Citizens!
That tsar has a most awful maw!
VOICES: True!
True, citizen and orator!
INTELLIGENT: The cursed glutton will eat all,
And leave us nothing, not a rat!
VOICE: True!
INTELLIGENT: And no one here
Will ever get to Ararat.
VOICES: True!
True!
INTELLIGENT: Enough!
Then break your rusty chains, you see!
GENERAL ROAR: Down!
Down with autocracy!

COMPROMISER: Against whom do you now rebel?
              Ah!
              A monarch he! One of the tsars!
              You will forever live imprisoned behind bars!
              For all authority
              Comes from the deity:
              'Tis sacred, then!
              So, gentlemen,
              Vote for a monarch bound
              To rule under a sound
              And legal constitution.
              He may be Grand Duke Nicholas,
              Or else
              The Grand Duke Michael.

THE UNCLEAN *and* THE CLEAN (*in chorus*) :
              Much we'll agree
              That he
              Shall swallow all!

GERMAN: I never will agree!

ALL (*in chorus*) : Never, not at all!

COMPROMISER (*pommeled and plaintive*) :
              How they wallop!
              How they pommel!
              It's easier to die
              Than bring them harmony.

MERCHANT (*pointing to the* NEGUS) :
              You've drunk enough of our blood!
              You've done dirt to the people! *

CLEMENCEAU (*pointing to the* NEGUS) :
              Look at that clown!—
              Along zongfong to drown!

(*With a united effort the assembly displaces the* NEGUS *and casts him overboard. Then the* CLEAN *lock arms with the* UNCLEAN *and they scatter in couples, whispering.*)

DIPLOMAT (*to the* MINER) :
              O comrades brave and true,
              How I rejoice with you,
              You scarcely can imagine!
              Those ancient bonds have vanished
              And we start life anew.

---

* Slogans popular after March, 1917.

CLEMENCEAU (*to the* BLACKSMITH):
        Accept felicitations
        On joining the free nations!

BLACKSMITH (*not committing himself*):
        Well, well!

CLEMENCEAU: The rest we will set right;
        The labor will be slight.

PRIEST (*to the* SEAMSTRESS):
        Now we will work for you, you for our benefit.

MERCHANT (*with satisfaction*):
        Yes, lead 'em by the nose to it!

LADY: Now was I ever a partisan
        Of the Negus, that black man?
        I live,
        I breathe for the Constituent!
        With all my heart you see me bent
        To serve the Provisional Government!
        To be pregnant I'll even consent
        For two whole years!
        At once I'll put on my red ribbons.
        Now we must adopt a more
        Revolutionary style.
        Excuse me, while
        I prepare to return
        To the people whom I love and adore.

(*Runs to her bandboxes.*)

CLEMENCEAU (*on the roundhouse*):
        Well, citizens, for long enough
        We have lived without authority.
        Now we will establish democratic society.
        Citizens,
        Let all be done with due celerity.
        Now we—may the Lord give rest to the soul of the
            Negus!—we thirteen
        Will be the ministers and their assistant ministers,
        And you—as citizens of a republic democratic—
        You will catch walruses, make boots, bake buns, and
            live in the attic.
        No objections?
        Have I convinced you every one to-day?

FARM HAND: Fine!—
        So long as the water is not far away.

ALL (*in chorus*) : Long live, long live our democratic republic!
CLEMENCEAU :   And now I
  (*To the* UNCLEAN.)
          Suggest you set to work.
  (*To the* CLEAN.)
          You take your pens.
  (*To the* UNCLEAN *once more.*)
          Work,
          Bring in your goods,
          We will divide them evenly for you—
          The last shirt shall be torn in two.
(*The* CLEAN *arrange a table and busy themselves with papers. When the* UNCLEAN *bring in edibles, they enter them as "goods received," and after their departure eat them up with gusto. The* BAKER, *coming for a second time, tries to glance under the papers.*)
LLOYD GEORGE : Why are you peeping?
          Stand aside from the papers!
          None of such capers!
          This task is not for lowly minds.
CLEMENCEAU :   Of government administration
          You do not have the smallest notion.
          Every plate that is brought in
          And each plate that goes out
          Must be provided with a number.
BLACKSMITH :   Before you set down the number and the date,
          We unclean workmen may have met our fate.
BAKER :   Come, you have promised to divide the goods.
PRIEST (*indignantly*) :
          Brethren!
          It is too soon for us to think of food!
RAJAH (*leading the* UNCLEAN *away from the table*) :
          Look at that shark!
          Hark!
          Does it not lay good eggs?
          And will it not give milk?
BLACKSMITH :   Hey, Rajah, maybe you're a pasha too:
          Think of the Turkish proverb:
          "Pasha, do not push too far"!
  (*Returning with the rest of the* UNCLEAN.)
          They give us lessons rare!
          However much you milk a shark,
          The shark will not give milk.

SHOEMAKER (*to the men who are writing*):
        It's time to dine; finish your job!
AMERICAN: But pray you give attention
        How beautiful the view,
        The waves and sea gull too!
FARM HAND: It's soup and tea you'd better mention.
        Now to the point!
        The point, my dear moguls!
        We have no time for gulls!
CLEMENÇEAU: Look! Look!
        On the sea
        Is a whale!
SOLDIER OF THE
RED ARMY: Send the whale
        To hell!
        You are a whale yourself,
        You ape!
THE UNCLEAN (*in a chorus, overturning the table*).
        You need not bother us with any government red tape!
(*The empty plates crash on the deck.*)
SEAMSTRESS *and* LAUNDRESS (*sadly*):
        The cabinet has gobbled all the menu.
CARPENTER (*jumping upon the overturned table*):
        Comrades!
        This is a knife plunged in our backs!
VOICES: And a fork too!
MINER: Comrades,
        How's this for you!
        One maw consumed before,
        But thirteen mouths swill more!
        The republic
        Turned out a tsar,
        But it turns out
        Itself to be a tsar with a full hundred mouths.
CLEMENCEAU (*picking his teeth*):
        Don't get excited!
        To divide we're delighted
        As we have promised.
        One man has got the doughnut;
        The next will get the doughnut's hole:
        And so the whole
        Is just a democratic republic.
MERCHANT: Some one must have the small seeds;

	The melon can't serve all needs.
THE UNCLEAN:	We'll show you the class conflict!
COMPROMISER:	Again,
	Again the roof collapses from the flood!
	Again,
	Again confusion and still more
	Uproar!
	Enough!
	Enough!
	Do not shed blood!
	Just listen, please!
	This is beyond my powers!
	All that is very good—
	The commune and so forth—
	But centuries must pass before
	We see it on this earth.
	Comrades and workingmen,
	Be at concord with the Clean!
	And hearken to an old man speak,
	A much-experienced Menshevik!
LLOYD GEORGE:	At concord?
	But then I shall lose all my hoard
	Of capital.
	Of harmony no word!
SOLDIER OF THE RED ARMY:	I'll show you concord!
COMPROMISER:	Why, what a pickle for my mouth!
	Again besieged from north and south!

(*The* UNCLEAN *advance upon the* CLEAN.)

THE CLEAN:	Hold, citizens, our policy decides—
THE UNCLEAN:	Come now, singe them on all four sides!
	We'll show them a real policy!
	Hold up your hands, you crew of robbers!
	You will remember long October
	The Twenty-fifth! *

(*The* UNCLEAN *arm themselves with the weapons dropped by the* CLEAN *while eating their dinner. They drive the* CLEAN *to the stern, then throw them overboard. The heels of the* CLEAN *twinkle in the air. But the* MERCHANT, *who on his way has snatched a slab of walrus meat, wedges himself into a chest in the corner. In another the* INTELLIGENT *and the* LADY *find a refuge.*

---

* Of 1917: the date of the Bolshevik Revolution, according to the Julian calendar.

The COMPROMISER *seizes the* FARM HAND *by the arm and tries to pull him away from the other* UNCLEAN, *sobbing bitterly meanwhile.**)

FARM HAND: Oh, what a little
           Idiot, drooling spittle!
           This is a revolution, my good man, and not a dress
              parade.

(*The* COMPROMISER *plunges his teeth into the hand of the* FARM HAND.)

BLACKSMITH: What a temper!
           Just you watch!
           Tumble him, lads,
           Beneath the hatch!

(*They do so.*)

CHIMNEY
SWEEPER: †   He may choke down there!
           His body's fat and fair,
           Just like a lady's.

FARM HAND: Why waste words?
           They are no loss.
           If they came back
           They'd nail us to a cross.
           We are too mild by half—
           Hurrah for Ararat!

THE UNCLEAN: True!
           True!
           We or they!

FARM HAND: Now for the terror!

BLACKSMITH: Comrades,
           Kick overboard the bawlers!
           Come, lads, why do you not rejoice?
           Rejoice!

(*But the voices of the* UNCLEAN *are stern; the Republic has consumed the very last supplies.*)

BAKER: Rejoice!
           But have you thought of bread and grain?

FARM HAND: Rejoice!
           How can we plant our meadows?

LAMPLIGHTER: Rejoice!
           There are no fields, but the angry main!

FISHERMAN: Nor can we fish; the nets are broken.

---

* A reference to the efforts of the moderate factions to find support among the peasants.

† Not mentioned in the list of characters; another relic of the "First Variant"!

CHAUFFEUR:	How can you cross those angry billows?
	If only it would dry up, fellows!
HUNTER:	The ark begins to crack.
CHAUFFEUR:	A compass is the thing we lack.
ALL:	Confusion and disorder!
BLACKSMITH:	We must not stop when we're not halfway over.
	Provisions from within the drowned
	We never can recover.
	Now for one thing we must by all means strive,
	That all of us remain strong and alive
	Till we reach Ararat.
	Suppose that storms beat on us,
	Suppose the sun may scorch us,
	Suppose that famine loom—
	We'll look straight in its eyes,
	We'll feed on naught but ocean foam.
	But we're masters here, at home!
LAUNDRESS:	To-day we'll eat a bit,
	To-morrow we'll feel pain.
	In all the ark but two stale biscuits now remain.
FARM HAND:	Hey!
	Comrades!
	Without a card give out no biscuits.

(*The* LADY *and the* INTELLIGENT *peep out from the corner chest.*)

INTELLIGENT:	Hark!
	They say:
	"Give biscuits"!
	And here we suffer cold and want and misery!
LADY:	So let's support Soviet authority! (*Crawls out.*)
THE UNCLEAN:	What's this?
	Men from beyond the grave?
INTELLIGENT:	No! No!
	We're yours, you see;
	Non-party men are we.
	We're from the corner chest;
	We're ready to maintain the power of the Soviets.
LADY:	I hate the sleek bourgeois,
	Rank rascals are they all!
	I long have been expecting
	That the bourgeoisie would fall.
	Now if you will allow,
	I too will work with you;

                        On a machine I'll type
                        Even with one finger.
INTELLIGENT: And take me too
                        With you.
                        You need a specialist.
                        Without some expert aid
                        You'll always feel afraid.
                        You will go down
                        And drown.
BLACKSMITH: We will not drown:
                        Don't croak!

  (*To the* LADY.)
                        Comrade, take a seat!

  (*To the* INTELLIGENT.)
                        Get down, you poor dead-beat,
                        And wield a poker!
CHAUFFEUR: A body without food
                        Is an engine without wood.
MINER: I too must now surrender;
                        My belly's feeling tender.
SOLDIER OF THE
RED ARMY: To slay the Clean was not enough to do.
                        We need some bread;
                        We need some water too.
THE UNCLEAN: Where can we flee?
                        What can we do?
SEAMSTRESS: But God will never leave us to our fate.
                        Let's fold our hands and simply wait.
HUNTER: My muscles have grown thin
                        From lack of food within.
SEAMSTRESS (*listening*):
                        What's that?
                        Do you hear?
                        Do you hear the music?
CARPENTER: That Antichrist related to us stories
                        Of Ararat and Paradise's glories.

  (*Jumping up in alarm, and pointing out to sea.*)
                        Who's there, fellows,
                        Treading the billows
                        And playing on his bones?
CHIMNEY
SWEEPER: Quit!
                        The sea

Is bare.
What creature could appear
To greet us?
SHOEMAKER: It
Is he
Out there,
Famine who comes to eat us.
FARM HAND: Well, let him come!
Here not a man will fail us.
Comrades, the foe attacks!
Quick!
Now all men to the decks!
Famine will now assail us.

(*They run forward, tottering, armed with anything that they can pick up. It grows light. A pause.*)
ALL: Well, then come!
What, not one?
And again,
Again we shall survey the barren waste of the main.
HUNTER: So you pray for a shadow in the fiery wastes of the desert;
And dying, you fancy the hot sands are cool—
A mirage, you poor fool!
CHAUFFEUR (*becomes fearfully excited, adjusts his glasses, looks out, and shouts to the* BLACKSMITH):
There
In the west—
Do you not see a little speck?
BLACKSMITH: Why gaze?
You might as well pound up your specs
Or hang them on your neck.
CHAUFFEUR (*runs off, rummages, and climbs to the lookout with a spyglass. In a moment his voice is heard, quivering with joy*):
Ararat! Ararat! Ararat!
ALL (*from every side*):
Oh, how glad I am!
How glad I am of that!

(*They snatch the spyglass from the* CHAUFFEUR *and huddle together.*)
CARPENTER: Where is it?
Where?
BLACKSMITH: There!
You can see it.

CARPENTER: What's that?
             It rises,
             Straightens,
             Approaches.
CHAUFFEUR: Approaches? How you talk!
             Ararat is a mountain that can't walk.
             Rub your eyes!
CARPENTER: Rub them yourself
             And gaze!
CHAUFFEUR: Yes, there comes
             A man of some sort.
             An old man with a cane.
             A young man with no cane.
             Aha, he walks the water like a lane!
SEAMSTRESS: Now peal, ye joyful bells!
             The music rolls and swells!
             'Tis he
             Who walked the sea
             Of Galilee.
BLACKSMITH: God has apples,
             Oranges,
             Cherries,
             And can bring spring seven times in a day;
             But from us only, us toilers, he's turned away.
             Now he sends Christ to entrap us.
FARM HAND: We don't want him.
             Send off the tramp!
             Hungry men have no time to pray.
             Don't you stir,
             Or I'll strike you, I say.
             Hey!
             Who are you?

(A man of the most ordinary sort steps upon the frozen deck.)

MAN: Who am I?
             I am of no class,
             No nation,
             No race.
             I have seen thirty,
             Forty centuries pass.
             I am simply
             The Man of the Future.
             I have come to blow
             The furnaces of souls,

For I know
How hard is human life.
Hearken!
A new
Sermon
On the Mount!
You await Ararats?
There are no Ararats.
None.
You but dreamed of them.
And if the mountain
Comes not to Mohammed—
Then damn it!
Not of Christ's Paradise I cry to you,
Where foolish fasters drink unsweetened tea.
But I cry of the true
And earthly Heavens.
Judge for yourselves: Is it Christ's Heaven,
That hungry, paltry Heaven of the Gospel story?
My Paradise has halls equipped most rarely,
Where electricity will serve you fairly.
In it the pleasant toil will not make hard your hands;
Work blooms like roses in those blessed lands.
There the bright sun effects such constant marvels
That every step is through glad beds of flowers.
Here the poor gardener must slave forever
With frames of glass and soil mixed with manure.
But in my Paradise,
On roots of common radish
Six times a year
Ripe pineapples appear.

ALL (*in chorus*): We'll all go to that land!
We've naught to lose!
But will they let in such a sinful band?

MAN: My Heaven is for all
Except the poor in spirit,
Through strenuous fasts turned lunatics.
A camel may pass through the needle's eye
More easily
Than such an elephant can come to me.
To me the man
Who's plunged a dagger calmly in his foe
And gone upon his way with a blithe song!

                    Come, come, and look not back!
                    You have the right to make
                    Your dwelling in my kingdom fair,
                    Of Earth—
                    And not of Heaven.
                    Come all
                    Who are not mere pack mules,
                    All those cramped and confined!
                    Know this:
                    For such
                    My Kingdom is designed
                    Of Earth—and not of Heaven.
ALL (*in chorus*): Isn't he laughing at the poor beggars!
                    Where are they?
                    What lands do you beckon us to?
MAN: Long is the road.
                    We must pass through the clouds.
ALL (*in chorus*): We'll smash each cloud, each fog!
MAN: But if Hell upon Hell attacks?
ALL (*in chorus*): We'll go there too!
                    We'll never turn our backs.
                    Lead us!
                    Where is it?
MAN: Where?
                    You wish another man to tell you where!
                    But it
                    Is here,
                    Beneath your hands.
                    Where are your hands?
                    You've folded them and know not what to do!
                    You huddle like mere beggars.
                    But you are rich.
                    Behold!
                    What wealth encircles you!
                    How dares the wind sport with the ark!
                    Away the crushing yoke of nature!
                    You will live in warmth
                    And light;
                    Electricity you'll force to move the waves.
                    And if
                    You are cast down beneath them,
                    Then do not fear—
                    The bottom of the sea

Is fair as any meadow.
Our daily bread
Is growing there—
Sea coal.
The wind may roar with the floods,
The walls of arks may split.
Your left hand and your right:
Those two
Will save you now.
I'm done.
Speak for yourselves.
I've said my say.

(*He disappears. On the deck there is an atmosphere of bewilderment and delight.*)

SHOEMAKER: Where is he?
BLACKSMITH: I think he is in me.
FARM HAND: I think that he
Has also entered into me.
VOICES: Who is he,
That spirit irresponsible and free?
Who is he—
Without a name?
Who is he—
Without a fatherland?
Why did he come our way?
What prophecies has he put forth to-day?
Though the fierce ocean's flood surrounds our tiny
band,
Fear not, my lads!
We'll find the Promised Land!
FARM HAND: So after all there is a Paradise.
And so to seek for happiness is wise.
VOICES: That we may reach that goal sooner,
Let every man now lift his hammer!
Up with the axes!
Straighten your ranks!
No crooked line!
The ark now cracks.
Salvation is in discipline.
BLACKSMITH (*his hand on the shrouds*):
The open gulf of the abyss bodes ill.
One path remains:
Up on the shrouds!

Up through the clouds!
Forward!

(*All rush to the mast.*)

ALL (*in chorus*):Forward through the sky!

(*On the shrouds their battle song peals forth.*)

ALL (*in chorus*):Hey, up aloft!
Up on the shrouds!
On through the clouds,
Commissars of the sea!
On, commissars of the sea!

SHOEMAKER: There the victors may rest from the fight and the fray.
If our feet ever tire, we'll make boots of the sky.

ALL (*in chorus*) : Though our feet may be bloody,
We'll make boots of the sky.

CARPENTER: The firmament splits
And the heavens are open.
Up along sunbeams,
By ladders of rainbows!

ALL (*in chorus*) : Up by the sunny steps,
Treading firm upon rainbows!

FISHERMAN: We need prophets no longer!
Ourselves are from Nazareth!
We've done with all popes!
Climb the masts!
Clutch the ropes!

ALL (*in chorus*) : To the masts!
To the masts!
To the shrouds!
To the shrouds!

(*While the last of the* UNCLEAN *is disappearing, the* LADY *and the* INTELLIGENT *clamber up the shrouds after him. The* MENSHEVIK [COMPROMISER] *stands for a moment, reflecting.*)

COMPROMISER: Whither are you bound?
To the Commune?
You're daft for such a distant goal to strive.

(*He looks around. The ark cracks ominously.*)
Forward, comrades!
Better go forward—and remain alive!

(*The* MENSHEVIK *disappears. Finally the* MERCHANT *crawls out of the corner chest, grinning.*)

MERCHANT: What idiots they are!
The ark is worth four hundred millions,
Minimum,

```
                Even as flotsam.
                Well,
                I'll speculate.
                What's that?
                It's breaking,
                Cracking.
                Save yourselves!
                We're sinking!
                Comrades!
                Comrades!
                Wait a minute!
                Comrades!
                Alone I perish on this spot!
                This is past all expression!
COMPROMISER:    Come on! Come on!
                You too, you know,
                May win a fat concession!
```

ACT III

Hell. In the center of the stage is a huge door; on it is the inscription: NO ADMITTANCE WITHOUT BEING ANNOUNCED. *Above are banks of smoky-yellow clouds, marked* PURGATORY.*

On the sides of the stage stand DEVIL WATCHMEN. *Two* DEVIL COURIERS *exchange calls across the theatre. Low singing is heard from behind the door.*

CHORUS:	We're devils, devils, devils, devils!
	Upon the spits we turn the sinful souls.
FIRST COURIER:	Yes, brother, damn it all!
	This is a scabby life!
SECOND COURIER:	Yes, these last months I've suffered grievous dole.
FIRST COURIER:	I tell you, it's a hole! †
CHORUS:	They have turned out those grafting cassocked priests;
	So now we have a crisis in supplies.
SECOND COURIER:	We nativeborn in Hell are in disgrace.
	Now foreign gentledevils rule the place.

---

* This detail is added from the "First Variant" of the original.

† Literally, "third category" of the supplies distributed during military communism.

"Give this!" they shout;
"Give that!"

FIRST COURIER: That Abyssinian Negus is the worst.
His mug is black;
His appetite would crack
A pig.

CHORUS: Alas, alas! Woe! Woe! We groan
Unfed! We'll croak here very soon!

FIRST COURIER: A devil's cheek was once like a watermelon.

SECOND
COURIER: That's true.

FIRST COURIER: But since the priests are gone, we've naught:
No sinners, not a felon.

SECOND
COURIER: Small portions here are brought!

FIRST COURIER: Most wretched rations!

SECOND
COURIER: Devils were once as they should be,
But now, disgusting to behold:
That is, both bald
And bobtailed!

FIRST COURIER: The day will come
When we too will revolt,
Raise hell!

SECOND
COURIER: Sh!
I hear a bell!

BOTH COURIERS: We run full tilt. (*They rush across the stage.*)

(*The* WATCHMEN *question the* COURIERS *and, after making a brief report to headquarters, throw open the door, admitting* LLOYD GEORGE, CLEMENCEAU, *the* PASHA, *the* GERMAN, *the* PRIEST, *the* CHINAMAN, *the* NEGUS, *and numerous other devils.**)

LLOYD GEORGE: Hey, you demons!
Hey, you Satan's pets!
Why do you catch no sinners in your nets?

PRIEST (*shaking his fist at the* COURIERS):
Have I toiled for you all my life so well,
To feed on scanty rations down in Hell?

COURIERS (*sullenly*):
Each of you should take a fork
And set about the work
Of catching sinners.

---

* The stage direction is amplified from the original.

CLEMENCEAU: Shut up!
Quit all such repartee!
We are white devils of high degree.
Not sparing sweat,
Black devils must work for the white
With all their might.

SECOND
COURIER: They've brought in their own schism.
Among the devils too they have begun
To start their class antagonism.

PASHA: Oh, how you talk!
How prone to strife!
I'll stick you with a fork!
You with a knife!

MASTER OF
CEREMONIES: His Majesty Beelzebub
Would talk with his own faithful realm of Hell.

GERMAN: Stand up!
Attention!
Each man must stand stock-still!

BEELZEBUB (*coming in*):
Demons and faithful subjects mine,
No longer shall you peak and pine!
Proclaim with joyful cries,
Our Lent is over!
Here we have full supplies;
We'll live in clover!
Flourish your tails on high!
Full fifteen sinners now are coming from the boat.

PRIEST (*crossing himself*):
Thank God!
No longer shall I sing with a dry throat.

CHINAMAN: They are a serious lot,
Though they are *sans culottes.*

NEGUS: Oh, I will gorge and swill,
Until the devils all feel ill!

LLOYD GEORGE: Now I my horns will whet.
They'll rue the day when I got wet.

BEELZEBUB (*to the* COURIERS):
Make haste
Each to his appointed place!
With your field glasses there
Look out and take care

> That not a man of them contrive to escape!
> Or else you'll get a whack
> On the nape
> Of your neck!

(*The* COURIERS, *equipped with field glasses, run into the auditorium, listening. The door flies open.*)

FIRST COURIER: Just let 'em come nigh!
> I'll show 'em!
> I'll lower my horns
> And raise my tail high!

SECOND
COURIER: I'll give 'em hell! Oo oo!

FIRST COURIER: Their feathers I will pluck.
> I would not wish my foes such luck.
> I like juicy sinners in ragout.

SECOND
COURIER: I eat 'em plain!
> I need no cook.
> Sh!
> Do you hear?
> Tuk-tuk-tuk!
> Tuk-tuk-tuk!

(*He listens. The racket of the* UNCLEAN *is heard, as they smash up the limbo of Hell.*)

FIRST COURIER: Our boss
> Will burst for joy.

SECOND
COURIER: Make 'em calm down, my boy!
> They must not raise such a hubbub.
> Go run and warn
> The staff of Lord Beelzebub.

(*The* FIRST COURIER *runs off.* BEELZEBUB *appears on high. He shades his eyes with his palm. All the* DEVILS *stand erect.*)

BEELZEBUB (*after assuring himself of the news, yells*):
> Hey, you!
> My devils!
> Bring on your kettles!
> Heap up the wood!
> Higher!
> Drier!
> Now hide behind the clouds, and pay
> Heed, lest some may stray
> Away!

(*The* DEVILS *hide themselves. From below are heard the words:*
"To the masts! To the masts! To the shrouds! To the shrouds!"
The throng of the UNCLEAN *rushes in, and a moment later the* DEVILS
pour forth, their pitchforks held ready for action.)

DEVILS: Oo-oo-oo-oo-oo-oo-oo!
A-a-a-a-a-a-ah!

BLACKSMITH (*to the* SEAMSTRESS, *laughing and pointing to the nearest
of the* DEVILS):
Old acquaintances!
How do you like that rabble?
We've settled those who had no horns;
Now with the hornèd we shall have no trouble.

(*The uproar begins to grow tiresome. The* UNCLEAN *hiss.*)

THE UNCLEAN: Sh-h-h-h!

(*The* DEVILS *lose their nerve and become quiet.*)

THE UNCLEAN: Is this Hell?

DEVILS (*hesitatingly*):
Y-y-yes.

FARM HAND (*pointing upward, to Purgatory*):
Comrades,
We must not pause!
There is the path that we must go by.

BEELZEBUB: Ah ha!
Devils to the fore!
Let them not enter Purgatory!

FARM HAND: Listen!
What is this poor story?

BLACKSMITH (*to* BEELZEBUB):
Quit all that!

BEELZEBUB (*in an injured tone*):
What! Quit, you say?

BLACKSMITH: Yes, certainly.
For shame!
Is this your game?
An ancient devil, you!
And gray-haired, too!
And yet you think to scare us so!
The iron smelting works
You've never visited, I know.

BEELZEBUB (*indifferently*):
I've never been inside your foundry!

BLACKSMITH: That's it, you see!
That would have made

> You shed
> Your fur
> Soon enough.
> You live here now
> Like any dude:
> So fat and fair,
> And yet so rude
> And rough.

BEELZEBUB: Much I am fat and fair!
> I'll show you rude and rough!
> Quit your prating!
> Mount the grating!

BAKER: Do tell!
> You think to scare us well!
> It makes me laugh, I vow!
> Now
> At home in old Moscow,
> You know,
> They'd pay high for your wood,
> They would!
> We have chilblains from the cold,
> But you, my host,
> Are warm as toast.
> It's blessed to be bakèd here!
> We could go naked here.

BEELZEBUB: Jest not nor dissemble!
> But tremble
> For your souls, for
> We'll stifle you with sulphur!

BLACKSMITH (*growing angry*):
> You brag like hell!
> What have you here?—
> A bit of sulphur smell.
> At home when they send poisonous gas around,
> Then all the plain grows gray with overcoats:
> A whole division topples to the ground.

BEELZEBUB: I tell you, dread that iron pot,
> Red-hot!
> Those prongs will stick through you
> Before you can say, "Boo!"

FARM HAND (*beside himself*):
> Why do you boast of rusty prongs?
> Your silly Hell is honey to our wrongs!

     During the War
     On an attack
     Machine-gun fire
     Would mow down three men out of four.
 (*The* Devils *prick up their ears.*)
Beelzebub (*trying to maintain discipline*) :
     Why stand you so
     With staring eyes?
     Perhaps all that he says is lies.
Farm Hand (*growing furious*) :
     I lie?
     You just sit here
     And guard your dens—
     But think of men's,
     You devils!
     Just let me speak—
Devils :   Silence!
Farm Hand : —of our earthly woe!
     Why should Beelzebub alarm us so?
     With a pitchfork he rambles throughout Hell.
     But for a moment I will tell
     Of earth.
     Do you know, devils, the meaning of blockade?
     The English tanks besiege the workingmen,
     And capital's armies and ships have made
     The Workingmen's Republic gasp for breath.
     At least no children and no righteous men are here;
     No tortures from your gridirons they need fear.
     But among us they too!
     No, devils, among you
     Men live a happier life!
     Like any savage Turk, you take
     And set a sinner on a stake;
     But we have our machines,
     And we have our *kultur*—
     And strife.
Voice (*from the throng of* Devils) :
     Hear! Hear!
Farm Hand : What if you do drink blood!
     It's tasteless raw!
     If I had time I'd guide you to a mill
     Where they distill
     It into chocolate for the bourgeois to swill.

VOICE (*from the throng of* DEVILS):
Whe-e-ew!
Honest?

FARM HAND: And if you saw a slave from the English colonies,
You devils would disperse with wails and cries.
They skin the niggers,
And they tan their hides,
To bind their precious books for London sales.
You stick nails in the ear;
But that, dear sirs, is mild!
They force swine's bristles underneath the nails.
Go gaze upon the soldiers in the trenches!
Compared to them your martyr's but a loafer
Upon a sofa.

VOICE (*from the throng of* DEVILS):
Enough!
Our hair's erect with terror!
These stories make us stifle.

FARM HAND: You think to scare us
With your bonfires
And your steel wires?
You think that you are devils?
Playful pups, naught else!
Have you been torn in half by factory belts?

BEELZEBUB (*taken aback*):
Well now!
They come into a house that is not theirs
And try to infect us with their new ideas.

PRIEST (*nudging* BEELZEBUB):
Tell 'em,
Tell 'em about our hellish furnace.

BEELZEBUB: I spoke of it.
They will not listen.
I cannot polish our rough surface!

FARM HAND (*advancing at him*):
Why do you gnash your fangs only at feeble men?

BEELZEBUB: What are you kicking at? Be civil!
A devil, sirs, must always be a devil!

COMPROMISER (*trying to calm down the* DEVILS *and the* UNCLEAN):
Oh, Lord!
More trouble coming!
Can I not pacify you?
Will not two revolutions satisfy you?

My comrades from the ocean,
Here do not raise another such commotion!

(*To* DEVILS.)

Have you no better food?
Such grub
Is not for you!
That is the rub!

(*To the* UNCLEAN.)

And you too are a healthy lot
If you will not concede a jot!
You see Beelzebub is old,
A venerable devil.
Cease every wrangling word!
Establish sweet concord!

BEELZEBUB: Oh, you poor toady!

FARM HAND: Oh, you tricky fox!

(*Both factions pommel the* COMPROMISER.)

COMPROMISER (*appealing to the audience*):

Citizens!
I never have had justice in my life!
I summon them to lay aside
Their strife,
And all I get is thumps from either side.

BEELZEBUB (*sadly, to the* UNCLEAN):

I would invite you to my private table,
To dine with me within;
But I cannot be very hospitable—
I've only bones and skin.
You know yourselves what men are like of late:
When roasted, you can't see 'em on the plate.
The other day they brought a workman here,
A cesspool worker, he!
So can't you understand?
We've naught to feed your band!

FARM HAND (*contemptuously, to the* UNCLEAN, *who have long been waiting impatiently*):

Let him go to his devils!
Come on, comrades!

(*The* UNCLEAN *start forward;* BEELZEBUB *catches at the last of them.*)

BEELZEBUB: A happy journey!
Call again!
I am a devil of *savoir faire.*

    Arrange your business then—
    And pray invite me there!
    I will be head commissar
    Of the fuel commissariat.
    Here we sit and starve, you see,
    For five days in a row;
    And we devils have, you know,
    A devilish appetite.

(*The* UNCLEAN *move onward and upward. The clouds are shattered by their blows. Darkness. From the darkness and the fragments of the abandoned stage emerges the following scene. Meanwhile the song of the* UNCLEAN *resounds through Hell.*)

BLACKSMITH: Break through with your bodies the hot
    And heavy doors of Hell!
    Tear Purgatory into shreds!
    Forward, my lads!
    Fear not!

ALL (*in chorus*) : Purgatory into fragments!
    Strike hard!
    Fear not!

MINER: Forward!
    We'll teach our bodies to do without rest.
    Higher!
    Aspire!
    Close ranks!
    Storm the banks
    Of clouds!

ALL (*in chorus*) : Higher!
    Tread the banks
    Of clouds!

LADY (*suddenly making her appearance and throwing herself on the bosom of* BEELZEBUB) :
    My dear Beelzebub!
    My darling tootsey-wootsey!
    My father dear!
    Let not a lady perish here
    Alone!
    Let me go!
    Let me go to my own!
    Let me go, dear, to your hall,
    For these Unclean appall
    My very soul!

BEELZEBUB: All right.
I offer shelter.
Pray enter!
Be happy quite,
Madame.

(*He points to the door, from which in an instant two* DEVILS *leap forth with pitchforks and drag away the* LADY. BEELZEBUB *rubs his hands.*)

BEELZEBUB: There's *one* to damn!
She's a deserter.
We shall delight
To eat for dessert her.

ACT IV

Paradise. Clouds are piled upon clouds. A general whitish tint pervades the scene. In the very center the inhabitants of Paradise are seated on the masses of clouds. METHUSELAH *is delivering an oration.*

METHUSELAH: Most saintly!
Go polish up our relics brightly!
Go clean your holy days right up!
For Gabriel announces to us
There advance here to us
More than a dozen of the righteous.
Most saintly!
Receive them in your midst!
Hunger plays with them as cats with mice.
They are sick of Hell.
They will be here in a trice.

INHABITANTS OF PARADISE (*with dignity*):
We see at once that they must be most worthy men.
We will bid them in.
We will welcome them by all means.

METHUSELAH: So we must set the table,
And meet them at the door.
We must receive them in most solemn style.

INHABITANTS
OF PARADISE: You are the eldest here: so be
The master of the ceremony.

METHUSELAH: I am not able—

ALL: No no!
You'll do!

METHUSELAH (*bows and goes to make arrangements at the table.   He
  arranges the SAINTS *in their places*):
             Chrysostom, pray stand here.
             Meanwhile you may prepare
             An eloquent toast of greeting
             In some such style as this:
             "We greet you all, and so does Christ."
             You know the way, so care
             For it yourself.
             Come here, Tolstoy! So, so!
             Your mien is fine and decorative;
             Stand as you have been standing.
             You here, Jean Jacques Rousseau!
             Now dress your ranks and stand in state,
             While I shall contemplate
             Our ceremonial table.—
             Have you begun
             To milk the clouds, my son?
ANGEL: I have.
METHUSELAH: When you have done,
             Just set it on the board.
             Then you may carve
             One little tiny bit of cloud
             For each of this our saintly crowd.
             It is not food that makes
             Us blessed fathers comfortable,
             But discourse edifying to the soul,
             Flowing across the table.
SAINTS: Well,
             Have they not yet been sighted?
             One cloud's edge is suspiciously inflated.
             They come! They come! They come upon their
                way!
             Can these be they?
             They come to Paradise, but look
             Like chimney sweepers caked with soot.
             We'll wash their faces.
             Well, saints, it seems, may be of various sorts and
                races.
 (*Shouts rise from below.*)
THE UNCLEAN: Let the guns roar,
             The cannons bellow!
             We for ourselves are Christ and savior!

(*The* UNCLEAN *rush in, breaking through the cloud of the floor.*)
THE UNCLEAN (*in chorus*):
Ugh! What a bearded throng!
Full three hundred strong!
METHUSELAH: Come in! Come in!
Come in to our peaceful abode!
VOICE OF AN ANGEL:
They have let in a madcap brood!
ANGELS: How do! How do!
Good day to you!
METHUSELAH: Now then, Chrysostom!
Speak your toast of welcome!
THE UNCLEAN: Send old Chrysostom down to Hell! Is
There nothing for our bellies?
We cannot hear orations
Until we get some rations.
METHUSELAH: Patience, brethren!
At once, without delay,
Your hunger we'll allay.
(*He leads the* UNCLEAN *to the spot where on the table of clouds
are spread forth cloud milk and cloud bread.*)
CARPENTER: I'm tired with my march.
Could I not have a chair?
METHUSELAH: No, sir, not here!
There are none in Paradise.
CARPENTER: You might some way devise
To ease our wonder-worker
Over there.
(*Pointing to* MINER.)
See how he stoops!
MINER: Don't call me names!
The main thing is to repair
Our vigor when it droops.
(*The* UNCLEAN *apply themselves to the cups and crusts. At first
they are startled; then, in great discontent, they fling away all the
flummery.*)
METHUSELAH: Well, have you had a taste?
CARPENTER (*threateningly*):
It's not to our own taste!
Is there nothing more substantial here?
METHUSELAH: Can incorporeal creatures bathe in wine or beer?
THE UNCLEAN: Have we been waiting for such damned poor fare!
Humbly we perish, perish there

                    Below!
                    If men but knew that such are your devices!
                    Why, we ourselves can show
                    A million of such paradises!

METHUSELAH (*pointing to a* SAINT *at whom the* BLACKSMITH *has been*
    yelling):   Do not yell! That is most impolite.
                    He is quite
                    Of archangelic station.

FISHERMAN: You'd better answer straight!
                    Can your archangels not serve up
                    For us some cabbage soup?

VOICES OF THE UNCLEAN:
                    We had no such idea of Heaven as this!

HUNTER: A pen!
                    A veritable den!

CHAUFFEUR: Not a fit Paradise for men!

SHOEMAKER: Well, my darlings,
                    We have attained the abode of blessed souls!

SERVANT: I tell you, it's the worst of holes!

FARM HAND: Do you do nothing but sit here on high?

ONE OF THE
ANGELS: Not exactly.— Why,
                    Oft we descend to earth's hard soil
                    And visit there a righteous brother or a sister.
                    Then we return, when we have poured our precious
                        oil.

SERVANT: So you let those white clouds wear off your plumes?
                    What freaks you are!
                    You might have elevators to your rooms.

SECOND ANGEL: Then we embroider fair and broad
                    Upon the clouds the letters I H S—
                    Initials of our Lord.

SERVANT: You'd better far
                    Be munching sunflower seeds— *
                    Provincials that you are,
                    And rank hayseeds!

FARM HAND: I wish they'd visit me upon the earth!
                    I'd cure those loafers of their sloth.
                    They sing down there below:
                    "The bonds are broken and the tyrants fall!"

---

* The peanuts and pop corn of the Russian peasants.

And when they get to work,
Not even your lofty station will aid you here at all.

SEAMSTRESS: It's just like Petersburg:
People packed up tight,
And victuals eaten up quite.

ONE OF THE
UNCLEAN: A dull life this of yours!
Most terribly it bores!

METHUSELAH: There is no help for it! Such are our occupations.
Of course
Even Paradise would benefit by alterations.

INTELLIGENT (*looks first at* LEV TOLSTOY, *then at* ROUSSEAU. *He addresses the latter*):

Continually I gaze with all my eyes
At you
And at Lev Nikolayevich.
Your features well I know!
You?
Aren't you Jean Jacques Rousseau?
Ah!
Permit me to impart
What joy now floods my heart!
'Twas you that wrote of liberty,
Equality, fraternity?
You wrote *The Social Contract?*
Just think!
Since I was a mere boy
I've known your books by rote—
Every word you wrote!
Let me express my deepest reverence,
For my sincerest pleasures
Are reading liberal sentiments:
Your writings are my treasures!
I never will go hence.
These coarse Unclean may go their ways,
But I shall venture to remain.
Yet not for long will I detain
You with my words of praise.
Your *Social Contract* says—

FARM HAND: How can we get out of here?
METHUSELAH: Ask Gabriel.
FARM HAND: But which might Gabriel be?
They're all alike to me!

METHUSELAH (*proudly stroking his beard*):
    Oh, don't say that!
    There are distinctions.
    For instance, if the beard be long—as thus.

THE UNCLEAN: Why waste talk!
    Smash the whole thing!
    This institution don't belong to us.

COMPROMISER: Hush! Hush!
    Comrades, agree,
    And quit your clashes!
    Let there arise no difference of classes!

(*To the* ANGELS.)
    Look!
    Each is a strapping lad!
    Were I
    In your own circumstances,
    Then I should be most happy.
    The best part of society
    Is the proletariat!

(*To the* UNCLEAN.)
    You too are a most dull conglomeration!
    Consider his high station!

(*Pointing to* METHUSELAH.)
    This is no Vrangel—*
    But an angel!

METHUSELAH: Agree with him!
    May God prevent it!

BLACKSMITH: Agree with you!
    You are demented!

(*Both parties pommel the* COMPROMISER.)

COMPROMISER (*weeping*):
    You offer pleasant words and tasty,
    And the result is something nasty!
    Again I get it from both sides!
    Ugh!
    One more attempt at harmony
    Will be the very death of me!

FARM HAND: To the Promised Land!
    Seek it beyond this Paradise!
    March on!
    With our strong tread we'll overturn

---

* See note on page 812.

        And spurn

        This Paradise!

ALL (*in chorus*): We'll find it though we overturn

        The universe!

METHUSELAH (*gazing at the destruction wrought in Paradise by the* UNCLEAN, *he wails in despairing tones*):

        Help!

        Catch them!

        Hold them!

        May lightning and the Lord of Hosts consume them!

  (*With a terrific peal of thunder the* LORD OF HOSTS *himself appears in the clouds, holding a bundle of thunderbolts in his hand.*)

LORD OF HOSTS: I'll crush you with my bolts of thunder!

SOLDIER OF THE RED ARMY (*reproachfully*):

        Like kids who blunder,

        They've gone and told mamma.

  (*His face contorted, seeing a fracas of untold dimensions approaching, the* COMPROMISER *starts to whimper.*)

COMPROMISER: Oof!

        Woof!

        Dear me, I see

        The Lord appear before me!

        I tremble!

        I fall flat!

        My legs are weak beneath me!

  (*To the* UNCLEAN.)

        Collect your wits!

        Agree!

        Can you make good your boasts

        Against the Lord of Hosts!

LORD OF HOSTS (*shaking his fist at the* COMPROMISER):

        If I were not all-merciful and peaceful,

        I'd give you of such harmony a fistful!

BLACKSMITH: We,

        Workmen, here

        To compromise with God?

        Your harmony will cost you dear!

  (*They thump the* COMPROMISER.)

COMPROMISER (*tearfully, yet with respect*):

        My principles begin to tarnish.

        What fists you have!

        If much more I compromise,

        I'll lose my menshevikish varnish.

LOCOMOTIVE ENGINEER (*points to the* LORD OF HOSTS, *who is brandish-ing the arrows of his lightnings, but does not care to use them, for fear of striking* METHUSELAH *or others of his company.*)
          Now we must snatch away God's lightnings!
          Grab 'em! To us
          They'll be of use
          For our
          Electric power!
          Such valuable thunder must
          Not go to waste!

(*The* UNCLEAN *throw themselves on the* LORD OF HOSTS *and snatch away his lightnings.*)

LORD OF HOSTS (*sadly*):
          They've plucked me bare
          Of down and hair!

METHUSELAH: Now what remains for us to chastise sinners with?

(*The* UNCLEAN, *carrying the lightnings, mount upward, smashing Paradise as they proceed on their way.*)

BLACKSMITH: The dawn is breaking fast.
          Onward! Rise
          To our true Paradise!
          There we will break our fast.

(*However, when, treading over the fragments, they have reached the summit, the* SEAMSTRESS *interrupts the* BLACKSMITH.)

SEAMSTRESS: But, tell me, what is there before us,
          To still the hunger pangs that gnaw us!

LAUNDRESS (*wearily*):
          We break, we break, we break
          These clouds!
          Is it not time to pass by these defiles!
          Shall we not soon with dew
          Wash off the dirt that now
          Defiles our weary bodies here below?

OTHER VOICES: Where is our way?
          Shall we not be once more in Hell?
          They've duped us!
          Duped us well!
          What will come next?
          The more we toil, the worse we're vext!

VOICE (*after a moment of reflection*):
          Forward the chimney sweep!
          Our spy will take a peep!

(*From the darkness of the fragments of Paradise a new scene rises.*

The COMPROMISER, *deep in meditation, separates from the* UNCLEAN, *who still proceed forward.*)

COMPROMISER: They've gone through Hell,
And then through Paradise,
And still they rise.
But shall not I at least turn back?
That angel brood
Are after all a good
And compromising pack
Of fellows.
Let those Unclean proceed, if they're not lazy;
(*Waves his hand after the* UNCLEAN *as they depart.*)
But I'll return
To Lev Tolstoy.
He's an aristocrat without alloy,
And civil!
I'll practice non-resistance now
To evil.*

ACT V

The Land of Fragments †

BLACKSMITH: Hey!
Why have you stopped?
Get on!
LAMPLIGHTER: No passing by!
Mountains are heaped along the road.
To travel such a highway we're not fitted.
SEAMSTRESS: During three years what rubbish has accumulated.
(*They survey the fragments.*)
SEAMSTRESS: See! A bit of our own ark!
SOLDIER OF THE
RED ARMY: The relics of the dark
Negus of Abyssinia.
SHOEMAKER: Morsels of Paradise.
FARM HAND: A shard of Hell.
LAMPLIGHTER: Well, well!
What can we do to-day?
We surely can't go on!
And we've no place to sit us down.

---

* See Introduction, pages 12, 13.   † No such heading in original.

BLACKSMITH: What shall we do, you say!
               Why, we must clear the way!
FARM HAND: So we need not deliberate.
               Comrade, we must organize
               And set to work, not prate.
SOLDIER OF THE RED ARMY (*with dignity*):
               Organization is of various sorts.
               At first, if we are wise, it
               Is necessary to decide
               What must be done—
               And then take our organization
               And revise it.
MINER (*with vexation*):
               A wise man, as I live!
               What bright advice you give!
               Revision is all tommyrot!
               We need commanders to instruct us what
               We need to do.
LAUNDRESS (*with a teasing air*):
               Commanders!
               Are you duffers!
               We need buffers!*
(*The* UNCLEAN *crowd together, scolding at one another.*)
HUNTER: I think
               All these reforms
               Are not according to the Marxian forms.
               I must support
               A program of a radically different sort.
               It is my wish to aid our toiling Russians
               To break the bonds of poverty and famine.
FARM HAND (*hopelessly*):
               Now they have started on their old discussions!
BLACKSMITH (*separating those advancing to the fray*):
               Comrades,
               Quit all this talking and disunion!
               We here are no trade union.
LOCOMOTIVE
ENGINEER: Buffers! Hark! Hark!
               Her talk is all beside the mark.
               The laundress' breasts are buffers!

---

* The reference is probably to buffer states; the laundress uses a catchword
without understanding its meaning.

But the poor locomotive has no wheels
And much less buffers!

BLACKSMITH: We drown in words
And reach no fords.
Leave newspaper talk
And set to work!
Forward!
Why float
On streams of debate?
The spade let us ply
And make the dirt fly!

ALL (*in chorus, as they clear away the fragments*):
Now then!
One blow!
And then two!
Why count!
One stroke!
And then more!

COMPROMISER (*appearing from a cloud marked* BERLIN): *
Oh! oh! oh!
Comrades!
Quit your work!
You all will understand
I counsel naught that has not been well planned.
From my own Paradise beyond the border
I can make projects in most perfect order.
Quit working, my good comrades!
From all this no results will come, lads.
Agree with me! . . .

BLACKSMITH: You've stuck out
Your phiz.
Look out
Lest all of a sudden my hammer may whiz
Against your brow!

COMPROMISER: Ow!
(*In a trice he shuts up the cloud.*)

MINER (*pausing with his mattock raised*):
Comrades,
Hearken
To those wailing cries!
Some one is crushed by the fragments

---

* A reference to the *Socialist Herald*, published in Berlin.

And dies!
Rush to his call
One and all.

(At the conclusion of his speech all dig with tenfold strength, and from the clouds appear a LOCOMOTIVE *and a* STEAMBOAT.*)*

LOCOMOTIVE: Hey!
Hark to the groan of the locomotive!
Let me live!
I cannot raise steam!
Give me black bread
From the Don! *
On!
Let me be fed!

LOCOMOTIVE
ENGINEER: No!
No death for you!
No, friend most true!
Have hope!
In the depths of the earth we will grope:
Coal we will bring to you,
Which will give wings to you!

STEAMBOAT: Oh! oh! oh!
Give me to drink from the springs and the river!
With holes in my sides I now shiver!
And lead me to the docks!
Give me but oil from Baku!
Oo! oo! oo!

MINER: Hey, comrades,
Follow me!
Why do you stand,
Hand rested upon hand?
For coal beneath the earth!
For oil!
The wells of oil
Will well reward our toil!

ALL (*in chorus*): Raise the spade!
Wield it well!
Strike, be not afraid!
Drive the drill!

CONFUSION: † Back!
Why do your hammers ring?

---

* The great coal basin of Russia.
† Not mentioned in the list of characters.

Back! Who can contend with me!
With Confusion!
Here I reign—
Empress Confusion!
I eat the locomotives.
Machines do I devour.
When I blow,
I blow away a factory like smoke.
When I but look,
The foundry will not strike a stroke.
I gnaw—
The railway train will run no more.
The city writhes with hunger
And with cold;
The village dies with cold
And lack of food.
Back!
I hate courageous toil.
Back!
All your endeavors I will spoil.
To me my host, sharpers and slackers!
To me my faithful horde of speculators!

(CONFUSION'S *"host" flocks about her.*)

HOST (*in chorus*):

Back!
Why do your hammers ring?
Back!
Who can contend with her!
With Confusion!

CONFUSION: Bow down! I am Confusion, empress mighty!
Your throats with hunger I will strangle tightly.

BLACKSMITH: Quit!—
Hit
The empress with a hammer!
To arms!

MINER (*advancing against* CONFUSION *and her army of profiteers*):
Seize the coal!
And seize those rogues as well!—
You long enough have ridden on top.*
Now we'll drive you all to work!

---

* Refers to stolen rides on top of railway cars, by "bootleggers" with sacks of goods.

BLACKSMITH : Catch the sharpers!
Down with the slackers!
All to work!
Work till you drop!

(*The* UNCLEAN *move forward;* CONFUSION'S *"host" withdraws.*)

MINER (*cutting in under* CONFUSION) :
Beneath Confusion shall we lower
Our heads?
Comrades,
Come, undermine her power!
Capture the trenches of the mines!

FARM HAND : Our battle lines are furrows in the field!

FARM HAND
and MINER :   Our arms
Are bread and coal!

BLACKSMITH (*slays* CONFUSION. *The end of his speech is spoken over her corpse.*)
Hurrah!
They've fled!
Confusion yields to us!
One more,
One more great stroke remains for us.
She's past and gone.
Enough!
Come on!
Descend!
Open is now the way,
The door into the future.

(*He points to the open shaft of the mine.*)
There!
Advance!
Drive gallery on gallery!
Sing :
"This will be our final conflict :
Let each stand at his place!" *

(*They enter the shaft. Their voices die away in the distance.*)

MINER (*wheeling out a truck of coal*) :
Here is the first
From the Moscow mines.

LOCOMOTIVE : Thanks!
I'm glad!

---

* From *The International.*

My boiler works.
Jack me up!

LOCOMOTIVE ENGINEER (*rolling in a cask of crude oil*):
From Baku!
Receive our gift!

STEAMBOAT: Ready.
In my side
No hole is left.

MINER (*with another truck*):
More has come on
From the basin of the Don.

LOCOMOTIVE: *   Thanks!
Now I'll summon steam.

LOCOMOTIVE ENGINEER (*with another cask*):
Another tank we've brought for *you*.

STEAMBOAT: Thanks:
Now my connecting rods can go.

LOCOMOTIVE ENGINEER (*with another cask*):
One present more from Ukhta.

MINER (*with another truck*):
And this from the Ural.

STEAMBOAT *and*
LOCOMOTIVE: Now we revive.
Hurrah, all!

LOCOMOTIVE: My wheels are moving.
STEAMBOAT: I am alive.
Straightway the rivers I'll be roving.

(*From the mouths of the shafts the* UNCLEAN *run forth and rush to embrace one another.*)

LOCOMOTIVE ENGINEER (*to* MINER):
I will help you!

MINER (*to* LOCOMOTIVE ENGINEER):
I will help you!

BLACKSMITH: I'll help you both!
LAUNDRESS: I'll help you both!
SOLDIER OF THE
RED ARMY: Extraordinary!
SEAMSTRESS: Beyond belief!
HUNTER: Fantastic news!
MINER: Look there beyond the farthest height!

---

* "Steamboat" in the original.

MINER *and* LOCOMOTIVE ENGINEER:
There's something there!

MINER: I'm drilling my last hole.

LOCOMOTIVE
ENGINEER: And I—
This is the last cask that I need to roll.

MINER: I hear
Far, far away . . .

LOCOMOTIVE
ENGINEER: I see
Far, far away . . .
Almost beyond my vision . . .

MINER: I hear a song,
Rumbling of wheels,
The peaceful breath of factories.

LOCOMOTIVE
ENGINEER: I see the sun.
The early dawn is fair.
A city must be there.

SOLDIER OF THE
RED ARMY: I think that victory is ours.
I think we are
Before the door
That opens to the bowers
Of our true Paradise of plenty.

LOCOMOTIVE: The locomotive's ready.

STEAMBOAT: The steamboat's ready too.

LOCOMOTIVE
ENGINEER: Set forth, now, all of you.
With their aid
We'll rush into the future,
Undismayed!

SOLDIER OF THE RED ARMY (*mounts the cab of the* LOCOMOTIVE;
he is followed by the others, some to the LOCOMOTIVE, *others to the*
STEAMBOAT): The path is plain,
Level and clean.
Now be the first there!
Forward, engineer!
To the waves!
To the rails!
Earned by hard toil,
It is at hand—
The future's joyous land,

A home for us!
Fly over space
On the wings of the machines!
Only they
Are the way
To the future's happiness!
Step after step,
Mount aloft!

ALL (*repeating after him in chorus*):
Forward!
On the wings of the machines!

ACT VI

The Promised Land. A huge gate. From behind certain projecting corners are dimly visible the streets and squares of earthly settlements. Over the gate are seen rainbows and the flower-like roofs of huge structures. At the gate is a LOOKOUT, *who calls by name to the* UNCLEAN *as they clamber upward.*

MINER: Comrades, this way!
                Come here!
                Now disembark!

(*The* UNCLEAN *ascend; and, tremendously astonished, gaze at the gate.*)

MINER: Marvels appear!
CARPENTER: But this seems like Ivanovo-Voznesensk! *
                Can there be marvels there!
SERVANT: How can we trust such rogues, pray tell me!
BLACKSMITH: This is not Voznesensk—
                I tell you. Ah,
                It is Marseilles!
SHOEMAKER: I think it's Shuya.†
CHAUFFEUR: Not Shuya, not at all!
                It's Manchester.
LOCOMOTIVE
ENGINEER: Aren't you ashamed to talk such nonsense?
                No Manchester is this!
                It is just Moscow.
                Why are you all blind?
                There, see, is the Tverskaya,

---

* A factory town in Russia.   † Also a factory town in Russia.

And there the Sadovaya,
And there the theatre
Of the Resefeser.*

FARM HAND: Whether it's Shuya, Manchester, or Moscow,
It matters not.
The important thing is now
That once again we are on earth,
Once more on our own ground.

ALL: Round is the damned old earth:
Oh, it is round!

LAUNDRESS: The earth, but changed!
I think
That for the earth
There's too small stink
Of slops!

SERVANT: What's that in the air that floats?
Fragrance of apricots!

SHOEMAKER: What! In Shuya
Can apricots appear?
And yet it is the autumn of the year.

(*They raise their heads. The rainbow dazzles their eyes.*)

SOLDIER OF THE
RED ARMY: Hey, lamplighter,
You have a ladder!
Climb
And take a look!

LAMPLIGHTER (*climbs and stops in stupefaction. He can do nothing but stammer*):
We're fools! Just fools!

SOLDIER OF THE
RED ARMY: But tell us!—
He's gazing like a goose upon the lightning!—
Tell us,
You owl!

LAMPLIGHTER: I can't!
Tight is my tongue!
Give me,
Give me a tongue sixty miles long!
A tongue that's bright
And white
As the sun's rays!

* That is, RSFSR, the initials of "Russian Socialist Federated Soviet Republic."
The Tverskaya and Sadovaya are streets in Moscow.

That hangs not like a rag,
But wags
And peals forth like a lyre!
And let that tongue
Be swung
By jewelers of oratory,
That words may fly forth from my mouth
Like nightingales
Of fairy tales! . . .
But what's the use!
Even then I could not tell a bit
Of it!
Buildings a hundred stories high
Cover the earth!
Between those houses
Hang graceful bridges!
Under the houses
Are all things that man eats,
Piled mountain high!
Over the bridges
Long rows of swift trains ply!

ALL (*in chorus*): Whole rows of trains?

LAMPLIGHTER: Yes, rows of trains!
The lamps
Glow with electric eyes!
Into those eyes
Motors a millionfold
More powerful than ours
Pour forth their powers
And radiant streams!
All the earth shines
And gleams!

ALL (*in chorus*): Shines?

LAMPLIGHTER: Yes, shines!

SOLDIER OF THE
RED ARMY: You've worked on them yourselves.
Why is he so surprised?

LOCOMOTIVE
ENGINEER: We've worked, I know,
But this is past belief!
What man of us can show
That wonders of such sort
Reward his toil and woe!

FARM HAND: Enough of lies!
This lecturer's too wise!
Thorny acacia roots
Never bore figs as fruits.

LAMPLIGHTER: Stop your brawling!
This is
Electrification!

ALL (*in chorus*): Electrification?

LAMPLIGHTER: Yes,
Electrification.
Forks stuck on knobs set in the earth.

LOCOMOTIVE
ENGINEER: Marvels!
No learned men would credit such a notion.

LAMPLIGHTER: There goes an electric tractor!
An electric sower!
An electric thrasher!
And in a second
The bread's
Already baked.

ALL (*in chorus*): Baked?

LAMPLIGHTER: Yes, baked.

BAKER: But the lady with her gaudy rags,
And the boss with his pug-dog face—
Do they still stroll about the place?
Are they still making hideous
The sidewalks for the rest of us?

LAMPLIGHTER: No,
No such people soil this town:
Nothing such I see below.—
There goes a sugar loaf!
Two more!

SEAMSTRESS: Sugar?
Do you hear?
What's to be done?
Before the deluge came I lost my cards,
The last one! *

ALL (*in chorus*): Do speak a little more exactly!

LAMPLIGHTER: There walk all sorts
Of victuals
And goods.

---

* A reference to the distribution of sugar by cards during the War and later.

Each has a hand,
Each has a foot.
Factories decked with flags.
Mile upon mile.
Wherever my eyes may roam—
Covered with flowers,
The lathe
And the loom
Stand
Without work.

THE UNCLEAN (*uneasily*):
Stand?
Without work?
And here we're wasting words upon the winds!
Perhaps the rain may come
And spoil all the machines!
Break in!
Shout!
Hey!
Who's there, I say!

LAMPLIGHTER (*sliding down*):
They're on the way!

ALL: Who?

LAMPLIGHTER: They,
The Things.

(*The doors fly open and the city is disclosed. But what a city! The wide-open frames of transparent factories and lodging houses tower up to the sky. Trains of railway cars, tram cars, and automobiles stand wrapped in rainbows. In the midst of the city is a garden of stars and moons, surmounted by the shining crown of the sun. From the show windows the best goods emerge, and, headed by the Sickle and the Hammer,* advance to the gate to offer Bread and Salt.†*)

Exclamations burst forth from the dumb ranks of the UNCLEAN, *who are huddled close together.*

THE UNCLEAN: A-a-a-a-a-ah!

THINGS: Ha! ha! ha! ha! ha! ha!

FARM HAND: Who are you?
And whose?

THINGS: Why whose?

FARM HAND: What is your master's name?

THINGS: No master us can claim.
No man's are we.

---

* Emblems of the Soviet Republic.   † Emblems of hospitality.

	Each is a delegate. The Sickle and the Hammer Greet you— The emblems of our socialistic state.
FARM HAND:	But for whom is the Bread? The Salt? The Sugar Loaf? Do you come to greet your governor?
THINGS:	No! You! All is yours!
LAUNDRESS:	Don't lie! We are not babes or blind. It must be, They sell you on the sly. It must be, A horde of speculators Hide behind.
THINGS:	No speculators! Look!
SERVANT:	I understand the way. They'll store you in the Empeekay,* And in a year they'll deal you out by spoonfuls.
THINGS:	In no place do they store Us. Each of you may take A peck And more.
FISHERMAN:	We must be asleep And dream of this.
SEAMSTRESS:	Once I sat In the third gallery. And on the stage I saw a ball. *La Traviata.* They dined And wined. I left the hall— And then life outside seemed so bitter: Dirt, Mire.

* That is, MPK, the Russian initials of "Local Committee on Food Supplies."

THINGS:	But now such rare delight
	Will always meet your sight!
	This is the earth.
BLACKSMITH:	Stop all this foolery!
	Is this the earth!
	The earth is dirt,
	Is night and dearth.
	On earth you work and think to eat your mouthful;
	A fat man comes and filches every morsel.

LAUNDRESS (*pointing at the* BREAD):

It calls,
But it
No doubt
Will bite.
A hundred thousand rubles I will bet you,
A hundred thousand teeth await you
In every ovenful of that Bread.

LOCOMOTIVE ENGINEER (*pointing to the* MACHINES):

They too!
They come to us!
They creep like any mouse.
Those soft-stepping Machines have clawed us all like
 cats!—
For your sharp teeth the workmen were the rats!

MACHINES: Forgive us, workman!

Workman, forgive!
It is you that wrought us,
Assembled us,
Founded us.
But they seized us,
Enslaved us.—
"Run, Machine, run!
Cease not, ye steel slaves!
Rest not, nor falter!"—
They bade us bear the fat men on our tires.
They bade us work for them in factories.
Shaft upon shaft,
With belts of leather,
Year after year—
They made us tear
With flywheels of steel
Your bodies frail.
Shout, ye motors!

Great is our glee!
Crushed are the fat men;
Now we are free!
Roar in the factories, moving the wheels!
Rush over steel rails, coursing the fields!
Now the world makes holiday;
Now the night shines as the day!
Now until the end of time
Yours are we, workmen.

THINGS: We too, we too, the tools of your trades;
Hammers and Needles, Saws, Tongs, and Spades!
When daylight scarcely had banished the dark,
Bending beneath us, you went to your work.
Heeding no longer the bosses' commands,
All things we fashion and forge for your hands.
To you,
Whose backs broke beneath us—
To you we come, and beg you greet us
In the wide smithy of this Paradise of Joy.
Raise now the Hammer, wield it as a toy.

EDIBLES: And we, all things that man can drink and eat—
We caused the workers trouble and defeat.
Without his Bread no laborer has might,
Nor without Sugar sweetness and delight.
By man's hard toil we scarce were earned.
Our price increased a millionfold:
Barking like dogs, we spurned
Your hungry gaze from windows of the shop.
But of the idle parasites you made an end,
And Bread is now both free and sweet.
All that you eyed with gnashing of your teeth,
All now is yours: seize it and eat!

MACHINES, THINGS, *and* EDIBLES (*in chorus*):
Take what is yours!
Take!
Go!
All wherewith to work!
All that man can eat!
Go and take!
Go, conquerors!

BLACKSMITH: Of course we must present
An order for supplies!
But we have none to show.

	We're straight from Paradise, Which we reached from Hell below.
THINGS:	No orders are required. No such things are desired.
FARM HAND:	Our feet aren't sharper than a hoe— We cannot blunt them now. Come, brothers, let us try! Now let us eat or die!

(*The* UNCLEAN *advance. The* FARM HAND *touches the earth.*)

FARM HAND:	It is the earth! It is Our native motherland!
ALL:	Now we must sing! Must shout! Must raise a prayer To the air!
BAKER (*to the* CARPENTER):	It's sugar! I licked it.
CARPENTER:	Well!
BAKER:	Sweet as sweet.
SEVERAL VOICES:	Now we'll be jolly beyond compare!
FARM HAND (*growing tipsy*):	Comrade Things, Just let me say a word to you! To suffer woe we need No longer fear. Now we will manufacture you, And you our mouths will feed. And if the boss some plot contrive, We will not let him go alive! It's we that now begin to live!
ALL:	To live! To live!
MERCHANT (*elbowing his way through the crowd, he jumps out in indignation*):	What's that you say! Be moderate! A concessionaire deserves his pay And rebate!
BLACKSMITH:	Be off with you! Your work is over. You've earned enough For your babies' milk.

> We've studied all your skill,
> And now we've learned it well.— *
> So now you may retire!

(*The* MERCHANT *is thrown out headlong.   The* UNCLEAN *survey the* THINGS *greedily.*)

FARM HAND: I'd like to take a Saw!
　　　　　　My arms are slack
　　　　　　For lack
　　　　　　Of work. I'm young, you see!
SAW: Take me!
SEAMSTRESS: I'd like a Needle! I can handle ye.
BLACKSMITH: My fingers itch. Give me a Hammer!
HAMMER: Take me and dandle me!

(*The* UNCLEAN, *the* THINGS, *and the* MACHINES *form a ring around the sunny garden.*)

LOCOMOTIVE ENGINEER (*to the* MACHINES):
　　　　　　I'd like to make you go.
　　　　　　You won't begin to rush and bellow?
MACHINES: No, never!
　　　　　　Just press the lever!

(*The* LOCOMOTIVE ENGINEER *presses the lever.   The wheels begin to turn.   The* UNCLEAN *gaze with delight and amazement.*)

LOCOMOTIVE
ENGINEER: Never have I seen such a world!
　　　　　　Whence comes it?
　　　　　　It is not the earth—
　　　　　　It is a glowing comet
　　　　　　That appears
　　　　　　With a train of railway cars.
　　　　　　Why did we low
　　　　　　Like oxen at the plow?
　　　　　　We waited,
　　　　　　Waited,
　　　　　　Waited years,
　　　　　　And never even cast our eyes
　　　　　　At the blessing that appears
　　　　　　Here at our side.
　　　　　　And why do men seek pleasures
　　　　　　By visiting museums?
　　　　　　Around them stand rich treasures upon treasures!

---

* A reference to Lenin's advocacy of the New Economic Policy: "We must learn from the bourgeois how to do business."

Is that the sky or but a strip of calico?
If our hands have made it so,
Then what door is
Not open wide before us?
We are the architects of earths,
The planets' decorators;
We are the wonder-makers.
The sunbeams we shall tie
In radiant brooms, and sweep
Clouds from the sky
With electricity.
We shall make honey-sweet the rivers of the worlds.
The streets of earth we'll pave with radiant stars.
Dig!
Gouge!
Saw!
Bore!
All shout, "Hurrah!"
Hurrah for all
The things that are!
To-day
These are but doors of theatre properties;
To-morrow their poor stuff
Will be replaced by firm realities.
We know that well,
We trust in it,
And now we tell
The news to you.
Come to us from the hall!
Come hither, one and all!
Come hither, actor,
Poet,
Director!

(*All the spectators mount the stage.*)

ALL (*in chorus*): Sun-worshipers in the fair church
Of this our Paradise on earth,
Now we will show you well how we can sing.
Come, take your stand
In our choral band!
Let the psalms of the future ring!

(*The* COMPROMISER *suddenly bobs up and gazes with astonishment at the Commune. Understanding what is going on, he politely removes his hat.*)

COMPROMISER: No!
An energetic man is out of place in Heaven.
Those fasting mugs don't please me. No,
Our destiny is socialism.
I always told you so.

(*To the* UNCLEAN.)
Comrades, you must not so discordantly
With jangling voices shout and cry.
Singing requires sweet harmony.

(*He goes to one side and softly directs them with his hand.   The*
BLACKSMITH *leads him away courteously.*)

THE UNCLEAN (*sing*) : *

With workers' millions now we've crushed
The ancient prison's ghastly power.
The brand of bondage yields to us;
The world is free this day and hour.
As dust oppression flies away;
Our chains are snapped and thrown aside.
The fairy tale is true to-day;
The Commune's door stands open wide.

Sound of victory the call!
Sing, men of all the earth!
With *The International*
Behold mankind's new birth!

We waited not for Heaven's salvation;
Nor God nor Devil plead our cause.
In arms we fought with every nation,
Gained power for the working class.
In one Commune the world we've blended;
The workers' ring enfolds all lands.
Now come and try to snatch our splendid,
Majestic power from our hands!

Sound of victory the call!
Sing, men of all the earth!
With *The International*
Behold mankind's new birth!

All memory of the past shall perish;
The bourgeois rule is crushed and lost!
The earth we hold and aye shall cherish,
We, soldiers of the toilers' host!

---

* The following song is an imitation of *The International.*

From fields and factories ascend!
Come from the towns both great and small!
The world is ours from end to end;
We who were naught, to-day are all!

Sound of victory the call!
Sing, men of all the earth!
With *The International*
Behold mankind's new birth!

BIOGRAPHICAL NOTES
AND
READING LIST

BIOGRAPHICAL NOTES

LEONÍD NIKOLÁYEVICH ANDRÉYEV (1871-1919) was born at Orel in central Russia; his father was a surveyor who died early, leaving the family in poverty. He studied at the University of St. Petersburg, where he led a dissipated life; then transferred to the University of Moscow, where he graduated in 1897. As a student he had engaged in newspaper work; immediately after his graduation he won a reputation as a reporter of court cases and a writer of *feuilletons*. In 1898 his stories attracted attention, bringing him to the notice of Gorky, who encouraged him in his career. During the following decade he became the most popular of Russian writers; *Silence* (1900), *The Red Laugh* (1904), and *The Seven Who Were Hanged* (1908) are among his notable tales. In 1908 he built himself a "castle" at Vammelsu in Finland, where he lived in pretentious seclusion until his death. He worked irregularly, dictating his compositions and making much use of stimulants. Previously without positive convictions in politics, during the Great War he became a member of the patriotic party; later he was a vehement opponent of the Bolsheviks.

Andreyev began work as a dramatist in 1905; during his later years he showed a distinct preference for the dramatic form. The list of his plays is as follows:—

To the Stars (1905), *Savva, The Life of Man* (1906), *Tsar Hunger* (1907), *The Black Maskers, The Days of Our Life, Love of One's Neighbor, The Bat* (1908), *Anathema, Anfisa* (1909), *Gaudeamus* (1910), *The Ocean* (1911), *Honor, The Sabine Women, Professor Storitsyn, Ekaterina Ivanovna* (1912), *Thou Shalt Not Kill* (1913), *Samson Enchained; The Waltz of the Dogs; Thought; An Event; The Parrot; King, Law, Liberty; Youth* (1914), *War's Burden, He Who Gets Slapped* (1915), *Dear Phantoms* (1916), *Requiem* (1917).

ANTÓN PÁVLOVICH CHÉKHOV (1860-1904) was the son of a merchant whose father had been a serf. He was born in Taganrog on the Sea of Azov. In 1884 he was graduated from the Faculty of Medicine in the University of Moscow. He began his literary career in 1880, while still a student, by stories published in comic journals; from these he passed to more serious work and became a regular contributor to the *Novoye Vremya,* then the most influential of Russian newspapers. He speedily won financial success and, somewhat later, attained literary fame as the foremost writer of his generation. His kindly, generous personal temperament, in strange contrast to the gloomy, sometimes cynical tone of his stories and dramas, made him universally loved. In 1892-93 he took part in relief work during the cholera epidemic. Though he held himself aloof from politics, he became the friend and helper of men of revolutionary inclinations such as Gorky. He married Madame Olga Knipper, a noted actress of the Moscow Art Theatre. His early death was due to consumption.

It would be futile to give titles of Chekhov's stories; *Sleepyhead* and *The Darling* are among his brief masterpieces. The list of his dramas is as follows:—

Serious plays: *On the Highway* (1884), *That Worthless Fellow Platonov* (early play, published posthumously), *Ivanov* (1886), *Tatyana Repina* (1889, published posthumously), *The Wood Sprite* (1889, remodeled as *Uncle Vanya,* 1896), *The Seagull* (1896), *The Three Sisters* (1900), *The Cherry Orchard* (1904).

Farces: *The Sudden Death of a Horse, or the Greatness of the Russian Soul, The Bear, The Proposal, A Tragedian in Spite of Himself, The Swan Song, The Wedding, The Jubilee.*

DENÍS IVÁNOVICH FONVÍZIN (1744-92) came of a family of gentry. He received a good education at the University of Moscow, and while still a student won a reputation as a translator. On leaving the University in 1762 he entered the state service, where he remained until 1783. For his material prosperity he was indebted to his patron, Count Panin. He made three journeys abroad. During his last years he was an invalid.

Fonvizin attracted attention in 1766 by his comedy, *The Brigadier,* and became a member of literary society in St. Petersburg. The climax of his career came in 1782, with the striking success on the stage of his second comedy, *The Young Hopeful,* which established his position as the leading Russian dramatist of his time. He wrote but two other plays, *The Choice of a Tutor* (a brief imitation of his own *Young Hopeful*) and *Corion* (in verse, an adaptation from the French of Gresset).

Aside from his comedies, Fonvizin wrote a few verses and some prose articles, none of them of great merit. More noteworthy are his letters from France, in which, despite his intellectual debt to the West, he shows a strongly nationalistic temper. In his literary work, which is that of a dilettante, and in his personal character, he is an excellent representative of the Russian cultivated gentry of the later eighteenth century.

NIKOLÁY VASÍLYEVICH GÓGOL (1809-52) was born in a village in the province of Poltava, in southern Russia; his parents were middle-class gentry. After finishing his gymnasium course, he came in 1829 to St. Petersburg, where for a short time he was in the government service. His earliest literary efforts were unsuccessful, but in 1831 he became known for a volume of stories of provincial life, *Evenings on a Farm near Dikanka.* Two volumes entitled *Mirgorod,* published in 1835 and containing among other tales his *Old-Fashioned Farmers, The King of the Gnomes,* and *Taras Bulba,* established his reputation as a literary leader. In the next year his comedy, *The Inspector,* with its stinging attack on government dishonesty, made him the idol of the Russian liberals. During the next twelve years he lived abroad, where he completed the first part of his masterpiece, *Dead Souls,* a narrative satire on Russian society, published in 1842. Among his other works of the same period are *The Overcoat,* the most famous of all Russian short stories, and two comedies, *Marriage* and *The Gamblers.* In 1842 his artistic work came practically to an end. In 1847 he published *Selections from Correspondence with Friends,* in which he revealed himself as a political and religious conservative of the deepest dye, thereby destroying his influence with the liberals, whose sympathy he had won by his satiric genius. During his last years he became a religious enthusiast of a crude and narrow sort; he died almost insane. Fragments of a second part of *Dead Souls,* published after his death, did not add to his fame.

MAXÍM GORKY (pseudonym for Alexéy Maxímovich Péshkov) was born in Nizhny Novgorod in 1869, the son of an upholsterer. He grew up in poverty, working at all sorts of drudgery, which he later described in *My Childhood* and in various tales. He had the scantiest schooling, deriving his education, such as it was, from his own wide and miscellaneous reading. For years he led the life of a tramp. He published his first story in 1892; by 1895 he had acquired a reputation. A rebel by temperament, he was in constant difficulties with the government, which in 1902 refused to sanction his election to the Imperial Academy of Sciences. In 1906 he left Russia, not to return there until 1914. Since 1917 he has been a supporter of the Soviet Government, but has done active work in aid of the intellectual classes ruined by the Revolution.

Among Gorky's best short stories are *Chelkash* (1895), *Konovalov* (1896), *Orlov and His Wife* (1897), *Twenty-six Men and a Girl* (1899). His most notable longer narratives are *Foma Gordeyev* (1899), *My Childhood* (1913), *In the World* (1915), *Recollections of Tolstoy* (1919), *My University Days* (1923), *Notes from a Diary* (1924),

Klim Samgin (1928: translated as *The Bystander* and *The Magnet*). The list of his dramas is as follows:—

The Petty Bourgeois (1900), *Down and Out* (1902), *Children of the Sun* (1904), *Summer Folk* (1905), *The Barbarians, Enemies* (1906), *The Last* (1908), *Queer People* (1910), *Vassa Zheleznova* (1911), *The Zykovs, Children* (1913), *The Old Man* (1915: translated as *The Judge*), *False Coin* (1927).

ALEXANDER SERGÉYEVICH GRIBOYÉDOV (1795-1829) came of a well-to-do family and was educated at the University of Moscow. On his graduation in 1812 he served for four years in the army. In 1817 he entered the Ministry of Foreign Affairs and spent the following years, until 1826, mainly in Georgia and Persia. He was a man of wide culture and early became known for his wit and literary talent. He was intimate with some of the leaders of the Decembrist Conspiracy of 1825, and, although acquitted by the government investigators, he was probably at least cognizant of the conspirators' plans. His hero Chatsky, whose long harangues show both liberal sentiment and an attachment to old Russian manners and customs, is a typical Decembrist. In 1827 Griboyedov returned to Georgia; in 1828 he was sent to Persia as Russian minister. In 1829 he was slain by a Persian mob.

Aside from *Wit Works Woe,* Griboyedov wrote, or aided in writing, ten dramas, some of which were adaptations from the French. Neither they nor his short poems and prose articles are of literary importance. On his masterpiece, *Wit Works Woe,* he labored for at least ten years, completing it in 1823.

VLADÍMIR VLADÍMIROVICH MAYAKÓVSKY (1894-1930) was born at Bagdaly, in the province of Kutaïs, Transcaucasia; his father was a forester. In 1905 he became a member of a Marxian circle. In 1906 the family moved to Moscow; here Mayakovsky entered a gymnasium, but he never finished his course. As a boy he worked as a propagandist and spent eleven months in prison. He studied painting and became known as a "cubofuturist" leader; later he turned his talent to account as a maker of propagandist posters. He took part in both the revolutions of 1917. In 1925 he made a trip to Mexico and the United States.

In 1909 Mayakovsky began work as a writer of verse and soon became the acknowledged chief of the futurist school. After 1917 his poems had huge circulation and wide influence, both for their form and for their contents. He confidently expected that futurist methods would henceforth dominate Russian poetry. But in his last years his popularity declined; his rampant individualism was found not to harmonize with strict Marxian principles. In contrast to the triumph of his *Mystery-*

Bouffe (1918 and 1921) his two latter plays, *The Bedbug* and *The Bathhouse,* were flat failures.

On April 14, 1930, whether owing to a quarrel over a woman or in despair at his own waning fame, Mayakovsky shot himself. Though Bolshevik public opinion condemned his suicide as a cowardly and bourgeois act, unworthy of a revolutionist, he received a splendid funeral.

ALEXANDER NIKOLÁYEVICH OSTRÓVSKY (1823-86) was the son of a humble Moscow lawyer who practiced among the merchants. As a boy he developed a passion for the theatre. After being expelled from the University of Moscow he served for eight years as a clerk of the Commercial Court, leaving it in 1851. Henceforth his entire life, outwardly uneventful, was devoted to the theatre; he married an actress. In 1886 he was appointed part-director of the Moscow Imperial Theatres and head of a dramatic school, but he did not live to carry out his plans.

Ostrovsky wrote forty-one plays in prose and seven in verse; the most important titles are as follows:—

In prose, realistic: *It's a Family Affair—We'll Settle It Ourselves* (1850), *The Poor Bride* (1852), *Stick to Your Own Station* (1853), *Poverty Is No Crime, You Can't Live Just as You Please* (1854), *A Lucrative Post, A Holiday Dream—Till Dinner Time* (1857), *A Protégée of the Mistress, The Thunderstorm* (1859), *An Old Friend Is Better than Two New Ones, Unlucky Days* (1860), *We Won't Brook Interference, You'll Get What You Seek* (1861), *Sin and Sorrow Are Common to All* (1863), *The Jesters* (1864), *At the Jolly Spot* (1865), *The Abyss* (1866), *Enough Stupidity in Every Wise Man* (1868), *An Ardent Heart* (1869), *Fairy Gold* (1870), *A Cat Has Not Always Carnival, The Forest* (1871), *Not a Penny, and Then Threepence* (1872), *Late Love* (1873), *Hard-earned Bread, Rich Brides* (1874), *Wolves and Sheep* (1875), *Truth Is Good, but Luck Is Better* (1876), *A Last Sacrifice* (1877), *A Dowerless Maiden* (1878), *The Heart's Not a Stone* (1879), *Bondwomen* (1880), *Gifted Actresses and Their Adorers* (1881), *Guilty Without Blame* (1884), *Not of This World* (1885).

In verse, historical plays: *Kozma Zakharyich Minin* (1862), *Dmitry the Pretender and Vasily Shuysky, Tushino* (1867), *Vasilisa Melentyeva* (1868); of life in the seventeenth century, without historical foundation: *The Voyevoda* (1865, revised 1886), *A Comedian of the Seventeenth Century* (1873); folklore play: *The Snow Maiden* (1873).

ALEXÉY FEOFILÁKTOVICH PÍSEMSKY (1820-81) came of a family of the minor nobility in the province of Kostroma. While a student in the

University of Moscow he won a reputation as a reader and actor. On his graduation in 1844 he entered the state service, where, except for an interval of seven years, he remained until 1874. He was a prolific writer both in fiction and in the drama. His novels, of which the most famous are *A Thousand Souls* (1858) and *A Troubled Sea* (1863), are characterized by a dry, hard, pessimistic realism, and by the predominance in them of the sex interest; they lack the idealism and the sympathy found in the other great Russian novelists. His dramas show the same literary temper. *The Miraslavskys and the Naryshkins* (1886) is an historical tragedy of the year 1682. *Usurpers of Law* and *Lieutenant Gladkov* (1867) are melodramas of the eighteenth century. Pisemsky's other plays deal with contemporary life; those of his last years are of inferior merit. The titles are as follows: *The Hypochondriac* (1852), *The Division* (1853), *The Veteran and the Recruit* (1854), *A Bitter Fate* (1859), *Experienced Falcons* (1868), *Beasts of Prey, Baal* (1873), *Enlightened Times* (1875), *A Financial Genius* (1876), *The Last Fledglings, Warriors and Temporizers* (1886). The dates given above are those of first publication, not of composition.

COUNT ALEXÉY KONSTANTÍNOVICH TOLSTÓY (1817-75) came of a wealthy and noted family of the highest Russian aristocracy. Born in St. Petersburg, he was one of the children who formed the "Sunday society" of the heir to the throne. As a boy he traveled extensively with his parents in Germany and Italy. He entered the state service in 1836. In 1855 he joined an aristocratic regiment for service in the Crimean War, but did not reach the scene of action. From 1857 to his death he held the honorary title of Master of the Hunt of the Imperial Court.

During a period when realism and discussion of social questions dominated Russian literature, Tolstoy, a cultured aristocrat, remained faithful to the romantic tradition of earlier years. In his novel, *Prince Serebryany* (1861), a story of the times of Ivan the Terrible, he imitated the style of Sir Walter Scott. His dramatic trilogy, *The Death of Ivan the Terrible* (1865), *Tsar Fedor Ivanovich* (1868), and *Tsar Boris* (1870) deals with the same period; the figure of Boris Godunov unites the three plays. His unfinished drama, *The Posadnik (Burgomaster)*, has the scene laid in old Novgorod in the thirteenth century. In his dramatic poem, *Don Juan,* he handles a traditional theme of Western literature. Aside from his dramas and his novel, Tolstoy is famous for his ballads, lyrics, narrative poems, and humorous verse.

COUNT LEV NIKOLÁYEVICH TOLSTÓY (1828-1910) came of the same distinguished family as the author of *The Death of Ivan the Terrible*. He was born on the estate of Yasnaya Polyana, near Tula, in central

Russia. He attended first the University of Kazan, then that of St. Petersburg, but did not finish his course. In 1851 he entered the army, serving at the siege of Sevastopol in 1854-55; in 1856 he left the military service. He became famous by his works, *Childhood, Boyhood, and Youth* (1852-56) and *Sevastopol* (1855). In 1862 he married; most of the remainder of his life he spent on his estate of Yasnaya Polyana. In 1863-69 he wrote *War and Peace* and in 1873-77 *Anna Karenin*. In 1879 he experienced a religious conversion that transformed his ideas of conduct and led him gradually to assimilate his life to that of a peasant. His most important works of fiction in his later years are *The Death of Ivan Ilyich* (1886), *The Kreutzer Sonata* (1889), and *Resurrection* (1899). His chief works on religion and ethics are *A Harmony and Translation of the Four Gospels* (1881-82), *My Religion* (1883), *What Shall We Do Then?* (1886), *The Kingdom of God Is Within You* (1893). His critical work, *What Is Art?* (1898), is based in large part on his religious principles. In 1910 he left home in an effort to realize his religious ideals. He was taken ill on the journey and died in the house of the station-master at Astapovo.

Tolstoy himself published but three dramas: *The First Distiller, The Power of Darkness* (1886), *The Fruits of Enlightenment* (1889). The following plays, some of them unfinished, were printed after his death: *The Nihilist, A Contaminated Family* (1863), *Dramatic Scenes of the Lord Who Became a Beggar* (1886), *Peter the Publican* (1894), *The Living Corpse* (1900), *And the Light Shineth in Darkness* (1902), *The Cause of It All* (1910).

IVÁN SERGÉYEVICH TURGÉNEV (1818-83) was born at Orel in central Russia. He came of a prosperous family of landed gentry and was never dependent on his pen for support. After graduating from the University of St. Petersburg he studied for three years in Berlin. By temperament and training he was the most European of Russian authors; a large part of his later life he spent in France. His dearest friend was the French opera singer, Madame Viardot-Garcia; with her and with her family he remained in intimate relations until his death. He began his literary career as a dramatist (see Introduction) and poet; but, after the immense success of *A Sportsman's Sketches* (1847-51), which had not only literary but social significance, in furthering the movement for the emancipation of the serfs, he turned definitely to prose fiction. In 1852, owing to his obituary notice of Gogol, which was so enthusiastic that it displeased the authorities, he was arrested and exiled to his estate for eighteen months. His series of novels, *Rudin* (1856), *A House of Gentlefolk* (1859), *On the Eve* (1860), and *Fathers and Children* (1862), made him the leading figure in Russian literature. *Smoke*

(1867), written in a definitely satiric vein, was less successful, and *Virgin Soil* (1876), his longest and most ambitious novel, was a failure. In 1868-69 he returned to the theatre by writing four librettos for operettas in which Madame Viardot-Garcia had a part. Numerous short stories accompanied his novels. Of his few critical essays that on *Hamlet and Don Quixote* is the most important. Among his latest works his *Poems in Prose* are particularly notable.

READING LIST

The following list is intended to include (1) the most useful and accessible books on Russian literature and the Russian drama, and (2) translations of Russian dramas. It cites only books in English and, except for some translations, takes no account of periodical literature. It is not a bibliography, not approaching completeness, even within the limits stated above, except in the list of translations. More ample references, up to 1924, may be found in Wiener, *The Contemporary Drama of Russia*.

HISTORY OF RUSSIAN LITERATURE

BRÜCKNER, ALEXANDER.—*A Literary History of Russia* (London, F. Unwin; New York, Scribner, 1908).

FREEMAN, JOSEPH; KUNITZ, JOSHUA; LOZOWICK, LOUIS.—*Voices of October: Art and Literature in Soviet Russia* (New York, Vanguard Press, 1930).

KROPOTKIN, PETR.—*Russian Literature* (London, Duckworth; New York, McClure Phillips, 1905).

MIRSKY, PRINCE DMITRY SVYATOPOLK.—*A History of Russian Literature from the Earliest Times to the Death of Dostoyevsky (1881)* (London, Routledge; New York, Knopf, 1927).

———*Contemporary Russian Literature, 1881-1925* (London, Routledge; New York, Knopf, 1926). The two volumes by Mirsky are the most satisfactory treatment of the subject in English.

WIENER, LEO.—*Anthology of Russian Literature from the Earliest Period to the Present Time*, 2 vols. (New York, Putnam, 1902-3).

HISTORY OF THE RUSSIAN DRAMA

WIENER, LEO.—*The Contemporary Drama of Russia* (Boston, Little, Brown, 1924). The introductory chapters sketch the history of the drama from its origins.

THE RUSSIAN STAGE

BAKSHY, ALEXANDER.—*The Path of the Modern Russian Stage* (London, Palmer and Hayward, 1916; Boston, Luce, 1918).

CARTER, HUNTLY.—*The New Theatre and Cinema of Soviet Russia* (London, Chapman and Dodd, 1924).

—— *The New Spirit in the Russian Theatre, 1917-28* (London and New York, Brentano's, 1929).

FÜLÖP-MILLER, RENÉ; GREGOR, JOSEPH.—*The Russian Theatre, its character and history, with especial reference to the revolutionary period,* translated by P. England (London, Harrap; Philadelphia, Lippincott, 1930). Splendidly illustrated.

SAYLER, OLIVER MARTIN.—*The Russian Theatre under the Revolution* (Boston, Little, Brown, 1920).

—— *The Russian Theatre* (New York, Brentano's, 1922; London, Brentano's, 1923). An enlarged edition of the previous work.

—— *Inside the Moscow Art Theatre* (New York, Brentano's, 1925; London, Brentano's, 1928).

STANISLAVSKY, KONSTANTIN (ALEXEYEV).—*My Life in Art,* translated by J. J. Robbins (Boston, Little, Brown, 1924; London, Bles, 1925).

COLLECTIONS OF RUSSIAN DRAMAS

Five Russian Plays, with One from the Ukrainian, translated by C. E. Bechhofer (London, Kegan Paul; New York, Dutton, 1916). Contains Evreynov: *A Merry Death, The Beautiful Despot;* Fonvizin: *The Choice of a Tutor;* Chekhov: *The Wedding, The Jubilee.*

The Moscow Art Theatre Series of Russian Plays: First Series, translated by J. Covan (New York and London, Brentano's, 1923). Contents: A. K. Tolstoy: *Tsar Fyodor Ivanovitch;* Gorky: *The Lower Depths;* Chekhov: *The Cherry Orchard, The Three Sisters, Uncle Vanya.* The plays are also published separately by Brentano's.

The Moscow Art Theatre Series of Russian Plays: Second Series (New York, Brentano's, 1923; London, Brentano's, 1924). Contains Dostoyevsky: *The Brothers Karamazoff;* Chekhov: *Ivanoff;* Ostrovsky: *Enough Stupidity in Every Wise Man.* The plays are also published separately by Brentano's.

INDIVIDUAL DRAMATISTS

ANDREYEV (1871-1919)

Biography and Criticism

KAUN, ALEXANDER.—*Leonid Andreyev, a Critical Study* (New York, Huebsch, 1924).

Translations of Dramas

Plays: The Black Maskers, The Life of Man, The Sabine Women, translated by C. L. Meader and F. N. Scott (New York, Scribner; London, Duckworth, 1915).

Anathema, translated by H. Bernstein (New York and London, Macmillan, 1910).

He, the One Who Gets Slapped, translated by G. Zilboorg (New York, Dial, 1921).

He Who Gets Slapped, translated by G. Zilboorg (New York and London, Brentano's, 1922; New York, French, 1929). Also in *Chief Contemporary Dramatists, Third Series* (Boston, Houghton Mifflin, 1930).

An Incident, translated by L. Pasvolsky, in *Poet Lore* (Vol. 27, 1916). Also in *Representative One-Act Plays by Continental Authors* (Boston, Little, Brown, 1922).

Katerina, translated by H. Bernstein (New York and London, Brentano's, 1923).

King Hunger, translated by E. M. Kayden, in *Poet Lore* (Vol. 22, 1911).

The Life of Man, translated by C. J. Hogarth (London, Allen and Unwin; New York, Macmillan, 1915).

Love of One's Neighbor, translated by T. Seltzer (New York, A. and C. Boni, 1914; Shay, 1917). Also in *Fifty Contemporary One-Act Plays* (New York, Appleton, 1920).

The Dear Departing (same play), translated by J. West (London, Hendersons, 1916).

The Pretty Sabine Women, translated by T. Seltzer, in *Drama* (Vol. 4, No. 13, 1914).

Samson in Chains, translated by H. Bernstein (New York, Brentano's, 1923).

Savva, The Life of Man, translated by T. Seltzer (New York, Kennerley, 1914). *The Life of Man* is also in *Representative Continental Dramas* (Boston, Little, Brown, 1924).

The Sorrows of Belgium, translated by H. Bernstein (New York and London, Macmillan, 1915).

To the Stars, translated by A. Goudiss, in *Poet Lore* (Vol. 18, 1907).

To the Stars, translated by M. Magnus (London, Daniel; New York, Daniels, 1921).

The Waltz of the Dogs, translated by H. Bernstein (New York, Macmillan, 1922; London, Brentano's, 1924).

ARTSYBASHEV (1878-1927)

Jealousy, Enemies, The Law of the Savage (New York, Boni and Liveright, 1923).

War, translated by T. Seltzer (New York, Knopf, 1916). Also in *Drama* (Vol. 6, 1916).

War, translated by P. Pinkerton and I. Ozhol (London, Richards, 1918).

CHEKHOV (1860-1904)

Biography, Criticism, Letters

ELTON, OLIVER.—*Chekhov* (Oxford University Press, 1929). Lecture.

GERHARDI, WILLIAM.—*Anton Chehov, a Critical Study* (London, Cobden-Sanderson; New York, Duffield, 1923).

GORKY, M., AND OTHERS.—*Reminiscences of Anton Chekhov,* translated by
S. S. Koteliansky and L. Woolf (New York, Huebsch, 1921).

Anton Tchekhov: Literary and Theatrical Reminiscences, translated and
edited by S. S. Koteliansky (London, Routledge; New York, Doran,
1927). By various authors.

The Life and Letters of Anton Tchekhov, translated and edited by S. S.
Koteliansky and P. Tomlinson (London, Cassell, 1925 [pop. ed., 1928];
New York, Doran, 1925). By various authors.

Letters on the Short Story, the Drama and Other Literary Topics, edited
by L. S. Friedland (New York, Minton, Balch, 1924; London, Bles,
1925).

Letters to his Family and Friends, translated by C. Garnett (London, Chatto;
New York, Macmillan, 1920).

Letters to Olga Leonardovna Knipper, translated by C. Garnett (London,
Chatto; New York, Doran, 1926).

Translations of Dramas

Complete Plays, translated by C. Garnett, 2 vols. (New York, Seltzer, 1923).
Contents: Vol. I: *The Cherry Orchard, Uncle Vanya, The Sea-Gull,
The Bear, The Proposal.* Vol. II: *Three Sisters, Ivanov, A Swan-Song,
An Unwilling Martyr, The Anniversary, On the High Road, The Wed-
ding.*

The Cherry Orchard and Other Plays, translated by C. Garnett (London,
Chatto, 1923). Contents as in Vol. I above.

Three Sisters and Other Plays, translated by C. Garnett (London, Chatto,
1923). Contents as in Vol. II above.

Plays, translated by C. Garnett (New York, Modern Library, 1930). Contents: *The Sea-Gull, The Cherry Orchard, Three Sisters, Uncle Vanya,
The Anniversary, On the High Road, The Wedding.*

Plays, translated by M. Fell (New York, Scribner; London, Duckworth,
1912). Contents: *Uncle Vanya, Ivanoff, The Sea-Gull, The Swan
Song.*

Plays, Second Series, translated by J. West (New York, Scribner; London,
Duckworth, 1916). Contents: *On the High Road, The Proposal, The
Wedding, The Bear, A Tragedian in Spite of Himself, The Anniversary,
The Three Sisters, The Cherry Orchard.*

Two Plays, translated by G. Calderon (London, Richards; New York, Ken-
nerley, 1912; London, Cape, 1927). Contents: *The Cherry Orchard,
The Seagull. The Cherry Orchard* is also in *Chief Contemporary
Dramatists* (Boston, Houghton Mifflin, 1915); and *The Seagull* in
Representative Continental Dramas (Boston, Little, Brown, 1924).

A Bear, translated by R. T. A. House (New York, Moods, 1909).

The Boor (same play), translated by H. Baukhage (New York, French,
1915). Also in *Fifty Contemporary One-Act Plays* (New York, Appleton, 1920); and in *Contemporary One-Act Plays* (New York, Scribner,
1922).

The Cherry Garden, translated by M. S. Mandell (New Haven, Whaples, 1908).

The Jubilee, translated by O. F. Murphy, in *Poet Lore* (Vol. 31, 1920).

A Marriage Proposal, translated by H. Baukhage and B. H. Clark (New York, French, 1914).

On the Highway, translated by D. A. Modell, in *Drama* (Vol. 6, 1916). Also in *Twenty-Five Short Plays (International),* (New York, Appleton, 1925).

The Sea-Gull, translated by F. Eisemann, in *Poet Lore* (Vol. 24, 1913).

The Seagull (London, Hendersons, 1921).

That Worthless Fellow Platonov, translated by J. Cournos (London, Dent; New York, Dutton, 1930).

The Tragedian in Spite of Himself, translated by O. F. Murphy, in *Poet Lore* (Vol. 33, 1922).

Uncle Vania, translated by F. A. Saphro, in *Poet Lore* (Vol. 33, 1922).

Uncle Vanya, translated by R. Caylor (New York, Covici, 1930).

The Wood Demon, translated by S. S. Koteliansky (London, Chatto, 1926; New York, Macmillan, 1927). A play remodeled into *Uncle Vanya.*

See also above, p. 894, *Five Russian Plays* and *The Moscow Art Theatre Series of Russian Plays.*

DYMOV (PERELMAN: 1878—)

Nju, translated by R. Ivan (New York, Knopf, 1917).

EVREYNOV (1879—)

Translations of Dramas

The Chief Thing: a Comedy for Some, a Drama for Others, translated by H. Bernstein and L. Randole (New York, Doubleday, Doran, 1926).

A Merry Death, translated by C. E. Bechofer, in *Representative One-Act Plays by Continental Authors* (Boston, Little, Brown, 1922).

The Theatre of the Soul, translated by M. Potapenko and C. St. John (London, Hendersons, 1915). Also in *Chief Contemporary Dramatists, Third Series* (Boston, Houghton Mifflin, 1930).

See also above, p. 894, *Five Russian Plays.*

Translation of Critical Work.

The Theatre in Life, translated by A. I. Nazaroff (London, Harrap; New York, Brentano's, 1927).

FONVIZIN (1744-92)

See above, p. 894, *Five Russian Plays.*

GOGOL (1809-52)

Biography and Criticism

LAVRIN, JANKO.—*Gogol* (London, Routledge; New York, Dutton, 1926).

Translations of Dramas

The Government Inspector and Other Plays, translated by C. Garnett (London, Chatto, 1926 [pop. ed. 1930]; New York, Knopf, 1927). Contents: *The Government Inspector, Marriage, The Gamblers, Dramatic Sketches and Fragments.*

The Gamblers, and Marriage, translated by A. Berkman (New York, Macaulay, 1927).

The Inspector, translated by T. H. Davies (London, Thacker, 1892).

The Inspector-General (or "Revizór"), translated by A. A. Sykes (London, Walter Scott, 1892).

The Inspector-General, translated by T. Seltzer (New York, Knopf, 1916).

Marriage, translated by E. L. Voynich, in *The Humour of Russia* (London, Walter Scott; New York, Scribner, 1909).

GORKY (PESHKOV: 1869—)

Biography and Criticism

DILLON, E. J.—*Maxim Gorky, his Life and Writings* (London, Isbister; New York, McClure, Phillips, 1903).

KAUN, A.—*Maxim Gorky and His Russia* (New York, Cape and Smith, 1931).

OSTWALD, H.—*Maxim Gorky,* translated by F. A. Welby (London, Heinemann, 1905).

Translations of Dramas

At the Bottom, translated by W. L. Laurence (New York, French, 1930). Same play as *Down and Out* in present volume.

The Lower Depths (same play), translated by L. Irving (London, T. F. Unwin; New York, Duffield, 1912).

A Night's Lodging (same play), translated by E. Hopkins, in *Poet Lore* (Vol. 16, 1905). Also, under title *Submerged* (Boston, Badger, 1915); and, under title, *The Lower Depths,* in *Chief Contemporary Dramatists, Second Series* (Boston, Houghton Mifflin, 1921).

The Children of the Sun, translated by A. J. Wolfe, in *Poet Lore* (Vol. 17, 1906).

The Judge, translated by M. Zakrevsky and B. H. Clark (New York, McBride, 1924).

The Smug Citizen, translated by E. Hopkins, in *Poet Lore* (Vol. 17, 1906).

Summer-Folk, translated by A. Delano, in *Poet Lore* (Vol. 16, 1905).

See also above, p. 894, *The Moscow Art Theatre Series of Russian Plays.*

HIPPIUS (MME. MEREZHKOVSKY: 1867—)

The Green Ring, translated by S. S. Koteliansky (London, Daniel, 1920; New York, Daniels, 1921).

Lunacharsky (1876—)

Three Plays: Faust and the City, Vasilisa the Wise, The Magi, translated by L. A. Magnus and K. Walter (London, Routledge; New York, Dutton, 1923).

Vasilisa the Wise, translated by L. A. Magnus (London, Routledge, 1922).

Ostrovsky (1823-86)

Plays: A Protégée of the Mistress, Poverty is No Crime, Sin and Sorrow Are Common to All, It's a Family Affair—We'll Settle it Ourselves, translation edited by G. R. Noyes (New York, Scribner, 1917).

At the Jolly Spot, translated by J. P. Campbell and G. R. Noyes, in *Poet Lore* (Vol. 36, 1925).

Bondwomen, translated by S. C. Kurlandzik and G. R. Noyes, in *Poet Lore* (Vol. 36, 1925).

A Cat Has Not Always Carnival, translated by J. P. Campbell and G. R. Noyes, in *Poet Lore* (Vol. 40, 1929).

A Domestic Picture, translated by E. L. Voynich, in *The Humour of Russia* (London, Walter Scott; New York, Scribner, 1909).

Fairy Gold, translated by C. C. Daniels and G. R. Noyes, in *Poet Lore* (Vol. 40, 1929).

The Forest, translated by C. V. Winlow and G. R. Noyes (New York, French, 1926).

Incompatibility of Temper, translated by E. L. Voynich, in *The Humour of Russia* (London, Walter Scott; New York, Scribner, 1909).

A Last Sacrifice, translated by E. Korvin-Kroukovsky and G. R. Noyes, in *Poet Lore* (Vol. 39, 1928).

The Storm, translated by C. Garnett (London, Duckworth, 1899, 1930; Chicago, Sergel, 1899, 1911; Boston, Luce, 1907).

The Storm, translated by G. F. Holland and M. Morley (London, G. Allen and Unwin, 1930).

The Thunderstorm (same play), translated by F. Whyte and G. R. Noyes (New York, French, 1927).

Wolves and Sheep, translated by I. S. Colby and G. R. Noyes, in *Poet Lore* (Vol. 37, 1926).

See also above, p. 894, *The Moscow Art Theatre Series of Russian Plays: Second Series.*

Pushkin (1799-1837)

Biography and Criticism

Mirsky, Prince Dmitry Svyatopolk.—*Pushkin* (London, Routledge; New York, Dutton, 1926).

Translation of Drama

Boris Godunov, translated by A. Hayes (London, Kegan Paul; New York, Dutton, 1918).

SHPAZHINSKY (1848-1917)

Madame Major, translated by F. H. Snow and B. M. Mekota, in *Poet Lore* (Vol. 28, 1917).

V. A. SOLLOGUB (1814-82)

His Hat and Cane, The Serenade, in *Plays for Private Acting* (New York, Holt, 1878).
His Hat and Cane (reprinted, Boston, 1902).

F. SOLOGUB (TETERNIKOV: 1863—)

The Triumph of Death, translated by J. Cournos, in *Drama* (Vol. 6, 1916).

STEPNIAK (KRAVCHINSKY: 1853-95)

The New Convert, translated by T. B. Eyges (Boston, Stratford, 1917).

A. K. TOLSTOY (1817-75)

The Death of Ivan the Terrible, translated by I. H. Harrison (London, 1869).
The Death of Ivan the Terrible, translated by A. Hayes (London, Kegan Paul, 1926).
    The translation of this play made by Mme. Sophie de Meissner for Richard Mansfield has never been published.
Czar Feodor Ivannovitch, translated by A. Hayes (London, Kegan Paul, 1924).
See also above, p. 894, *The Moscow Art Theatre Series of Russian Plays.*

L. N. TOLSTOY (1828-1910)

Biography and Criticism

FAUSSET, HUGH I'ANSON.—*Tolstoy, the Inner Drama* (London, Cape, 1927; New York, Harcourt, Brace, 1928). Mainly a psychological study.
MAUDE, AYLMER.—*The Life of Tolstoy,* 2 vols. (London, Constable, 1908, 1910; New York, Dodd, Mead, 1910). Revised edition (Oxford University Press, 1929, 1930). The most complete account in English of the events of Tolstoy's life.

Nazaroff, Alexander I.—*Tolstoy, the Inconstant Genius* (New York, Stokes, 1929; London, Harrap, 1930).

Noyes, George Rapall.—*Tolstoy* (New York, Duffield, 1918; London, Murray, 1919).

Rolland, Romain.—*Tolstoy*, translated by B. Miall (London, T. F. Unwin; New York, Dutton, 1911).

Translations of Dramas

Novels and Other Works, 22 vols. (New York, Scribner, 1899). Volume XVI contains dramas.

Complete Works, translated by L. Wiener, 24 vols. (Boston, Estes, 1904-5). Volume XVIII contains *The Power of Darkness* and *The Fruits of Enlightenment*.

Works, Tolstóy Centenary Edition, translated by A. and L. Maude (Oxford University Press, 1928–). Volume XVII, *Plays*, contains *The First Distiller, The Power of Darkness, The Fruits of Enlightenment, The Live Corpse, The Cause of it All, The Light Shines in Darkness*.

Dramatic Works, translated by N. H. Dole (New York, Crowell, 1923; London, Harrap, 1924). Contents: *The Power of Darkness, The First Distiller, The Fruits of Enlightenment, The Live Corpse, The Light Shines in the Darkness, The Root of All Evil, The Wisdom of Children*. *The Root of All Evil* is the same play as *The Cause of It All*.

Plays: The Power of Darkness, The First Distiller, Fruits of Culture, translated by L. and A. Maude (New York, Funk and Wagnalls, 1904).

Plays, translated by L. and A. Maude (complete edition, including the posthumous plays, London, Constable, 1914; New York, Funk and Wagnalls, 1919). Also in The World's Classics, Vol. 243 (Oxford University Press, 1923). Contents same as of Vol. XVII of *Tolstóy Centenary Edition*.

Posthumous Works, translated by A. J. Wolfe, 3 vols. (New York, International Book Publishing Co., 1920). Volume II contains *And a Light Shineth in the Darkness* and *The Living Corpse;* Volume III contains *The Wisdom of Children* and *The Cause of It All*.

The Dominion of Darkness (London, Vizetelly, 1888; Chicago, Sergel, 1890). Same play as *The Power of Darkness*.

The Fruits of Culture, translated by G. Schumm (Boston, Tucker, 1891).

The Fruits of Enlightenment (same play), (New York, Munro, 1891; Seaside Lib.).

The Fruits of Enlightenment (New York, United States Book Co., 1891).

The Fruits of Enlightenment (Boston, Luce, 1911).

The Light that Shines in Darkness, edited by Dr. H. Wright (New York, Dodd, Mead, 1912).

The Light that Shines in Darkness, The Man Who Was Dead, The Cause of It All, edited by Dr. H. Wright (Boston, Estes, n. d.).

The Light that Shines in Darkness, The Wisdom of Children, in *Father Sergius and Other Stories and Plays*, edited by Dr. H. Wright (London, Nelson, 1912). *The Wisdom of Children* is also contained in *Father*

Sergius and Other Stories, edited by Dr. H. Wright (New York, Dodd, Mead, 1912). This volume is also issued by Estes, Boston, under title, *Father Sergius, The Wisdom of Children, Miscellaneous Stories.*
Literary Fragments, Letters and Reminiscences Not Previously Published, edited by R. Fülöp-Miller, translated by P. England (New York, Dial Press, 1931). Contains *The Nihilist* and *The Progressives.*
The Living Corpse, translated by Mrs. E. M. Evarts (Philadelphia, Brown Bros., 1912).
The Man Who Was Dead (The Living Corpse), The Cause of It All, edited by Dr. H. Wright (New York, Dodd, Mead, 1912). Also in *The Forged Coupon and Other Stories and Dramas,* edited by Dr. H. Wright (London, Nelson, 1911).
Redemption and Two Other Plays (New York, Boni and Liveright, 1919). In the Modern Library. Contents: *Redemption, The Power of Darkness, The Fruits of Culture. Redemption* is the same play as *The Man Who Was Dead* and *The Living Corpse.*
Stories and Dramas, translated by L. Turin, H. M. Lucas, C. J. Hogarth (London, Dent; New York, Dutton, 1926). Contains *The Nihilist, The Contaminated Family, Dramatic Scenes about the Pan Who Became a Beggar, Peter the Publican. The Contaminated Family* is the same play as *The Progressives.*

TURGENEV (1818-83)

Biography and Criticism

GARNETT, EDWARD WILLIAM.—*Turgenev, a Study* (London, Collins, 1917).
HALPERINE-KAMINSKY, ELY (Editor).—*Tourguéneff and his French Circle,* translated by E. M. Arnold (London, T. F. Unwin, 1898).
YARMOLINSKY, AVRAHM.—*Turgenev, the Man, his Art and his Age* (New York, Century, 1926; London, Hodder and Stoughton, 1927).

Translations of Dramas

Plays, translated by M. S. Mandell (New York, Macmillan; London, Heinemann, 1924). Contents: *Carelessness, Broke, Where It Is Thin, There It Breaks, The Family Charge, The Bachelor, An Amicable Settlement, A Month in the Country, The Country Woman, A Conversation on the Highway, An Evening in Sorrento.* These titles do not always agree with those used in the Introduction to the present volume.
One May Spin a Thread Too Finely, translated by M. Gough. In *Fortnightly Review* (Vol. 91, 1909). Same play as *Where It Is Thin, There It Breaks.*

(1)

CATALOGUE OF DOVER BOOKS

Literature, History of Literature

ARISTOTLE'S THEORY OF POETRY AND THE FINE ARTS, edited by S. H. Butcher. The celebrated Butcher translation of this great classic faced, page by page, with the complete Greek text. A 300 page introduction discussing Aristotle's ideas and their influence in the history of thought and literature, and covering art and nature, imitation as an aesthetic form, poetic truth, art and morality, tragedy, comedy, and similar topics. Modern Aristotelian criticism discussed by John Gassner. lxxvi + 421pp. 5⅜ x 8. **T42 Paperbound $2.00**

INTRODUCTIONS TO ENGLISH LITERATURE, edited by B. Dobrée. Goes far beyond ordinary histories, ranging from the 7th century up to 1914 (to the 1940's in some cases.) The first half of each volume is a specific detailed study of historical and economic background of the period and a general survey of poetry and prose, including trends of thought, influences, etc. The second and larger half is devoted to a detailed study of more than 5000 poets, novelists, dramatists; also economists, historians, biographers, religious writers, philosophers, travellers, and scientists of literary stature, with dates, lists of major works and their dates, keypoint critical bibliography, and evaluating comments. The most compendious bibliographic and literary aid within its price range.

Vol. I. THE BEGINNINGS OF ENGLISH LITERATURE TO SKELTON, (1509), W. L. Renwick, H. Orton. 450pp. 5⅛ x 7⅞. **T75 Clothbound $4.50**

Vol. II. THE ENGLISH RENAISSANCE, 1510-1688, V. de Sola Pinto. 381pp. 5⅛ x 7⅞. **T76 Clothbound $4.50**

Vol. III. AUGUSTANS AND ROMANTICS, 1689-1830, H. Dyson, J. Butt. 320pp. 5⅛ x 7⅞. **T77 Clothbound $4.50**

Vol. IV. THE VICTORIANS AND AFTER, 1830-1940's, E. Batho, B. Dobrée. 360pp. 5⅛ x 7⅞. **T78 Clothbound $4.50**

EPIC AND ROMANCE, W. P. Ker. Written by one of the foremost authorities on medieval literature, this is the standard survey of medieval epic and romance. It covers Teutonic epics, Icelandic sagas, Beowulf, French chansons de geste, the Roman de Troie, and many other important works of literature. It is an excellent account for a body of literature whose beauty and value has only recently come to be recognized. Index. xxiv + 398pp. 5⅜ x 8. **T355 Paperbound $2.25**

THE POPULAR BALLAD, F. B. Gummere. Most useful factual introduction; fund of descriptive material; quotes, cites over 260 ballads. Examines, from folkloristic view, structure; choral, ritual elements; meter, diction, fusion; effects of tradition, editors; almost every other aspect of border, riddle, kinship, sea, ribald, supernatural, etc., ballads. Bibliography. 2 indexes. 374pp. 5⅜ x 8. **T548 Paperbound $1.85**

MASTERS OF THE DRAMA, John Gassner. The most comprehensive history of the drama in print, covering drama in every important tradition from the Greeks to the Near East, China, Japan, Medieval Europe, England, Russia, Italy, Spain, Germany, and dozens of other drama producing nations. This unsurpassed reading and reference work encompasses more than 800 dramatists and over 2000 plays, with biographical material, plot summaries, theatre history, etc. "Has no competitors in its field," THEATRE ARTS. "Best of its kind in English," NEW REPUBLIC. Exhaustive 35 page bibliography. 77 photographs and drawings. Deluxe edition with reinforced cloth binding, headbands, stained top. xxii + 890pp. 5⅜ x 8. **T100 Clothbound $6.95**

THE DEVELOPMENT OF DRAMATIC ART, D. C. Stuart. The basic work on the growth of Western drama from primitive beginnings to Eugene O'Neill, covering over 2500 years. Not a mere listing or survey, but a thorough analysis of changes, origins of style, and influences in each period; dramatic conventions, social pressures, choice of material, plot devices, stock situations, etc.; secular and religious works of all nations and epochs. "Generous and thoroughly documented researches," Outlook. "Solid studies of influences and playwrights and periods," London Times. Index. Bibliography. xi + 679pp. 5⅜ x 8. **T693 Paperbound $2.75**

A SOURCE BOOK IN THEATRICAL HISTORY (SOURCES OF THEATRICAL HISTORY), A. M. Nagler. Over 2000 years of actors, directors, designers, critics, and spectators speak for themselves in this potpourri of writings selected from the great and formative periods of western drama. On-the-spot descriptions of masks, costumes, makeup, rehearsals, special effects, acting methods, backstage squabbles, theatres, etc. Contemporary glimpses of Molière rehearsing his company, an exhortation to a Roman audience to buy refreshments and keep quiet, Goethe's rules for actors, Belasco telling of $6500 he spent building a river, Restoration actors being told to avoid "lewd, obscene, or indecent postures," and much more. Each selection has an introduction by Prof. Nagler. This extraordinary, lively collection is ideal as a source of otherwise difficult to obtain material, as well as a fine book for browsing. Over 80 illustrations. 10 diagrams. xxiii + 611pp. 5⅜ x 8. **T515 Paperbound $3.00**

CATALOGUE OF DOVER BOOKS

WORLD DRAMA, B. H. Clark. The dramatic creativity of a score of ages and eras — all in two handy compact volumes. Over ⅓ of this material is unavailable in any other current edition! 46 plays from Ancient Greece, Rome, Medieval Europe, France, Germany, Italy, England, Russia, Scandinavia, India, China, Japan, etc. — including classic authors like Aeschylus, Sophocles, Euripides, Aristophanes, Plautus, Marlowe, Jonson, Farquhar, Goldsmith, Cervantes, Molière, Dumas, Goethe, Schiller, Ibsen, and many others. This creative collection avoids hackneyed material and includes only completely first-rate works which are relatively little known or difficult to obtain. "The most comprehensive collection of important plays from all literature available in English," SAT. REV. OF LITERATURE. Introduction. Reading lists. 2 volumes. 1364pp. 5⅜ x 8.

Vol. 1, T57 Paperbound **$2.50**
Vol. 2, T59 Paperbound **$2.50**

MASTERPIECES OF THE RUSSIAN DRAMA, edited with introduction by G. R. Noyes. This only comprehensive anthology of Russian drama ever published in English offers complete texts, in 1st-rate modern translations, of 12 plays covering 200 years. Vol. 1: "The Young Hopeful," Fonvisin; "Wit Works Woe," Griboyedov; "The Inspector General," Gogol; "A Month in the Country," Turgenev; "The Poor Bride," Ostrovsky; "A Bitter Fate," Pisemsky. Vol. 2: "The Death of Ivan the Terrible," Alexey Tolstoy "The Power of Darkness," Lev Tolstoy; "The Lower Depths," Gorky; "The Cherry Orchard," Chekhov; "Professor Storitsyn," Andreyev; "Mystery Bouffe," Mayakovsky. Bibliography. Total of 902pp. 5⅜ x 8.

Vol. 1 T647 Paperbound **$2.25**
Vol. 2 T648 Paperbound **$2.00**

EUGENE O'NEILL: THE MAN AND HIS PLAYS, B. H. Clark. Introduction to O'Neill's life and work. Clark analyzes each play from the early THE WEB to the recently produced MOON FOR THE MISBEGOTTEN and THE ICEMAN COMETH revealing the environmental and dramatic influences necessary for a complete understanding of these important works. Bibliography. Appendices. Index. ix + 182pp. 5⅜ x 8.

T379 Paperbound **$1.35**

THE HEART OF THOREAU'S JOURNALS, edited by O. Shepard. The best general selection from Thoreau's voluminous (and rare) journals. This intimate record of thoughts and observations reveals the full Thoreau and his intellectual development more accurately than any of his published works: self-conflict between the scientific observer and the poet, reflections on transcendental philosophy, involvement in the tragedies of neighbors and national causes, etc. New preface, notes, introductions. xii + 228pp. 5⅜ x 8.

T741 Paperbound **$1.50**

H. D. THOREAU: A WRITER'S JOURNAL, edited by L. Stapleton. A unique new selection from the Journals concentrating on Thoreau's growth as a conscious literary artist, the ideals and purposes of his art. Most of the material has never before appeared outside of the complete 14-volume edition. Contains vital insights on Thoreau's projected book on Concord, thoughts on the nature of men and government, indignation with slavery, sources of inspiration, goals in life. Index. xxxiii + 234pp. 5⅜ x 8.

T678 Paperbound **$1.65**

THE HEART OF EMERSON'S JOURNALS, edited by Bliss Perry. Best of these revealing Journals, originally 10 volumes, presented in a one volume edition. Talks with Channing, Hawthorne, Thoreau, and Bronson Alcott; impressions of Webster, Everett, John Brown, and Lincoln; records of moments of sudden understanding, vision, and solitary ecstasy. "The essays do not reveal the power of Emerson's mind . . . as do these hasty and informal writings," N.Y. Times. Preface by Bliss Perry. Index. xiii + 357pp. 5⅜ x 8.

T477 Paperbound **$1.85**

FOUNDERS OF THE MIDDLE AGES, E. K. Rand. This is the best non-technical discussion of the transformation of Latin pagan culture into medieval civilization. Covering such figures as Tertullian, Gregory, Jerome, Boethius, Augustine, the Neoplatonists, and many other literary men, educators, classicists, and humanists, this book is a storehouse of information presented clearly and simply for the intelligent non-specialist. "Thoughtful, beautifully written," AMERICAN HISTORICAL REVIEW. "Extraordinarily accurate," Richard McKeon, THE NATION. ix + 365pp. 5⅜ x 8.

T369 Paperbound **$2.00**

PLAY-MAKING: A MANUAL OF CRAFTSMANSHIP, William Archer. With an extensive, new introduction by John Gassner, Yale Univ. The permanently essential requirements of solid play construction are set down in clear, practical language: theme, exposition, foreshadowing, tension, obligatory scene, peripety, dialogue, character, psychology, other topics. This book has been one of the most influential elements in the modern theatre, and almost everything said on the subject since is contained explicitly or implicitly within its covers. Bibliography. Index. xlii + 277pp. 5⅜ x 8.

T651 Paperbound **$1.75**

HAMBURG DRAMATURGY, G. E. Lessing. One of the most brilliant of German playwrights of the eighteenth-century age of criticism analyzes the complex of theory and tradition that constitutes the world of theater. These 104 essays on aesthetic theory helped demolish the regime of French classicism, opening the door to psychological and social realism, romanticism. Subjects include the original functions of tragedy; drama as the rational world; the meaning of pity and fear, pity and fear as means for purgation and other Aristotelian concepts; genius and creative force; interdependence of poet's language and actor's interpretation; truth and authenticity; etc. A basic and enlightening study for anyone interested in aesthetics and ideas, from the philosopher to the theatergoer. Introduction by Prof. Victor Lange. xxii + 265pp. 4½ x 6⅜.

T32 Paperbound **$1.45**

Philosophy, Religion

GUIDE TO PHILOSOPHY, C. E. M. Joad. A modern classic which examines many crucial problems which man has pondered through the ages: Does free will exist? Is there plan in the universe? How do we know and validate our knowledge? Such opposed solutions as subjective idealism and realism, chance and teleology, vitalism and logical positivism, are evaluated and the contributions of the great philosophers from the Greeks to moderns like Russell, Whitehead, and others, are considered in the context of each problem. "The finest introduction," BOSTON TRANSCRIPT. Index. Classified bibliography. 592pp. 5⅜ x 8.
T297 Paperbound **$2.00**

HISTORY OF ANCIENT PHILOSOPHY, W. Windelband. One of the clearest, most accurate comprehensive surveys of Greek and Roman philosophy. Discusses ancient philosophy in general, intellectual life in Greece in the 7th and 6th centuries B.C., Thales, Anaximander, Anaximenes, Heraclitus, the Eleatics, Empedocles, Anaxagoras, Leucippus, the Pythagoreans, the Sophists, Socrates, Democritus (20 pages), Plato (50 pages), Aristotle (70 pages), the Peripatetics, Stoics, Epicureans, Sceptics, Neo-platonists, Christian Apologists, etc. 2nd German edition translated by H. E. Cushman. xv + 393pp. 5⅜ x 8. T357 Paperbound **$1.85**

ILLUSTRATIONS OF THE HISTORY OF MEDIEVAL THOUGHT AND LEARNING, R. L. Poole. Basic analysis of the thought and lives of the leading philosophers and ecclesiastics from the 8th to the 14th century—Abailard, Ockham, Wycliffe, Marsiglio of Padua, and many other great thinkers who carried the torch of Western culture and learning through the "Dark Ages": political, religious, and metaphysical views. Long a standard work for scholars and one of the best introductions to medieval thought for beginners. Index. 10 Appendices. xiii + 327pp. 5⅜ x 8. T674 Paperbound **$2.00**

PHILOSOPHY AND CIVILIZATION IN THE MIDDLE AGES, M. de Wulf. This semi-popular survey covers aspects of medieval intellectual life such as religion, philosophy, science, the arts, etc. It also covers feudalism vs. Catholicism, rise of the universities, mendicant orders, monastic centers, and similar topics. Unabridged. Bibliography. Index. viii + 320pp. 5⅜ x 8.
T284 Paperbound **$1.85**

AN INTRODUCTION TO SCHOLASTIC PHILOSOPHY, Prof. M. de Wulf. Formerly entitled SCHOLASTICISM OLD AND NEW, this volume examines the central scholastic tradition from St. Anselm, Albertus Magnus, Thomas Aquinas, up to Suarez in the 17th century. The relation of scholasticism to ancient and medieval philosophy and science in general is clear and easily followed. The second part of the book considers the modern revival of scholasticism, the Louvain position, relations with Kantianism and Positivism. Unabridged. xvi + 271pp. 5⅜ x 8.
T296 Clothbound **$3.50**
T283 Paperbound **$1.75**

A HISTORY OF MODERN PHILOSOPHY, H. Höffding. An exceptionally clear and detailed coverage of western philosophy from the Renaissance to the end of the 19th century. Major and minor men such as Pomponazzi, Bodin, Boehme, Telesius, Bruno, Copernicus, da Vinci, Kepler, Galileo, Bacon, Descartes, Hobbes, Spinoza, Leibniz, Wolff, Locke, Newton, Berkeley, Hume, Erasmus, Montesquieu, Voltaire, Diderot, Rousseau, Lessing, Kant, Herder, Fichte, Schelling, Hegel, Schopenhauer, Comte, Mill, Darwin, Spencer, Hartmann, Lange, and many others, are discussed in terms of theory of knowledge, logic, cosmology, and psychology. Index. 2 volumes, total of 1159pp. 5⅜ x 8.
T117 Vol. 1, Paperbound **$2.25**
T118 Vol. 2, Paperbound **$2.25**

ARISTOTLE, A. E. Taylor. A brilliant, searching non-technical account of Aristotle and his thought written by a foremost Platonist. It covers the life and works of Aristotle; classification of the sciences; logic; first philosophy; matter and form; causes; motion and eternity; God; physics; metaphysics; and similar topics. Bibliography. New Index compiled for this edition. 128pp. 5⅜ x 8. T280 Paperbound **$1.00**

THE SYSTEM OF THOMAS AQUINAS, M. de Wulf. Leading Neo-Thomist, one of founders of University of Louvain, gives concise exposition to central doctrines of Aquinas, as a means toward determining his value to modern philosophy, religion. Formerly "Medieval Philosophy Illustrated from the System of Thomas Aquinas." Trans. by E. Messenger. Introduction. 151pp. 5⅜ x 8. T568 Paperbound **$1.25**

LEIBNIZ, H. W. Carr. Most stimulating middle-level coverage of basic philosophical thought of Leibniz. Easily understood discussion, analysis of major works: "Theodicy," "Principles of Nature and Grace," "Monadology"; Leibniz's influence; intellectual growth; correspondence; disputes with Bayle, Malebranche, Newton; importance of his thought today, with reinterpretation in modern terminology. "Power and mastery," London Times. Bibliography. Index. 226pp. 5⅜ x 8. T624 Paperbound **$1.35**

THE SENSE OF BEAUTY, G. Santayana. A revelation of the beauty of language as well as an important philosophic treatise, this work studies the "why, when, and how beauty appears, what conditions an object must fulfill to be beautiful, what elements of our nature make us sensible of beauty, and what the relation is between the constitution of the object and the excitement of our susceptibility." "It is doubtful if a better treatment of the subject has since been published," PEABODY JOURNAL. Index. ix + 275pp. 5⅜ x 8.
T238 Paperbound **$1.00**

PROBLEMS OF ETHICS, Moritz Schlick. The renowned leader of the "Vienna Circle" applies the logical positivist approach to a wide variety of ethical problems: the source and means of attaining knowledge, the formal and material characteristics of the good, moral norms and principles, absolute vs. relative values, free will and responsibility, comparative importance of pleasure and suffering as ethical values, etc. Disarmingly simple and straightforward despite complexity of subject. First English translation, authorized by author before his death, of a thirty-year old classic. Translated and with an introduction by David Rynin. Index. Foreword by Prof. George P. Adams. xxi + 209pp. 5⅜ x 8.
T946 Paperbound **$1.60**

AN INTRODUCTION TO EXISTENTIALISM, Robert G. Olson. A new and indispensable guide to one of the major thought systems of our century, the movement that is central to the thinking of some of the most creative figures of the past hundred years. Stresses Heidegger and Sartre, with careful and objective examination of the existentialist position, values—freedom of choice, individual dignity, personal love, creative effort—and answers to the eternal questions of the human condition. Scholarly, unbiased, analytic, unlike most studies of this difficult subject, Prof. Olson's book is aimed at the student of philosophy as well as at the reader with no formal training who is looking for an absorbing, accessible, and thorough introduction to the basic texts. Index. xv + 221pp. 5⅜ x 8½.
T55 Paperbound **$1.65**

SYMBOLIC LOGIC, C. I. Lewis and C. H. Langford. Since first publication in 1932, this has been among most frequently cited works on symbolic logic. Still one of the best introductions both for beginners and for mathematicians, philosophers. First part covers basic topics which easily lend themselves to beginning study. Second part is rigorous, thorough development of logistic method, examination of some of most difficult and abstract aspects of symbolic logic, including modal logic, logical paradoxes, many-valued logic, with Prof. Lewis' own contributions. 2nd revised (corrected) edition. 3 appendixes, one new to this edition. 524pp. 5⅜ x 8.
S170 Paperbound **$2.00**

WHITEHEAD'S PHILOSOPHY OF CIVILIZATION, A. H. Johnson. A leading authority on Alfred North Whitehead synthesizes the great philosopher's thought on civilization, scattered throughout various writings, into unified whole. Analysis of Whitehead's general definition of civilization, his reflections on history and influences on its development, his religion, including his analysis of Christianity, concept of solitariness as first requirement of personal religion, and so on. Other chapters cover views on minority groups, society, civil liberties, education. Also critical comments on Whitehead's philosophy. Written with general reader in mind. A perceptive introduction to important area of the thought of a leading philosopher of our century. Revised index and bibliography. xii + 211pp. 5⅜ x 8½.
T996 Paperbound **$1.50**

WHITEHEAD'S THEORY OF REALITY, A. H. Johnson. Introductory outline of Whitehead's theory of actual entities, the heart of his philosophy of reality, followed by his views on nature of God, philosophy of mind, theory of value (truth, beauty, goodness and their opposites), analyses of other philosophers, attitude toward science. A perspicacious lucid introduction by author of dissertation on Whitehead, written under the subject's supervision at Harvard. Good basic view for beginning students of philosophy and for those who are simply interested in important contemporary ideas. Revised index and bibliography. xiii + 267pp. 5⅜ x 8½.
T989 Paperbound **$2.00**

MIND AND THE WORLD-ORDER, C. I. Lewis. Building upon the work of Peirce, James, and Dewey, Professor Lewis outlines a theory of knowledge in terms of "conceptual pragmatism." Dividing truth into abstract mathematical certainty and empirical truth, the author demonstrates that the traditional understanding of the a priori must be abandoned. Detailed analyses of philosophy, metaphysics, method, the "given" in experience, knowledge of objects, nature of the a priori, experience and order, and many others. Appendices. xiv + 446pp. 5⅜ x 8.
T359 Paperbound **$2.25**

SCEPTICISM AND ANIMAL FAITH, G. Santayana. To eliminate difficulties in the traditional theory of knowledge, Santayana distinguishes between the independent existence of objects and the essence our mind attributes to them. Scepticism is thereby established as a form of belief, and animal faith is shown to be a necessary condition of knowledge. Belief, classical idealism, intuition, memory, symbols, literary psychology, and much more, discussed with unusual clarity and depth. Index. xii + 314pp. 5⅜ x 8.
T235 Clothbound **$3.50**
T236 Paperbound **$1.75**

LANGUAGE AND MYTH, E. Cassirer. Analyzing the non-rational thought processes which go to make up culture, Cassirer demonstrates that beneath both language and myth there lies a dominant unconscious "grammar" of experience whose categories and canons are not those of logical thought. His analyses of seemingly diverse phenomena such as Indian metaphysics, the Melanesian "mana," the Naturphilosophie of Schelling, modern poetry, etc., are profound without being pedantic. Introduction and translation by Susanne Langer. Index. x + 103pp. 5⅜ x 8.
T51 Paperbound **$1.25**

CATALOGUE OF DOVER BOOKS

AN ESSAY CONCERNING HUMAN UNDERSTANDING, John Locke. Edited by A. C. Fraser. Unabridged reprinting of definitive edition; only complete edition of "Essay" in print. Marginal analyses of almost every paragraph; hundreds of footnotes; authoritative 140-page biographical, critical, historical prolegomena. Indexes. 1170pp. 5⅜ x 8.

T530 Vol. 1 (Books 1, 2) Paperbound **$2.50**
T531 Vol. 2 (Books 3, 4) Paperbound **$2.50**
2 volume set **$5.00**

THE PHILOSOPHY OF HISTORY, G. W. F. Hegel. One of the great classics of western thought which reveals Hegel's basic principle: that history is not chance but a rational process, the realization of the Spirit of Freedom. Ranges from the oriental cultures of subjective thought to the classical subjective cultures, to the modern absolute synthesis where spiritual and secular may be reconciled. Translation and introduction by J. Sibree. Introduction by C. Hegel. Special introduction for this edition by Prof. Carl Friedrich. xxxix + 447pp. 5⅜ x 8.

T112 Paperbound **$2.25**

THE PHILOSOPHY OF HEGEL, W. T. Stace. The first detailed analysis of Hegel's thought in English, this is especially valuable since so many of Hegel's works are out of print. Dr. Stace examines Hegel's debt to Greek idealists and the 18th century and then proceeds to a careful description and analysis of Hegel's first principles, categories, reason, dialectic method, his logic, philosophy of nature and spirit, etc. Index. Special 14 x 20 chart of Hegelian system. x + 526pp. 5⅜ x 8.

T254 Paperbound **$2.45**

THE WILL TO BELIEVE and HUMAN IMMORTALITY, W. James. Two complete books bound as one. THE WILL TO BELIEVE discusses the interrelations of belief, will, and intellect in man; chance vs. determinism, free will vs. determinism, free will vs. fate, pluralism vs. monism; the philosophies of Hegel and Spencer, and more. HUMAN IMMORTALITY examines the question of survival after death and develops an unusual and powerful argument for immortality. Two prefaces. Index. Total of 429pp. 5⅜ x 8.

T291 Paperbound **$2.00**

THE WORLD AND THE INDIVIDUAL, Josiah Royce. Only major effort by an American philosopher to interpret nature of things in systematic, comprehensive manner. Royce's formulation of an absolute voluntarism remains one of the original and profound solutions to the problems involved. Part One, Four Historical Conceptions of Being, inquires into first principles, true meaning and place of individuality. Part Two, Nature, Man, and the Moral Order, is application of first principles to problems concerning religion, evil, moral order. Introduction by J. E. Smith, Yale Univ. Index. 1070pp. 5⅜ x 8.

T561 Vol. 1 Paperbound **$2.75**
T562 Vol. 2 Paperbound **$2.75**
Two volume set **$5.50**

THE PHILOSOPHICAL WRITINGS OF PEIRCE, edited by J. Buchler. This book (formerly THE PHILOSOPHY OF PEIRCE) is a carefully integrated exposition of Peirce's complete system composed of selections from his own work. Symbolic logic, scientific method, theory of signs, pragmatism, epistemology, chance, cosmology, ethics, and many other topics are treated by one of the greatest philosophers of modern times. This is the only inexpensive compilation of his key ideas. xvi + 386pp. 5⅜ x 8.

T217 Paperbound **$2.00**

EXPERIENCE AND NATURE, John Dewey. An enlarged, revised edition of the Paul Carus lectures which Dewey delivered in 1925. It covers Dewey's basic formulation of the problem of knowledge, with a full discussion of other systems, and a detailing of his own concepts of the relationship of external world, mind, and knowledge. Starts with a thorough examination of the philosophical method; examines the interrelationship of experience and nature; analyzes experience on basis of empirical naturalism, the formulation of law, role of language and social factors in knowledge; etc. Dewey's treatment of central problems in philosophy is profound but extremely easy to follow. ix + 448pp. 5⅜ x 8.

T471 Paperbound **$2.00**

THE PHILOSOPHICAL WORKS OF DESCARTES. The definitive English edition of all the major philosophical works and letters of René Descartes. All of his revolutionary insights, from his famous "Cogito ergo sum" to his detailed account of contemporary science and his astonishingly fruitful concept that all phenomena of the universe (except mind) could be reduced to clear laws by the use of mathematics. An excellent source for the thought of men like Hobbes, Arnauld, Gassendi, etc., who were Descarte's contemporaries. Translated by E. S. Haldane and G. Ross. Introductory notes. Index. Total of 842pp. 5⅜ x 8.

T71 Vol. 1, Paperbound **$2.00**
T72 Vol. 2, Paperbound **$2.00**

THE CHIEF WORKS OF SPINOZA. An unabridged reprint of the famous Bohn edition containing all of Spinoza's most important works: Vol. I: The Theologico-Political Treatise and the Political Treatise. Vol. II: On The Improvement Of Understanding, The Ethics, Selected Letters. Profound and enduring ideas on God, the universe, pantheism, society, religion, the state, democracy, the mind, emotions, freedom and the nature of man, which influenced Goethe, Hegel, Schelling, Coleridge, Whitehead, and many others. Introduction. 2 volumes. 826pp. 5⅜ x 8.

T249 Vol. I, Paperbound **$1.50**
T250 Vol. II, Paperbound **$1.50**

CATALOGUE OF DOVER BOOKS

THE ANALYSIS OF MATTER, Bertrand Russell. A classic which has retained its importance in understanding the relation between modern physical theory and human perception. Logical analysis of physics, prerelativity physics, causality, scientific inference, Weyl's theory, tensors, invariants and physical interpretations, periodicity, and much more is treated with Russell's usual brilliance. "Masterly piece of clear thinking and clear writing," NATION AND ATHENAEUM. "Most thorough treatment of the subject," THE NATION. Introduction. Index. 8 figures. viii + 408pp. 5⅜ x 8. S231 Paperbound **$1.95**

CONCEPTUAL THINKING (A LOGICAL INQUIRY), S. Körner. Discusses origin, use of general concepts on which language is based, and the light they shed on basic philosophical questions. Rigorously examines how different concepts are related; how they are linked to experience; problems in the field of contact between exact logical, mathematical, and scientific concepts, and the inexactness of everyday experience (studied at length). This work elaborates many new approaches to the traditional problems of philosophy—epistemology, value theories, metaphysics, aesthetics, morality. "Rare originality . . . brings a new rigour into philosophical argument," Philosophical Quarterly. New corrected second edition. Index. vii + 301pp. 5⅜ x 8 T516 Paperbound **$1.75**

INTRODUCTION TO SYMBOLIC LOGIC, S. Langer. No special knowledge of math required — probably the clearest book ever written on symbolic logic, suitable for the layman, general scientist, and philosopher. You start with simple symbols and advance to a knowledge of the Boole-Schroeder and Russell-Whitehead systems. Forms, logical structure, classes, the calculus of propositions, logic of the syllogism, etc., are all covered. "One of the clearest and simplest introductions," MATHEMATICS GAZETTE. Second enlarged, revised edition. 368pp. 5⅜ x 8. S164 Paperbound **$1.85**

LANGUAGE, TRUTH AND LOGIC, A. J. Ayer. A clear, careful analysis of the basic ideas of Logical Positivism. Building on the work of Schlick, Russell, Carnap, and the Viennese School, Mr. Ayer develops a detailed exposition of the nature of philosophy, science, and metaphysics; the Self and the World; logic and common sense, and other philosophic concepts. An aid to clarity of thought as well as the first full-length development of Logical Positivism in English. Introduction by Bertrand Russell. Index. 160pp. 5⅜ x 8. T10 Paperbound **$1.25**

ESSAYS IN EXPERIMENTAL LOGIC, J. Dewey. Based upon the theory that knowledge implies a judgment which in turn implies an inquiry, these papers consider the inquiry stage in terms of: the relationship of thought and subject matter, antecedents of thought, data and meanings. 3 papers examine Bertrand Russell's thought, while 2 others discuss pragmatism and a final essay presents a new theory of the logic of values. Index. viii + 444pp. 5⅜ x 8. T73 Paperbound **$2.25**

TRAGIC SENSE OF LIFE, M. de Unamuno. The acknowledged masterpiece of one of Spain's most influential thinkers. Between the despair at the inevitable death of man and all his works and the desire for something better, Unamuno finds that "saving incertitude" that alone can console us. This dynamic appraisal of man's faith in God and in himself has been called "a masterpiece" by the ENCYCLOPAEDIA BRITANNICA. xxx + 332pp. 5⅜ x 8. T257 Paperbound **$2.00**

HISTORY OF DOGMA, A. Harnack. Adolph Harnack, who died in 1930, was perhaps the greatest Church historian of all time. In this epoch-making history, which has never been surpassed in comprehensiveness and wealth of learning, he traces the development of the authoritative Christian doctrinal system from its first crystallization in the 4th century down through the Reformation, including also a brief survey of the later developments through the Infallibility decree of 1870. He reveals the enormous influence of Greek thought on the early Fathers, and discusses such topics as the Apologists, the great councils, Manichaeism, the historical position of Augustine, the medieval opposition to indulgences, the rise of Protestantism, the relations of Luther's doctrines with modern tendencies of thought, and much more. "Monumental work; still the most valuable history of dogma . . . luminous analysis of the problems . . . abounds in suggestion and stimulus and can be neglected by no one who desires to understand the history of thought in this most important field," Dutcher's Guide to Historical Literature. Translated by Neil Buchanan. Index. Unabridged reprint in 4 volumes. Vol I: Beginnings to the Gnostics and Marcion. Vol II & III: 2nd century to the 4th century Fathers. Vol IV & V: 4th century Councils to the Carlovingian Renaissance. Vol VI & VII: Period of Clugny (c. 1000) to the Reformation, and after. Total of cii + 2407pp. 5⅜ x 8.

T904 Vol I	Paperbound	**$2.50**
T905 Vol II & III	Paperbound	**$2.75**
T906 Vol IV & V	Paperbound	**$2.75**
T907 Vol VI & VII	Paperbound	**$2.75**
	The set	**$10.75**

THE GUIDE FOR THE PERPLEXED, Maimonides. One of the great philosophical works of all time and a necessity for everyone interested in the philosophy of the Middle Ages in the Jewish, Christian, and Moslem traditions. Maimonides develops a common meeting-point for the Old Testament and the Aristotelian thought which pervaded the medieval world. His ideas and methods predate such scholastics as Aquinas and Scotus and throw light on the entire problem of philosophy or science vs. religion. 2nd revised edition. Complete unabridged Friedländer translation. 55 page introduction to Maimonides's life, period, etc., with an important summary of the GUIDE. Index. lix + 414pp. 5⅜ x 8. T351 Paperbound **$2.00**

Art, History of Art, Antiques, Graphic Arts, Handcrafts

ART STUDENTS' ANATOMY, E. J. Farris. Outstanding art anatomy that uses chiefly living objects for its illustrations. 71 photos of undraped men, women, children are accompanied by carefully labeled matching sketches to illustrate the skeletal system, articulations and movements, bony landmarks, the muscular system, skin, fasciae, fat, etc. 9 x-ray photos show movement of joints. Undraped models are shown in such actions as serving in tennis, drawing a bow in archery, playing football, dancing, preparing to spring and to dive. Also discussed and illustrated are proportions, age and sex differences, the anatomy of the smile, etc. 8 plates by the great early 18th century anatomic illustrator Siegfried Albinus are also included. Glossary. 158 figures, 7 in color. x + 159pp. 5⅝ x 8⅜.   T744 Paperbound **$1.50**

AN ATLAS OF ANATOMY FOR ARTISTS, F Schider. A new 3rd edition of this standard text enlarged by 52 new illustrations of hands, anatomical studies by Cloquet, and expressive life studies of the body by Barcsay. 189 clear, detailed plates offer you precise information of impeccable accuracy. 29 plates show all aspects of the skeleton, with closeups of special areas, while 54 full-page plates, mostly in two colors, give human musculature as seen from four different points of view, with cutaways for important portions of the body. 14 full-page plates provide photographs of hand forms, eyelids, female breasts, and indicate the location of muscles upon models. 59 additional plates show how great artists of the past utilized human anatomy. They reproduce sketches and finished work by such artists as Michelangelo, Leonardo da Vinci, Goya, and 15 others. This is a lifetime reference work which will be one of the most important books in any artist's library. "The standard reference tool," AMERICAN LIBRARY ASSOCIATION. "Excellent," AMERICAN ARTIST. Third enlarged edition. 189 plates, 647 illustrations. xxvi + 192pp. 7⅞ x 10⅝.   T241 Clothbound **$6.00**

AN ATLAS OF ANIMAL ANATOMY FOR ARTISTS, W. Ellenberger, H. Baum, H. Dittrich. The largest, richest animal anatomy for artists available in English. 99 detailed anatomical plates of such animals as the horse, dog, cat, lion, deer, seal, kangaroo, flying squirrel, cow, bull, goat, monkey, hare, and bat. Surface features are clearly indicated, while progressive beneath-the-skin pictures show musculature, tendons, and bone structure. Rest and action are exhibited in terms of musculature and skeletal structure and detailed cross-sections are given for heads and important features. The animals chosen are representative of specific families so that a study of these anatomies will provide knowledge of hundreds of related species. "Highly recommended as one of the very few books on the subject worthy of being used as an authoritative guide," DESIGN. "Gives a fundamental knowledge," AMERICAN ARTIST. Second revised, enlarged edition with new plates from Cuvier, Stubbs, etc. 288 illustrations. 153pp. 11⅜ x 9.   T82 Clothbound **$6.00**

THE HUMAN FIGURE IN MOTION, Eadweard Muybridge. The largest selection in print of Muybridge's famous high-speed action photos of the human figure in motion. 4789 photographs illustrate 162 different actions: men, women, children—mostly undraped—are shown walking, running, carrying various objects, sitting, lying down, climbing, throwing, arising, and performing over 150 other actions. Some actions are shown in as many as 150 photographs each. All in all there are more than 500 action strips in this enormous volume, series shots taken at shutter speeds of as high as 1/6000th of a second! These are not posed shots, but true stopped motion. They show bone and muscle in situations that the human eye is not fast enough to capture. Earlier, smaller editions of these prints have brought $40 and more on the out-of-print market. "A must for artists," ART IN FOCUS. "An unparalleled dictionary of action for all artists," AMERICAN ARTIST. 390 full-page plates, with 4789 photographs. Printed on heavy glossy stock. Reinforced binding with headbands. xxi + 390pp. 7⅞ x 10⅝.
T204 Clothbound **$10.00**

ANIMALS IN MOTION, Eadweard Muybridge. This is the largest collection of animal action photos in print. 34 different animals (horses, mules, oxen, goats, camels, pigs, cats, guanacos, lions, gnus, deer, monkeys, eagles—and 21 others) in 132 characteristic actions. The horse alone is shown in more than 40 different actions. All 3919 photographs are taken in series at speeds up to 1/6000th of a second. The secrets of leg motion, spinal patterns, head movements, strains and contortions shown nowhere else are captured. You will see exactly how a lion sets his foot down; how an elephant's knees are like a human's—and how they differ; the position of a kangaroo's legs in mid-leap; how an ostrich's head bobs; details of the flight of birds—and thousands of facets of motion only the fastest cameras can catch. Photographed from domestic animals and animals in the Philadelphia zoo, it contains neither semiposed artificial shots nor distorted telephoto shots taken under adverse conditions. Artists, biologists, decorators, cartoonists, will find this book indispensable for understanding animals in motion. "A really marvelous series of plates," NATURE (London). "The dry plate's most spectacular early use was by Eadweard Muybridge," LIFE. 3919 photographs; 380 full pages of plates. 440pp. Printed on heavy glossy paper. Deluxe binding with headbands. 7⅞ x 10⅝.   T203 Clothbound **$10.00**

ART ANATOMY, William Rimmer, M.D. Often called one of America's foremost contributions to art instruction, a work of art in its own right. More than 700 line drawings by the author, first-rate anatomist and dissector as well as artist, with a non-technical anatomical text. Impeccably accurate drawings of muscles, skeletal structure, surface features, other aspects of males and females, children, adults and aged persons show not only form, size, insertion and articulation but personality and emotion as reflected by physical features usually ignored in modern anatomical works. Complete unabridged reproduction of 1876 edition slightly rearranged. Introduction by Robert Hutchinson. 722 illustrations. xiii + 153pp. 7¾ x 10¾.
T908 Paperbound **$2.00**

ANIMAL DRAWING: ANATOMY AND ACTION FOR ARTISTS, C. R. Knight. The author and illustrator of this work was "the most distinguished painter of animal life." This extensive course in animal drawing discusses musculature, bone structure, animal psychology, movements, habits, habitats. Innumerable tips on proportions, light and shadow play, coloring, hair formation, feather arrangement, scales, how animals lie down, animal expressions, etc., from great apes to birds. Pointers on avoiding gracelessness in horses, deer; on introducing proper power and bulk to heavier animals; on giving proper grace and subtle expression to members of the cat family. Originally titled "Animal Anatomy and Psychology for the Artist and Layman." Over 123 illustrations. 149pp. 8¼ x 10½.
T426 Paperbound **$2.00**

DESIGN FOR ARTISTS AND CRAFTSMEN, L. Wolchonok. The most thorough course ever prepared on the creation of art motifs and designs. It teaches you to create your own designs out of things around you — from geometric patterns, plants, birds, animals, humans, landscapes, and man-made objects. It leads you step by step through the creation of more than 1300 designs, and shows you how to create design that is fresh, well-founded, and original. Mr. Wolchonok, whose text is used by scores of art schools, shows you how the same idea can be developed into many different forms, ranging from near representationalism to the most advanced forms of abstraction. The material in this book is entirely new, and combines full awareness of traditional design with the work of such men as Miro, Léger, Picasso, Moore, and others. 113 detailed exercises, with instruction hints, diagrams, and details to enable you to apply Wolchonok's methods to your own work. "A great contribution to the field of design and crafts," N. Y. SOCIETY OF CRAFTSMEN. More than 1300 Illustrations. xv + 207pp. 7⅞ x 10¾.
T274 Clothbound **$4.95**

HAWTHORNE ON PAINTING. A vivid recreation, from students' notes, of instruction by Charles W. Hawthorne, given for over 31 years at his famous Cape Cod School of Art. Divided into sections on the outdoor model, still life, landscape, the indoor model, and water color, each section begins with a concise essay, followed by epigrammatic comments on color, form, seeing, etc. Not a formal course, but comments of a great teacher-painter on specific student works, which will solve problems in your own painting and understanding of art. "An excellent introduction for laymen and students alike," Time. Introduction. 100pp. 5⅜ x 8.
T653 Paperbound **$1.00**

THE ENJOYMENT AND USE OF COLOR, Walter Sargent. This book explains fascinating relations among colors, between colors in nature and art; describes experiments that you can perform to understand these relations more thoroughly; points out hundreds of little known facts about color values, intensities, effects of high and low illumination, complementary colors, color harmonies. Practical hints for painters, references to techniques of masters, questions at chapter ends for self-testing all make this a valuable book for artists, professional and amateur, and for general readers interested in world of color. Republication of 1923 edition. 35 illustrations, 6 full-page plates. New color frontispiece. Index. xii + 274pp. 5⅜ x 8.
T944 Paperbound **$2.25**

DECORATIVE ALPHABETS AND INITIALS, ed. by Alexander Nesbitt. No payment, no permission needed to reproduce any one of these 3924 different letters, covering 1000 years. Crisp, clear letters all in line, from Anglo-Saxon mss., Luebeck Cathedral, 15th century Augsburg; the work of Dürer, Holbein, Cresci, Beardsley, Rossing Wadsworth, John Moylin, etc. Every imaginable style. 91 complete alphabets. 123 full-page plates. 192pp. 7¾ x 10¾.
T544 Paperbound **$2.25**

THREE CLASSICS OF ITALIAN CALLIGRAPHY, edited by Oscar Ogg. Here, combined in a single volume, are complete reproductions of three famous calligraphic works written by the greatest writing masters of the Renaissance: Arrighi's OPERINA and IL MODO, Tagliente's LO PRESENTE LIBRO, and Palatino's LIBRO NUOVO. These books present more than 200 complete alphabets and thousands of lettered specimens. The basic hand is Papal Chancery, but scores of other alphabets are also given: European and Asiatic local alphabets, foliated and art alphabets, scrolls, cartouches, borders, etc. Text is in Italian. Introduction. 245 plates. x + 272pp. 6⅛ x 9¼.
T212 Paperbound **$2.25**

CALLIGRAPHY, J. G. Schwandner. One of the legendary books in the graphic arts, copies of which brought $500 each on the rare book market, now reprinted for the first time in over 200 years. A beautiful plate book of graceful calligraphy, and an inexhaustible source of first-rate material copyright-free, for artists, and directors, craftsmen, commercial artists, etc. More than 300 ornamental initials forming 12 complete alphabets, over 150 ornate frames and panels, over 200 flourishes, over 75 calligraphic pictures including a temple, cherubs, cocks, dodos, stags, chamois, foliated lions, greyhounds, etc. Thousand of calligraphic elements to be used for suggestions of quality, sophistication, antiquity, and sheer beauty. Historical introduction. 158 full-page plates. 368pp. 9 x 13.
T475 Clothbound **$10.00**

CATALOGUE OF DOVER BOOKS

THE HISTORY AND TECHNIQUE OF LETTERING, A. Nesbitt. The only thorough inexpensive history of letter forms from the point of view of the artist. Mr. Nesbitt covers every major development in lettering from the ancient Egyptians to the present and illustrates each development with a complete alphabet. Such masters as Baskerville, Bell, Bodoni, Caslon, Koch, Kilian, Morris, Garamont, Jenson, and dozens of others are analyzed in terms of artistry and historical development. The author also presents a 65-page practical course in lettering, besides the full historical text. 89 complete alphabets; 165 additional lettered specimens. xvii + 300pp. 5⅜ x 8. T427 Paperbound **$2.00**

FOOT-HIGH LETTERS: A GUIDE TO LETTERING (A PRACTICAL SYLLABUS FOR TEACHERS), M. Price. A complete alphabet of Classic Roman letters, each a foot high, each on a separate 16 x 22 plate—perfect for use in lettering classes. In addition to an accompanying description, each plate also contains 9 two-inch-high forms of letter in various type faces, such as "Caslon," "Empire," "Onyx," and "Neuland," illustrating the many possible derivations from the standard classical forms. One plate contains 21 additional forms of the letter A. The fully illustrated 16-page syllabus by Mr. Price, formerly of the Pratt Institute and the Rhode Island School of Design, contains dozens of useful suggestions for student and teacher alike. An indispensable teaching aid. Extensively revised. 16-page syllabus and 30 plates in slip cover, 16 x 22. T239 Clothbound **$6.00**

THE STYLES OF ORNAMENT, Alexander Speltz. Largest collection of ornaments in print— 3765 illustrations of prehistoric, Lombard, Gothic, Frank, Romanesque, Mohammedan, Renaissance, Polish, Swiss, Rococo, Sheraton, Empire, U. S. Colonial, etc., ornament. Gargoyles, dragons, columns, necklaces, urns, friezes, furniture, buildings, keyholes, tapestries, fantastic animals, armor, religious objects, much more, all in line. Reproduce any one free. Index. Bibliography. 400 plates. 656pp. 5⅝ x 8⅜. T557 Paperbound **$2.50**

HANDBOOK OF DESIGNS AND DEVICES, C. P. Hornung. This unique book is indispensable to the designer, commercial artist, and hobbyist. It is not a textbook but a working collection of 1836 basic designs and variations, carefully reproduced, which may be used without permission. Variations of circle, line, band, triangle, square, cross, diamond, swastika, pentagon, octagon, hexagon, star, scroll, interlacement, shields, etc. Supplementary notes on the background and symbolism of the figures. "A necessity to every designer who would be original without having to labor heavily," ARTIST AND ADVERTISER. 204 plates. 240pp. 5⅜ x 8. T125 Paperbound **$2.00**

THE UNIVERSAL PENMAN, George Bickham. This beautiful book, which first appeared in 1743, is the largest collection of calligraphic specimens, flourishes, alphabets, and calligraphic illustrations ever published. 212 full-page plates are drawn from the work of such 18th century masters of English roundhand as Dove, Champion, Bland, and 20 others. They contain 22 complete alphabets, over 2,000 flourishes, and 122 illustrations, each drawn with a stylistic grace impossible to describe. This book is invaluable to anyone interested in the beauties of calligraphy, or to any artist, hobbyist, or craftsman who wishes to use the very best ornamental handwriting and flourishes for decorative purposes. Commercial artists, advertising artists, have found it unexcelled as a source of material suggesting quality. "An essential part of any art library, and a book of permanent value," AMERICAN ARTIST. 212 plates. 224pp. 9 x 13¾. T20 Clothbound **$10.00**

1800 WOODCUTS BY THOMAS BEWICK AND HIS SCHOOL. Prepared by Dover's editorial staff, this is the largest collection of woodcuts by Bewick and his school ever compiled. Contains the complete engravings from all his major works and a wide range of illustrations from lesser-known collections, all photographed from clear copies of the original books and reproduced in line. Carefully and conveniently organized into sections on Nature (animals and birds, scenery and landscapes, plants, insects, etc.), People (love and courtship, social life, school and domestic scenes, misfortunes, costumes, etc.), Business and Trade, and illustrations from primers, fairytales, spelling books, frontispieces, borders, fables and allegories, etc. In addition to technical proficiency and simple beauty, Bewick's work is remarkable as a mode of pictorial symbolism, reflecting rustic tranquility, an atmosphere of rest, simplicity, idyllic contentment. A delight for the eye, an inexhaustible source of illustrative material for art studios, commercial artists, advertising agencies. Individual illustrations (up to 10 for any one use) are copyright free. Classified index. Bibliography and sources. Introduction by Robert Hutchinson. 1800 woodcuts. xiv + 247pp. 9 x 12. T766 Clothbound **$10.00**

A HANDBOOK OF EARLY ADVERTISING ART, C. P. Hornung. The largest collection of copyright-free early advertising art ever compiled. Vol. I contains some 2,000 illustrations of agricultural devices, animals, old automobiles, birds, buildings, Christmas decorations (with 7 Santa Clauses by Nast), allegorical figures, fire engines, horses and vehicles, Indians, portraits, sailing ships, trains, sports, trade cuts — and 30 other categories! Vol. II, devoted to typography, has over 4000 specimens: 600 different Roman, Gothic, Barnum, Old English faces; 630 ornamental type faces; 1115 initials, hundreds of scrolls, flourishes, etc. This third edition is enlarged by 78 additional plates containing all new material. "A remarkable collection," PRINTERS' INK. "A rich contribution to the history of American design," GRAPHIS. Volume I, Pictorial. Over 2000 illustrations. xiv + 242pp. 9 x 12. T122 Clothbound **$10.00** Volume II, Typographical. Over 4000 specimens. vii + 312pp. 9 x 12. T123 Clothbound **$10.00** Two volume set, T121 Clothbound, only **$18.50**

CATALOGUE OF DOVER BOOKS

THE 100 GREATEST ADVERTISEMENTS, WHO WROTE THEM AND WHAT THEY DID, J. L. Watkins. 100 (plus 13 added for this edition) of most successful ads ever to appear. "Do You Make These Mistakes in English," "They laughed when I sat down," "A Hog Can Cross the Country," "The Man in the Hathaway Shirt," over 100 more ads that changed habits of a nation, gave new expressions to the language, built reputations. Also salient facts behind ads, often in words of their creators. "Useful . . . valuable . . . enlightening," Printers' Ink. 2nd revised edition. Introduction. Foreword by Raymond Rubicam. Index. 130 illustrations. 252pp. 7¾ x 10¾.
T540 Paperbound **$2.50**

THE DIDEROT PICTORIAL ENCYCLOPEDIA OF TRADES AND INDUSTRY, MANUFACTURING AND THE TECHNICAL ARTS IN PLATES SELECTED FROM "L'ENCYCLOPEDIE OU DICTIONNAIRE RAISONNE DES SCIENCES, DES ARTS, ET DES METIERS" OF DENIS DIDEROT, edited with text by C. Gillispie. The first modern selection of plates from the high point of 18th century French engraving, Diderot's famous Encyclopedia. Over 2000 illustrations on 485 full-page plates, most of them original size, illustrating the trades and industries of one of the most fascinating periods of modern history, 18th century France. These magnificent engravings provide an invaluable source of fresh, copyright-free material to artists and illustrators, a lively and accurate social document to students of cultures, an outstanding find to the lover of fine engravings. The plates teem with life, with men, women, and children performing all of the thousands of operations necessary to the trades before and during the early stages of the industrial revolution. Plates are in sequence, and show general operations, closeups of difficult operations, and details of complex machinery. Such important and interesting trades and industries are illustrated as sowing, harvesting, beekeeping, cheesemaking, operating windmills, milling flour, charcoal burning, tobacco processing, indigo, fishing, arts of war, salt extraction, mining, smelting iron, casting iron steel, extracting mercury, zinc, sulphur, copper, etc., slating, tinning, silverplating, gilding, making gunpowder, cannons, bells, shoeing horses, tanning, papermaking, printing, dying, and more than 40 other categories. Besides being a work of remarkable beauty and skill, this is also one of the largest collections of working figures in print. 920pp. 9 x 12. Heavy library cloth.
T421 Two volume set **$18.50**

THE HANDBOOK OF PLANT AND FLORAL ORNAMENT, R. G. Hatton. One of the truly great collections of plant drawings for reproduction: 1200 different figures of flowering or fruiting plants—line drawings that will reproduce excellently. Selected from superb woodcuts and copperplate engravings appearing mostly in 16th and 17th century herbals including the fabulously rare "Kreuter Büch" (Bock) "Cruijde Boeck" (Dodoens), etc. Plants classified according to botanical groups. Also excellent reading for anyone interested in home gardening or any phase of horticulture. Formerly "The Craftsman's Plant-Book: or Figures of Plants." Introductions. Over 1200 illustrations. Index. 548pp. 6⅛ x 9¼.
T649 Paperbound **$3.00**

HANDBOOK OF ORNAMENT, F. S. Meyer. One of the largest collections of copyright-free traditional art in print. It contains over 3300 line cuts from Greek, Roman, Medieval, Islamic, Renaissance, Baroque, 18th and 19th century sources. 180 plates illustrate elements of design with networks, Gothic tracery, geometric elements, flower and animal motifs, etc., while 100 plates illustrate decorative objects: chairs, thrones, daises, cabinets, crowns, weapons, utensils, vases, jewelry, armor, heraldry, bottles, altars, and scores of other objects. Indispensable for artists, illustrators, designers, handicrafters, etc. Full text. 3300 illustrations. xiv + 548pp. 5⅜ x 8.
T302 Paperbound **$2.50**

COSTUMES OF THE GREEKS AND ROMANS, Thomas Hope. Authentic costumes from all walks of life in Roman, Greek civilizations, including Phrygia, Egypt, Persia, Parthia, Etruria, in finely drawn, detailed engravings by Thomas Hope (1770-1831). Scores of additional engravings of ancient musical instruments, furniture, jewelry, sarcophagi, other adjuncts to ancient life. All carefully copied from ancient vases and statuary. Textual introduction by author. Art and advertising personnel, costume and stage designers, students of fashion design will find these copyright-free engravings a source of ideas and inspiration and a valuable reference. Republication of 1st (1812) edition. 300 full-page plates, over 700 illustrations. xliv + 300pp. 5⅝ x 8⅜.
T21 Paperbound **$2.00**

PRINCIPLES OF ART HISTORY, H. Wölfflin. Analyzing such terms as "baroque," "classic," "neoclassic," "primitive," "picturesque," and 164 different works by artists like Botticelli, van Cleve, Dürer, Hobbema, Holbein, Hals, Rembrandt, Titian, Brueghel, Vermeer, and many others, the author establishes the classifications of art history and style on a firm, concrete basis. This classic of art criticism shows what really occurred between the 14th century primitives and the sophistication of the 18th century in terms of basic attitudes and philosophies. "A remarkable lesson in the art of seeing," SAT. REV. OF LITERATURE. Translated from the 7th German edition. 150 illustrations. 254pp. 6⅛ x 9¼.
T276 Paperbound **$2.00**

AFRICAN SCULPTURE, Ladislas Segy. First publication of a new book by the author of critically acclaimed AFRICAN SCULPTURE SPEAKS. It contains 163 full-page plates illustrating masks, fertility figures, ceremonial objects, etc., representing the culture of 50 tribes of West and Central Africa. Over 85% of these works of art have never been illustrated before, and each is an authentic and fascinating tribal artifact. A 34-page Introduction explains the anthropological, psychological, and artistic values of African sculpture. "Mr. Segy is one of its top authorities," NEW YORKER. 164 full-page photographic plates. Bibliography. 244pp. 6 x 9.
T396 Paperbound **$2.00**

DESIGN MOTIFS OF ANCIENT MEXICO, J. Enciso. This unique collection of pre-Columbian stamps for textiles and pottery contains 766 superb designs from Aztec, Olmec, Totonac, Maya, and Toltec origins. Plumed serpents, calendrical elements, wind gods, animals, flowers, demons, dancers, monsters, abstract ornament, and other designs. More than 90% of these illustrations are completely unobtainable elsewhere. Use this work to bring new barbaric beauty into your crafts or drawing. Originally $17.50. Printed in three colors. 766 illustrations, thousands of motifs. 192pp. 7⅞ x 10¾. T84 Paperbound **$1.85**

DECORATIVE ART OF THE SOUTHWEST INDIANS, D. S. Sides. A magnificent album of authentic designs (both pre- and post-Conquest) from the pottery, textiles, and basketry of the Navaho, Hopi, Mohave, Santo Domingo, and over 20 other Southwestern groups. Designs include birds, clouds, butterflies, quadrupeds, geometric forms, etc. A valuable book for folklorists, and a treasury for artists, designers, advertisers, and craftsmen, who may use without payment or permission any of the vigorous, colorful, and strongly rhythmic designs. Aesthetic and archeological notes. 50 plates. Bibliography of over 50 items. xviii + 101pp. 5⅝ x 8⅜. T139 Paperbound **$1.00**

PAINTING IN THE FAR EAST, Laurence Binyon. Excellent introduction by one of greatest authorities on subject studies 1500 years of oriental art (China, Japan; also Tibet, Persia), over 250 painters. Examines works, schools, influence of Wu Tao-tzu, Kanaoka, Toba Sojo, Masanobu, Okio, etc.; early traditions; Kamakura epoch; the Great Decorators; T'ang Dynasty; Matabei, beginnings of genre; Japanese woodcut, color print; much more, all chronological, in cultural context. 42 photos. Bibliography. 317pp. 6 x 9¼. T520 Paperbound **$2.25**

ON THE LAWS OF JAPANESE PAINTING, H. Bowie. This unusual book, based on 9 years of profound study-experience in the Late Kano art of Japan, remains the most authentic guide in English to the spirit and technique of Japanese painting. A wealth of interesting and useful data on control of the brush; practise exercises; manufacture of ink, brushes, colors; the use of various lines and dots to express moods. It is the best possible substitute for a series of lessons from a great oriental master. 66 plates with 220 illustrations. Index. xv + 177pp. 6⅛ x 9¼. T30 Paperbound **$2.00**

THE MATERIALS AND TECHNIQUES OF MEDIEVAL PAINTING, D. V. Thompson. Based on years of study of medieval manuscripts and laboratory analysis of medieval paintings, this book discusses carriers and grounds, binding media, pigments, metals used in painting, etc. Considers relative merits of painting al fresco and al secco, the procession of coloring materials, burnishing, and many other matters. Preface by Bernard Berenson. Index. 239pp. 5⅜ x 8. T327 Paperbound **$1.85**

THE CRAFTSMAN'S HANDBOOK, Cennino Cennini. This is considered the finest English translation of IL LIBRO DELL' ARTE, a 15th century Florentine introduction to art technique. It is both fascinating reading and a wonderful mirror of another culture for artists, art students, historians, social scientists, or anyone interested in details of life some 500 years ago. While it is not an exact recipe book, it gives directions for such matters as tinting papers, gilding stone, preparation of various hues of black, and many other useful but nearly forgotten facets of the painter's art. As a human document reflecting the ideas of a practising medieval artist it is particularly important. 4 illustrations. xxvii + 142pp. D. V. Thompson translator. 6⅛ x 9¼. T54 Paperbound **$1.35**

VASARI ON TECHNIQUE, G. Vasari. Pupil of Michelangelo and outstanding biographer of the Renaissance artists, Vasari also wrote this priceless treatise on the technical methods of the painters, architects, and sculptors of his day. This is the only English translation of this practical, informative, and highly readable work. Scholars, artists, and general readers will welcome these authentic discussions of marble statues, bronze casting, fresco painting, oil painting, engraving, stained glass, rustic fountains and grottoes, etc. Introduction and notes by G. B. Brown. Index. 18 plates, 11 figures. xxiv + 328pp. 5⅜ x 8. T717 Paperbound **$2.25**

METHODS AND MATERIALS OF PAINTING OF THE GREAT SCHOOLS AND MASTERS, C. L. Eastlake. A vast, complete, and authentic reconstruction of the secret techniques of the masters of painting, collected from hundreds of forgotten manuscripts by the eminent President of the British Royal Academy: Greek, Roman, and medieval techniques; fresco and tempera; varnishes and encaustics; the secrets of Leonardo, Van Eyck, Raphael, and many others. Art historians, students, teachers, critics, and laymen will gain new insights into the creation of the great masterpieces; while artists and craftsmen will have a treasury of valuable techniques. Index. Two volume set. Total of 1025pp. 5⅜ x 8. T718 Paperbound **$2.25**
T719 Paperbound **$2.25**
The set **$4.50**

BYZANTINE ART AND ARCHAEOLOGY, O. M. Dalton. Still the most thorough work in English—both in breadth and in depth—on the astounding multiplicity of Byzantine art forms throughout Europe, North Africa, and Western Asia from the 4th to the 15th century. Analyzes hundreds of individual pieces from over 160 public and private museums, libraries, and collections all over the world. Full treatment of Byzantine sculpture, painting, mosaic, jewelry, textiles, etc., including historical development, symbolism, and aesthetics. Chapters on iconography and ornament. Indispensable for study of Christian symbolism and medieval art. 457 illustrations, many full-page. Bibliography of over 2500 references. 4 Indexes. xx + 727pp. 6⅛ x 9¼. T776 Clothbound **$8.50**

CATALOGUE OF DOVER BOOKS

METALWORK AND ENAMELLING, H. Maryon. This is probably the best book ever written on the subject. Prepared by Herbert Maryon, F.S.A., of the British Museum, it tells everything necessary for home manufacture of jewelry, rings, ear pendants, bowls, and dozens of other objects. Clearly written chapters provide precise information on such topics as materials, tools, soldering, filigree, setting stones, raising patterns, spinning metal, repoussé work, hinges and joints, metal inlaying, damascening, overlaying, niello, Japanese alloys, enamelling, cloisonné, painted enamels, casting, polishing, coloring, assaying, and dozens of other techniques. This is the next best thing to apprenticeship to a master metalworker. 363 photographs and figures. 374pp. 5½ x 8½. T183 Clothbound **$8.50**

SILK SCREEN TECHNIQUES, J. I. Biegeleisen, Max A. Cohn. A complete-to-the-last-detail copiously illustrated home course in this fast growing modern art form. Full directions for building silk screen out of inexpensive materials; explanations of five basic methods of stencil preparation—paper, blockout, tusche, film, photographic—and effects possible: light and shade, washes, dry brush, oil paint type impastos, gouaches, pastels. Detailed coverage of multicolor printing, illustrated by proofs showing the stages of a 4 color print. Special section on common difficulties. 149 illustrations, 8 in color. Sources of supply. xiv + 187pp. 6⅛ x 9¼. T433 Paperbound **$1.75**

A HANDBOOK OF WEAVES, G. H. Oelsner. Now back in print! Probably the most complete book of weaves ever printed, fully explained, differentiated, and illustrated. Includes plain weaves; irregular, double-stitched, and filling satins; derivative, basket, and rib weaves; steep, undulating, broken, offset, corkscrew, interlocking, herringbone, and fancy twills; honeycomb, lace, and crepe weaves; tricot, matelassé, and montagnac weaves; and much more. Translated and revised by S. S. Dale, with supplement on the analysis of weaves and fabrics. 1875 illustrations. vii + 402pp. 6 x 9¼. T209 Clothbound **$5.00**

BASIC BOOKBINDING, A. W. Lewis. Enables the beginner and the expert to apply the latest and most simplified techniques to rebinding old favorites and binding new paperback books. Complete lists of all necessary materials and guides to the selection of proper tools, paper, glue, boards, cloth, leather, or sheepskin covering fabrics, lettering inks and pigments, etc. You are shown how to collate a book, sew it, back it, trim it, make boards and attach them in easy step-by-step stages. Author's preface. 261 illustrations with appendix. Index. xi + 144pp. 5⅜ x 8. T169 Paperbound **$1.45**

BASKETRY, F. J. Christopher. Basic introductions cover selection of materials, use and care of tools, equipment. Easy-to-follow instructions for preparation of oval, oblong trays, lidded baskets, rush mats, tumbler holders, bicycle baskets, waste paper baskets, many other useful, beautiful articles made of coiled and woven reed, willow, rushes, raffia. Special sections present in clear, simple language and numerous illustrations all the how-to information you could need: linings, skein wire, varieties of stitching, simplified construction of handles, dying processes. For beginner and skilled craftsman alike. Edited by Majorie O'Shaugnessy. Bibliography. Sources of supply. Index. 112 illustrations. 108pp. 5 x 7¼. T903 Paperbound **$1.00**

THE ART OF ETCHING, E. S. Lumsden. Everything you need to know to do etching yourself. First two sections devoted to technique of etching and engraving, covering such essentials as relative merits of zinc and copper, cleaning and grounding plates, gravers, acids, arrangement of etching-room, methods of biting, types of inks and oils, mounting, stretching and framing, preserving and restoring plates, size and color of printing papers, much more. A review of the history of the art includes separate chapters on Dürer and Lucas van Leyden, Rembrandt and Van Dyck, Goya, Meryon, Haden and Whistler, British masters of nineteenth century, modern etchers. Final section is a collection of prints by contemporary etchers with comments by the artists. Professional etchers and engravers will find this a highly useful source of examples. Beginners and teachers, students of art and printing will find it a valuable tool. Index. 208 illustrations. 384pp. 5⅜ x 8. T49 Paperbound **$2.50**

WHITTLING AND WOODCARVING, E. J. Tangerman. What to make and how to make it for even a moderately handy beginner. One of the few works that bridge gap between whittling and serious carving. History of the art, background information on selection and use of woods, grips, types of strokes and cuts, handling of tools and chapters on rustic work, flat toys and windmills, puzzles, chains, ships in bottle, nested spheres, fans, more than 100 useful, entertaining objects. Second half covers carving proper: woodcuts, low relief, sculpture in the round, lettering, inlay and marquetry, indoor and outdoor decorations, pierced designs, much more. Final chapter describes finishing, care of tools. Sixth edition. Index. 464 illustrations. x + 239pp. 5½ x 8⅛. T965 Paperbound **$1.75**

THE PRACTICE OF TEMPERA PAINTING, Daniel V. Thompson, Jr. A careful exposition of all aspects of tempera painting, including sections on many possible modern uses, propensities of various woods, choice of material for panel, making and applying the gesso, pigments and brushes, technique of the actual painting, gilding and so on—everything one need know to try a hand at this proven but neglected art. The author is unquestionably the world's leading authority on tempera methods and processes and his treatment is based on exhaustive study of manuscript material. Drawings and diagrams increase clarity of text. No one interested in tempera painting can afford to be without this book. Appendix, "Tempera Practice in Yale Art School," by Lewis E. York. 85 illustrations by York; 4 full-page plates. ix x 149pp. 5⅜ x 8½. T343 Paperbound **$1.50**

SHAKER FURNITURE, E. D. Andrews and F. Andrews. The most illuminating study on what many scholars consider the best examples of functional furniture ever made. Includes the history of the sect and the development of Shaker style. The 48 magnificent plates show tables, chairs, cupboards, chests, boxes, desks, beds, woodenware, and much more, and are accompanied by detailed commentary. For all antique collectors and dealers, designers and decorators, historians and folklorists. "Distinguished in scholarship, in pictorial illumination, and in all the essentials of fine book making," Antiques. 3 Appendixes. Bibliography. Index. 192pp. 7⅞ x 10¾.   T679 Paperbound **$2.00**

JAPANESE HOMES AND THEIR SURROUNDINGS, E. S. Morse. Every aspect of the purely traditional Japanese home, from general plan and major structural features to ceremonial and traditional appointments—tatami, hibachi, shoji, tokonoma, etc. The most exhaustive discussion in English, this book is equally honored for its strikingly modern conception of architecture. First published in 1886, before the contamination of the Japanese traditions, it preserves the authentic features of an ideal of construction that is steadily gaining devotees in the Western world. 307 illustrations by the author. Index. Glossary. xxxvi + 372pp. 5⅝ x 8⅜.   T746 Paperbound **$2.25**

COLONIAL LIGHTING, Arthur H. Hayward. The largest selection of antique lamps ever illustrated anywhere, from rush light-holders of earliest settlers to 1880's—with main emphasis on Colonial era. Primitive attempts at illumination ("Betty" lamps, variations of open wick design, candle molds, reflectors, etc.), whale oil lamps, painted and japanned hand lamps, Sandwich glass candlesticks, astral lamps, Bennington ware and chandeliers of wood, iron, pewter, brass, crystal, bronze and silver. Hundreds of illustrations, loads of information on colonial life, customs, habits, place of acquisition of lamps illustrated. A unique, thoroughgoing survey of an interesting aspect of Americana. Enlarged (1962) edition. New Introduction by James R. Marsh. Supplement "Colonial Chandeliers," photographs with descriptive notes. 169 illustrations, 647 lamps. xxxi + 312pp. 5⅝ x 8¼.   T975 Paperbound **$2.00**

CHINESE HOUSEHOLD FURNITURE, George N. Kates. The first book-length study of authentic Chinese domestic furniture in Western language. Summarises practically everything known about Chinese furniture in pure state, uninfluenced by West. History of style, unusual woods used, craftsmanship, principles of design, specific forms like wardrobes, chests and boxes, beds, chairs, tables, stools, cupboards and other pieces. Based on author's own investigation into scanty Chinese historical sources and surviving pieces in private collections and museums. Will reveal a new dimension of simple, beautiful work to all interior decorators, furniture designers, craftsmen. 123 illustrations; 112 photographs. Bibliography. xiii + 205pp. 5¼ x 7¾.   T958 Paperbound **$1.50**

ART AND THE SOCIAL ORDER, Professor D. W. Gotshalk, University of Illinois. One of the most profound and most influential studies of aesthetics written in our generation, this work is unusual in considering art from the relational point of view, as a transaction consisting of creation-object-apprehension. Discussing material from the fine arts, literature, music, and related disciplines, it analyzes the aesthetic experience, fine art, the creative process, art materials, form, expression, function, art criticism, art and social life and living. Graceful and fluent in expression, it requires no previous background in aesthetics and will be read with considerable enjoyment by anyone interested in the theory of art. "Clear, interesting, the soundest and most penetrating work in recent years," C. J. Ducasse, Brown University. New preface by Professor Gotshalk. xvi + 248pp. 5⅝ x 8½.
                                                                     T294 Paperbound **$1.65**

FOUNDATIONS OF MODERN ART, A. Ozenfant. An illuminating discussion by a great artist of the interrelationship of all forms of human creativity, from painting to science, writing to religion. The creative process is explored in all facets of art, from paleolithic cave painting to modern French painting and architecture, and the great universals of art are isolated. Expressing its countless insights in aphorisms accompanied by carefully selected illustrations, this book is itself an embodiment in prose of the creative process. Enlarged by 4 new chapters. 226 illustrations. 368pp. 6⅛ x 9¼.   T215 Paperbound **$2.00**

VITRUVIUS: TEN BOOKS ON ARCHITECTURE. Book by 1st century Roman architect, engineer, is oldest, most influential work on architecture in existence; for hundreds of years his specific instructions were followed all over the world, by such men as Bramante, Michelangelo, Palladio, etc., and are reflected in major buildings. He describes classic principles of symmetry, harmony; design of treasury, prison, etc.; methods of durability; much more. He wrote in a fascinating manner, and often digressed to give interesting sidelights, making this volume appealing reading even to the non-professional. Standard English translation, by Prof. M. H. Morgan, Harvard U. Index. 6 illus. 334pp. 5⅜ x 8.   T645 Paperbound **$2.00**

THE BROWN DECADES, Lewis Mumford. In this now classic study of the arts in America, Lewis Mumford resurrects the "buried renaissance" of the post-Civil War period. He demonstrates that it contained the seeds of a new integrity and power and documents his study with detailed accounts of the founding of modern architecture in the work of Sullivan, Richardson, Root, Roebling; landscape development of Marsh, Olmstead, and Eliot; the graphic arts of Homer, Eakins, and Ryder. 2nd revised enlarged edition. Bibliography. 12 illustrations. Index. xiv + 266pp. 5⅜ x 8.   T200 Paperbound **$1.75**

CATALOGUE OF DOVER BOOKS

THE AUTOBIOGRAPHY OF AN IDEA, Louis Sullivan. The pioneer architect whom Frank Lloyd Wright called "the master" reveals an acute sensitivity to social forces and values in this passionately honest account. He records the crystallization of his opinions and theories, the growth of his organic theory of architecture that still influences American designers and architects, contemporary ideas, etc. This volume contains the first appearance of 34 full-page plates of his finest architecture. Unabridged reissue of 1924 edition. New introduction by R. M. Line. Index. xiv + 335pp. 5⅜ x 8. T281 Paperbound **$2.00**

THE DRAWINGS OF HEINRICH KLEY. The first uncut republication of both of Kley's devastating sketchbooks, which first appeared in pre-World War I Germany. One of the greatest cartoonists and social satirists of modern times, his exuberant and iconoclastic fantasy and his extraordinary technique place him in the great tradition of Bosch, Breughel, and Goya, while his subject matter has all the immediacy and tension of our century. 200 drawings. viii + 128pp. 7¾ x 10¾. T24 Paperbound **$1.85**

MORE DRAWINGS BY HEINRICH KLEY. All the sketches from Leut' Und Viecher (1912) and Sammel-Album (1923) not included in the previous Dover edition of Drawings. More of the bizarre, mercilessly iconoclastic sketches that shocked and amused on their original publication. Nothing was too sacred, no one too eminent for satirization by this imaginative, individual and accomplished master cartoonist. A total of 158 illustrations. Iv + 104pp. 7¾ x 10¾. T41 Paperbound **$1.85**

PINE FURNITURE OF EARLY NEW ENGLAND, R. H. Kettell. A rich understanding of one of America's most original folk arts that collectors of antiques, interior decorators, craftsmen, woodworkers, and everyone interested in American history and art will find fascinating and immensely useful. 413 illustrations of more than 300 chairs, benches, racks, beds, cupboards, mirrors, shelves, tables, and other furniture will show all the simple beauty and character of early New England furniture. 55 detailed drawings carefully analyze outstanding pieces. "With its rich store of illustrations, this book emphasizes the individuality and varied design of early American pine furniture. It should be welcomed," ANTIQUES. 413 illustrations and 55 working drawings. 475. 8 x 10¾. T145 Clothbound **$10.00**

THE HUMAN FIGURE, J. H. Vanderpoel. Every important artistic element of the human figure is pointed out in minutely detailed word descriptions in this classic text and illustrated as well in 430 pencil and charcoal drawings. Thus the text of this book directs your attention to all the characteristic features and subtle differences of the male and female (adults, children, and aged persons), as though a master artist were telling you what to look for at each stage. 2nd edition, revised and enlarged by George Bridgman. Foreword. 430 illustrations. 143pp. 6⅛ x 9¼. T432 Paperbound **$1.50**

LETTERING AND ALPHABETS, J. A. Cavanagh. This unabridged reissue of LETTERING offers a full discussion, analysis, illustration of 89 basic hand lettering styles — styles derived from Caslons, Bodonis, Garamonds, Gothic, Black Letter, Oriental, and many others. Upper and lower cases, numerals and common signs pictured. Hundreds of technical hints on make-up, construction, artistic validity, strokes, pens, brushes, white areas, etc. May be reproduced without permission! 89 complete alphabets; 72 lettered specimens. 121pp. 9¾ x 8. T53 Paperbound **$1.35**

STICKS AND STONES, Lewis Mumford. A survey of the forces that have conditioned American architecture and altered its forms. The author discusses the medieval tradition in early New England villages; the Renaissance influence which developed with the rise of the merchant class; the classical influence of Jefferson's time; the "Mechanicsvilles" of Poe's generation; the Brown Decades; the philosophy of the Imperial facade; and finally the modern machine age. "A truly remarkable book," SAT. REV. OF LITERATURE. 2nd revised edition. 21 illustrations. xvii + 228pp. 5⅜ x 8. T202 Paperbound **$1.65**

THE STANDARD BOOK OF QUILT MAKING AND COLLECTING, Marguerite Ickis. A complete easy-to-follow guide with all the information you need to make beautiful, useful quilts. How to plan, design, cut, sew, appliqué, avoid sewing problems, use rag bag, make borders, tuft, every other aspect. Over 100 traditional quilts shown, including over 40 full-size patterns. At-home hobby for fun, profit. Index. 483 illus. 1 color plate. 287pp. 6¾ x 9½. T582 Paperbound **$2.00**

THE BOOK OF SIGNS, Rudolf Koch. Formerly $20 to $25 on the out-of-print market, now only $1.00 in this unabridged new edition! 493 symbols from ancient manuscripts, medieval cathedrals, coins, catacombs, pottery, etc. Crosses, monograms of Roman emperors, astrological, chemical, botanical, runes, housemarks, and 7 other categories. Invaluable for handicraft workers, illustrators, scholars, etc., this material may be reproduced without permission. 493 illustrations by Fritz Kredel. 104pp. 6½ x 9¼. T162 Paperbound **$1.00**

PRIMITIVE ART, Franz Boas. This authoritative and exhaustive work by a great American anthropologist covers the entire gamut of primitive art. Pottery, leatherwork, metal work, stone work, wood, basketry, are treated in detail. Theories of primitive art, historical depth in art history, technical virtuosity, unconscious levels of patterning, symbolism, styles, literature, music, dance, etc. A must book for the interested layman, the anthropologist, artist, handicrafter (hundreds of unusual motifs), and the historian. Over 900 illustrations (50 ceramic vessels, 12 totem poles, etc.). 376pp. 5⅜ x 8. T25 Paperbound **$2.00**

Teach Yourself

These British books are the most effective series of home study books on the market! With no outside help they will teach you as much as is necessary to have a good background in each subject, in many cases offering as much material as a similar high school or college course. They are carefully planned, written by foremost British educators, and amply provided with test questions and problems for you to check your progress; the mathematics books are especially rich in examples and problems. Do not confuse them with skimpy outlines or ordinary school texts or vague generalized popularizations; each book is complete in itself, full without being overdetailed, and designed to give you an easily-acquired branch of knowledge.

TEACH YOURSELF ALGEBRA, P. Abbott. The equivalent of a thorough high school course, up through logarithms. 52 illus. 307pp. 4¼ x 7. T680 Clothbound **$2.00**

TEACH YOURSELF GEOMETRY, P. Abbott. Plane and solid geometry, covering about a year of plane and six months of solid. 268 illus. 344pp. 4½ x 7. T681 Clothbound **$2.00**

TEACH YOURSELF TRIGONOMETRY, P. Abbott. Background of algebra and geometry will enable you to get equivalent of elementary college course. Tables. 102 illus. 204pp. 4½ x 7. T682 Clothbound **$2.00**

TEACH YOURSELF THE CALCULUS, P. Abbott. With algebra and trigonometry you will be able to acquire a good working knowledge of elementary integral calculus and differential calculus. Excellent supplement to any course textbook. 380pp. 4¼ x 7. T683 Clothbound **$2.00**

TEACH YOURSELF THE SLIDE RULE, B. Snodgrass. Basic principles clearly explained, with many applications in engineering, business, general figuring, will enable you to pick up very useful skill. 10 illus. 207pp. 4¼ x 7. T684 Clothbound **$2.00**

TEACH YOURSELF MECHANICS, P. Abbott. Equivalent of part course on elementary college level, with lever, parallelogram of force, friction, laws of motion, gases, etc. Fine introduction before more advanced course. 163 illus. 271pp. 4½ x 7. T685 Clothbound **$2.00**

TEACH YOURSELF ELECTRICITY, C. W. Wilman. Current, resistance, voltage, Ohm's law, circuits, generators, motors, transformers, etc. Non-mathematical as much as possible. 115 illus. 184pp. 4¼ x 7. T230 Clothbound **$2.00**

TEACH YOURSELF HEAT ENGINES E. DeVille. Steam and internal combustion engines; non-mathematical introduction for student, for layman wishing background, refresher for advanced student. 76 illus. 217pp. 4¼ x 7. T237 Clothbound **$2.00**

TEACH YOURSELF TO PLAY THE PIANO, King Palmer. Companion and supplement to lessons or self study. Handy reference, too. Nature of instrument, elementary musical theory, technique of playing, interpretation, etc. 60 illus. 144pp. 4¼ x 7. T959 Clothbound **$2.00**

TEACH YOURSELF HERALDRY AND GENEALOGY, L. G. Pine. Modern work, avoiding romantic and overpopular misconceptions. Editor of new Burke presents detailed information and commentary down to present. Best general survey. 50 illus. glossary; 129pp. 4¼ x 7. T962 Clothbound **$2.00**

TEACH YOURSELF HANDWRITING, John L. Dumpleton. Basic Chancery cursive style is popular and easy to learn. Many diagrams. 114 illus. 192pp. 4¼ x 7. T960 Clothbound **$2.00**

TEACH YOURSELF CARD GAMES FOR TWO, Kenneth Konstam. Many first-rate games, including old favorites like cribbage and gin and canasta as well as new lesser-known games. Extremely interesting for cards enthusiast. 60 illus. 150pp. 4¼ x 7. T963 Clothbound **$2.00**

TEACH YOURSELF GUIDEBOOK TO THE DRAMA, Luis Vargas. Clear, rapid survey of changing fashions and forms from Aeschylus to Tennessee Williams, in all major European traditions. Plot summaries, critical comments, etc. Equivalent of a college drama course; fine cultural background 224pp. 4¼ x 7. T961 Clothbound **$2.00**

TEACH YOURSELF THE ORGAN, Francis Routh. Excellent compendium of background material for everyone interested in organ music, whether as listener or player. 27 musical illus. 158pp. 4¼ x 7. T977 Clothbound **$2.00**

TEACH YOURSELF TO STUDY SCULPTURE, William Gaunt. Noted British cultural historian surveys culture from Greeks, primitive world, to moderns. Equivalent of college survey course. 23 figures, 40 photos. 158pp. 4¼ x 7. T976 Clothbound **$2.00**

Fiction

FLATLAND, E. A. Abbott. A science-fiction classic of life in a 2-dimensional world that is also a first-rate introduction to such aspects of modern science as relativity and hyperspace. Political, moral, satirical, and humorous overtones have made FLATLAND fascinating reading for thousands. 7th edition. New introduction by Banesh Hoffmann. 16 illustrations. 128pp. 5⅜ x 8. **T1 Paperbound $1.00**

THE WONDERFUL WIZARD OF OZ, L. F. Baum. Only edition in print with all the original W. W. Denslow illustrations in full color—as much a part of "The Wizard" as Tenniel's drawings are of "Alice in Wonderland." "The Wizard" is still America's best-loved fairy tale, in which, as the author expresses it, "The wonderment and joy are retained and the heartaches and nightmares left out." Now today's young readers can enjoy every word and wonderful picture of the original book. New introduction by Martin Gardner. A Baum bibliography. 23 full-page color plates. viii + 268pp. 5⅜ x 8. **T691 Paperbound $1.50**

THE MARVELOUS LAND OF OZ, L. F. Baum. This is the equally enchanting sequel to the "Wizard," continuing the adventures of the Scarecrow and the Tin Woodman. The hero this time is a little boy named Tip, and all the delightful Oz magic is still present. This is the Oz book with the Animated Saw-Horse, the Woggle-Bug, and Jack Pumpkinhead. All the original John R. Neill illustrations, 10 in full color. 287 pp. 5⅜ x 8. **T692 Paperbound $1.50**

28 SCIENCE FICTION STORIES OF H. G. WELLS. Two full unabridged novels, MEN LIKE GODS and STAR BEGOTTEN, plus 26 short stories by the master science-fiction writer of all time! Stories of space, time, invention, exploration, future adventure—an indispensable part of the library of everyone interested in science and adventure. PARTIAL CONTENTS: Men Like Gods, The Country of the Blind, In the Abyss, The Crystal Egg, The Man Who Could Work Miracles, A Story of the Days to Come, The Valley of Spiders, and 21 more! 928pp. 5⅜ x 8. **T265 Clothbound $4.50**

THREE MARTIAN NOVELS, Edgar Rice Burroughs. Contains: Thuvia, Maid of Mars; The Chessmen of Mars; and The Master Mind of Mars. High adventure set in an imaginative and intricate conception of the Red Planet. Mars is peopled with an intelligent, heroic human race which lives in densely populated cities and with fierce barbarians who inhabit dead sea bottoms. Other exciting creatures abound amidst an inventive framework of Martian history and geography. Complete unabridged reprintings of the first edition. 16 illustrations by J. Allen St. John. vi + 499pp. 5⅜ x 8½. **T39 Paperbound $1.85**

SEVEN SCIENCE FICTION NOVELS, H. G. Wells. Full unabridged texts of 7 science-fiction novels of the master. Ranging from biology, physics, chemistry, astronomy to sociology and other studies, Mr. Wells extrapolates whole worlds of strange and intriguing character. "One will have to go far to match this for entertainment, excitement, and sheer pleasure . . . ," NEW YORK TIMES. Contents: The Time Machine, The Island of Dr. Moreau, First Men in the Moon, The Invisible Man, The War of the Worlds, The Food of the Gods, In the Days of the Comet. 1015pp. 5⅜ x 8. **T264 Clothbound $4.50**

THE LAND THAT TIME FORGOT and THE MOON MAID, Edgar Rice Burroughs. In the opinion of many, Burroughs' best work. The first concerns a strange island where evolution is individual rather than phylogenetic. Speechless anthropoids develop into intelligent human beings within a single generation. The second projects the reader far into the future and describes the first voyage to the Moon (in the year 2025), the conquest of the Earth by the Moon, and years of violence and adventure as the enslaved Earthmen try to regain possession of their planet. "An imaginative tour de force that keeps the reader keyed up and expectant," NEW YORK TIMES. Complete, unabridged text of the original two novels (three parts in each). 5 illustrations by J. Allen St. John. vi + 552pp. 5⅜ x 8½.
T1020 Clothbound $3.75
T358 Paperbound $2.00

3 ADVENTURE NOVELS by H. Rider Haggard. Complete texts of "She," "King Solomon's Mines," "Allan Quatermain." Qualities of discovery; desire for immortality; search for primitive, for what is unadorned by civilization, have kept these novels of African adventure exciting, alive to readers from R. L. Stevenson to George Orwell. 636pp. 5⅜ x 8. **T584 Paperbound $2.00**

A PRINCESS OF MARS and A FIGHTING MAN OF MARS: TWO MARTIAN NOVELS BY EDGAR RICE BURROUGHS. "Princess of Mars" is the very first of the great Martian novels written by Burroughs, and it is probably the best of them all; it set the pattern for all of his later fantasy novels and contains a thrilling cast of strange peoples and creatures and the formula of Olympian heroism amidst ever-fluctuating fortunes which Burroughs carries off so successfully. "Fighting Man" returns to the same scenes and cities—many years later. A mad scientist, a degenerate dictator, and an indomitable defender of the right clash—with the fate of the Red Planet at stake! Complete, unabridged reprinting of original editions. Illustrations by F. E. Schoonover and Hugh Hutton. v + 356pp. 5⅜ x 8½. **T1140 Paperbound $1.75**

THE PIRATES OF VENUS and LOST ON VENUS: TWO VENUS NOVELS BY EDGAR RICE BURROUGHS. Two related novels, complete and unabridged. Exciting adventure on the planet Venus with Earthman Carson Napier broken-field running through one dangerous episode after another. All lovers of swashbuckling science fiction will enjoy these two stories set in a world of fascinating societies, fierce beasts, 5000-ft. trees, lush vegetation, and wide seas. Illustrations by Fortunino Matania. Total of vi + 340pp. 5⅜ x 8½. T1053 Paperbound **$1.75**

RURITANIA COMPLETE: THE PRISONER OF ZENDA and RUPERT OF HENTZAU, Anthony Hope. The first edition to include in one volume both the continually-popular "Prisoner of Zenda" and its equally-absorbing sequel. Hope's mythical country of Ruritania has become a household word and the activities of its inhabitants almost a common heritage. Unabridged reprinting. 14 illustrations by Charles Dana Gibson. vi + 414pp. 5⅜ x 8. T69 Paperbound **$1.35**

GHOST AND HORROR STORIES OF AMBROSE BIERCE, Selected and introduced by E. F. Bleiler. 24 morbid, eerie tales—the cream of Bierce's fiction output. Contains such memorable pieces as "The Moonlit Road," "The Damned Thing," "An Inhabitant of Carcosa," "The Eyes of the Panther," "The Famous Gilson Bequest," "The Middle Toe of the Right Foot," and other chilling stories, plus the essay, "Visions of the Night" in which Bierce gives us a kind of rationale for his aesthetic of horror. New collection (1964). xxii + 199pp. 5⅜ x 8⅜. T767 Paperbound **$1.00**

BEST GHOST STORIES OF J. S. LE FANU, Selected and introduced by E. F. Bleiler. LeFanu is deemed the greatest name in Victorian supernatural fiction. Here are 16 of his best horror stories, including 2 nouvelles: "Carmilla," a classic vampire tale couched in a perverse eroticism, and "The Haunted Baronet." Also: "Sir Toby's Will," "Green Tea," "Schalken the Painter," "Ultor de Lacy," "The Familiar," etc. The first American publication of about half of this material: a long-overdue opportunity to get a choice sampling of LeFanu's work. New selection (1964). 8 illustrations. 5⅜ x 8⅜. T415 Paperbound **$1.85**

FIVE GREAT DOG NOVELS, edited by Blanche Cirker. The complete original texts of five classic dog novels that have delighted and thrilled millions of children and adults throughout the world with stories of loyalty, adventure, and courage. Full texts of Jack London's "The Call of the Wild"; John Brown's "Rab and His Friends"; Alfred Ollivant's "Bob, Son of Battle"; Marshall Saunders' "Beautiful Joe"; and Ouida's "A Dog of Flanders." 21 illustrations from the original editions. 495pp. 5⅜ x 8. T777 Paperbound **$1.75**

THE CASTING AWAY OF MRS. LECKS AND MRS. ALESHINE, F. R. Stockton. A charming light novel by Frank Stockton, one of America's finest humorists (and author of "The Lady, or the Tiger?"). This book has made millions of Americans laugh at the reflection of themselves in two middle-aged American women involved in some of the strangest adventures on record. You will laugh, too, as they endure shipwreck, desert island, and blizzard with maddening tranquility. Also contains complete text of "The Dusantes," sequel to "The Casting Away." 49 original illustrations by F. D. Steele. vii + 142pp. 5⅜ x 8. T743 Paperbound **$1.00**

AT THE EARTH'S CORE, PELLUCIDAR, TANAR OF PELLUCIDAR: THREE SCIENCE FICTION NOVELS BY EDGAR RICE BURROUGHS. Complete, unabridged texts of the first three Pellucidar novels. Tales of derring-do by the famous master of science fiction. The locale for these three related stories is the inner surface of the hollow Earth where we discover the world of Pellucidar, complete with all types of bizarre, menacing creatures, strange peoples, and alluring maidens—guaranteed to delight all Burroughs fans and a wide circle of adventure lovers. Illustrated by J. Allen St. John and P. F. Berdanier. vi + 433pp. 5⅜ x 8½. T1051 Paperbound **$2.00**

THE WAR IN THE AIR, IN THE DAYS OF THE COMET, THE FOOD OF THE GODS: THREE SCIENCE FICTION NOVELS BY H. G. WELLS. Three exciting Wells offerings bearing on vital social and philosophical issues of his and our own day. Here are tales of air power, strategic bombing, East vs. West, the potential miracles of science, the potential disasters from outer space, the relationship between scientific advancement and moral progress, etc. First reprinting of "War in the Air" in almost 50 years. An excellent sampling of Wells at his storytelling best. Complete, unabridged reprintings. 16 illustrations. 645pp. 5⅜ x 8½. T1135 Paperbound **$2.00**

DAVID HARUM, E. N. Westcott. This novel of one of the most lovable, humorous characters in American literature is a prime example of regional humor. It continues to delight people who like their humor dry, their characters quaint, and their plots ingenuous. First book edition to contain complete novel plus chapter found after author's death. Illustrations from first illustrated edition. 192pp. 5⅜ x 8. T580 Paperbound **$1.15**

TO THE SUN? and OFF ON A COMET!, Jules Verne. Complete texts of two of the most imaginative flights into fancy in world literature display the high adventure that have kept Verne's novels read for nearly a century. Only unabridged edition of the best translation, by Edward Roth. Large, easily readable type. 50 illustrations selected from first editions. 462pp. 5⅜ x 8. T634 Paperbound **$1.75**

CATALOGUE OF DOVER BOOKS

FROM THE EARTH TO THE MOON and ALL AROUND THE MOON, Jules Verne. Complete editions of two of Verne's most successful novels, in finest Edward Roth translations, now available after many years out of print. Verne's visions of submarines, airplanes, television, rockets, interplanetary travel; of scientific and not-so-scientific beliefs; of peculiarities of Americans; all delight and engross us today as much as when they first appeared. Large, easily readable type. 42 illus. from first French edition. 476pp. 5⅜ x 8.   T633 Paperbound **$1.75**

THREE PROPHETIC NOVELS BY H. G. WELLS, edited by E. F. Bleiler. Complete texts of "When the Sleeper Wakes" (1st book printing in 50 years), "A Story of the Days to Come," "The Time Machine" (1st complete printing in book form). Exciting adventures in the future are as enjoyable today as 50 years ago when first printed. Predict TV, movies, intercontinental airplanes, prefabricated houses, air-conditioned cities, etc. First important author to foresee problems of mind control, technological dictatorships. "Absolute best of imaginative fiction," N. Y. Times. Introduction. 335pp. 5⅜ x 8.   T605 Paperbound **$1.50**

GESTA ROMANORUM, trans. by Charles Swan, ed. by Wynnard Hooper. 181 tales of Greeks, Romans, Britons, Biblical characters, comprise one of greatest medieval story collections, source of plots for writers including Shakespeare, Chaucer, Gower, etc. Imaginative tales of wars, incest, thwarted love, magic, fantasy, allegory, humor, tell about kings, prostitutes, philosophers, fair damsels, knights, Noah, pirates, all walks, stations of life. Introduction. Notes. 500pp. 5⅜ x 8.   T535 Paperbound **$1.85**

Prices subject to change without notice.

Dover publishes books on art, music, philosophy, literature, languages, history, social sciences, psychology, handcrafts, orientalia, puzzles and entertainments, chess, pets and gardens, books explaining science, intermediate and higher mathematics, mathematical physics, engineering, biological sciences, earth sciences, classics of science, etc. Write to:

Dept. catrr.
Dover Publications, Inc.
180 Varick Street, N.Y. 14, N.Y.